Advanced Mac OS X Programming

Mark Dalrymple
Aaron Hillegass

To order copies of this book:
Atlas Books
(800) 247-6553
http://www.atlasbooks.com/

For more information about this book or the class it is based upon, contact;
Big Nerd Ranch, Inc.
931 Monroe Drive
Suite 102, PMB 254
Atlanta, GA 30030
(678) 595 - 6773
http://www.bignerdranch.com/

Publishers Cataloging-in-Publication Data

Dalrymple, Mark
    Advanced Mac OS X Programming / Mark Dalrymple, Aaron Hillegass
        p. cm.
    ISBN 0-9740785-1-4
        1. Mac OS. 2. Operating Systems (Computers) 3.Macintosh
        I. Hillegass, Aaron
    QA76.76.063 D635 2003

ISBN 0-9740785-1-4
Second edition (First edition was titled *Core Mac OS X and Unix Programming*)
First printing   September 2005

To Glenn, Mary Jo, and Enna — Mark

To my parents, Tom and Suzanna — Aaron

Table of Contents

Acknowledgements

This book is based upon our experiences teaching a five-day class at the Big Nerd Ranch called *Core Mac OS X and Unix Programming* course. The patience and curiousity of our students has made this a more complete and comprehensible introduction to the plumbing that makes Mac OS X a reliable, flexible, and high-performance system.

Assisting us through the entire process, Chris Campbell has shown himself to be a great proofreader and DocBook markup master. Chris also helped develop some of the tools that we used to write and improve the book.

Thanks to Mark's associates in the Western Pennsylvania Linux User's group and the Pittsburgh chapter of CocoaHeads: Zach Paine helped us enormously by doing much of the original DocBook markup, James O'Kane and Kolt Loughran provided many suggestions on early drafts of the manuscript after a trial run of some chapters at a WPLUG tutorial. Also thanks go to Curtis Galloway for answering many low-level questions and Wayne Hasley for his encouragement and providing access to his stable of Mac Hardware.

In preparing this book, several people reviewed the drafts and brought errors to our attention. The most astonishing quantity of corrections came from Bill Monk. It would be difficult overstate Bill's contributions. Other technical reviewers who submitted errors: Eric Peyton, Jeremy Wyld, Dave Zarzycki, Carl-Johan Kihlborn, Juan Pablo Claude, Richard Wolf, and Michael Simmons. They made this book better with their useful corrections and suggestions. Any errors that remain in this book are completely our fault.

Sarah Hillegass did our copyediting. Courtney Garvin designed the cover.

Emily Herman is handling all the marketing for this book.

All the layout for this book was done using OpenJade, TeX, and Norm Walsh's DSSSL stylesheets for the DocBook DTD. We appreciate the efforts of all the volunteers who have worked on these projects.

We also wish to thank our wives, Sharlotte DeVere and Michele Hillegass, for their support, patience and understanding.

Chapter 1. Introduction

Unix: Built to Evolve

Complex systems come into existence in only two ways: through careful planning or through evolution. An airport is an example of something that is planned carefully beforehand, built, and then undergoes only minor changes for the rest of its existence. Complex organisms (like humans) are an example of something that has evolved continually from something simple.

In the end, organisms that are well suited to evolution will always win out over organisms that are less suited to evolve. For example, sexual reproduction helps create smooth and continuous evolution. As a result, nearly all complex organisms reproduce sexually.

An operating system evolves. Of course, the programmer who creates a new operating system designs it carefully, but in the end, an operating system that is well suited to evolution will replace an operating system that is not. It is, then, an interesting exercise to think about what traits make an operating system capable of evolution.

The first version of Unix was developed by Ken Thompson at Bell Laboratories in 1969. It was written in assembly language to run on a PDP-7. Dennis Ritchie, also at Bell Labs, invented the C programming language. Among computer languages, C is pretty low level, but it is still much more portable than assembly language. Together, Thompson and Ritchie completely rewrote Unix in C. By 1978, Unix was running on several different architectures. Portability, then, was the first indication that Unix is well suited to evolution.

In 1976, Bell Labs began giving the source code for Unix to research facilities. The Computer Systems Research Group at UC Berkeley got a copy and began tinkering with it. The design of Unix was exceedingly elegant and was deemed a perfect platform upon which to build two important technologies: virtual memory and TCP/IP networking. By freely distributing the source code, Bell Labs was inviting people to extend Unix. Extensibility was the second indication that Unix is well suited to evolution.

It should be noted here that Berkeley's work on Unix was funded by DARPA. Without the warm glow of government grants for basic research, there would be no internet. These grants would be much more difficult to get in today's political climate. In fact, not so long ago, the NSA discontinued all work to improve the security of Linux because of complaints that it was creating unfair competition for Microsoft.

4.4BSD was the last release of Unix produced by Berkeley. It was used as the basis for FreeBSD, OpenBSD, NetBSD, and Mac OS X. Today, Unix is used as an operating system for cellular phones and supercomputers. It is the most popular operating system for web servers, mail servers, and engineering workstations. The manner in which it has found a home in so many niches is yet another indication that Unix is capable of evolution.

Mac OS X is based upon 4.4BSD, but notice that this new niche, a desktop operating system that your grandmother will love, is very different from Unix's previous purposes. To reach this goal, Apple has made several important additions to its Unix core.

The Unix part of Mac OS X is called *Darwin*. The large additions to Darwin that Apple has made are known as the *core technologies*. Apple, recognizing that Unix must continue to evolve, has released the source code to Darwin and most of the core technologies.

This Book

As Unix has evolved into this new niche, existing books have fallen behind. While there are several books on the graphical aspects of Mac programming, this is the only explanation of the plumbing that makes it all work. This is where you will learn the nitty-gritty that separates the experienced programmer from the beginners.

As someone who develops applications and servers for Mac OS X, there are large chunks of Unix that you probably do not care about. For example, do you need to know how to neatly format your text on a VT100 terminal? We will do our best to steer clear of historical curiosities and focus on technologies that you will actually need to understand.

When you finish this book, you will be able to:

- Create applications that leverage the full power of the Unix APIs.
- Use advanced ideas like multithreading and interprocess communications to increase the performance and reliability of your application.
- Add networking capabilities to event-driven applications.
- Make networked applications Bonjour-aware.
- Use the keychain and authorization capabilities of the security framework.
- Use distributed objects to create client/server applications.
- Understand and use gcc, the linker, the debugger, and cvs.
- Use the performance tools to evaluate and improve the responsiveness of your existing applications.

The ideas in this book can be broken into three basic groups:

Unix APIs

> There are a set of standard Unix APIs that every programmer should know how to use. Even if higher-level abstractions alleviate the need to ever call them directly, understanding these functions and structures will give you a much deeper knowledge of how your system works. Much of what is said here will also be true for Linux.

Framework APIs

> There is a whole set of daemons and frameworks that Apple has added to its version of Unix. These frameworks are exceedingly powerful and Apple has been slow to document how they work and how they are to be used.

Tools

Many of the most commonly used developer tools for Mac OS X come straight from its Unix roots: gcc, gdb, the linker, cvs, and make. We have done our best to give clear, simple examples of how these tools can be used to their full potential. We have also documented some tools that Apple provides for performance analysis.

The majority of the code in this book is ANSI C. Some of the chapters use the Cocoa APIs, so you should have a basic understanding of Cocoa and Objective-C. You can get the necessary expertise by reading the first nine chapters of Aaron Hillegass' *Cocoa Programming for Mac OS X*.

Typographical Conventions

To make the book easier to comprehend, we have used several typographical conventions.

Function names will appear in a bold, fixed-width font. All standard Unix functions are completely lowercase. Functions developed by Apple are often mixed case. To make it clear that it is a function, the name will be followed by a set of parentheses. For example, you might see, "Use **NSLog()** or **printf()** to display the computed value."

In Objective-C, class names are always capitalized. In this book, they will also appear in a bold, fixed-width font. In Objective-C, method names start with a lowercase letter. Method names will also appear in a fixed-width, bold font. So, for example, you might see, "The class **NSObject** has the method **dealloc**."

Other literals that you would see in code will appear in a regular fixed-width font. Also, filenames will appear in this same font. Thus, you might see "In `SomeCode.c`, set the variable `foo` to `null`."

Occasionally, there will be an excerpt from a terminal window. What you should type will appear in a bold fixed-width font. The computer's response will appear in a regular fixed-width font. Example:

```
$ ls /var
at        cron    empty   mail    named    root   tmp     yp
backups db        log     msgs    netboot  run    spool   vm
```

Online Materials

The code in this book should be downloaded from http://www.borkware.com/corebook/. This website also includes a message board where you can find errata, suggestions, and comments from other readers. We hope that this website will be a valuable addition to the book.

Chapter 2. The Compiler

The C compiler is probably the central-most tool in your programming arsenal. No matter what editor you use for source code, no matter if you build your programs with Xcode or make,, the C compiler is involved. The *GNU C compiler* (called gcc, but can be invoked with the command cc) is what ships with Apple's developer tools. The Mac OS X 10.4 development tools in code both gcc versions 3.3 and 4.0. The older compiler is available if you have code that will not compile with the newer compiler, or if you need to support versions of Mac OS X prior to version 10.3.9.

You can switch between the two by running /usr/sbin/gcc_select command, described later.

The compiler supports a number of languages, which you can choose from with different file extensions:

.c

> Regular C

.m

> Objective-C

.C

> C++ (but do not use on HFS+ file systems since it is not case sensitive)

.cpp

> C++

.mm

> Objective-C++, a blend of C++ and Objective-C

Handy Flags

The documentation for gcc is included with Xcode. Beware that gcc is huge, with lots of options, lots of features, lots of flags, and lots of extensions to the languages it compiles. It also has lots of cool stuff. Here are some flags that I find useful on a regular basis:

-g

> Add debugging symbols.

-E

> See preprocessor output.

-S

> See generated assembly code.

-save-temps

> Keep temporary files around.

```
-Wall, -Wmost
```

Show more warnings.

```
-Werror
```

Treat warnings as errors.

```
-DSYMBOL
```

#define from the command line.

```
-DSYMBOL=value
```

#define with a value from the command line.

```
-O#
```

Set optimization levels.

Debugging

-g Turns on debugging symbols, which are chunks of extra data that allow debuggers to map an arbitrary address in your executable code back to the source that generated it. It also contains information on variable names, data structures, and types. Enabling debugging symbols also makes your program bigger, and also may expose some implementation details that you might prefer to be hidden. The strip command will remove these symbols. The downside of stripping your executables (or not building your application with -g) means that you will not have symbolic stack traces when looking at errors in the field, and you will not be able to easily analyze core files that people email you. The atos command can help map addresses back to program symbols. During development, it is always a good idea to use -g. It only adds debugging symbols and does not affect the code generation.

Warnings

I am a big fan of compiler warnings. If the compiler is complaining about something I wrote, most likely the code I am writing is questionable and could lead to errors somewhere down the line. I try to have my code to always compile cleanly without warnings. -Wall will show a lot of warnings for most everything the gcc developers consider questionable. -Wmost is a good middle ground when using the Cocoa frameworks.

Specific warnings can be turned on and off independently depending on your specific coding style. For example, say you are using a library which uses macros that leave unused variables around. Messy, but pretty much harmless since the compiler will not allocate space for them. Example 2-1 shows some warnings when compiling.

Example 2-1. warning.m

```
// warning.m -- show generation of compiler warnings

/* compile with:
cc -Wall -o warning warning.m
```

```
*/

int main (int argc, char *argv)
{
    int i;
} // main
```

Then if you build it:

```
$ cc -Wall -o warning warning.m
warning.m:2: warning: second argument of 'main' should be 'char **'
warning.m: In function 'main':
warning.m:3: warning: unused variable 'i'
warning.m:4: warning: control reaches end of non-void function
```

Two of those warnings are really interesting since they are actually errors: I messed up the parameters to **main()**, and I did not return anything from **main()**. But (in this case) the unused variable is not a show-stopper. I fix my code otherwise:

```
int main (int argc, char *argv[])
{
    int i;
    return (0);
} // main
```

```
$ cc -Wall warning.m
warning.m: In function 'main':
warning.m:3: warning: unused variable 'i'
```

You can turn that warning off with

```
$ cc -Wall -Wno-unused warning.m
(no complaints)
```

So you will still get other warnings if you make mistakes. If you wanted to only see unused variables, and no other errors, use -Wunused (drop the no-):

```
$ cc -Wunused warning.m
warning.m: In function 'main':
warning.m:3: warning: unused variable 'i'
```

The gcc documentation have the full set of warnings described in detail.

It is worth your time to reduce your warning count. If you have a lot of warnings that you "just ignore all the time," useful warnings will get lost in the noise. So either fix them or suppress the ones you consider useless. Another downside with lots of warnings that whiz by is when building a large project, particularly when building from the command line with make or xcodebuild, is that it is easy to miss them and spend time debugging an error that also raised a warning. You can configure your projects to pass the -Werror flag to gcc. This will treat warnings as errors, halting the build process when using makefiles or Xcode. You can enable this in Xcode by looking at the project's build settings.

And lastly, for a quick syntax check (no code generation), give gcc the -fsyntax-only flag.

Defining Preprocessor Symbols

You can define preprocessor symbols in your code with #define. These set values (or just that a symbol exists) in the preprocessor. These symbols can be checked with the #ifdef, #ifndef, or #if directives. The symbol values will also be used for substitution or other preprocessor directives. You can define these preprocessor symbols as arguments to the compiler via -D. Example 2-2 shows preprocessor macros used for conditional compilation. Conditional compilation means that sections of code are included or excluded based on preprocessor symbol values.

Example 2-2. define.m

```
// define.m -- conditional compilation

/* compile with:
cc -g -Wall -o define define.m
*/

#include <stdio.h>

#define THING_3

int main (int arg, char *argv[])
{
#ifdef THING_1
    printf ("thing1\n");
#endif

#if THING_2 == 23
    printf ("thing2\n");
#endif

#ifdef THING_3
    printf ("thing3\n");
#endif

    return (0);

} // main
```

Build it:

```
$ cc -g -Wall -o define define.m
```

and run it:

```
$ ./define
thing3
```

Defining the other two symbols will get the other two messages printed. You could either add to the code

```
#define THING_2 23
#define THING_1
```

and that will work. You can also tell the compiler to do it for you

```
$ cc -g -Wall -o define -DTHING_1 -DTHING_2=23 define.m
```

The definition of THING_1 just sets the existence of the preprocessor symbol, the second sets a value.

Running it gives all three messages now:

```
$ ./define
thing1
thing2
thing3
```

Conditional compilation is a handy technique to use when you have multi-platform code that you use to turn on or off compatibility features. It also can be used for turning features on or off with just a compiler flag. For instance, the source files for a web server communications driver that could include or exclude encryption.

Be very careful what you decide to #define, especially if you define commonly used tokens like if. You can run into situations where, for instance, a structure field was #defined to another name (presumably to hack around an error in an API), but this macro could end up clobbering a variable name used elsewhere. Remember that the preprocessor knows nothing about the C language. It just does blind textual replacements.

Seeing Preprocessor Output

Sometimes you get an inscrutable error from the compiler and you have no idea why the compiler is complaining. Or you may have code that looks reasonable and compiles OK, but behaves in a way that defies sanity, even when you take the phase of the moon into account. At times like this examining the preprocessor output can prove fruitful so you can see *exactly* what the compiler is seeing. The -E flag tells gcc to send the preprocessed source code to standard out.

Example 2-3 looks simple enough. It will read a line from standard in and print it back out.

Example 2-3. preprocTest.m

```
// preprocTest -- a program to show preprocessor output

/* compile with:
cc -g -Wall -o preprocTest preprocTest.m
or
cc -Wall -E preprocTest.m > junk.i
*/

#import <stdio.h>

#define BUFFER_SIZE 2048

int main (int argc, char *argv[])
{
    char buffer[BUFFER_SIZE];    /* this is a comment */
    char *thing;

    thing = fgets (buffer, BUFFER_SIZE, stdin);
```

```
    printf ("%s", thing);

    /* some other comment */
    return (0);

} // main
```

Compile it and run it:

```
$ cc -g -Wall -o preprocTest preprocTest.m
$ ./preprocTest
hello[return]
hello
$
```

Now dig into its preprocessed output. Compile your program like this now:

```
$ cc -g -Wall -E preprocTest.m > junk.i
```

This command tells gcc to preprocess the source file and write the results to junk.i (the .i extension is for preprocessed output). junk.i will be a couple of hundred lines long due to the size and complexity of the header files it includes. Open it up in your favorite text editor and scroll to the end. You will see something like this:

```
int main (int argc, char *argv[])
{
    char buffer[2048];
    char *thing;

    thing = fgets (buffer, 2048, (&__sF[0]));
    printf ("%s", thing);


    return (0);

}
```

It is somewhat recognizable as the original program. Notice that all the comments are gone. he #define BUFFER_SIZE 2048 is gone also, but you can see where 2048 has been substituted into the text stream. Notice that stdin has been expanded into the address of the zero element of an array named __sF. What is __sF? Search in junk.i for it. About half-way through you will see

```
extern FILE __sF [ ] ;
```

An array of FILE structures. Because you are seeing exactly what the compiler is seeing, you can look at the guts of FILE (search for __sFILE). There are all sorts of goodies like function pointers, buffers, and block size variables in there. This is not the kind of information you would want your code to depend on, but it can be a big help when debugging. Plus it is fun to dig into things and see how they work.

You can this preprocessed output when you are debugging macros. Write your macro, run it through the preprocessor and see if it has the effect you want.

Seeing the Generated Assembly Code

For the real hard-core hackers, you can look at the assembly code generated by the compiler. Sometimes you need this to track down compiler problems, OS problems, or so you can browse around just for general amusement and education. To get the assembly code compile with the -S flag, and the results will be put into an .s file based on the name of your source file. For instance, running

```
$ cc -g -Wall -S preprocTest.m
```

will create a preprocTest.s. If you want to assemble the resulting file, feed it to the compiler like this:

```
$ cc -o preprocTest preprocTest.s
```

You can also use otool to disassemble existing programs if you do not want to muck around with compiler flags. If you want to save all the intermediate elements (including some not covered here), you can use the -save-temps flag.

Preprocessor Hints and Tricks

The C compilation process happens in several stages. The preprocessor performs text substitutions on your source code and strips out comments. The compiler takes the preprocessed output and generates an assembly language file, which is then assembled into the machine code. If you do not tell gcc to just leave the object file sitting around, the linker will also be invoked to complete the build process.

The preprocessor is a pretty simple straight-text substitution mechanism, with some conditional inclusion features. It is not as powerful and full-featured as something like the GNU m4 macro processor, but it has plenty of power.

Predefined macros

One use the preprocessor features is with conditional compilation so that you only include code for particular platforms. How can you tell what platform you are on? Compilers define some built-in macros to let you decide what code to include or not:

__APPLE__

Defined for an Apple Platform, such as OS X.

__APPLE_CC__

This is an integer value representing the version of the compiler.

__OBJC__

Defined if the compiler is compiling in Objective-C mode.

__cplusplus

Defined if the compiler is compiling in C++ mode.

__MACH__

Defined if the Mach system calls are available.

The preprocessor also defines some special macros that expand to the current location in the file being compiled, and the current date and time:

__DATE__

>The current date.

__TIME__

>The current time.

__FILE__

>The name of the file.

__LINE__

>The line number of the file (before preprocessing).

__FUNCTION__

>The name of the function or Objective C method being compiled. This is a gcc extension and might not be available on all compilers, if code portability is important to you. This also not a macro, but something that comes from the compiler. Remember that the preprocessor does not know anything about the C or Objective-C language.

Example 2-4 shows some of the predefined macros.

Example 2-4. predef.m

```
// predef.m -- show compiler pre-defined macros

/* compile with:
cc -g -Wall -o predef predef.m
*/

#import <Foundation/Foundation.h>
#import <stdio.h>

void someFunc (void)
{
    printf ("file %s, line %d, function %s\n",
            __FILE__, __LINE__, __FUNCTION__);
} // someFunc

@interface SomeClass : NSObject { }
+ (void) someMethod;
@end

@implementation SomeClass
+ (void) someMethod
{
    printf ("file %s, line %d, function %s\n",
            __FILE__, __LINE__, __FUNCTION__);
} // someMethod
@end
```

```
int main (int argc, char *argv[])
{
    printf ("__APPLE__: %d,  __APPLE_CC__: %d\n",
            __APPLE__, __APPLE_CC__);
    printf ("today is %s, the time is %s\n",
            __DATE__, __TIME__);
    printf ("file %s, line %d, function %s\n",
            __FILE__, __LINE__, __FUNCTION__);
    someFunc ();
    [SomeClass someMethod];
    return (0);
} // main
```

Compile it with:

```
$ cc -g -Wall -o predef -framework Foundation predef.m
```

The `-framework` flag automatically figures out where to find the headers and libraries you need to link against. Most other Unixes do not have frameworks, which can make compiling and linking against sophisticated libraries (like the Foundation kit) more tedious.

Run it:

```
$ ./predef
__APPLE__: 1,  __APPLE_CC__: 5026
today is Aug 13 2005, the time is 19:58:09
file predef.m, line 32, function main
file predef.m, line 13, function someFunc
file predef.m, line 23, function +[SomeClass someMethod]
```

The __DATE__ and __TIME__ macros are useful for date and time stamping a program or module when it is compiled. This can be very helpful when you are going through a debug/test cycle with a bunch of plug-ins and it is easy to get confused about which development version of the code you are working with. It is also useful when diagnosing customer problems in the field to know exactly which version of the code you are dealing with.

Macro hygiene

One of the problems with the C Preprocessor is that it is pretty stupid. It has no clue about the context it is working in, so it cannot do what you mean, just what you say. So be careful of how you say things.

For example, you might have a preprocessor macro that looks like this:

```
#define SQUARE(x)    x*x
```

Pretty simple. SQUARE(5) turns into 5*5, which yields the result desired. If someone uses SQUARE(2+3), it will get fed to the compiler as 2+3*2+3, which due to precedence rules is actually 2 + (3*2) + 3, which is 11, not 25. Oops. If you parenthesize the arguments instead:

```
#define SQUARE(x)    (x) * (x)
```

SQUARE(2+3) will turn into (2+3) * (2+3), the correct result.

It is generally a good idea to surround the whole macro result in parentheses as, such as:

```
#define SQUARE(x)    ((x)*(x))
```

to prevent problems if the macro expands into an expression with operators of higher precedence next to it.

Beware of side effects in macros. The preprocessor is strictly textual substitution. The code SQUARE(i++) will expand to (i++)*(i++), which actually is undefined in the C standard, but it could cause i to be incremented twice, which probably is not the intended behavior. Similarly, using functions with side effects in a macro like this could be bad news.

Multiline macros

Sometimes you want a macro to be more than one line of code, such as this one which increases a global error count and then displays an error for the user.

```
#define FOUND_AN_ERROR(desc)    \
    error_count++;    \
    fprintf(stderr, "found an error '%s' at file %s, line %n\n", \
            desc, __FILE__, __LINE__);
```

The macro can be used like:

```
    if (something_bad_happened) {
        FOUND_AN_ERROR("something really bad happened")
    }
```

Example 2-5 uses the macro:

Example 2-5. multilineMacro.m

```
// multilineMacro.m -- multi-line macro hygiene

/* compile with:
cc -g -Wall -o multilineMacro multilineMacro.m
*/

#import <stdio.h>

#define FOUND_AN_ERROR(desc)    \
    error_count++;    \
    fprintf(stderr, "found an error '%s' at file %s, line %d\n", \
            desc, __FILE__, __LINE__);

int error_count;

int main (int argc, char *argv[])
{
    if (argc == 2) {
        FOUND_AN_ERROR ("something bad happened");
    }
    printf ("done\n");
    return (0);
```

```
} // main
```

Compile it:

```
$ cc -g -Wall -o multilineMacro multilineMacro.m
```

And run it:

```
$ ./multilineMacro
done
```

Now run it with an argument (which is considered to be the error condition):

```
$ ./multilineMacro bork
found an error 'something bad happened' at file
    multilineMacro.m, line 13
done
```

Looks like it works fine. There is one lurking problem: what if a programmer on your team that does not fully brace the `if` statement uses the macro?

Remove the braces from your `if`. The code itself innocent enough.

```
if (argc == 2)
    FOUND_AN_ERROR ("something bad happened");
```

Build it and run the program without an argument (which is the "non-error" case)

```
$ ./multilineMacro
found an error 'something bad happened' at file
    multilineMacro.m, line 13
done
```

Oops! Correct code is now considered to be in error. Take a look at what is happening. The C preprocessor is mutating your code from

```
if (argc == 2)
    FOUND_AN_ERROR ("something bad happened");
```

to

```
if (argc == 2)
    error_count++;
    fprintf(stderr, "found an error '%s' at file %s, line %d\n",
            "something bad happened", "multilineMacro.m", 13);
```

Or, if indented the way that it is actually being executed:

```
if (argc == 2)
    error_count++;
fprintf(stderr, "found an error '%s' at file %s, line %d\n",
        "something bad happened", "multilineMacro.m", 13);
```

Here is the problem. You need to wrap these multiline macros in curly braces so that they are essentially one statement. It will then become one statement as far as the compiler is concerned.

Change your macro to read:

```
#define FOUND_AN_ERROR(desc)     \
    do {    \
        error_count++;    \
        fprintf(stderr, "found an error '%s' at file %s, line %d\n", \
                desc, __FILE__, __LINE__);  \
    } while (0)
```

and recompile (leaving the unbraced if statement). Run it:

```
$ ./multilineMacro
done
```

and it works properly. Double-check the error case (just to make sure it did not get broken in the process of making the fix):

```
$ ./multilineMacro bork
found an error 'something bad happened' at file
    multilineMacro.m, line 15
done
```

The macro is wrapped with a `do { } while (0)` statement. The code inside of the loop will get executed only once. This idiom also has the nice side-effect of turning the multi-line operation into a single statement which makes the unbraced `if` behave as expected. This is a technique known as "eating the semicolon." Just plain braces will not work because you will end up with stray semicolons that will confuse the compiler if you have an `else` clause.

Variable Arguments

Functions that take variable arguments are a flexible and powerful interface. The **printf()** family is such an example. One function, an expressive mini command language, and a variable number of arguments leads to an incredibly powerful tool. The stdarg manpage has all the details on using variable arguments.

To handle variable arguments in your own functions, you first declare a variable of type va_list, which acts like a pointer to argument values on the call stack, as shown in Figure 2-1. Initialize it with **va_start()**, giving it the name of the last declared function argument. Then call **va_arg()**, giving it the type of data you expect. Each time you call **va_arg()** an internal pointer moves to point to the next argument on the call stack. Because you are giving **va_arg()** the type of data you are using, **va_arg()** can figure out the size of the data. The function knows how much data you are expecting to get back, as well as how far it needs to to advance its pointer when walking the stack.

Figure 2-1. Memory Layout of Variable Arguments

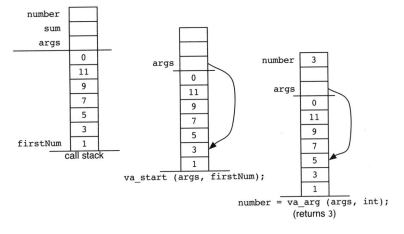

```
int addemUp (int firstNum, ...);
```

result = addemUp (1, 3, 5, 7, 9, 11, 0);

How does **va_arg()** know when to stop? It does not. There is no magic that plants a flag at the end of function's parameters. Your code will need to know when to stop, either by having some kind of pre-supplied format (like **printf()** and friends), or by having some sentinel value (zero or NULL, like with [NSArray arrayWithObjects:]) to signal the end. This is a major source of run-time errors. If you supply a bad format string to **printf()**, or do not include the terminating sentinel value, the function processing the call stack could wander off into random data, causing a crash or data corruption.

va_end() cleans up any internal state being used.

Example 2-6 provides a function function that adds up the integers that are passed to it, using zero as a sentinel value to stop processing:

Example 2-6. vararg.m

```
// vararg.m -- demonstrate variable argument lists

/* compile with:
cc -g -Wall -o vararg vararg.m
*/

#import <stdio.h>    // for printf
#import <stdarg.h>   // varargs stuff

// sum all the integers passed in.  Stopping if it is zero

int addemUp (int firstNum, ...)
{
    va_list args;

    int sum = firstNum;
    int number;
```

```
        va_start (args, firstNum);

        while (1) { // just keep spinning until we are done
            number = va_arg (args, int);
            sum += number;
            if (number == 0) {
                break;
            }
        }

        va_end (args);

        return (sum);

} // addemUp

int main (int argc, char *argv[])
{
    int sumbody;

    sumbody = addemUp (1,2,3,4,5,6,7,8,9,0);
    printf ("sum of 1..9 is %d\n", sumbody);

    sumbody = addemUp (1,3,5,7,9,11,0);
    printf ("sum of odds from 1..11 is %d\n", sumbody);

    return (0);

} // main
```

Build it:

```
$ cc -g -Wall -o vararg vararg.m
```

And run it:

```
$ ./vararg
sum of 1..9 is 45
sum of odds from 1..11 is 36
```

Another use of variable argument functions is adding value to functions that already take variable arguments. You may want a version of **printf()** that took a debug level and only printed out text if the level exceeds some globally set value. To do this, you can write a function to accept the debug level, the format string, the arguments, and then turn around and call **vprintf()**, the varargs-savvy workhorse of **printf()**, like in Example 2-7

Example 2-7. debuglog.m

```
// deubglog.m -- conditional debug logging

/* compile with:
cc -g -Wall -o debuglog debuglog.m
*/
```

```
#import <stdio.h>      // for printf
#import <stdarg.h>     // varargs stuff

int globalLevel = 50;

void debugLog (int logLevel, const char *format, ...)
{
    if (logLevel > globalLevel) {
        va_list args;
        va_start (args, format);
        vprintf (format, args);
        va_end (args);
    }

} // debugLog

int main (int argc, char *argv[])
{
    debugLog (10, "this will not be seen: %d, %s, %d\n", 10,
              "hello", 23);

    debugLog (87, "this should be seen: %s, %d\n", "bork", 42);

    return (0);

} // main
```

Compile and run it as usual:

```
$ cc -g -Wall -o debuglog debuglog.m
$ ./debuglog
this should be seen: bork, 42
```

Cocoa programmers can create variable argument functions in Objective-C. It works in exactly the same way, but aware you cannot create **NSInvocation**s that reference variable argument methods. Example 2-8 has a **SomeClass** object has a weird little method that takes an arbitrary number of objects (terminated by nil) and prints out their description.

Example 2-8. describeObjects.m

```
// describeObjects -- variable arguments in Objective-C

/* compile with:
cc -g -Wall -o describeObjects \
    -framework Foundation describeObjects.m
*/

#import <Foundation/Foundation.h>

@interface ObjectDescriber : NSObject { }

- (void) describeObjects: (id) firstObject, ...;

@end // ObjectDescriber
```

```
@implementation ObjectDescriber

- (void) describeObjects: (id) firstObject, ...
{
    va_list args;
    id obj = firstObject;

    va_start (args, firstObject);

    while (obj) {
        NSString *string = [obj description];
        NSLog (@"the description is:\n     %@", string);
        // get the next object
        obj = va_arg (args, id);
    }

    va_end (args);

} // describeObjects

@end // ObjectDescriber


int main (int argc, char *argv[])
{
    NSAutoreleasePool *pool = [[NSAutoreleasePool alloc] init];

    ObjectDescriber *describer = [[ObjectDescriber alloc] init];

    NSString *someString = @"someString";
    NSNumber *num = [NSNumber numberWithInt: 23];
    NSDate *date = [NSCalendarDate calendarDate];

    [describer describeObjects:someString, num, date, nil];

    [pool release];

    return (0);

} // main
```

Compile it:

```
    $ cc -g -Wall -o describeObjects \
-framework Foundation describeObjects.m
    $ ./describeObjects
    2005-08-13 20:15:17.277 describeObjects[2622] the description is:
        someString
    2005-08-13 20:15:17.287 describeObjects[2622] the description is:
        23
    2005-08-13 20:15:17.313 describeObjects[2622] the description is:
        2005-08-13 20:15:17 -0400
```

There are also a handful of Cocoa methods that accept `va_lists` much like
vprintf() did above, like **NSString**'s **initWithFormat**: arguments, and **NSLogv**..

Varargs Gotchas

One common mistake is making assumptions on sizes of data that get passed to functions that take varying arguments. For example:

```
size_t mysize = somevalue();
printf ("mysize is %d\n", mysize);
```

This code is making the assumption that `sizeof(size_t) == sizeof(int)`, which could be correct, but also could break in the case if a `size_t` is 8 bytes and an `int` is just 4. The function call here will push 8 bytes of data, but **printf()** (having been told to expect an `int`) only pulls off 4 bytes. You will probably crash if there are subsequent arguments: **printf()** pulls off the next 4 bytes expecting a character pointer but actually gets the lower 4 bytes of your `size_t` (which is unlikely to be a valid address). One way to fix this is to cast your `size_t` argument to the type specified in the format string. If >`size_t` grows in subsequent versions of the OS, you will get a compiler warning about losing precision, which sure beats a crash:

```
size_t mysize = somevalue();
printf ("mysize is %d\n", (int)mysize);
```

Compiler Optimization

There are two classes of argument flags for controlling optimization, which controls how the compiler generates machine code from your C code, as well as how it rewrites your code to behave more optimally. You can use -o with a number or letter to control the optimization level.

-O0

Means do no optimize.

-O1

Means do some optimization (also what is used if you use -o without a number).

-O2 and -O3

Use yet more optimization.

-Os

Optimize for size. It does the same optimizations as -O2, but does not do function inlining.

Higher optimization levels can make code unstable as more and more mechanical operations happen to it, so be sure to test when changing levels. Sometimes failures that happen at higher optimization levels can actually be indications of programming errors, so if you have the time it may be worthwhile to pursue any failures that happen at higher optimization levels.

If you know of specific optimizations that you want to enable (like strength reduction, or common subexpression evaluation) or disable, you can turn them on or off individually. For example:

`-fstrength-reduce`

> Will enable strength reduction.

`-fno-strength-reduce`

> Will turn off strength reduction, even if the `-O#` setting would have it enabled otherwise.

The `gcc` documentation describes all the available control flags, and there are a lot of them.

Having an optimization level set to `-O2` or higher will issue a warning (when `-Wall` is engaged) if a variable is used before initialization. The compiler needs to do flow analysis to determine if this happens, and that analysis only happens with `-O` levels of 2 or higher.

`gcc` is unique amongst compilers because it supports both `-g` (debugging) and `-O` (optimization) at the same time. This combination usually is not supported in C compilers. You can use `gdb` on an optimized program, but there may be unexpected results because code can be re-ordered and variables may be eliminated. If you are single-stepping through some code in the debugger and your current line is bouncing all over the place, you are most likely dealing with code that has been run through the optimizer.

Apple recommends using `-Os` to optimize for size, even on fast new machines. It might not produce the best optimization for a specific program, but it gives the best overall system performance since the system working set seems to be a big constraint on performance.

GCC Extensions

One of the constants of GNU products are large number of features. `gcc` has an incredible number of extensions available. They can help improve your code, but they also destroy portability if you are wanting to target a platform that does not have `gcc` or you are not using `gcc`.

Here are a couple of interesting extensions:

- `long long` and `unsigned long long`: `double` word (e.g. 64 bit) integers, are treated as first class citizens. You can perform basic math (+,-,*,/), modular arithmetic, and bitwise operations with them.

- Complex numbers: in C++ you can create complex numbers as a first class type, but `gcc` C has them built in.

- Variable length automatic arrays: like you can use in C++, declaring the size of a stack-based array at run time:

      ```
      int size = some_function();
      char buffer[size];
      ```

  The array also gets deallocated when the brace level the array was declared in is exited.

- Inline functions (like in C++).

- Macros with variable number of arguments, very handy for wrappers around `printf` and friends.
- Packed structures, which remove any alignment padding the compiler might otherwise include. Add `__attribute((packed))__` at the end of your structure definition.

A number of these extensions have made their way into C99 (the most recent version of the ISO C standard), such as variable automatic arrays and complex numbers. Also, Objective-C with the `gcc` compiler lets you declare variables anywhere, just like in C++.

gcc 4.0

All actively maintained software marches onward. This includes the compiler. Each new revision of Mac OS X seems to be accompanied by a new revision of `gcc`. Panther brought us `gcc` 3.3, and Tiger has brought us `gcc` 4.0. Along with the new compilers are new features and new compiler flags to control them.

When you install the Tiger Xcode development package, `gcc` 4.0 is installed automatically, and `gcc` 3.3 is installed for backwards compatibility. You may also need to use `gcc` 3.3 for those cases where `gcc` 4.0's and your code do not get along. `gcc` 4.0 is a pickier compiler than 3.3, and emits more warnings. It has also become more "standards conformant" when compiling C++. It is a point-oh version of the compiler, so sometimes it will reject valid code, and sometimes it will reject invalid code that was happily consumed by previous versions.

You can access a particular compiler version directly using the commands `/usr/bin/gcc-3.3` and `/usr/bin/gcc-4.0`, or you can use the `gcc_select` program to change versions of the compiler system-wide:

```
$ sudo gcc_select 3.3
Default compiler has been set to:
gcc version 3.3 20030304 (Apple Computer, Inc. build 1809)

$ sudo gcc_select 4.0
Default compiler has been set to:
gcc version 4.0.0 (Apple Computer, Inc. build 5026)
```

Like previous versions of `gcc`, 4.0 changes the C++ ABI. The ABI is the Application Binary Interface, which describes details like function calling conventions, name mangling conventions, and default structure layout. You should use libraries and frameworks that have been built with `gcc` 4.x with new code built on the same family of compilers. Programs might link without incident when mixing the older and newer C++ ABI, but problems can manifest themselves at run-time.

long double

`gcc` 4.0 includes a new data type, `long double`, which uses twice the storage space of a double, so you get approximately double the precision. Prior to Mac OS X 10.3.9, the system C library did not support a true `long double` type, so passing a `long double` to any system C library routine might lead to problems. To create a `long double` constant in code, follow it with a capital L, and use `%Lf` when printing out long doubles with printf(). Example 2-9 assigns the fist 50 digits of pi to a float, double, and long double, and prints out the results along with the size of each type:

Example 2-9. long-double.m

```
#import <stdio.h>    // for printf()

/* compile with
gcc -g -Wall -o long-double long-double.m
*/

int main (void)
{
    float thing1;
    double thing2;
    long double thing3;

    thing1 = 3.14159265358979323846264338327950288419716939937510L;
    thing2 = 3.14159265358979323846264338327950288419716939937510L;
    thing3 = 3.14159265358979323846264338327950288419716939937510L;

    printf ("thing1: (%2lu) %36.35f\n", sizeof(thing1), thing1);
    printf ("thing2: (%2lu) %36.35lf\n", sizeof(thing2), thing2);
    printf ("thing3: (%2lu) %36.35Lf\n", sizeof(thing3), thing3);

    return (0);

} // main
```

When run, it generates this output:

```
$ ./long-double
thing1: ( 4) 3.14159274101257324218750000000000000
thing2: ( 8) 3.14159265358979311599796346854418516
thing3: (16) 3.14159265358979323846264338327948123
```

float loses precision at about 7 places after the decimal point, double about 15, long double about 30. You can see that they consume 4, 8, and 16 bytes of memory respectively.

Testing the Compiler Version

gcc supplies a number of preprocessor macros that you can use in your code to test what version of the compiler you are using, and enable or disable code based on it. For instance, you could use long doubles if the code is being compiled with gcc 4, but fall back and use regular doubles on gcc 3. The version macros are:

__GNUC__

The major revision number. For gcc 3.2.1, __GNUC__ would be 3.

__GNUC_MINOR__

The minor revision number. For gcc 3.2.1, __GNUC_MINOR__ would be 2.

`__GNUC_PATCHLEVEL__`

The patch level number. For gcc 3.2.1, __GNUC_PATCHLEVEL__ would be 1.

New Optimizer

The optimizer has been changed for gcc 4.0. Many of the same optimizer flags work as they did before, and new flags have been added. Because it is a new optimizer, it is possible there are compiler bugs related to aggressive optimization of correct code. As with any change to the toolchain for building a program, it pays to do appropriate testing to make sure new problems are not introduced.

The usual optimization flags from previous version of `gcc` still apply. `-O0` for no optimization and a maximally debuggable application. `-O` is a tradeoff of compile speed and execution speed. `-O2` performs the optimizations that do not involve a space-for-time tradeoff, but it does attempt function inlining when specified. `-O3` is best for code that makes heavy use of loops and lots of computation. It considers all functions in the current compilation unit (source file) for inlining, even those not declared inline. `-Os` optimizes for code size rather than speed. There is no loop unrolling, but performance should still be about `-O2` levels. Apple still recommends using `-Os`, which will lead to smaller executables, and so there will be less paging from disk for large programs.

`-fast` is a new optimization flag which changes the overall optimization strategy for gcc. Use this for fastest possible running code for G4 and G5 processors. The optimzations happen at the expense of code size. `-fast` sets the optimization level to `-O3`, and ignores any specific compiler optimization flags, except for those that specify the target architecture.

`-fastcp`, which does not do anything different than `-fast` in `gcc` 4.0, is for C++ users only. It will change in the future to add optimizations to C++ code. `-fastf` is for C code made from fortran-to-C translators, or if your code has fortran semantics.

The `-fast` family of flags can break IEEE-754 conformance for floating point math. Round-off errors can grow if you are doing lots of calculations so you will need to decide if your floating point calculations need IEEE-754's guarantees of accuracy. It also changes the alignment mode of data types (such as the layout of members of a struct), which can create binary compatibility issues. Code compiled with `-fast` cannot always be linked against code compiled without it.

Vectorization

`gcc` 4.0 also includes an autovectorizer. The compiler attempts to convert code, such as loops, or sequences of similar operations over chunks of data, into code for the vector processor (PowerPC Altivec, or Intel SSE2/SSE3). To use the vectorizer, you need to supply the `-ftree-vectorize` compiler flag. This only works at optimization levels `-O2` or higher (`gcc` only computes a probable data flow graph using `-O2` and higher), and where the target architecture has vector instructions (not the G3).

`-ftree-vectorize` also enables the `-fstrict-aliasing` compiler flag, which lets the compiler make some assumptions based on the type of expressions it sees. In particular, an object of one type is assumed never to reside at the same address as an object of a different type (unless they are "almost the same"). An `unsigned int` can alias an `int`, but not a pointer or a double. Doing something like taking the address of an `int` and storing a `double` there breaks the strict-aliasing assumptions. The `-Wstrict-aliasing` flag will cause the compiler to emit warnings about most places that might break the strict aliasing rules.

Even More Compiler Flags

`gcc` has always had a lot of command-line flags that can control many aspects of the compiler, such as the dialect of the language being compiled, the manipulations performed on the resulting object code, and controlling what warnings are emitted.

In `Xcode`, you can pass these flags to the compiler by setting the "Other C Flags" (for optimization, and other general flags) and "Other Warning Flags" (for flags related to warnings) in the target inspector, as shown in Figure 2-2. It really does not matter where they go because they are both concatenated before being put on the command line that invokes the compiler during the build process. The warning flags are placed before the other C flags, in case there is any order dependency between a set of flags.

Figure 2-2. Setting Xcode's Compiler Flags

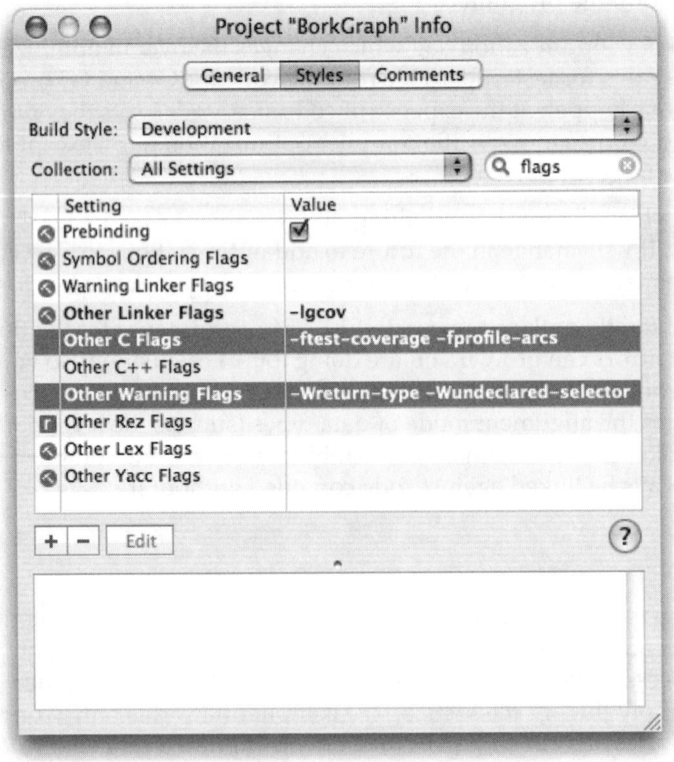

Here are some flags that might be of interest to you:

`-Wstrict-selector-matching`

The compiler automatically emits warnings about type inconsistencies between methods in Objective-C that have the same name but different argument or return types. Apple has relaxed some of the more paranoid warnings generated by the compiler, but you can make the compiler paranoid again by adding this flag.

`-Wno-protocol`

This flag makes Objective-C's `@protocol` feature more useful in some circumstances. The default behavior of `@protocol` is to issue a warning for every method declared in the protocol that is not defined in the class that is adopting the protocol, even if the methods are implemented by a superclass. By giving `gcc` this flag, methods from the superclass will be considered to be implemented and no warning will be issued.

`-fobjc-call-cxx-cdtors`

For the longest time, Objective-C++ has had a limitation regarding C++ objects that are embedded in Objective-C objects: constructors for the C++ objects never get called when the Objective-C object was allocated and initialized. The whole block of memory for the Objective-C object was zeroed as usual by the **alloc** method, and so the C++ object also was cleared out to all zeros. But its constructor is not called, so the C++ object might be in a broken state having not been constructed properly. Likewise, destructors were never invoked on the embedded C++ object when the Objective-C object is deallocated, so the C++ object could leak memory.

By adding this flag, the compiler will create a pair of Objective-C methods (called **.cxx_construct** and **.cxx_destruct**) that are called by the Objective-C run-time to construct and destruct the C++ objects.

`-Wundeclared-selector`

This flag tells the compiler to warn you if you use a `@selector()` that the it has not seen yet. You might have an NSTimer callback method called moveMonsterTowardsPlayer:, and you accidentally use @selector(moveMonsterToPlayer:). If you use this flag, the compiler will issue a warning. Needless to say This can save you some headaches by catching typos at compile-time rather than run-time.

`-fobjc-direct-dispatch`

Objective-C direct dispatch is also called "accelerated Objective-C dispatch". Special entry points exist in high memory for commonly-used functions, like **objc_msgSend()** (which is what Objective-C boils the `[object message]` syntax down to during compilation). When this flag is supplied, the compiler can emit instructions that jump directly to that high-memory address (using the `bla` instruction on the PowerPC, for example)) for improved performance. In some dirt-simple benchmarks I ran, this mechanism takes 10-20% off of message send overhead. The downside is that programs will only run on Mac OS X versions 10.4 or later.

`-Q`

This last one is purely for geeky fun. It tells the compiler to display the name of functions and methods as they are compiled, along with random statistics about the compilation:

```
-[BWCrossStitchChangeList addStitchWithThread:atRow:column:]
-[BWCrossStitchChangeList markRemovedAtRow:column:]
-[BWCrossStitchChangeList changeEnumerator]
-[BWCrossStitchChangeList isChangeAtRow:column:]
-[BWCrossStitchChangeList count]

Execution times (seconds)
preprocessing         :    0.02 ( 1%) wall
lexical analysis      :    0.01 ( 0%) wall
parser                :    0.98 (61%) wall
tree gimplify         :    0.01 ( 1%) wall
expand                :    0.01 ( 1%) wall
global alloc          :    0.02 ( 1%) wall
final                 :    0.01 ( 0%) wall
symout                :    0.05 ( 3%) wall
TOTAL                 :           1.61
```

64-Bit Computing

With the advent of the PowerPC G5 processor and Mac OS X 10.4, 64-bit computing is readily available to the programmers who need it. 64-bit computing means that a process can directly address more than the 4 gigs of memory that 32-bit computing allows. The process might not actually *get* more than 4 gigs of memory, depending on what the user has installed in the machine, per-process limits, different operating system settings, and so on. At the time this is being written, the 64-bit question on the Mac Intel platform has not been announced.

How much bigger is the 64-bit address space compared to the 32-bit one? A common analogy is this: if a byte is a dot the size of the period at the end of this sentence, then a 32-bit address space would cover the surface of the Golden Gate Bridge. A 64-bit address space would cover the entire land surface of the Earth.

The 64-bit Programming Model

The 64-bit programming model used by Mac OS X is called LP64. This means that ints are 32 bits, longs are 64 bits, and pointers are 64 bits. long long is still 64 bits. To make 64-bit programs, you must use gcc 4.0 or later, or use a commercial compiler that supports Mac OS X 64-bit programming.

Code compiled with the 32-bit model is not compatible with code compiled with the 64-bit model. There are changes to the Mach-O ABI to support 64-bit computing. bools are still one byte in size, and the alignment in structs is "natural", so fields like pointers will be padded so that the pointers are 8-byte aligned. In a 64-bit world, More kinds of structs are passed by value in registers, such as a struct composed of three doubles will be passed using three floating point registers.

This also means that 64-bit programs can only use 64-bit frameworks. Initially, Mac OS X 10.4 only supplies the System and Accelerate frameworks with 64-bit versions. None of the user interface frameworks are supplied in a 64-bit version. Also, only C and C++ are supported in 64-bit code, not Objective-C. Supplying a user interface to your 64-bit programs requires you to split the program into 32-bit client part and a

64-bit server parts and have them communicate via shared memory, sockets, pipes, or whatever mechanism you prefer.

There are some consequences from these two bits of information. You cannot use 32-bit plug-ins in a 64-bit program, for instance. Plus there is a code impact from the change in the sizes of the primitive data types.

When using interprocess communication, networking, and binary data files, you should be careful when you choosing your data types Explicitly sized data types (like `uint32_t`) will stay the same size in both 32-bit and 64-bit worlds, and are more predictable than generic types (like `long`) which can change.

Alignment of data also changes between the two worlds. Pointers and longs will need to have 64-bit alignment vs 32-bit alignment, which can make structures larger. The general rule of thumb of putting the larger elements early in the structure should give you good use of space vs. padding caused by data alignment.

64-bit Cleanliness

Be careful of mixing 64 bit (`long`) and 32 bit (`int`) values. You can get unexpected results, such as truncation of values. If you assign a pointer to a 64-bit `long`, pass it as a 32-bit `int` function argument, and then convert the function result back into a pointer, the upper 4 bytes will be stripped off due to the int argument.

If you are seeing problems with data truncation, try using the `-Wconversion` compiler flag. It will cause the compiler to warn you about any data conversions it thinks are suspect. This will flag some legitimate conversions, but it will be a place to start looking for the problem.

There are also some pre-defined types to hold values that might overflow an int:

`uintptr_t`

> Use this as the destination when casting 64-bit pointers to integer types.

`ptrdiff_t`

> An integer sufficiently large to hold the result of pointer arithmatic.

`size_t`

> The type that `sizeof` returns. This has become a 64 bit value.

`pos_t`

> An integer sufficiently large to hold a file position.

`off_t`

> An integer sufficiently large to hold a file offset.

Also, never assume you know the size of any structure. Always use `sizeof`.

Bitmasks of type `long` have some gotchas. By default, masks expressed in code as constants are treated as an `unsigned int`, meaning that any significant digits implicitly added by the compiler will be zeros. If you want zeros in the upper bits of your mask, that is fine. If you want ones in the upper part of your mask, you will want to write the mask as the bitwise inverse of the mask's inverse. For instance, if you are wanting the mask 0xfffc to be sign-extended through all 64 bits, you will

want to do something like the second line (the first line shows you what bitmask
would result without using this inversion trick):

```
0xfffffffc // 0x00000000fffffffc (64 bits)
~0x3       // 0xfffffffc (32 bits) or 0xfffffffffffffffc (64 bits)
```

be careful of making assumptions about how many bits are in a `long` if you are
shifting through its bits. Use the `LONG_BIT` constant to figure out the number of bits
involved.

Should You Go 64-bit?

So, should you immediately go for 64-bits? Sure, if you need it now, but for most
developers, 64-bit computing will not have much of an immediate impact.

You truly *need* a 64-bit address space when you need random access to huge data
objects (greater than 2 gig), or you need concurrent access to a quantity of data that
will not fit into a 32-bit address space, like multi-gig data modeling, data mining,
web caches, large-scale 3-D rendering, very large databases, etc.

If your app uses a streaming data access model, or just uses 64-bit integer math, you
do not absolutely need 64-bit computing. When compiled for the G5 architecture,
32-bit programs that use 64-bit integer math (`long longs`) will use the 64-bit math
instructions and take advantage of the extra bits in the processor's registers. You
also do not need 64-bit computing when dealing with very large files. The file
system API is capable of handling 64-bit offsets.

You will not get an automatic performance increase going to 64-bits, like what
Windows users are. The Intel family of processors are register starved, so the
increase in registers going to 64-bit computing is a huge performance boost. The
PowerPC was designed from the outset for 64-bitness. Also, there is no story yet on
what 64-bit support the Intel-based Mac family will have.

If anything, you could see a performance decrease. 64-bit code is larger, and it deals
with larger data, so cache misses will happen more often. Larger apps and larger
data can require more memory, so may end up paging if there is not enough
physical RAM on the machine.

Instruction sequences to get an address or constant into a register is longer on 64-bit
code. And some situations, like using a 32-bit signed integer for an array index, if it
is not stored in a register it will require the value to be sign-extended on every
access.

Universally Fat Binaries

Mach-O supports "fat" files (which have been recently renamed as "universal" files,
but I will be using the original fat term through here), which let you have 32-bit,
64-bit, and Intel 386 architecture code in the same file, allowing for a single
application or a single framework to service all computing worlds.

Fat Binaries from the Command Line

You can use the `gcc` on the command-line (or in `makefiles`) to generate object code
for any of the supported architectures. You can also build fat binaries using these
command-line tools.

Give gcc the -arch ppc64 flag to compile the code in 64-bit mode. Example 2-10 will get compiled and run in a couple of different ways, starting out with -arch ppc64, which causes the emitted code to use the LP64 model. Use -arch ppc to indicate you want the 32-bit model. -arch i386 will give you Intel code.

Example 2-10. sizeprinter.c

```
#include <stdio.h>  // for printf()

int main (void)
{
    printf ("sizeof(int*) is %ld\n", sizeof(int*));

    return (0);

} // main
```

When I compile it in 64-bit mode and run it on my G4 machine (which is only 32-bits) like this, I get rejected

```
g4$ gcc -arch ppc64 -g -Wall -o sizeprinter sizeprinter.c
g4$ ./sizeprinter
bash: ./sizeprinter: cannot execute binary file
```

It works when copied over to a G5 and run:

```
g5$ ./sizeprinter
sizeof(int*) is 8
```

To compile an Intel binary on a PowerPC system, you need to specify the Universal SDK on the command-line. The -Wl flag passes arguments on to the linker telling it to use /Devleoper/SDKs/MacOSX10.4u.sdk as the system library root. Otherwise you will get a lot of linker errors because the installed system libraries do not have Intel code in them.

```
g4$ gcc -arch i386 -g -Wall -o sizeprinter sizeprinter.c \
        -Wl,-syslibroot,/Developer/SDKs/MacOSX10.4u.sdk
```

You will still get rejected if you try running it on the wrong architecture:

```
g4$ ./sizeprinter
bash: ./sizeprinter: cannot execute binary file
```

But it works when copied to an Intel Mac.

The easy way to create a fat binary is to give gcc all of architectures on the command line. Here is how to make a fat binary using the code from Example 2-10.

```
g4$ gcc -arch ppc64 -arch ppc -arch i386 \
  -g -Wall -Wl,-syslibroot,/Developer/SDKs/MacOSX10.4u.sdk \
  -o sizeprinter sizeprinter.c
```

If you do not need the Intel version, you can leave off the -arch i386 flag and remove the -Wl jazz. The program gets run on a G4:

```
g4$ ./sizeprinter
sizeof(int*) is 4
```

and the same executable run on a G5:

```
g5$ ./sizeprinter
sizeof(int*) is 8
```

and the same executable run on the Intel developer preview machine:

```
386$ ./sizeprinter
sizeof(int*) is 4
```

The `file` command will tell you about the fatness of a program:

```
$ file sizeprinter
sizeprinter: Mach-O fat file with 3 architectures
sizeprinter (for architecture ppc): Mach-O executable ppc
sizeprinter (for architecture ppc64): Mach-O 64-bit executable ppc64
sizeprinter (for architecture i386): Mach-O executable i386
```

When you specify multiple architectures, your file actually gets compiled multiple times, with resulting sets of object code getting merged into one file. Example 2-11 uses some preprocessor macros to determine what mode the compiler is currently in. __ppc__ is defined when compiling in 32-bit PowerPC mode, __ppc64__ when compiling in PPC 64-bit mode, __i386__ when compiling for Intel, and __LP64__ when using the LP64 model. When compiling Mac OS X 64-bit PPC programs, both __ppc64__ and __LP64__ will be defined. In the code, the `#warning` preprocessor directive is used to tell us what bits of code are being compiled at any particular point in time.

Example 2-11. fat-macro-warn.c

```
/* compile with
gcc -o fat-macro-warn fat-macro-warn.c
or
gcc -arch ppc64 -o fat-macro-warn fat-macro-warn.c
or
gcc -arch ppc64 -arch ppc -arch i386 -o fat-macro-warn fat-macro-warn.c
*/

int main (void)
{
#warning compiling the file

#ifdef __LP64__
#warning in LP64
#endif

#ifdef __ppc64__
#warning in __ppc64__
#endif

#ifdef __ppc__
#warning in __ppc__
#endif
```

```
#ifdef __i386__
#warning in __i386__
#endif

    return (0);

} // main
```

Compiling it without extra flags tells us the __ppc__ section gets compiled. At least on a G4 or G5. On an Intel system it will be compiling with __i386__ defined.

```
g4$ gcc -o fat-macro-warn fat-macro-warn.c
fat-macro-warn.c:12:2: warning: #warning compiling the file
fat-macro-warn.c:23:2: warning: #warning in __ppc__
```

Compiling it with -arch ppc64 tells us it finds the __ppc64__ and __LP64__ sections:

```
g4$ gcc -arch ppc64 -o fat-macro-warn fat-macro-warn.c
fat-macro-warn.c:12:2: warning: #warning compiling the file
fat-macro-warn.c:15:2: warning: #warning in LP64
fat-macro-warn.c:19:2: warning: #warning in __ppc64__
```

And finally compiling for all three architectures will show all the warnings. Notice the order. It looks like gcc is compiling the 32-bit version first, then compiling the 64-bit version. Sometimes when you run this command line, the i386 warnings may be intermixed. It seems like gcc is parallelizing the non-PowerPC compilation.

```
% gcc -arch ppc64 -arch ppc -o fat-macro-warn fat-macro-warn.c
fat-macro-warn.c:12:2: warning: #warning compiling the file
fat-macro-warn.c:15:2: warning: #warning in LP64
fat-macro-warn.c:19:2: warning: #warning in __ppc64__
fat-macro-warn.c:12:2: warning: #warning compiling the file
fat-macro-warn.c:23:2: warning: #warning in __ppc__
fat-macro-warn.c:12:2: warning: #warning compiling the file
fat-macro-warn.c:27:2: warning: #warning in __i386__
# ... snipped link warnings and errors about i386
```

You do not have to compile multiple architectures at the same time. Instead, you can compile them separately and then use the lipo command to assemble individual files (object files, libraries, executables) into fat versions. "lipo" comes from the Greek word for "fat". Using the code from Example 2-10, these steps will create three object files and one fat binary. Here is the 32-bit PPC version:

```
$ gcc -g -o sizeprinter-32 sizeprinter.c
```

And the 64-bit PPC version:

```
$ gcc -arch ppc64 -g -o sizeprinter-64 sizeprinter.c
```

And the i386 version:

```
$ gcc -arch i386 -g -o sizeprinter-64 sizeprinter.c \
    -Wl,-syslibroot,/Developer/SDKs/MacOSX10.4u.sdk
```

And then the join them with lipo, using file to verify that it is indeed a fat binary:

```
$ lipo -create -output sizeprinter-fat \
sizeprinter-32 sizeprinter-64 sizeprinter-386
$ file sizeprinter-fat
sizeprinter-fat: Mach-O fat file with 3 architectures
sizeprinter-fat (for architecture ppc): Mach-O executable ppc
sizeprinter-fat (for architecture ppc64): Mach-O 64-bit executable ppc64
sizeprinter-fat (for architecture i386): Mach-O executable i386
```

Fat Binaries in Xcode

You can use Xcode to make fat binaries. If you will be wanting to make Intel binaries, you need to set the cross-development target SDK to be the Mac OS X 10.4 (Universal) SDK. Figure 2-3 shows this setting in the General tab of the project inspector.

Figure 2-3. Setting The Cross-Development Target SDK

Once you have set up your cross-development SDK, you specify the architectures you want using the Build tab. The Architectures setting specifies the processor architectures that will be used. If you double-click on the Setting side of the setting, a sheet will drop down with checkboxes for PowerPC (32-bit) and Intel. Figure 2-4 shows that If you double-click on the Value side of the setting, it lets you type in the architectures you want.

Figure 2-4. Setting Architectures in Xcode

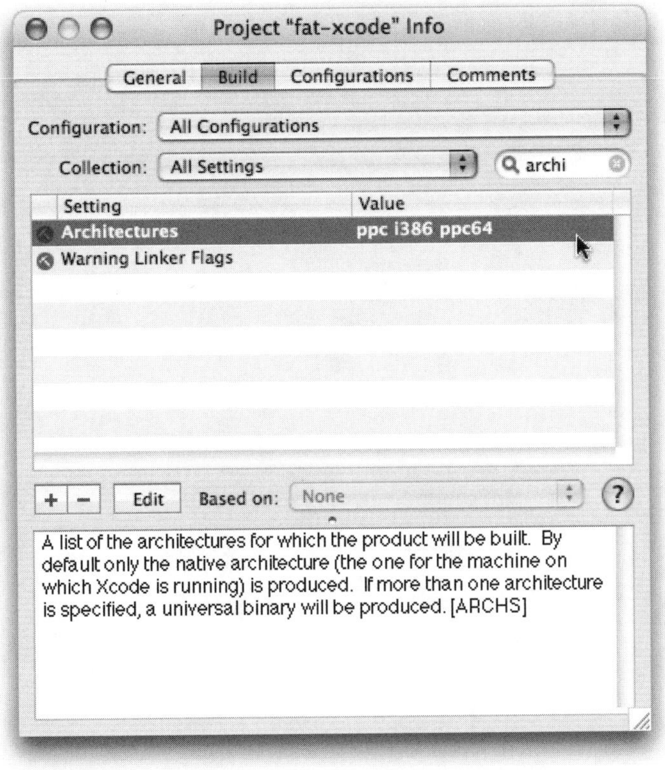

Once you have these settings configured, you can build your projects and end up with fat binaries.

Chapter 3. Libraries

A library is a packaged collection of object files that programs can then link against to make use of the features it provides. Traditional Unix has two kinds of libraries: static libraries where the linker packages the object code into the application, and shared libraries where the linker just stores a reference to a library and the symbols the application needs. Mac OS X brings frameworks to the table also, which package shared libraries with other resources, like header files, documentation, and subframeworks.

Static Libraries

Static libraries are the simplest libraries to work with. Many open source projects that you can download will frequently build static libraries, whether for your programs to link against, or for internal use to simplify the build system where each major module is put into its own static library. All of these libararies are then linked together to make the final executable program. Figure 3-1 shows the object code that lives in shared libraries is physically copied into the final executable.

Figure 3-1. Static Libraries

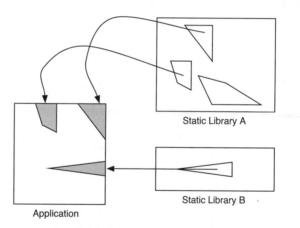

The `ar` program is what is used to create libraries, or in `ar`'s terminology, archives. `ar` can create an archive, add new files to it, and existing files can be extracted, deleted, or replaced. Files are named in the archive by their file name (any files specified with a path just use the file name).

In the materials from the website, you will find five source files that look like Example 3-1:

Example 3-1. src0.c

```
// src0.c : a simple source file so we can fill a library

/* compile with:
cc -g -Wall -c src0.c
*/

int add_0 (int number)
```

```
{
    return (number + 0);
} // add_0
```

These are little functions that do not actually do anything useful. You can compile them all into object files by this command:

```
$ cc -g -c src*.c
```

You can see the source files:

```
$ ls *.c
src0.c   src1.c   src2.c   src3.c   src4.c
```

and the associated object files:

```
$ ls *.o
src0.o   src1.o   src2.o   src3.o   src4.o
```

And this is how you create the archive:

```
$ ar crl libaddum.a *.o
```

With the final result looking like Figure 3-2

Figure 3-2. Inside a library

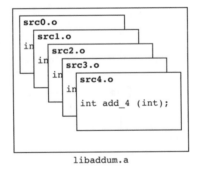

libaddum.a

The flags are:

c

Create if the archive does not exist.

r

'Replace or add the specified files to the archive.

l

The next argument is the name of the library file.

After you create or modify an archive, you need to run the `ranlib` command, which builds the table of contents for the archive. The linker needs this table of contents to locate the object files it actually needs to link in. Frequently `ranlib` can be used to "fix" broken libraries. If you get strange linker errors (particularly if you're not using Apple's development tools) when using a static library, run `ranlib` on it and see if it that helps things.

```
$ ranlib libaddum.a
```

To actually use a static library in your program, you need to use two compiler flags. `-L` tells the linker what directory to look in. `-l` (lower case Ell) tells the linker what files to look for. By convention, library file names are of the form `libfoo.a`, where `foo` is some descriptive name for the features the library provides. If you specify `-lfoo`, the linker knows to look for `libfoo.a`.

Example 3-2 is a program that uses some of the functions from the library:

Example 3-2. useadd.m

```
// useadd.m -- use functions from a library

/* compile with:
cc -g -Wall -o useadd useadd.m -L. -laddum
*/

#import <stdlib.h>      // for EXIT_SUCCESS
#import <stdio.h>       // for printf

int main (int argc, char *argv[])
{
    int i;

    i = 5;
    printf ("i is %d\n", i);

    i = add_1 (i);
    printf ("i after add_1: %d\n", i);

    i = add_4 (i);
    printf ("i after add_4: %d\n", i);

    exit (EXIT_SUCCESS);
} // main
```

If you just try to compile like other programs, you will (understandably) get a complaint about the missing functions:

```
$ cc -g -o useadd useadd.m
/usr/bin/ld: Undefined symbols:
_add_1
_add_4
```

BSD systems frequently prepend an underscore to symbols during linking. The missing symbol names are actually "add_1" and "add_4" Now add the flags to tell the linker where to look, and what library to use:

```
$ cc -g -o useadd useadd.m -L. -laddum
```

A sample run:

```
$ ./useadd
i is 5
i after add_1:  6
i after add_4:  10
```

Note that the library stuff is specified after the source file name. If it were the other way around:

```
$ cc -g -o useadd -L. -laddum useadd.m
/usr/bin/ld: Undefined symbols:
_add_1
_add_4
```

You still get the errors since the linker scans files left to right. It looks at the library, sees that nobody so far needs those symbols to link, and so discards the file. It then goes on to resolve the symbols for the useadd program itself. Since it already discarded the library, the linker complains about the missing symbols. Depending on the complexity of your libraries (e.g., circular references), you may need to specify a library more than once.

When using libraries provided by other parties, it can be a real hassle figuring out where a symbol lives when you get one of these undefined symbol errors. The nm command can come in handy, since it shows you information about the symbols that live in applications, libraries, and object files.

Compile the program, but generate an object file instead of a program (the -c flag):

```
$ cc -g -c  useadd.m
$ ls -l useadd.o
-rw-r--r--  1 markd  staff  7532 Aug 25 14:03 useadd.o
```

And now nm it:

```
$ nm useadd.o
         U _add_1
         U _add_4
         U _exit
00000000 T _main
         U _printf
         U dyld_stub_binding_helper
```

The U is for "undefined" and the T stands for a defined text section symbol. You can see the two add functions that were used, and **printf**, plus a little housekeeping.

You can nm libraries too:

```
$ nm libaddum.a
libaddum.a(src0.o):
00000000 T _add_0

libaddum.a(src1.o):
00000000 T _add_1

libaddum.a(src2.o):
00000000 T _add_2
```

```
libaddum.a(src3.o):
00000000 T _add_3

libaddum.a(src4.o):
00000000 T _add_4
```

Which shows each object file that has been put into the archive, as well as what symbols are present.

Using static libraries in Xcode is really easy. Just drag the libfoo.a file into your project. Xcode will automatically link it in.

Shared Libraries

When you use static libraries, the code is linked physically into your executable program. If you have a big library, say 1 megabyte, which is linked into a dozen programs, you will have 12 megabytes of disk space consumed. With today's huge hard drives that is not too big of a deal. You also have the libraries taking up that megabyte of space in each program's memory. This is a much bigger problem. Memory is a scarce shared resource, so having duplicate copies of library code each occupying their own pages in memory can put stress on the memory system and cause paging.

Shared libraries were created to address this problem. Instead of copying the code into the programs, just a reference is included. When the program needs a feature out of a shared library, the linker just includes the name of the symbol and a pointer to the library, as shown in Figure 3-3.

Figure 3-3. Shared Libraries

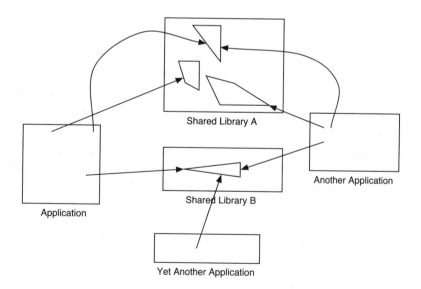

When the program is executed, the loader finds the shared libraries, loads them into memory and fixes up the references (resolves the symbols) so that they point to the now-loaded shared library. The shared library code can be loaded into shared pages of memory and shared among many different processes. In the example above, the dozen programs linking to a 1 megabyte shared library will not take up any extra space on disk, plus the library will only appear once in physical RAM and will be shared amongst the dozen processes. Of course, any space for variable data the shared library uses will be duplicated in each process. You may have heard the term "two level namespaces" bandied about during the transition from Mac OS X 10.0.x to 10.1.x. All that means is that the name of the library is stored along with the symbol. In the "flat namespace" model just the symbol was stored and the loader would search amongst various libraries for the symbol. That caused problems, for instance, if the `log()` function was defined in a math library and someone else defined a `log()` function to output text to a logfile. The math library function user might get the file logging function instead. The two level namespaces handle this case for you so that the two `log()` can coexist. You can sometimes run into difficulty when building code from other Unix platforms. Adding the flag `-flat_namespace` to the link lines can fix many problems.

To build a shared library, use `ld`, the linker, rather than `ar`. To build the little adder function shared library, use a command like

```
$ ld -dynamic -o libaddum.dylib *.o
```

And link it into your program like this:

```
$ cc -g -o useadd useadd.m libaddum.dylib
```

As an aside, you can specify a static library like this as well:

```
$ cc -g -o useadd useadd.m libaddum.a
```

and you can use the linker search paths with shared libraries:

```
$ cc -g -o useadd useadd.m -L. -laddum
```

The linker, when given a choice between a shared library and a static library will choose the shared library.

When you run the program, the loader searches for the shared libraries to load. It looks in a number of default places (like `/usr/lib`), and it also looks at the environment variable `LD_LIBRARY_PATH`. Any paths specified there (multiple paths can be separated by colons) are searched in order, looking for the library.

By convention on Mac OS X, shared libraries have an extension of `.dylib`, for Dynamic Library. On most other Unix systems, the extension is `.so`, for Shared Object, so do not be confused if you go to another system and see lots of `.so` files lying around.

`nm` can also be used to see what dynamic libraries an application links against by using `-mg` flags. In this case, nm is being run against a Cocoa application:

```
$ nm -mg BigShow
00000000 (absolute) external .objc_class_name_AppController
         (undefined [lazy bound]) external .objc_class_name_BigElement
(from BigShowBase)
         (undefined [lazy bound]) external .objc_class_name_NSArray (from
Cocoa)
         (undefined [lazy bound]) external .objc_class_name_NSBezierPath
(from Cocoa)
```

```
          (undefined [lazy bound]) external .objc_class_name_NSBundle (from
Cocoa)
          (undefined [lazy bound]) external .objc_class_name_NSColor (from
Cocoa)
...
          (undefined) external __objcInit (from Cocoa)
          (undefined [lazy bound]) external _abort (from libSystem)
          (undefined [lazy bound]) external _atexit (from libSystem)
          (undefined [lazy bound]) external _calloc (from libSystem)
...
00007008 (__DATA,__data) [referenced dynamically] external _environ
          (undefined) external _errno (from libSystem)
          (undefined [lazy bound]) external _exit (from libSystem)
          (undefined [lazy bound]) external _free (from libSystem)
          (undefined) external _mach_init_routine (from libSystem)
```

Which shows the symbols from Cocoa that are being used (**NSArray, NSBezierPath**, some of the standard C library symbols (**abort(), calloc()**), and some housekeeping calls (_objcInit).

Shared libraries can be loaded on demand after your program has started, and are the standard Unix way for building a plug-in architecture to your program.

If you want to see all the shared libraries a program pulls in, run the program from the command line and set the DYLD_PRINT_LIBRARIES environment variable to 1. You can use this to peek into a program and see how it does some stuff. For instance:

```
$ setenv DYLD_PRINT_LIBRARIES 1
$ /Applications/iTunes.app/Contents/MacOS/iTunes
loading libraries for image: /Applications/iTunes.app/
Contents/MacOS/iTunes
loading library: /usr/lib/libz.1.1.3.dylib
loading library: /usr/lib/libSystem.B.dylib
loading library: /System/Library/Frameworks/Carbon.framework/
Versions/A/Carbon
loading library: /System/Library/Frameworks/IOKit.framework/
Versions/A/IOKit
...
loading library: /System/Library/QuickTime/\
QuickTimeFirewireDV.component/Contents/MacOS/QuickTimeFirewireDV
loading libraries for image: /System/Library/QuickTime/\
QuickTimeFirewireDV.component/Contents/MacOS/QuickTimeFirewireDV
loading libraries for image: /System/Library/Extensions/\
IOUSBFamily.kext/Contents/PlugIns/IOUSBLib.bundle/Contents/MacOS/\
IOUSBLib
loading library:/System/Library/Frameworks/\
ApplicationServices.framework/Versions/A/Frameworks/\
CoreGraphics.framework/Resources/libCGATS.A.dylib
```

In all, a total of 136 libraries. It is pretty interesting some of the stuff in there, like Speech Synthesis, a cryptography library, and some of the private frameworks like iPod framework and DesktopServicesPriv.

Frameworks

Shared libraries are nice from a system implementation point of view, but straight shared libraries are a pretty inconvenient way to package and ship a complete product. When you are providing some kind of software library, like database access API, you will want to provide not only the shared library that has the executable code, but also the header files that describe the API provided, the documentation, and any additional resources like images or sounds. With plain old shared libraries (on plain old Unix), you will need to cook up your own packaging format, or use whatever platform specific delivery mechanisms (like RPMs on Red Hat Linux). Even then, the pieces of your product will probably get split up: libraries into `/usr/lib`, header files into `/usr/include`, etc.

NeXT came up with the framework idea to address these issues. Figure 3-4 shows a framework, which is a bundle that contains the shared library as well as subdirectories for headers and other resources.

Figure 3-4. A Framework

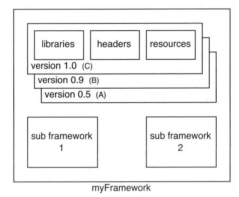

Since the framework has a somewhat complex internal structure (including a directory hierarchy for versions and a set of symbolic links to indicate which version is current) which is also being changed by Apple, it is best to just let `Xcode` do the work.

Building a framework in `Xcode`:

1. Launch `Xcode`
2. File > New Project
3. Framework > Cocoa Framework
4. Drag in your source files
5. If you wish, you can remove the Cocoa, Foundation, and AppKit frameworks from the External Frameworks and Libraries folder, since you will not need them.

Now make a header file for the adder functions:

Example 3-3. adder.h

```
// adder.h -- header file for the little adder functions we have

int add_0 (int number);
int add_1 (int number);
int add_2 (int number);
int add_3 (int number);
int add_4 (int number);
```

Since it is a public header file, you need to tell Xcode that this header is public so that it will be added to the Headers directory of the framework:

1. Launch Xcode

2. Drag in the header file

3. Build > Build

When you are done, the project window should look like Figure 3-5

Figure 3-5. Framework Source Files

Now to build the useadd program:

```
$ cc -g -o useadd -F./Adder/build  -framework Adder useadd.m
```

Note the use of -F to specify where the linker should search for the framework when linking. It works just like the -L flag for static and shared libraries. If you run it now, you will get an error, though:

```
dyld: ./useadd can't open library: /Users/markd/Library/Frameworks/
    Adder.framework/Versions/A/Adder (No such file or directory, errno = 2)
```

That is because the -F flag only affects compile time behavior (finding the framework so the linker can make sure all the symbols are there). At run time, if the framework is not embedded in the program's bundle, the system looks in these directories in this order:

1. `~/Library/Frameworks`

2. `/Library/Frameworks`

3. `/Network/Library/Frameworks`

4. `/System/Library/Frameworks`

So copy the `Adder.framework` into your `~/Library/Frameworks` (which you may need to manually create), and re-run the program:

```
$ ./useadd
i is 5
i after add_1: 6
i after add_4: 10
```

If you turn on `DYLD_PRINT_LIBRARIES`, you can see the program using the new framework:

```
$ setenv DYLD_PRINT_LIBRARIES 1
$ ./useadd
loading libraries for image: ./useadd
loading library: /Users/markd/Library/Frameworks/Adder.framework/
Versions/A/Adder
loading library: /usr/lib/libSystem.B.dylib
loading libraries for image: /Users/markd/Library/
Frameworks/Adder.framework/Versions/A/Adder
loading libraries for image: /usr/lib/libSystem.B.dylib
loading library: /usr/lib/system/libmathCommon.A.dylib
loading libraries for image: /usr/lib/system/libmathCommon.A.dylib
i is 5
i after add_1: 6
i after add_4: 10
```

You can see the framework being loaded in the beginning.

Framework Versioning

Frameworks include major and minor versioning so that you can update your library and not negatively impact the programs that use the framework. A major version change is one that breaks existing programs that end up usising the newer version, but are linked against an older version. This can happen when an API is removed, a function signature is changed, a method is added to a C++ class, or the size or layout of a class or structure is changed.

A minor version change is one where programs that use newer versions of the library will break when using an older version of the library. This can happen when an API or new structure is added. Older programs can continue to use this newer (minor) version of the library since stuff was only added and nothing removed, but programs that link against this newer version cannot be run against the older library since the new API or structure will not be there.

The inside of a framework is a hierarchy of directories and symbolic links. As shown in Figure 3-6, the top level is a directory named `Versions` which contains directories for each of the major versions. Traditionally they're named with letters, like A, B, C, but they can be any name. Inside of the `Versions` directory is a symbolic link, named `Current`, which points to the current version (which is usually the newest one, the one wih the highest letter).

Figure 3-6. Inside a framework.

At the top level of the framework are symbolic links to the shared library (without the `.dylib` extension), the `Headers` directory, and the `Resources` directory. These are actually symbolic links to `Current/Headers` and `Current/Resources`. This means that you can just change the `Current` symbolic link to another version and the other symbolic links will automatically point to that other version.

To create a new version directory in `Xcode`, set the `FRAMEWORK_VERSION` setting of the framework target in Project > Edit Active Build Style, as shown in Figure 3-7 When you build the project a new version directory will be added to the framework. This won't update the `Current` symbolic link, though. One thing to watch out for if you end up supporting multiple versions of the framework is to not do a "Clean all;" that will wipe out the older versions, and `Xcode` will only rebuild the most current version. Or else keep older versions of the framework's guts elsewhere so you can construct the framework for new versions.

Figure 3-7. Setting framework major version

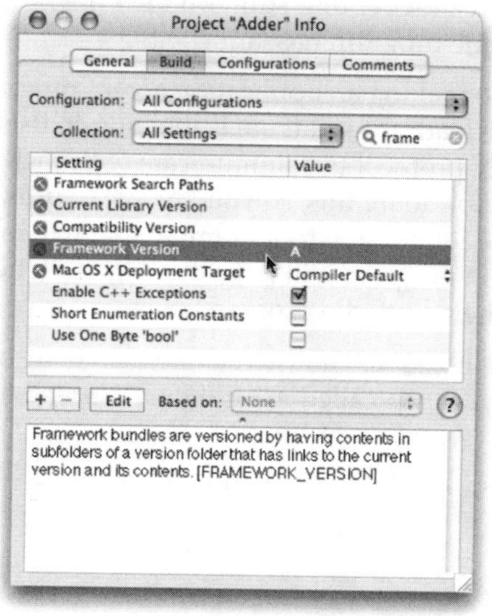

When you link against a framework, the linker will link against the `Current` version. If you want to link against an older version of a framework, you'll need to change the `Current` symbolic link to point to the version you want to link against. At runtime, the loader will choose the correct version of the library. You can see what versions of libraries a program links against by using `otool -Lv`. Here you can see that `iPhoto` links againt the B version of `libSystem`, and uses the A version of the Cocoa frameworks.

```
$ otool -Lv /Applications/iPhoto.app/Contents/MacOS/iPhoto
/Applications/iPhoto.app/Contents/MacOS/iPhoto:
    /usr/lib/libSystem.B.dylib
            (compatibility version 1.0.0, current version 55.0.0)
    time stamp 1039863485 Sat Dec 14 05:58:05 2002
    /System/Library/Frameworks/Cocoa.framework/Versions/A/Cocoa
            (compatibility version 1.0.0, current version 7.0.0)
    time stamp 1045684082 Wed Feb 19 14:48:02 2003
    . . .
```

Writing Plug-ins

Shared libraries can be loaded on demand after the program has started running. They are the mechanism used to add plug-in features: build a shared library and have the program load it. Generic Unix applications can use the `dyld` functions to load shared libraries and get the addresses of symbols (including function pointers to executable code). Higher-level applications can load bundles at runtime. Cocoa can use the **NSBundle** class, and there are Carbon and Core Foundation bundle loading APIs as well.

Bundles in Cocoa

A bundle is a directory containing some executable code (whether it is a shared library or an executable program) and the various resources that support the code. Cocoa applications are bundles, as are frameworks, screensavers, `Interface Builder` plug-ins, and a lot of other stuff. Bundles are how Cocoa handles plug-ins that are loaded after the program has launched.

There are two sides to making an application accept plug-ins, namely there is the application doing the loading, and there is the plug-in itself. They both need to agree on some kind of protocol to communicate with each other. There is not any pre-defined protocol for doing this, so you are free to use whatever mechanism you care to. Here is a little foundation tool example that will load plug-ins that return a string, which the main program will print out. Once all the plug-ins have had a chance to print out their stuff, the program exits.

Create three projects in `Xcode`. First, a `Foundation Tool` called `BundlePrinter`. Then create a `Cocoa Bundle` called `SimpleMessage`, and a `Cocoa Bundle` called `ComplexMessage`.

Add a header file to `BundlePrinter` that looks like this:

Example 3-4. BundlePrinter.h

```
// BundlePrinter.h -- protocol for BundlePrinter plugins to use

@protocol BundlePrinterProtocol

+ (BOOL)activate;
+ (void)deactivate;

- (NSString *)message;

@end
```

A very simple protocol. The class is given an opportunity to do stuff when activated and deactivated (perhaps it needs to create and destroy a big image or load an mp3 file), and then an object method for getting a string message to print.

Add this header file to the two bundle projects. Now go ahead and implement the plug-ins to conform to this protocol. Add a `SimpleMessage.m` file to the `SimpleMessage` project. Also set the `Principal Class` for the project to `SimpleMessage` (go to the Targets pane, select `SimpleMessage` target, select the `Cocoa-Specific` entry under `Info.plist Entries`, and put in `SimpleMessage` for the `Principal Class`).

Here is what `SimpleMessage.m` looks like:

Example 3-5. SimpleMessage.m

```
// SimpleMessage.m -- a simple plug-in that returns a simple,
//                    hard-coded message

#import <Foundation/Foundation.h>
#import "BundlePrinter.h"

@interface SimpleMessage : NSObject <BundlePrinterProtocol>
{
}

@end


@implementation SimpleMessage

+ (BOOL)activate
{
    NSLog (@"SimpleMessage plug-in activated");
    return (YES);

} // activate

+ (void)deactivate
{
    NSLog (@"SimpleMessage plug-in deactivated");
} // deactivate

- (NSString *)message
{
```

```
          return (@"This is a Simple Message");
} // message

@end // SimpleMessage
```

Build it and fix any errors.

Do the same thing for ComplexMessage (set the ComplexMessage **Principal class**, and add the ComplexMessage.m **source file**).

Example 3-6. ComplexMessage.m

```
// ComplexMessage -- a plug-in that returns a message
//                    using some stored state

#import <Foundation/Foundation.h>
#import "BundlePrinter.h"
#import <stdlib.h>        // for random number routines
#import <time.h>          // for time() to seed the random generator

@interface ComplexMessage : NSObject <BundlePrinterProtocol>
{
    int randomValue;
}

@end


@implementation ComplexMessage

+ (BOOL)activate
{
    NSLog (@"ComplexMessage plug-in activated");
    return (YES);

} // activate

+ (void)deactivate
{
    NSLog (@"ComplexMessage plug-in deactivated");
} // deactivate

- (id)init
{
    if (self = [super init]) {
        srandom (time(NULL));
        randomValue = random () % 500;
    }

    return (self);

} // init

- (NSString *)message
{
    return ([NSString stringWithFormat:
              @"Here is a random number: %d", randomValue]);
```

```
} // messagee

@end // ComplexMessage
```

This is more complex in that it stores some state at initialization time and uses it later.

Build this and fix any errors.

Now, in the `BundlePrinter` project, edit `main.m` so that it looks like this:

Example 3-7. main.m

```
// main.m -- the main BundlePrinter program

#import <Foundation/Foundation.h>
#import "BundlePrinter.h"

NSString *processPlugin (NSString *path)
{
    NSBundle *plugin;
    Class principalClass;
    id pluginInstance;
    NSString *message = nil;

    NSLog (@"processing plug-in: %@", path);

    plugin = [NSBundle bundleWithPath:path];

    if (plugin == nil) {
        NSLog (@"could not load plug-in at path %@", path);
        goto bailout;
    }

    principalClass = [plugin principalClass];

    if (principalClass == nil) {
        NSLog (@"could not load principal class for plug-in at path %@",
                path);
        NSLog (@"make sure the PrincipalClass target setting is correct");
        goto bailout;
    }

    if (![principalClass conformsToProtocol:
            @protocol(BundlePrinterProtocol)]) {
        NSLog (@"plug-in must conform the BundlePrinterProtocol");
    }

    // tell the plug-in that it's being activated
    if (![principalClass activate]) {
        NSLog (@"could not activate class for plug-in at path %@",
                path);
        goto bailout;
    }

    // make an instance of the plug-in and ask it for a message
    pluginInstance = [[principalClass alloc] init];
```

```
    message = [pluginInstance message];
    [pluginInstance release];

    // ok, we're done with it
    [principalClass deactivate];

 bailout:

    return (message);

} // processPlugin

int main (int argc, const char *argv[])
{
    NSAutoreleasePool *pool = [[NSAutoreleasePool alloc] init];
    NSDirectoryEnumerator *enumerator;
    NSString *path, *message;

    // walk the current directory looking for bundles

    enumerator = [[NSFileManager defaultManager] enumeratorAtPath:@"."];

    while (path = [enumerator nextObject]) {

        if ([[path pathExtension] isEqualToString:@"bundle"]) {
            message = processPlugin (path);

            if (message != nil) { // plugin succeeded
                printf ("\nmessage is: '%s'\n\n", [message cString]);
            }
        }
    }

    [pool release];

    return (0);

} // main
```

main () looks in the directory you invoke the program from searching for entries
that end in ".bundle." If it finds one, it attemps to load it and invoke methods on
the class it finds there.

Here is a sample run, after copying (or symlinking) the SimpleMessage and
ComplexMessage bundles into a directory and run the program. In this case copy
them to the BundlePrinter project directory.

```
    $ build/BundlePrinter
    ... BundlePrinter[4458] processing plug-in: ComplexMessage.bundle
    ... BundlePrinter[4458] ComplexMessage plug-in activated
    ... BundlePrinter[4458] ComplexMessage plug-in deactivated

    message is: 'Here is a random number: 198'

    ... BundlePrinter[4458] processing plug-in: SimpleMessage.bundle
    ... BundlePrinter[4458] SimpleMessage plug-in loaded
    ... BundlePrinter[4458] SimpleMessage plug-in unloaded
```

```
message is: 'This is a Simple Message'
```

There are a couple of limitations that are glossed over here. One is that you cannot load the same bundle twice. You will get a message from the Objective-C runtime about duplicate classes. The other is you cannot unload an Objective-C bundle. The Objective-C runtime gets its claws into the shared library and refuses to let go.

Bundles With Dylib

If you do not want to use (or cannot use) **NSBundle** for loading plug-ins, you can load a special kind of shared library (also called a bundle, but it is different from the collection of files in a directory meaning) documented in the **NSModule** manpage. (Even though these calls have the NS prefix, they are not part of the Cocoa framework.)

The various calls to load plug-ins take some flag arguments to tell it how to handle error conditions. It can either print a message to stderr and exit (which is the default), or you can provide some callback functions to try to resolve the problem. Sometimes you can have the call return an error code and use **NSLinkEditError** to get the specifics.

You build a bundle with cc by giving it the -bundle flag:

```
$ cc -g -o simplemessage.msg -bundle simplemessage.m
```

(.msg is a suffix just pulled out of the air for this sample.)

Then in the program you wish to load the bundle into, you create an NSObjectFileImage using **NSCreateObjectFileImageFromFile** giving it the path to the shared library. Then **NSLinkModule** to actually have the loader pull in the shared library. **NSLookupSymbolInImage** is used to find the symbol, and then **NSAddressOfSymbol** is used to (finally!) get the address of the symbol.

Here is the same program (printing out messages) but done using shared libraries.

First the plug-ins themselves:

Example 3-8. simplemessage.m

```
// simplemessage.m -- return a malloc'd block of memory to a
//                    simple message

/* compile with:
cc -g -Wall -o simplemessage.msg -bundle simplemessage.m
*/

#import <string.h>      // for strdup
#import <stdio.h>       // for printf

int BNRMessageActivate (void)
{
    printf ("simple message activate\n");
    return (1);
} // BNRMessageActivate

void BNRMessageDeactivate (void)
```

```
{
    printf ("simple message deactivate\n");
} // BNRMessageDeactivate

char *BNRMessageMessage (void)
{
    return (strdup("This is a simple message"));
} // BNRMessageMessage
```

Example 3-9. complexmessage.m

```
// complexmessage.m -- return a malloc'd block of memory
//                     to a complex message

/* compile with:
cc -g -Wall -o complexmessage.msg -bundle complexmessage.m
*/

#import <stdlib.h>      // for random number routines
#import <time.h>        // for time() to seed the random generator
#import <stdio.h>       // for printf
#import <string.h>      // for strdup, and snprintf

static int g_randomValue;

int BNRMessageActivate (void)
{
    printf ("complex message activate\n");

    srandom (time(NULL));
    g_randomValue = random () % 500;

    return (1);

} // BNRMessageActivate

void BNRMessageDeactivate (void)
{
    printf ("complex message deactivate\n");
} // BNRMessageDeactivate

char *BNRMessageMessage (void)
{
    char buffer[2048];

    snprintf (buffer, 2048, "Here is a random number: %d", g_randomValue);

    return (strdup(buffer));

} // BNRMessageMessage
```

And finally the program to load these plug-ins:

Example 3-10. bundleprinter.m

```
// bundleprinter.m -- dynamically load some plugins and invoke functions
//                    on them

/* compile with:
cc -g -Wall -o bundleprinter bundleprinter.m
*/

#import <mach-o/dyld.h> // for dynamic loading API
#import <sys/types.h>   // for random type definition
#import <sys/dirent.h>  // for struct dirent
#import <dirent.h>      // for opendir and friends
#import <stdlib.h>      // for EXIT_SUCCESS
#import <stdio.h>       // for printf
#import <errno.h>       // for errno/strerror
#import <string.h>      // for strdup

// we need a type to coerce a void pointer to the function pointer we
// need to jump through.  Having a type makes things a bit easier
// to read

typedef int (*BNRMessageActivateFP) (void);
typedef void (*BNRMessageDeactivateFP) (void);
typedef char * (*BNRMessageMessageFP) (void);

// given a module and a symbol, look it up and return the address
// NULL returned if the symbol couldn't be found

void *addressOfSymbol (NSModule *module, const char *symbolName)
{
    NSSymbol    symbol;
    void        *address = NULL;

    symbol = NSLookupSymbolInModule (module, symbolName);

    if (symbol == NULL) {
        fprintf (stderr, "Could not find symbol\n");
        goto bailout;
    }

    address = NSAddressOfSymbol (symbol);

  bailout:
    return (address);

} // addressOfSymbol

// given a path to a plugin, load it, activate it, get the message,
// deactivate it, and unload it

char *processPlugin (const char *path)
{
    NSObjectFileImage    image;
    NSObjectFileImageReturnCode status;
    NSModule    module = NULL;
    char *message = NULL;
```

```
    status = NSCreateObjectFileImageFromFile (path, &image);

    if (status != NSObjectFileImageSuccess) {
        fprintf (stderr, "couldn't load plugin %s. Error = %d\n",
                path, status);
        goto bailout;
    }

    // this will abort the program if an error happens.
    // which we don't want.
    // _OPTION_PRIVATE is necessary so we can use NSLookupSymbolInModule
    // _RETURN_ON_ERROR is so we don't abort the program if a module
    //                  happens to have a problem loading (say undefined
    //                  symbols)

    module = NSLinkModule (image, path,
                        NSLINKMODULE_OPTION_PRIVATE
                        | NSLINKMODULE_OPTION_RETURN_ON_ERROR);

    if (module == NULL) {
        fprintf (stderr, "couldn't load module from plug-in at path %s.",
                path);
        goto bailout;
    }

    // ok, we have the module loaded.  Look up the symbols and call them
    // if they exist.
    {
        BNRMessageActivateFP activator;
        BNRMessageDeactivateFP deactivator;
        BNRMessageMessageFP messagator;

        activator = addressOfSymbol (module, "_BNRMessageActivate");
        if (activator != NULL) {
            int result = (activator)();
            if (!result) { // the module didn't consider itself loaded
                goto bailout;
            }
        }

        messagator = addressOfSymbol (module, "_BNRMessageMessage");
        if (messagator != NULL) {
            message = (messagator)();
        }

        deactivator = addressOfSymbol (module, "_BNRMessageDeactivate");
        if (deactivator != NULL) {
            (deactivator)();
        }
    }

bailout:

    // clean up no matter what
    if (module != NULL) {
        (void) NSUnLinkModule (module, 0);
```

```
    }

    // couldn't find a cleanup counterpart to
    // NSCreateObjectFileImageFromFile

    return (message);

} // processPlugin

int main (int argc, char *argv[])
{
    DIR *directory;
    struct dirent *entry;

    // walk through the current directory

    directory = opendir (".");

    if (directory == NULL) {
        fprintf (stderr,
            "could not open current directory to look for plugins\n");
        fprintf (stderr, "error: %d (%s)\n", errno, strerror(errno));
        exit (EXIT_FAILURE);
    }

    while ( (entry = readdir(directory)) != NULL) {

        // if this is a file of type .msg (an extension made up for this
        // sample), process it like a plug-in

        if (strstr(entry->d_name, ".msg") != NULL) {
            char *message;
            message = processPlugin (entry->d_name);

            printf ("\nmessage is: '%s'\n\n", message);
            if (message != NULL) {
                free (message);
            }
        }
    }

    closedir (directory);

    return (EXIT_SUCCESS);

} // main
```

Shared Libraries and dlopen

Mac OS X has been somewhat unique with its API for manually loading bundles and shared libraries, using the the dyld API (NSCreateObjectFileImageFromFile() and friends). Most other unix platforms have a much simpler API, consisting of dlopen(), dlsym(), dlclose(), and dlerror(). The "dl" prefix is for "Dynamic Library". Mac OS X 10.3 had a compatibility library that provided these calls, and 10.4 they are a native API.

dlopen()

dlopen() is used to open a shared library or a bundle at a given path:

```
void* dlopen (const char* path, int mode);
```

dlopen() opens the library and resolves any symbols it contains. It returns an opaque handle to the library which can be used in subsequent calls, or it returns NULL if the library could not be opened. The function dlerror() returns a string describing the error.

The path can be a full path or a relative path. If the path is just a leaf name (having no slash in the path, just a library name), dlopen() uses this algorithm to find the library:

1. The LD_LIBRARY_PATH environment variable (a colon-separated list of directories) is consulted, and the directories searched (in order) to find the library

2. If the DYLD_LIBRARY_PATH environment variable is set, those directories are searched for the leaf

3. If the DYLD_FALLBACK_LIBRARY_PATH environemnt variable is set, those directories are searched. If this environment variable is not set, $HOME/lib, /usr/local/lib, and then /usr/lib are searched

4. Finally the path is treated like a regular path

Because Mac OS X has fat binary files, there are no separate 32-bit and 64-bit search paths.

The mode parameter can take one of two options, which control the binding of external functions. (external as in functions not defined in the shared library that was just loaded):

RTLD_NOW

Each external function is bound immediately. You can use this flag to make sure that any undefined symbols are discovered at load-time.

RTLD_LAZY

Each external function is bound the first time it is called. You will usually use this form because it is more efficient, by not needing to bind functions that might never be called.

RTLD_GLOBAL

This is an optional bitwise-OR-in flag. Symbols exported from the loaded library will be available to any other libraries that are loaded, in addition to being available through calls to dlsym(). This is the default behavior.

RTLD_LOCAL

This is also an optional bitwise-OR-in flag. Symbols exported from the loaded library are generally hidden and only available to dlsym() when using the module handle for this library.

dlsym()

Once you have a module handle from dlopen(), you can use dlsym() to get the address of code or data at the location specified by a given symbol.

```
void* dlsym (void *module, const char *symbol);
```

module is a module pointer returned by dlopen(). Unlike the dyld family of calls, you do not prepend the symbol with an underscore. If the symbol cannot be found, dlsym() returns NULL and you can query dlerror() to see what the problem was.

There are two constants you can give to dlsym() instead of a module handle: RTLD_DEFAULT to search through every Mach-O image in the process in the order they were loaded. This can be an expensive operation since it will have to slog through all of the system frameworks. You can also use RTLD_NEXT to search for the symbol in any Mach-O images that were loaded after the one calling dlsym(). So, if you call dlsym() in your main program using RTLD_NEXT, it will look in any libraries loaded after your program started running.

BundleLoader Revisited

Example 3-11 has taken the processPlugin() function from bundleprinter.m from the Libraries chapter, but it has been ported to use dlopen() rather than the dylib calls. As you can see, it is a good deal shorter and simpler than the dylib version. The rest of the program (and the plugins) is unchanged from Chapter 5 in the book.

Example 3-11. processPlugin() from bundleprinter-dl.m

```
// bundleprinter-dl.m -- dynamically load some plugins and invoke
//                       functions on them, using the dlopen()
//                       family of calls

/* compile with
cc -g -o bundleprinter-dl bundleprinter-dl.m
*/

#import <dlfcn.h> // for dlopen() and friends

...

char *processPlugin (const char *path)
{
    char *message = NULL;

    void *module;
    module = dlopen (path, RTLD_LAZY);

    if (module == NULL) {
        fprintf (stderr,
                 "couldn't load plugin at path %s.  error is %s\n",
                 path, dlerror());
        goto bailout;
    }

    BNRMessageActivateFP activator;
    BNRMessageDeactivateFP deactivator;
```

```
    BNRMessageMessageFP messagator;

    activator = dlsym (module, "BNRMessageActivate");
    deactivator = dlsym (module, "BNRMessageDeactivate");
    messagator = dlsym (module, "BNRMessageMessage");

    if (activator == NULL || deactivator == NULL
        || messagator == NULL) {
        fprintf (stderr,
                "could not find BNRMessage* symbol (%p %p %p)\n",
                activator, deactivator, messagator);
        goto bailout;
    }

    int result;
    result = (activator)();
    if (!result) { // the module didn't consider itself loaded
        goto bailout;
    }

    message = (messagator)();

    (deactivator)();

  bailout:

    if (module != NULL) {
  result = (dlclose (module));
        if (result != 0) {
            fprintf (stderr, "could not dlclose %s.  Error is %s\n",
                    path, dlerror());
        }
    }

    return (message);

} // processPlugin
```

And the run is the same as the dylib version's output:

```
$ ./bundleprinter-dl
complex message activate
complex message deactivate

message is: 'Here is a random number: 230'

simple message activate
simple message deactivate

message is: 'This is a simple message'
```

Embedding Frameworks in Applications

Frameworks are wonderful mechanisms for packaging libraries, header files, and other resources. It is common for a development shop (even a single person) to have a handy collection of utility classes and functions that get used in a number of different programs. You can put all of that common code into a framework, and then embed that framework into your applications. This keeps the common code in one place (the framework) rather than having multiple copies in all the different projects, getting out of sync with each other.

The technique provided here of creating embeddable frameworks with Xcode, as well as automatic cross-project dependency management, is courtesy of Jonathan "Wolf" Rentzch. Wolf has a quicktime movie at http://rentzsch.com/cocoa/embeddedFrameworks which walks through this procedure interactively.

Creating the Framework

The first step in the process is creating the framework. We will use a framework called SimpleFramework, which has a single class providing a single method. Use Xcode to create a new project, a new Cocoa Framework, as shown in Figure 3-8. Give it the name "SimpleFramework" as shown in Figure 3-9

Figure 3-8. Create a new Cocoa Framework

Figure 3-9. Name the new Cocoa Framework

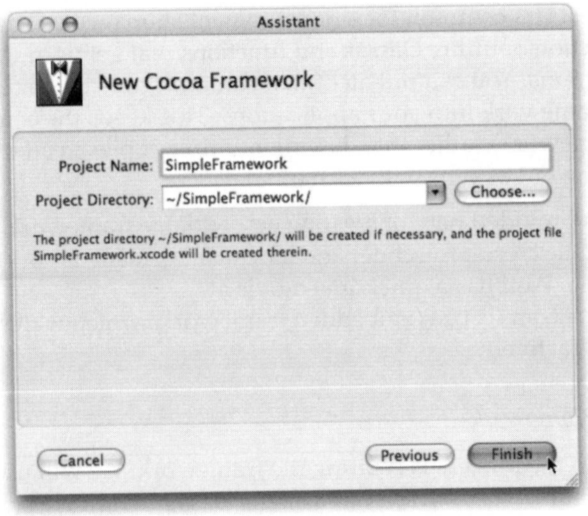

Add a class to the framework called Stuff. The Stuff.h header file should look like Example 3-12 and the Stuff.m implementation file should look like Example 3-13

Example 3-12. Stuff.h

```
// Stuff.h -- interface to a minimal class for the SimpleFramework

#import <Cocoa/Cocoa.h>

@interface Stuff : NSObject
{
}

+ (void) doStuff;

@end // Stuff
```

Example 3-13. Stuff.m

```
// Stuff.m -- implementation of a minimal class for the SimpleFramework

#import "Stuff.h"

@implementation Stuff

+ (void) doStuff
{
    NSLog (@"doing stuff.");
} // doStuff

@end // Stuff
```

The next step is to make the header file for the framework public. Select the SimpleFramework target in the Targets portion of the Xcode Groups & Files pane, and change the Stuff.h Role to be "public", as shown in Figure 3-10. Headers marked as public will be copied into the Headers directory of the framework. Header files that are private to the framework should be left untouched.

Figure 3-10. Make the Framework Header Public

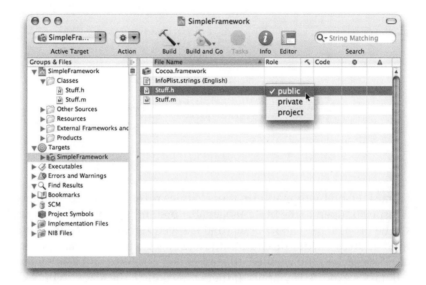

Next comes the magic. Select the SimpleFramework target again in the Targets portion of the Xcode Groups & Files pane, and open the inspector. It is very important that you perform the next steps on the *target*, not the top-level project. There are similar settings there, but they will break when you use the cross-project dependency trick shown later. Select the Build tab of the inspector, and edit the Installation Directory setting to be `@executable_path/../Frameworks`.

Mach-O dynamic libraries have the path where they live hard-coded into them. This is OK for libraries that will be living in /System/Library/Frameworks, but it will not work for a library that lives in an Application that can be moved around at the user's whim. The `@executable_path` refers to the path to the application's executable. This can change from run to run of the program. `/../` backs you up out of the directory in the application bundle that contains the program's executable, and `Frameworks` is the directory where the application will copy its Frameworks.

Yes, the framework will have to know where the application will be wanting to put its frameworks. Another way to think of it is that the application can only put the framework where the framework wants to go. This is shown in Figure 3-11.

Figure 3-11. Set the Framework Installation Directory

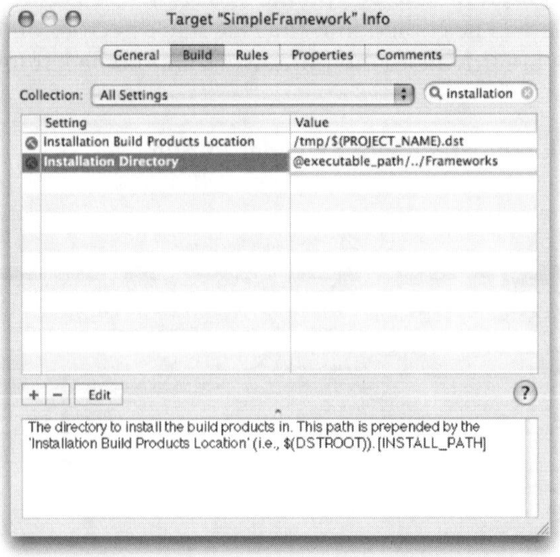

Next comes the prebinding information. While you still have the SimpleFramework target inspector open to the build tab, enable prebinding and set the Other Linker Flags to be `-seg1addr 0xc0000000` (that is seven zeros). -seg1addr specifies the preferred address in your program's address space where the framework should be loaded. With prebinding enabled, the linker will go ahead and resolve the addresses of the library's exported symbols. If there is a conflict, the loader will re-do that resolution. If you can get that work done at link-time, you will save a little bit of launch time.

Unfortunately, if -seg1addr is not specified, it defaults to NULL, which tells the loader to resolve the exported symbols every time. Apple recommends that third-party libraries use prebinding addresses starting with 0xc0000000, which is what is shown in Figure 3-12

Figure 3-12. Set the Framework Prebinding Information

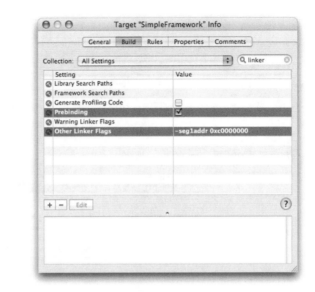

Now build the framework. You should have a SimpleFramework.framework in the build directory.

Creating the Application

Now it is time to make the application that will use (and embed) SimpleFramework. Make a new Cocoa application and call it SimpleApplication. Drag the SimpleFramework.framework bundle from the Finder into the Linked Frameworks folder into the Xcode Groups & Files pane.

Write the code that uses the framework. Example 3-14 shows main.m with the inclusion of the Stuff.h header file (notice the name of the framework in the path to the header), and the use of the doStuff method.

Example 3-14. main.m

```
#import <Cocoa/Cocoa.h>
#import <SimpleFramework/Stuff.h>

int main (int argc, char *argv[])
{
    [Stuff doStuff];

    return (NSApplicationMain(argc,  (const char **) argv));

} // main
```

The next step is to make a copy files phase. After your program has finished compiling and linking, the copy files phase will make a copy of the framework and put it into the application bundle. Select the SimpleApplication target, and bring up the contextual menu to add a New Copy Files Build Phase, as shown in Figure 3-13. This will add a new gray square underneath the SimpleApplication target.

Figure 3-13. Add a Copy Files Build Phase

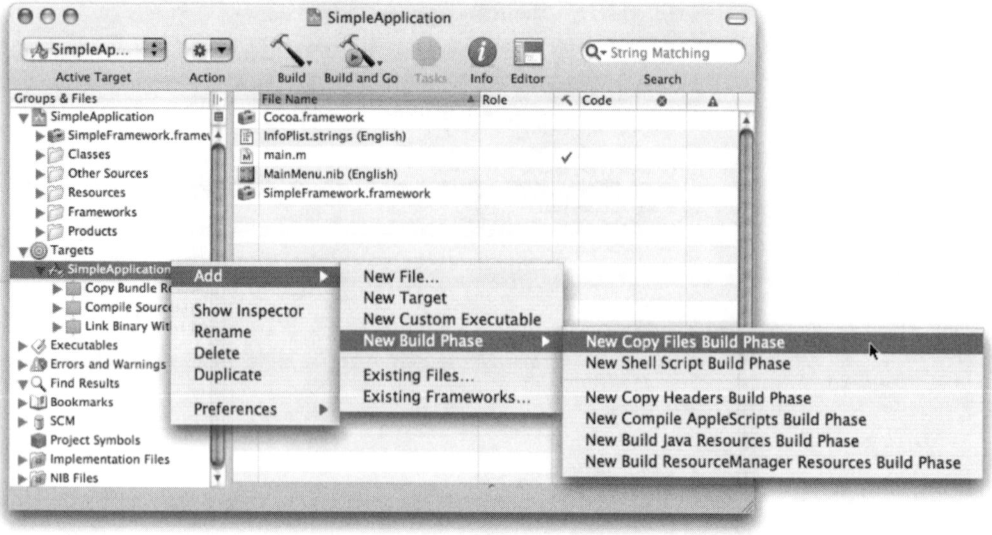

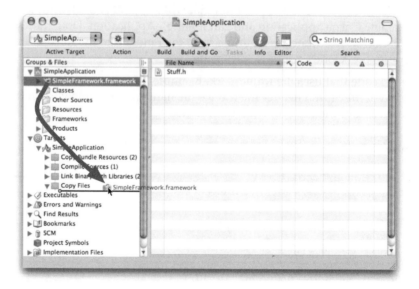

Drag SimpleFramework.framework into the copy phase, as shown in Figure 3-14.

Figure 3-14. Drag SimpleFramework Into the Copy Phase

Finally, tell the copy phase where to put its files. Each copy phase can put the files it copies into one directory. If you want to copy files into different directories into the application bundle (such as the executables directory if you have helper apps), you need to add a new copy phase. Select the Copy Files phase and open its inspector, which looks like Figure 3-15. Choose "Frameworks" from the pop-up menu.

Figure 3-15. Copy Files to the Frameworks Directory

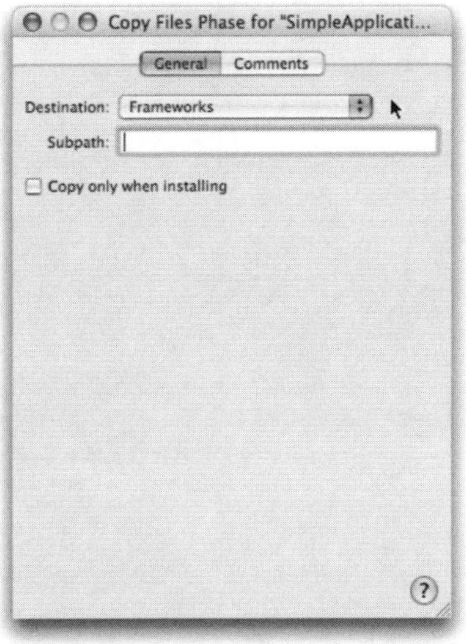

Now build the application. If you look in the application's bundle, you will see Frameworks living inside of the Contents directory:

```
$ ls build/SimpleApplication.app/Contents/Frameworks/
SimpleFramework.framework/
```

When you run the program, you will see this in your console:

```
2005-05-23 23:42:22.471 SimpleApplication[29538] doing stuff.
```

There is one piece of mop-up left to do. The frameworks that get copied into the application bundle still have their header files intact. That means anyone with the gumption to dig into your application bundle can see your headers, which may contain trade secrets, or an #ifdef HORRID_HACK macro you do not want the world to see.

To fix this, add a Shell Script Build Phase to the SimpleApplication target. You add it just like adding a copy files phase (as shown in Figure 3-13), but select the shell script build phase menu item. Select the new script phase and open the inspector and add the script to the Script box as shown in Figure 3-16. The script itself is

```
find $BUILD_ROOT/$CONFIGURATION/$WRAPPER_NAME -name '*.h' -exec rm {} \;
```

Figure 3-16. Script to Remove Header Files from the Application Bundle

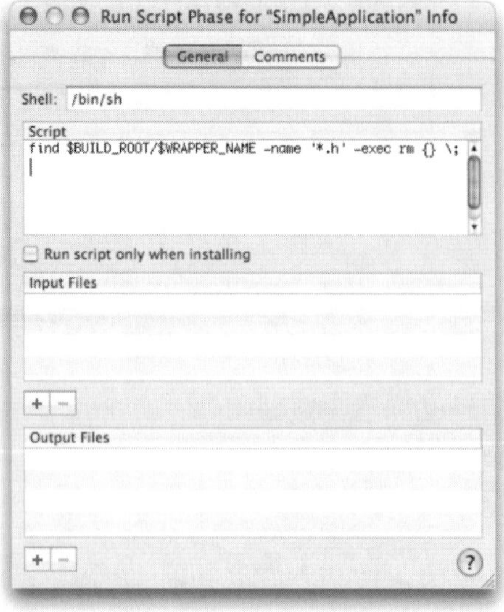

Cross-Project Dependencies

If you change a file in the framework, you will need to rebuild the framework so that the application can pick up the change. That can be inconvenient if you have a lot of frameworks, or if you are making changes to both the application and framework at the same time. You can set up dependencies in Xcode so that the framework will get built (if needed) when you build your application.

The first step is to get the framework project into the application project. You can drag the project file from the Finder, or you can drag the framework project's proxy icon, as shown in Figure 3-17.

Figure 3-17. Dragging the Framework Project's Proxy Icon

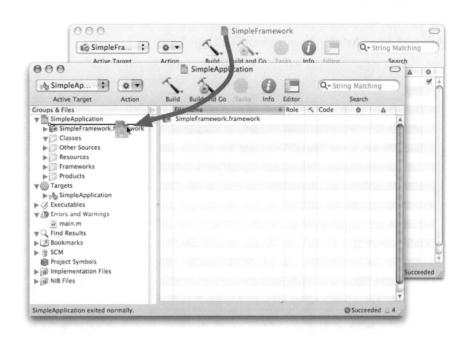

Once the framework project file is in your application project, it is time to establish the dependency. Select the SimpleApplication target and open its inspector. Select the General tab. It should look like Figure 3-18. Click the Plus button at the bottom of the inspector.

Figure 3-18. Start Adding the Framework Depedency

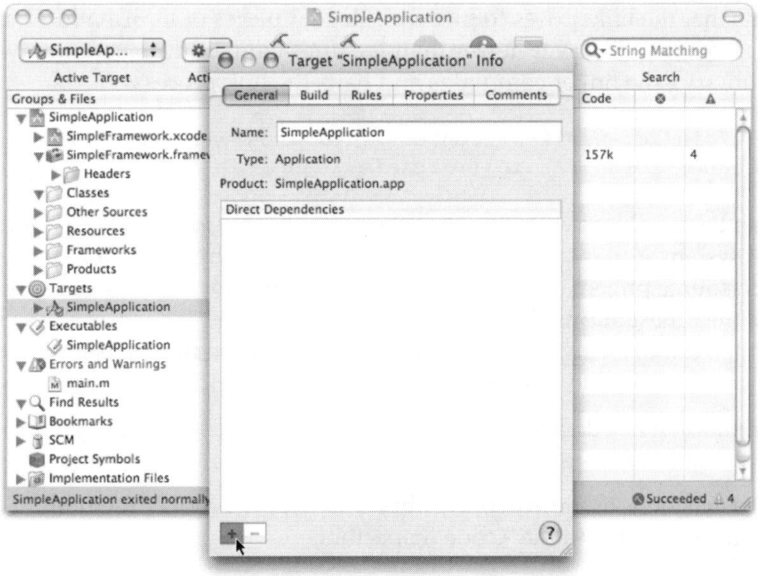

A sheet will drop down, showing the different items you can make the application depedent upon. Select SimpleFramework and add it, as shown in Figure 3-19.

Figure 3-19. Start Adding the Framework Depedency

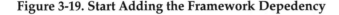

You can now edit Stuff.m, kick off a build from SimpleApplication, and the SimpleFramework will be rebuilt automatically.

ranlib and Source Code Management

The ranlib command takes the contents of a static library and creates a table of contents that the linker uses to find the relevant pieces of information it needs. If the timestamp of the library is newer than the timestamp of the last ranlib (which stored in the library), the linker complains and halts the link process:

```
/usr/bin/ld: table of contents for archive: ./libthing.a is out of
    date; rerun ranlib(1) (can't load from it)
```

This can be a problem when you have a static library stored in your source code control system. You may have a library from a commercial vendor, or acquired from an open source project. When you check the library out of your source code control system the timestamp will be wrong as far as the linker is concerned. So you have to run ranlib. ranlib changes the file, so your SCM system thinks its modified and wants you to check in your changes. That is a pretty vicious cycle to get into.

Eric Friendman has developed a technique to solve this problem. The solution is to copy any static libraries into the build area and run ranlib and link to them there.

These instructions assume that the library lives at the root of the project, so no path qualifiers are needed in the Xcode inspectors.

First, add a new shell script phase to the application target in the same way it was added in the previous section. Make sure the Run Script phase happens before the Link Binary WIth Library phase.

The second step is to list the input files, which will be fed to the script, and list the output files, which is what will be used by Xcode for further processing. The script will take the libraries listed in the input files and do its work of copying and ranlibbing. The script does not return anything (outside of a zero/one success result), but Xcode uses the file names listed in the script phase inspector.

Figure 3-20 shows the inspector for the script phase. It will take the file named libthing.a and do the copy and ranlib. After the script phase, Xcode will use the file $(TARGET_TEMP_DIR)/libthing.a for linking. Xcode will do proper dependency analysis: if the original library has not changed, it will not run the script.

Figure 3-20. Script Phase For Copy and Ranlib

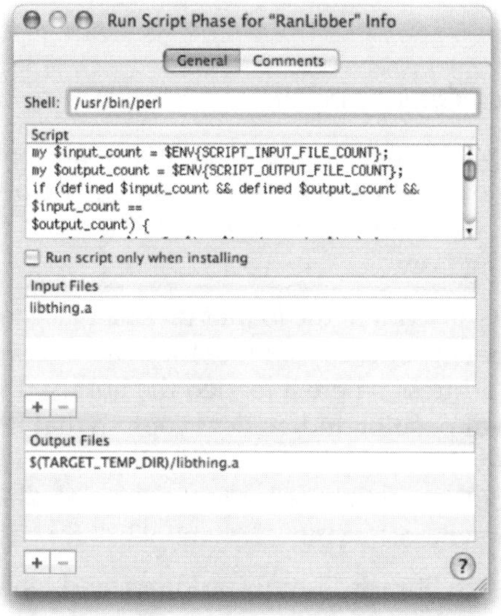

Now for the script itself. This is a perl script, so make sure that /usr/bin/perl is in the Shell textfield, and enter the script shown in Example 3-15

Example 3-15. Shell Phase Copy/Ranlib Perl Script

```
# get the number of entries listed in the input and output file panes
my $input_count = $ENV{SCRIPT_INPUT_FILE_COUNT};
my $output_count = $ENV{SCRIPT_OUTPUT_FILE_COUNT};

# make sure the values are sane.  The number of input and output
# files should match
if (defined $input_count && defined $output_count
    && $input_count == $output_count) {

    # for each file in the list of input and output files,
    # copy from the input (src) to the output (dest)
    # and ranlib it
```

```
    for (my $i = 0; $i < $input_count; $i++) {

        my $src = $ENV{"SCRIPT_INPUT_FILE_$i"};
        my $dest = $ENV{"SCRIPT_OUTPUT_FILE_$i"};

        system ('/bin/cp', $src, $dest);
        system ('/usr/bin/ranlib', $dest);
    }

    # successful run
    exit 0;

} else {
    # otherwise there was a user configuration error
    print STDERR "Input/output count either undefined or not equal";
    exit 1;
}
```

For The More Curious: Optimizing the system

You have seen the Apple installers spend an inordinate amount of time "Optimizing your system." What exactly is it doing? It is running the program update_prebinding which performs some modifications to shared libraries to make program loading faster.

When a shared library is loaded, the loader picks a place in memory to stick the code. It then calculates the address of all of the symbols exported by the shared library based on the address where it loaded the library (this is also why libraries need to be made out of position indepedent code so that they can be placed at any address). If you have a lot of libraries, or really big libraries, this can take a non-trivial amount of time as the loader chugs through "load at address xyz, calculate address for symbol1, symbol2, symbol3..." for each library.

Prebinding assigns each library a unique address, and when the library is loaded, the system attempts to place the library there. The calculations of symbol addresses can be done just once during the prebinding step and stored in the shared library. Then the loader just has to load the library at the indicated address and the symbols will already have their correct address without any additional work. If there happens to be a conflict (like someone else got loaded at that address), the loader falls back to its default behavior and loads the library at another address and mops up the symbols.

The only thing that gets sped up by this prebinding is application launch times. That is why it is usually OK to interrupt the optimization step, especially if you are doing a lot of individual installs.

Challenge

Take the Cocoa plug-in example and include it in a GUI program, putting the plug-in name and the message into an **NSTableView**.

Chapter 4. Command Line Programs

Much of the power that Unix brings to the user is in the command line tools, where the user can set up pipelines of independent programs that manipulate data. It is time to take a peek under the hood of a typical command line tool and see how it works, as many of the concepts (handling arguments, checking the environment, handling command line flags) have application to any Unix program. Here you are going to write a program that filters its input by changing any letters it finds to upper or lower case.

Figure 4-1 shows a typical command-line program, along with its three communication streams. The standard-in stream (also called "stdin") supplies data to the program. You read the data you are to process from standard-in. Once you run out of data, you are done. After you process the data, write new data to the standard-out stream (also called "stdout"). If you need to report any errors, or report some information that is not directly related to the processing of the data, you can write that information to the standard-error stream (also called "stderr").

When you create a pipeline command in a shell, like `cat words.txt | wc -l`, the shell creates two new processes, one for `cat` and one for `wc`. The shell then hooks the standard-out of `cat` to the standard-in of `wc`, and also hooks the standard-out of `ls` back to the shell so that the shell can read the output from `wc`. By using shell redirection features, you can pour a file's contents into the standard-in of a program, and save the standard-out output to a file.

Figure 4-1. The Standard File Streams

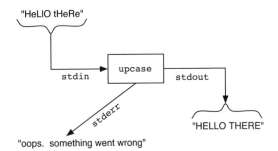

The Basic Program

When you `#import` the `stdio.h` header file, it defines some global symbols that represent the three file streams: `stdin`, `stdout`, and `stderr` (which represent standard-in, standard-out, and standard-error).

Use your favorite text editor (`vi`, `emacs`, `TextEdit.app`, `Xcode`, `BBEdit`) and create a file called `upcase.m`.

First the preliminaries. Import the header files. You will always need some kind of header files:

```
#import <Foundation/Foundation.h>      // for BOOL
#import <stdlib.h>                      // for EXIT_FAILURE/SUCCESS
```

```
#import <stdio.h>                    // for standard I/O stuff
```

`Foundation.h` is the Cocoa Foundation Kit which makes available a lot of nice features. For now you are just going to be using the BOOL type.

`stdlib.h` brings in a whole bunch of stuff, in particular the EXIT_FAILURE / EXIT_SUCCESS macros.

`stdio.h` provides the declarations for the Standard Input/Output types and functions.

Next you need a function to change the case of all the characters in a buffer:

```
void changecaseBuffer (char buffer[], size_t length, BOOL upcase)
{
    char *scan, *stop;

    scan = buffer;
    stop = buffer + length;

    while (scan < stop) {
        if (upcase) {
            *scan = toupper (*scan);
        } else {
            *scan = tolower (*scan);
        }
        scan++;
    }

} // changecaseBuffer
```

changecaseBuffer() scans over every byte in the buffer and uses the standard C library **toupper()** or **tolower()** functions on each one, and changes a character's case appropriately if it is a letter and leaves it alone if not.

Picking a number out of the air, say 2K, define a buffer size symbolic constant.

```
#define BUFFER_SIZE 2048
```

Finally your main function (which is where program control flow starts when the program is run) reads and processes the input:

```
int main (int argc, char *argv[])
{
    char buffer[BUFFER_SIZE];
    size_t length;
    BOOL upcase = YES;

    while (!feof(stdin)) {
        length = fread (buffer, 1, BUFFER_SIZE, stdin);
        changecaseBuffer (buffer, length, upcase);
        fwrite (buffer, 1, length, stdout);
    }
    return (0);
} // main
```

For now, let us compile this on the command line with:

```
$ cc -o upcase upcase.m
```

and run it. (The command is saying to run the c compiler on upcase.m, and generate an executable program with the name upcase. If you did not include the **–o upcase**, the compiler would use the name a.out by default. Not very intuitive.) Invoke your new program with ./**upcase**, type some stuff, a return, and press control-D (which is the end of file key sequence). So,

```
$ ./upcase
HooVeR Ni BOrK
HOOVER NI BORK
^D
```

This program also works in simple pipelines:

```
$ echo "HooVeR" | ./upcase
HOOVER
```

It works for more complex pipelines as well:

```
$ cat /usr/share/dict/words | ./upcase | grep LENS
ANTILENS
CAMALDOLENSIAN
DECLENSION
...
(and about 18 more LENS-like words).
```

Inside the Central Loop

Take a look at the central loop there:

```
while (!feof(stdin)) {
```

Loop over the body of the while loop until you reach the EOF (end of file) for the standard in stream. The end of file happens when you explicitly enter that control-D if you are typing text into the program. When in a pipeline, the standard in stream will be closed when the program ahead exits or decides to close the outgoing pipe on its end.

```
length = fread (buffer, 1, BUFFER_SIZE, stdin);
```

Read in no more than BUFFER_SIZE bytes. The arguments look pretty obvious (where to put the data read, how much to read, and where to read it from). What is that "1" hanging around there? This particular family of functions can read uniformly sized blocks of data from a file. (A technique known as record-oriented storage). Say you had a file that had a bunch of 50 byte records that stored people's names, shoe sizes, and blood types. If you wanted to read in a dozen of these records at once, you would have a call like

```
length = fread (buffer, 50, 12, stdin);
```

The system would read 50 * 12 = 600 bytes, and length would be 12, signifying the number of records read. The interesting information for the character-case mangling example is the number of bytes read (assuming one byte per character. A pretty safe assumption when dealing with "classic" Unix), you are saying to read BUFFER_SIZE records of one byte each, e.g., a maximum of 2048 bytes. If you reversed the order of the arguments, as BUFFER_SIZE, 1, that would tell the system to read one record of

2048 bytes. If there were only a dozen bytes available to read, the length would be returned as zero (since there is not enough data for one 2048 byte record) and the code would not do any processing.

```
changecaseBuffer (buffer, length, upcase);
```

Call **changecaseBuffer** to process the buffer. Note that the length is passed as an argument. **fread** will not append a trailing zero (hex `0x00`) terminating character to the string, so the receiving function will not know where to stop processing unless you tell it where to stop.

Finally, write to the standard out pipe:

```
fwrite (buffer, 1, length, stdout);
```

Using the same idea of "writing length records of 1 byte each."

Changing by Name

Now it is time to let the user change the program behavior. One way is to look at the name of the program. There is a Linux utility called BusyBox that implements many of the standard Unix command line programs in one small executable, changing its behavior based on the name. On your system you probably have a /usr/bin/ranlib which is a symbolic link to the libtool program. In this case libtool will work like ranlib when called that.

In Example 4-1 you will choose your behavior if we are run as "upcase" or "downcase". To do this, you need to look at the argv array that gets passed to **main**. argv is the typical contraction of the phrase "argument vector". You could call that parameter anything you wanted to, but typically it will just be argv.

The argv array has all of the command line arguments passed to the program. The shell breaks up the command the user typed in, usually at white space characters (but that can be overridden with quotes). One handy thing is that the program invocation is in the first element of the array, at argv. Note that this is the command as entered by the user. If the program was run with **./upcase**, argv[0] would be "./upcase." If the program was started with **/Users/bork/projects/book/chapter2/upcase**, that is what argv[0] would be. So you cannot really depend on a specific string there. Luckily there is a little convenience function called **fnmatch** that does shell-style filename matching. If the string in argv matches "*upcase" or "*downcase," that will be sufficient to tell the difference.

Example 4-1. upcase.m

```
// upcase.m -- convert text to upper case

/* compile with
cc -g -Wall -o upcase upcase.m
*/
#import <Foundation/Foundation.h>    // for BOOL
#import <stdlib.h>                    // for EXIT_FAILURE
#import <stdio.h>                     // for standard I/O stuff
#import <fnmatch.h>                   // for fnmatch()
```

```
#define BUFFER_SIZE 2048

// changecaseBuffer is unchanged

int main (int argc, char *argv[])
{
    char buffer[BUFFER_SIZE];
    size_t length;
    BOOL upcase = YES;

    if (fnmatch ("*upcase", argv[0], 0) == 0) {
        printf ("upcase!\n");
        upcase = YES;
    }
    if (fnmatch ("*downcase", argv[0], 0) == 0) {
        printf ("downcase!\n");
        upcase = NO;
    }

    while (!feof(stdin)) {
        length = fread (buffer, 1, BUFFER_SIZE, stdin);
        changecaseBuffer (buffer, length, upcase);
        fwrite (buffer, 1, length, stdout);
    }

    return (EXIT_SUCCESS);

} // main
```

Compile your program like before with:

```
$ cc -g -Wall -o upcase upcase.m
```

Here is a sample run:

```
$ echo "bLaRg" | ./upcase
upcase!
BLARG
```

Now make a symbolic link that points to upcase:

```
$ ln -s upcase downcase
```

and run the program like this:

```
$ echo "bLaRg" | ./downcase
downcase!
blarg
```

Looking at the Environment

Another way to influence program behavior is through environment variables, which are key/value pairs that are under user control via the shell, as shown in

Figure 4-2. The `getenv()` function is used to read the variables the user has set (directly or indirectly) in the environment from which your program has been run.

Figure 4-2. Environment Variables

SHELL	/bin/tcsh
HOME	/Users/markd
USER	markd
LANG	en_US
MACHTPE	powerpc
HOST	ilamp.local.

getenv ("HOME"); ⟶ "/Users/markd"

You give `getenv()` the name of the environment variable you want. If the variable does not exist in the environment you get NULL back. If it does exist you will get a string back with the value. Memory issues like ownership of returned values will be covered in Chapter 5 (Memory). Here, the system owns the memory so you do not need to free it.

To control your case conversion program, you will use the CASE_CONV variable. The value of LOWER will have it massage strings to lower case, and UPPER to massage it to upper case (and if it is not set, it will default to upper case).

You will want to remove the

```
#import <fnmatch.h>
```

The declarations for `getenv()` and family live in stdlib.h, which you already have included.

Also remove the two if blocks that use **fnmatch()** and replace them with:

```
char *envSetting;

envSetting = getenv ("CASE_CONV");

if (envSetting != NULL) {
    if (strcmp(envSetting, "UPPER") == 0) {
        printf ("upper!\n");
        upcase = YES;
    }
    if (strcmp(envSetting, "LOWER") == 0) {
        printf ("lower!\n");
        upcase = NO;
    }
}
```

Recompile it with:

```
$ cc -o upcase upcase.m
```

and give it a whirl:

```
$ setenv CASE_CONV LOWER
$ ./upcase
```

```
lower!
GrEEblE
greeble
```

And verify that it works:

```
$ setenv CASE_CONV UPPER
$ ./upcase
upper!
GrEEblE
GREEBLE
```

Parsing the Command Line

The last way to influence program behavior (outside of reading some configuration files yourself) is by reading command line arguments. This is actually the most common way to do it as well.

Recall earlier that the "choose behavior based on program name" version of your upcase program looked at the first element of argv to get the program name. The argv array also has all of the program's arguments in addition to the name used to start the program.

Example 4-2 is a quick little program that prints out command line arguments:

Example 4-2. dumpargs.m

```
// dumpargs.m -- show program arguments

/* compile with:
cc -g -Wall -o dumpargs dumpargs.m
*/

#include <stdio.h>
#include <stdlib.h>

int main (int argc, char *argv[])
{
    int i;

    for (i = 0; i < argc; i++) {
        printf ("%d: %s\n", i, argv[i]);
    }

    return (EXIT_SUCCESS);

} // main
```

Now feed this program various arguments:

```
$ ./dumpargs
0: ./dumpargs
```

As expected, the name of the program lives in the 0th element of the argv array.

```
$ ./dumpargs -oop -ack -blarg
0: ./dumpargs
```

```
1: -oop
2: -ack
3: -blarg
```

You can also see the effect of shell file name globbing, and of quotation marks.

```
$ ./dumpargs "dump*" dump*
0: ./dumpargs
1: dump*
2: dumpargs
3: dumpargs.m
```

The first argument, since it is in quotes is given to you explicitly as "dump*." The second dump* was intercepted by the shell and expanded to be all of the files that start up with dump (in this case just the name of the program and the name of the .m file).

Now back to upcase.m. Use the -u flag for uppercase and -l (ell) for lowercase.

Remove the code you added for handling the environment variables and add this:

```
if (argc >= 2) {
    if (strcmp(argv[1], "-u") == 0) {
        printf ("upper!\n");
        upcase = YES;
    }
    if (strcmp(argv[1], "-l") == 0) {
        printf ("lower!\n");
        upcase = NO;
    }
}
```

Recompile and try it out:

```
$ ./upcase -u
upper!
GrEEbLe
GREEBLE

$ ./upcase -l
lower!
GrEEbLe
greeble
```

One thing some experienced programmers will notice is the distinct lack of error checking going on. Much of the work of programming Unix is catching and handling errors, whether they are user errors (typing invalid or conflicting command arguments) or system errors (a disk fills up). You may have noticed the return (EXIT_SUCCESS); at the end of each of the **main()** functions. EXIT_SUCCESS is a macro that expands to zero, which when returned, tells the shell that the command succeeded. Any non-zero return value tells the shell that the command failed. The shell uses this return value to decide whether to continue with the work it is doing (whether running a shell script or just a command pipeline). For upcase, you should do a little checking of arguments, such as whether the user entered entered too many, or entered one that is invalid.

EXIT_FAILURE (a macro that expands to the value one) is a handy constant; return it to signal the shell that something went wrong. Here is upcase with some error checking (replace the argv code you entered above with this):

```
if (argc > 2) {
    fprintf (stderr, "bad argument count.  Must be zero or one\n");
    return (EXIT_FAILURE);

} else if (argc == 2) {
    BOOL found = NO;

    if (strcmp(argv[1], "-u") == 0) {
        upcase = YES;
        found = YES;
    }
    if (strcmp(argv[1], "-l") == 0) {
        upcase = NO;
        found = YES;
    }
    if (!found) {
        fprintf (stderr, "bad command line argument: '%s'\n",
                 argv[1]);
        fprintf (stderr, "expecting -u or -l\n");
        return (EXIT_FAILURE);
    }
}
```

Any time you discover something is wrong, print out a complaint message (to the standard error stream, where errors belong) and bail out with an error code.

In real life programs there is usually some cleanup work that would need to be done, like closing files or freeing memory.

> Personally, I like keeping all of my cleanup code in one place, right before the function ends. I also like to keep a single exit from any function. That means there's a single place to put cleanup code. Therefore I use the venerable and much maligned goto statement. If something goes wrong, jump to the bailout point and clean up any messes made, then return.

For example in pseudo-code:

```
{
    my_result = failure;
    blah = allocate_some_memory ();
    if (do_something(blah) == failure) {
        goto bailout;
    }
    ack = open_a_file ();
    if (process_file (blah, ack) == failure) {
        goto bailout;
    }
    hoover = do_something_else ();
    if (have_fun (blah, hoover) == failure) {
        goto bailout;
    }
    // we survived! yay
    my_result = success;
```

```
bailout:
    if (blah) {
        free_the_memory (blah);
    }
    if (ack) {
        close_the_file (ack);
    }
    if (hoover) {
        clean_this_up (hoover);
    }
    return (my_result);
}
```

If you are using C++ you can use exception handling (which is really just a fancy goto) and stack-based cleanup objects to simplify cleanup, but in C you have to either have a bunch of nested ifs or use goto.

Here is my final **main()** with error checking of the command line arguments and a single exit point:

```
int main (int argc, char *argv[])
{
    char buffer[BUFFER_SIZE];
    size_t length;
    BOOL upcase = YES;
    int exitReturn = EXIT_FAILURE;

    if (argc > 2) {
        fprintf (stderr, "bad argument count.  Must be zero or one\n");
        goto bailout;

    } else if (argc == 2) {
        BOOL found = NO;

        if (strcmp(argv[1], "-u") == 0) {
            upcase = YES;
            found = YES;
        }
        if (strcmp(argv[1], "-l") == 0) {
            upcase = NO;
            found = YES;
        }
        if (!found) {
            fprintf (stderr,
                    "bad command line argument: '%s'\n", argv[1]);
            fprintf (stderr, "expecting -u or -l\n");
            goto bailout;
        }
    }

    while (!feof(stdin)) {
        length = fread (buffer, 1, BUFFER_SIZE, stdin);
        changecaseBuffer (buffer, length, upcase);
        fwrite (buffer, 1, length, stdout);
    }
```

```
        exitReturn = EXIT_SUCCESS;

bailout:
        return (exitReturn);

} // main
```

For the More Curious: getopt()

Parsing command line options can be tedious, messy code. Let us say you have a program that takes these command line arguments:

```
$ ./myprog
  -f                : run in a fast mode
  -k                : kill other processes with our name
  -t file-name      : twiddle the file named file-name
  -u file-name      : uppercase the file name file-name
  -V                : print out version stuff and exit
```

and then an arbitrary number of additional arguments (file names) to do some other stuff to.

You would have to scan through all of arguments, see if they match the ones you accept, double-check to make sure that -t and -u have a following argument, and complain otherwise. It would also be nice to support the user entering `-fkt oopack` as well as `-f -k -t oopack`.

The **getopt()** function walks through `argv` for you and returns a character for each argument, as well as sets some global variables that contain information on what it has found.

getopt() takes a string that describes what arguments you want. If a command line argument takes an additional parameter (like the -u file-name above), put in a colon. So, for this contrived example, you would use the string `"fkt:u:V"`. Order of arguments in the string does not matter. **getopt()** also takes argc and argv:

```
int getopt (int argc, char * const *argv, const char *optstring);
```

The global `char *optarg` points to the option argument. For instance, upon seeing -u, `optarg` would point to the file name. If **getopt** sees an argument it does not understand, it returns "?". When **getopt** runs out of command line arguments (that is, it finds a "--" argument, or one that does not start with a leading dash), the `optind` global variable has the count of the number of `argv` entries it has looked at. That value can then be used to adjust `argc` and `argv` so that you know what additional arguments there are.

Here is a little program that parses the arguments that you see above. (The code for setting of flags and processing of files has been omitted.)

```
int main (int argc, char *argv[])
{
    int ch;

    while ( (ch = getopt(argc, argv, "fkt:u:V")) != -1) {
        switch (ch) {
            case 'f':
                printf ("found an 'f' flag\n");
```

```
                    break;
              case 'k':
                printf ("found a 'k' flag\n");
                break;
              case 't':
                printf ("found a 't' flag, and the argument is %s\n",
                        optarg);
                break;
              case 'u':
                printf ("found a 'u' flag, and the argument is %s\n",
                        optarg);
                break;
              case 'V':
                printf ("found a 'V' flag");
                break;
              case '?':
              default:
                printf ("d'oh!  use these flags: f, k, t (file),
                        u(file), V\n");
                return (EXIT_FAILURE);
          }
      }

      // bias the argv/argc to skip over the processed args
      argc -= optind;
      argv += optind;

      {
          int i;
          for (i = 0; i < argc; i++) {
              printf ("found file argument: %s\n", argv[i]);
          }
      }

      return (EXIT_SUCCESS);

} // main
```

Chapter 5. Memory

Introduction

Many of the early Mac OS X marketing buzzwords revolved around the memory management practices of the OS, especially as compared to classic Mac OS. It employed terms such as "protected memory" and "virtual memory," plus the ability for programs to crash and die in horrible ways and not affect other running programs. Mac OS X typically makes better use of available memory than previous Mac OS versions due to these features.

Virtual Memory

Virtual memory is a way for the computer to fake having more memory than it actually has. A machine might have 128 megabytes of RAM, but programs can be written that manipulate data several times that amount. The when available amount of memory overflows, portions of the data is saved out to disk and read back in when the program needs it.

The operating system handles the grungy details of keeping data that is currently being worked on physically in memory, and keeping data that has not been touched in a while saved to the disk, as well as doing the work to bring data from disk and into memory so the program can work on it.

At a fundamental level, the operating system deals with pages, which are 4k chunks of memory that the operating system addresses. Programs are given pages as they request memory. As pages are used, they are kept on a list of recently used pages. As programs request more and more memory from the system, the least recently used pages are written to disk (termed "paging" or "swapping") and the chunk of physical memory is reused.

Pages can be written out and then read back in at different physical addresses. For instance, a 4k page starting at address 0x5000 might be paged out and given to another program. The program that needs the data that was at 0x5000 now needs it again, so the OS reads the page from disk. The chunk of memory at 0x5000 may now in use by the second program. Oops. To fix this, virtual addresses are used.

Figure 5-1 shows virtual memory in action. Virtual addresses are the memory addresses a program sees, and each program has its own address space. The virtual address gets mapped by the OS (and hardware in the CPU) to the physical address of a chunk of a page of RAM. Program A and program B each have a page of data at 0x5000. In physical memory, A's might live at address 0x15020 and B's might live at address 0x3150, but the address translation lets each program live with the fantasy of having their data at address 0x5000.

Figure 5-1. Virtual Memory

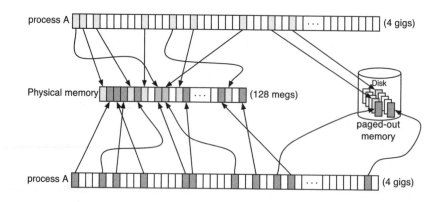

The total amount of memory that a program has allocated to it at a particular time is called its *virtual set*. The amount of memory that is actually located in RAM is called a process' *resident set*. The difference between the virtual set and the resident set is stored out on disk in a swap file (or a dedicated swap partition). "Swap" derives its name from the pages that are swapped for each other when paging happens. You can also lock (a.k.a. "wire") memory down so it does not get swapped out. Some pages you absolutely do not want to be swapped out, such as pages containing decryped passwords. These pages should be wired down with the `mlock()` function before decrypting the password.

Pages can have permissions, such as read-only, read/write, and executable. That helps keep you from scribbling over your own code, as well as helps prevent some exploits that try to execute code from a page that is not marked executable.

Differences From Classic Mac OS Memory Management

The classic Mac memory model presents RAM as one very large (single) address space that is shared between the OS and all the programs that are running, as shown in Figure 5-2. It has a form of virtual memory that uses disk space in addition to physical RAM for all the programs to share (and has the same kinds of virtual address translation working behind the scenes).

Figure 5-2. Classic Mac Memory Map

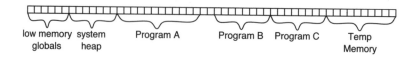

Where classic Mac OS and Mac OS X differ is that the OS and each program live in their own address space. Now, instead of every program sharing the same 32-bit address space (4 gigs), each program now has its *own* 32-bit address space, independent of all the other programs running on the system.

This opens new possibilities with each program having its own 4 gigabytes of independent addressable space. (Well, minus a gigabyte or so of the address space that belongs to the operating system.) You can map files into memory and treat them like any other piece of memory (memory mapped files are discussed in Chapter 8 (Files)). You can also have large but sparse allocations of memory. (Allocate a a gig of memory but only use a couple of megabytes. Handy for dealing with very large sparse matrices.)

Each program having its own address space also adds a layer of security that does not exist in the classic Mac OS memory model. One program cannot see the memory of another program except under very controlled circumstances, such as with superuser privileges, or through explicit cooperative sharing via shared memory. It becomes impossible for program A to have a pointer error and scribble bad data into program B's memory range. (This is what is known as "protected memory.")

Separate address spaces also removes the need for the user to manually configure memory partitions. The OS, rather than the user, optimizes the amount of physical memory allocated to a particular program based on actual usage, and the user does not have the headache of changing partition sizes or having to quit existing programs to free up enough memory to run a new one.

Some of the curiosities of Mac memory management (hold-overs from the Mac 128K days) such as Handles (pointers to pointers such that the memory ultimately being pointed to can be moved around and free space compacted), the System Heap, and temporary memory are no longer necessary (and in fact are not used in pure Unix programming) because there is no real need to move memory around. Just allocate it and let virtual addressing and paging handle the details.

Program Memory Model

The memory model of individual programs are similar in Classic Mac OS and OS X. There is space for the executable code, a stack, and a heap, although the heaps differ somewhat in the two worlds. Figure 5-3 shows the different chunks of memory consumed in a typical program:

Figure 5-3. Unix Program Memory Model

The "Text" Segment

This is the executable program code. At program launch time the code is mapped into memory from the executable as read-only pages (so no self-modifying code unless you jump through some hoops). Since these pages are read-only they can be easily shared among multiple programs so the pages only have to appear in memory once and can still be shared among multiple users. This is especially handy for shared libraries that are loaded into each program. Since the data is read-only, some Unix operating systems will swap directly from the program's executable file, saving a little space in the swapfile.

Initialized Data Segment

These are initialized global and static variables. e.g. things like `float pi = 3.1415` outside of any functions, or `static int blah = 25` inside of a function. The initialized data is stored in the data segment itself, which is just copied into memory into a read/write page which the program can then modify (and this segment is very fast to load and initialize all of the globals. No real explicit initialization happens, just bulk data loads.)

Uninitialized Data Segment

This is all the stuff that lives in global space but is not given an explicit initializer, like `int bork` or `char buffer[5000]` that all gets cleared out to zero on program launch. These are not treated like the initialized data segment (which would mean lots of zero blocks in the executable, and is wasteful of disk space). Just the size of this data segment is stored. On program load, the OS allocates that amount of space and zero-fills it.

This is also referred to as the "bss" segment in man pages and the historical literature. "bss" comes from an assembler instruction that means "block started by symbol."

Heap

The Unix heap is similar to the Classic Mac construct of the same name. It is the area where dynamic (run-time) allocations happen. If you ask for 40K, that 40K will come from the heap. The Unix heap differs from the classic Mac heap is that the Unix heap is just a big arena of memory. There is not any visible auxiliary overhead such as master pointers or handles.

The Program Stack

This is the program call stack. Local (automatic) variables are stored here, as are the stack frames for each function call. When a function calls another function, the processor registers and other assorted bookkeeping need to be stored before the new function is called, and they need to be restored when the new function exits. To support recursion (and an arbitrary depth of function calls) a stack is used.

Memory "allocation" using the program stack is very fast. Internally a pointer is used to indicate where the end of the stack is. Reserving space on the stack just involves adding a value to this stack pointer, whether it be five bytes or five thousand. You do not want to store *too* much stuff on the stack (big buffers and whatnot) since some systems have a limit on how big the stack can be. Also when you get into threaded programming, stack space is frequently very limited since each thread has its own chunk of memory to use for a stack. This is discussed in Chapter 22 (Threads).

There is also an additional segment for Objective-C bookkeeping.

The `size` command will show the size of numerous segments of programs. Here is one without any Objective-C stuff:

```
$ size /bin/ls
__TEXT __DATA __OBJC others dec hex
24576 4096 0 7884 36556 8ecc
```

Here is one with Objective-C stuff:

```
$ size /Applications/Mail.app/Contents/MacOS/Mail
__TEXT __DATA __OBJC others dec hex
1667072 69632 139264 71548 1947516 1db77c
```

You can see you have to give `size` the path to the actual executable that lives inside of an application bundle

Example 5-1 is a program that has 8K of initialized data, and a meg of uninitialized data:

Example 5-1. dataseg.m

```
// dataseg.m -- show size of data segments

/* compile with:
cc -g -Wall -o dataseg dataseg.m
*/

#import <stdio.h>   // for printf()
#import <stdlib.h>  // for exit()

// about 8K doubles. lives in the initialized data segment.
double x[] = {
    0.0, 1.0, 2.0, 3.0, 4.0, 5.0, 6.0, 7.0, 8.0, 9.0,
    10.0, 11.0, 12.0, 13.0, 14.0, 15.0, 16.0, 17.0, 18.0, 19.0,
    ...
    1010.0, 1011.0, 1012.0, 1013.0, 1014.0, 1015.0,
    1016.0, 1017.0, 1018.0, 1019.0
};

// one meg, all zeros.  Lives in the uninitialzed data segment
char buffer[1048576];

int main (int argc, char *argv[])
{
    printf ("hi!\n");
    return (0);
} // main
```

Running `size` on this program yields:

```
$ size dataseg
__TEXT __DATA __OBJC others dec hex
8192 1060864 0 12288 1081344 108000
```

Here `size` combines the size of initialized and uninitialized data. Note that 1060864 (the data segment size) minus 1048576 (the zero-filled uninitialized data) is 12288, which is 8192 (the 8K of double data) plus 4096 (4K of overhead and bookkeeping).

Note finally that the application size is small:

```
$ ls -l dataseg
-rwxr-xr-x  1 markd  markd  25728 Aug 10 20:56 dataseg*
```

`size -m` (which shows some extra stuff from the Mach-O segments) will show some additional details:

```
$ size -m dataseg
Segment __PAGEZERO: 4096
Segment __TEXT: 8192
 Section __text: 2420
 Section __picsymbol_stub: 0
 Section __symbol_stub: 0
 Section __picsymbolstub1: 384
 Section __cstring: 312
 total 3116
Segment __DATA: 1060864
 Section __data: 8184
 Section __nl_symbol_ptr: 16
 Section __la_symbol_ptr: 48
 Section __dyld: 28
 Section __common: 1048640
 total 1056916
Segment __LINKEDIT: 8192
 total 1081344
```

Memory Lifetime

There are some nuances regarding lifetime of variables and memory in some of the different memory areas of a running Unix process.

Initialized and uninitialized data segment variables are around during the entire run time of the program. They will not go away. Memory on the heap is explicitly asked for and is explicitly released. Memory here can be deallocated, but it is under program control. Memory on the stack goes away (meaning that it can be reused by someone else) as soon as it goes out of scope (even before a function exits). The stack memory behavior causes errors for some programmers who assume that some memory will be valid longer than it is. A classic error is something like:

```
char *borkulize (void)
{
    char buffer[5000];

    // work on buffer

    return (buffer);

} // borkulize
```

buffer is allocated on the stack. Once buffer goes out of scope, that memory becomes available for other functions. Anyone working with the return result of **borkulize()** is taking a chance that someone will clobber the values (potentially much later in time after this function exits).

Dynamic Memory Allocation

Dynamic memory allocation concerns memory that comes from the heap. The heap of the program starts off at an OS-defined default amount of space available for program consumption. As you allocate memory from the heap, it fills up. When it does, your program is given more memory from the OS until the system either runs out of memory or reaches a (configurable) maximum size for allocated memory. You can release memory you have allocated to allow it to be reused by your program. As an aside, memory allocated and subsequently freed is still counted as part of your program. So if you allocate 50 megabytes for temporary workspace and then free it all, your program will still have 50 megabytes of memory allocated to it (which will eventually get swapped out since you might not be using it). The total amount of memory can be considered a high water mark.

The primary functions for allocation and deallocating memory are:

```
void *malloc (size_t size);

void free (void *ptr);

void *realloc (void *ptr, size_t size);
```

These functions give you memory from the heap.

malloc()

malloc() allocates a chunk of memory with the address of the block aligned to the strictest boundary required in the OS. E.g. if an 8-byte double had the strictest alignment, **malloc()** would return addresses that were evenly divisible by 8. Example 5-2 allocates blocks of different sizes and shows the address of the returned memory.

Example 5-2. mallocalign.m

```
// mallocalign.m -- see how malloc aligns its pointers

/* compile with
cc -Wall -g -o mallocalign mallocalign.m
*/

#import <stdio.h>    // for printf()
#import <stdlib.h>   // for malloc()

void allocprint (size_t size)
{
    void *memory;

    memory = malloc (size);
    printf ("malloc(%ld) == %p\n", size, memory);
    // intentionally don't free so we get a new malloced block of memory

} // allocprint

int main (int argc, char *argv[])
{
    allocprint (1);
    allocprint (2);
    allocprint (sizeof(double));
    allocprint (1024 * 1024);
    allocprint (1);
    allocprint (1);

    return (0);

} // main
```

has a run of

```
$ ./mallocalign
malloc(1) == 0x500150
malloc(2) == 0x5001a0
malloc(8) == 0x5001b0
malloc(1048576) == 0x605000
malloc(1) == 0x5001c0
malloc(1) == 0x5001d0
```

which are all addresses evenly divisible by 16. This is good to know when doing Altivec work, because Altivec works best when data is aligned on 16-byte boundaries.

Generally you use the C sizeof operator to determine how much memory to allocate for specific data structures:

```
typedef struct Node {
    int blah; // 4 bytes
    int bork; // 4 bytes
} Node;

Node *mynode = malloc (sizeof(Node));   // 8 bytes
```

and for arrays

```
Node mynode[] = malloc (sizeof(Node) * 100);   // 800 bytes
```

Note that **malloc()** is free to give you a block of memory that is larger than what you ask for. You are only guaranteed of having as much memory that you ask for.

Example 5-3 allocates a number of blocks, and then uses **malloc_size()** to see how much space is actually allocated.

Example 5-3. mallocsize.m

```
// mallocsize.m -- see what kind of block sizes malloc is
//                 actually giving us

/* compile with:
cc -g -Wall -o mallocsize mallocsize.m
*/

#import <stdlib.h>       // for malloc()
#import <stdio.h>        // for printf()
#import <malloc/malloc.h> // for malloc_size()

void allocprint (size_t size)
{
    void *memory;

    memory = malloc (size);
    printf ("malloc(%ld) has a block size of %ld\n",
      size, malloc_size(memory));
} // allocprint

int main (int argc, char *argv[])
```

```
{
    allocprint (1);
    allocprint (sizeof(double)); // 8 bytes
    allocprint (14);
    allocprint (16);
    allocprint (32);
    allocprint (48);
    allocprint (64);
    allocprint (100);

    return (0);

} // main
```

Yields:

```
$ ./mallocsize
malloc(1) has a block size of 16
malloc(8) has a block size of 16
malloc(14) has a block size of 16
malloc(16) has a block size of 16
malloc(32) has a block size of 32
malloc(48) has a block size of 48
malloc(64) has a block size of 64
malloc(100) has a block size of 112
```

You can see that the actual block size is smaller than what was asked for. Memory allocation algorithms are an interesting area of computer science, and most any operating systems textbook will describe a number of different algorithms for managing dynamic memory. Usually, the system has a bunch of buckets that each contain uniform-sized blocks of memory. The system chooses the smallest block size that will contain the requested amount of memory. Rather than have a whole bunch of 9-byte blocks, and a whole bunch of 10-byte blocks, and a whole bunch of 11-byte blocks (and so on and so on), it will have larger increments. In the above case it has 16 bytes, 32 bytes, 48 bytes, 64 bytes, and so on, which seem to be powers of two or sums of powers of two. Previous versions of Mac OS X had different block sizes for the allocated blocks, like 14 bytes, 30 bytes, 46 bytes, and so on.

Even though **malloc_size()** reports sizes (possibly) larger that what was initially allocated, you should not use it to see "how much memory is allocated to this pointer." That is, if a function is passed a pointer that had been allocated using malloc(8), but you used **malloc_size()** on the pointer and subsequently treaded the pointer like it had come from malloc(14). Doing that would certainly cause problems. **malloc_size()** also won't work for pointers to stack memory. You will still need to pass around sizes of buffers.

The memory returned by **malloc()** has some bookkeeping information associated with it, which s (usually stored as a negative offset from the pointer returned to you so that the system can find its bookkeeping information easily. This, along with the previous note on allocation block sizes, means you cannot make any assumptions about memory placement with multiple calls to **malloc()**.

E.g., you cannot depend on this:

```
x = malloc (10);
y = malloc (10);
```

to look like Figure 5-4 in memory

Figure 5-4. Incorrect Memory Layout

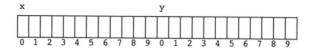

There are actually some web pages out there that assert that this *must* be true. It actually looks something Figure 5-5

Figure 5-5. How blocks are actually laid out

One last corollary of the above observation. There is no guarantee of locality of reference (a fancy term meaning data that is frequently used together is near each other in memory, leading to fewer cache misses and less paging activity) either. You could do

```
x = malloc (10);
y = malloc (10);
```

and it is perfectly legal for **malloc()** to give you a pointer to x from one end of your address space and y to be an address way on the other side.

Finally, **malloc()** on Mac OS X is always thread safe, as opposed to **malloc()** on some other Unix variants (like Linux) which is only thread safe if you link in the thread libraries, so there is always going to be a little extra overhead when using **malloc()** and friends on Mac OS X compared to some other Unix operating systems.

free()

free() tells the system that you are done with a block of memory and that it can be reused by a subsequent call to **malloc()**. In the earlier examples, especially mallocalign.m, the allocated memory is purposely never freed since the same block would keep getting returned, and it is hard to draw conclusions about memory alignment if you get the same starting address for a block of memory each time.

Not freeing allocated memory is termed a "memory leak," since the memory just kind of leaks away and is not available for use any more. There is a discussion about memory leaks and memory leak detection tools later on.

Lastly, make sure you only feed **free()** addresses you get from **malloc()**. You will get unpredictable results (crash) if you give **free()** addresses of stack buffers or other memory not allocated by **malloc()**.

realloc()

`realloc()` resizes a chunk of memory that has been previously allocated. Programmers familiar with classic Mac OS memory management will rightfully ask, "How can it resize memory? These are pointers, not handles." Essentially, `realloc()` does something like:

```
void *cheesyRealloc (void *ptr, size_t size)
{
    void *newMem = malloc (size);
    memcpy (newMem, ptr, size);
    free (ptr);
    return (newMem);
} // cheesyRealloc
```

So these blocks can move in the heap. Handles have the nice property that when they move you do not need to update everyone that points to the handle since the double indirection takes care of that for you. In standard Unix memory management you have to do that bookkeeping yourself, usually by just having the pointer be in one place and wrap an API around it, or by using two memory objects: a smaller one that will not move (like a tree node), and a larger one that the smaller one points to (like the user-editable label for the tree node). The larger one can be reallocated and only the tree node needs to update the address change.

As you would expect, `realloc()` has optimizations so that it does not have to do the allocate/copy/free procedure every time a block is reallocated. As noted above, sometimes the block returned from `malloc()` is actually larger than what you asked for. `realloc()` can just say, "OK, you can now use the rest of the block." There are also games `realloc()` can play, like if there is a free block in another bucket that is contiguous with the block of memory you want to reallocate. `realloc()` behind the scenes can glom that second block onto the first and let you use that space.

But in any case, be sure to assign the return value of `realloc()` back to your pointer. (This is a mistake I personally make all too often). E.g., this is a lurking problem:

```
void *blah = malloc (sizeof(Node) * 20);
...
realloc (blah, sizeof(Node) * 40); // this is bad!
...
```

Sometimes it will work, sometimes not. Always do this:

```
blah = realloc (blah, sizeof(Node) * 40);
```

calloc()

`malloc()` does not initialize the memory it returns to you, so you will probably have a bunch of stale junk in the memory you get. A pretty common idiom is to allocate a chunk of memory and zero it out so that it is pretty safe to use:

```
void *memory = malloc (sizeof(Node) * 50);
memset (memory, 0, sizeof(Node) * 50);
```

You can also use `calloc()` to do this in one operation:

```
void *calloc(size_t nelem, size_t elsize);
```

The arguments are a little odd compared to **malloc()** in that it is assuming you are allocating an array. It is just doing a multiplication behind the scenes. So,

```
memory = calloc (sizeof(Node), 50);
```

gives identical results to the two-step sequence above. In general, it is better to use **calloc()** because the OS can do some optimizations behind the scenes, like allowing the kernel to reserve the memory, but not actually allocate it. It can then give you zero-filled pages when it is actually accessed.

alloca()

Even though the man page for **alloca()** says, "This is machine dependent, its use is discouraged," it is still a documented API you can use, which can be useful at times.

```
void *alloca(size_t size);
```

alloca() (for alloc automatic) allocates memory for you on the call stack. This means that allocation is very fast (just some pointer adjustments), and you do not need to perform an explicit **free()** on your memory to release it. When the function ends, the stack frame just goes away and with it the chunk of the frame that contains the alloca memory. As with stuff that appears too good to be true, there is always a catch. Do not go nuts and overflow your stack with lots of local storage, especially if you use lots of recursion, or if your code could be run in a threaded environment where stack sizes are much more limited.

Memory Ownership Issues

One of the details involved with dynamic memory is determining who is responsible for a piece of allocated memory and making sure that the memory is freed when nobody else is using it. This is one of those parts of programming that has lots of different solutions, each with their own tradeoffs (as witnessed by Java garbage collection, C++ destructors, and Cocoa's retain/release/autorelease technique).

There are no real rules for ownership of memory that is passed back and forth between Unix and C function calls, so you pretty much need to check the man page for the calls in question (which is usually a good idea anyway). For instance:

- **getenv()** returns a char *, but you do not need to free it since the environment variables are all stored in a global array and **getenv()** just returns a string contained in that array.

- **strdup()** returns a char *, which you do need to free since it allocates memory on your behalf.

- Some calls take buffers, which you can **malloc** or create on the stack and you are responsible for **free**ing the memory when you are done. A subset of these calls can be given NULL for the buffer argument and they will allocate memory on your behalf. **getcwd()** behaves like this.

- Some other calls will give you reference to memory that they own (usually some kind of global buffer), such as **ctime()** for converting a Unix time into a character constant.

- Finally, there are some APIs that wrap dynamic memory allocation in an API, and depend on you to use that API to create and destroy objects, such as **opendir()** and **closedir()** for iterating through the contents of directories.

And, of course, you can use any of these techniques for modules and APIs that you create, as seems appropriate. It is perfectly fine for you to do your own memory allocation out of a big block if that gives you better behavior. Example 5-4 shows one of my favorite suballocation techniques using a memory pool. A memory pool is an allocator for vending identically sized objects, which can be handy for things like tree nodes.

Example 5-4. nodepool.m

```
// nodepool.m -- a simple memory pool for vending like-size pieces of
//               memory.  An example of custom memory management

/* build with:
cc -g -Wall -O1 -framework Foundation -o nodepool nodepool.m
*/

#import <Foundation/Foundation.h>
#import <stdlib.h>
#import <stdio.h>

// this is the free list that gets weaved through all the blocks

typedef struct BWPoolElement {
    struct BWPoolElement *next;
} BWPoolElement;

@interface BWNodePool : NSObject
{
    unsigned char        *memblock; // a big blob of bytes
    BWPoolElement        *freelist;
    size_t                nodeSize;
    size_t                count;
}

- (id) initWithNodeSize: (size_t) nodeSize   count: (size_t) count;
- (void *) allocNode;
- (void) freeNode: (void *) nodePtr;

@end // BWNodePool


@implementation BWNodePool

- (void) weaveFreeListFrom: (unsigned char *) startAddress
                  forCount: (size_t) theCount
{
    unsigned char *scan = startAddress;
    int i;

    for (i = 0; i < theCount; i++) {
        if (freelist == NULL) {
            freelist = (BWPoolElement *) scan;
            freelist->next = NULL;
```

```
            } else {
                BWPoolElement *temp = (BWPoolElement*) scan;
                temp->next = freelist;
                freelist = temp;
            }
            scan += nodeSize;
    }

} // weaveFreeListFrom

- (id)initWithNodeSize:(size_t)theNodeSize   count:(size_t)theCount
{
    if ((self = [super init])) {
        nodeSize = theNodeSize;
        count = theCount;

        // make sure there's enough space to store the pointers
        // for the freelist

        if (nodeSize < sizeof(BWPoolElement)) {
            nodeSize = sizeof(BWPoolElement);
        }

        // allocate memory for the block
        memblock = malloc (nodeSize * count);

        // walk through the block building the freelist
        [self weaveFreeListFrom:memblock  forCount:theCount];
    }

    return (self);

} // initWithNodeSize

- (void)dealloc
{
    free (memblock);
    [super dealloc];
} // dealloc

- (void *)allocNode
{
    void *newNode = NULL;

    if (freelist == NULL) {
        // out of space. just give up and surrender for now.
        // you can add pool growing by keeping an array of memblocks
        // and creating a new one when the previous block fills up.
        fprintf (stderr, "out of space in node pool.  Giving up\n");
        abort ();
    }

    // take a new node off of the freelist
    newNode = freelist;
    freelist = freelist->next;

    return (newNode);
```

```
} // allocNode

- (void) freeNode: (void *) nodePtr
{
    // stick freed node at the head of the freelist
    ((BWPoolElement*)nodePtr)->next = freelist;
    freelist = nodePtr;
} // freeNode

@end // BWNodePool


#define NODE_BUF_SIZE 137
typedef struct ListNode {
    int                 someData;
    struct ListNode     *next;
} ListNode;

void haveFunWithPool (int nodeCount)
{
    int i;
    ListNode *head, *node, *prev;
    BWNodePool *nodePool;

    NSLog (@"fun with pool");

    nodePool = [[BWNodePool alloc] initWithNodeSize:sizeof(ListNode)
                                   count:nodeCount];
    head = node = prev = NULL;
    for (i = 0; i < nodeCount; i++) {
        node = [nodePool allocNode];
        node->someData = i;

        // and bookkeeping
        node->next = prev;
        prev = node;
    }
    head = node;

    // clean up the list
    [nodePool release];

} // haveFunWithPool

void haveFunWithMalloc (int nodeCount)
{
    int i;
    ListNode *head, *node, *prev;

    NSLog (@"fun with malloc");

    head = node = prev = NULL;

    for (i = 0; i < nodeCount; i++) {
        node = malloc (sizeof(ListNode));
        node->someData = i;
```

```
            // and bookkeeping
            node->next = prev;
            prev = node;
        }
        head = node;

        // now clean it up
        while (head != NULL) {
            ListNode *node = head;
            head = head->next;
            free (node);
        }

} // haveFunWithMalloc

int main (int argc, char *argv[])
{
    int count;

    if (argc != 3) {
        fprintf (stderr, "usage: %s -p|-m #\n", argv[0]);
        fprintf (stderr, "          program to exercise memory "
                          "allocation\n");
        fprintf (stderr, "          -p to use a memory pool\n");
        fprintf (stderr, "          -m to use malloc\n");
        fprintf (stderr, "          #   number of nodes to play "
                          "with\n");
        return (1);
    }
    count = atoi (argv[2]);

    if (strcmp(argv[1], "-p") == 0) {
        haveFunWithPool (count);
    } else {
        haveFunWithMalloc (count);
    }

    return (0);

} // main
```

One thing to note is that once the pool is created, allocations and frees are constant time (just a pointer assignment). **malloc()** usually takes longer due to the complexity of its internal data structures. Also note that the pool can free everything at once (handy since these list nodes do not reference any other objects that need to be cleaned up). Here are some timings (in seconds) of runs of the program (from the time command):

Count	Pool	malloc()
1,000,000	0.10	1.00
5,000,000	0.60	7.61
10,000,000	1.86	20.23

This shows there can be, under some circumstances, benefit to doing your own allocation. Generally it is better to test first to find out what your bottlenecks are before implementing your own allocator, but it is nice to have the option when you need it. If you are using C++, you can override the new operator to use a pool for allocations. (Objective-C doesn't give you this kind of control, unfortunately). In one C++ project I worked on, we had a class that supported chained array subscriptis for digging into a compacted dictionary, with code performing access like flavor['page']['sect']['styl'][5]. Very convenient coding-wise, but this technique caused a lot of temporary objects to be created and destroyed. A pool was put under new and sped things up by an order of magnitude.

One thing to note in the nodepool.m code is that it does not handle the pool growing case. You cannot just **realloc()** the memblock since it could move in memory, leaving the freelist pointers dangling (as well as any pointers the objects being allocated might have, such as the linked list pointers). This can be fixed by having an array of memory pointers, when you run out of memory create a new block, add it to the array, and weave the freelist through the new block.

One last note, operations on the nodepool are not thread safe. A challenge is to make it safe in Chapter 22 (Threads).

Debugging Memory Problems

Errors in memory management cause a huge number of problems when programming in C, and can lead to difficult to track down bugs since the manifestation of a problem can happen long after the actual program error happened.

Common API issues

When **malloc()** cannot allocate memory it returns NULL. Many programmers tend to ignore NULL results from **malloc()**, because if memory is really exhausted the system is in some pretty serious trouble (swapping heavily) and it is just easier to crash and restart (plus it can be tedious checking the return value of **malloc()** all the time). There is no equivalent of the classic Mac OS **GrowZoneProc** that gets called when the heap is full and lets you free temporary resources. So if you want to do something similar you will need to implement it yourself.

The typical Cocoa idiom of allocation and initialization

```
NSArray *array = [[NSArray alloc] init];
[array addObject: myObject];
```

glosses over allocation problems. **alloc** may return a nil object, and since Objective-C messages to nil are legal, in the face of an allocation problem this code will propagate this nil object without complaint.

If you are paranoid, and/or want to be robust in low memory conditions for your own allocations, you can put a wrapper around **malloc()** (say a **safeMalloc()**, or use preprocessor tricks to rename **malloc()** itself) that on a NULL return from **malloc()** will attempt to free memory and try the allocation again, and perhaps call **abort()** when things are in complete dire straits.

You can get garbage collectors for C and C++ to do automatic cleanup of memory. There are some tantalizing hints about garbage collection in Cocoa, but the feature was not ready for prime time by the time Mac OS X 10.4 was released. This may appear in a later version of the operating system.

Another common API issue is not assigning the return value of **realloc()**. Your program can work fine until the block of memory moves, and then you are pointing to old memory. If that old memory does not get reused right away, things will seem to work fine until the most inconvenient moment, when things will fall apart.

Only free allocated memory once: do not try to free the same pointer twice. That will usually lead to a crash as the **malloc()** data structures get confused. Also do not try to free memory you got from some other API, unless it explicitly says you can call **free()** on it. For instance, **opendir()** allocates a chunk of memory and returns it to you, but do not **free()** that memory, use **closedir()**.

Lastly, do not access memory you have just freed. The old (stale) data may still be there, but that is something you do not want to depend on, especially in a threaded environment.

Memory corruption

Memory corruption happens when a piece of code writes data into the wrong location in memory. At best you will try writing into memory you do not have access to and will crash. At worst you will slightly corrupt some data structure which will manifest itself in an error millions of instructions in the future.

The most common kinds of memory errors in C are buffer overruns and dangling pointers.

Buffer overruns are when you think you have a certain amount of memory at your disposal but you actually have less than that allocated. A classic example is forgetting to account for the trailing zero byte for C string termination.

For instance:

```
char *stringCopy = malloc (strlen(mystring));
strcpy (stringCopy, mystring);
```

You have just written one byte past the end of your allocated block of memory. To correct this, you need to account for that extra byte:

```
char *stringCopy = malloc (strlen(mystring) + 1);
strcpy (stringCopy, mystring);
```

Off-by-one errors (also called "obiwans" or "fence-post errors") can also cause a buffer overrun. For instance:

```
void myFunction ()
{
    int i;
    ListNode mynodes[20];
    char stringBuffer[1024];

    for (i = 0; i <= 20; i++) {
        mynodes[i].stuff = i;
        ...
    }

} // myFunction
```

Note that the loop runs from 0 through 20, which is 21 times through the loop. The last time through the loop is indexing past the end of the `mynodes` array and (most likely) has just trashed the beginning of the `stringBuffer` array. What can make buffer overruns like this so nasty is that **malloc()** stores bookkeeping information in memory immediately before the pointer it gives you. If you overrun a buffer off the beginning of the buffer you will smash that information. If you overrun off the end it could smash the **malloc()** information of another buffer. When you go to free that second piece of memory, you might crash inside of **free()**, and then spend a while on a wild goose chase wondering why some piece of good code just failed.

Another nasty side effect of buffer overruns like this is that malicious data could clobber the stack in such a way that when the function returns, program control will jump to an unexpected place. Many Windows platform exploits work like this.

Dangling pointers are memory addresses stored in pointer variables that do not have any correlation with the memory they should be pointing to. Uninitialized pointers can cause this, as can forgetting to assign the return value of **realloc()**, as well as not propagating the address when memory moves or is changed. For instance:

```
char *g_username;

const char *getUserName ()
{
    return (g_username);
}

void setUserName (const char *newName)
{
    free (g_username);
    g_username = strdup (newName); // performs a malloc
}
```

Now consider this scenario:

```
name = getUserName(); // say it is address 0x1000, "markd"
setUserName ("bork"); // the memory at address 0x1000 has been freed
printf (name);        // using a dangling pointer now
```

The OS X **malloc()** libraries have some built-in tools to help track down some of these conditions. You control it by setting environment variables and then running your program. (If you are debugging a GUI app, you can run it from the command line by doing "`open /path/to/your/AppBundle.app`".)

```
$ export MallocHelp=1
```

will display help. (C Shell users would use `setenv MallocHelp 1`). When you are done using MallocHelp, you can remove the environment variable by using the `unset` command. (C Shell users would use `unsetenv`) To turn off `MallocHelp` you would execute `unset MallocHelp`. The next few sections will cover what some of the different environment variables are and what they do when set. All are case-sensitive.

MallocGuardEdges

For large blocks, this puts a 4k page with no permissions before and after the allocation. This will catch buffer overruns before and after the allocated block. The size of a "large block" is undefined, but experimentally 12K and larger seem to be considered large blocks.

Example 5-5 is a little program to show it in action:

Example 5-5. mallocguard.m

```
// mallocguard.m -- exercise MallocGuardEdges.

/* compile with:
cc -g -Wall -o mallocguard mallocguard.m
*/

#import <stdlib.h>

int main (int argc, char *argv[])
{
    unsigned char *memory = malloc (1024 * 16);
    unsigned char *dummy = malloc (1024 * 16);

    unsigned char *offTheEnd = memory + (1024 * 16) + 1;

    *offTheEnd = 'x';

    return (0);

} // main
```

The first **malloc()** gets us 16K of memory. The second one is there to provide some more pages of memory that can be clobbered with the bad assignment to offTheEnd.

Running it normally gives us this:

```
$ ./mallocguard
$
```

Like nothing happend. Let us turn on the guard:

```
$ export MallocGuardEdges=1
$ ./mallocguard
(9436) malloc: protecting edges
Bus error
```

A program error found for us. gdb can tell us exactly where the error happened.

MallocScribble

This writes over freed blocks with a known value (0x55) which will catch attempts to reuse memory blocks. That is a bad pointer value (an odd address) which will cause addressing errors if it gets used. Judging from experiments, **free()** will always clear the first 8 or so bytes to zero on a free which will catch some errors, but not all. Also, MallocScribble is broken in some versions of Mac OS X 10.3 and 10.4. It does not scribble on small blocks, and causes crashes on larger blocks.

Example 5-6 is a little example that you can use to exercise MallocScribble.

Example 5-6. mallocscribble.m

```
// mallocscribble.m -- exercise MallocScribble

/* compile wth:
cc -g -Wall -o mallocscribble mallocscribble.m
*/

#import <stdlib.h>      // for malloc()
#import <stdio.h>       // for printf()
#import <string.h>      // for strcpy()

typedef struct Thingie {
    char blah[16];
    char string[30];
} Thingie;

int main (int argc, char *argv[])
{
    Thingie *thing = malloc (sizeof(Thingie));

    strcpy (thing->string, "hello there");
    printf ("before free: %s\n", thing->string);
    free (thing);
    printf ("after free: %s\n", thing->string);

    return (0);

} // main
```

(The 16-character `blah` entry is to work around **free()**'s zeroing of the data so the code can show what it is doing with `MallocScribble` enabled.)

Here is the run without anything set in the environment:

```
$ ./mallocscribble
before free: hello there
after free: hello there
```

And after, on an older system before MallocScribble broke:

```
$ export MallocScribble=1
$ ./mallocscribble
malloc[20701]: enabling scribbling to detect mods to free blocks
before free: hello there
after free: UUUUUUUUUUUUUUUUUUUUUUUUUUUUUUU
```

MallocStackLogging and MallocStackLoggingNoCompact

Records stacks on memory management calls for later use by tools like `malloc_history`.

MallocCheckHeapStart

After *n* dynamic memory operations, start performing sanity checks of the **malloc()** data structures for any signs of corruption.. Example 5-7 lets you play with MallocCheckHeapStart.

Example 5-7. malloccheckstart.m

```
// malloccheckstart.m -- play with MallocCheckHeapStart

/* compile wth:
cc -g -Wall -o malloccheckstart malloccheckstart.m
*/

#import <stdlib.h>    // for malloc()
#import <string.h>    // for memset()

int main (int argc, char *argv[])
{
    int i;
    unsigned char *memory;

    for (i = 0; i < 10000; i++) {
        memory = malloc (10);

        if (i == 3783) {
            // smash some memory
            memset (memory-16, 0x55, 26);
        }
    }
    return (0);
} // main
```

If you just run it, it seems to work OK:

```
$ ./malloccheckstart
$
```

But export MallocCheckHeapStart=100 and you get a lot of information. (This is another debugging aid that has become broken in later versions of Mac OS X, at least in version 10.4.2. Hopefully it will fixed in a later version)

```
$ ./malloccheckstart
malloc[20765]: checks heap after 100th operation and each \
1000 operations
MallocCheckHeap: PASSED check at 100th operation
MallocCheckHeap: PASSED check at 1100th operation
MallocCheckHeap: PASSED check at 2100th operation
MallocCheckHeap: PASSED check at 3100th operation
*** malloc[20765]: invariant broken for 0x52f20 (prev_free=0) this
msize=21845
*** malloc[20765]: Region 0 incorrect szone_check_all() counter=5
*** malloc[20765]: error: Check: region incorrect
*** MallocCheckHeap: FAILED check at 4100th operation
Stack for last operation where the malloc check succeeded:
0x70056c80 0x700042b0 ...
(Use 'atos' for a symbolic stack)
```

```
*** Recommend using 'setenv MallocCheckHeapStart 3100;
setenv MallocCheckHeapEach 100' to narrow down failure
*** Sleeping for 100 seconds to leave time to attach
```

Then use gdb to attach to the running program and poke around to see what is going on.

These are really handy utilities. They do not pinpoint exactly what went wrong, but they are useful for narrowing down the error possibilities.

Guard Malloc

Xcode comes with libgmalloc (Guard Malloc), which is an aggressive debugging malloc library, geared to catch memory overrun errors like reading or writing off the end of an array.

When libgmalloc is enabled, each memory allocation is placed on its own virtual memory, with the end of the buffer placed at the end of the page's memory. The next page is kept unallocated. You will generate a signal if you try to access beyond the end of the buffer. This will immediately catch thee kinds of errors.

When memory is freed, libgmalloc deallocates its virtual memory, causing reads or writes to cause a bus error. Because of all of the extra pressure put on the virtual memory system, your application can run ten to one hundred times slower, so you probably do not want to run this all of the time, but when you need help tracking down nasty memory corruption problems, this can be a life-saver.

To enable libgmalloc, set the environment variable DYLD_INSERT_LIBRARIES to have the value /usr/lib/libgmalloc.dylib. This will cause the libgmalloc library to be loaded, and override the existing definitions of **malloc()** and **free()**. You can either set this in your environment before running the program:

```
$ export DYLD_INSERT_LIBRARIES=/usr/lib/libgmalloc.dylib
```

Or set it in gdb before running your program:

```
$ set env DYLD_INSERT_LIBRARIES /usr/local/libgmalloc.dylib
```

When your program reads or writes off of the end of a dynamically allocated chunk of memory, the debugger will halt execution of your program, and you can then poke around and see what went wrong.

Memory Leaks

Another common set of memory-related errors are memory leaks. These are bits of memory that get allocated and never deallocated. Frequently, memory leaks happen when you assign a pointer to a new value but do not free the old value:

```
char *mystring;
mystring = strdup ("hello"); // performs a malloc() and a string copy
mystring = strdup ("there");
```

The first string ("hello") has been leaked. Because the address of that memory was never preserved, it can never be freed. A little memory leaked here or there, aside from being a bit sloppy, is not all that bad in today's systems with gobs of RAM. What is the real killer are leaks that happen often, like inside of a loop, or every time the user does a common operation. Leaking 100 bytes is not too bad. Leaking 100 bytes every time the user presses a key in a word processor can be deadly. Applications in Mac OS X tend to stay running for long periods of time. The user may forget about an app, then click on it in the Dock to do something with it. A small memory leak can really add up when your program can be running for weeks between restarts.

One easy way to tell if your program is leaking is to run the `top` program, find your application in the list, and watch the right-most column. If that number is continually increasing, you probably have a memory leak.

OS X comes with a utility called `leaks` that will grovel around in your program's address space and find unreferenced memory. `leaks` is a good quick check to see if there are any leaks. It walks your programs address space like a garbage collector, looking for pointers into **malloc()** blocks. If it cannot find one, `leaks` will report a leak, along with a dump of some of the bytes near start of the block. If the leaked chunk of memory is an instance of an an Objective-C object, `leaks` will show the name of the class:

```
$ leaks BorkGraph
Process 21669: 26306 nodes malloced for 2042 KB
Process 21669: 154 leaks for 5120 total leaked bytes.
Leak: 0x011f3c50  size=40
  0x77eb239b 0x00000020 0x011f3ca0 0x00000001      w.#.... ..X.....
  0x00000065 0x00000065 0x00000065 0x00000000      ...e...e...e....
  0x011b8de0 0x011b8e30 0x00000000 0x00000000      .......o........
Leak: 0x011f3ca0  size=48          string 'xrvt'
Leak: 0x02634eb0  size=32          instance of 'NSAffineTransform'
  0xa287e7ac 0x40ccb65b 0x80000000 0x80000000      ....@..[........
  0x40ccb65b 0xc226542a 0xc2f88fc7 0x00000000      @..[.xT*........
```

Memory Leaks in Cocoa

In addition to **malloc()**-related memory leaks, you can also leak memory in Cocoa programs by not being careful with your `retain` and `release` calls. Example 5-8 intentionally leaks some objects.

For instance:

Example 5-8. objectleak.m

```
// objectleak.m -- leak some Cocoa objects

/* compile with:
cc -g -Wall -framework Foundation -o objectleak objectleak.m
*/

#import <Foundation/Foundation.h>

int main (int argc, char *argv[])
{
    NSAutoreleasePool *pool = [[NSAutoreleasePool alloc] init];
    NSMutableArray *array = [[NSMutableArray alloc] init];
    NSNumber *number;
```

```
    int i;

    for (i = 0; i < 20; i++) {
        // alloc creates an object with a retain count of 1
        number = [[NSNumber alloc] initWithInt: i];
        [array addObject: number]; // number has retain count of 2
    }

    [array release]; // each of the numbers have retain counts of 1

    [pool release];

    return (0);

} // main
```

Each of the `NSNumber` objects still has a retain count of one after the array is released, therefore they have been leaked. `MallocDebug.app` can show some information about the leaks. `ObjectAlloc.app`, discussed in Chapter 25 (Performance), can show you Cocoa object leaks as well.

For the More Curious

ps and top

The `ps` command ("process status") command has some features for keeping tabs on your program's memory use. Here is a handy use of `ps`:

```
$ ps -auxw | grep something-interesting
```

where `something-interesting` is the PID or program name of interest. So, something like

```
$ ps -auxw | grep Finder
```

will show some information about the Finder process:

```
markd   229   0.0  1.9    84160  10096  ??  S   0:43.11 /System/ \
Library/CoreServices/Finder.app/Contents/MacOS/Finder -psn_0_2621
```

In order, the columns are:

1. Owner of the process (markd).

2. Process ID (229).

3. CPU currently taken (0.0%).

4. Real memory in use (1.9%).

5. Virtual size, the total footprint of the program (84160K, or 84 megs).

6. Resident set size, how much is living in RAM right now. (This is 10096K, or about 10 megs, which for a 512 meg machine is about 1.9%. It is nice when those things work out.)

7. Controlling terminal (not important).

8. Process state (more about this in Chapter 13 (Multiprocessing)).

9. Total CPU time consumed by the process (43 seconds).

10. Command with arguments that started the process.

Relating to memory, the fifth and sixth columns are the most interesting. You can look at just those with the command

```
ps -ax -o user,pid,vsz,rss,command
```

Which will show the owner, the PID, the virtual size,the resident size, and the command. ps can show a wealth of information about what is running on your system. Check out the man page for more.

You can run this repeatedly to see if your program (or any other) seems to be growing without bound.

The top program, referenced a little earlier, also shows a wealth of information, and it updates stuff in real time.

Here is a sample snapshot during the writing this chapter:

```
Processes: 42 total, 3 running, 39 sleeping. 124 threads        15:00:28
Load Avg: 0.27, 0.18, 0.01 CPU usage: 14.2% user, 12.4% sys, 73.5% idle
SharedLibs: num = 113, resident = 20.7M code, 2.31M data, 5.99M LinkEdit
MemRegions:num = 3733, resident = 52.5M + 3.58M private, 41.7M shared
PhysMem:  44.5M wired, 78.2M active, 81.9M inactive, 205M used, 307M free
VM: 2.19G + 56.0M   59120(0) pageins, 254239(0) pageouts
```

PID	COMMAND	%CPU	TIME	#TH	#PRTS	#MREGS	RPRVT	RSHRD	RSIZE	VSIZE
21013	top	9.7%	0:00.81	1	14	15	212K	372K	468K	1.62M
21007	tcsh	0.0%	0:00.12	1	24	16	488K	700K	960K	5.76M
21001	tcsh	0.0%	0:00.15	1	24	16	488K	700K	956K	5.76M
20467	Mozilla	0.0%	2:32.92	6	87	368	17.7M	21.8M	31.4M	86.4M
20318	tcsh	0.0%	0:00.11	1	16	16	0K	648K	0K	9.46M
19895	BorkPad	0.0%	0:03.03	2	113	99	804K	6.04M	764K	56.0M
18612	TruBlueEn	2.6%	84:27.76	18	177	231	10.7M	3.55M	12.8M	1.05G
17407	tcsh	0.0%	0:00.31	1	16	16	288K	668K	384K	9.46M
6779	tcsh	0.0%	0:00.13	1	16	16	0K	648K	0K	9.46M
1086	tcsh	0.0%	0:01.17	1	16	17	296K	668K	504K	9.71M
327	emacs	0.0%	2:09.06	1	13	558	4.27M	1.72M	5.61M	13.1M
297	SecurityA	0.0%	0:01.34	2	88	86	696K	4.95M	748K	54.2M
270	tcsh	0.0%	0:00.21	1	24	17	0K	648K	0K	5.74M
259	Terminal	3.5%	12:43.40	8	133	582	3.65M	8.28M	7.30M	64.0M
254	automount	0.0%	0:00.04	2	11	19	48K	432K	124K	2.14M

The stuff related to memory is bolded.

```
MemRegions: num = 3733, resident = 52.5M + 3.58M private, 41.7M shared
```

This line tells us the number of memory regions (blocks of allocated memory from the kernel), how much RAM is currently swapped in, how much is private to the kernel, and how much is shared between processes (like for text segments of programs).

```
PhysMem:44.5M wired, 78.2M active, 81.9M inactive, 205M used, 307M free
```

This describes the physical memory:

wired memory

> Memory that will not be swapped out to disk.

active memory

> Physical memory that is resident and mapped (a process has active use of the memory), and it has been recently accessed.

inactive memory

> Pages currently resident in physical memory, but have not been recently accessed. They contain valid data. These pages are ripe for being swapped out to disk.

used memory

> The sum of wired, active, and inactive memory.

free memory

> Pages no longer containing valid data. The system can use these to cache disk blocks.

The numbers (44.5 + 78.2 + 81.9 + 307) add up to 511.6, which is close enough to the 512M of RAM installed on the machine.

```
VM: 2.19G + 56.0M   59120(0) pageins, 254239(0) pageouts
```

2.19 gigs of cumulative virtual address space are being consumed on machine. Along with 56 megs of virtual address space consumed by the kernel.

There have been 59,120 pageins (bringing pages from swap into memory) and 254,239 pageouts (moving pages from memory into swap). Recently there have not been any pageins or pageouts. (There was a whole lot of virtual memory activity with some sample programs that ran amok allocating huge reams of memory.)

The columns RPRVT, RSHRD, RSIZE, and VSIZE all relate to memory.

RPRVT

> Resident private memory.

RSHRD

> Resident shared memory.

RSIZE

> Total resident memory. Total number of real pages that this process currently has associated with it. Includes pages that may be shared with other processes. RPRVT does not include pages that are shared.

VSIZE

> Total address space currently mapped, but not necessarily allocated. If you were to touch every page of the mapped address space, RSIZE would be the same as VSIZE.

RSIZE and VSIZE are the most interesting ones, especially if they are increasing, or are huge.

Resource limits

Since Unix is a a multi-user system, there are safeguards in the OS to keep processes from dominating (and possibly bringing down) the system by consuming too many resources. There are a number of different resources that are controlled:

RLIMIT_DATA

Maximum size (bytes) of the data segment for a process (that is, the maximum size of the heap plus initialized + uninitialized data segments).

RLIMIT_RSS

Maximum size (bytes) which a processes resident set may grow (e.g., maximum amount of physical RAM to be given). If memory becomes scare, the system will first take memory away from processes that have exceeded their RSS limit.

RLIMIT_STACK

Maximum size (bytes) of the stack segment. How deep your program stack can get.

RLIMIT_MEMLOCK

Maximum size (bytes) which a process can lock (wire) into memory with the **mlock()** function.

There are also resources not related to memory:

RLIMIT_FSIZE

Maximum size (bytes) of a file that may be created.

RLIMIT_NOFILE

Maximum number of simultaneously open files.

RLIMIT_NPROC

Maximum number of simultaneous processes for the current user.

RLIMIT_CPU

Maximum amount of CPU time (in seconds).

RLIMIT_CORE

Largest size (in bytes) of core files.

Resource limits are expressed as a soft limit and a hard limit. When the soft limit is exceeded, the program may receive a signal (like a software interrupt. Signals are discussed in depth in Chapter 7 (Exceptions)) but it will be allowed to continue execution until it reaches the hard limit. The soft limits are usually set lower, but you can raise them to the hard limit. You can lower the hard limit, but you can never raise the hard limit unless you are running with superuser privileges.

Example 5-9 shows you the hard and soft limits currently in force:

Example 5-9. limits.m

```
// limits.m -- see the resource limits in force

/* compile with:
cc -g -Wall -o limits limits.m
*/

#import <sys/types.h>
#import <sys/time.h>
#import <sys/resource.h>
#import <stdio.h>
#import <string.h>
#import <errno.h>

typedef struct Limit {
    int resource;
    const char *name;
} Limit;

Limit limits[] = {
    { RLIMIT_DATA,      "data segment maximum (bytes)" },
    { RLIMIT_RSS,       "resident size maximum (bytes)" },
    { RLIMIT_STACK,     "stack size maximum (bytes)" },
    { RLIMIT_MEMLOCK,   "wired memory maximum (bytes)" },
    { RLIMIT_FSIZE,     "file size maximum (bytes)" },
    { RLIMIT_NOFILE,    "max number of simultaneously open files" },
    { RLIMIT_NPROC,     "max number of simultaneous processes" },
    { RLIMIT_CPU,       "cpu time maximum (seconds)" },
    { RLIMIT_CORE,      "core file maximum (bytes)" }
};

// turn the rlim_t value in to a string, also translating the magic
// "infinity" value to something human readable
void stringValue (rlim_t value, char *buffer, size_t buffersize)
{
    if (value == RLIM_INFINITY) {
        strcpy (buffer, "infinite");
    } else {
        snprintf (buffer, buffersize, "%lld", value);
    }
} // stringValue

// right-justify the first entry in a field width of 45, then display
// two more strings

#define FORMAT_STRING "%45s: %-10s (%s)\n"

int main (int argc, char *argv[])
{
    struct rlimit rl;
    Limit *scan, *stop;

    scan = limits;
    stop = scan + (sizeof(limits) / sizeof(Limit));

    printf (FORMAT_STRING, "limit name", "soft-limit", "hard-limit");
```

```
    while (scan < stop) {
        if (getrlimit (scan->resource, &rl) == -1) {
            fprintf (stderr, "error in getrlimit for %s: %d/%s\n",
                        scan->name, errno, strerror(errno));
        } else {
            char soft[20];
            char hard[20];

            stringValue (rl.rlim_cur, soft, 20);
            stringValue (rl.rlim_max, hard, 20);

            printf (FORMAT_STRING, scan->name, soft, hard);
        }
        scan++;
    }
    return (0);
} // main
```

And here is the output on my system:

```
                             limit name: soft-limit (hard-limit)
           data segment maximum (bytes): 6291456    (infinite)
          resident size maximum (bytes): infinite   (infinite)
             stack size maximum (bytes): 8388608    (67108864)
           wired memory maximum (bytes): infinite   (infinite)
              file size maximum (bytes): infinite   (infinite)
    max number of simultaneously open files: 256     (infinite)
        max number of simultaneous processes: 100    (532)
             cpu time maximum (seconds): infinite   (infinite)
              core file maximum (bytes): 0          (infinite)
```

All things considered, the system is pretty kind to us.

You read the current resource limits by using **getrlimit()** as shown in the code above, and you can change the resource limits by using **setrlimit()** and passing it an appropriately filled in struct rlimit.

Example 5-10 is a program that will attempt to open the same file over and over. (It is easier to show resource limits with files than trying to overflow the stack.)

Example 5-10. openfiles.m

```
// openfiles.m -- see what happens when we open a lot of files

/* compile with:
cc -g -Wall -o openfiles openfiles.m
*/

#import <fcntl.h>
#import <stdio.h>

int main (int argc, char *argv[])
{
    int fd, i;
```

```
    for (i = 0; i < 260; i++) {
        fd = open ("/usr/include/stdio.h", O_RDONLY);
        printf ("%d: fd is %d\n", i, fd);
    }

    return (0);

} // main
```

When run, this happens:

```
$ ./openfiles
0: fd is 3
1: fd is 4
2: fd is 5
...
250: fd is 253
251: fd is 254
252: fd is 255
253: fd is -1
254: fd is -1
```

Note that the fd variable starts becoming -1 (cannot open the file) after a value of 255 (which correlates with what the result of limits.m up above). There are already the 3 files opened for us, stdin, stdout, stderror, which count as open files against the resource limit.

Example 5-11 is a modification to openfiles.m to set the soft limit:

Example 5-11. openfiles.m (revised)

```
// openfiles.m -- see what happens when we open a lot of files

/* compile with:
cc -g -Wall -o openfiles openfiles.m
*/

#import <sys/types.h>
#import <sys/time.h>
#import <sys/resource.h>
#import <fcntl.h>
#import <stdio.h>
#import <errno.h>

int main (int argc, char *argv[])
{
    int fd, i;
    int limit;
    struct rlimit rl;

    if (argc != 2) {
        fprintf (stderr, "usage:  %s open-file-rlimit\n", argv[0]);
        exit (1);
    }
    limit = atoi (argv[1]);
    rl.rlim_cur = limit;
    rl.rlim_max = RLIM_INFINITY;
```

```
    if (setrlimit(RLIMIT_NOFILE, &rl) == -1) {
        fprintf (stderr, "error in setrlimit, RLIM_NOFILE: %d/%s\n",
                errno, strerror(errno));
        exit (1);
    }

    for (i = 0; i < 260; i++) {
        fd = open ("/usr/include/stdio.h", O_RDONLY);
        printf ("%d: fd is %d\n", i, fd);
    }

    return (0);

} // main
```

Here are some sample runs:

```
$ ./openfiles 10
0: fd is 3
1: fd is 4
2: fd is 5
3: fd is 6
4: fd is 7
5: fd is 8
6: fd is 9
7: fd is -1
8: fd is -1

$ ./openfiles 1000000
0: fd is 3
1: fd is 4
2: fd is 5
...
257: fd is 260
258: fd is 261
259: fd is 262
```

Setting lower resource limits can be handy when you are spawning off other programs (which is talked about in Chapter 13 (Multiprocessing)). If you do not trust the other programs, or want to constrain their limits, you can use **setrlimit()** on yourself, then launch your child process who will run under the reduced limits.

Some other tools

The heap command lists all the **malloc()**-allocated buffers in the heap of a program. Give it the PID of the program to look at.

heap is interesting when pointed at a Cocoa program because it shows Objective-C classes. Here is stuff from objectleak.m (edited down):

```
Process 6999: 4 zones
All zones: 1139 nodes malloced - 103KB
...
All zones: 1139 nodes malloced - Sizes: 32KB[1] 16KB[1]
  4KB[1] 2062[1] 2046[1] 1806[1] 878[1] 862[1] 638[1] 558[1]
  526[2] 398[1] 270[1] 254[2] 238[1] 222[1] 206[1] 190[3]
```

```
174[2] 158[4] 142[3] 126[4] 110[3] 94[9] 78[10] 62[40]
46[186]  30[787] 14[69]
...
Found 232 ObjC classes in process 6999
...
Zone DefaultMallocZone_0x8b1d0: 1139 nodes (105054 bytes)

<not Objective C object>  = 1103 (104438 bytes)
NSshortNumber             = 20 (280 bytes)
NSRandomSpecifier         = 1 (14 bytes)
NSAutoreleasePool         = 1 (30 bytes)
NSPlaceholderValue        = 1 (14 bytes)
NSunsignedIntNumber       = 1 (14 bytes)
NSHTTPURLHandle           = 1 (14 bytes)
NSPlaceholderMutableArray = 1 (14 bytes)
NSCFBoolean               = 1 (14 bytes)
NSPlaceholderNumber       = 1 (14 bytes)
NSMachPort                = 1 (14 bytes)
NSMiddleSpecifier         = 1 (14 bytes)
NSFormatter               = 1 (14 bytes)
NSNotificationCenter      = 1 (62 bytes)
NSValue                   = 1 (14 bytes)
NSMoveCommand             = 1 (14 bytes)
NSThread                  = 1 (62 bytes)
NSTerminologyRegistry     = 1 (14 bytes)
```

All sorts of cool stuff that is lurking under the hood, such as the notification center, a Mach port, a thread, and the 20 NSshortNumbers.

malloc_history will show you a history of memory activity. This requires that you set MallocStackLogging to 1 in your environment before running.

Example 5-12 is a program that does some memory manipulations, and then sleeps:

Example 5-12. mallochistory.m

```
// mallochistory.m -- do some mallocation so we can use malloc_history
// be sure to the environment variable MallocStackLogging or
// MallocStackLoggingNoCompact to 1. Then run this program, and while
// it sleeps at the end, run 'malloc_history pid -all_by_size' or
// 'malloc_history pid -all_by_count'

/* compile with:
cc -g -Wall -o mallochistory mallochistory.m
*/

#import <unistd.h>   // for getpid(), sleep()
#import <stdlib.h>   // for malloc()
#import <stdio.h>    // for printf

void func2 ()
{
    char *stuff;
    int i;

    for (i = 0; i < 3; i++) {
        stuff = malloc (50);
        free (stuff);
```

```
        }
        stuff = malloc (50);
        // so we can use the malloc_history address feature
        printf ("address of stuff is %p\n", stuff);

        // intentionally leak stuff

    } // func2

    void func1 ()
    {
        int *numbers;

        numbers = malloc (sizeof(int) * 100);
        func2 ();

        // intentionally leak numbers

    } // func1

    int main (int argc, char *argv[])
    {
        printf ("my process id is %d\n", getpid());
        func1 ();

        sleep (600);
        return (0);
    } // main
```

When run, this program does:

```
$ export MallocStackLogging=1
$ ./mallochistory
malloc[7090]: recording stacks using standard recorder
my process id is 7098
address of stuff is 0x45490
```

Then in another terminal, see who has manipulated the block:

```
$ malloc_history 7098 0x45490

Call [2] [arg=50]: thread_800013b8 |0xbffffc80 | start | _start
    | main | func1 | func2 | malloc | malloc_zone_malloc
```

You can also see what stuff is currently allocated and who did it. In this case, the stack entries are ordered by size. Stuff that is purely overhead has been removed.

```
$ malloc_history 7098 -all_by_size
1 calls for 131072 bytes: thread_800013b8 |0xbffffc80 | start
    | _start | main | printf | vfprintf | __swsetup | __smakebuf
    | malloc | malloc_zone_malloc
```

Looks like **printf()** and friends need a big (128K) buffer to do their work:

```
1 calls for 400 bytes: thread_800013b8 |0xbffffc80 | start | _start
    | main | func1 | malloc | malloc_zone_malloc
```

Here is the numbers array:

```
1 calls for 50 bytes: thread_800013b8 |0xbffffc80 | start | _start
    | main | func1 | func2 | malloc | malloc_zone_malloc
```

And the final **malloc()** from **func2()**.

vm_stat

vm_stat shows some Mach virtual memory statistics. Here it is for my system right now:

```
Mach Virtual Memory Statistics: (page size of 4096 bytes)
Pages free:                      62921.
Pages active:                    19655.
Pages inactive:                  36597.
Pages wired down:                11899.
"Translation faults":         20246163.
Pages copy-on-write:           1330902.
Pages zero filled:             4738887.
Pages reactivated:              595761.
Pageins:                         60044.
Pageouts:                       254239.
Object cache: 412841 hits of 484419 lookups (85% hit rate)
```

You could run vm_stat at different points in time to see if your system is swapping (lots of pageins and pageouts). The man page has information on each of the entries.

vmmap

vmmap is like leaks and heap in that it looks into a running program. In this case, it shows all the mapped pages in memory, including permissions on the pages. There is a lot of output from this command.

Remember earlier when MallocGuardEdges considered a "large block" to be 12K? I used vmmap to figure that out, using a program like Example 5-13

Example 5-13. mallochelp.m

```
// mallochelp.m -- try to figure out the "large" block size

/* compile with
cc -g -Wall -o mallochelp mallochelp.m
*/

#import <sys/types.h>   // for random types
#import <unistd.h>      // for getpid(), sleep()
#import <stdlib.h>      // for malloc()
#import <stdio.h>       // for printf()

int main (int argc, char *argv[])
{
    malloc (1024 * 16);
    printf ("my process ID is %d\n", getpid());
    sleep (30);
    return (0);
```

```
} // main
```

will run, print its process ID, and sleep. I ran vmmap on it and directed its output to a file:

```
$ ./mallochelp
my process ID is 7139
```

and in another terminal window:

```
$ vmmap 7139 > tmp1
```

Then set the MallocGuardEdges environment variable and run mallochelp again:

```
$ export MallocGuardEdges=1
$ ./mallochelp
malloc[7141]: protecting edges
my process ID is 7141
```

and run in the other terminal window:

```
$ vmmap 7141 > tmp2
```

And then diff the two:

```
$ diff tmp1 tmp2
```

And the interesting lines are:

```
> GUARD                    84000 [    4K] ---/rwx SM=NUL
> GUARD                    ab000 [    4K] ---/rwx SM=NUL
```

These are two new guard pages of 4K in size, with no user permissions (---) on them. I just kept lowering the amount of memory allocated until these guard pages did not appear.

Challenge

Find all the errors in Example 5-14, some of which are memory related (I found nine of them).

Example 5-14. memerror.m

```
// memerror.h -- try to find (and fix!) all the memory-related errors
//                in this program

// Take a string from the command line.  Make a linked-list out of it
// in reverse order. Traverse it to construct a string in reverse.
// Then clean up afterwards.

/* compile with
cc -g -o memerror memerror.m
*/

#import <stdio.h>
#import <stdlib.h>
```

```
typedef struct CharNode {
    char theChar;
    struct CharNode *next;
} CharNode;


// build a linked list backwards, then walk the list.

void reverseIt (char *stringbuffer)
{
    CharNode *head, *node;
    char *scan, *stop;

    // clear out local vars
    head = node = NULL;

    // find the start and end of the string so we can walk it
    scan = stringbuffer;
    stop = stringbuffer + strlen(stringbuffer) + 1;

    // walk the string
    while (scan < stop) {
        if (head == NULL) {
            head = malloc (sizeof(CharNode*));
            head->theChar = *scan;
            head->next = NULL;
        } else {
            node = malloc (sizeof(CharNode*));
            node->theChar = *scan;
            node->next = head;
            head = node;
        }
        scan++;
    }

     // ok, re-point to the buffer so we can drop the characters
    scan = stringbuffer;

    // walk the nodes and add them to the string
    while (head != NULL) {
        *scan = head->theChar;
        free (head);
        node = head->next;
        head = node;
        scan++;
    }

    // clean up the head
    free (head);

} // reverseIt


int main (int argc, char *argv[])
{
    char *stringbuffer;
```

```
        // make sure the user supplied enough arguments.  If not, complain
        if (argc != 2) {
            fprintf (stderr, "usage: %s string.  This reverses the string "
                    "given on the command line\n");
            exit (1);
        }

        // make a copy of the argument so we can make changes to it
        stringbuffer = malloc (strlen(argv[1]));
        strcpy (argv[1], stringbuffer);

        // reverse the string
        reverseIt (stringbuffer);

        // and print it out
        printf ("the reversed string is '%s'\n", *stringbuffer);

        return (0);

    } // main
```

Chapter 6. Debugging With GDB

What is a Debugger?

A debugger is a program that runs your program and has the power to suspend its execution and poke around in memory, examining and changing memory values. It can catch your program after it runs into trouble so you can investigate the problem. Debuggers know about the data structures you are using and can display those structures in an intelligent way. You can experiment with your program, and you can also step through someone else's code to figure out how it works.

Mac OS X comes with gdb, the GNU project's debugger, which has a long heritage dating back to 1988. It is fundamentally a command-line oriented tool, but it has been extended over the years to make integration into IDEs (like Xcode and emacs) pretty easy.

To effectively use the debugger, your program needs to be compiled with debugging symbols enabled (usually by giving the -g flag to the compiler). These debugging symbols include lookup tables that map addresses in memory to the appropriate source file and line of code as well as data type information for the program's custom data structures. You can freely mix code which has debug symbols and no debug symbols. gdb will try its best it can to present a reasonable view of the world. Understandably, you will not be able to do much with code that has not been compiled with debug symbols.

Documentation for gdb can be found at
/Developers/Documentation/DeveloperTools/gdb/gdb/gdb_toc.html. gdb has a positively huge feature list, but you will hit the highlights here.

Using GDB From The Command Line

First, look at driving gdb from the command line. Why waste time with gdb's command line mode? Historically gdb has been a command line program. You have access to all of gdb's features, both common and esoteric. The GUIs that are layered on top of gdb never export all of the features and so can limit some of the power that is lurking under the hood. Luckily, Xcode gives you a console pane to interact with gdb's command line, so you have the best of both worlds there.

Being comfortable at the gdb command line also makes gdb more useful when you want to do remote debugging, that is, running your program and the debugger on another machine over an ssh connection. Xcode has some remote debugging facilities, but it requires that Xcode be installed on both the local and remote machines. gdb is also available for many Unix platforms, so it you become comfortable with the gdb command line, you can apply your debugging skills to those other platforms.

A Sample GDB Session

At the end of Chapter 5 (Memory) is a challenge to find all nine errors in the program memerror, which reverses a string given to the program as a command line argument.

Here we will use gdb and track down some of the errors.

Compile the program and make sure the -g flag is used to turn on debug symbols:

```
$ cc -g -o memerror memerror.m
```

If you are using Xcode, make sure that no optimizations are turned on. Otherwise, single-stepping will behave erratically.

Trying to run the program gives this:

```
$ ./memerror blargle
the reversed string is '(null)'
```

Which is not the desired result.

Start gdb and tell it to use memerror for the target program:

```
$ gdb ./memerror
GNU gdb 6.1-20040303 (Apple version gdb-413)(Wed May 18 10:17:02 GMT 200
Copyright 2004 Free Software Foundation, Inc.
[...]
(gdb)
```

Here gdb gives you its prompt. Since this is a small program, you will single-step over some code. Set a breakpoint on the **main()** function. A breakpoint is a spot in your code where gdb will halt your program's execution and give control to gdb so you can look around.

Use the break command to set a a breakpoint at the beginning of a function. This breakpoint will get triggered before any code in the function gets executed:

```
(gdb) break main
Breakpoint 1 at 0x2b98: file memerror.m, line 73.
```

and run the program:

```
(gdb) run
Starting program: /Users/markd/Projects/core-osx/gdb-chap/memerror
Reading symbols for shared libraries . done

Breakpoint 1, main (argc=1, argv=0xbffff254) at memerror.m:73
73        if (argc != 2) {
```

You can see that the breakpoint on **main()** was triggered. Single-stepping, executing the program one line of code at a time, is performed by using the next command.

```
(gdb) next
74              fprintf (stderr, "usage: %s string.  This reverses the string
```

Hmmm, that is interesting. You are on the usage line. You get in this case if argc is not two. What is argc's value?

```
(gdb) print argc
$1 = 1
```

argchas a value of one because you did not specify any arguments to the program (oops). The "$1" printed in the above statement can be ignored for now. It is just a convenience variable you can use to refer to the value later.

So, just single step on out to finish the program:

```
(gdb) next
```

```
usage: kmewrkmfijq348tdrnmg8i34jtnragujnttns string. This reverses the
string given on the command line.

76            exit (1);
```

Wow. A lot of garbage there. Looks like you stumbled across the first bug (bug #1) unexpectedly:

```
fprintf (stderr, "usage: %s string.  This reverses the string "
              "given on the command line\n");
```

Note that **fprintf()** has a %s format specifier in the string, but no corresponding value to plug in there, so the function picked up some garbage from the stack. Looks like this **fprintf()** is expecting to use the name of the program as specified by the user in the message. That is an easy enough fix:

```
fprintf (stderr, "usage: %s string.  This reverses the string "
              "given on the command line\n", argv[0]);
```

You could quit gdb and run your compilation command again, or you could tell gdb to run a shell command for you:

```
(gdb) shell cc -g -o memerror memerror.m
```

Now restart the program with a command-line argument:

```
(gdb) run blargle
The program being debugged has been started already.
Start it from the beginning? (y or n)
```

and answer y and press return. It will print out:

```
'/Users/markd/Projects/core-osx/gdb-chap/memerror' has changed;
re-reading symbols.
    rereading symbols.
```

to let you know that it realizes the program is different and needs to be reloaded.

Since you did not quit gdb, the breakpoint on **main()** is still active.

```
Breakpoint 1, main (argc=2, argv=0xbffff240) at memerror.m:73
73      if (argc != 2) {
```

And double-check argc for paranoia's sake:

```
(gdb) print argc
$1 = 2
```

A value of two. Good. And for fun look at the argument vector:

```
(gdb) print argv
$2 = (char **) 0xbffff240

(gdb) print argv[0]
$3 = 0xbffff324 "/Users/markd/Projects/core-osx/gdb-chap/memerror"

(gdb) print argv[1]
$4 = 0xbffff355 "blargle"
```

That looks good. So single-step

```
(gdb) next
80      stringbuffer = malloc (strlen(argv[1]));
```

and see how big that is going to be. You can call your program's functions from inside the debugger.

```
(gdb) call (int) strlen(argv[1])
$5 = 7
```

So this will allocate 7 bytes of memory. So single-step over the allocation:

```
(gdb) n
```

You can abbreviate commands so long as they do not become ambiguous. In this case, n is the same as next.

```
(gdb) n
81      strcpy (argv[1], stringbuffer);
```

Hmmm.. wait a minute. Strings in C are null-terminated, meaning that you need an extra byte at the end. The call to **malloc()** did not allocate enough memory, so this call to **strcpy()** (which you have not executed yet) will clobber an extra byte of memory. That is easy enough to fix in code. You would change

```
stringbuffer = malloc (strlen(argv[1]));
```

to be

```
stringbuffer = malloc (strlen(argv[1]) + 1);
```

Go ahead and change the code (bug #2). No need to recompile and rerun, you can patch this error for this session immediately.

```
(gdb) set var stringbuffer = (void *)malloc ((int)strlen(argv[1]) + 1)
```

You can see that there are explicit casts for return values from the **strlen()** and **malloc()** functions. These casts are necessary when you call a function that does not have debug info, like these library functions.

OK, with that done, execute the next line of code (the **strcpy()**):

```
(gdb) n
85              reverseIt (stringbuffer);
```

Look at stringbuffer to make sure it has a resonable value:

```
(gdb) print stringbuffer
$6 = 0x300160 ""
```

What? The line of code in question is:

```
strcpy (argv[1], stringbuffer);
```

Checking the man page, it looks like the arguments are reversed. **strcpy()** takes *destination* first, then the source (bug #3). This is also an easy code change to make:

```
strcpy (stringbuffer, argv[1]);
```

Unfortunately, you cannot fix this up as easily as you did with the **malloc()** error, since the bad **strcpy()** clobbered argv[1]. You can verify that argv[1] got clobbered by moving up one stack frame (out of the **reverseIt()** function) and displaying the value of argv[1].

```
(gdb) up
(gdb) print argv[1]
$9 = 0xbffffc16 "\000"...
```

So, fix the code, and rebuild:

```
(gdb) shell cc -g -o memerror memerror.m
```

You are reasonably sure now that the code up until the call to **reverseIt()** is pretty good. So add a new breakpoint on **reverseIt()**:

```
(gdb) break reverseIt
Breakpoint 2 at 0x2a34: file memerror.m, line 29.
```

and rerun the program. You do not need to respecify the arguments given to the program, gdb will remember them.

```
(gdb) run
The program being debugged has been started already.
Start it from the beginning? (y or n) y
'/Users/markd/Projects/core-osx/gdb-chap/memerror' has changed;
re-reading symbols.
Breakpoint 1 at 0x2b74: file memerror.m, line 69.
Breakpoint 2 at 0x2a1c: file memerror.m, line 24.

Breakpoint 1, main (argc=2, argv=0xbffff240) at memerror.m:73
73      if (argc != 2) {
(gdb)
```

Thus, you can see that your first breakpoint is still there. Doing continue will resume execution until the program exits, or a breakpoint is hit.

```
(gdb) continue
Continuing.

Breakpoint 2, reverseIt (stringbuffer=0x300150 "blargle") at memerror.m:29
29      head = node = NULL;
```

You are in **reverseIt()**. You can ask gdb for a listing to remind yourself what code is involved:

```
(gdb) list
25          {
26              CharNode *head, *node;
27              char *scan, *stop;
28
29              // clear out local vars
30              head = node = NULL;
31
32              // find the start and end of the string so we can walk it
```

127

```
33              scan = stringbuffer;
34              stop = stringbuffer + strlen(stringbuffer) + 1;
```

So you are about ready to execute line 30. So some more single-stepping

```
(gdb) n
32      scan = stringbuffer;
(gdb) n
33      stop = stringbuffer + strlen(stringbuffer) + 1;
(gdb) n
36      while (scan < stop) {
```

and take a look at the pointer chase variables

```
(gdb) print scan
$1 = 0x300150 "blargle"

(gdb) print stop
$2 = 0x300158 ""
```

That looks OK. Looking at the address that `stop` has, 0x62b8, is 8 bytes past 0x62b0, the contents of `scan`. "Blargle" is 7 characters, plus the null byte is 8. You can use gdb to verify that.

```
(gdb) print 0x300158 - 0x300150
$3 = 8
```

If you do not want to type out those addresses, you can use the dollar-variable labels:

```
(gdb) print $2 - $1
$4 = 8
```

That looks good. More single stepping:

```
(gdb) n
38                      if (head == NULL) {

(gdb) n
39                          head = malloc (sizeof(CharNode*));
```

To sanity check the amount of memory being allocated:

```
(gdb) print sizeof(CharNode*)
$5 = 4
```

4 bytes. Pull apart the types here:

```
(gdb) whatis head
type = CharNode *
```

`head` is a pointer to a `CharNode`. What is a `CharNode`?

```
(gdb) ptype CharNode
type = struct CharNode {
    char theChar;
    CharNode *next;
```

```
}
```

A `CharNode` is a `char` plus a pointer. That sounds like it should be more than 4 bytes.

```
(gdb) print sizeof(CharNode)
$6 = 8
```

Sure enough, you are not allocating enough memory. Here is the line of code again:

```
head = malloc (sizeof(CharNode*));
```

Looks like a common C beginner's mistake, confusing a pointer to what it points to. The **malloc()** here is allocating enough memory for a pointer to a `CharNode`, not a full `CharNode`. To fix this, it should be

```
head = malloc (sizeof(CharNode));
```

(bug #4). Looking at the code, there is a nearly identical line of code in the `else` branch. That should be fixed too.

```
node = malloc (sizeof(CharNode*));
```

becomes

```
node = malloc (sizeof(CharNode));
```

(bug #5).

You will need to recompile and restart things to fix this. Before doing that, clean up the breakpoints. You do not need the one on **main()**, and probably do not need the one at the top of **reverseIt()** since you are pretty sure the beginning of that function is good.

For fun, do the `where` command to see the call stack.

```
(gdb) where
#0  reverseIt (stringbuffer=0x300150 "blargle") at memerror.m:38
#1  0x00002c1c in main (argc=2, argv=0xbffff240) at memerror.m:84
```

so you are at line 38 of `memerror.m` in **reverseIt()**, and at line 84 of `memerror.m`, inside of **main()**. Do a `list` to see exactly what `gdb` thinks is line 38.

```
(gdb) list
33          stop = stringbuffer + strlen(stringbuffer) + 1;
34
35          // walk the string
36          while (scan < stop) {
37              if (head == NULL) {
38                  head = malloc (sizeof(CharNode));
39                  head->theChar = *scan;
40                  head->next = NULL;
41              } else {
42                  node = malloc (sizeof(CharNode));
```

A good place to break would be on line 36, right before entering the loop.

```
(gdb) break memerror.m:36
Breakpoint 3 at 0x2a6c: file memerror.m, line 36.
```

To see all the current breakpoints, info breakpoints will show them and their ID number:

```
(gdb) info breakpoints
Num Type           Disp Enb Address    What
1   breakpoint     keep y   0x00002b98 in main at memerror.m:73
 breakpoint already hit 1 time
2   breakpoint     keep y   0x00002a34 in reverseIt at memerror.m:29
 breakpoint already hit 1 time
3   breakpoint     keep y   0x00002a6c in reverseIt at memerror.m:36
```

Disable the first two.

```
(gdb) disable 1
(gdb) disable 2
```

and double-check that they are disabled:

```
(gdb) info breakpoints
Num Type           Disp Enb Address    What
1   breakpoint     keep n   0x00002b98 in main at memerror.m:73
 breakpoint already hit 1 time
2   breakpoint     keep n   0x00002a34 in reverseIt at memerror.m:29
 breakpoint already hit 1 time
3   breakpoint     keep y   0x00002a6c in reverseIt at memerror.m:36
```

The "enabled" column now reads n for the first two breakpoints. So, assuming you have fixed the above **mallocs**, rebuild the program

```
(gdb) shell cc -g -o memerror memerror.m
```

and run it

```
(gdb) run
The program being debugged has been started already.
...

Breakpoint 3, reverseIt (stringbuffer=0x300150 "blargle") at memerror.m:
36      while (scan < stop) {
```

And sure enough, you are at the beginning of the loop. Time to step again.

```
(gdb) n
37               if (head == NULL) {
```

```
(gdb) print head
$1 = (CharNode *) 0x0
```

So you will go into the first branch of the if.

```
(gdb) n
38               head = malloc (sizeof(CharNode));
(gdb) n
39               head->theChar = *scan;
(gdb) n
40               head->next = NULL;
(gdb) n
```

```
47          scan++;
```

And for fun, print out head to make sure it is sane:

```
(gdb) print *head
$9 = {
  theChar = 98 'b',
  next = 0x0
}
```

Looks good. Now step back through the top of the loop:

```
(gdb) n
36      while (scan < stop) {
```

And you are back at the top. For fun, double-check the value of scan:

```
(gdb) print scan
$10 = 0x300151 "largle"
```

This is good: you are one character into the string. Step a couple of more times.

```
(gdb) n
37              if (head == NULL) {
(gdb) n
42                  node = malloc (sizeof(CharNode));
```

Now you are into the else clause (notice the line number jump from 38 to 43).

```
(gdb) n
43                  node->theChar = *scan;
(gdb) n
44                  node->next = head;
(gdb) n
45                  head = node;
(gdb) n
47              scan++;
```

And sanity check stuff:

```
(gdb) print *node
$11 = {
  theChar = 108 'l',
  next = 0x300160
}
```

```
(gdb) print *node->next
$12 = {
  theChar = 98 'b',
  next = 0x0
}
```

So the linked list looks pretty good.

Step over the scan++:

```
(gdb) n
36      while (scan < stop) {
```

So you are reasonably sure the loop is good. The gdb command until will resume execution until the line of code after the current one. Even though gdb shows us poised at the beginning of the loop, it knows that we have just finished an iteration of the loop. So if you issue the until command now, execution will continue until the loop finishes (no need to single-step through everything).

So, disable the breakpoint at the top of the loop (breakpoint 3 above)

```
(gdb) dis 3
```

and do until

```
(gdb) until
51              scan = stringbuffer;
```

Which just so happens to be after the loop.

Take a look at the linked list just to be sure:

```
(gdb) print *head
$13 = {
  theChar = 0 '\000',
  next = 0x3001c0
}

(gdb) print head-gt;next
$14 = (struct CharNode *) 0x3001c0

(gdb) print *head->next
$15 = {
  theChar = 101 'e',
  next = 0x3001b0
}

(gdb) print *head->next->next
$16 = {
  theChar = 108 'l',
  next = 0x3001a0
}

(gdb) print *head->next->next->next
$17 = {
  theChar = 103 'g',
  next = 0x300190
}
```

Looks like a reversed string. That is a good sign. That leading zero value at the head looks a bit odd, though. You might or might not want that in there. So, continuing on:

```
(gdb) n
54              while (head != NULL) {

(gdb) n
55                  *scan = head->theChar;

(gdb) n
56                  free (head);
```

```
(gdb) n
57                     node = head->next;
```

Something does not look right there. Print out ∗head again:

```
(gdb) print *head
$18 = {
  theChar = 0 '\000',
  next = 0x3001c0
}
```

Still looks the same, but something smells wrong with the code. Oops. The head gets freed, and then the memory gets used after the **free()** (bug #6). That is pretty bad. So fix it. Change

```
        free (head);
        node = head->next;
```

to

```
        node = head->next;
        free (head);
```

Step a couple of times to go back to the top of the loop

```
(gdb) n
58                     head = node;
(gdb) n
59                     scan++;
(gdb) n
54              while (head != NULL) {
```

and set a breakpoint here

```
(gdb) break
Breakpoint 4 at 0x2b4c: file memerror.m, line 54.
```

Just break by itself sets a breakpoint at the current position.

So, rebuild

```
(gdb) shell cc -g -o memerror memerror.m
```

and restart. (I know I get a little peeved at "The program being debugged has been started already. Start it from the beginning? (y or n)" messages, so I am going to turn them off, and then restart):

```
(gdb) set confirm off

(gdb) run
'/Users/markd/Projects/core-osx/gdb-chap/memerror' has changed;
re-reading symbols.

Breakpoint 4, reverseIt (stringbuffer=0x62b0 "blargle\000"...)
    at memerror.m:55
54              while (head != NULL) {
```

and then single-step some more and verify that the code is doing what you want, and then finish the loop:

```
54              while (head != NULL) {
(gdb) n
55                  *scan = head->theChar;
(gdb) n
56                  node = head->next;
(gdb) n
57                  free (head);
(gdb) n
58                  head = node;
(gdb) n
59                  scan++;

(gdb) disable 4
(gdb) until
64                  free (head);
```

Now take a look at the buffer

```
(gdb) print stringbuffer
$1 = 0x300150 ""
```

That does not look very promising. Maybe the leading zero byte in the linked list is messing things up. Look at the memory one byte into the string:

```
(gdb) print (char *)(stringbuffer + 1)
$2 = 0x300151 "elgralb"
```

Sure enough, that is "blargle" spelled backwards. So it looks like bug #7 is that extra zero byte. Where would that have come from? The code is walking the string from beginning to end, and building a reversed linked list, so the *last* character of the string becomes the *head* of the linked list, and it is the head where that zero byte is. So it looks like the first loop is going one byte too far. Revisit this line of code:

```
stop = stringbuffer + strlen(stringbuffer) + 1;
```

There it is right there! It explicitly includes the trailing zero byte, but you do not want it. Change this line of code to

```
stop = stringbuffer + strlen(stringbuffer);
```

So, it looks like you found the problem! We must be done. Time to send the program over to QA and also put some T-shirts on order before the product launch. Fix the code and quit gdb gdb:

```
(gdb) quit
$
```

and rebuild the program:

```
$ cc -g -o memerror memerror.m
```

and run it:

```
$ ./memerror blargle
```

```
Bus error
```

Ack! You crashed. You were, like most programmers, a little too optimistic. gdb is pretty handy for catching crashes like these. When there is a crash like this, there is usually a smoking gun pointing to the problem. So, gdb the program again:

```
$ gdb ./memerror
[... copyright stuff ...]
```

You have to re specify the command line arguments since you exited gdb earlier.

```
(gdb) run blargle
Starting program: /Users/markd/Projects/core-osx/gdb-chap/memerror blargle
Reading symbols for shared libraries . done

Program received signal EXC_BAD_ACCESS, Could not access memory.
Reason: KERN_PROTECTION_FAILURE at address: 0x00000064
0x90003248 in strlen ()
```

and look at the stack:

```
(gdb) where
#0   0x90003248 in strlen ()
#1   0x9000cd9c in __vfprintf$LDBL128 ()
#2   0x900fbcb8 in vfprintf_l$LDBL128 ()
#3   0x900fe38c in printf$LDBL128 ()
#4   0x00002c34 in main (argc=2, argv=0xbffff240) at memerror.m:87
```

Looks like something bad is happening at line 87 in memerror.m, stack frame number 4. Go to that frame:

```
(gdb) frame 4
#4   0x00002c34 in main (argc=2, argv=0xbffff240) at memerror.m:87
87          printf ("the reversed string is '%s'\n", *stringbuffer);
```

What is stringbuffer?

```
(gdb) print stringbuffer
$1 = 0x300150 "elgralb"
```

That looks OK. Of course, looking closer at the code, why did the programmer dereference the stringbuffer pointer?

```
(gdb) print *stringbuffer
$2 = 101 'e'
```

So printf() is trying to interpret the number 101 as an address of a string. That is not a valid address, so eventually some function deep in the standard library will use that bad address and choke. Generally, if you see standard library functions on the stack, there is not anything really wrong with them. The code calling them has messed something up. This is an easy enough fix. Change

```
printf ("the reversed string is '%s'\n", *stringbuffer);
```

to

```
printf ("the reversed string is '%s'\n", stringbuffer);
```

Get out of gdb:

```
(gdb) quit
The program is running.  Exit anyway? (y or n) y
```

Fix the code and rebuild:

```
$ cc -g -o memerror memerror.m
```

and run it:

```
$ ./memerror blargle
the reversed string is 'elgralb'
```

Hooray! It works! You found eight errors. There are actually nine. The last one does not affect the program's output, but is a little bit of sloppiness. The string buffer gets memory from **malloc()**, but that memory is never explicitly freed.

GDB Specifics

The above walk through hits on the major things you can do with gdb in command-line mode:

- See program listings
- See the stack trace and move around in the stack looking at the variables in various functions
- Set and disable breakpoints
- Display data
- Change data
- Change execution flow

Here is some reference stuff of different commands that could be useful. This is still a very small subset of what gdb is capable of.

Help

gdb has extensive online help. Just doing help shows you the top-level classes of help available:

```
(gdb) help
List of classes of commands:

aliases -- Aliases of other commands
breakpoints -- Making program stop at certain points
data -- Examining data
files -- Specifying and examining files
internals -- Maintenance commands
obscure -- Obscure features
running -- Running the program
stack -- Examining the stack
status -- Status inquiries
support -- Support facilities
```

```
tracepoints -- Tracing of program execution without
               stopping the program
user-defined -- User-defined commands
```

You can look at a particular class of stuff:

```
(gdb) help breakpoints

Making program stop at certain points.

List of commands:

awatch -- Set a watchpoint for an expression
break -- Set breakpoint at specified line or function
catch -- Set catchpoints to catch events
clear -- Clear breakpoint at specified line or function
[...]
thbreak -- Set a temporary hardware assisted breakpoint
txbreak -- Set temporary breakpoint at procedure exit
watch -- Set a watchpoint for an expression
xbreak -- Set breakpoint at procedure exit
```

as well as help on a particular command:

```
(gdb) help until
Execute until the program reaches a source line greater than the
current or a specified line or address or function (same args as
break command). Execution will also stop upon exit from the current
stack frame.
```

The `apropos` command lets you search through the help if you do not know the
exact name or class of a command.

```
(gdb) apropos thread
catch -- Set catchpoints to catch events
info mach-thread -- Get info on a specific thread
info mach-threads -- Get list of threads in a task
info thread -- Get information on thread
info threads -- IDs of currently known threads
[...]
thread -- Use this command to switch between threads
thread apply -- Apply a command to a list of threads
apply all -- Apply a command to all threads
thread resume -- Resume a thread
thread suspend -- Suspend a thread
```

Stack Traces

You can see a stack trace, that is, all of the currently active functions, with the `where`
command (also `backtrace` and `bt`). It will show you the stack frames currently
active:

```
(gdb) where
#0  0x70000a50 in strlen ()
#1  0x70001b14 in vfprintf ()
#2  0x700129f0 in printf ()
#3  0x00001d9c in main (argc=2, argv=0xbfffffb38) at memerror.m:88
```

```
#4    0x00001aec in _start ()
#5    0x0000191c in start ()
```

The bottom-most frame, **start()** in this case is termed the "innermost" stack frame. The top of the stack is the "outermost" frame (good to know for some gdb documentation). You can move up and down the stack using up and down, up being towards the innermost frame, and down being towards the outermost. Unfortunately that is backwards from the way the stack is listed in the backtrace. Specifically, if you were at frame #3 (**main()**), doing down would put you into frame 2, doing up would put you into frame 4.

You can look at the local variables or arguments with a single operation:

```
info args
```

Show all the arguments to the function.

```
info locals
```

Show the local variables and their values.

```
info catch
```

Show any active C++ exception handlers.

Program Listings

You can see around where you are by using the list command. You can see the first 10 lines around the beginning of a function by doing list function-name. To change the number of lines listed, use set listsize:

```
(gdb) set listsize 17
(gdb) list reverseIt
17            char theChar;
18            struct CharNode *next;
19        } CharNode;
20
21
22        // build a linked list backwards, then walk the list.
23
24        void reverseIt (char *stringbuffer)
25        {
26            CharNode *head, *node;
27            char *scan, *stop;
28
29            // clear out local vars
30            head = node = NULL;
31
32            // find the start and end of the string so we can walk it
33            scan = stringbuffer;
```

(Note that gdb lists lines centered on the given line.)

If you are very curious, you can see a disassembly of your code:

```
(gdb) break main
Note: breakpoint 1 also set at pc 0x1d1c.
```

```
Breakpoint 3 at 0x1d1c: file memerror.m, line 74.
(gdb) run
Starting program:/Users/markd/BNRunix/gdb-chapter/./memerror blargle
[Switching to thread 1 (process 916 thread 0x2107)]

Breakpoint 1, main (argc=2, argv=0xbffffb38) at memerror.m:74
74              if (argc != 2) {
(gdb) disassemble
Dump of assembler code for function main:
0x1cf8 <main>:          mflr    r0
0x1cfc <main+4>:        stmw    r30,-8(r1)
0x1d00 <main+8>:        stw     r0,8(r1)
0x1d04 <main+12>:       stwu    r1,-80(r1)
0x1d08 <main+16>:       mr      r30,r1
[...]
0x1d98 <main+160>:      bl      0x1f28 <dyld_stub_printf>
0x1d9c <main+164>:      li      r3,0
0x1da0 <main+168>:      bl      0x1ee0 <dyld_stub_exit>
0x1da4 <main+172>:      lwz     r1,0(r1)
0x1da8 <main+176>:      lwz     r0,8(r1)
0x1dac <main+180>:      mtlr    r0
0x1db0 <main+184>:      lmw     r30,-8(r1)
0x1db4 <main+188>:      blr
End of assembler dump.
```

Breakpoints

Use break to set a breakpoint. You can break on a function name, or you can give a filename:line specification to stop in a specific place.

Breakpoints can have conditions attached to them:

```
(gdb) break memerror.m:74 if argc != 2
Breakpoint 1 at 0x1d1c: file memerror.m, line 74.
```

This breakpoint will only be triggered if argc is not 2. You can also attach conditions after the breakpoint has been created by using the cond command. You specify the condition using the syntax of whatever language you are debugging. If you are debugging an Ada or a FORTRAN program, you would use the logical syntax of those languages.

```
(gdb) cond 2 (argc != 2)
```

rbreak lets you use a regular expression to stop on a bunch of functions. Very handy for overloaded functions in C++.

```
(gdb) rbreak .*printf.*
(sets about 35 breakpoints for me)
```

You can also put a breakpoint on a specific template instantiation:

```
(gdb) break StitchFiend<int>::blargle
```

info breakpoints will show you all the currently active breakpoints.

You saw the next command previously. That steps one line of code at a time, but does not step into function calls. You can use step to go into function calls.

Breakpoints can be disabled (so they do not fire) or enabled (to wake up a disabled breakpoint). You can set an ignore count on a breakpoint which gets decremented every time the breakpoint is hit by using `ignore breakpoint# count`. When the ignore count reaches zero the breakpoint will trigger. You would use this when you know that the first 700 pieces of data process OK but item 701 fails.

You can also attach commands to breakpoints. When you put a command on a breakpoint, those commands will be run by `gdb`. Any `gdb` command can be used on a breakpoint, even the `continue` command, which will resume execution, and enabling or disabling other breakpoints. To attach commands to a breakpoint, use the `commands` command:

```
(gdb) break walkTreePostorder
Breakpoint 2 at 0x1d80: file treefunc.c, line 6

(gdb) commands 2
Type commands for when breakpoint 2 is hit, one per line.
End with a line saying just "end".
>where
>print node
>continue
>end
```

These commands will print out the value of the node parameter every time the **walkTreePostorder** function is called.

Displaying Data

`print` can be used to display variables and the result of function calls. You can control the format of the displayed data by adding a format flag after the command:

```
(gdb) print i
$1 = 17263812

(gdb) print/x i
$2 = 0x1076cc4

(gdb) print /o i
$3 = 0101666304

(gdb) print/t i
$4 = 1000001110110110011000100
```

Here are some of the format flags:

`/x`

Hexadecimal

`/d`

Signed decimal

`/u`

Unsigned decimal

`/o`

Octal

`/t`

Binary (t for "two")

`/c`

Print as a character constant

`/f`

Floating point

You can use these in ad-hoc expressions too:

```
(gdb) print/o 0xfeedface
$5 = 037673375316

(gdb) print/d "help"
$7 = {104, 101, 108, 112, 0}

(gdb) print /x 0644
$8 = 0x1a4
```

These are a life saver if your HP-16C calculator is not handy to do base conversions.

You can also use gdb to display arrays. There was a billboard in Silicon Valley that showed something like this:

```
int imsg[] = {78, 111, 119, 32, 72, 105, 114, 105, 110, 103, 0};
```

I wonder what that means? The gdb array display features can help us out. By putting a type in curly braces you tell gdb that you are interested in seeing data shown as an array. You can show a certain number of elements in the array:

```
(gdb) print {int} imsg @ 10
$2 = {78, 111, 119, 32, 72, 105, 114, 105, 110, 103}
```

You can also show a slice of an array. This shows two elements, starting at the third index (which is actually the fourth element):

```
(gdb) print {int}(imsg + 3)@2
$3 = {32, 72}
```

and you can print each of the elements of the array as a specific type:

```
(gdb) print/c {int} imsg @ 10
$4 = {78 'N', 111 'o', 119 'w', 32 ' ', 72 'H', 105 'i', 114 'r',
     105 'i', 110 'n', 103 'g'}
```

Which spells out "Now Hiring" in ASCII.

You can look at static/global variables in other scopes by qualifying the variable name with a scope:

by file

```
"file"::variable-name
```

by function

```
function-name::variable-name
```

If you want to see all of the processor's registers, use `info registers`, which shows all registers except the floating point ones. `info all registers` shows all of them, including the AltiVec registers.

For Objective-C programs, there are a couple of commands:

`info classes`

> Show all classes that have debugging symbols.

`info selectors`

> Show all selectors.

If you are looking at a variable, `whatis variable-name` will show you the type of the variable name. `ptype type-name` will show you the data structure for that type.

Lastly, you can call functions in your program with `call function-name`, independent of the main flow of execution that `gdb` currently has interrupted. This is nice if you have a complex data structure - you can write a program to look at the data structure and return a string that presents it in a more readable form. This is pretty much what the `po` (print object) command does. It invokes the **-description** method for the given object. One thing to look out for is that this function could crash `gdb` itself if the program state is bad or your function generates an access exception.

Changing Data

This is really easy. Use `set var varname = expression`, where `expression` can include standard C operators (+, -, |, &, etc) and can call functions in your program.

Changing Execution Flow

You can bail out of a function early with `return`. For functions that return values, you can also specify a return value. This is very useful if you know the function is going to return a bad value and you know what it should be returning.

`finish` will continue execution until the current function ends, then `gdb` will break back in again. `until` will resume execution and break after the next instruction when until was invoked. This is useful (as seen above) for letting a loop finish.

Handy Tricks

Sometimes you are running and you get an error like this:

```
*** malloc[1064]: Deallocation of a pointer not malloced: 0x442b0;
This could be a double free(), or free() called with the
middle of an allocated block; Try setting environment
variable MallocHelp to see tools to help debug
```

But usually by the time you can react, your program has moved far past that. You can set a breakpoint on **malloc_printf()**, which is what generates that particular message.

Another even more common occurrence in Cocoa programming is this error:

```
2002-08-20 18:33:04.545 badmessage[1082] ***-[NSCFArray frobulate:]:
selector not recognized
2002-08-20 18:33:04.545 badmessage[1082] *** Uncaught exception:
<NSInvalidArgumentException> ***-[NSCFArray frobulate:]: selector
not recognized
```

And by the time you see this, your program is long past the point of the error. You can set a breakpoint on **-[NSException raise]** to break every time this happens. If you are using native Objective-C exceptions, discussed in Chapter 7 (Exceptions), you can put a breakpoint on the **objc_exception_throw()** function to catch @throws when they happen.

It would be really handy to have a breakpoint put on **-[NSException raise]** every time you run gdb. You could add it to your Xcode project and to the project templates. But that would not help you if you get someone else's project and they have this error. When gdb starts up, it looks for a file in your home directory called .gdbinit. It will read each line and execute it as if you had typed it in yourself. My .gdbinit contains:

Example 6-1. .gdbinit

```
fb -[NSException raise]
fb malloc_printf
```

fb stands for future break. gdb attempts to set the breakpoint whenever it loads a shared library or a framework. Eventually it will load the framework that contains **-[NSException raise]** or **malloc_printf** and set the breakpoint there.

What's nice is that this sets stuff for every gdb session you have no matter what is or is not set in an Xcode project.

When you are dealing with Objective-C code you can poke around the processor registers to see some information about a method's arguments even if you do not have debugging symbols for that method (such as something from Cocoa). For the PowerPC, register r3, referenced in gdb with $r3, has the value of self. Register r4 ($r4) has the selector, which currently is actually a pointer to a string, so you can see what selector is being used. Integer and pointer arguments then go up from there.

```
(gdb) po $r3
<BWStitchView: 0x1a6670>

(gdb) print (char *) $r4
$5 = 0x90874160 "drawRect:"
```

Lastly, you can debug programs remotely, meaning that you do not have to physically be at the machine where the program being debugged is running. For embedded systems and kernel programming, you can set up a network connection or a serial line. For ordinary, every day programs, it is much easier to just ssh into the box (which means you need a login) and run the program. You can also attach `gdb` to a program that is already running. This is very useful for the user who always has some kind of bad problem but it never happens when you are around watching. In this case, `ssh` into their machine, attach to the program, set some breakpoints, do a `continue`, and leave it. Eventually the problem will manifest itself and you can poke around and see what is going wrong.

Debugging Techniques

Being able to use debugging tools is only part of the debugging battle. Becoming an effective debugger is a holistic, never-ending process. I have been debugging software for over twenty years, and I am still learning new ways of producing (and finding) program errors. Here are some things I have learned over the years.

One of the most important things to remember is that bugs are just errors. They are mistakes that people, either you or others, have made. They are not things that randomly crawl into your code. Some programmers don't call bugs "bugs", but instead use the more accurate (but less fun) term "defect", to emphasize that bugs are just mistakes. Knowing that a bug can be tracked down to a mistake that has been made along the line takes some of the mystery out of them. One of the nice things about being human is that we get to make mistakes, and I find that most of my best learning happens in the context of having made a mistake. So long as you do not make the same mistake again and again, there is no shame in messing up every now and then.

One piece of advice I wish I had received early on in my career was "try not to get too debugger happy". Debuggers are great tools, but they are not the hammer to use to pound all nails. When you see a bug, the debugger might not be the most effective way to find the problem. Sometimes inspecting code or writing a test program can isolate the program faster than cranking up the debugger. Robert C. Martin, a long-time regular in the `comp.object` newsgroup and author of a number of excellent books, posted an article on a website claiming that "Debuggers are a Wasteful Timesink." He noticed that in classes that he teaches that some students waste a lot of time in debuggers when inspection or some caveman debugging can find the problems more quickly.

"Wasteful Timesink" is a bit of an extreme position, but it did elicit a very interesting discussion. The Java and script crowd (perl, python, etc) frequently said that they almost never used debuggers, and wondered why they are such a big issue. The C and C++ crowd, on the other hand, use debuggers all the time due to the low-level nature of the languages. Because most Mac applications are coded in C, C++, or Objective-C, we do have a need for debuggers, but there are other techniques that can be employed.

Many of us have had the experience of going to a co-worker, start explaining a bug, and about half way through the description say "Never mind, I know what it is now". The act of having to explain the problem to another person helps solidify the evidence you have gathered about the bug, and also helps your subconscious mind work on the problem and move toward a solution. I have worked with programmers that keep a teddy bear, rubber duck, or Bill the Cat doll on their desk and regularly use them as a sounding-board for debugging.

Sometimes you come across "code smells". You look at some code, and something just does not smell right. There may be conditionals that are very deeply nested, or you see a lot of copy and paste with minor tweaks, or thousand line functions with nested switch statements and gotos that go backwards. Code like this frequently is the source of bugs, and can be a good first place to start tracking down problems.

If you have a particularly nasty problem, keep a log of what you have tried, and what results you got. You can use a piece of paper or even just a plain text file to keep the log. You may find yourself in the third or fourth day of tracking down a problem and have forgotten about a vital piece of data you found on the first day. You can also look at your accumulated data for patterns.

Because C, C++, and Objective-C programmers are particularly dependent on debuggers, you should write code with debugging in mind. Objective-C is particularly bad by making it very easy to deeply chain method calls. New Cocoa programmers, and macho "see how studly I am" programmers like to deeply nest their Objective-C code. It does look pretty cool, and does reduce the amount of vertical space consumed by the code. Here is a contrived, but representative example:

```
[document objectAtIndex: [tableView selectedRow]]
    setFont: [[NSUserDefaults standardDefaults] labelFont]
```

Now suppose you have a problem on this line of code. It is difficult to use a debugger on this statement because you cannot place a breakpoint on the interior method calls. Is the selectedRow a sane value? What is the document object that is being accessed and having its font set? When I am given code like this to debug, I break it apart:

```
int selectedRow;
selectedRow = [tableView selectedRow];

Paragraph *paragraph;
paragraph = [document objectAtIndex: selectedRow];

Font *labelFont;
labelFont = [[NSUserDefaults standardDefaults] labelFont];

[paragraph setFont: labelFont];
```

You can now put a breakpoint on any of these lines of code. You can also through them and inspect intermediate results. The usual complaint upon seeing code like this is "but that's inefficient!". Until you have actually measured this code and the original code, you do not know that for sure. The compiler is free, in an optimized build, to remove variables and shuffle code around. Both versions can run equally as fast, but the second is easier to read, and certainly easier to debug.

Tracking Down Problems

You have to find the problem before you can fix it. In terms of finding problems, crashers are my favorite kind of bug. Usually the cause is very simple, and usually debuggers can give you a pointer directly to the smoking gun that caused the problem, or at least it is the start of the trail to the ultimate problem.

If a problem is reproducible, it is dead. If you have a reproducible test case, you can, with enough tenacity, work the problem back to its origins. If you do not have a reproducible test case, do not give up. It just means you have more work ahead of you. Try to get as much information about reproducing the problem as you can. If you have the luxury of a lot of different bug reports about the sample problem, you may be able to glean enough data to construct a way to reproduce the bug.

Intermittent problems are some of the hardest to fix. You might have a server that misbehaves every couple of days, or you may have one user that makes your program crash. In situations like this, you can "camp" on the program. Attach to the program with a debugger, and just let it sit until the program crashes or triggers a conditional breakpoint. A lot of times you can remotely log into another machine and attach to the misbehaving program, and then let it sit there until the problem happens. In the mean time you can continue doing work rather than sitting and watching over someone's shoulder for hours.

You can apply the binary search algorithm to debugging. Delete a chunk of code from a misbehaving program. If the problem still happens, you can ignore the code you just deleted. If the problem goes away, you can focus your attention to the code you just removed. It is situations like this where having a source code control system comes in *very* handy. Mutilate some code, gather some data about the problem, and then revert to a pristine version of the program. Then use the data you just collected to mutilate some other code and gather some more data. We talk about source code control in general, and the Subversion source version control system in particular, in Chapter 24.

Lastly, be consistent with your test data. If you use a different file in every iteration of your debugging, you can send yourself on wild goose chases if there are actually several different problems. On the other hand, try to use good test data that streamlines your debugging process. You may have a reproducible test case that involves a 300 megabyte 3D model that takes five minutes to load. If you can reproduce the problem with a 30K model that takes under a second to load, you can spend more time debugging and less time waiting for the data to load.

Debugger Techniques

Sometimes it can be faster to compile and link in some **printf()** or **NSLog()** statements than to crank up a big program in gdb and set up cascading breakpoints. I like to call this technique "Caveman Debugging". It is a pretty primitive way to do things, but sometimes the simplest techniques can be the most effective.

Become aware of your debugger's features. gdb has a huge feature set, with features ranging from very basic to arcane and obscure. I try to read through the gdb documentation at least every year. Features that originally looked weird might now look useful, and new features are getting added to gdb all the time. Personally, I do not end up using a whole lot of esoteric debugger features. Setting breakpoints, getting stack traces, and doing some single-stepping is the most of my day-to-day work using gdb.

You can use gdb for code exploration, especially when you are first wrapping your mind around a new code base. Pick an interesting function and put a breakpoint on it. Run the program and see who is calling that function, and under what circumstances. Sometimes you find out that a function you think is the cause of a problem never actually gets called.

You can also use a debugger to single-step through brand new code. Bugs are generally introduced by new code, so it makes sense to really scrutinize new code that is added to a program. A common technique is to single-step through all new code and verify that it is behaving properly.

For The More Curious

Core files

Core files are a Unixism where a program that has crashed (usually by trying to read or write into memory it does not have access to) will write out its address space to disk. You can then poke around this core file with gdb and see what was happening when the program crashed, kind of like a software autopsy.

By default on Mac OS X, core files are not dropped when your program crashes. Core files take a *long* time to write on OS X, and on machines with less-than-stellar disk throughput, it can hose your machine for a fair number of seconds while the core file is being written. So in general you will not get core files unless you ask for them.

Example 6-2 is a program that can generate errors that can drop core files:

Example 6-2. assert.m

```
// assert.m -- invoke assert, thereby dropping a core file

/* compile with:
cc -g -Wall -o assert assert.m
*/

#import <assert.h>       // for assert
#import <stdio.h>        // for printf() and friends
#import <string.h>       // for strlen()
#import <stdlib.h>       // for EXIT_SUCCESS

void anotherFunction (char *ook)
{
    assert (strlen(ook) > 0);

    printf ("wheeee! Got string %s\n", ook);

} // anotherFunction


void someFunction (char *blah)
{
    anotherFunction (blah);
} // someFunction


int main (int argc, char *argv[])
{
    someFunction (argv[1]);
    return (EXIT_SUCCESS);
} // main
```

If you run this with no arguments, you will get a bus error (since `anotherFunction()` tries to print a NULL pointer). If it is run with an argument of `""`, an assertion will be raised that causes a core dump. If run with a non-empty argument, it will get printed out.

If you run it using the default environment, no core file is dropped. You can tell your shell to allow programs to drop cores. The ulimit command (or the limit command in the C shell) lets you control resource limits. The –a command flag shows the current limits.

```
$ ulimit -a
core file size          (blocks, -c) 0
data seg size           (kbytes, -d) 6144
file size               (blocks, -f) unlimited
max locked memory       (kbytes, -l) unlimited
max memory size         (kbytes, -m) unlimited
open files                      (-n) 256
pipe size        (512 bytes, -p) 1
stack size              (kbytes, -s) 8192
cpu time             (seconds, -t) unlimited
max user processes              (-u) 100
virtual memory          (kbytes, -v) unlimited
```

Note that core file size is zero kbytes. You can increase the limit with

```
$ ulimit -c unlimited
```

Now, if you run the program

```
$ ./assert ""
assert.m:13: failed assertion 'strlen(ook) > 0'
Abort (core dumped)
```

core files get dropped in the /cores directory with the name core.process-id.

Then you can look at it in gdb:

```
$ gdb ./assert /cores/core.1104
[... copyright stuff ...]
warning: core file may not match specified executable file.
#0  0x7001a70c in kill ()
```

So the program terminated in the **kill()** function. Look at the whole stack trace:

```
(gdb) where
#0  0x7001a70c in kill ()
#1  0x7006f990 in abort ()
#2  0x00001df0 in __eprintf ()
#3  0x00001d00 in anotherFunction(ook=0xbffffc85 "\000"...)
         at assert.m:13
#4  0x00001d48 in someFunction (blah=0xbffffc85 "\000"...)
         at assert.m:21
#5  0x00001d84 in main (argc=2, argv=0xbffffbec) at assert.m:27
#6  0x00001bf8 in _start ()
#7  0x00001a28 in start ()
```

Move to the third stack frame:

```
(gdb) up 3
#3  0x00001d00 in anotherFunction(ook=0xbffffc85 "\000"...)
         at assert.m:13
13              assert (strlen(ook) > 0);
```

This is the assert. The smoking gun, so you know exactly what happened.

You can turn off core dumps by doing

```
$ ulimit -c 0
```

One place where core files are very useful is for crashes that happen out in the field, where the user can send you the core file for later dissection. However, having them run a shell and set limits might not be practical. You can programmatically tell the system you want to drop a core file even if the shell limit is zero. Recall from Chapter 5 (Memory) about process resource limits. One of the resource limits is RLIMIT_CORE, the largest size (in bytes) of core files. You can manaully use the resource limit calls to increase the coredump size. Example 6-3 is a modified assert.m:

Example 6-3. assert2.m

```
// assert2.m -- invoke assert, thereby dropping a core file

/* compile with:
cc -g -Wall -o assert2 assert2.m
*/

#import <assert.h>        // for assert()
#import <stdio.h>         // for printf() and firends
#import <sys/types.h>     // for random types
#import <sys/time.h>      // for random types
#import <sys/resource.h>  // for setrlimit()
#import <errno.h>         // for errno
#import <string.h>        // for strlen()
#import <stdlib.h>        // for EXIT_SUCCESS

void anotherFunction (char *ook)
{
    assert (strlen(ook) > 0);

    printf ("wheeee! Got string %s\n", ook);

} // anotherFunction

void someFunction (char *blah)
{
    anotherFunction (blah);
} // someFunction

void enableCoreDumps ()
{
    struct rlimit rl;

    rl.rlim_cur = RLIM_INFINITY;
    rl.rlim_max = RLIM_INFINITY;


    if (setrlimit (RLIMIT_CORE, &rl) == -1) {
        fprintf (stderr, "error in setrlimit for RLIMIT_CORE: %d (%s)\n",
                errno, strerror(errno));
```

```
        }

    } // enableCoreDumps

int main (int argc, char *argv[])
{
    enableCoreDumps ();

    someFunction (argv[1]);
    return (EXIT_SUCCESS);
} // main
```

If you run it now, you get a core file:

```
$ ./assert2 ""
assert2.m:19: failed assertion 'strlen(ook) > 0'
Abort (core dumped)
```

To use this in a real program, you might want to put in some secret way that the user can execute that function to allow core dumping. Like, "Command-shift-option-click the about box OK button and you will get a debug panel. Check the core dump check box, then do whatever it is that crashes the program."

Stripping

Debugging symbols are pretty big and can bloat up your executable. A simple Cocoa application of mine weighs in at 262K with debug symbols, whereas without the symbols it is about 30K. Depending on the application, keeping debug symbols around might not be a bad thing. For a high-traffic web server application, we kept the debug symbols to make diagnosing production problems easier (and it really came in handy sometimes). If your program has 500 megs of graphics and support files, a couple of hundred K of debug symbols probably is not too bad. On the other hand, if you are writing smaller downloadable applications, the extra hundred K or a meg could be a significant barrier to your program being used. Having debug symbols also makes it easier for people to reverse-engineer your code. You can either rebuild your program using the Deployment target in Xcode, or you can just run the strip program against the executable. For instance:

```
$ ls -l BorkPad
-rwxr-xr-x  1 markd   staff   262780 Aug 19 21:10 BorkPad
$ strip BorkPad
$ ls -l BorkPad
-rwxr-xr-x  1 markd   staff   30608 Aug 20 21:37 BorkPad
```

So what happens then if your program crashes out in the field? If you can get a core file, you can load the core file into a gdb session with an unstripped version of your executable and be able to debug symbolically. For example, use the assert2 program, make a stripped copy, and generate a core file:

```
$ cp assert2 stripped
$ strip stripped
$ ./stripped ""
assert2.m:19: failed assertion 'strlen(ook) > 0'
Abort (core dumped)
```

If you gdb the stripped program, thestack traces are not very useful:

```
$ gdb stripped /cores/core.2342
...
(gdb) where
#0   0x9001b52c in kill ()
#1   0x9005ceec in abort ()
#2   0x00001d18 in dyld_stub_exit ()
#3   0x00001c20 in ?? ()
#4   0x00001c64 in ?? ()
#5   0x00001ca4 in ?? ()
#6   0x00001978 in ?? ()
#7   0x000017f8 in ?? ()
```

But if you use the original, unstripped file, you have good stack traces:

```
$ gdb assert2 /cores/core.2342
...
(gdb) where
#0   0x9001b52c in kill ()
#1   0x9005ceec in abort ()
#2   0x00001d18 in dyld_stub_exit ()
#3   0x00001c20 in anotherFunction (ook=0xbffffb87 "\000"...)
     at assert2.m:19
#4   0x00001c64 in someFunction (blah=0xbffffb87 "\000"...)
     at assert2.m:27
#5   0x00001ca4 in main (argc=2, argv=0xbffffadc) at assert2.m:37
#6   0x00001978 in _start (argc=2, argv=0xbffffadc, envp=0xbffffae8)
     at /SourceCache/Csu/Csu-45/crt.c:267
#7   0x000017f8 in start ()
```

If you do not want to mess with gdb, or the user emails you a stack trace from the crash reporter, you can use atos to map the address to a symbol to see what function and line caused the problem.

```
$ atos -o assert2 0x00001ca4
_main (assert2.m:38)

$ atos -o assert2 0x00001c20
_anotherFunction (assert2.m:21)
```

More Advanced GDB Commands

Threads

gdb supports debugging threaded programs (we have lots to say about threading issues in Chapter 22 (Threads)) but here are some useful commands relating to threads.

info threads

> Shows information about all the currently active threads. Here is something from a simple Cocoa program while the **Page Setup** dialog is active:

```
(gdb) info threads
  3 process 128 thread 0x213 0x70978 in mach_msg_overwrite_trap()
```

```
 2 process 128 thread 0x1f7 0x70978 in mach_msg_overwrite_trap()
*1 process 128 thread 0x163 0x70978 in mach_msg_overwrite_trap()
```

You can change between threads with the `thread` command, and then poke around and see what it is doing:

```
(gdb) thread 3
[Switching to thread 3 (process 1208 thread 0x2123)]
#0  0x70000978 in mach_msg_overwrite_trap ()

(gdb) where
#0  0x70000978 in mach_msg_overwrite_trap ()
#1  0x70005a04 in mach_msg ()
#2  0x7017bf84 in __CFRunLoopRun ()
#3  0x701b70ec in CFRunLoopRunSpecific ()
#4  0x7017b8cc in CFRunLoopRunInMode ()
#5  0x7061be08 in XIOAudioDeviceManager::NotificationThread ()
#6  0x706141c0 in CAPThread::Entry ()
#7  0x7002054c in _pthread_body ()
```

thread apply

Run a command for every thread.

```
(gdb) thread apply all where

[... took out the same stack trace as above ...]

Thread 2 (process 1208 thread 0x1f07):
#0  0x70000978 in mach_msg_overwrite_trap ()
#1  0x70005a04 in mach_msg ()
#2  0x70026a2c in _pthread_become_available ()
#3  0x70026724 in pthread_exit ()
#4  0x70020550 in _pthread_body ()


Thread 1 (process 1208 thread 0x1603):
#0  0x70000978 in mach_msg_overwrite_trap ()
#1  0x70005a04 in mach_msg ()
#2  0x7017bf84 in __CFRunLoopRun ()
#3  0x701b70ec in CFRunLoopRunSpecific ()
#4  0x7017b8cc in CFRunLoopRunInMode ()
...
#23 0x7938bed0 in NSApplicationMain ()
#24 0x000036b4 in _start ()
#25 0x000034e4 in start ()
#0  0x70000978 in mach_msg_overwrite_trap ()
```

When debugging, one thread is always the focus for the debugging, known as the current thread. You can break in particular threads if you wish, using `thread apply # break` .... When the program stops, all threads stop, and when the program starts (even just doing a step), all threads potentially start as well. Note that during the time of the single-step, the other threads will run full bore. The single-stepping only applies to the current thread.

Chapter 7. Exceptions, Error Handling, and Signals

One of the grisly facts of programming life is that errors can happen, and program code must react to those errors and deal with them appropriately. With the Unix APIs, there are two primary ways that exceptional conditions are communicated to programs. One is through return codes from function calls plus a global variable that describes the error in more detail. The other is through signals sent to the program from the OS. The Objective-C compiler and Cocoa framework in Mac OS X also provides an exception-handling architecture that programs can take advantage of.

errno

Most of the library functions and system calls provided by Unix systems have a return value that signifies that an error happened during the execution of the call. The global integer variable `errno` will be set to a value to indicate what went wrong.

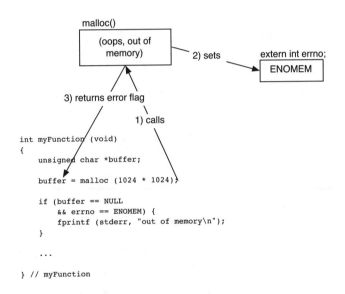

You can use the function **strerror()** to get a human description of the error. It is necessary to `#include <errno.h>` to get the definition of `errno`. The prototype for **strerror()** lives in `<string.h>`. You can look in `/usr/include/sys/errno.h` for the complete set of `errno` values. It is important to include `errno.h` rather than providing your own `extern int errno`, since `errno` is implemented in a thread-safe manner that is more than just a simple global `int`.

The man pages for Unix calls spell out in detail what the error code is and what specific `errno` values are set. For example, from the `open(2)` man page:

```
OPEN(2)                   System Calls Manual                   OPEN(2)


NAME
     open - open or create a file for reading or writing

SYNOPSIS
     #include <fcntl.h>
```

```
int
open (char *path, int flags, mode_t mode);
```

DESCRIPTION

The file name specified by path is opened for reading and/or
writing as specified by the argument flags and the file
descriptor returned to the calling process. The flags argument
may indicate the file is to be created if it does not exist (by
....
If successful, open() returns a non-negative integer, termed a
file descriptor. It returns -1 on failure. The file pointer
used to mark the current position within the file is set to the
beginning of the file.

ERRORS

The named file is opened unless:

[ENOTDIR]	A component of the path prefix is not a directory.
[ENAMETOOLONG]	A component of a pathname exceeded {NAME_MAX} characters, or an entire path name exceeded {PATH_MAX} characters.
[ENOENT]	O_CREAT is not set and the named file does not exist.
[ENOENT]	A component of the path name that must exist does not exist.
...	
[EFAULT]	Path points outside the process's allocated address space.
[EEXIST]	O_CREAT and O_EXCL were specified and the file exists.
[EOPNOTSUPP]	An attempt was made to open a socket (not currently implemented).

The symbols in square brackets are the errno value. Example 7-1 has code that
looks for specific errors. A real life program would handle these errors in an
appropriate manner.

Example 7-1. open.m

```
// open.m -- try opening files and getting different errors.

/* compile with:
cc -g -Wall -o open open.m
*/

#import <fcntl.h>        // for open()
#import <unistd.h>       // for close()
#import <sys/stat.h>     // for permission flags
```

```
#import <stdlib.h>      // for EXIT_SUCCESS, etc
#import <stdio.h>       // for printf() and friends
#import <errno.h>       // for errno
#import <string.h>      // for strerror()

// given a path and access flags, try to open the file.
// if an error happens, write it out to standard error.

void tryOpen (const char *path, int flags)
{
    int result;

    result = open (path, flags,
                   S_IRUSR | S_IWUSR | S_IRGRP  | S_IWGRP);

    if (result == -1) {
        fprintf (stderr, "an error happened opening %s\n", path);

        switch (errno) {

          case ENOTDIR:
            fprintf (stderr,
                    "    part of the path is not a directory\n");
            break;

          case ENOENT:
            fprintf (stderr, "    something doesn't exist, "
                    "like part of a path, or O_CREAT is not set and "
                    "the file doesn't exist\n");
              break;

          case EISDIR:
            fprintf (stderr,
                    "    tried to open directory for writing\n");
            break;

          default:
            fprintf (stderr, "    another error happened:    "
                    "errno %d, strerror: %s\n",
                    errno, strerror(errno));
        }

    } else {
        close (result);
    }

    fprintf (stderr, "\n");

} // tryOpen


int main (int argc, char *argv[])
{
    // trigger ENOTDIR
    tryOpen ("/mach.sym/blah/blah", O_RDONLY);

    // trigger ENOENT, part of the path doesn't exist
```

```
    tryOpen ("/System/Frameworks/bork/my-file", O_RDONLY);

    // trigger ENOENT, O_CREAT not set and file doesn't exist
    tryOpen ("/tmp/my-file", O_RDONLY);

    // trigger EISDIR
    tryOpen ("/dev", O_WRONLY);

    // trigger EEXIST
    tryOpen ("/private/var/log/system.log", O_CREAT | O_EXCL);

    return (EXIT_SUCCESS);

} // main
```

In most cases it is not possible to handle *every* possible error condition (like ENFILE: System file table is full). But in general try to handle what error makes sense and have a catch-all case that will log the error. The main downside with this return code/errno reporting technique is that it is necessary to check the result code of *every* library function call which can get tedious pretty quickly. Plus all of the error-handling code obscures the flow of control. Some programmers write error-handling wrappers around library functions so that return codes do not pollute the mainline code.

With that caveat in mind, you are free to use this convention for your own code, which can be nice when you are supplying a library to programmers familiar with the Unix conventions. There is no standard way to add your own error strings to **strerror()**, unfortunately.

setjmp, longjmp

Languages like C++ and Java have exception-handling features built in. This is where code can happily go about its business, ignoring anything that might go wrong with the functions it is calling. But if something does go wrong, an exception can be thrown which will terminate the current flow of execution. Control resumes execution at a previously registered exception handler which can then decide how best to recover from the problem and resume the work.

C has a primitive form of exception handling that can be used in a similar manner. The **setjmp** and **longjmp** functions are used like a super-goto:

```
int setjmp(jmp_buf env);

void longjmp(jmp_buf env, int value);
```

The jmp_buf is a data structure that holds the current execution context (the current program counter, stack pointer, etc). You **setjmp** where you want execution to return (equivalent to your exception handler), and call **longjmp()** when you want to branch back to that point (equivalent to throwing an exception).

Example 7-2 shows how to use **longjmp()**.

Example 7-2. longjmp.m

```
// longjmp.m -- use setjmp, longjmp

/* compile with:
cc -g -Wall -o longjmp longjmp.m
*/

#import <setjmp.h>      // for setjmp / longjmp
#import <stdio.h>       // for printf
#import <stdlib.h>      // for EXIT_SUCCESS

static jmp_buf handler;

void doEvenMoreStuff ()
{
    printf ("      entering doEvenMoreStuff\n");
    printf ("      done with doEvenMoreStuff\n");

} // doEvenMoreStuff

void doMoreStuff ()
{
    printf ("    entering doMoreStuff\n");
    doEvenMoreStuff ();
    longjmp (handler, 23);
    printf ("    done with doMoreStuff\n");
} // doMoreStuff

void doStuff ()
{
    printf ("entering doStuff\n");
    doMoreStuff ();
    printf ("done with doStuff\n");
} // doStuff

int main (int argc, char *argv[])
{
    int result;

    if ( (result = setjmp(handler)) ) {
        printf ("longjump called, result of %d\n", result);
    } else {
        doStuff ();
    }

    return (EXIT_SUCCESS);

} // main
```

A sample run:

```
$ ./longjmp
entering doStuff
    entering doMoreStuff
        entering doEvenMoreStuff
        done with doEvenMoreStuff
```

```
longjump called, result of 23
```

Two of the functions never get to print out their "done with" statements. They just get jumped over.

The interesting piece here is the `if` statement. When **setjmp()** is called, it returns zero so the second branch of the `if` is taken. When **longjmp()** is called, that `if` statement is essentially evaluated again and execution begins again at that point. The `value` argument to **longjmp()** is what is returned from **setjmp()** the second time it returns.

Any number of **setjmp()** calls can be active at any point in time, so long as they use different memory locations for their `jmp_bufs`. You can maintain a stack of `jmp_bufs` so that **longjmp** knows to jump to the closest **setjmp()**. This is what Cocoa uses for its "classic" exception handling mechanism (discussed after Signals).

There is one rule to remember when using **setjmp()** and **longjmp()**: any local variables in the function that calls **setjmp()** and that might be used after a **longjmp()** must be declared `volatile`. That will force the compiler to read the variables from memory each time rather than using processor registers. **setjmp** saves some processor state, but it does not save every register. When **longjmp()** branches back to its matching **setjmp()**, any garbage in the registers can give you wrong values in variables.

Signals

Signals are like software interrupts, they can be delivered to your program at any time due to a number of well-defined conditions, like when you write outside of your mapped memory pages you will get sent a SIGBUS (bus error) or a SIGSEGV (segmentation violation) signal. If a subprocess of yours terminates you will get a SIGCHLD (child stopped) signal. If your controlling terminal goes away, there is SIGHUP (terminal hung up), and if you use the **alarm()** function, you will get sent SIGALRM when the time expires. The system defines about 31 different signals, many of which deal with job control or specific hardware issues.

A signal is delivered to your program asynchronously whenever it enters the operating system, whether it be via a system call or just regular process scheduling. This means that your code can be interrupted by a signal at pretty much any time.

As you saw above, signals are named with SIG plus an abbreviation of what the signal does. These are defined in `<sys/signal.h>` if you are curious as to what is there. The `signal` man page has the complete list of signals. The **signal()** function (which is a simplified form of `sigaction`, which will be discussed shortly) is used to provide a handler for a signal.

Handling A Signal

Use the **signal** function to register a signal handler.

```
typedef void (*sig_t) (int);

sig_t signal (int sig, sig_t func);
```

where `sig` is the signal number (e.g., SIGHUP) and **func** is the handler function. If you do not call **signal()** for a particular signal, the system default handler is used.

Depending on the signal, the default handler will either ignore the signal or terminate the process. Check the `signal(2)` man page for details on which is which.

Example 7-3 shows a program that registers signal handlers for three signals. The program will catch the signals and either print out that the signal was caught (SIGHUP and SIGUSR1), or exit (SIGUSR2). By the way, SIGUSR1 and SIGUSR2 are signals that your program can use for its own purposes. The OS will not send you those signals unless explicitly told to.

Example 7-3. catch.m

```
// catch.m -- catch some signals

/* compile with:
cc -g -Wall -o catch catch.m
*/

#import <signal.h>      // for signal functions and types
#import <stdio.h>       // printf and friends
#import <stdlib.h>      // for EXIT_SUCCESS
#import <unistd.h>      // for sleep
#import <string.h>      // for strlen

static void writeString (const char *string)
{
    int length = strlen (string);
    write (STDOUT_FILENO, string, length);
} // writeString

void handleHUP (int signo)
{
    writeString ("got a HUP!\n");
} // handleHUP

void handleUsr1Usr2 (int signo)
{
    if (signo == SIGUSR1) {
        writeString ("got a SIGUSR1\n");

    } else if (signo == SIGUSR2) {
        writeString ("got a SIGUSR2. exiting\n");
        exit (EXIT_SUCCESS);
    }

} // handleUsr1Usr2

int main (int argc, char *argv[])
{
    int i;

    // register our signal handlers

    (void) signal (SIGHUP, handleHUP);
    (void) signal (SIGUSR1, handleUsr1Usr2);
    (void) signal (SIGUSR2, handleUsr1Usr2);

    // now do our Real Work
```

```
    for (i = 0; i < 500000; i++) {
        printf ("i is %d\n", i);
        sleep (1);
    }

    return (EXIT_SUCCESS);

} // main
```

Here is a sample run using two terminals: one to see the output and the other to run the `kill` command, which sends signals to programs.

```
Terminal 1                          Terminal 2
$ ./catch &
[1] 7429   (this is the process ID)
1
2
3
4
5
6
7                                   kill -HUP 7429
got a HUP!
8
9
10
11
12                                  kill -USR1 7429
got a SIGUSR1
13
14
15
16
17
18                                  kill -USR2 7429
got a SIGUSR2, exiting
[1]   Done   ./catch
```

A signal handler can handle more than one signal. Also, the return value of **signal()** is the previously registered function. If you are adding a signal handler to a library, or know that more than one handler will be registered for a signal, you should hang on to that return value and call that when your handler is invoked. If you want to register the same function for a bunch of signals you will need to call **signal()** a bunch of times.

To ignore a signal, use the constant SIG_IGN instead of a function address. To restore the default behavior, use SIG_DFL. You cannot ignore or block the SIGKILL or SIGSTOP. That gives system adminstrators the ability to kill any process that has run amok.

Use the **raise()** system call to send yourself a signal.

```
int raise (int sig);
```

sig is the numbero f the signal to raise. Your program can terminate itself by raising SIGKILL.

Blocking Signals

Sometimes it is inconvenient to have a signal handler called during a critical piece of code. You may using a signal to interrupt a long-running process but you do not want to stop in the middle of a complex data structure change and leave your program's environment in an inconsistent state.

Every running program has a signal mask associated with it. This is a bitmask that specifies what signals are blocked from delivery, as shown in Figure 7-1. When you block a signal, that tells the kernel to kernel keeps track of which blocked signals have been sent to the application (but not how many times a signal has been sent). The signal gets delivered when it gets unblocked.

Figure 7-1. Blocking Signals

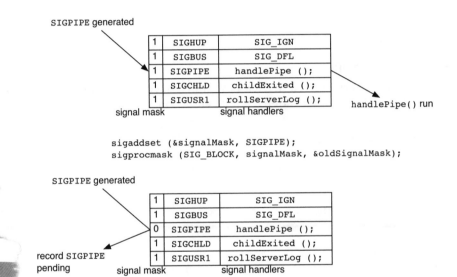

You use **sigprocmask()** to control the signal mask:

```
int sigprocmask (int how, const sigset_t *set, sigset_t *oset);
```

how is one of

SIG_BLOCK

Add the given signals to the program's signal mask (union).

SIG_UNBLOCK

Remove the signals from the program's signal mask (intersection).

SIG_SETMASK

Replace the program's signal mask with the new one.

sigset_t is an abstract type that represents the signal mask. set is the set of signals you want to add or remove, and oset is the original set. (handy for feeding back into **sigprocmask** with SIG_SETMASK). You manipulate sigset_t with these functions (defined in man sigsetops(3)).

```
int sigemptyset (sigset_t *set);
```

Clear a signal set to all zeros (no signals).

```
int sigfillset (sigset_t *set);
```

Fill it with all 1s (all signals).

```
int sigaddset (sigset_t *set, int signo);
```

Add a specific signal to the set.

```
int sigdelset (sigset_t *set, int signo);
```

Remove a specific signal from the set.

```
int sigismember (const sigset_t *set, int signo);
```

Test membership

Example 7-4 is a variation of the catch program above, but instances in which i is not a multiple of five are considered a critical section.

Example 7-4. catchblock.m

```
// catchblock.m -- catch and block some signals

/* compile with:
cc -g -Wall -o catchblock catchblock.m
*/

#import <signal.h>      // for signal functions and types
#import <stdio.h>       // printf and friends
#import <stdlib.h>      // for EXIT_SUCCESS
#import <unistd.h>      // for sleep
#import <string.h>      // for strlen

static void writeString (const char *string)
{
    int length = strlen (string);
    write (STDOUT_FILENO, string, length);

} // writeString

void handleHUP (int signo)
{
    writeString ("got a HUP!\n");

} // handleHUP

void handleUsr1Usr2 (int signo)
{
    if (signo == SIGUSR1) {
        writeString ("got a SIGUSR1\n");

    } else if (signo == SIGUSR2) {
```

```
            writeString ("got a SIGUSR2. exiting\n");
            exit (EXIT_SUCCESS);
    }

} // handleUsr1Usr2

int main (int argc, char *argv[])
{
    int i;
    sigset_t signalMask, oldSignalMask;

    // register our signal handlers

    (void) signal (SIGHUP, handleHUP);
    (void) signal (SIGUSR1, handleUsr1Usr2);
    (void) signal (SIGUSR2, handleUsr1Usr2);

    // construct our signal mask.  We don't want to be bothered
    // by SIGUSR1 or SIGUSR2 in our critical section.
    // but we will leave SIGHUP out of the mask so that it will get
    // delivered

    sigemptyset (&signalMask);
    sigaddset (&signalMask, SIGUSR1);
    sigaddset (&signalMask, SIGUSR2);

    // now do our Real Work

    for (i = 0; i < 500000; i++) {
        printf ("i is %d\n", i);

        if ( (i % 5) == 0) {
            printf ("blocking at %i\n", i);
            sigprocmask (SIG_BLOCK, &signalMask,
                         &oldSignalMask);
        }

        if ( (i % 5) == 4) {
            printf ("unblocking at %i\n", i);
            sigprocmask(SIG_SETMASK, &oldSignalMask, NULL);
        }

        sleep (1);
    }

    return (EXIT_SUCCESS);

} // main
```

A sample run:

```
Terminal 1                              Terminal 2
./catchblock &
[1] 7533
i is 0
blocking at 0
i is 1
```

```
i is 2
i is 3
i is 4
unblocking at 4
i is 5
blocking at 5
i is 6                                              kill -HUP 7533
got a HUP!
i is 7
i is 8                                              kill -HUP 7533
got a HUP!
i is 9
unblocking at 9
i is 10
blocking at 10
i is 11                                             kill -USR1 7533
i is 12
i is 13
i is 14
unblocking at 14
got a SIGUSR1
i is 15
blocking at 15
i is 16                                             kill -USR1 7533
i is 17                                             kill -USR1 7533
i is 18                                             kill -USR1 7533
i is 19
unblocking at 19
got a SIGUSR1
i is 20
blocking at 20
i is 21
i is 22                                             kill -USR2 7533
i is 23
i is 24
unblocking at 24
got a SIGUSR2. exiting
```

It works as expected: HUPs make it through immediately, and USR1 and USR2 are only handled once at the unblocking no matter how many times they are sent.

You can use **sigpending()** to see if a signal of interest is pending:

```
int sigpending (sigset_t *set);
```

Which returns a mask of the pending signals.

Handling signals with *sigaction()*

sigaction() is the full-featured way of handling signals:

```
struct sigaction {
    void      (*sa_handler)();
    sigset_t  sa_mask;
    int       sa_flags;
};

int sigaction (int sig, const struct sigaction *act,
```

```
struct sigaction *oact);
```

Instead of just passing in a handler function, you pass in a structure containing the handler function, the set of signals that should be added to the process signal mask, and some flags. Usually you just set them to zero. The **sigaction()** man page describes them (mainly used for some SIGCHLD signals, or for controlling which stack is used when signals are handled).

Like **signal()**, the previous setting is returned, this time in the oact parameter if it is non-NULL.

Signal Issues

Reentrancy

There are a number of difficult programming issues involved with signals which sometimes make them more difficult to deal with than they are worth. The first is reentrancy, and the second concerns race conditions.

A reentrant function is one that will work if there are two execution streams active in it at one time. This can happen even without threads. For example, consider this code:

```
...
ptr = malloc (50);
...
```

The program is in the middle of calling **malloc()** and **malloc()** is messing with its internal data structures and is in an inconsistent state. Then a signal happens. Because signals happen asynchronously, your program is interrupted and the signal handler runs:

```
...
tempPtr = malloc (20);
...
```

Because **malloc()** is in the middle of its previous work you will most likely crash.

In your signal handlers you should only use reentrant functions. The **sigaction()** man page has a list of functions that are either reentrant or are not interruptable by signals.

In general, these are safe:

- **longjmp()**
- Reentrant versions of functions, like **strtok_r()**
- Program terminators like **abort()** and **exit()**
- Unbuffered I/O (**read()**, **write()**, **open()**, etc)
- Interrogative functions (**getgid()**, **getpid()**, **getuid()**)
- Signal functions (**sigaction()**, **sigprocmask()**)
- Any of your own reentrant functions

These are unsafe:

- Buffered I/O printf and friends. That is why a custom writeString function was used earlier

- `malloc()` and `free()`

- Anything using static buffer space, like `strtok()`

- Any of your own non reentrant functions

You do not need to make your signal handler reentrant. When a signal handler is entered, the signal that triggered the handler is automatically added to the process signal mask. The handler will not get triggered again until it returns. Note that if a handler is registered for more than one signal using `signal()` or `sigaction()`, you will need to make it reentrant.

You may notice that `longjmp()` is on the set of safe functions. You are free to `longjmp()` out of a signal handler to wherever the matching `setjmp()` was placed. This is a way of handling the interruption of a long running process. You may wonder about the process signal mask. If you `longjmp()` out of a handler, is the signal still being blocked? `longjmp()` automatically restores the signal mask when jumping out of a signal handler. If you do not want this behavior (like what exists on some other Unixes) you can use the `_setjmp()` and `_longjmp()` functions.

Example 7-5 is an example of breaking out of a long-running process.

Example 7-5. interrupt.m

```
// interrupt.m -- show interruption of a long-running process

/* compile with:
cc -g -Wall -o interrupt interrupt.m
*/

#import <signal.h>       // for signal functions and types
#import <unistd.h>       // for sleep
#import <string.h>       // for strerror
#import <setjmp.h>       // for setjmp / longjmp
#import <stdio.h>        // for printf
#import <stdlib.h>       // for EXIT_SUCCESS
#import <errno.h>

static jmp_buf handler;

void handleSignal (int signo)
{
    longjmp (handler, 1);
} // handleSignal

void doLotsOfWork ()
{
    int i;

    for (i = 0; i < 50000; i++) {
        printf ("i is %d\n", i);
        sleep (1);
    }

} // doLotsOfWork
```

```
int main (int argc, char *argv[])
{
    volatile int handlerSet = 0;

    struct sigaction action;

    sigemptyset (&action.sa_mask);
    sigaddset (&action.sa_mask, SIGTERM);

    action.sa_handler = handleSignal;
    action.sa_flags = 0;

    if (sigaction (SIGUSR1, &action, NULL) == -1) {
        fprintf (stderr, "error in sigaction: %d / %s\n",
                 errno, strerror(errno));
        return (EXIT_FAILURE);
    }

    while (1) {

        if (!handlerSet) {
            if (setjmp (handler)) {
                // we longjmp'd to here.  Reset our handler
                // next time around
                handlerSet = 0;
                continue;
            } else {
                handlerSet = 1;
            }
        }

        printf("starting lots of work\n");
        doLotsOfWork ();
    }

    return (EXIT_SUCCESS);

} // main
```

A sample run:

```
Terminal 1                              Terminal 2
$ ./interrupt &
[1] 7625
starting lots of work
i is 0
i is 1
i is 2
i is 3
i is 4
i is 5
i is 6                                  kill -USR1 7625
starting lots of work
i is 0
i is 1
i is 2                                  kill -USR1 7625
```

```
starting lots of work
i is 0
i is 1
i is 2
i is 3
i is 4                                                kill 7625

[1]    Terminated                          ./interrupt
```

The last kill sends a SIGTERM, which terminates the process if not handled.

Race conditions

The other bugaboo with signals are race conditions (a subject revisited in Chapter 22 (Threads)). A race condition happens when two different streams of execution hit an ambiguous area of code and the code's behavior changes depending on the order in which the two streams execute.

A piece of code as simple as

```
i = 5;
i = i + 7;
```

can be subject to race conditions. Depending on order of operations, you can get different results:

```
thread 1                    thread 2
 i = 5
 copy i to register
 add 7 to 5
 store 12 into i
                            i = 12
                            copy i to register
                            add 7 to 12
                            store 19 into i

Final value: 19


thread 1                    thread 2
 i = 5
 copy i to register
                            i = 5
                            copy i to register
                            add 7 to 5
                            store 12 into i
 add 7 to 5
 store 12 into i

Final value : 12
```

The interrupt.m program has a couple of race conditions in it. The first happens after you register the signal handler but before the call to **setjmp()** on the jump_buf. If a SIGUSR1 signal happens any time after the **sigaction()** and **setjmp()**, you will crash by trying to **longjmp()** with an invalid jump buffer.

Likewise, if a SIGUSR1 signal happens between the time that the code returns from **set jmp()** and you call **set jmp()** again, you will crash from using an out-of-date jmp_buf. You can use **sigprocmask()** to block the signals during these vulnerable times.

Signal handling is a dangerous and ugly task. The kqueue interface (discussed in Chapter 15) provides an easy-to-use and safe way of handling signals.

Exception-Handling in Cocoa

Cocoa provides two exception-handling mechanisms similar to what C++ and Java offer. The older, "classic" way to handle exceptions is to wrap a body of code with a set of macros. The newer way, the "native" way, was introduced in Mac OS X 10.3 and adds language support for exceptions.

Classic Exception-Handling

To handle exceptions, wrap your code in an NS_DURING clause. Any exceptional conditions will raise an exception which can then be caught by an NS_HANDLER clause.

The way you work it is:

```
NS_DURING
    ... code that might throw an exception
NS_HANDLER
    ... code to examine the exception and possibly handle it
NS_ENDHANDLER
```

If any code between NS_DURING and NS_HANDLER raises an exception, execution immediately resumes with the first instruction after NS_HANDLER, as shown in Figure 7-2

Figure 7-2. Exception flow of control

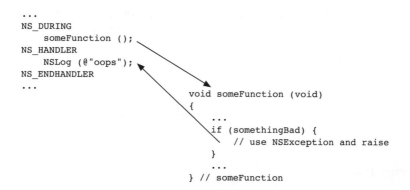

Handlers can be arbitrarily nested, so you could call a function that is in an NS_DURING handler, and it can set up its own NS_DURING handler. When someone finally raises an exception, flow of control will jump to the closest NS_HANDLER.

The macro for NS_HANDLER declares a local variable called localException that you can query for details about the exception - specifically, its name and the reason it happened. You can also use localException to "rethrow" the exception, y using [localException raise].

Example 7-6 is a little foundation tool to show exception-handling in action. **-[NSString characterAtIndex:]** will raise an exception if you try to get a character that is beyond the length of the string.

Example 7-6. exception.m

```
// exception.m -- show simple exception handling in Cocoa

/* compile with:
cc -g -Wall -o exception -framework Foundation exception.m
*/

#import <Foundation/Foundation.h>
#import <stdlib.h>                          // for EXIT_SUCCESS

int main (int argc, char *argv[])
{
    NSAutoreleasePool *pool = [[NSAutoreleasePool alloc] init];
    NSString *string = @"hello";

    NS_DURING
        NSLog (@"character at index 0: %c",
                [string characterAtIndex:0]);
        NSLog (@"character at index 1: %c",
                [string characterAtIndex:1]);
        NSLog (@"character at index 2000: %c",
                [string characterAtIndex: 2000]);
        NSLog (@"character at index 2: %c",
                [string characterAtIndex:2]);

    NS_HANDLER
        NSLog (@"inside of exception handler.");
        NSLog (@"name is : %@", [localException name]);
        NSLog (@"reason is : %@", [localException reason]);
        NSLog (@"userInfo dict: %@", [localException userInfo]);

    NS_ENDHANDLER

    [pool release];

    return (EXIT_SUCCESS);

} // main
```

A sample run:

```
$ ./exception
2002-09-03 16:17:31.433 exception[7700] character at index 0: h
2002-09-03 16:17:31.433 exception[7700] character at index 1: e
2002-09-03 16:17:31.435 exception[7700] inside of exception handler.
2002-09-03 16:17:31.435 exception[7700] name is : NSRangeException
2002-09-03 16:17:31.435 exception[7700] reason is:
```

```
 [NSConstantString characterAtIndex:]: Range or index out of bounds
 2002-09-03 16:17:31.435 exception[7700] userInfo dict: (null)
```

The first two **characterAtIndex** method calls succeed, and the third raised an exception, terminating the code in the NS_DURING section of code.

Specific Cocoa methods document whether they raise exceptions. Unfortunately there is not a centralized list of all methods that can raise exceptions.

Cocoa classic exception-handling is based on **setjmp()**/**longjmp()**, so you again must use volatile variables if they might be used after the **longjmp()** to your NS_HANDLER. Also, there is no automatic cleanup of allocated objects when exceptions happen (like with stack objects in C++). Also, there are some restrictions in what you can do during the NS_HANDLER portion. Specifically, you should not **goto** or **return** out of an exception-handling domain (anywhere between NS_DURING and NS_HANDLER), otherwise the exception handler stack will be left in a bad state. Also, **setjmp()**/**longjmp()** should not be used if it crosses an NS_DURING statement. In general, if you are using Cocoa exception handling, you will not need to use **setjmp()**/**longjmp()**.

Cocoa exception-handling is a heavy-weight operation, so do not use it for normal flow of control. It is better test a string's length when processing characters rather than falling off the string's end and depending on an exception to terminate your processing.

Cocoa provides the **NSException** object. You can allocate your own instances of this object and use them to raise your own exceptions. You can supply your own name and reason strings or use some of the built-in ones.

Example 7-7 is a foundation tool that raises a custom exception:

Example 7-7. raise-classic.m

```
// raise-classic.m -- raise an exception

/* compile with:
cc -g -Wall -o raise-classic -framework Foundation raise-classic.m
*/

#import <Foundation/Foundation.h>
#import <stdlib.h>                      // for EXIT_SUCCESS

void doSomethingElse ()
{
    NSDictionary *userInfo;
    userInfo = [NSDictionary dictionaryWithObjectsAndKeys:
                                    @"hello", @"thing1",
                                    @"bork", @"thing2",
                                    nil];
    NSException *exception;
    exception = [NSException exceptionWithName: @"MyException"
                        reason: @"doSomethingElse raised MyException"
                     userInfo: userInfo];
    [exception raise];

    NSLog (@"after the raise.  This will not be executed");
```

```
} // doSomethingElse

void doSomething ()
{
    doSomethingElse ();
} // doSomething

int main (int argc, char *argv[])
{
    NSAutoreleasePool *pool = [[NSAutoreleasePool alloc] init];

    NS_DURING
        doSomething ();

    NS_HANDLER
        NSLog (@"inside of exception handler.");
        NSLog (@"name is : %@", [localException name]);
        NSLog (@"reason is : %@", [localException reason]);
        NSLog (@"userInfo dict: %@", [localException userInfo]);

    NS_ENDHANDLER

    [pool release];

    return (EXIT_SUCCESS);

} // main
```

A sample run:

```
$ ./raise-classic
... [876] inside of exception handler.
... [876] name is : MyException
... [876] reason is : doSomethingElse raised a MyException
... [876] userInfo dict:  {thing1 = hello; thing2 = bork; }
```

The Cocoa classic exception-handling mechanism is fundamentally string based. There is no a hierarchy of exception classes like there is in Java and C++. When code throws a built-in exception (like **NSGenericException**), is is actually just an NSString that gets put into an **NSException** object.

You can use gdb to halt execution when exceptions are thrown. Put a breakpoint on **-[NSException raise]**.

Native Exception-Handling

Starting with Mac OS X 10.3, native exception handling was added to the Objective-C language. You need to turn it on before you can use it. You can provide gcc the -fobjc-exceptions flag when compiling on the command line or with `makefiles`, and in `Xcode` you check the **Enable Objective-C Exceptions** checkbox, as shown in Figure 7-3

Figure 7-3. Enabling Native Objective-C Exceptions

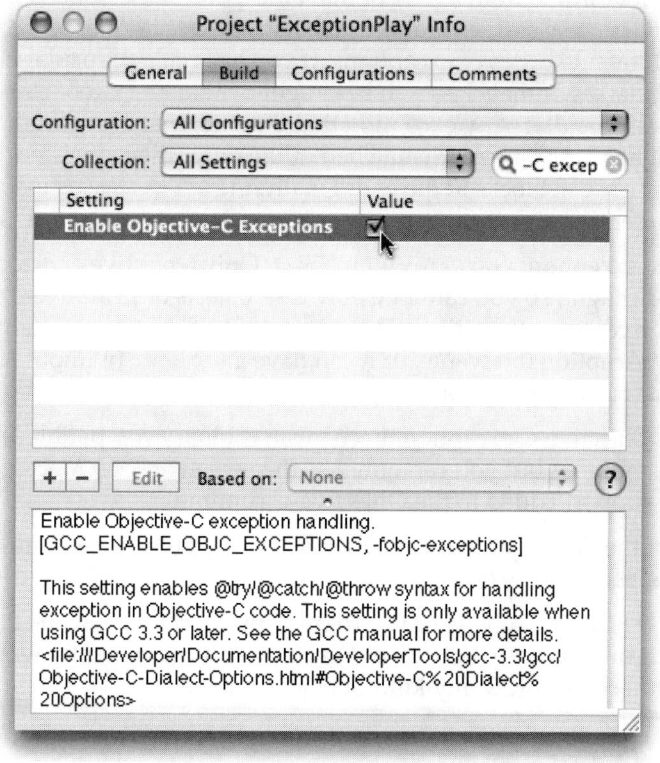

Enabling native exceptions also enables some native thread-safety tools that will be discussed in Chapter 22 (Multithreading).

Example 7-8 shows the syntax for native Objective-C exceptions.

Example 7-8. Objective-C Exception Syntax

```
@try {
    ...
    @throw expr;
}
@catch (SomeClass *exception) {
    ...
    @throw expr;
    ...
    @throw
}
@catch (AnotherClass *exception) {
    ...
}
@catch (id allOthers) {
    ...
}
```

```
@finally {
    ...
    @throw expr;
}
```

You wrap the code that might throw an exception inside of a @try block. If any exceptions are thrown from inside of that block, one of the @catch handlers may be entered. Unlike the classic exceptions, the native exceptions are object based, so you can catch different classes of exceptions. If you @catch a particular class, any objects that are subclasses of that class will be caught by that block too. Use id to designate the "catch-all" handler. Any exception that does not match any of the other classes will be caught here. Classes are matched in the order they are listed, so be sure to have any id @catch blocks at the end. Finally, the @finally section is run, whether or not an exception was thrown or the @try block completed successfully.

To throw an exception, you @throw an object. Only Objective-C objects can be thrown and caught, so you cannot throw C++ objects or primitive C types. You can @throw an exception at any time. The code inside of a @catch section can throw a brand new exception if it wants, or it can have a @throw; (without an object) to re-throw the current exception.

The native Objective-C exception mechanism is binary compatible with the NS_HANDLER idioms, but you can only use the new syntax on Mac OS X 10.3 or later because of support added to the Objective-C runtime.

If you want the debugger to break when a @throw, put a breakpoint on **objc_exception_throw()**.

Example 7-9 is the raise-classic program, but ported to use the native exception syntax. It throws an NSException object because it conveniently wraps some useful data, but you could throw any kind of object you want.

Example 7-9. raise-native.m

```
// raise-native.m -- raise an exception

/* compile with
cc -g -Wmost -fobjc-exceptions -o raise-native \
    -framework Foundation raise-native.m
*/

#import <:Foundation/Foundation.h>
#import <stdlib.h>           // for EXIT_SUCCESS

void doSomethingElse ()
{
    NSDictionary *userInfo;
    userInfo = [NSDictionary dictionaryWithObjectsAndKeys:
                                @"hello", @"thing1",
                                @"bork", @"thing2", nil];
    NSException *exception;
    exception = [NSException
                    exceptionWithName: @"MyException"
                    reason: @"doSomethingElse raised a MyException"
                    userInfo: userInfo];
    @throw exception;
```

```
    NSLog (@"after the raise.  This won't be executed");

} // doSomethingElse

void doSomething ()
{
    doSomethingElse ();
} // doSomething

int main (int argc, char *argv[])
{
    NSAutoreleasePool *pool = [[NSAutoreleasePool alloc] init];

    @try {
        doSomething ();
    }
    @catch (NSException *exception) {
        NSLog (@"inside of exception handler.");
        NSLog (@"name is : %@", [exception name]);
        NSLog (@"reason is : %@", [exception reason]);
        NSLog (@"userInfo dict: %@", [exception userInfo]);
    }
    @finally {
        [pool release];
    }

    return (EXIT_SUCCESS);

} // main
```

And the results are the same as `raise-classic`:

```
$ ./raise-native
... [21540] inside of exception handler.
... [21540] name is : MyException
... [21540] reason is : doSomethingElse raised a MyException
... [21540] userInfo dict: {thing1 = hello; thing2 = bork; }
```

Subclassing NSApplication to catch exceptions

In some applications, Xcode for example, when an exception falls through the stack all the way to the run loop, the user is shown the exception in a panel. (Often, the panel just says something like "Something has gone wrong. You may want to save what you are working on and restart this application.") How is this done?

When an exception falls through the stack all the way to the run loop, the instance of **NSApplication** gets sent the following message:

```
- (void) reportException: (NSException *) theException
```

This method simply logs the exception using **NSLog()** and the run loop begins again. If you would like to alter this behavior, you must subclass **NSApplication** and override **reportException:**.

If you do this, make sure that you also alter the `Info.plist` for your application so that it uses your subclass instead of **NSApplication**:

```
<key>NSPrincipalClass</key>
<string>MyExceptionReportingApplication</string>
```

Note that this only works if your Objective-C code is in a Cocoa application. If you have written a tool, you will call **NSSetUncaughtExceptionHandler()** and supply it with a pointer to a function with this signature:

```
void MyHandler(NSException *e);
```

Logging

In our development careers at one time or another we have all done "caveman debugging", putting in lots of print statements to see program flow and to see what values our variables have. Putting in **fprintf()** and **NSLog()** to print to the terminal and using the stuff from Chapter 8 (Files) you can redirect those print statements to log files.

There are also times when you are logging and it is not debugging related, like server programs keeping a log of connections or printing information that may be of interest to administrators (such as that the disk is filling up). Most Unix systems have a daemon running called `syslogd`, the system logging daemon. System administrators can configure `syslogd` to log to a file or to send the log information from many machines to a central location (very useful if you have a lot of machines to keep an eye on).

syslog()

One programmatic interface to `syslogd`, the **syslog()** function, is:

```
void syslog (int priority, const char *message, ...);
```

The message is a **printf()**-style string. You can use any **printf()** token in there you want. There is also an added format string, "%m", to put in the current error message from `strerror()`. **syslog()** also adds a trailing newline if one is not already specified in the message string.

The priority controls if the logging will be seen or not. Here is their order high to low

LOG_EMERG

A panic condition. This is normally broadcast to all users.

LOG_ALERT

A condition that should be corrected immediately, such as a corrupted system database.

LOG_CRIT

Critical conditions, e.g., hard device errors.

LOG_ERR

> Errors.

LOG_WARNING

> Warning messages.

LOG_NOTICE

> Conditions that are not error conditions, but should possibly be handled specially.

LOG_INFO

> Informational messages.

LOG_DEBUG

> Messages that contain information normally of use only when debugging a program.

The configuration file for `syslogd`, `/etc/syslogd.conf`, contains the controls for setting the threshold where logging will occur. By default, `LOG_DEBUG` messages are not shown, but everything else is.

You can control some of the syslog behavior of the logging output by using **openlog()**.

```
void openlog (const char *ident, int logopt, int facility);
```

`ident` is the name to use for the program in the log. By default, the executable name is used. `logopt` is any one of these flags bitwise-OR'd together.

LOG_CONS

> If **syslog()** cannot pass the message to `syslogd`, it will attempt to write the message to the console (`/dev/console`).

LOG_NDELAY

> Open the connection to **syslogd(8)** immediately. Normally the open is delayed until the first message is logged. This is useful for programs that need to manage the order in which file descriptors are allocated.

LOG_PERROR

> Write the message to standard error output as well as to the system log.

LOG_PID

> Log the process ID with each message; this is useful for identifying instantiations of daemons.

The facility parameter tells `syslogd` that the program is a member of a standard facility, like being a daemon, or are part of the security subsystem. For example, if you were writing a daemon that was part of the mail system, you would call **openlog()** with a facility of `LOG_MAIL`. These constants are listed in the man page.

Example 7-10 is a sample that logs to `syslog`, which by default gets written locally to `/var/log/system.log`. This is the one of the logs that the `Console.app` looks at.

Example 7-10. syslog.m

```
// syslog.m -- use the syslog functions

/* compile with:
cc -g -Wall -o syslog syslog.m
*/

#import <syslog.h>      // for syslog and firneds
#import <stdlib.h>      // for EXIT_SUCCESS
#import <errno.h>       // for errno

int main (int argc, char *argv[])
{
    syslog (LOG_WARNING, "this is a warning message");
    errno = EINVAL;
    syslog (LOG_ERR, "this is an error, %m", errno);
    syslog (LOG_EMERG, "WHOOP!! WHOOP!!");

    openlog ("BNRsyslogTest", LOG_PID | LOG_NDELAY | LOG_CONS,
             LOG_DAEMON);

    syslog (LOG_DEBUG, "Debug message");
    syslog (LOG_NOTICE, "Notice message");

    return (EXIT_SUCCESS);

} // main
```

A run of this produces in the log:

```
$ tail -f /private/var/log/system.log
(and run ./syslog in another terminal)

(beep)Message from syslogd@borkopolis at Tue Sep  3 20:27:53 2002...
borkopolis ./syslog: WHOOP!! WHOOP!!
Sep  3 20:27:53 borkopolis ./syslog: this is a warning message
Sep  3 20:27:53 borkopolis ./syslog: this is an error, Invalid argument
Sep  3 20:27:53 borkopolis ./syslog: WHOOP!! WHOOP!!
Sep  3 20:27:53 borkopolis BNRsyslogTest[7855]: Notice message
```

Here you can see the LOG_EMERG getting broadcast to all the open terminals, then the various syslog messages. You can call **openlog()** at anytime. You can see how the LOG_PID and "BNRsyslogTest" settings appear.

ASL

The **syslog()** function is very portable and works on all modern Unix-flavored systems. Apple has introduced its own API that adds some value on top of syslogd. ASL, the Apple System Log facility, provides an alternate API for sending messages to syslogd, as well as a capability for querying syslogd for information about previously logged items.

ASL Messages

ASL is based on messages, and these messages are an opaque type called `aslmsg`. A message is a container for key / value pairs, with a number of pre-defined keys that have meaning for launchd. You create a new message **asl_new()**:

```
aslmsg asl_new (uint32_t type);
```

asl_new() creates a new `aslmsg` and returns it to you. The `type` parameter can either be `ASL_TYPE_MSG` to create a new message, or `ASL_TYPE_QUERY` to create a new search query.

When you are done with an `aslmsg`, release its resources using **asl_free()**, which takes an `aslmsg` as its only argument.

Add keys and values to a message by using asl_set:

```
int asl_set (aslmsg message, const char *key, const char *value);
```

`message` is the `aslmsg` you are filling out. `key` and `value` are zero-terminated strings (ASCII or UTF-8). The function returns zero on success, non-zero for failure. There are a number of pre-defined keys that have defaults set, and you are also allowed to add your own keys. The predefined keys are: `ASL_KEY_TIME`, `ASL_KEY_HOST`, `ASL_KEY_SENDER` (defaults to the process name), `ASL_KEY_PID`, `ASL_KEY_UID`, `ASL_KEY_GID`, `ASL_KEY_LEVEL`, `ASL_KEY_MSG` (the text to actually log).

You can get a value out of a message for a specific key by using **asl_get()**, and iterate through a message's contents by using **asl_key()**.

```
const char *asl_get (aslmsg message, const char *key);
```

Given a `message` and a `key`, this returns the value, or NULL if there is no value under that key.

```
const char *asl_key (aslmsg message, uint32_t index);
```

Given a `message`, this returns the key at the position indicated by `index`. The function returns NULL If `index` falls off the end of the list of keys You can spin through the keys by starting at 0 and incrementing an index. When the function returns NULL, you have reached the end. You can give the returned key to **asl_get()** to retrieve the value.

Once you have constructed a message you can send it off to `syslogd` by using **asl_send()**:

```
int asl_send (aslclient client, aslmsg message);
```

The first argument, `client`, is an `aslclient`. Your application gets one client created for free. If you want to log messages from threads other than the main one you will need to create additional clients using **asl_open()**. **asl_open()** is not described here. Check the `asl` man page for details. The second argument, `message` is the message that has already been constructed.

ASL supplies two convenience functions, **asl_log()** and **asl_vlog()**, so that you do not have to create a new `aslmsg` every time you want to log something:

```
int asl_log (aslclient client, aslmsg message, int level,
             const char *format, ...);
```

```
int asl_vlog (aslclient client, aslmsg message, int level,
              const char *format, val_list args);
```

You can pass NULL for the first argument, `client`. You only need additional clients for multi-threaded applications. The `message` argument is a template message that has some key/value pairs already added to it. The template will get merged with default values for the message. You can pass NULL if you do not have a template message you want to use. You can use the standard printf-style strings and arguments with **asl_log()**. If you have a `va_list` handy, you can pass that instead of a string of arguments.

There is one bizarre gotcha relating to linking programs that use **asl_log()** and **asl_vlog()**, at least with Mac OS X 10.4. You have to define an environment variable, MACOSX_DEPLOYMENT_TARGET and set it to the value 10.4 before compiling your program. Otherwise you will get a linker error like o/usr/bin/ld: Undefined symbols: _asl_log$LDBLStub You can also work aroudn this by gcc 3.3 rather than the 4.x family. This seems to allow it to link correctly.

ASL Queries

Using ASL messages seems like a lot of work over when you can just use **syslog()**. ASL also provides a way to query `syslogd` for information about previously logged entries, turning `syslogd` into a mini-database of sorts. To construct a query you make a new message of type ASL_TYPE_QUERY, and then use the **asl_set_query()** function to add predicates. You can set multiple predicates, which will be hooked together using logical ANDs.

```
int asl_set_query (alsmsg query, const char *key, const char *value,
                   uint32_t operation);
```

The `query` parameter is an `aslmsg` that was created with a ASL_TYPE_QUERY type. `key` is the key you want to search for. `value` is the value you want to search for, and `operation` is the way to search, along with some optional flags.

Here are the different query operations:

ASL_QUERY_OP_EQUAL

> Compare values for equality. If the value for `key` in a logged message is equal to the `value` parameter, that message will be returned from the query.

ASL_QUERY_OP_GREATER

> If the value for `key` in a logged message is strictly greater than the `value` parameter, that message will be returned from the query.

ASL_QUERY_OP_GREATER_EQUAL

> If the value for `key` in a logged message is greater than or equal to the `value` parameter, that message will be returned from the query.

ASL_QUERY_OP_LESS

> If the value for `key` in a logged message is strictly less than the `value` parameter, that message will be returned from the query.

ASL_QUERY_OP_LESS_EQUAL

If the value for `key` in a logged message is less greater than or equal to the `value` parameter, that message will be returned from the query.

ASL_QUERY_OP_NOT_EQUAL

If the value for `key` in a logged message is not equal to the to the `value` parameter, that message will be returned from the query.

ASL_QUERY_OP_REGEX

If the value for `key` in a logged message matches the regular expression specified by `value` parameter, that message will be returned from the query. Regular expression searches use `regex`. Check the `regex(3)` man page for details. Patterns are compiled using the `REG_EXTENDED` (use "modern" regular expressions) and `REG_NOSUB` (compile the regular expression for matching that only reports success or failure, not what was matched) options.

ASL_QUERY_OP_TRUE

Always true. Use this to test for the existence of a key.

There are also a number of modifiers you can bitwise-OR into the **asl_set_query()**'s `operation` parameter:

ASL_QUERY_OP_CASEFOLD

Compare strings in a case-insensitive manner. This is the only modifier that is checked for the ASL_QUERY_OP_REGEX operation.

ASL_QUERY_OP_PREFIX

Match a leading substring.

ASL_QUERY_OP_SUFFIX

Match a trailing substring

ASL_QUERY_OP_SUBSTRING

Match any substring.

ASL_QUERY_OP_NUMERIC

Convert values to integers using **atoi()**. By including this option to one of the relative operations (greater, greater_equal, etc), you can do numeric comparisons instead of string comparisons. This is very handy when you are wanting a specific range of message levels.

After you have constructed the query message, you send it off to `syslogd` by using **asl_search()**:

```
aslresponse asl_search (aslclient client, aslmsg query);
```

The `client` can be NULL unless you are calling this from multiple threads. `query` is the query message you constructed with **asl_set_query**. The return value, an `aslresponse`, is an opaque iterator type that you feed to **aslresponse_next()** until it returns NULL. Release the query's resources by using **aslresponse_free()**. Both of these functions take an aslresponse from **asl_search()**

Example 7-11 will list all of the messages that syslogd has recently displayed. It uses a query using ASL_QUERY_OP_TRUE to match everything.

Example 7-11. asl-list.m

```
// asl-list.m -- show what asl messages have been logged so far

#import <asl.h>      // for ASL API
#import <stdio.h>    // for printf()

/* compile with
cc -g -Wmost -o asl-list asl-list.m
*/

void dumpAslMsg (aslmsg message)
{
    // walk the keys and values in each message
    const char *key, *value;
    int i = 0;
    while (key = asl_key (message, i)) {
        value = asl_get (message, key);
        printf ("%d: %s => %s\n", i, key, value);
        i++;
    }

} // dumpAslMsg

int main (void)
{
    // construct a query for all senders using a regular expression
    // that matches everything
    aslmsg query;
    query = asl_new (ASL_TYPE_QUERY);
    asl_set_query (query, ASL_KEY_SENDER, "", ASL_QUERY_OP_TRUE);

    // perform the search
    aslresponse results = asl_search (NULL, query);

    // walk the returned messages
    aslmsg message;
    while (message = aslresponse_next (results)) {
        dumpAslMsg (message);
        printf ("-------------------------------------------\n");
    }

    aslresponse_free (results);
    asl_free (query);

    return (0);

} // main
```

And here is a sample run:

```
$ ./asl-list
----------------------------------------
0: Time => 2005.08.02 13:21:51 UTC
1: Facility => daemon
2: Sender => configd
3: PID => 53
4: Message => posting notification \
com.apple.system.config.network_change
5: Level => 5
6: UID => -2
7: GID => -2
8: Host => borkopolis
----------------------------------------
0: Time => 2005.08.02 13:21:51 UTC
1: Facility => netinfo
2: Sender => lookupd
3: PID => 19441
4: Message => lookupd (version 365) starting - \
Tue Aug  2 09:21:51 2005
5: Level => 5
6: UID => -2
7: GID => -2
8: Host => borkopolis
----------------------------------------
0: Time => 2005.08.04 16:27:24 UTC
1: Facility => user
2: Sender => cp
3: PID => -1
4: Message => error processing extended attributes: \
Operation not permitted
5: Level => 4
6: UID => -2
7: GID => -2
8: Host => borkopolis
```

There actually was a *lot* more output. This is just a representative sample.

Example 7-12 logs a simple message with **asl_log()**, then builds a template message, and uses that for a couple of logs. The template has a custom key in it, "Suit", presumably because the organization running this program wants to log when someone enters the research lab while wearing a specific kind of protective suit. Two people are logged having been suited up. After the logs, a query is made to get the log messages for when Alex wears his suit. Because this uses **asl_log()**, you have to set the MACOSX_DEPLOYMENT_TARGET environment variable for it to link correctly.

Example 7-12. asl-log-n-query.m

```
// asl-log-n-query.m -- do some logs and some queries

#import <asl.h>       // for ASL function
#import <stdio.h>     // for printf()
#import <syslog.h>    // for LOG_ constants

/* compile with this.  Need to set the env var otherwise
 * asl_log() won't link
export MACOSX_DEPLOYMENT_TARGET=10.4
```

```
cc -g -Wmost -o asl-log-n-query asl-log-n-query.m
*/

void dumpAslMsg (aslmsg message)
{
    // walk the keys and values in each message
    const char *key, *value;
    int i = 0;
    while (key = asl_key (message, i)) {
        value = asl_get (message, key);
        printf ("%d: %s => %s\n", i, key, value);
        i++;
    }

} // dumpAslMsg

int main (void)
{
    // do a simple log
    asl_log (NULL, NULL, LOG_NOTICE, "hello how are %s today?", "you");

    // make a template message with our custom tags
    aslmsg template = asl_new (ASL_TYPE_MSG);
    asl_set (template, "Suit", "(4A)CGS");

    // log some messages
    asl_log (NULL, template, LOG_NOTICE, "Laurel has suited up");
    asl_log (NULL, template, LOG_NOTICE, "Alex has suited up");

    // do a query to see how many times Alex has worn his
    // (4A)CGS suit

    aslmsg query;
    query = asl_new (ASL_TYPE_QUERY);

    asl_set_query (query, "Suit", "(4A)CGS", ASL_QUERY_OP_EQUAL);
    asl_set_query (query, ASL_KEY_MSG, "Alex", ASL_QUERY_OP_REGEX);

    // perform the search
    aslresponse results = asl_search (NULL, query);

    // walk the returned messages
    aslmsg message;
    while (message = aslresponse_next(results)) {
        dumpAslMsg (message);
        printf ("---------------------------------------\n");
    }

    aslresponse_free (results);
    asl_free (query);

    asl_free (template);

    return (0);

} // main
```

When you run the program, have a `tail -f` pointed at `/var/system.log` so you can see the three log messages:

```
$ tail -f /var/system.log
Aug 6 15:20:57 borkopolis asl-log-n-query[99]: hello how are you today?
Aug 6 15:20:57 borkopolis asl-log-n-query[99]: Laurel has suited up
Aug 6 15:20:57 borkopolis asl-log-n-query[99]: Alex has suited up
```

Then the program displays the results from its query. It shows an earlier notice from 17:45:45, and the one from 19:20:57. The descripancy in time stamps that the program displays and what `syslogd` displays is because of time zones. The time returned from the query is UTC (universal time), and and the output in the log file is the current time zone (Eastern Daylight Time in my case).

```
$ ./asl-log-n-query
0: Time => 2005.08.06 17:45:45 UTC
1: Host => borkopolis
2: Sender => asl-log-n-query
3: PID => 22812
4: UID => 501
5: GID => 501
6: Level => 5
7: Message => Alex has suited up
8: Suit => (4A)CGS
-----------------------------------------
0: Time => 2005.08.06 19:20:57 UTC
1: Host => borkopolis
2: Sender => asl-log-n-query
3: PID => 22877
4: UID => 501
5: GID => 501
6: Level => 5
7: Message => Alex has suited up
8: Suit => (4A)CGS
-----------------------------------------
```

ASL also has some features that allow you to change the logging level of applications remotely, allowing you as a user or an administrator to crank up or down the volume of logging from an application. Check out the `asl` man page.

For The More Curious

Assertions

Assertions are a programming technique where tests are put in for conditions that cannot happen. If the program does get into such a state, the program kills itself, dropping a core file if it is configured to do so.

The assert macro

```
assert(expression);
```

evaluates the expression. If the expression is false, the process is terminated, a diagnostic message is written to the standard error stream, and the **abort ()** function is called, which terminates the program by raising the signal `SIGABRT`. Because most programmers use asserts for debugging purposes, you can compile them out of a production program by using the preprocessor flag -DNDEBUG. Be aware of side effects due to code called in the **assert()** macro. This could cause your program to fail in a non-debug build. Personally, I am the sort that likes to leave that stuff in (so long as it is not computationally expensive) since we are much more likely to run into problems with our programs out in the field where disabled assertions will not do us much good, but that is an individual decision. This is a point of some debate. Users of GUI apps might not want their whole work session blown away because of a failed assert somewhere.

Cocoa also has an assertion mechanism, **NSAssertionHandler**. There you use macros like **NSAssert** (when in a method) and **NSCAssert** (when in a regular old C function) to evaluate a condition. If it evaluates to false, the message is passed to an **NSAssertionHandler** (one associated with each thread). When invoked, this object prints an error message, and raises an NSInternalInconsitencyException, which can be caught using NS_DURING/NS_HANDLER.

Challenges

1. Fix the race conditions in interrupt.m by using **sigprocmask()**. Is the behavior of **longjump()** appropriate, or should **_setjmp()** and **_longjmp()** be used instead?

2. Tweak /etc/syslogd.conf to display the debug message from syslog.m in the system.log file.

Chapter 8. Files, Part 1: I/O and Permissions

Files are the permanent storage for the data that your programs generate. The semantics of handling files are similar to most every other common platform (open, read, write, seek to a particular location, close), with some added nuances that live in the details.

The idea of a file is a fundamental Unix concept. Pretty much everything is treated as a file. Ordinary "write the bits for a jpeg graphic" go to files in the file system. Network connections are treated as files. Accessing physical devices is done with file operations. Interacting with the terminal is with file operations. This has the nice side effect of using the same API for reading and writing data to all of these disparate machine entities. The downside is that there is some additional complexity in the API to handle the different corner cases involved with accessing all of these OS features.

Unbuffered I/O

The unbuffered I/O APIs are the fundamental system calls (function calls that go into the kernel) upon which other APIs (like the buffered I/O ones) can be built.

Opening a file

open opens a file:

```
int open (const char *path, int flags, mode_t mode);
```

The mode argument deals with default permissions on newly created files (which person has authority to read and write to the file), the details of which will be talked about a little later. The flags field is used to control the behavior of the file. Bitwise-OR in one of these flags

O_RDONLY

> Open read-only

O_WRONLY

> Open write-only

O_RDWR

> Open read/write

and any of these flags:

O_APPEND

> Append on every write. This does an implicit seek to the end before writing, but is atomic.

O_NONBLOCK

> Do not block for an open, and do not block when waiting for data.

O_CREAT

> Create the file if it does not exist.

O_TRUNC

> Truncate the file to zero bytes when opening it.

O_EXCL

> Generate an error if the file already exists.

O_SHLOCK

> Obtain a shared lock.

O_EXLOCK

> Obtain an exclusive lock (more on locks later).

If there was an error, **open()** returns -1 and sets the errno global variable to the appropriate value. This "returning -1 and setting errno on an error" is common to most of the file I/O functions (unfortunately not all).

If **open()** was successful, the return value is a non-negative integer called a *file descriptor*, frequently shortened to just fd. This integer value is the index into a per-process table that references open files. This file descriptor is used as a handle to the file for subsequent calls.

The three standard streams that shells establish for programs are located at file descriptor values zero (for standard in), one (for standard out), and two (for standard error). You can pass these numbers to the **read()** and **write()** functions, or you can use the symbolic constants STDIN_FILENO, STDOUT_FILENO, or STDERR_FILENO, as shown in Figure 8-1.

Figure 8-1. File Descriptors

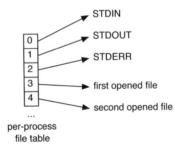

One piece of trivia, when you open a file, the file descriptor returned is guaranteed to be the lowest numbered unused descriptor. This can be useful when you are reopening a file on one of the standard streams (although the **dup2()** call is better for that).

Example 8-1 is a program that closes stdout and reopens it to a logfile, set in append-only mode. Note that **printf()** writes to the standard out.

Example 8-1. append.m

```
// append.m -- show an opening of a logfile, replacing a
//              standard stream.
```

```
/* compile with:
cc -g -Wall -o append append.m
*/

#import <unistd.h>      // for STDOUT_FILENO
#import <stdlib.h>      // for EXIT_SUCCESS
#import <fcntl.h>       // for OPEN
#import <stdio.h>       // for printf() and friends
#import <errno.h>       // for errno
#import <string.h>      // for strerror()
#import <sys/stat.h>     // for permission constants

int main (int argc, char *argv[])
{
    int fd;

    close (STDOUT_FILENO);

    // open a log file, write only, and to always automatically append.
    // oh, and create the file if it does not exist already
    fd = open ("/tmp/logthingie.txt", O_WRONLY | O_CREAT | O_APPEND,
            S_IRUSR | S_IWUSR);

    if (fd == -1) {
        fprintf (stderr, "cannot open log file.  Error %d (%s)\n",
                errno, strerror(errno));
        exit (EXIT_FAILURE);
    }

    printf ("wheee, we have a log file open\n");

    exit (EXIT_SUCCESS);

} // main
```

Here are some runs of the program:

```
$ ls -l /tmp/logthingie.txt
ls: /tmp/logthingie.txt: No such file or directory


$ ./append

$ ls -l /tmp/logthingie.txt
-rwxr-xr--  1 markd  wheel  31 Aug 10 11:55 /tmp/logthingie.txt*

$ cat /tmp/logthingie.txt
wheee, we have a log file open

$ ./append
$ ./append

$ cat /tmp/logthingie.txt
wheee, we have a log file open
wheee, we have a log file open
wheee, we have a log file open
```

Some things to note about the code. That is a lot of header files to include for such a small program. Things are pretty scattered about in the headers, but the man pages usually tell you what files to include to use particular features. For others, (like finding where STDOUT_FILENO live) you can resort to just grepping the files:

```
$ cd /usr/include
$ grep STDOUT_FILENO *.h
unistd.h:#define STDOUT_FILENO 1 /* standard output file */
```

Another thing to note is the manual writing to standard error. Since standard out was closed you could not use **printf()** to complain about the error opening the file. After all, the file opening failed.

Lastly, note the file permissions of the file:

```
-rwxr-xr--  1 markd  wheel  31 Aug 10 11:55 /tmp/logthingie.txt*
```

Plain old text files should not be executable. This can be fixed by explicitly setting the file permissions (described later).

Writing to a file

The **write()** system call is what is used to move bytes from memory to the disk:

```
ssize_t write (int fd, const void *buf, size_t nbytes);
```

Give it an address and a number of bytes to write, and the bytes will make it out to the file.

The return value is -1 in the case of an error (in which errno is set to whatever complaint the system is having), or else the number of bytes written. Note that the number of bytes written could be less than nbytes, such as in the case of writing a whole lot of data to a network connection or to a pipe (you could be filling up kernel buffers). The samples here will just call **write()** without a loop. Chapter 11 (Networking) will demonstrate the paranoid way of calling **write()**.

Each open file has an offset associated with it. This is the location within the file where writing and reading happen. This offset is automatically updated on each read or write, and can be explicitly set by **lseek()**. The O_APPEND flag overrides this and forces all writing to happen at the end of the file.

Example 8-2 is a little program that uses **write()** to create a file that contains a string the user passed in when invoking the program. To add a little interest, you will write out the length of the string first, and not have the traditional trailing zero byte that terminates string:

Example 8-2. writestring.m

```
// writestring.m -- take argv[1] and write it to a file,
//                  prepending the length of the string

/* compile with:
cc -g -Wall -o writestring writestring.m
*/

#import <fcntl.h>        // for open()
#import <sys/stat.h>     // for permission flags
```

```
#import <stdlib.h>        // for EXIT_SUCCESS et. al.
#import <stdio.h>         // for printf() and friends
#import <errno.h>         // for errno
#import <string.h>         // for strerror()
#import <unistd.h>         // for write()

int main (int argc, char *argv[])
{
    int fd;
    int stringLength;
    ssize_t result;

    if (argc != 2) {
        fprintf (stderr, "usage:  %s string-to-log\n", argv[0]);
        exit (EXIT_FAILURE);
    }

    fd = open ("/tmp/stringfile.txt", O_WRONLY | O_CREAT | O_TRUNC,
               S_IRUSR | S_IWUSR);

    if (fd == -1) {
        fprintf (stderr, "cannot open file.  Error %d (%s)\n",
                 errno, strerror(errno));
        exit (EXIT_FAILURE);
    }

    // write the length
    stringLength = strlen (argv[1]);
    result = write (fd, &stringLength, sizeof(stringLength));

    if (result == -1) {
        fprintf (stderr, "cannot write to file.  Error %d (%s)\n",
                 errno, strerror(errno));
        exit (EXIT_FAILURE);
    }

    // now write the string
    result = write (fd, argv[1], stringLength);

    if (result == -1) {
        fprintf (stderr, "cannot write to file.  Error %d (%s)\n",
                 errno, strerror(errno));
        exit (EXIT_FAILURE);
    }

    close (fd);

    exit (EXIT_SUCCESS);

} // main
```

Here it is in action:

```
$ ./writestring "I seem to be a fish"
$
```

Looking at the size of the file:

```
$ ls -l /tmp/stringfile.txt
-rw-------  1 markd  wheel  23 Aug 10 12:24 /tmp/stringfile.txt
```

Note that the permissions are much more reasonable. That is what the S_IRUSR | S_IWUSR did. The file is 23 bytes, which is the exact size it should be: 4 bytes for the length, plus 19 for the text.

The hexdump program is useful for seeing inside of files:

```
$ hexdump -C /tmp/stringfile.txt
0000   00 00 00 13 49 20 73 65   65 6d 20 74 6f 20 62 65
         |....I seem to be|
0010   20 61 20 66 69 73 68
         | a fish|
0017
```

How to parse the output: The left-hand column is the number of bytes into the file that the particular line starts on. The bytes of hex are the contents of the file, 16 bytes per line. The right-hand column shows the ASCII interpretation, with unprintable characters replaced by periods.

So, the first couple of bytes:

```
00000000   00 00 00 13
```

Starting at offset zero are four bytes of 00000013, which is decimal 19 (the length of the string). Following that are 19 bytes of the actual string data.

Reading From a File

Reading is the inverse of writing: it moves bytes from the file into memory. The prototype is nearly identical to **write()**:

```
ssize_t read (int d, void *buf, size_t nbytes);
```

Note that buf is not a const void *, but just a void *, meaning that the function could change the contents of the buffer. Of course, that is the whole point of the function call.

Like the other calls around here, **read()** returns -1 on an error (setting errno as appropriate). For a successful read, it will return the number of bytes actually read, and return zero on end of file (EOF). When run from an interactive terminal, some magic happens under the hood and **read()** reads entire lines. Note that **read()** can return fewer bytes than asked for, such as when it reaches EOF, or due to networking buffering, reading from the terminal, or when dealing with record-oriented devices like tape drives. Like **write()**, **read()** also updates the current location.

Example 8-3 is the counterpart to writestring, which takes the specially formatted file and reads it back in.

Example 8-3. readstring.m

```
// readstring.m -- open /tmp/stringfile.txt and write out
//                 its contents

/* compile with:
cc -g -Wall -o readstring readstring.m
```

```
*/

#import <fcntl.h>          // for open()
#import <stdlib.h>         // for EXIT_SUCCESS et. al.
#import <stdio.h>          // for printf() and friends
#import <errno.h>          // for errno and strerror()
#import <string.h>         // for strerror()
#import <unistd.h>         // for close() and read()

int main (int argc, char *argv[])
{
    int fd;
    int stringLength;
    ssize_t result;
    char *buffer;

    fd = open ("/tmp/stringfile.txt", O_RDONLY);

    if (fd == -1) {
        fprintf (stderr, "cannot open file.  Error %d (%s)\n",
                errno, strerror(errno));
        exit (EXIT_FAILURE);
    }

    result = read (fd, &stringLength, sizeof(stringLength));

    if (result == -1) {
        fprintf (stderr, "cannot read file.  Error %d (%s)\n",
                errno, strerror(errno));
        exit (EXIT_FAILURE);
    }

    buffer = malloc (stringLength + 1);  // account for trailing 0 byte

    result = read (fd, buffer, stringLength);

    if (result == -1) {
        fprintf (stderr, "cannot read file.  Error %d (%s)\n",
                errno, strerror(errno));
        exit (EXIT_FAILURE);
    }

    buffer[stringLength] = '\000';

    close (fd);

    printf ("our string is '%s'\n", buffer);

    free (buffer); // clean up our mess

    exit (EXIT_SUCCESS);

} // main
```

And the program in action:

```
$ ./readstring
```

```
our string is 'I seem to be a fish'
```

Closing files

To close a file, you use `close()`:

```
int close (int fd);
```

This removes the file descriptor from the per-process file table and frees up system resources associated with this open file. This has a return value of -1 to indicate error, otherwise it returns a zero on successful completion. In the above samples, the return value from `close()` is not checked. That is primarily just laziness, since errors should not happen on close, and if they do, there is not a lot you can do about it.

When a process exits, all open files are automatically closed, and any blocks waiting in kernel buffers are queued for writing.

Changing the Read/Write Offset

The read/write offset is the number of bytes from the beginning of the file where the next read or write operation will take place. This offset is an attribute of the open file, so if you open the same file twice you will get two file descriptors, each with an independent file offset. The offset starts at zero unless O_APPEND was used to open the file.

The `lseek()` call is what is used to change the offset:

```
off_t lseek (int fd, off_t offset, int whence);
```

`offset`, in combination with `whence`, is used to locate a particular byte in the file. `whence` can have one of three values:

SEEK_SET

   Offset is an absolute position.

SEEK_CUR

   Offset is a delta from the current location.

SEEK_END

   Offset is relative off the end of the file.

The offset can be negative for SEEK_CUR and SEEK_END. So, if you wanted to start writing five bytes from the end of the file, you would do something like:

```
blah = lseek (fd, -5, SEEK_END);
```

Note that the offset itself can never go negative. It will get pinned to zero. Different seeking scenarios can be seen in Figure 8-2.

Figure 8-2. lseek()

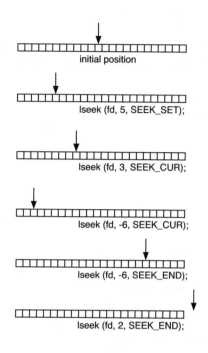

The return value from **lseek()** is the resulting offset location in bytes from the beginning of the file. Otherwise a -1 return value and errno are used to communicate back the error.

You are quite welcome to seek off the end of the file. Any bytes not explicitly written will default to zero. Note also that some devices are incapable of seeking, like a pipe or a network connection.

lseek() is a logical operation, not a physical one. It is just updating a value in the kernel, so no actual I/O takes place until you perform a read or write.

To get the current offset, do:

```
off_t offset = lseek (fd, 0, SEEK_CUR);
```

This will also tell you if the device is capable of seeking. If you get an error, you know you cannot seek with this kind of file.

Why is it called **lseek()**? Back in the misty past, the function to perform this work was originally called just seek, but it took an int parameter, which could be 16 or 32 bit. When seek was extended to support larger files, a long argument was used, hence the "L."

Atomic operations

In man pages (and around this chapter), you will see references to "atomic operations." These are operations that do multiple things, but all happen within one system call, thereby preventing race condition errors with other programs.

For example, **open()** has the O_APPEND flag, which makes the append be an atomic operation. You just **write()** to the file descriptor and the output happens in the end.

Without `O_APPEND`, you would have to do two operations:

```
lseek (fd, 0, SEEK_END); // seek to the end
write (fd, buffer, datasize);
```

The race condition happens if your program gets pre-empted by the kernel after the **lseek()**, but before the **write()**, and someone else happens to be writing to the file as well.

Figure 8-3. Race condition start

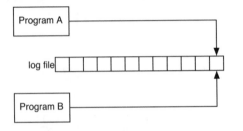

each performs lseek (fd, 0, SEEK_END);

Figure 8-4. Program A writes its data

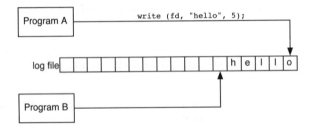

Figure 8-5. Program B clobbers it

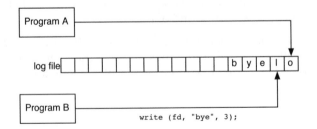

So say the file `log.txt` looks like

```
finished frobulating the bork\nadded a hoover\n
```

and the last position is at offset 50,000.

- Program A does the lseek to 50,000, and gets pre-empted.
- Program B does an **lseek()** to 50,000, and writes "removed the wikkit\n".
- Program A is scheduled again, and writes "ack ack\n".

The file now looks like

```
finished frobulating the bork\nadded a hoover\nack ack\nhe wikkit\n
```

in short, it is been trashed. Atomic operations were introduced to prevent such errors.

Another example of an atomic operation is doing an open with O_CREAT and O_EXCL. The open will fail if the file exists. This is a handy way to check whether your program is already running, if you only want one copy to be active, like many internet server programs.

Scatter / gather I/O

Frequently when writing, you will be doing multiple **write()** calls for a logical piece of data. For instance, in the writestring.m program above, there were two writes: one for a size and one for the string. Web server software has two distinct chunks of data involved when responding to any request: the reply headers and the actual data, which are usually kept in distinct data structures. In these cases you can do multiple writes (which have the overhead of multiple system calls), or copy all the data into a different buffer and then write it in one call (which has data copying overhead, and possibly involves dynamic memory, which is another performance hit). Or you can use the scatter/gather read functions **readv()** and **writev()** to package up your data and have the kernel write it all in one operation. From the receiver's point of view (whether the bytes are from a file or from the program on the other end of a network connection), all three are equivalent.

```
ssize_t readv (int fd, const struct iovec *iov, int iovcnt);

ssize_t writev (int fd, const struct iovec *iov, int iovcnt);
```

Rather than taking a buffer, these two take an array of struct iovec

```
struct iovec {
    void *iov_base;
    size_t iov_len;
};
```

where iov_base is the buffer location and iov_len is how much data to read and write, shown in Figure 8-6.

Figure 8-6. Scatter / Gather I/O

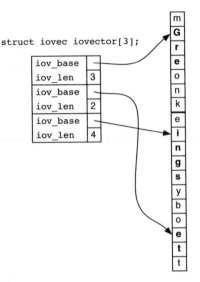

Example 8-4 and Example 8-5 updated to use scatter/gather I/O:

Example 8-4. writevecstring.m

```
// writevecstring.m -- take argv[1] and write it to a file, prepending
//                     the length of the string.  and using
//                     scatter/gather I/O

/* compile with:
cc -g -Wall -o writevecstring writevecstring.m
*/

#import <sys/types.h>    // for ssize_t
#import <sys/uio.h>      // for writev() and struct iovec
#import <fcntl.h>        // for open()
#import <sys/stat.h>     // for permission flags
#import <stdlib.h>       // for EXIT_SUCCESS et. al.
#import <stdio.h>        // for printf() and friends
#import <errno.h>        // for errno
#import <string.h>       // for strerror()
#import <unistd.h>       // for close()

int main (int argc, char *argv[])
{
    int fd;
    int stringLength;
    ssize_t result;
    struct iovec vector[2]; // one for size, one for string

    if (argc != 2) {
        fprintf (stderr, "usage:  %s string-to-log\n", argv[0]);
        exit (EXIT_FAILURE);
    }
```

```
fd = open ("/tmp/stringfile.txt", O_WRONLY | O_CREAT | O_TRUNC,
            S_IRUSR | S_IWUSR);

if (fd == -1) {
    fprintf (stderr, "cannot open file.  Error %d (%s)\n",
            errno, strerror(errno));
    exit (EXIT_FAILURE);
}

stringLength = strlen (argv[1]);
vector[0].iov_base = (void *) &stringLength;
vector[0].iov_len = sizeof(stringLength);
vector[1].iov_base = argv[1];
vector[1].iov_len = stringLength;

result = writev (fd, vector, 2);

if (result == -1) {
    fprintf (stderr, "cannot write to file.  Error %d (%s)\n",
            errno, strerror(errno));
    exit (EXIT_FAILURE);
}

close (fd);

exit (EXIT_SUCCESS);

} // main
```

Note the cast here:

```
vector[0].iov_base = (void *) &stringLength;
```

Unfortunately, the man page and the header file do not always agree. In the header file `sys/uio.h` is this:

```
/*
 * XXX
 * iov_base should be a void *.
 */
struct iovec {
    char    *iov_base;      /* Base address. */
    size_t  iov_len;        /* Length. */
};
```

So in this case you need to cast `(int *)` to something that is compatible with a `(char *)`.

Here is the equivalent on the read side:

Example 8-5. readvecstring.m

```
// readvecstring.m -- open /tmp/stringfile.txt and write out
//                    its contents using scatter/gather reads

/* compile with:
cc -g -Wall -o readvecstring readvecstring.m
```

```
*/

#import <sys/types.h>    // for ssize_t
#import <sys/uio.h>      // for readv() and struct iovec
#import <fcntl.h>        // for open()
#import <sys/stat.h>     // for permission flags
#import <stdlib.h>       // for EXIT_SUCCESS et. al.
#import <stdio.h>        // for printf() and friends
#import <errno.h>        // for errno
#import <string.h>       // for strerror()
#import <unistd.h>       // for close()

int main (int argc, char *argv[])
{
    int fd;
    int stringLength;
    ssize_t result;
    char buffer[4096];
    struct iovec vector[2];

    fd = open ("/tmp/stringfile.txt", O_RDONLY);

    if (fd == -1) {
        fprintf (stderr, "cannot open file.  Error %d (%s)\n",
                errno, strerror(errno));
        exit (EXIT_FAILURE);
    }

    vector[0].iov_base = (void *) &stringLength;
    vector[0].iov_len = sizeof(stringLength);
    vector[1].iov_base = buffer;
    vector[1].iov_len = 4096;

    result = readv (fd, vector, 2);

    if (result == -1) {
        fprintf (stderr, "cannot read file.  Error %d (%s)\n",
                errno, strerror(errno));
        exit (EXIT_FAILURE);
    }

    buffer[stringLength] = '\000'; // need to zero-terminate it

    close (fd);

    printf ("our string is '%s'\n", buffer);

    exit (EXIT_SUCCESS);

} // main
```

Unfortunately, the reading side of things is not as pretty as the writing side. Since the size of the string is unknown, a guess was made at the maximum size of the string. Hard-coded limits like this will be the source of errors in the future (as soon as someone writes a 4K+1 string to one of these files). In general the **writev()** will be the most convenient way to write scattered data like this, but you will still do multiple reads to pull apart the data - either that or read a lot of stuff into a buffer and process the data.

creat()

Just a historical note, there is also a the **creat()** function which you might see in your travels through other people's code:

```
int creat (const char *path, mode_t mode);
```

This creates files, and has been superceded by **open()**. creat(path, mode) is equivalent to

```
open(path, O_CREAT | O_TRUNC | O_WRONLY, mode);
```

Blocking I/O

By default, file I/O is blocking. The function call will wait until the I/O completes. If you open with the O_NONBLOCK flag, reads will return immediately with an error (errno of EAGAIN). You can also use the **select()** or **poll()** functions (discussed in detail in Chapter 11 (Networking)) to see if I/O is possible for a particular file descriptor.

Buffered I/O

The preceeding calls are generally considered "unbuffered I/O". There is a little bit of buffering that happens the kernel (probably no more than a couple of disk blocks) so that a physical I/O is not performed for every byte read, but for the most part what you read is what you get in terms of physical I/O. If you want to read in large blocks of data and process the data out of that buffer, you will have to do the work yourself (refilling the buffer when it gets low, remembering your place in the buffer, handling reading and writing, etc). It is not hard work, just kind of tedious.

The Standard C I/O functions are known as buffered I/O. The library handles the details of buffer allocation I/O in optimally sized chunks, only doing real physical I/O when the buffer is empty (for reading) or is full (for writing), or is explicitly flushed to the disk.

Rather than passing file descriptors around, buffered I/O has an opaque type called FILE (also known as a stream), and you pass pointers to FILEs around. Wrapped in that FILE is the file descriptor, the buffer, and other pieces of housekeeping.

There are three kinds of buffering that buffered I/O can use:

Fully Buffered

Actual I/O only happens when the buffer gets full, and is the default for files associated with non-interactive devices.

Line Buffered

I/O happens when a newline character is encountered on input or output. You can use a function to write one character at a time to a stream, but the actual I/O only happens on a newline (or when the buffer is getting full).

Unbuffered

> No buffering happens, calls just turn around and invoke **read()** or **write()**. The Standard Error stream is usually unbuffered so that error messages appear instantly. The other two standard streams are either fully or line buffered, depending on whether they are attached to an interactive device (like a terminal).

You can use **setbuf()** or **setvbuf()** to change the buffering behavior.

Opening files

The buffered I/O functions (with a few exceptions) begin with "f." So, for instance, opening files is done with **fopen()**:

```
FILE *fopen (char *path, char *mode);
```

fopen() returns a pointer to newly allocated FILE structure (you do not need to worry about allocating it, but be sure to dispose of it with **fclose()**). It is an opaque type, but you can look at it anyway (hint: stdio.h, or print out a FILE structure in gdb).

There are buffered I/O versions of the three standard streams, called stdin, stdout, stderr, and you can pass any of these to the buffered I/O functions.

Back to **fopen()**. It takes a pathname to the file, and a mode, which is a character string.

Here are the modes:

"r"

> Open file for reading.

"r+"

> Open for reading and writing.

"w"

> Truncate file to zero length, or create if it does not exist, and then open for writing.

"w+"

> Truncate file to zero length, or create if it does not exist, and then open for reading and writing.

"a"

> File is created if it does not exist, then open it for writing in append mode.

"a+"

> File is created if it does not exist, then open it for reading, and writing in append mode.

Or, put another way,

"r"   Open for reading, file must exist.

"w"   Truncate or create if necessary, file does not need to exist.

"a"   Create if necessary, file does not need to exist. Append mode.

And stick on a "+" to have both reading and writing possible.

There are some subtleties with "+" modes. Output cannot be followed by input without an explicit **fflush()** or something that flushes the buffer (like an **fseek()**, **fsetpos()**, **rewind()**). Similarly input cannot be directly followed by output without calling of the above calls.

Since buffered I/O comes from the portable standard C library, it has support for a distinction between binary files and text files because some operating systems have that distinction. Unix makes no such distinction, so any special binary flags (sticking a "b" onto a/a+/w/w+, etc.) passed for the mode are ignored.

Files created with **fopen()** have permissions rw-rw-rw-. You cannot change that directly with **fopen()**, but instead use the **chmod()** or **fchmod()** system calls.

There are two companion calls to **fopen()**:

```
FILE *fdopen (int fd, char *mode);

FILE *freopen (char *path, char *mode, FILE *stream);
```

fdopen() takes an existing file descriptor (gotten from **open()**, or from a networking call) and wraps a FILE stream around it.

freopen() closes and reopens a given file pointer, but using the new path instead of what was used before. **freopen()** is very handy if you are redirecting the standard streams. You can do something like stdin = freopen ("/my/new/stdin.file", "w+", stdin); to redirect standard in.

Closing Files

```
int fclose (FILE *stream);
```

Dissociates the stream from its underlying file. Any buffered data is queued to the kernel using **fflush()** and the enclosed file descriptor is closed. If the program terminates abnormally, any buffered data will not be flushed to the kernel, and will be lost.

Text I/O

The buffered I/O API has two concepts of I/O when it comes to reading and writing: one is text oriented, the other is binary oriented.

Text I/O can be done a character-at-a-time, or a line at a time. Here are the character at a time functions:

```
int getc (FILE *stream);

int getchar ();

int fgetc (FILE *stream);
```

Each will try to get the next input character from the given stream (or from stdin for **getchar()**). It is interesting that these functions return an int rather than a char. The return value is overloaded so that it returns both the function data or a status value. Since char's useful values cover the entire expressible range of values, some other extra bits are needed to store a unique result values. If end of file or a read error occurs, the return returns the constant EOF (usually -1). You need to use the routines **feof()** and **ferror()** to distinguish between end of file and an error. In the case of error, errno is set like in the unbuffered I/O function. On a successful read, the return value is the character data. You can use the function **clearerr()** to clear the end of file and error indicators on the FILE stream.

The implementation of **getc()** and **fgetc()** are defined by the ANSI C standard. **getc()** is implemented by a macro, and **fgetc()** is implemented as a function. The implications of this specification are that the argument to **getc()** should not have any side effects since it could get evaluated more than once by the macro. It also means that if you want to stash something in a function pointer, you can use **fgetc()**. The actual time difference between **getc()** and **fgetc()** is negligible, so just use **fgetc()**, unless you can measure that the function call overhead is a problem.

Example 8-6 is how to check for EOF, and discriminate between error and end of file:

Example 8-6. buffread.m

```
// buffread.m -- show how to read using buffered I/O, including
//                 error / eof handling

/* compile with:
cc -g -Wall -o buffread buffread.m
*/

#import <stdlib.h>       // for EXIT_SUCCESS, etc
#import <stdio.h>        // all the buffered I/O API
#import <errno.h>        // for errno
#import <string.h>       // for strerror()

int main (int argc, char *argv[])
{
    FILE *file;
    int result;

    file = fopen ("/etc/motd", "r");

    while (1) {
        result = fgetc (file);
        if (result == EOF) {
            if (feof(file)) {
                printf ("EOF found\n");
            }
            if (ferror(file)) {
                printf ("error reading file: %d (%s)\n",
                        errno, strerror(errno));
            }
            break;
        } else {
            printf ("got a character: '%c'\n", (char) result);
        }
```

```
    }

    fclose (file);

    return (EXIT_SUCCESS);

} // main
```

Not only can you read characters from the stream, you can push them back onto the stream with **ungetc()**:

```
int ungetc (int c, FILE *stream);
```

ANSI C only guarantees one character of pushback, but the OS X man pages says you can push back an arbitrary amount. Being able to push back characters is handy in some parsers. You can peek a character ahead to see if this particular chunk of text is interesting. If not, push that character back and let some other piece of code handle the parsing. **ungetc()** clears the EOF flag so you can unget a character on an EOF and then read it later. Note that calls to a positioning function (**fseek()**, **fsetpos()**, or **rewind()**) will discard the pushed-back characters.

So those are the character-at-a-time read functions. To actually write to a stream character-wise, use one of these:

```
int fputc (int c, FILE *stream);

int putchar (int c);

int putc (int c, FILE *stream);
```

These are exactly analogous to the reading functions. **fputc()** is a function, **putc()** is a macro, **putchar()** implicitly uses stdout.

For line-at-a-time I/O, use these functions:

```
char *fgets (char *str, int size, FILE *stream);

char *gets (char *str); // do not use this one

int fputs (const char *str, FILE *stream);

int puts (const char *str);
```

You give **fgets()** and **gets()** an already allocated character buffer. The functions will return when they see an end of line character, or they fill up the buffer. Note that **gets()** does not accept a size so there is no way to really control how much will get put into the buffer, making buffer overflows really easy (so do not use it). **fgets()** stores the newline character in the buffer, while **gets()** does not. If an end of file or an error occurs they return NULL, and you need to check **feof()** and **ferror()** to see what happened. In both cases, a zero byte is appended to the end of the string.

puts() writes to standard out. **fputs()** does not automatically put a newline to the stream, while **puts()** does.

Binary I/O

Binary I/O is not limited to just binary data: you can use it for blocks of text too. (block I/O would probably be a better name). These calls are handy for writing arrays of structures to disk. Beware of portability problems when blindly writing structures like this. If any of the data types should change size you can end up breaking your file format.

```
size_t fread (void *ptr, size_t size, size_t nmemb, FILE *stream);

size_t fwrite (const void *ptr, size_t size, size_t nmemb, FILE *stream);
```

Each function has a pointer to memory, the size of the struct, and the number of elements in an array of these structs. The return value is the number of actual *elements* written, not the number of bytes written. Internally it is just doing the multiplication and writing that number of bytes. These functions do not stop at zero bytes or newlines like the text I/O functions do. If the number of elements read or written is less than expected, check `ferror()` and `feof()`.

Example 8-7 shows binary reading:

Example 8-7. fbinaryio.m

```
// fbinaryio.m -- do some binary reading and writing using buffered I/O

/* compile with:
cc -g -Wall -o fbinaryio fbinaryio.m
*/

#import <stdlib.h>      // for EXIT_SUCCESS, etc
#import <stdio.h>       // for the buffered I/O API
#import <errno.h>       // for errno and strerror()
#import <string.h>       // for strerror()

typedef struct Thing {
    int         thing1;
    float       thing2;
    char        thing3[8];
} Thing;

Thing things[] = {
    { 3, 3.14159, "hello" },
    { 4, 4.29301, "bye" },
    { 2, 2.14214, "bork" },
    { 5, 5.55556, "elf up" }
};

int main (int argc, char *argv[])
{
    size_t thingCount;
    size_t numWrote;
    FILE *file;

    thingCount = sizeof(things) / sizeof(Thing); //how many we have

    file = fopen ("/tmp/thingfile", "w");
```

```
    if (file == NULL) {
        fprintf (stderr, "error opening file: %d (%s)\n",
                 errno, strerror(errno));
        exit (EXIT_FAILURE);
    }

    numWrote = fwrite (things, sizeof(Thing), thingCount, file);

    if (numWrote != thingCount) {
        fprintf (stderr,
                 "incomplete write (%d of %d). Error %d (%s)\n",
                 (int)numWrote, (int)thingCount, errno,
                 strerror(errno));
        exit (EXIT_FAILURE);
    }

    fclose (file);

    // now re-open and re-read and make sure everything is groovy
    file = fopen ("/tmp/thingfile", "r");

    if (file == NULL) {
        fprintf (stderr, "error opening file: %d (%s)\n",
                 errno, strerror(errno));
        exit (EXIT_FAILURE);
    }

    {
        // we know we are reading in thingCount, so we can go ahead and
        // allocate that much space
        Thing readThings[sizeof(things) / sizeof(Thing)];
        ssize_t numRead;

        numRead = fread (readThings, sizeof(Thing), thingCount, file);
        if (numRead != thingCount) {
            fprintf (stderr, "short read.  Got %d, expected %d\n",
                     (int)numRead, (int)thingCount);
            if (feof(file)) {
                fprintf (stderr, "we got an end of file\n");
            }
            if (ferror(file)) {
                fprintf (stderr, "we got an error: %d (%s)\n",
                         errno, strerror(errno));
            }
        } else {
            // just for fun, compare the newly read ones with the ones
            // we have statically declared
            int i;
            for (i = 0; i < thingCount; i++) {
                if (   (things[i].thing1 != readThings[i].thing1)
                    || (things[i].thing2 != readThings[i].thing2)
                    || (strcmp(things[i].thing3, readThings[i].thing3)
                        != 0)) {
                    fprintf (stderr, "mismatch with element %d\n", i);
                } else {
                    printf ("successfully compared element %d\n", i);
                }
```

```
                }
            }
        }

        fclose (file);

        exit (EXIT_SUCCESS);

    } // main
```

Here is a sample run:

```
$ ./fbinaryio
successfully compared element 0
successfully compared element 1
successfully compared element 2
successfully compared element 3
```

And just for fun, look at the file itself:

```
$ hexdump -C /tmp/thingfile
0000  00 00 00 03 40 49 0f d0  68 65 6c 6c 6f 00 00 00
          |....@I..hello...|
0010  00 00 00 04 40 89 60 57  62 79 65 00 00 00 00 00
          |....@.`Wbye.....|
0020  00 00 00 02 40 09 18 d2  62 6f 72 6b 00 00 00 00
          |....@...bork....|
0030  00 00 00 05 40 b1 c7 26  65 6c 66 20 75 70 00 00
          |....@..&elf up..|
```

You can see that there are 4 bytes of integer, 4 bytes of float, and 8 bytes of character data. It just so happens to line up with the struct Thing definition.

Positioning

Like unbuffered I/O, the buffered I/O FILE streams have a current position.

```
long ftell (FILE *stream);

int fseek (FILE *stream, long offset, int whence);
```

ftell() returns the current location in the file. **fseek()** is like lseek(). It has the same use of offset and whence (SEEK_SET, SEEK_CUR, SEEK_END). The return value of **fseek()** is zero on successful completion, otherwise -1 is returned and errno is set appropriately. Note that the offset type of these functions are longs, which can limit file sizes. There are also versions that take off_t types, which could be larger than longs:

```
off_t ftello (FILE *stream);

int fseeko (FILE *stream, off_t offset, int whence);
```

An alternate interface is

```
int fgetpos (FILE *stream, fpos_t *pos);

int fsetpos (FILE *stream, const fpos_t *pos);
```

using the opaque `fpos_t` type. On some platforms it is the same as an `off_t`. On other platforms it is an 8-byte array.

```
void rewind (FILE *stream);
```

will reset the current location in the file to the very beginning, also clearing the error flag.

Formatted I/O

The **printf** family of calls live under standard / buffered I/O since they write out to `FILE` streams, either explicitly or implicitly (or in the case of **s[n]printf** which writes to a buffer, but it has the same syntax as its I/O companions).

```
int printf (const char *format, ...);

int fprintf (FILE *stream, const char *format, ...);

int sprintf (char *str, const char *format, ...);

int snprintf (char *str, size_t size, const char *format, ...);

int asprintf (char **ret, const char *format, ...);
```

printf() writes to the `stdout` file. **fprintf()** writes to any `FILE`. **sprintf()** writes into a buffer, and **snprintf()** writes into a buffer but it is given the size of the buffer. Always use **snprintf()** instead of **sprintf()**. There is no prevention of buffer overruns in **sprintf()**, especially if any user-entered data gets fed into the function. With **snprintf()** buffer overruns will not happen. **asprintf()** takes **snprintf()** to the next level by automatically allocating a buffer for you that is the correct size (which you will need to **free()** once you are done with it).

The specifics of the **printf**-style of formatting are covered in opaque detail in the man page, and in most every C-101 book out there.

You can do formatted input as well, using

```
int scanf (const char *format, ...);

int fscanf (FILE *stream, const char *format, ...);

int sscanf (const char *str, const char *format, ...);
```

These take format strings like **printf()**, but instead of just regular arguments in the ... section of the parameter list, you need to provide pointers to appropriate-sized areas of memory. The **scanf()** functions will not allocate memory for you. There is not much in the way of error detection or recovery when using the functions. Outside of toy programs, you will probably want to write your own parsing code, use `lex/yacc`, or use a regular expression library.

Misc Functions

Here are miscellaneous buffered I/O functions.

```
int fileno (FILE *stream);
```

Returns the file descriptor that the stream is wrapped around. This is handy if you need to use `fcntl()`, `fchmod()`, `fstat()`, or the `dup()` functions.

```
int getw(FILE *stream);

int putw(int w, FILE *stream);
```

These are like `getc()`/`putc()`, but read or write an integer. The integers are not written in a canonical form (discussed in Chapter 11 (Networking)), so if you want to be portable, you will need to put the bytes into a known byte order.

Buffered I/O vs. Unbuffered I/O

With buffered I/O, there is a lot of data copying happening:

program structures -> FILE buffer -> kernel buffer -> disk.

With unbuffered I/O, the copy to the FILE buffer is avoided, and with scatter/gather I/O, the kernel might be able to avoid a copy into its own buffers.

Since `read()`/`write()` are not buffered (save for a disk block or two in the kernel data structures) they can be slow when dealing with lots of smaller reads and writes. Buffered I/O would be a win here.

When doing big reads and writes (dozens of K of image data, for instance), there is a win to using plain `read()` and `write()` calls to avoid the buffering step in between.

Fundamentally everything boils down to the file descriptor. Even FILEs have a file descriptor at their heart. Be careful when mixing buffered and unbuffered I/O with the same file descriptor. The FILE part of the world does not get notified if you do I/O with the file descriptor, leading to some confusing synchronization errors.

In both the buffered and unbuffered I/O cases, there is some magic that happens when input or output are going to a terminal device. `read()` takes on per-line semantics, and the buffered I/O calls take on line buffering behavior.

Lastly, when both buffered and unbuffered I/O perform a write operation, the data does not necessarily end up on disk immediately. The kernel will buffer the writing to reduce the number of physical I/O operations it has to do. This means that you can dutifully write your data, have the OS crash, and your data is lost. If you are truly paranoid about having data written to disk (like in a database system), you can use one of the sync calls:

```
void sync (void);
```

This forces the queuing of modified buffers in the block buffer for I/O. This call will return immediately and the kernel will write the blocks at its leisure. This will force writing for all modified blocks system wide.

```
int fsync (int fd);
```

causes all modified data and metadata for a file to be flushed out to the physical disk. This is applies to just one file. The call will block for all I/O to complete before returning.

Removing Files

Removing files is pretty easy. Use the `unlink()` system call:

```
int unlink (const char *path);
```

This returns zero on successful completion or -1 if there was an error (with `errno` set to the error that actually happened). A file can have multiple references to itself (hard links, which will be discussed in a bit), and a file is removed when all references to it have been eliminated.

There is one subtly when unlinking files that are currently open. The directory entry for the file is removed immediately (so if you do an `ls` on the directory you will not see the file), but the file's contents still exist on the disk, still consume space, and are still available to the program that has the file open. The actual space is reclaimed by the OS once all programs close the file. This is useful for temporary files, ones you do not want to hang around after the program goes away. By unlinking the temporary file immediately after opening it, you do not need to worry about deleting the file once your program is over. The space occupied by the file will be reclaimed even if your program crashes.

This behavior can occasionally lead to puzzling system administration issues. Imagine the scenario where a web server has a 100-meg log file open and the disk it is on is filling up. Someone deletes the file hoping to reclaim the space. Since the log file is still open, those 100 megs are still being used, but they will not show up using any command (like `du`).

Rather than deleting the file, you can truncate it with the command:

```
$ sudo cp /dev/null /the/log/file/name
```

If you have already deleted the file, you can use the command `lsof`, to "ls Open Files" and see what is there. `lsof` is pretty handy anyway to peek inside the system and see what is going on.

```
$ sudo lsof
(Huge amount of output.  Here are a couple lines.)

pbs    266 markd cwd   VDIR  14,9      1486      2 / (/dev/disk0s9)
pbs    266 markd   0u  VCHR   0,0   0t4015 262628 /dev/console
pbs    266 markd   1u  VCHR   0,0   0t4015 262628 /dev/console
pbs    266 markd   2u  VCHR   0,0   0t4015 262628 /dev/console
```

This is the pasteboard server, process ID 266, owned by user `markd`. It has three files open on `fd` 0, 1, 2, all open for read/write, and all going to `/dev/console`. It also has the directory / (the unix root directory) open, as the current working directory.

```
Adium    1269 markd   7u  inet 0x0240d7bc   0t0     TCP
10.0.1.142:49249->toc-m04.blue.aol.com:9898 (ESTABLISHED)
```

`Adium`, an AIM client that is running with `pid` 1269, has `fd` 7 being an internet connection. On the local side the IP address 10.0.1.142 port 49249, is connected to toc-m04.blue.aol.com, port 9898.

```
lsof   1361 markd   3r  VCHR   3,0        0t0 26234372 /dev/mem
lsof   1361 markd   4r  VCHR   3,1 0t26432612 26234244 /dev/kmem
lsof   1361 markd   5r  VREG  14,9    3169824    66862 /mach_kernel
```

Finally, this run of `lsof` has file descriptors 3, 4, 5 open, reading `/dev/mem`, `/dev/kmem` (kernel memory), and also has the `mach_kernel` file open, so it can resolve the data it finds in the memory devices.

Temporary Files

Temporary files, as the name implies, are files that are used by a program as it is running and then are not useful once the program goes away. Unix systems typically store temp files in a well known location so that people know where to clean out files that are left over accidentally, and some systems will clear out the directory that holds the temp files on startup.

When a program wants to create a temporary file it, needs a unique name so that it does not clash with what is already in the temp directory. If two programs ended up using the same temporary file, they would both probably fail in weird and wonderful ways.

Where is this temporary directory? There is an algorithm used when determining where the temp directory is. First, the environment variable TMPDIR is used (if it exists). Then, the directory P_tmpdir defined in `/usr/include/stdio.h` (which on OS X is `/var/tmp`), and then the directory `/tmp` is tried.

Here are the functions for dealing with temporary file names.

These functions generate the file name:

```
char *tmpnam (char *str);

char *tempnam (const char *tmpdir, const char *prefix);

char *mktemp (char *template);
```

And these functions will open the file for you automatically:

```
int mkstemp (char *template);

FILE *tmpfile (void);
```

First the file name generation functions.

`tmpnam()` returns a pointer to a file name in the P_tmpdir (a global variable declared in `stdio.h`) directory. If you pass NULL for the `str` argument the file name will be returned out of a static buffer (not very good for thread safety). You can also pass in a buffer and `tmpnam()` will write into that.

`tempnam()` is similar to `tmpnam()`, but lets you specify the directory to put the file into, as well as a prefix to the name. This function will allocate memory, which you will need to `free()`. If the prefix is NULL, the P_tmpdir value will be used instead.

`mktemp()` uses a template you supply, replacing any X characters with something unique. The passed in template gets modified, so keep a copy of your template if you want to use it again.

Example 8-8 shows all of them in action:

Example 8-8. tempfun.m

```
// tempfun.m -- see how different temp file names are generated

/* compile with:
cc -g -Wall -o tempfun tempfun.m
*/

#import <stdlib.h>       // for EXIT_SUCCESS, etc
#import <stdio.h>        // for the temp name functions
#import <unistd.h>       // for mk[s]temp
#import <string.h>       // for strcpy()

int main (int argc, char *argv[])
{
    char *name;
    char buffer[1024];

    printf ("my process ID is %d\n", getpid());

    name = tmpnam (NULL);
    printf ("tmpnam(NULL) is '%s'\n", name);

    name = tmpnam (buffer);
    printf ("tmpnam(buffer) is '%s'\n", buffer);

    name = tempnam ("/System/Library", "my_prefix");
    printf ("tempnam(/System/Library, my_prefix) is '%s'\n", name);
    free (name);

    name = tempnam ("/does/not/exist", "my_prefix");
    printf ("tempnam(/does/not/exist, my_prefix) is '%s'\n", name);
    free (name);

    strcpy (buffer, "templateXXXXXX");
    name = mktemp (buffer);
    printf ("mktemp(templateXXXXXX) is '%s'\n", name);

    return (0);

} // main
```

And some output:

```
$ ./tempfun
my process ID is 1482
tmpnam(NULL) is '/var/tmp/tmp.0.001482'
tmpnam(buffer) is '/var/tmp/tmp.1.001482'
tempnam(/System/Library, my_prefix) is
                '/System/Library/my_prefix001482'
tempnam(/does/not/exist, my_prefix) is '/var/tmp/my_prefix001482'
mktemp(templateXXXXXX) is 'template001482'
```

Note that the temporary file name is related to the process ID of the running program.

Some of the calls do take precautions if a file name already exists:

```
$ sudo touch /var/tmp/tmp.0.001505 /var/tmp/tmp.1.001505 \
/System/Library/my_prefix001505 /var/tmp/my_prefix001505 \
template001505

$ ./tempfun
my process ID is 1505
tmpnam(NULL) is '/var/tmp/tmp.0.a01505'
tmpnam(buffer) is '/var/tmp/tmp.1.a01505'
tempnam(/System/Library, my_prefix) is
                    '/System/Library/my_prefixa01505'
tempnam(/does/not/exist, my_prefix) is '/var/tmp/my_prefixa01505'
mktemp(templateXXXXXX) is 'templatea01505'
```

The functions plugged in an extra "a" for the file names.

Remember the discussion a little earlier on atomic operations and race conditions? Unfortunately they can happen here. You generate the temporary name with one function call, then another call to open the file. In the intervening time, a rogue program could create a file of the same name, which could prevent your program from running, or entice it to operate on bad data.

The other two functions, **mkstemp()** and **tmpfile()** generate the temp file name and open the file for you. **mkstemp()** uses the same template idea that **mktemp()** uses, and creates the file with permission mode rw-------, and returns a file descriptor for it.

tmpfile() uses **mkstemp()** and opens a buffered I/O stream to a new file. This file is automatically unlinked so you do not need to worry about cleaning up after it.

File Permissions

The classic Macintosh has a one user, one computer mindset. The user at the computer is pretty much free to do what they want, whether it be simply copying files around or mucking around in the system folder. All of that has changed in OS X. Because OS X has the Unix heritage, it has a multi-user permission model on the file system, and as users and developers, you need to get used to it.

Users and groups

Every user on the system has a user ID (an integer). Each user belongs to one or more named groups and each group has an ID. For instance:

```
$ ls -l chapter.txt
-rw-r--r--  1 markd  staff  48827 Aug 11 14:14 chapter.txt
```

The user is markd, the group is staff.

```
$ ls -l /bin/ls
-r-xr-xr-x  1 root  wheel  27160 Dec  8  2001 /bin/ls*
```

ls is owned by the user root, the group wheel.

You can see what users and groups are configured on your machine with nidump. On my PowerBook G4, I have

```
$ nidump passwd .
nobody:*:-2:-2::0:0:Unprivileged User:/dev/null:/dev/null
```

```
root:*:0:0::0:0:System Administrator:/var/root:/bin/tcsh
daemon:*:1:1::0:0:System Services:/var/root:/dev/null
unknown:*:99:99::0:0:Unknown User:/dev/null:/dev/null
www:*:70:70::0:0:World Wide Web Server:/Library/WebServer:/dev/null
markd:39.dxiwzIfvlU:501:20::0:0:markd:/Users/markd:/bin/tcsh
smmsp:*:25:25::0:0:Sendmail User:/private/etc/mail:/dev/null
bork:EB0mNxAcVD2wY:502:20::0:0:bork:/Users/bork:/bin/tcsh
```

The accounts `markd` and `bork` are accounts that were added to the machine. The rest come with the OS. The order of the fields (separated by colons above, are):

- username

- one-way hashed password, "*" if there is no password

- user id (in this case, the user ID is 501)

- group id (20 is `staff`)

- The next three are esoteric (password change time, user access class, and the Gecos field which can be used for general information)

- the full name of the user

- the user's home directory

- the user's login shell

You can see groups with `nidump` also:

```
$ nidump group .
(edited)
wheel:*:0:markd,bork
...
staff:*:20:root
...
admin:*:80:root,markd,bork
```

The fields here are the group name, the group's password (which rarely gets used), the group's ID (gid), and any group members. This way a user can be in more than one group. The user's primary group is what is listed in the `nidump passwd` listing, then they can be added to other groups here. Groups are a way to aggregate users that should have similar access permissions on sets of files. For instance, you would want your developers to be able edit files on a shared documentation tree. Specifically, the user `markd` is in group `staff` (due to the passwd entry), and is also a member of the group `wheel` and `admin`.

On other systems that do not use `NetInfo` (which would be just about every other flavor of Unix out there), the files `/etc/passwd` and `/etc/group` have the above information.

You use the `chown` command line program to change the ownership of a file. You must have superuser privilege to give away one of your own files to another user (otherwise you could use that to defeat disk space quotas).

For instance:

```
$ touch spoon
```

```
$ ls -l spoon
-rw-r--r--  1 markd  staff  0 Aug 11 14:40 spoon

$ chown bork spoon
chown: spoon: Operation not permitted

$ sudo chown bork spoon

$ ls -l spoon
-rw-r--r--  1 bork  staff  0 Aug 11 14:40 spoon
```

You can change groups with `chgrp`:

```
$ chgrp wheel spoon
chgrp: spoon: Operation not permitted

$ sudo chgrp wheel spoon

$ ls -l spoon
-rw-r--r--  1 bork  wheel  0 Aug 11 14:40 spoon
```

You can combine these two operations into one `chmod` command if you wish:

```
$ sudo chown markd:staff spoon

$ ls -l spoon
-rw-r--r--  1 markd  staff  0 Aug 11 14:40 spoon
```

There are system calls for manually changing the owner and group of a file:

```
int chown (const char *path, uid_t owner, gid_t group);

int lchown (const char *path, uid_t owner, gid_t group);

int fchown(int fd, uid_t owner, gid_t group);
```

chown() changes the owner and group of a file, **lchown()** changes it for a symbolic link, and **fchown()** operates on a file that is already open.

If you need to look up the owner and group IDs:

```
struct passwd *getpwent (void);

struct passwd *getpwnam (const char *login);

struct passwd *getpwuid (uid_t uid);
```

There are equivalent operations (like **getgrent()**, **getgrnam()**, **getgrgid()**) for getting group information.

`struct passwd` has all of the elements seen in the `passwd` entries above, like `pw_name` (login name), `pw_uid` (their user id), `pw_gid` (their group id), and others. **getpwent()** can be used to iterate through the password list. **getpwnam()** maps a login name to the `passwd` entry. **getpwuid()** maps a numeric userID to the appropriate `passwd` entry.

File permissions

Associated with each file and directory are a number of bits of information. The nine most important of those bits are the file permissions. When you `ls -l` a file, you will see them:

```
$ ls -l chapter.txt
-rw-r--r--  1 markd   staff   52655 Aug 11 15:11 chapter.txt
```

In particular, look at rw- r-- r-- three sets of three bits. The first set are permissions for the user who owns the file (`markd`, who can read from and write to the file). The second set are permissions for the group of the file (staff, who can read the file). Anyone who is a member of the staff group can read this file. The last set of bits are the permissions for all the others (anyone who is not `markd` and is not in the staff group)

Each of owner, group, and world can have these bits set:

r

   Read

w

   Write

x

   Execute

The clue to the OS that a file is actually an executable program is that the execute bit is set. There is not a magic file name suffix (like .EXE) that tells the OS that this file is executable.

Here are the permissions from some arbitrarily picked files from my file system:

```
$ ls -l /bin/ls
-r-xr-xr-x 1 root   wheel   27160 Dec  8  2001 /bin/ls*
```

The user (`root`) group (`wheel`), and others can all read and execute the file. Nobody can write to it. (The `wheel` group is used to designate system administrators on BSD systems)

```
$ ls -l /Developer/Documentation/Cocoa/helpviewericon.gif
-rw-rw-r-- 1 root   admin   631 Jul 19  2001 \
/Developer/Documentation/Cocoa/helpviewericon.gif
```

The user (root), group (admin) can each read and write the file. All the others can only read it.

```
$ ls -l /var/tmp/console.log
-rw-------  1 markd   wheel   39093 Aug 11 15:04 /var/tmp/console.log
```

The user (`markd`) can read and write the file. Neither the group nor anyone else can do anything to it.

You will sometimes see file permissions expressed numerically. Since each chunk of permissions is three bits, octal is how numbers are usually expressed.

```
r : 100
w : 010
x : 001
```

So a permission of `rw` is binary 110, which is octal value of 6. A permission of `rwx` is binary 111, which is octal value of 7.

`rwx rw- r--` is the same as 111 110 100, which is 764 in octal. Figure 8-7 shows some permission values, their octal representation, and what `ls -l` would show you.

Figure 8-7. Permission Bits

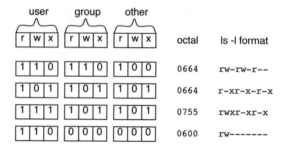

The `chmod` command lets you change these permission bits, either in octal or symbolically.

For instance:

```
$ touch test
$ ls -l test
-rw-r--r--  1 markd   staff   0 Aug 11 15:23 test

$ chmod 775 test
$ ls -l test
-rwxr-xr-x  1 markd   staff   0 Aug 11 15:23 test

$ chmod 400 test
$ ls -l test
-r--------  1 markd   staff   0 Aug 11 15:23 test
```

Most people do not tend to think in octal, so you can use symbols instead.

u

Modify user permissions.

g

Modify group permissions.

o

Modify other permissions.

+

Set the bits that follow.

–

Clear the bits that follow.

r

Read.

w

Write.

x

Execute.

```
$ chmod ugo+rw test
```

(For user, group, other, turn on the read and write bits.)

```
$ ls -l test
-rw-rw-rw-  1 markd   staff   0 Aug 11 15:23 test
```

```
$ chmod +x test
```

(This is shorthand for everything.)

```
$ ls -l test
-rwxrwxrwx  1 markd   staff   0 Aug 11 15:23 test*
```

```
$ chmod g-wx test
```

(Turn off write and execute for group.)

```
$ ls -l test
-rwxr--rwx  1 markd   staff   0 Aug 11 15:23 test*
```

There is also an API for affecting the permission bits:

```
int chmod (const char *path, mode_t mode);
```

```
int fchmod (int fd, mode_t mode);
```

where **chmod()** affects a file in the file system, and **fchmod()** changes the permissions on a file you already have open.

There is a whole slew of unpronounceable constants for specifying the mode:

```
#define S_IRWXU 0000700     /* RWX mask for owner */
#define S_IRUSR 0000400     /* R for owner */
#define S_IWUSR 0000200     /* W for owner */
#define S_IXUSR 0000100     /* X for owner */

#define S_IRWXG 0000070     /* RWX mask for group */
#define S_IRGRP 0000040     /* R for group */
#define S_IWGRP 0000020     /* W for group */
#define S_IXGRP 0000010     /* X for group */

#define S_IRWXO 0000007     /* RWX mask for other */
#define S_IROTH 0000004     /* R for other */
```

```
#define S_IWOTH 0000002    /* W for other */
#define S_IXOTH 0000001    /* X for other */
```

So, to specify rwxrw-r--, you would do something like this:

```
    user              group            other
    rwx               rw-               r--
     7                 6                 4
  S_IRWXU |   (S_IRGRP | S_IWGRP)   | S_IROTH
```

There is one more complication that gets thrown into the mix, the umask set by the user. The user has control over what permissions get used when creating new files by using the umask command to specify a numeric (octal) value to specify the bits that should be left unset, as shown in Figure 8-8.

Figure 8-8. umask

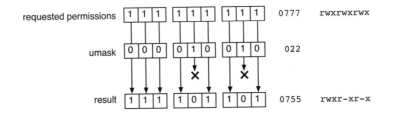

For example:

```
$ umask
22
$ touch test
$ ls -l test
-rw-r--r--  1 markd  staff  0 Aug 11 15:47 test
```

The umask of "22" is binary 000 010 010. The middle bit is the "w" write bit. So a umask of 22 will remove the write bit for group and others. If I change my umask

```
$ umask 002
$ umask
2
$ rm test
$ touch test
$ ls -l test
-rw-rw-r--  1 markd  staff  0 Aug 11 15:48 test
```

now only the "other" group of permissions has the write bit stripped out. If you are truly paranoid, you can use something like this:

```
$ umask 077
$ umask
77
$ rm test
$ touch test
$ ls -l test
-rw-------  1 markd  staff  0 Aug 11 15:49 test
```

The 77 (all bits set for group and other) causes all of those permission bits to be stripped out, so now only the user has any access to the files.

If you are using groups to control permissions, a umask of 002 is most friendly. You will not be creating files that cannot be written to by the group (which can temporarily mess up your project tree if you are using CVS).

There is also a **umask()** system call where you can change the umask used on the fly.

```
mode_t umask (mode_t numask);
```

The umask is inherited by child processes, which is handy if you want to make the umask more restrictive before spawning off a subprocess.

One interesting implementation detail in the Unix file system is that if you chmod a file, the modification date does not change. The file itself is not affected, just the metadata.

There is one last commonly used permission bit associated with files, the "set-uid" bit. There are some operations that can only be performed with the permission of root, the superuser, such as modifying the password file. But some of these operations (like changing a password) you want ordinary mortals to be able to do. The way Unix works around this problem is by having a bit that says, "when you run this program, run it as if the user were the same user as the file's owner, rather than running the program as the logged in user."

If you look at /usr/bin/passwd:

```
$ ls -l /usr/bin/passwd
-r-sr-xr-x  1 root  wheel  29756 Dec  8  2001 /usr/bin/passwd*
```

Notice the "s" in the user execute bit. That means when /usr/bin/passwd is run, it runs as root rather than as the logged-in user markd.

If you look something like one of the program files in the Oracle database:

```
$ cd $ORACLE_HOME/bin
$ ls -l oracle
-rwsr-s--x  1  oracle  oinstall 23389261 May 13 1997 oracle*
```

This is suid-oracle. When you run this program, it runs as if the logged in user were oracle. Also notice the second "s" in the group execute bit. That means the program will run as the group oinstall.

When a program runs, there are actually 6 (or more) IDs associated with it:

The real user ID and real group ID.

> This is who you really are, who you were when you logged in. These typically do not change during the life of a running program.

The effective user ID, effective group ID, supplementary group IDs.

> These are used for file permission checks. When you run an suid-root binary, your effective user ID is root.

The saved set-group-ID and saved set-user-ID

These are used by the exec functions, which will be discussed in Chapter 13 (Multiprocessing).

Example 8-9. uid.m

```
// uid.m -- experiment with user and group ids.
//           run as normal, then change this to be suid, and run again

/* compile with:
cc -g -Wall -o uid uid.m
*/

#import <sys/types.h>    // for struct group/struct passwd
#import <grp.h>          // for getgrgid()
#import <pwd.h>          // for getpwuid()
#import <stdio.h>        // for printf() and friends
#import <stdlib.h>       // EXIT_SUCCESS
#import <unistd.h>       // for getuid() and friends

int main (int argc, char *argv[])
{
    uid_t user_id;
    uid_t effective_user_id;
    gid_t group_id;
    gid_t effective_group_id;
    struct group *group;
    struct passwd *user;

    user_id = getuid ();
    effective_user_id = geteuid ();

    group_id = getgid ();
    effective_group_id = getegid ();

    user = getpwuid (user_id);
    printf ("real user ID is '%s'\n", user->pw_name);

    user = getpwuid (effective_user_id);
    printf ("effective user ID is '%s'\n", user->pw_name);

    group = getgrgid (group_id);
    printf ("real group is '%s'\n", group->gr_name);

    group = getgrgid (effective_group_id);
    printf ("effective group is '%s'\n", group->gr_name);

    exit (EXIT_SUCCESS);

} // main
```

Here is a run just as `markd`:

```
$ ls -l uid
-rwxrwxr-x  1 markd  staff  16692 Aug 11 16:35 uid*
$ ./uid
```

```
real user ID is 'markd'
effective user ID is 'markd'
real group is 'staff'
effective group is 'staff'
```

Now make it suid root:

```
$ sudo chown root:wheel uid
$ sudo chmod ug+s uid
$ ls -l uid
-rwsrwsr-x  1 root   wheel  16692 Aug 11 16:37 uid*
(note the s bits)
$ ./uid
real user ID is 'markd'
effective user ID is 'root'
real group is 'staff'
effective group is 'wheel'
```

So now this program is running with privileges of root.

Finally, let is try it as another ordinary user:

```
$ sudo chown bork:admin uid
$ ls -l uid
-rwsrwsr-x  1 bork   admin  16692 Aug 11 16:37 uid*

$ ./uid
real user ID is 'markd'
effective user ID is 'bork'
real group is 'staff'
effective group is 'admin'
```

One thing to note is that the setuid bits get cleared if a non-privileged program writes to the setuid file.

```
$ ls -l uid
-rwsrwsr-x  1 bork   admin  16692 Aug 11 16:37 uid*
$ cat >> uid
1 [control-D for end of file]
$ ls -l uid
-rwxrwxr-x  1 bork   admin  16694 Aug 11 16:40 uid*
```

That is a security measure to keep some malicious program from replacing a setuid program and running hostile code with root privileges.

Directory Permissions

Directories have the same permission bits as files (rwx for user, group, and other), but with slightly different interpretations. Because you cannot run directories as programs, the execute bit takes on a different meaning: it acts like a search bit. When opening any type of file by name, the user in question must have execute permission on every directory mentioned in the path (whether they match the user, group, or are other). Read permission is different from the execute/search permission. Read permission lets you read the directory itself, like with the ls command, to obtain a list of all the file names in the directory. Execute just means that you can pass through, or execute programs in that directory. You do not need read permissions along the way.

As an example, you create a directory, and copy a program into it

```
$ mkdir permtest
$ cp /bin/hostname permtest
$ chmod -rw permtest
$ ls -ld permtest
d--x--x--x  3 markd  staff  58 Aug 11 16:52 permtest/
```

Now you have turned off everything but the search bits.

```
$ ls permtest
ls: permtest: Permission denied
```

No read permission, so you get an error.

```
$ ./permtest/hostname
localhost
```

But you can still run programs in there.

Permission-Check Algorithms

Here is the quick overview of how permissions interact with the file operations discussed earlier:

- Must have read permission to open a file for reading with O_RDONLY or O_RDWR.
- Must have write permission to open a file for writing with O_WRONLY and O_RDWR.
- Must have write permission to O_TRUNCate a file.
- Must have write and execute permission on a directory to create a new file (write permission so you can modify the directory entry, and execute permission so the file can be searched).
- Must have write and execute permission on a directory to delete a file. You do not actually need read/write permissions on the file itself since the operation is actually just on the directory data structures.
- Must have the execute bit set to run a file program as a program.
- For accessing a file:
  - If the effective user ID is zero (root), access is allowed.
  - If the effective user ID is the same as the owner ID of the file, check the appropriate permission bit and allow access.
  - If the effective group ID or supplementary group ID is the same as the group ID of the file, check the appropriate permission bit and allow access.
  - If the appropriate access permission bit is set, allow access.
  - Otherwise do not allow access.

The whole effective user ID and real user ID brings up some interesting questions regarding file permissions. What if the user is running a setuid program but that program does not want to modify any files the user could not ordinarily be able to modify. The **access()** system call comes to the rescue:

```
int access (const char *path, int mode);
```

This checks the accessibility of the file named by the path, using the mode, and as the *real* userID and groupID of the user. The mode is the bitwise OR of the permissions to check:

R_OK

Read permission.

W_OK

Write permission.

X_OK

Execute/search permission.

F_OK

The file exists.

All components of the path are checked for access permissions.

Example 8-10. access.m

```
// access.m -- use the access() call to check permissions
//              run this as normal person, then make suid-root
//              and try again

/* compile with:
cc -g -Wall -o access access.m
*/

#import <unistd.h>      // for access()
#import <stdio.h>       // for printf()
#import <stdlib.h>      // for EXIT_SUCCESS
#import <errno.h>       // for errno
#import <string.h>      // for strerror()

int main (int argc, char *argv[])
{
    int result;

    result = access ("/etc/motd", R_OK);

    if (result == 0) {
        printf ("read access to /etc/motd\n");
    } else {
        printf ("no read access to /etc/motd: %d (%s)\n",
                errno, strerror(errno));
    }
```

```
    result = access ("/etc/motd", W_OK);

    if (result == 0) {
        printf ("write access to /etc/motd\n");
    } else {
        printf ("no write access to /etc/motd: %d (%s)\n",
                errno, strerror(errno));
    }

    return (EXIT_SUCCESS);

} // main
```

Run as just `markd`:

```
$ ./access
read access to /etc/motd
no write access to /etc/motd: 13 (Permission denied)
```

Run as root:

```
$ sudo ./access
read access to /etc/motd
write access to /etc/motd
```

Run setuid-root:

```
$ sudo chown root:wheel access
$ sudo chmod ug+s access
$ ls -l access
-rwsrwsr-x  1 root  wheel  9644 Aug 11 17:10 access*

$ ./access
read access to /etc/motd
no write access to /etc/motd: 13 (Permission denied)
```

So it works as expected.

For the More Curious: Memory-Mapped files

Memory mapped files are a blend of the virtual memory system and the file system, where a file's contents are mapped onto a range of bytes in memory. When you get bytes from that range of memory, you are reading from the file. When you change bytes in that range of memory, you are writing to the file. In essence you are doing I/O without using **read()** and **write()**. The virtual memory system gets to do the work of buffering, reading, and writing, only bringing in the blocks from disk that are actually used. To use memory-mapped files, you need to open the file, then call

```
caddr_t mmap (caddr_t addr, size_t len, int prot, int flags, int fd,
              off_t offset);
```

The return value is the address where the mapped file starts. Otherwise -1 is returned and `errno` is set.

Here are the arguments:

`addr`

> If non-zero, it is used as a hint to the system where in memory to start mapping to the file. **mmap()** is free to use or ignore this value. Usually you just pass in zero.

`len`

> How many bytes to map from the file. If you have a huge file, you can map just a portion of it to make things a little faster. Plus, it looks like there is a 1 gig limit to the amount of address space that will be mapped with this call.

`prot`

> Protection on the mapped memory. Pass a bitwise OR of one or more of these values:

> `PROT_EXEC`

>> Code may be executed on the mapped pages.

> `PROT_READ`

>> You can read from the pages.

> `PROT_WRITE`

>> You can write to the pages.

> These flags need to match the open mode of the file. For instance, you cannot `PROT_WRITE` a read-only file.

`flags`

> specifies various options. Here are the commonly used flags:

> `MAP_FIXED`

>> Return value must equal addr. If that is not possible an error is returned.

> `MAP_SHARED`

>> Storing bytes in memory will modify the mapped file. Be sure to set this if you expect your memory writes to be reflected back in the file.

> `MAP_PRIVATE`

>> Storing bytes in memory causes a copy of the mapped pages to be made, and all subsequent references reference the copy.

> `MAP_FILE`

>> Map from a regular file or a character special device. This is the default and does not need to be specified.

> `MAP_INHERIT`

>> Permit mapped regions to be mapped across **exec()** system calls so you can pass the mapped regions onto child processes.

```
fd
```

The file descriptor for the open file.

```
offset
```

The number of bytes into the file to start mapping. Usually you just pass in zero.

To unmap pages, use

```
int munmap (caddr_t addr, size_t len);
```

Returns zero on success, -1/setting `errno` on error. If you try to access this memory after the `munmap()`, you will generate invalid memory references. Note that `close()` does not unmap pages, but pages will get unmapped when your program exits.

`addr` and `offset` should be multiples of the system's virtual memory page size (use `sysconf()` to figure it out).

To flush modified pages back to the file system, use `msync()`:

```
int msync (void *addr, size_t len, int flags);
```

If `len` is zero, all modified pages will be flushed. Possible flag values are

```
MS_ASYNC
```

Return immediately and let the write happen at the kernel's convenience.

```
MS_SYNC
```

Perform synchronous writes.

```
MS_INVALIDATE
```

Invalidate all cached data (presumably to force a re-read from the file).

Some rules to remember:

- You can memory-map regular files, not networked file descriptors or device files.
- You need to be careful if the size of the underlying file could change after it gets mapped, otherwise memory access errors might be triggered.
- You cannot use `mmap()` and memory writes to memory to extend files. You will need to seek and write to accomplish that.

Example 8-11 is a program that opens files, `mmap()`s them, then walks the memory performing the "rot-13" encryption on them. Rot-13 (short for "rotate 13") is a simple letter substitution cypher. It replaces letters with those that are 13 positions head of it in the alphabet. rot-13 is reversible. If you rot-13 text, you can rot-13 it again to get the original text back.

Example 8-11. mmap-rot13.m

```
// mmap-rot13.m -- use memory mapped I/O to apply the rot 13
//                 'encryption' algorithm to a file.

/* compile with:
cc -g -Wall -o mmap-rot13 mmap-rot13.m
```

```
*/

#import <sys/fcntl.h>     // for O_RDWR and open()
#import <sys/stat.h>      // for fstat() and struct stat
#import <sys/mman.h>      // for mmap, etc
#import <stdio.h>         // printf, etc
#import <errno.h>         // for errno
#import <stdlib.h>        // EXIT_SUCCESS, etc
#import <ctype.h>         // for isalpha()
#import <string.h>        // for strerror()
#import <unistd.h>        // for close()

// walk the buffer shifting alphabetic characters 13 places
void rot13 (caddr_t base, size_t length)
{
    char *scan, *stop;

    scan = base;
    stop = scan + length;

    while (scan < stop) {
        // there are tons of implementations of rot13 out on the net
        // much more compact than this
        if (isalpha(*scan)) {
            if (   (*scan >= 'A' && *scan <= 'M')
                || (*scan >= 'a' && *scan <= 'm')) {
                *scan += 13;
            } else if (   (*scan >= 'N' && *scan <= 'Z')
                || (*scan >= 'n' && *scan <= 'z')) {
                *scan -= 13;
            }
        }
        scan++;
    }

} // rot13

void processFile (const char *filename)
{
    int fd = -1;
    int result;
    caddr_t base = (caddr_t) -1;
    size_t length;
    struct stat statbuf;

    // open the file first
    fd = open (filename, O_RDWR);
    if (fd == -1) {
        fprintf (stderr, "could not open %s: error %d (%s)\n",
                 filename, errno, strerror(errno));
        goto bailout;
    }

    // figure out how big it is
    result = fstat (fd, &statbuf);
    if (result == -1) {
        fprintf (stderr, "fstat of %s failed: error %d (%s)\n",
```

```
                            filename, errno, strerror(errno));
            goto bailout;
        }
        length = statbuf.st_size;

        // mmap it
        base = mmap (NULL, length, PROT_READ | PROT_WRITE,
                     MAP_SHARED, fd, 0);
        if (base == (caddr_t) -1) {
            fprintf (stderr, "could not mmap %s: error %d (%s)\n",
                     filename, errno, strerror(errno));
            goto bailout;
        }

        // actually perform the rot13 algorithm
        rot13 (base, length);

        // flush the results
        result = msync (base, length, MS_SYNC);
        if (result == -1) {
            fprintf (stderr, "msync failed for %s: error %d (%s)\n",
                     filename, errno, strerror(errno));
            goto bailout;
        }

  bailout:
        // clean up any messes we have made
        if (base != (caddr_t) -1) {
            munmap (base, length);
        }
        if (fd != -1) {
            close (fd);
        }

} // processFile

int main (int argc, char *argv[])
{
    int i;

    if (argc == 1) {
        fprintf (stderr, "usage: %s /path/to/file ... \n"
                 "rot-13s files in-place using memory mapped I/O\n",
                 argv[0]);
        exit (EXIT_FAILURE);
    }

    for (i = 1; i < argc; i++) {
        processFile (argv[i]);
    }

    exit (EXIT_SUCCESS);

} // main
```

And of course, a sample run or two:

```
$ cat > blorf
Blorf is the name of a bunny rabbit.

$ ./mmap-rot13 blorf
$ cat blorf
Oybes vf gur anzr bs n ohaal enoovg.

$ ./mmap-rot13 blorf
$ cat blorf
Blorf is the name of a bunny rabbit.
```

Chapter 9. Files, Part 2: Directories, File Systems, and Links

Directories are the counterparts to files. They are the locations that store the files and give a hierarchical structure to the file system. The file system itself is built upon inodes and data blocks, which are both used by files and directories to store their data. Links (hard links and symbolic links) use features of the file system implementation to give indirect access to files.

Directories

Compared to files, there is comparatively very little that can be done to them. You can create directories, remove them, and iterate through their contents.

Creation and destruction

```
int mkdir (const char *path, mode_t mode);
```

mkdir() creates a new directory at the path. The permissions on the directory are specified in mode (using the S_I* constants discussed back with **chmod()**). The umask is applied (clearing bits in the mode that are set in the umask). Do not forget to set the execution bits! This returns zero on success, -1 on error with errno set as appropriate.

```
int rmdir (const char *path);
```

td This will remove the directory at the path. The directory must be empty of any files or subdirectories, otherwise an error will be removed. Like **mkdir()**, zero is returned on success, -1 on error, and errno is set.

Directory iteration

The opendir() Family

These are the functions you use to iterate through the contents of a directory:

```
DIR *opendir (const char *filename);

struct dirent *readdir(DIR *dirp);

long telldir (const DIR *dirp);

void seekdir (DIR *dirp, long loc);

void rewinddir(DIR *dirp);

int closedir(DIR *dirp);
```

The usual use of this API is to use **opendir()** on a path. **opendir()** returns an opaque DIR handle whose resources will be freed when **closedir()** is called. Call **readdir()** in a loop until it returns NULL. **telldir()** lets you know what location you are in a directory stream. **seekdir()** will move the position of the directory stream to the indicated location, and **rewinddir()** will reset the position to the beginning of the directory. The struct dirent returned from **readdir()** looks like:

```
struct dirent {
    u_int32_t  d_fileno;      /* file number (inode) of entry */
    u_int16_t  d_reclen;      /* length of this record */
    u_int_8_t  d_type;        /* the type of the file */
    u_int8_t   d_namlen;      /* length of string in d_name */
    char       d_name[MAXNAMLEN + 1];  /* maximum name length */
};
```

Usually the d_name is the piece of information that is most interesting.

There is no guarantee of the order in which the files will be returned by readdir().
On HFS+ file systems, they seem to be returned in alphabetical order, but you
shouldn't assume that this is always the case.

Example 9-1 is a little program that acts like a cheap version of ls, without any
features:

Example 9-1. cheapls.m

```
// cheapls.m -- a cheap-o ls program using the directory'
//               iteration functions

/* compile with:
cc -g -Wall -o cheapls cheapls.m
*/

#import <sys/types.h>     // for random type definition
#import <sys/dirent.h>    // for struct dirent
#import <dirent.h>        // for opendir and friends
#import <stdlib.h>        // for EXIT_SUCCESS
#import <stdio.h>         // for printf
#import <errno.h>         // for errno
#import <string.h>        // for strerror()

int main (int argc, char *argv[])
{
    DIR *directory;
    struct dirent *entry;
    int result;

    if (argc != 2) {
        fprintf (stderr, "usage:  %s /path/to/directory\n", argv[0]);
        exit (EXIT_FAILURE);
    }

    directory = opendir (argv[1]);
    if (directory == NULL) {
        fprintf (stderr, "could not open directory '%s'\n", argv[1]);
        fprintf (stderr, "let's see if errno is useful: %d (%s)\n",
                 errno, strerror(errno));
        exit (EXIT_FAILURE);
    }

    while ( (entry = readdir(directory)) != NULL) {
        long position = telldir (directory);
        printf ("%3ld: %s\n", position, entry->d_name);
    }
```

```
    result = closedir (directory);
    if (result == -1) {
        fprintf (stderr, "error closing directory: %d (%s)\n",
                 errno, strerror(errno));
        exit (EXIT_FAILURE);
    }
    return (0);
} // main
```

And some sample runs (edited):

```
$ ./cheapls .
   1: .
   2: ..
   3: #uid.m#
   4: .#chapter.txt
   5: .#uid.m
   6: .DS_Store
   7: .gdb_history
   8: access
   9: access.m
  10: access.m~
  11: append
  12: append.m
       . . .
  49: writestring.m
  50: writevecstring
  51: writevecstring.m

$ ./cheapls /Developer/Applications
   1: .
   2: ..
   3: .DS_Store
   4: Apple Help Indexing Tool.app
   5: AppleScript Studio
   6: DebugNubController.app
   7: Extras
       . . .
  23: Quartz Debug.app
  24: Sampler.app
  25: Thread Viewer.app
```

getdirentries()

opendir() and friends form the POSIX API for directory iteration. They are also portable to all of the different Unix flavored systems out there. BSD also provides its own directory reading function called **getdirentries()**. **getdirentries()** returns file name information like **readdir()**, but rather than being called in a loop for each file **getdirentries()** returns the file name information in the form of a bunch of dirent structures laid end-to-end in a buffer that you supply. This reduces the number of function calls you have to make. In some cases, walking a buffer can be more convenient than processing **readdir()** continually in a loop. **getdirentries()** is marginally faster than **opendir()** and **readdir()**, but the actual performance differences are minor, so you should choose your directory iteration API based on what is most convenient for your code, and whether cross-Unix compatibility is important to you.

```
int getdirentries (int fd, char *buffer, int bufferLength,
                   long *basePointer)
```

This function takes a file descriptor for an directory that has been **open()**ed. You supply a chunk of memory, `buffer`, which should be at least as large as the blocksize of the file. Example 9-2 will be using **stat()** to determine this (and also to make sure that the directory name given by the user actually is a directory). **stat()**, which returns a chunk of metadata about a file, will be discussed in detail later in this chapter.

You pass the buffer's length in the `bufferLength` parameter. **getdirentries()** will write as much data into the buffer as will fit. `basePointer` is where **getdirentries()** jots down how far it has read into the directory. If you manipulate the file descriptor and want to resume the directory traversal, you can **lseek()** to this location and continue. Otherwise you can ignore the value (but you still need to pass in the `basePointer` argument.)

On a successful read, **getdirentries()** returns the number of bytes that it placed into the buffer. When it has run out of directory entries, it returns zero. If an error happens, it returns -1 and sets `errno` to an appropriate error value.

Figure 9-1 shows how the data is packed into the buffer supplied to **getdirentries()**. The `struct dirent`s are packed end to end, taking up only as much space as necessary accommodate the four header fields and the name data. There is some padding between the entries to keep them aligned on four-byte boundaries. To process the data you need to use some pointer techniques. I like having a `scan` variable that points to the item currently being processed. When you are done with that item, add the value of the `d_reclen` field to the `scan` pointer, which takes you to the beginning of the next item. Because **getdirentries()** returns how many bytes it put into your buffer, you know to stop looking when `scan` falls outside of that range of bytes.

Figure 9-1. Packed Direntries

Example 9-2 is the same as the `cheapls` program, but using **getdirentries()** instead of **opendir()** and **readdir()**.

Example 9-2. cheapls-direntries.m

```
// cheapls-direntries -- cheapls, but using getdirentries()

/* compile with
cc -g -o cheapls-direntries cheapls-direntries.m
*/
```

```
#import <sys/types.h> // for random type definition
#import <sys/dirent.h> // for struct dirent
#import <dirent.h> // for getdirentries()
#import <stdlib.h> // for EXIT_SUCCESS
#import <stdio.h> // for printf
#import <errno.h> // for errno
#import <string.h> // for strerror
#import <fcntl.h> // for O_RDONLY
#import <sys/stat.h> // for struct statbuf and stat()

int main (int argc, char *argv[])
{
    // sanity check the program argument first
    if (argc != 2) {
 fprintf (stderr, "usage:  %s /path/to/directory\n", argv[0]);
 exit (EXIT_FAILURE);
    }

    int fd;
    fd = open (argv[1], O_RDONLY);

    if (fd == -1) {
        fprintf (stderr, "could not open directory '%s'\n", argv[1]);
        fprintf (stderr, "error: %d/%s\n", errno, strerror(errno));
        exit (EXIT_FAILURE);
    }

    // make sure it is actually a directory
    // also gives us the blocksize for the getdirentries call
    struct stat statbuf;
    int result;
    result = fstat (fd, &statbuf);

    if (result == -1) {
        fprintf (stderr, "could not stat directory '%s'\n", argv[1]);
        fprintf (stderr, "error: %d/%s\n", errno, strerror(errno));
        exit (EXIT_FAILURE);
    }

    if (! (statbuf.st_mode & S_IFDIR)) {
        fprintf (stderr, "%s is not a directory\n", argv[1]);
        exit (EXIT_FAILURE);
    }

#define BLOCK_COUNT 10
    char *buffer;
    buffer = malloc (statbuf.st_blksize * BLOCK_COUNT);
    long base = 0; // all of these are belong to us

    // get first batch of directory entries
    result = getdirentries (fd, buffer,
                            statbuf.st_blksize * BLOCK_COUNT,
                            &base);

    int position = 1;

    while (result > 0) {
        // walk through the returned buffer
```

```
            char *scan, *stop;
            scan = buffer;
            stop = scan + result;

            while (scan < stop) {
                struct dirent *entry = (struct dirent *) scan;

                printf ("%3ld: %s\n", position, entry->d_name);

                scan += entry->d_reclen;
                position++;
            }

            // get the next batch (or zero when we run out)
            result = getdirentries (fd, buffer,
                                    statbuf.st_blksize * BLOCK_COUNT,
                                    &base);
        }
        free (buffer);

        if (result == -1) {
            fprintf (stderr, "error using getdirentries: %d/%s\n",
                    errno, strerror(errno));
            exit (EXIT_FAILURE);
        }

        close (fd);

        return (EXIT_SUCCESS);

} // main
```

and a sample run, which should be identical to `cheapls`.

```
$ ./cheapls-direntries .
 1: .
 2: ..
 3: #uid.m#
 4: .#chapter.txt
 5: .#uid.m
 6: .DS_Store
 7: .gdb_history
 8: access
 9: access.m
10: access.m~
11: append
12: append.m
    ...
49: writestring.m
50: writevecstring
51: writevecstring.m
```

`cheapls` and `cheapls-direntries` were used to compare the run time of both techniques. The output of the program was sent to `/dev/null` and timed with the `time` command in the C Shell. For a directory with 19,900 file names, `cheapls` took (on average, on my machine) 0.34 seconds. `cheapls-direntries` took 0.25 seconds.

Practically, not a whole lot of difference. Presumably **opendir()** uses **getdirentries()** under the hood and adds a tiny bit of overhead of its own.

Current working directory

There is a piece of global state in every program which is the current working directory. If you try to do any file operations without specifying a full path, the operation constructs a path by appending the arguments to **open()**, etc., with the current working directory. You use this concept all the time in the shell when you cd to a directory and perform operations without specifying a full path (that is, a path beginning with a slash character).

```
int chdir (const char *path);

int fchdir (int fd);
```

The **chdir()** function sets your current working directory to the given path, while **fchdir()** uses a file descriptor of an open directory. On success it returns zero, and it returns -1 on error with errno set appropriately.

Use **getcwd()** to get the current directory:

```
char *getcwd (char *buf, size_t size);
```

Pass it in a buffer and the size of the buffer. You should make sure that buf is MAXPATHLEN bytes or larger. On successful completion, the address buf is returned, NULL in case of error (with errno set) The **getcwd()** man page warns not to use **getcwd()** to save a directory for the purpose of returning to it (like when using the shell's pushd command). Instead you should open the current directory ("."), stash away the file descriptor, and then use **fchdir()** to return to it.

Be aware that the current working directory is not a thread-safe concept. One thread could change the working directory and then get pre-empted by another thread, which then changes the working directory. When the first thread gets control, the current working directory will be wrong. If you are going to be dealing with multiple directories in a threaded app, use full path names. (More on similar issues in Chapter 13 (Multiprocessing).)

Inside The File System

Figure 9-2 shows that the physical disk is divided up into partitions:

Figure 9-2. Partitions

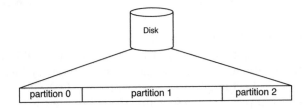

And when you make a filesystem on a particular partition, it looks something like Figure 9-3

Figure 9-3. Filesystem

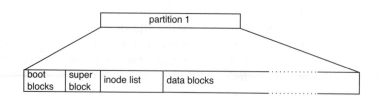

The superblock is a block in a known location that has pointers to the rest of the on-disk data structures. Frequently there are redundant copies of the superblock in case the primary superblock gets destroyed.

An inode (an indirect block) is the handle used to hold onto an individual file, as shown in Figure 9-4. Each file has an inode, and that inode has in it the metadata for the file (the size, modification dates, etc.), as well as a list of datablocks that compose the file. The inode also has a link count, which is a reference count of the number of directory entries that point to the inode. The file is only deleted when the count goes to zero, as noted with **unlink()**.

Figure 9-4. inodes

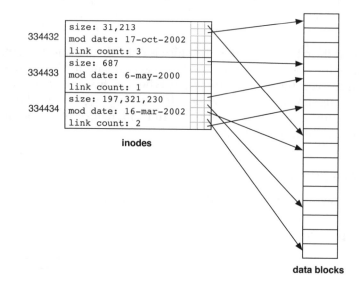

The data blocks can contain either file data or they can be directory blocks (a data block with a flag saying it is a directory), as shown in Figure 9-5. A directory is a list of file names and inode numbers. (The number of an inode is the inode's address. The directory does not actually store a copy of the inode itself.) When you iterate through a directory, it picks up the filename from the directory and can then find the actual file by using the inode.

Figure 9-5. Directory Structure

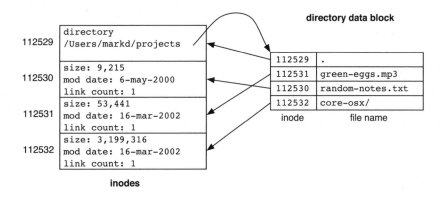

The special files in directories are just inode numbers. For instance, "." is the inode that references the directory, and ".." is the directory's parent. Since the inode points within a particular file system, you cannot have a directory with files that cross file system boundaries. This has the side effect of that if you move a file on to a new place on the same file system, the move is just a couple of directory block manipulations. No data is actually copied.

There are some points to be taken from this. Since files are referenced by their inode number (which you can see when you do an `ls -i`), a file can physically appear in more than one place (known as hard links, which are talked about in a bit). It also means that there is a finite pool of inodes available. You can use `df -i` to see the number of inodes in use and free. If you run out of inodes you will not be able to create any more files on that file system even if there is plenty of space. When you create new file systems from scratch (via the `newfs` command), you need to decide on the inode density. For a file system that will primarily be storing digital video, you do not need a whole lot of inodes since you will have relatively few individual files. If you are creating a file system to store a usenet newsfeed, you will want to have a much higher density of inodes, since newsfeeds tend to have a huge number of tiny files.

Unlike most other Unix systems, you can work around some of these problems by creating disk images with the `DiskCopy`. When mounted, the disk images are treated just like disk devices. You can even `newfs` a mounted disk image to have the inode density you need.

There are some hard-coded limits regarding the filesystem, particularly things like file names and path names. Path names are limited to the constant PATH_MAX, which is defined as 1024 bytes. This can really stink for languages like Korean with 3-byte characters in UTF-8. Likewise, the maximum size for a file name is 1024 bytes.

Standard Unix file systems are not journaled (in a journaled filesystem, the metadata on the disk is always consistent). In the event of an abnormal reboot, the program `fsck` does a disk consistency check and cleans up any erroneous metadata. There exists an add-on that turns HFS+ into a journaled file system.

Links

Unix has two kinds of links: hard links and symbolic links. OS X brings the classic

Mac concept of an alias to the table as well. Links are ways of referencing a file from more than one place, which can be handy when you are faced with software that makes assumptions about what path something lives in, or when you want a particular file to live in multiple places (say a README placed in each users home directory), but to only occupy disk space for one copy.

Hard links

As mentioned earlier in the brief overview of the file system, hard links are entries in multiple directories that all refer to the same inode. The file appears in multiple places at once. Use the `ln` command to create a hard link:

```
$ mkdir linktest
$ cd linktest
$ touch spoon
(create a new file)

$ ln spoon spoon2
(make a hard link)

$ ls -li
total 0
571668 -rw-rw-r--  2 markd  staff  0 Aug 12 11:52 spoon
571668 -rw-rw-r--  2 markd  staff  0 Aug 12 11:52 spoon2
```

The left-hand column shows the inode of the file. Note that the inodes are the same. Also notice the third column. It says that there are two hard links to this file.

```
$ ln spoon spoon3
$ ls -li
total 0
571668 -rw-rw-r--  3 markd  staff  0 Aug 12 11:52 spoon
571668 -rw-rw-r--  3 markd  staff  0 Aug 12 11:52 spoon2
571668 -rw-rw-r--  3 markd  staff  0 Aug 12 11:52 spoon3
```

Now there are three hard links to the same file.

Since hard links refer to inodes, they cannot cross file system boundaries. If you `mv` a hard linked file to another file system, the data will get copied, the original removed, and the link count will go down by one.

Users cannot create hard links to directories. On some file systems the superuser can make hard links to directories, but in general that is not advisable because hard links can form cycles in the directories, which the kernel really is not designed to handle.

Symbolic links

A symbolic link is a file that contains the path to another file, and this path can be relative or absolute. Symbolic links are not included in the reference count of a file, and in fact do not have to actually point to a real file at all (in which case they become dangling links). Use `ln -s` to create a symbolic link:

```
$ mkdir symlinktest
$ cd symlinktest
$ touch spoon
(make an empty file)
```

```
$ ln -s spoon spoon2
(make a relative symbolic link)

$ ls -l
total 8
-rw-rw-r--  1 markd  staff  0 Aug 12 12:08 spoon
lrwxrwxr-x  1 markd  staff  5 Aug 12 12:08 spoon2@ -> spoon

$ ln -s `pwd`/spoon spoon3
(use the backtick shell operator to run pwd, then paste that into the
command, which will give us a full path)

$ ls -l
total 16
-rw-rw-r--  1 markd  staff   0 Aug 12 12:08 spoon
lrwxrwxr-x  1 markd  staff   5 Aug 12 12:08 spoon2 -> spoon
lrwxrwxr-x  1 markd  staff  49 Aug 12 12:08 spoon3 -> /Users/markd/\
BNRUnix/files2-chap/symlinktest/spoon
```

Note the size column. It is the number of characters in the symlink. Also notice the leading character over there in the permissions - a lower case L, signifying this is a link.

If you add the -F flag, you can see some extra symbols attached to file names:

```
$ ls -F
spoon    spoon2@ spoon3@
```

The at sign says it is a symbolic link. Additional character suffixes that -F brings are "/" for directories, and "*" for executable files. A trick is to alias ls to be ls -F so that you can see these little clues.

Symlinks are like pointers to files, as shown in Figure 9-6. They were created to work around some of the problems with hard links, such as crossing file systems and making links to directories. You can make a symbolic link to a directory and not cause problems. You can generate loops with symlinks, but function calls that try to resolve them will generate an error.

Figure 9-6. Hard and Symbolic Links

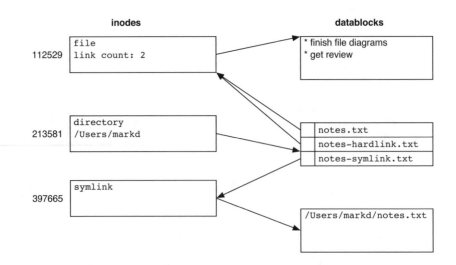

The real power of symbolic links comes in when you are moving things around in the file system. Say your webserver log files in /home/nsadmin/logs/borkware is filling up your drive. You can copy all the log files to another place, like /Volumes/BigDisk/logs/borkware, and then point the first path to the second. No need to change any configuration files, and existing paths to the logs still work. Granted, things can get out of hand and can become unmaintainable if you have too many layers of symlink indirection.

Most of the file API you have seen so far will follow symbolic links automatically, like **chmod()**, **chown()**, **open()**, and **stat()** (discussed a bit later).

There are some function calls that let you manipulate the link directly.

```
int lchown (const char *path, uid_t owner, gid_t group);
```

This changes the owner

```
int readlink (const char *path, char *buf, int bufsiz);
```

places the contents of the symbolic link path into the buffer. This does not append the terminating zero byte. It returns the number of characters it wrote into the buffer, or -1 on error (with errno set appropriately).

And other functions **lstat()**.

And finally, some API will deal with the link directly, like **rename()** and **unlink()**.

This reading through of links (like with **open()**) can lead to some confusion:

```
$ ln -s /no/such/file oopack
$ ls oopack
oopack
(It is there)
$ cat oopack
cat: oopack: No such file or directory
(no, it is not there.  huh?)
```

```
$ ls -l oopack
lrwxr-xr-x  1 markd  staff  13 Aug 12 12:30 oopack@ -> /no/such/file
(oh, it is a symlink that points to nowhere)
```

This is another reason to alias `ls` to include the `-F` flag.

```
$ ls -F oopack
oopack@
```

This makes it obvious `oopack` is a symlink.

Mac OS aliases

Users can create aliases in the `Finder` by explicitly making an alias or performing some mouse dragging operations. Like symbolic links, aliases are not included in a file's reference count, and they can dangle, pointing nowhere. On HFS+, an alias contains the file's file number (similar to an inode number), so the alias can find the file anywhere on the disk. The path to the file is also stored in case the file is deleted and replaced with a new one.

Differences between the kinds of links:

- Hardlinks always point to valid files.
- Symlinks do not track file moves, but aliases do.
- Symlinks survive file deletions, aliases do not always.
- Symlinks can make loops.

API for links

```
int link (const char *name1, const char *name2);

int symlink (const char *name1, const char *name2);
```

This creates a hardlink (or symlink) with `name2` referring to the same file as `name1`. Zero is returned on success, -1 on error with `errno` set appropriately. When making a symlink, use **`readlink()`** to get the file name stored in the link.

You will need to use the Carbon API if you want to deal with aliases.

File Metadata

File Metadata is data about the file, but is not the file's data itself. This includes stuff like the file's size, the file's type, the last access times, etc.

stat()

Three functions can be used to access the metadata:

```
int stat (const char *path, struct stat *sb);

int lstat (const char *path, struct stat *sb);
```

```
int fstat (int fd, struct stat *sb);
```

stat() gets information about the file at a path, following any intervening symbolic links. **lstat()** gets information about the symbolic link itself. **fstat()** gives you metadata about open files. As with most Unix file functions, a return value of zero indicates success, a value of -1 indicates an error and `errno` is set appropriately.

You do not need read, write, or execute permissions on a file to **stat()** it, but all directories listed in the path name need to be searchable.

`struct stat` is the focal point for all of the data returned by these calls. You allocate a `struct stat` either on the stack or dynamically, and pass that to the function.

```
struct stat {
    dev_t     st_dev;     /* device inode resides on */
    ino_t     st_ino;     /* inode's number */
    mode_t    st_mode;    /* inode protection mode */
    nlink_t   st_nlink;   /* number or hard links to the file */
    uid_t     st_uid;     /* user-id of owner */
    gid_t     st_gid;     /* group-id of owner */
    dev_t     st_rdev;    /* device type, for special file inode */
    struct timespec st_atimespec; /* time of last access */
    struct timespec st_mtimespec; /* time of last data modification */
    struct timespec st_ctimespec; /* time of last file status change */
    off_t     st_size;    /* file size, in bytes */
    quad_t    st_blocks;  /* blocks allocated for file */
    u_long    st_blksize;/* optimal file sys I/O ops blocksize */
    u_long    st_flags;   /* user defined flags for file */
    u_long    st_gen;     /* file generation number */
};
```

Here is a breakdown of the more common fields:

`st_mode` contains the file type and permissions. The lower nine bits have the user, group, and other permissions. You can focus in on those by using the mask `ACCESSPERMS` (0777). You can also bitwise-and things using the macros listed back when **chmod()** was discussed (`S_IRWXU`, `S_IRUSR`, etc.).

There are also bits for determining the type of file being looked at.

Table 9-1. File Types

Mask	Convenience Macro	What it is
S_IFIFO	S_ISFIFO()	FIFO (named pipe, an IPC mechanism)
S_IFCHR	S_ISCHR()	character special device (like terminals and serial lines)
S_IFDIR	S_ISDIR()	directory
S_IFBLK	S_ISBLK()	block special device (like disks and tapes)
S_IFREG	S_ISREG()	plain old regular file
S_IFLNK	S_ISLNK()	symbolic link

Mask	Convenience Macro	What it is
S_IFSOCK	S_ISSOCK()	socket (network communication)

The `st_uid` and `st_gid` fields tell you the user that owns the file, as well as the group associated with the file.

`st_size` has the file size in bytes.

There are three file times associated with each file:

`st_atimespec`

> The last access time. That is, the last time the file was opened for reading. You can see this with `ls -lu`. You can also access just the `tv_sec` field by using `st_atime`.

`st_mtimespec`

> The last modification time. This is the date displayed by `ls -l`. You can also access just the `tv_sec` field by using `st_mtime`.

`st_ctime`

> Last change in inode status, like by using `chmod` or `chown`. `ls -lc` shows this time. You can also access just the `tv_sec` field by using `st_ctime`.

These file times are of type `time_t`, which is the number of seconds since midnight, Jan 1, 1970 (the start of the Unix epoch)

The **utimes()** system call can be used to change access and modification times of a file. This is handy if you are writing something like `tar` and need to preserve access times when you expand an archive.

Example 9-3 is a little program that will print out a whole bunch of stuff from `struct stat`:

Example 9-3. permtype.m

```
// permtype.m -- use stat to discover the type and permissions
//                for a file

/* compile with:
cc -g -Wall -o permtype permtype.m
*/

#import <sys/stat.h>    // for stat() and struct stat
#import <stdlib.h>      // for EXIT_SUCCESS
#import <stdio.h>       // for printf
#import <errno.h>       // for errno
#import <grp.h>         // for group file access routines
#import <pwd.h>         // for passwd file access routines
#import <sys/time.h>    // for struct tm, localtime, etc
#import <string.h>      // for strerror


// cheesy little lookup table for mapping perm value to the
// familiar character string
```

```
static const char *g_perms[]  = {
    "---", "--x", "-w-", "-wx", "r--", "r-x", "rw-", "rwx"
};

typedef struct StatType {
    unsigned long      mask;
    const char         *type;
} StatType;

static StatType g_types[] = {
    { S_IFREG, "Regular File" },
    { S_IFDIR, "Directory" },
    { S_IFLNK, "Symbolic Link" },
    { S_IFCHR, "Character Special Device" },
    { S_IFBLK, "Block Special Device" },
    { S_IFIFO, "FIFO" },
    { S_IFSOCK, "Socket" },
};

void displayInfo (const char *filename)
{
    int result;
    struct stat statbuf;
    StatType *scan, *stop;

    result = lstat (filename, &statbuf);

    if (result == -1) {
        fprintf (stderr, "error with stat(%s) :  %d (%s)\n",
                 filename, errno, strerror(errno));
        return;
    }

    printf ("%s:\n", filename);

    printf (" permissions: %s%s%s\n",
            g_perms[(statbuf.st_mode & S_IRWXU) >> 6],
            g_perms[(statbuf.st_mode & S_IRWXG) >> 3],
            g_perms[(statbuf.st_mode & S_IRWXO)]);

    // figure out the type
    scan = g_types;
    stop = scan + (sizeof(g_types) / sizeof(StatType));

    while (scan < stop) {
        if ((statbuf.st_mode & S_IFMT) == scan->mask) {
            printf (" type: %s\n", scan->type);
            break;
        }
        scan++;
    }

    // any special bits sets?
    if ((statbuf.st_mode & S_ISUID) == S_ISUID) {
        printf (" set-uid!\n");
    }
    if ((statbuf.st_mode & S_ISGID) == S_ISUID) {
```

```c
        printf ("  set-group-id!\n");
    }

    // file size
    printf ("  file is %ld bytes (%f K)\n",
            (long)statbuf.st_size,
            (float) (statbuf.st_size / 1024.0));

    // owning user / group
    {
        struct passwd *passwd;
        struct group *group;

        passwd = getpwuid (statbuf.st_uid);
        group = getgrgid (statbuf.st_gid);

        printf ("  user: %s (%d)\n", passwd->pw_name, statbuf.st_uid);
        printf ("  group: %s (%d)\n", group->gr_name, statbuf.st_gid);
    }

    // now the dates
    {
        char buffer[1024];
        struct tm *tm;

        tm = localtime (&statbuf.st_atime);
        strftime (buffer, 1024, "%m/%d/%Y", tm);
        printf ("  last access: %s\n", buffer);

        tm = localtime (&statbuf.st_mtime);
        strftime (buffer, 1024, "%m/%d/%Y", tm);
        printf ("  last modification: %s\n", buffer);

        tm = localtime (&statbuf.st_ctime);
        strftime (buffer, 1024, "%m/%d/%Y", tm);
        printf ("  last inode change: %s\n", buffer);
    }

    // double-space output
    printf ("\n");

} // displayInfo

int main (int argc, char *argv[])
{
    int i;

    if (argc == 1) {
        fprintf (stderr, "usage:  %s /path/to/file ... \n", argv[0]);
        exit (EXIT_FAILURE);
    }

    for (i = 1; i < argc; i++) {
        displayInfo (argv[i]);
    }

    exit (EXIT_SUCCESS);
```

```
} // main
```

A sample run

```
$ ./permtype permtype / oopack /dev/kmem /usr/bin/passwd
(where oopack is a symbolic link)

permtype:
  permissions: rwxrwxr-x
  type: Regular File
  file is 23924 bytes (23.363281 K)
  user: markd (501)
  group: staff (20)
  last access: 08/12/2002 15:04:30
  last modification: 08/12/2002 15:04:11
  last inode change: 08/12/2002 15:04:11

/:
  permissions: rwxrwxr-x
  type: Directory
  file is 1452 bytes (1.417969 K)
  user: root (0)
  group: admin (80)
  last access: 08/12/2002 15:04:30
  last modification: 08/10/2002 22:41:04
  last inode change: 08/10/2002 22:41:04

oopack:
  permissions: rwxr-xr-x
  type: Symbolic Link
  file is 13 bytes (0.012695 K)
  user: markd (501)
  group: staff (20)
  last access: 08/12/2002 15:03:24
  last modification: 08/12/2002 15:04:28
  last inode change: 08/12/2002 15:04:28

/dev/kmem:
  permissions: rw-r-----
  type: Character Special Device
  file is 0 bytes (0.000000 K)
  user: root (0)
  group: kmem (2)
  last access: 08/12/2002 14:37:36
  last modification: 08/08/2002 21:44:32
  last inode change: 08/08/2002 21:44:32

/usr/bin/passwd:
  permissions: r-xr-xr-x
  type: Regular File
  set-uid!
  file is 29756 bytes (29.058594 K)
  user: root (0)
  group: wheel (0)
  last access: 07/06/2002 11:37:31
  last modification: 12/08/2001 13:58:34
```

```
last inode change: 06/19/2002 15:40:57
```

Now, just to make your life a little more complicated, both Cocoa and Carbon have different kinds of metadata they bring to the table, including things like the HFS+ Creator and Type code for files, and whether the file extension should be hidden.

NSFileManager has a number of constants for use in the attribute dictionary returned by -[NSFileManager fileAttributesAtPath: traverseLink:]. There is some overlap with what you get from struct stat:

* NSFileSize

* NSFileModificationDate

* NSFileOwnerAccountName

* NSFileGroupOwnerAccountName

* NSFileReferenceCount (# of hard links)

* NSFileIdentifier

* NSFilePosixPermissions (the rwx permissions)

* NSFileExtensionHidden

* NSFileHFSCreatorCode

* HSFileHFSTypeCode

* NSFileType (This is a string that says whether it is of type Directory, Regular, Symbolic Link, etc.)

In Carbon, you can use calls like **FSGetCatalogInfo()** to get an FSCatalogInfo structure that has information like AppleShare sharing flags, the creation date, the backup date, Finder information, the logical and physical size of the data and resource fork, as well as a text encoding hint.

getattrlist()

Darwin introduces a new function, **getattrlist()**, that returns file metadata. In addition to the metadata that **stat()** gives you, **getattrlist()** can give you a whole lot more. You can pick and choose the individual pieces of metadata that you want to look at. If you are only interested in seeing a file's size and last access time, **getattrlist()** can be told to just return those two pieces of metadata and not worry about anything else.

One caveat before we dig into **getattrlist()**: this function has existed since Mac OS X 10.0, but was first documented in Mac OS X 10.4. The man page is full of caveats and a bit of humor, such as "For reasons that are not at all obvious" and "Generally not a useful value." **getattrlist()** is not defined to work for all file system types. We will be hitting the highlights here, and you can find the full description in the **getattrlist()** manpage.

```
int getattrlist (const char *path, struct attrlist *attrList,
                 void *attrBuf, size_t attrBufSize,
                 unsigned long options)
```

You supply the `path` of the file for which you want the metadata. `attrBuf` and `attrBufSize` are where the metadata will stored. The return value from **getattrlist()** is zero on success, -1 on error, with the actual error placed in `errno`.

One word of warning: if you ask for too much data, **getattrlist()** will silenty truncate the data it places in the buffer. There are some structures, that you will see later, that reference data in other places in the buffer, which could end up referencing memory off the end of the buffer. There is no easy way to determine if **getattrlist()** truncates data, so be sure make your buffers large enough. Each of the different attributes has either a defined size, or a maximum size on the data that can be returned.

The `options` argument can be zero, or `FSOPT_NOFOLLOW` to not follow a symbolic link if it occurs as the last component of `path`.

Describing the Attributes

A `struct attrlist` is used to tell **getattrlist()** which bits of metadata you are interested in:

```
struct attrlist {
    u_short        bitmapcount; /* number of bit sets here */
    u_int16_t      padding;     /* for 4-byte alignment */
    attrgroup_t    commonattr;  /* common attributes */
    attrgroup_t    volattr;     /* volume attributes */
    attrgroup_t    dirattr;     /* directory attributes */
    attrgroup_t    fileattr;    /* file attributes */
    attrgroup_t    forkattr;    /* fork attributes */
};
```

The structure starts out with `bitmapcount`, which is the number of `attrgroup_t`s that the structure contains. An `attrgroup_t` is just an unsigned 32-bit integer. The current version of `struct attrlist` has five entries. There is a handy define, `ATTR_BIT_MAP_COUNT`, available to use for this value. After a bit of padding to keep everything on 4-byte alignment, the five bitmaps follow. Set bits in these bitmaps using the bitwise-OR operator, to indicate the attributes you are interested in. Be sure to zero out the entire structure before setting any specific attribute flags.

`commonattr` contains bitmap flags for attributes that relate to all types of file system objects. Here are some common attributes you may be interested in. The typenames mentioned in each attribute are what get placed into your `attrBuf`:

ATTR_CMN_NAME

> The name of the file, represented by an `attrreference_t` structure. It is a zero-terminated UTF-8 C string. The `attrreference_t` structure will be described in the section below that talks about parsing the returned attributes.

ATTR_CMN_OBJTYPE

> The type of the file. The values are taken from `enum vtype` that is defined in `<sys/vnode.h>`. Common values include VREG (regular file), VDIR (directory), VLNK (symbolic link)

ATTR_CMN_MODTIME

> The modification time of the file, represented as a `struct timespec`. This is equivalent to `st_mtimespec` in `struct stat`. You can access other file times by using `ATTR_CMN_CRTIME` (creation time), `ATTR_CMN_CHGTIME` (last attribute modification time), and `ATTR_CMN_ACCTIME` (time of last access).

ATTR_CMN_OWNERID

> The owner of the file, represented as a `uid_t`. You can get the group name with `ATTR_CMD_GRPID`, which places a `gid_t` into the attributes buffer.

ATTR_ACCESSMASK

> The access permissions of the file represented as a `mode_t`. This is equivalent to `st_mode` in `struct stat`

`volattr` contains bitmap flags for attributes that relate to mounted volumes. The `path` should refer to the volume's mountpoint.

ATTR_VOL_INFO

> If you are wanting any volume attributes to be returned, you must include this value in the bitmask. This does not result in any attribute data actually being returned.

ATTR_VOL_SIZE

> The total size of the volume, in bytes, represented by an `off_t`.

ATTR_VOL_SPACEFREE

> The free space of the volume, in bytes, represented by an `off_t`.

ATTR_VOL_SPACEAVAIL

> The space, in bytes, on the volume that is available to non-privileged users. Volumes reserve an amount of free space to prevent disk exhaustion errors. You should report this value, and not `ATTR_VOL_SPACEFREE`, to users.

ATTR_VOL_IOBLOCKSIZE

> The optimal block size to use when reading or writing data. This is an `unsigned long`.

ATTR_VOL_FILECOUNT

> The number of files currently on the volume. Also an `unsigned long`.

ATTR_VOL_DIRCOUNT

> The number of directories currently on the volume. An unsigned long

ATTR_VOL_NAME

> An `attrreference_t` structure containing the name of the volume. This is a UTF-8 zero-terminated C string. The data length will not be greater than NAME_MAX + 1.

ATTR_VOL_CAPABILITIES

> A `vol_capabilities_attr_t` structure that describes the optional features supported by the volume. Consult the **getattrlist()** manpage for the `vol_capabilities_attr_t` and the different volume capabilities supported.

ATTR_VOL_ATTRIBUTES

> A `vol_attributes_attr_t` structure that describes the attributes supported by the volume. Likewise, consult the manpage for details on using this.

`dirattr` contains bitmap flags for attributes that relate to directories. There are two other flags, but they're documented as either "you should not always rely on this value being accurate" and "Due to a bug, this flag is never set on current systems". So this is the only directory attribute you should use:

ATTR_DIR_ENTRYCOUNT

> An `unsigned long` with the number of file system objects in the directory, not including things like . and .., termed "synthetic entries."

`fileattr` contains bitmap flags for attributes that relate to regular files.

ATTR_FILE_TOTALSIZE

> The total number of bytes of all forks of a file, represented by an `off_t`. This is the logical size of a file. If a text file had 40 characters in it, the logical size would be 40.

ATTR_FILE_ALLOCSIZE

> The total number of bytes on disk used by all of the file's forks. This is the physical size of a file. If the 40-character text file was living on a volume with a 4K block size, the physical size of the file would be 4K.

ATTR_FILE_IOBLOCKSIZE

> The optimal block size to use when reading or writing this file's data. This is an `unsigned long`

ATTR_FILE_DATALENGTH

> The logical size of the data fork for the file. This is an `off_t`. You can use `ATTR_FILE_DATAALLOCSIZE` to get the physical size of the data fork.

ATTR_FILE_RSRCLENGTH

> The logical size of the resource fork for the file. This is an `off_t`. You can use `ATTR_FILE_RSRCALLOCSIZE` to get the physical size of the resource fork.

The `forkattr` bitmap should be left empty. According to the manpage, "Fork attributes are not properly implemented by any current Mac OS X volume format implementation. We strongly recommend that client programs do not request fork attributes"

Parsing the Buffer

The data that is placed into your buffer by **getattrlist()** is placed in the order that the attribute bitmap flags are listed in the man page (and the order they are listed here). The scalar types, such as mode_t, off_t, unsigned long, are stacked end-to-end, sometimes with padding to align values to natural byte boundaries. Typically you will define a struct that lays out the data types you're expecting back, and then cast your buffer's address to a pointer of this type.

The variable-length attributes (particularly names) are accessed indirectly using an attrreference_t. If you are using the struct-overlay idiom, you would have an attrreference_t in your struct. An attrreference_t looks like this:

```
typedef struct attrreference {
    long        attr_dataoffset;
    size_t      attr_length;
} attrreference_t;
```

To get at the actual data, you would add attr_dataoffset to the address of the attrreference_t in the struct. For instance, you might be asking for the file name and the modification time. Your overlay struct might look like this:

```
typedef struct PermTypeAttributes {
    unsigned long length;
    attrreference_t name;
    struct timespec modTime;
} PermTypeAttributes;
```

After you call **getattrlist()**, set up your overlay:

```
PermTypeAttributes *permAttributes;
permAttributes = (PermTypeAttributes *) buffer;
```

Then you would access the name like this:

```
char *filenameFromAttrs;
filenameFromAttrs = ((char *)&permAttributes->name)
    + permAttributes->name.attr_dataoffset;
```

Example 9-4 is the permtype program, but implemented using **getattrlist()** rather than **stat()**.

Example 9-4. permtype-getattrlist.m

```
// permtype-getattrlist.m -- use getattrlist() to discover type and
//                           permissions for a file.

/* compile with
cc -g -o permtype-getattrlist permtype-getattrlist.m
*/

#import <sys/stat.h>    // for stat() and struct stat
#import <stdlib.h>      // for EXIT_SUCCESS
#import <stdio.h>       // for printf
#import <errno.h>       // for errno
#import <grp.h>         // for group file access routines
```

```
#import <pwd.h>          // for passwd file access routines
#import <sys/attr.h>     // for attribute structures
#import <unistd.h>       // for getattrlist()
#import <string.h>       // for memset()

// cheesy little lookup table for mapping perm value to the
// familiar character string
static const char *g_perms[]  = {
    "---", "--x", "-w-", "-wx", "r--", "r-x", "rw-", "rwx"
};

typedef struct StatType {
    unsigned long       mask;
    const char          *type;
} StatType;

static StatType g_types[] = {
    { S_IFREG, "Regular File" },
    { S_IFDIR, "Directory" },
    { S_IFLNK, "Symbolic Link" },
    { S_IFCHR, "Character Special Device" },
    { S_IFBLK, "Block Special Device" },
    { S_IFIFO, "FIFO" },
    { S_IFSOCK, "Socket" },
};

// structure of the data being returned by getattrlist()

typedef struct PermTypeAttributes {
    unsigned long       length;
    attrreference_t     name;
    struct timespec     modTime;
    struct timespec     changeTime;
    struct timespec     accessTime;
    uid_t               ownerId;
    gid_t               groupId;
    short               padding;
    mode_t              accessMask;
    off_t               fileLogicalSize;
} PermTypeAttributes;

void displayInfo (const char *filename)
{
    struct attrlist attrList;

    // must clear out the structure first, otherwise we'll get
    // undefined results
    memset (&attrList, 0, sizeof(attrList));
    attrList.bitmapcount = ATTR_BIT_MAP_COUNT;

    // get the name, the permissions, and the stat-style times
    attrList.commonattr = ATTR_CMN_NAME
        | ATTR_CMN_MODTIME | ATTR_CMN_CHGTIME | ATTR_CMN_ACCTIME
        | ATTR_CMN_OWNERID | ATTR_CMN_GRPID | ATTR_CMN_ACCESSMASK;

    // also get the size
    attrList.fileattr = ATTR_FILE_TOTALSIZE;
```

```
// the returned data cannot be larger than this, so we're safe
// as far as silent data truncation goes
char attrBuffer[sizeof(PermTypeAttributes) + NAME_MAX + 1];

int result = getattrlist (filename, &attrList, attrBuffer,
                          sizeof(attrBuffer), 0);

if (result == -1) {
    fprintf (stderr, "error with getattrlist(%s) : %d / %s\n",
             filename, errno, strerror(errno));
    return;
}

// overlay our structure on top of the returned bytes
PermTypeAttributes *permAttributes;
permAttributes = (PermTypeAttributes *) attrBuffer;

// get to the string data from the attribute
char *filenameFromAttrs;
filenameFromAttrs = ((char *)&permAttributes->name)
    + permAttributes->name.attr_dataoffset;

printf ("%s:\n", filenameFromAttrs);

printf ("  permissions: %s%s%s\n",
        g_perms[(permAttributes->accessMask & S_IRWXU) >> 6],
        g_perms[(permAttributes->accessMask & S_IRWXG) >> 3],
        g_perms[(permAttributes->accessMask & S_IRWXO)]);

// figure out the type
StatType *scan, *stop;
scan = g_types;
stop = scan + (sizeof(g_types) / sizeof(StatType));

while (scan < stop) {
    if ((permAttributes->accessMask & S_IFMT)
        == scan->mask) {
        printf ("  type: %s\n", scan->type);
        break;
    }
    scan++;
}

// any special bits sets?
if ((permAttributes->accessMask & S_ISUID) == S_ISUID) {
    printf ("  set-uid!\n");
}
if ((permAttributes->accessMask & S_ISGID) == S_ISUID) {
    printf ("  set-group-id!\n");
}

// file size
printf ("  file is %lld bytes (%lld K)\n",
        permAttributes->fileLogicalSize,
        permAttributes->fileLogicalSize / 1024);
```

```
            // owning user / group
            {
                struct passwd *passwd;
                struct group *group;

                passwd = getpwuid (permAttributes->ownerId);
                group = getgrgid (permAttributes->groupId);

                printf ("   user: %s (%d)\n", passwd->pw_name,
                        permAttributes->ownerId);
                printf ("  group: %s (%d)\n", group->gr_name,
                        permAttributes->groupId);
            }

            // now the dates
            {
                char buffer[1024];
                struct tm *tm;

                tm = localtime (&permAttributes->accessTime.tv_sec);
                strftime (buffer, 1024, "%c", tm);
                printf ("   last access: %s\n", buffer);

                tm = localtime (&permAttributes->modTime.tv_sec);
                strftime (buffer, 1024, "%c", tm);
                printf ("   last modification: %s\n", buffer);

                tm = localtime (&permAttributes->changeTime.tv_sec);
                strftime (buffer, 1024, "%c", tm);
                printf ("   last inode change: %s\n", buffer);
            }

            // double-space output
            printf ("\n");

        } // displayInfo

        int main (int argc, char *argv[])
        {
            int i;

            if (argc == 1) {
                fprintf (stderr, "usage:  %s /path/to/file ... \n", argv[0]);
                exit (EXIT_FAILURE);
            }

            for (i = 1; i < argc; i++) {
                displayInfo (argv[i]);
            }

            exit (EXIT_SUCCESS);

        } // main
```

The output from this program is identical to the output from permtype.

Metadata in Batches

So why talk about **getdirentries()** and **getattrlist()** when there are perfectly functional POSIX calls to do the same work? Both of those functions lead up to the somewhat unpronounceable **getdirentriesattr()** function that lets you get file attributes in bulk. You can get metadata for many files with a single call to **getdirentriesattr()**, which in some cases can make your program faster.

```
int getdirentriesattr (int fd, struct attrlist *attrList,
                       void *attrBuf, size_t attrBufSize,
                       unsigned long *count,
                       unsigned long *basePointer,
                       unsigned long *newState,
                       unsigned long options);
```

getdirentriesattr() reads directory entries, like with **readdir()** and **getdirentries()**, and returns their attributes, like with **stat()** and **getattrlist()**. fd is an open file descriptor for the directory you want to iterate through. Just open the directory using **open()**. attrList is the set of attributes you want for each file. This is constructed just like the attribute list for **getattrlist**. attrBuf is the chunk of memory where the attributes should be stored, and pass the length of this buffer in attrBufSize.

count is an in/out parameter. You pass in the number of directory entries you are interested in seeing, and the function will pass back through that parameter the number of entires it actually placed into the buffer. Unlike **getattrlist()**, this function will not silently truncate your data. The basePointer parameter is an out parameter, giving you the offset into the directory, in case you need to **lseek()** at a later time. Usually the value can be ignored, but you still have to pass a valid address here. newState is an out parameter too, which changes value if the directory has been modified since you started iterating through it. Finally, options should have zero passed. There is one option described in the man page, with the tantalizingly vague statement "This option allowed for specific performance optimizations for specific clients on older systems"

On a successful completion the function returns 0, and 1 if the call completed and it has returned the last entry. -1 returned on errors, and check errno.

The data is arranged in the buffer like it is with **getattrlist()**. Each file's run of attributes starts out with a 4-byte length value. This is the number of bytes of attributes for that file. Add this length to the attribute's starting address to find the next batch. Variable length attributes are stored like **getatrlist()** as well, by using the attr_dataoffset element to find the location in the buffer of the filename data.

Example 9-5 calculates the amount of disk space consumed by a folder. It uses both **stat()** and **getdirentriesattr()**.

Example 9-5. foldersize.m

```
// foldersize.m -- calculate the size of a folder

/* compile with
cc -g -Wmost -o foldersize foldersize.m
*/

#import <sys/types.h>   // for random type definition
```

```
#import <sys/dirent.h>   // for struct dirent
#import <dirent.h>       // for getdirentries()
#import <stdlib.h>       // for EXIT_SUCCESS
#import <stdio.h>        // for printf
#import <errno.h>        // for errno
#import <string.h>       // for strerror
#import <fcntl.h>        // for O_RDONLY
#import <sys/stat.h>     // for struct statbuf and stat()
#import <sys/param.h>    // for MAXPATHLEN
#import <sys/attr.h>     // for attrreference_t
#import <unistd.h>       // for getdirentriesattr()
#import <sys/vnode.h>    // for VDIR

// show the files and sizes of the files as they are processed
static int g_verbose = 0;

// -------------------------------------------------
// stat code

off_t sizeForFolderStat (char *path)
{
    off_t size = 0;

    DIR *directory;
    directory = opendir (path);

    if (directory == NULL) {
        fprintf (stderr, "could not open directory '%s'\n", path);
        fprintf (stderr, "error is %d/%s\n", errno, strerror(errno));
        exit (EXIT_FAILURE);
    }

    struct dirent *entry;
    while ( (entry = readdir(directory)) != NULL) {
        char filename[MAXPATHLEN];

        // don't mess with the metadirectories
        if (strcmp(entry->d_name, ".") == 0
            || strcmp(entry->d_name, "..") == 0) {
            continue;
        }

        // rather than changing the cwd each time through the loop,
        // construct the full path relative the given path.
        // since the original path is either absolute, or relative to
        // the current working directory, this should always give us
        // a stat-able path
        snprintf (filename, MAXPATHLEN, "%s/%s",
                  path, entry->d_name);

        struct stat statbuf;
        int result;

        // use lstat so we don't multiply-coun the sizes of files that
        // are pointed to by symlinks
        result = lstat (filename, &statbuf);
```

```
            if (result != 0) {
                fprintf (stderr, "could not stat '%s': %d/%s\n",
                          entry->d_name, errno, strerror(errno));
                continue;
            }

            if (S_ISDIR(statbuf.st_mode)) {
                size += sizeForFolderStat (filename);

            } else {
                if (g_verbose) {
                    printf ("%lld %s\n",
                              statbuf.st_size, entry->d_name);
                }

                size += statbuf.st_size;
            }
        }

    closedir (directory);

    return (size);

} // sizeForFolderStat

// -------------------------------------------------
// getdirentriesattr

// the attributes we want to get with each call to getdirentriesattr
static struct attrlist g_attrlist; // gets zeroed automatically

// this is the data being returned by each call

typedef struct fileinfo {
    unsigned long length;
    attrreference_t  name;
    fsobj_type_t objType;
    off_t logicalSize;
} fileinfo;

// try to pick up this many entries each time through
#define ENTRIES_COUNT 30

// don't know how long each file name is, so make a guess so
// we can size the results buffer
#define AVG_NAME_GUESSTIMATE 64

off_t sizeForFolderAttr (char *path)
{
    off_t size = 0;
    int fd = open (path, O_RDONLY);

    if (fd == -1) {
        fprintf (stderr,
                  "could not open directory '%s'.  Error %d %s\n",
                  path, errno, strerror(errno));
        goto bailout;
```

```
    }

    // a rough guess on the appropriate buffer size
    char attrbuf[ENTRIES_COUNT
                 * (sizeof(fileinfo) + AVG_NAME_GUESSTIMATE)];

    unsigned long count;
    unsigned long newState = 0;
    unsigned long base;

    int result;

    while (1) {
        count = ENTRIES_COUNT;
        result = getdirentriesattr (fd, &g_attrlist,
                                    attrbuf, sizeof(attrbuf),
                                    &count, &base,
                                    &newState, 0);
        if (result < 0) {
            fprintf (stderr,
                     "error with getdirentriesattr for '%s'. %d/%s\n",
                     path, errno, strerror(errno));
            goto bailout;
        }
        if (result == 1) {
            // we're done
            break;
        }

        // walk the returned buffer
        fileinfo *scan = (fileinfo *) attrbuf;

        for (; count > 0; count--) {
            if (scan->objType == VDIR) {
                char filename[MAXPATHLEN];

                // see comment about paths up in sizeForFolderStat()
                snprintf (filename, MAXPATHLEN, "%s/%s", path,
                          ((char *) &scan->name)
                          + scan->name.attr_dataoffset);

                size += sizeForFolderAttr (filename);

            } else {
                if (g_verbose) {
                    printf ("%lld %s\n", scan->logicalSize,
                            ((char *) &scan->name)
                            + scan->name.attr_dataoffset);
                }

                size += scan->logicalSize;
            }

            // move to the next attribute in the returned set.
            scan = (fileinfo*) (((char *) scan) + scan->length);
        }
    }
```

```
bailout:
    close (fd);

    return (size);

} // sizeForFolderAttr



int main (int argc, char *argv[])
{
    // sanity check the program argument first
    if (argc != 3) {
        fprintf (stderr,
                "usage:  %s {stat|attr} /path/to/directory\n",
                argv[0]);
        exit (EXIT_FAILURE);
    }
    off_t size = 0;

    if (strcmp(argv[1], "stat") == 0) {
        size = sizeForFolderStat (argv[2]);

    } else if (strcmp(argv[1], "attr") == 0) {

        // these are the attributes we're wanting.  Set them up in
        // global so we don't have to do a memset + this jazz
        // on every recursion

        g_attrlist.bitmapcount = ATTR_BIT_MAP_COUNT;
        g_attrlist.commonattr = ATTR_CMN_NAME | ATTR_CMN_OBJTYPE;
        g_attrlist.fileattr = ATTR_FILE_DATALENGTH;
        // using ATTR_FILE_TOTALSIZE would be better, so that we get
        // the space consumed by resource forks, but we're using this
        // code to parallel what stat gives us, which doesn't include
        // resource fork size.

        size = sizeForFolderAttr (argv[2]);

    } else {
        fprintf (stderr,
                "usage:  %s {stat|attr} /path/to/directory\n",
                argv[0]);
        exit (EXIT_FAILURE);
    }

    printf ("size is %lld bytes (%lld K).\n",
            size, size / 1024);

    return (EXIT_SUCCESS);

} // main
```

You run the program by telling it whether you want to run the "stat" or "attr" version of the code, and also give it a starting directory:

```
% ./foldersize stat ~/Projects/core-osx
size is 87608376 bytes (85555 K).

% ./foldersize attr ~/Projects/core-osx
size is 87608376 bytes (85555 K).
```

Things get interesting when you start timing the program.

```
% time ./foldersize stat ~
size is 2011237930 bytes (1964099 K).
0.727u 10.416s 0:31.22 35.6% 0+0k 3137+2io 0pf+0w

% time ./foldersize attr ~
size is 2011237930 bytes (1964099 K).
0.131u 3.534s 0:17.55 20.8% 0+0k 3285+0io 0pf+0w
```

The time command is discussed in Chapter 25 (Performance), but the thing to look for here is the time. It took 31 seconds to crawl through my home directory with the stat() version, but only 18 seconds with the getdirentriesattr() function.

Mac OS X Specific Weirdness

Since OS X is a hybrid between classic Mac OS and Unix, there are some peculiarities unique to OS X.

Resource forks

The first weirdness are resource forks, the additional stream that files have which store structured data. At the file system level, forks are really just two files that happen to share a name. Until Mac OS X 10.4, the Unix command line utilities did not know resource forks were there and so it was possible for the resource fork to get lost or corrupted. cp and tar, for instance, did not preserve the fork. You can get replacement programs (like hfstar) for older systems that will preserve the resource fork.

In the command line environment you cannot really see the resource fork unless you append /..namedfork/rsrc to the name of the file. For example, the outline processor used to outline big chunks of this book is a 1990's version of More running in the Classic environment. Here is a look at More in the terminal:

```
$ cd /Applications
$ ls -l MORE
-rw-r--r--  1 markd  unknown  0 Jun 23 12:18 MORE
```

Hmmm, nothing there. But back in the Old Days, almost nothing was put into an application's data fork. Everything went into the resource fork:

```
$ ls -l MORE/..namedfork/rsrc
-rw-r--r--  1 markd  unknown  607251 Jun 23 12:18 MORE/..namedfork/rsrc
```

Most of the calls you have seen in this chapter do not pay any attention to the resource fork, they just look at the data fork. If you need to support resource fork reading and writing, you will need to use the Carbon libraries. getattrlist() and getdirentriesattr() will give you metadata about the resource fork.

.DS_Store

If you `ls -a` in directories, you will probably find a file named `.DS_Store`. This is a cache file the `Finder` writes that contains file names and icon placement. When mounting network volumes, the `Finder` will scribble the files into any directory the user visits, which can sometimes lead to friction between the Mac users and with the people who run the file servers.

Disk I/O and sleep

A programmer on one of the mailing lists was describing a problem he was having with a program works like `tail -f`, which monitors log file and reads any new stuff that is appended. Much to his horror, machines that were running this program would never go to sleep. If a lot of I/O happens (say more than one physical disk I/O every couple of seconds) the OS considers the machine to be busy and will not go to sleep. In this particular case he was seeking to the end and attempting to read. The suggestion was to use **stat()** instead to see if the file changed size. **stat()** does not cause physical I/O once the inode for a file is cached in memory.

For The More Curious

Differences between HFS+ and UFS

The Apple engineers did a masterful job of integrating HFS+ (the default disk format) into the world of Unix. The above discussion about inodes is more accurate for UFS (the Unix file system, also known as the Berkeley Fast File System), but the general concepts apply to both worlds.

In HFS+, file name encoding is in unicode rather than ASCII. File names are also case preserving, but case insensitive. Traditional Unix file systems are case sensitive. The Apple teams originally thought this case preserving / case sensitive difference would cause lots of problems, but it turns out to be not so bad. There are not many examples in the real world where the case of letters in filenames are used to discriminate. Unfortunately, with the `make` command, `makefile` and `Makefile` are different beasts. There are also some parts of the CPAN Perl archive that have distinct files that differ only in the case of their names. A way around this limitation is to create a UFS partition for these malcontents, or else use `Disk Utility` to create a UFS disk image.

The path separator for UFS is `/`, but in HFS+ is `:`. This is addressed by the HFS+ file system implementation converting colons to slashes and vice versa. The file system sees colons, but everything above that is slashes. Carbon does another transform back into colons since that is the path separator used.

HFS+ lacks support for hard links. It is actually implemented by a kernel-level symbolic link visible only to the HFS+ file system. The behavior is very similar to hard links when viewed from above the kernel, but they are relatively inefficient in comparison.

UFS does not support file IDs. File IDs are persistent handles to files similar to inodes, and they can be used similar to path names in Unix. The nice thing about file IDs is that once the ID is obtained the file can be renamed or moved anywhere on disk and still be found and opened. Also, in HFS+, access by ID is faster than by path (since it avoids path parsing and traversal). These file IDs are part of how aliases do their thing.

HFS+ also allows for arbitrarily named file attributes. Mac OS X lets you get and set these attributes.

HFS+ filenames are at most 255 characters long, or 512 bytes. Files have a maximum size of 2^{63} bytes.

From running experiments, it does not look like HFS+ supports holes in files. In traditional Unix file systems, if you write a byte, seek 100 megs, then write another byte, your file will only occupy two disk blocks. The intervening zero-filled blocks will not actually be consuming space in the file system. This is a disk space optimization for files that could have large ranges of zeros in them (like core files).

There are differences in deletion semantics between classic Mac OS and OS X. In Mac OS, if you try to delete a file someone else currently has open, the delete fails. This is opposed to traditional Unix where the delete happens but the disk blocks do not get reclaimed until the file is closed. This behavior led some Mac developers to use open files as semaphores, controlling behavior among multiple programs. This difference is in part due to the implementation of the different file systems. In UFS, metadata is in the inode, stored separately from the data. In HFS+, the metadata is stored in with the file data, and there is no real inode. In either case, the kernel caches the metadata so that the **stat()** call will not cause physical I/O.

The differences in permission semantics are important. OS 9 totally ignores the Unix permission bits. Someone can boot into OS 9 and have free reign over a disk, bypassing all security. This is not a problem in Classic since Classic is just another program running as the current user.

Also, files that are created in OS 9 do not have these permission bits. If a file created in OS 9 is then looked at under OS X, the system plays some games. The owner, group, and mode are shown as some reasonable default (by looking at the permissions on the directory node on which the file system is mounted). The actual permission bits on disk remain unset unless the user sets them explicitly.

There are some cultural differences regarding file names. Mac OS users are used to spaces and special characters in their file names while Unix folks are not. This can lead to really bad situations like the iTunes installer wiping out entire disks because it did not consider that a volume name might have a space in it. So if you are doing any file name manipulations (especially in shell scripts), be sure to keep this in mind.

System directories that Unix folks are familiar with (/etc, /usr, /tmp, /var) are hidden at the application level, and some are hidden behind symlinks so that casual Mac users will not need to worry about them.

The usual Unix software install paradigm (put library files into */lib, program files into */bin, documentation int */share) does not work that well with individually administered systems like personal computers. One program can end up scattering junk everywhere, making uninstalling a real pain. NeXT bundles (the directories that behave like files) addressed a lot of problems here. The OS folks liked bundles so much, they followed the same scheme for system-wide libraries. Rather than put stuff into /usr/include and /usr/lib, it goes into framework bundles.

Other random calls

Here are some system calls that did not fit in well anyplace else.

```
int rename (const char *from, const char *to);
```

This causes `from` to be renamed to `to`. This is just inode/directory manipulation, so both `from` and `to` must live on the same file system, in which case you will need to copy the data. This returns zero on success, -1 / `errno` on error.

```
int dup (int fd);
```

```
int dup2 (int fd, int newfd);
```

These functions duplicate an existing file descriptor, as if you opened the file again. The return value of **dup()** is a file descriptor that is guaranteed to be the lowest numbered available (or -1 on error). The original file is not closed. A use for **dup()** is for reassigning one of the standard streams. You can close the file descriptor zero (standard in), open another file (say a log file), and then **dup()** that descriptor so that you get `fd` zero.

dup2() has slightly different semantics. It will create a duplicate file descriptor at a particular file descriptor value. If there is already a file open using that descriptor, it is closed first. This is another way of replacing the standard streams. Since it does a **close()** and **dup()** in one operation, it is atomic.

Note that duplicated file descriptors share the same reference in the per-process file table. So a write to one `fd` will move the current location of the second `fd`. If you want a true independent reference, reopen the file.

The **fcntl()** function is the kitchen-sink function for setting various attributes on file descriptors and for performing some operations as well:

```
int fcntl (int fd, int cmd, int arg);
```

`fd` is the file descriptor to manipulate. This can be an opened file, a network connection, or any other entity that is referred to by a file descriptor. `cmd` is the command to apply to the file descriptor, and `arg` is an argument to the command. Here are some **fcntl()** commands:

F_DUPFD

>   Duplicate a file descriptor. The new `fd` is the lowest numbered descriptor that is not open that is greater than or equal to the third argument (as an integer).

F_GETFD / F_SETFD

>   Get/set per-processor file descriptor flags (currently the only flag is FD_CLOEXEC, to close the file automatically in child processes).

F_GETFL / F_SETFL

>   Get/set kernel status flags: Such as O_RDONLY / O_WRONLY / O_APPEND, etc.

F_GETOWN / F_SETOWN

>   Get/set async i/o ownership.

Duplicating descriptors low with **dup()** and **dup2()** makes sense when redirecting streams. Why the F_DUPD behavior, then, of duplicating things higher? This actually came in really handy with AOLserver on older versions of IRIX, the Unix-like system that ran on Silicon Graphics workstations. AOLserver had an embedded Tcl interpreter that used buffered I/O FILEs for certain commands. Unfortunately, IRIX only used a 8-bit value to store the file descriptor value in these structures, so you could have at most 253 of these FILEs. Whenever a non-FILE fd was created (by a new connection from across the network, or opening a file to be returned to the web browser), the fd was duplicated to a value greater than 256 using **fcntl**(F_DUPFD), leaving the lower values free for the Tcl interpreter.

```
int truncate (const char *path, off_t length);

int ftruncate (int fd, off_t length);
```

These truncate a file (whether by path or an open file descriptor) to be at most the given length. Extra data is lost, but the file is not grown.

```
long pathconf (const char *path, int name);

long fpathconf (int fd, int name);
```

These provide applications a way to determine the current value of some system limits or options. Here are some possible names:

_PC_LINK_MAX

The maximum file link count.

_PC_NAME_MAX

The maximum number of bytes in a file name.

_PC_PATH_MAX

The maximum number of bytes in a pathname.

_PC_PIPE_BUF

The maximum number of bytes that will be written atomically to a pipe.

If the call fails, -1 is returned and errno is set. If the given variable does not have a limit, -1 is returned and errno is not modified. Otherwise, the current value is returned.

```
int sysctl (int *name, u_int namelen, void *oldp, size_t *oldlenp,
            void *newp, size_t newlen);
```

This retrieves system information and lets processes (with appropriate privileges) set system information. There are all sorts of information you can get from this, like kernel debug values, machine model, cpu count, native byte order, amount of physical memory, the kernel page size, etc. Check out the man page for more details.

Other random programs

You saw `lsof` earlier, which shows open files system wide.

The `chflags` program is similar to the linux `chattr` program. It lets you set some attributes on the file. Of particular interest are the `[no]schg` and `[no]uchg` flags, which set the system and user immutable flags. When these are set, the files cannot be modified even if their file permissions would allow it. This is handy for hardening a file system against attackers. Most "script-kiddie" system crackers are not prepared for immutable files. This is also the flag that the `Finder` sets when you select the Locked attribute of a file.

`/Developer/Tools/SetFile` sets attributes of HFS+ files, which include whether a file is an alias, it is a bundle, has a custom icon, is on the desktop, is locked, or is invisible. You can also use it to set the file type and creator.

Cocoa APIs of interest

The equivalent of **`getcwd()`** in Cocoa is `[[NSFileManager defaultManager] currentDirectoryPath]`. You do not need to worry about hardcoded `MAXPATHLEN` issues.

`NSFileManager`'s **`movePath: toPath:`** is a single function call to move and rename files. This will copy across file system boundaries. Note that this always does a copy, even on the same file system. In general, try **`rename()`** first. If that returns an `errno` of `EXDEV`, use this **`NSFileManager`** call. If you are worried about preserving the resource fork, ignore **`rename()`** and just use this.

Access Control Lists

Mac OS X 10.4 introduces access control lists, commonly abbreviated ACLs. An access control list is a set of permissions in addition to, and sometimes superseding, traditional unix permissions. This allows you to specify that a particular user has access (or is denied access) to a particular file with a particular kind of action. Mac OS X's ACLs are based on the Windows NTFS ACLs.

ACLs are not enabled by default on OS X client as of version 10.4, so you may have to enable them yourself by using `fsaclctl`:

```
# /usr/sbin/fsaclctl -e -p /
```

Once ACLs are enabled, you can use the `chmod` command to grant permissions:

```
$ chmod +a "markd allow read" spoon.txt
```

Use the `-le` flag to show the extra permissions:

```
$ ls -le spoon.txt
ls -le spoon
-r-------- + 1 oopack  wheel  12 Jun  6 16:58 spoon.txt
 0: user:markd allow read
```

For all file system objects you can specify permissions on who can delete the object, who can read or write attributes or extended attributes, who can read or write security information, and who can `chown` the file.

For files, you can put permissions on who can read, write, append, or execute a file. For directories you have control over who can list, search, add files to, add subdirectories to, or delete children. The ACL API has over 30 function calls in it, so we will not be discussing it here because the kernel will automatically apply ACLs when you try to open files or perform other file manipulations. Check the `acl` man page for details.

Extended Attributes

Extended attributes, introduced in Mac OS X 10.4, are name/data pairs associated with file system objects. The name is a zero-terminated UTF-8 string, with the value being any kind of data. You can set an extended attribute with **setxattr()**:

```
int setxattr (const char *path, const char *name, void *value,
              size_t size, u_int32_t position, int options);
```

`path` is the path to the file to set the attribute for. `name` is the extended attribute to set. The value of the attribute is specified by `value` and its `size`. The `position` is used as an offset into the attribute so you can change parts of an extended attribute in-place. `options` controls symlink following behavior (XATTR_NOFOLLOW), and flags to control creation and replacing behavior: XATTR_CREATE will fail if the named attribute already exists, and XATTR_REPLACE will fail if the named attribute does not to exist. If you don't specify either one of these flags, **setxattr()** will allow both creation and replacement. If you already have a file open, you can use **fsetxattr()**, which takes a file descriptor rather than a path name. This function returns zero on success, -1 on failure with `errno` set appropriately.

You can fetch extended attributes by using **getxattr()**:

```
ssize_t getxattr (const char *path, const char *name, void *value,
                  size_t size, u_int32_t position, int options);
```

This function retrieves up to `size` bytes from the attribute named `name` for the file specified by `path`. The `position` is the position within the attribute to start reading from, and `size` specifies how many bytes to read from the attribute. The only `option` available is XATTR_NOFOLLOW, which does not follow symbolic links. The function returns the amount of data actually read from the attribute, or -1 on error. In the error case, `errno` is set accordingly. If you already have an open file, you can use **fgetxattr()** to get attributes via an existing file descriptor.

When you are done with an extended attribute, you can remove it with **removexattr()**:

```
int removexattr (const char *path, const char *name, int options);
```

`path` is the path to the file, `name` is the name of the attribute to remove, and `option` can be zero, or XATTR_NOFOLLOW to not follow symbolic links. Returns zero on sucecss, -1 on failure, with `errno` set. If you already have an open file, you can use **fremovexattr()**.

To iterate through existing attributes, use **listxattr()**:

```
ssize_t listxattr (const char *path, char *namebuf, size_t size,
```

```
        int options);
```

listxattr() returns a list of names of extended attributes for the file referenced by path and deposits them into the buffer namebuf. If namebuf is NULL, the function returns the size of the list of extended attribute names so you can allocate enough memory. Of course, this is subject to race conditions: somebody else may change the attributes of the file between calling **listxattr()** with a NULL namebuf and the call with the actual buffer. options should either be zero, or XATTR_NOFOLLOW to not follow symbolic links. The size of the name list is returned. If there are no attributes, zero is returned. Otherwise -1 is returned and errno is set. As you might guess, there is a **flistxattr()** function that takes a file descriptor rather than a path.

Challenge

Using the directory enumeration and metadata functions, write a Cocoa program to descend into a directory hierarchy and build an **NSOutlineview** or **NSBrowser** view of the contents.

Chapter 10. NSFileManager

NSFileManager is a class in the Foundation framework that acts as a convenient wrapper for the Unix functions **unlink()**, **getdirentries()**, **stat()**, and **mkdir()**. In this chapter, you are going to create a simple file browser using **NSFileManager** and **NSTreeController**.

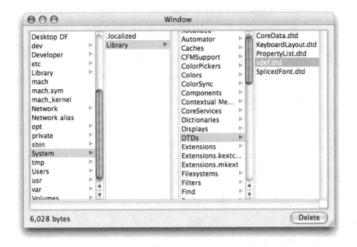

NSFileManager

Without going into too much detail, here are the basic types of methods that are in **NSFileManager**:

The method for getting the shared instance of **NSFileManager**:

+ (NSFileManager *)**defaultManager**

Wrappers for **stat()**:

- (NSDictionary *)**fileAttributesAtPath:**(NSString *)path
                             traverseLink:(BOOL)yorn

- (BOOL)**fileExistsAtPath:**(NSString *)path

- (BOOL)**fileExistsAtPath:**(NSString *)path
           isDirectory:(BOOL *)isDirectory

- (BOOL)**isReadableFileAtPath:**(NSString *)path

- (BOOL)**isWritableFileAtPath:**(NSString *)path

- (BOOL)**isExecutableFileAtPath:**(NSString *)path

- (BOOL)**isDeletableFileAtPath:**(NSString *)path

Change the file attributes:

- (BOOL)**changeFileAttributes:**(NSDictionary *)attributes
                      atPath:(NSString *)path

Linking, copying, and deleting files and directories:

- (BOOL)**linkPath:**(NSString *)src
          toPath:(NSString *)dest
        handler:(id)handler

- (BOOL)**copyPath:**(NSString *)src

```
            toPath: (NSString *)dest
          handler: (id)handler
```

- (BOOL)**movePath:** (NSString *)src
            toPath: (NSString *)dest
          handler: (id)handler

- (BOOL)**removeFileAtPath:** (NSString *)path
                  handler: (id)handler

Wrappers for getdirentries():

- (NSArray *)**directoryContentsAtPath:** (NSString *)path

- (NSDirectoryEnumerator *)**enumeratorAtPath:** (NSString *)path

- (NSArray *)**subpathsAtPath:** (NSString *)path;

Wrapper for **mkdir()**:

- (BOOL)**createDirectoryAtPath:** (NSString *)path
                  attributes: (NSDictionary *)attributes

Reading a file:

- (NSData *)**contentsAtPath:** (NSString *)path

Creating a file:

- (BOOL)**createFileAtPath:** (NSString *)path
              contents: (NSData *)data
            attributes: (NSDictionary *)attr

The display name (On Mac OS X, the display name and the filename may be different. For example, if the user has hidden extensions, the display name will not have the extension, but the filename will.):

- (NSString *)**displayNameAtPath:** (NSString *)path

Compare two files:

- (BOOL)**contentsEqualAtPath:** (NSString *)path1
                  andPath: (NSString *)path2

As you can see, **NSFileWrapper** has several very convenient methods. For example, **removeFileAtPath:handler:** will remove directories and their contents, thus it is often easier to use than **rmdir()** which only works on empty directories.

Make a File Browser

Create a new "Cocoa Application" project called **Remover**. (Besides browsing, your app will allow the user to delete files and directories.)

To represent the information about one directory entry (which may be a file or a directory), you will create a class called **DirEntry**. You will also have an **NSTreeController** and an **AppController**.

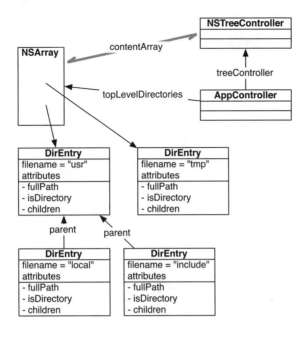

Create the DirEntry Class

The file system is essentially a tree; each node of the tree is a directory or a file. We are going to create a class to hold onto the information about one node, so create a class called **DirEntry**.

Each instance of **DirEntry** will know its parent, its file attributes, and its filename. If it is a directory, it will know how to create an array containing **DirEntry**s representing its children. Thus, make DirEntry.h look like this:

Example 10-1. DirEntry.h

```objc
#import <Cocoa/Cocoa.h>

@interface DirEntry : NSObject {
  NSDictionary *attributes;
  DirEntry *parent;
  NSString *filename;
}
+ (NSMutableArray *)entriesAtPath:(NSString *)path
                      withParent:(DirEntry *)d;
- (id)initWithFilename:(NSString *)fn
             parent:(DirEntry *)d;
- (NSString *)fullPath;
- (NSString *)filename;
- (NSDictionary *)attributes;
- (unsigned long long)fileSize;
- (BOOL)isDirectory;
- (BOOL)isLeaf;
- (NSArray *)children;
- (NSMutableArray *)components;
- (DirEntry *)parent;
@end
```

Now to implement these methods:

Example 10-2. DirEntry.m

```
#import "DirEntry.h"

@implementation DirEntry

#pragma mark Creation and Destruction

+ (NSMutableArray *)entriesAtPath:(NSString *)path
                       withParent:(DirEntry *)d
{
    NSMutableArray *result = [NSMutableArray array];
    NSArray *filenames;
    filenames = [[NSFileManager defaultManager] directoryContentsAtPath:pa
    if (filenames == nil) {
        NSRunAlertPanel(@"Read failed",
                        @"Unable to read \'%@\'",
                        nil, nil, nil,
                        path);
        return result;
    }
    int max, k;
    max = [filenames count];
    for (k = 0; k < max; k++) {
        DirEntry *newEntry;
        NSString *filename = [filenames objectAtIndex:k];
        newEntry = [[DirEntry alloc] initWithFilename:filename
                                               parent:d];
        [result addObject:newEntry];
        [newEntry release];
    }
    return result;
}

- (id)initWithFilename:(NSString *)fn
                parent:(DirEntry *)d
{
    [super init];
    parent = [d retain];
    filename = [fn copy];
    return self;
}

- (void)dealloc
{
    [attributes release];
    [filename release];
    [parent release];
    [super dealloc];
}

#pragma mark File info
```

```
- (NSMutableArray *)components
{
    NSMutableArray *result;
    if (!parent) {
        result = [NSMutableArray arrayWithObject:@"/"];
    } else {
        result = [parent components];
    }
    [result addObject:[self filename]];
    return result;
}

- (NSString *)fullPath
{
    return [NSString pathWithComponents:[self components]];
}

- (NSString *)filename
{
    return filename;
}

- (NSDictionary *)attributes
{
    if (!attributes) {
        NSString *path = [self fullPath];
        attributes = [[NSFileManager defaultManager] fileAttributesAtPath:path
                                                      traverseLink:YES];
        [attributes retain];
    }
    return attributes;
}

- (BOOL)isDirectory
{
    NSString *fileType = [[self attributes] fileType];
    return [fileType isEqual:NSFileTypeDirectory];
}

- (DirEntry *)parent
{
    return parent;
}

#pragma mark For use in bindings

- (BOOL)isLeaf
{
    return ![self isDirectory];
}

- (unsigned long long)fileSize
{
    return [[self attributes] fileSize];
}

- (NSArray *)children
```

```
    {
        NSString *path = [self fullPath];
        return [DirEntry entriesAtPath:path
                            withParent:self];
    }

@end
```

Notice that there is a category on **NSDictionary** that enables you to easily read information from the attributes dictionary. Here is the interface for that category:

```
@interface NSDictionary (NSFileAttributes)

- (unsigned long long) fileSize;
- (NSDate *) fileModificationDate;
- (NSString *) fileType;
- (unsigned long) filePosixPermissions;
- (NSString *) fileOwnerAccountName;
- (NSString *) fileGroupOwnerAccountName;
- (BOOL) fileExtensionHidden;
- (OSType) fileHFSCreatorCode;
- (OSType) fileHFSTypeCode;
- (BOOL) fileIsImmutable;
- (BOOL) fileIsAppendOnly;
- (NSDate *) fileCreationDate;
- (NSNumber *) fileOwnerAccountID;
- (NSNumber *) fileGroupOwnerAccountID;
@end
```

Create a nib file using NSTreeController

The **NSTreeController** is for displaying hierarchical data in an **NSBrowser** or an **NSOutlineView**. Besides setting the contentArray (as you would for an **NSArrayController**), you also define a childrenKeyPath and a leafKeyPath.

In our case, the **NSTreeController** will be displaying **DirEntry** objects. Note that the **DirEntry** objects have a **children** method and an **isLeaf** method. These will be our childrenKeyPath and our leafKeyPath respectively.

Open the MainMenu.nib file in Interface Builder. To instantiate a tree controller, drag one off the controller palette. Make it non-editable and allow the empty selection. Set the children key path to be children and set the leaf key path to be isLeaf. The objects being displayed are **DirEntry** objects. They have a filename attribute and a fileSize attribute.

Create a subclass of **NSObject** called **AppController**. **AppController** needs one action called **deleteSelection:** and one outlet of type **NSTreeController** called treeController.

Create the files `AppController.h` and `AppController.m`. Instantiate **AppController**.

Drop an **NSBrowser** and an **NSButton** on the window. In the inspector, set the **NSBrowser** so that it does not display titles. Make the **AppController** the target of the button and set the action to be **deleteSelection:**.

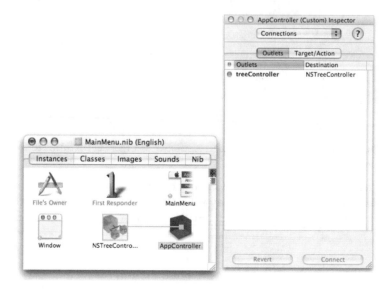

Set the autosizing for the **NSBrowser** to grow with the window and for the **NSButton** to remain in place. You may also want to set Column Resizing to User for the **NSBrowser**.

Set the `treeController` outlet of **AppController** to point to the **NSTreeController**.

Bind the `contentArray` of the tree controller to the `topLevelDirectories` attribute of the **AppController**. (Note that you will actually have to type "topLevelDirectories" into the combo box.)

Select the browser and view its bindings. Bind the `content` to the tree controller's `arrangedObjects`.

Bind the `contentValues` to the tree controller's `arrangedObjects` `filename`.

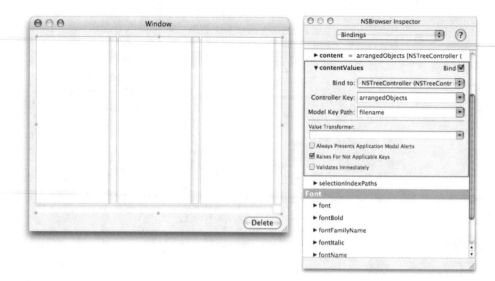

Bind the `selectionIndexPaths` to the tree controller's `selectionIndexPaths`.

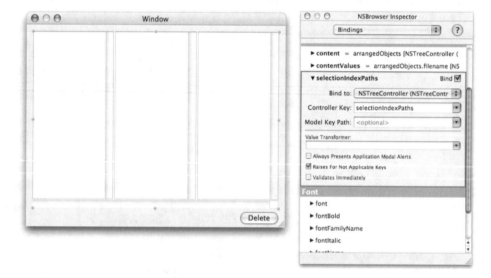

For fun, why don't we also show the size of the selected file. Drop a text field on the window. The size is a number of bytes, so give it a positive format that shows no decimal points and labels the number as bytes: "0 bytes". Tell it to add 1000 separators.

Bind the value of the text field to the tree controller's selection's fileSize.

Using NSBrowser and DirEntry

Now open AppController.h. You will need a pointer to the tree controller and an array of **DirEntry** objects to hold the top-level directory entries

Example 10-3. AppController.h

```
#import <Cocoa/Cocoa.h>
@interface AppController : NSObject {
    IBOutlet NSTreeController *treeController;
    NSMutableArray *topLevelDirectories;
}
- (void)setTopLevelDirectories:(NSMutableArray *)top;
- (IBAction)deleteSelection:(id)sender;
@end
```

In the `AppController.m` file, implement these methods:

Example 10-4. AppController.m

```
#import "AppController.h"
#import "DirEntry.h"

@implementation AppController

- (id)init
{
    [super init];
    NSMutableArray *top;
    top = [DirEntry entriesAtPath:@"/"
                       withParent:nil];
    [self setTopLevelDirectories:top];
    return self;
}

- (void)setTopLevelDirectories:(NSMutableArray *)top
{
    [top retain];
    [topLevelDirectories release];
    topLevelDirectories = top;
}

// You will implement this later
- (IBAction)deleteSelection:(id)sender
{
    NSLog(@"-[AppController deleteSelection:] to be implemented");
}
@end
```

Build and run the app. You should be able to browse, but not delete.

Adding deletion

Replace the deleteSelection: method in AppController to enable deletion:

Example 10-5. AppController.m

```
- (IBAction)deleteSelection:(id)sender
{
    // Get the selection
    NSArray *selection = [treeController selectedObjects];
    int count = [selection count];
    // Is nothing selected?
    if (count == 0) {
        NSRunAlertPanel(@"Delete",
                        @"Select something before deleting",
                        nil, nil, nil);
        return;
    }
```

```
    // Loop through each selected DirEntry, ask user to confirm, then delete
    int i;
    for (i = 0; i < count; i++){
        DirEntry *dirEntry = [selection objectAtIndex:i];
        NSString *path = [dirEntry fullPath];
        int choice = NSRunAlertPanel(@"Delete",
                                     @"Really delete \'%@\'?",
                                     @"Delete",
                                     @"Cancel",
                                     nil,
                                     path);
        if (choice == NSAlertDefaultReturn) {

            // Send notifications that trigger KVO to update browser
            [[dirEntry parent] willChangeValueForKey:@"children"];

            // Actually delete the file or directory
            BOOL good;
            good = [[NSFileManager defaultManager] removeFileAtPath:path
                                                            handler:self];
            [[dirEntry parent] didChangeValueForKey:@"children"];

            // Was the delete a failure?
            if (!good) {
                NSRunAlertPanel(@"Delete",
                                @"Delete was not successful",
                                nil, nil, nil);
            }
        }
    }
}
// This delegate method of NSFileManager gets called if something
// goes wrong with the delete
- (BOOL)fileManager:(NSFileManager *)manager
       shouldProceedAfterError:(NSDictionary *)errorInfo
{
    NSLog(@"error = %@", errorInfo);
    return NO;
}
```

Build and test this *carefully*. It really will delete entire directories.

NSWorkspace

On Mac OS X, many file-related activities are handled by the Finder. In the AppKit framework, **NSWorkspace** is an elegant interface to the Finder. For example, if you wanted to get the icon that would be displayed for a particular file, you would use **NSWorkspace**. Also, the **NSWorkspace** posts notifications when Finder-related activities occur. For example, when a device is mounted or unmounted, **NSWorkspace**'s notification center posts a notification.

Here are a few interesting methods in **NSWorkspace**:

+ (NSWorkspace *) **sharedWorkspace**

Returns the shared instance.

- (BOOL) **openFile:** (NSString *) fullPath

Opens the file at fullPath with its default application. The application is started if necessary. This method returns YES if the file was successfully opened.

- (BOOL) **openURL:** (NSURL *) url

Opens a URL with the user's default browser. Returns YES if successful.

- (BOOL) **launchApplication:** (NSString *) appName

appName is the name of the app or the full path to it. You can include . app or not. Returns YES if the app launches or is currently running.

- (NSNotificationCenter *) **notificationCenter**

Returns the notification center for the **NSWorkspace**. To receive notifications listed below, you will want to register with *this* notification center.

- (NSImage *) **iconForFile:** (NSString *) fullPath;

Returns the icon for the file at fullPath.

NSWorkspace posts the following notifications:

- NSWorkspaceWillLaunchApplicationNotification

- NSWorkspaceDidLaunchApplicationNotification

- NSWorkspaceDidTerminateApplicationNotification

- NSWorkspaceWillPowerOffNotification

- NSWorkspaceDidMountNotification (The device being mounted or unmounted is in the userInfo dictionary under NSDevicePath.)

- NSWorkspaceWillUnmountNotification

- NSWorkspaceDidUnmountNotification

- NSWorkspaceDidPerformFileOperationNotification (Only notifies your app about the completion of its own file operations performed using the **NSWorkspace** object!)

As an educational exercise, register for all notifications from the workspace in **init** and log them as they arrive. Add some code to AppController.m:

```
- (void) logThis: (NSNotification *) note
{
    NSLog(@"received: %@", note);
}
- (id) init
{
    [super init];
    NSMutableArray *top;
    top = [DirEntry entriesAtPath:@"/"
                      withParent:nil];
    [self setTopLevelDirectories:top];
    NSNotificationCenter *nc;
    nc = [[NSWorkspace sharedWorkspace] notificationCenter];
    [nc addObserver:self
           selector:@selector(logThis:)
               name:nil
             object:nil];
    return self;
}
```

Build and run the app. Start other applications. Insert and eject a CD. Note that you are informed of these activities.

Historical trivia: On NeXTSTEP, the equivalent of Finder was an application called Workspace. That is why this class is called **NSWorkspace**.

Challenge

1. Use the **NSDirectoryEnumerator** to calculate the true size of the selected directory.

2. Use **NSWorkspace** to find and display an icon for the selected file or directory in an **NSImageView**.

3. If the user double-clicks a file, open it. (This also uses **NSWorkspace**.)

Chapter 11. Network Programming With Sockets

The native Mac OS X networking API is Berkeley sockets, variants of which are available on just about every platform available today. The sockets API is simultaneously elegant (such as just needing a couple of calls to set up network communications) and ugly. The data structures involved are a bit awkward because there are few `typedef`s so you have to use the `struct` keyword frequently. The API predates ANSI C, and some of the techniques employed require a lot of casting.

One of the problems with networking in general, and sockets in particular, is that there is a lot of documentation and a lot of features of varying levels of complexity and obscurity. It is easy to get lost in the details and be unable to get the basics working. Here you are primarily going to be concerned with basic stream-oriented network communication.

Addresses

Network interfaces, such as ethernet cards or airport cards, are identified by an IP (Internet Protocol) address. An IP address is a numeric value which is used as the source (or destination) of a network message. A typical network message would be something like "An interface at IP address 10.0.1.123 is sending 30 bytes of data to another interface at IP 192.168.254.42". There are two major flavors of IP addresses: IPv4 and IPv6, which are ways of saying "Internet Protocol version 4" and "Internet Protocol version 6".

IPv4 is the current addressing mode of the internet, which 32-bit addresses. We have exhausted the 32-bit address space, meaning that there are not enough addresses available to address the current number of computers wanting to connect to the internet. There are some workarounds (such as Network Address Translation and local addressing) that allow multiple machines share the same public IP address, but it is not a sustainable solution. IPv6, the next generation of the internet protocol, uses 128-bit addresses. The magnitude of number representable in 128 bits is 340 undecillion, where undecillion is ten raised to the 36th power. Hopefully we will not be running out of IPv6 addresses any time soon.

IP addresses are numeric values. To make them a little easier to read, there are human-readable "presentation" formats. IPv4 addresses are usually represented in "dotted-quad" format, which are the four bytes of the address represented by decimal numbers, separated by periods. `127.0.0.2` is in dotted-quad format, as is `66.227.8.230`.

IPv6 addresses are represented by by sixteen-bit quantities separated by colons. `FDEC:BA98:7654:3210:FEDC:BA98:7654:3210` could be an IPv6 address, as well as `1080:0000:0000:0000:0008:0800:2000C:417A`. You can omit leading zeros in each group to reduce the amount of clutter (but there has to be at least one digit in every field). The previous address could be written as `1080:0:0:0:8:800:200C:417A`. If there are multiple consecutive 16-bit groups of zeros, they can be elided and replaced with `::`. The previous address can therefore be written `1080::8:800:200C:417A`. To prevent ambiguities, there can only be one `::` per address. The last 32 bits can also be written in dotted-quad format, leading to an IPv6 address like `1080::8:800:32.12.65.116`.

Because IPv4 and IPv6 need to interoperate, there are two special IPv6 address formats. The first is an IPv4-compatible IPv6 address of the form `::d.d.d.d`. That is, leading zeros, followed by a 32-bit IPv4 address in dotted-quad format. This is typically used for hosts and routers to dynamically tunnel IPv6 packets over IPv4 routing.

The other is an IPv4-mapped IPv6 address, which takes the form `::FFFF:d.d.d.d`. That is, leading zeros, followed by 16 bits of ones, followed by a 32-bit IPv4 address. This is how IPv4-only nodes (those that do not support IPv6) are represented to IPv6-aware software. This address format allows IPv6 systems to interoperate with IPv4-only systems.

The Address Data Structures

When dealing with network addresses, you will be using a number of data structures to represent the addresses, and a number of functions for converting addresses between different formats.

The fundamental data structure in the sockets API, which you will not actually use directly is `struct sockaddr`:

```
struct sockaddr {
    u_char      sa_len;
    u_char      sa_family;
    char        sa_data[];
};
```

`struct sockaddr` acts like an abstract base class in object-oriented languages. It defines two fields that are common amongst all of the different address types. By examining these fields you can see how large the address structure is (by looking at `sa_len`), and what kind of address it is (IPv4, IPv6, local address for unix sockets, X.25, or other kinds of addresses that have not been invented yet) by looking at the `sa_family` field. `sa_data` is there to say that there is address-specific data that follows.

IPv4 Address Structures

The address structure for IPv4 addresses is `struct sockaddr_in`, where the _in suffix means "Internet":

```
struct sockaddr_in {
    u_char      sin_len;
    u_char      sin_family;
    u_short     sin_port;
    struct      in_addr sin_addr;
    char        sin_zero[8];
};
```

The first two fields match the first two fields of `struct sockaddr`. `sin_family` should be `AF_INET` for IPv4 addresses. The last element, `sin_zero`, is padding so that `struct sockaddr` matches the size of `struct sockaddr`. It should be cleared to zero.

TCP/IP communication deals with addresses and ports. You saw the different address formats earlier. Every IP address has 65535 ports associated with it. Communication actually happens between address/port pairs. For example, communicating with the web server at `www.bignerdranch.com` involves going to address 66.227.8.230 and connecting to port 80. Locally your web browser will be communicating from a port on your local IP address. The `sin_port` field indicates which port should be used. The IP address lives in `sin_addr`.

`sin_addr` is a `struct in_addr`, which is one of the annoying parts of the sockets API:

```
struct in_addr {
    in_addr_t s_addr;
};
```

This is a structure with only a single element. The actual address type (`in_addr_t`) is actually an unsigned 32 bit integer.

There is one detail: both the port (2 bytes) and the address (4 bytes) need to be in network byte order.

IPv6 Address Structures

Because IPv6 addresses are quite a bit larger than IPv4 addresses, and there are some features that IPv6 has that IPv4 does not, a new address structure became necessary. `struct sockaddr_in6` looks like this:

```
struct sockaddr_in6 {
    uint8_t              sin6_len;
    sa_family_t          sin6_family;
    in_port_t            sin6_port;
    uint32_t             sin6_flowinfo;
    struct in6_addr      sin6_addr;
    uint32_t             sin6_scope_id;
};
```

Like `struct sockaddr_in`, the first field is the length and the second field is the family (which should be `AF_INET6`). After that follows the port, which is just like the port in IPv4. We will not talk about `sin6_flowinfo` or `sin6_scope_id`, which are more advanced IPv6 features that are not necessary to deal with on a daily basis. One interesting thing to notice is that `sockaddr_in6` uses more descriptive types than the older `sockaddr_in`.

`sin6_addr` is the actual IP address, of type `struct in6_addr`. Like `struct in_addr`, `struct in6_addr` is a structure that holds the address:

```
struct in6_addr {
    uint8_t      s6_addr[16];
}
```

Network Byte Order

The way bytes are ordered in multi-byte integers can vary from platform to platform. The bytes of the integer value of 0x12345678 could be stored in memory in that order, with the most significant byte occurring at a lower address. This is called "big endian" because the big part of the integer (most significant byte) occurs first. That value could also be stored stored as 0x78563412,(termed "little endian", having the least significant byte occurring first. The PowerPC stores its integers in big endian byte order, while Intel x86 machines store integers in little endian byte order.

Both parties must agree on what order the specific bytes will have when transferring integers between machines over the network. Usually you will use the "network byte order," which is defined to be big endian.

Because Mac developers support software on both architectures, we have to worry about network byte order, not only with regards to transferring data over a network, but also when writing binary files. It is always a good idea to store your integers in network byte order to prevent surprises later on. There are some useful functions provided that ensure that your data is in network byte order:

```
uint16_t htons (uint16_t hostshort);

uint32_t htonl (uint32_t hostlong);

uint16_t ntohs (uint16_t netshort);

uint32_t ntohl (uint32_t netlong);
```

A hint on parsing the names: h stands for "Host", n for "Network", s for "Short", and l for "Long".

So, **htonl()** is "host to network long,", and the converse is **ntohl()** "network to host long." You do not need to worry about network byte order when sending text data or single bytes.

Core Foundation provides a number of byte swapping routines as well. There are 15 functions for swapping the bytes of 16, 32, and 64 bit integers. The format of the functions are CFSwapInt + word size + direction of conversion. The word size is 16, 32, or 64. Direction of conversion can be omitted, in which case the bytes are swapped, or it can be one of BigToHost (big endian to the host's native byte order, similar to the toh functions), HostToBig (native byte order to big endian, similar to the ton functions), HostToLittle, and LittleToHost. The last two convert between the host's native format and little endan mode.

Some valid byte swapping functions would then be **CFSwapInt16()**, **CFSwap32BigToHost()**, **CFSwapInt64HostToLittle()**, and so on.

Address Conversions

There are two fundamental forms for IP addresses. The first is a human-readable "presentation" form, such as the IPv4 dotted-quad or the IPv6 colon-delimited hex address. The other is a binary format "network" form that can be used by the sockets API to actually send data across the network. The presentation address is what the user interacts with, and the network form is used by the program's code.

IPv4 and IPv6 Compatible Functions

The **inet_pton()** function converts from an address in presentation format to one in network format, hence the "P to N" in the function name.

```
int inet_pton (int addressFamily, const char *sourceBuffer, void
*destinationAddress);
```

Converts from an ascii representation to a network address. addressFamily is the family of the address being passed in, and should be either AF_INET or AF_INET6. sourceBuffer is a zero-terminated ascii string that holds the presentation address. `destinationAddress` should be a `struct in_addr` for an AF_INET address, or a `struct in6_addr` for an AF_INET6 address.

`inet_pton()` returns 1 if the address was valid for the specified address family, 0 if the address was not parsable in the specified address family, or -1 if some system error occurred. Consult `errno` for the specific error.

The `inet_ntop()` converts the other direction, from a network address to a presentation form.

```
const char *inet_ntop (int addressFamily, const void *sourceAddress,
char *destinationBuffer, socklent_t bufferSize);
```

Converts from a network address to an ascii representation. `addressFamily` is the family of the address, and should be either `AF_INET` or `AF_INET6`. The `sourceAddress` parameter is an address in network format, such as a `struct in_addr` or a `struct in6_addr`. The destination buffer is a character buffer that you provide (you cannot pass NULL here) which will be filled in with the presentation-format address. The buffer should be at least as large as `INET_ADDRSTRLEN` when using the `AF_INET` address family, or at least as large as `INET6_ADDRSTRLEN` when using `AF_INET6`. Using these constants guarantees that the buffer will be large enough to hold the largest possible presentation address.

Upon success, the `inet_ntop()` returns the address of your character buffer. On failure it returns NULL, in which case you should consult `errno` for what went wrong.

Example 11-1 shows **inet_pton** and **inet_ntop** in action. An address in ascii-presentation format is converted into a binary address and back again.

Example 11-1. ptontoa.m

```
// ptontoa.m -- use inet_pton and inet_ntoa

/* compile with
gcc -g -Wall -o ptontoa ptontoa.m
*/

#import <sys/types.h>   // for type definitions, like u_char
#import <sys/socket.h>  // for AF_INET[6]
#import <netinet/in.h>  // for in_addr and in6_addr
#import <arpa/inet.h>   // for inet_*
#import <errno.h>       // for errno
#import <string.h>      // for strerror
#import <stdio.h>       // for printf()

const char *in6ToChar (struct in6_addr *addr)
{
    static char s_address[INET6_ADDRSTRLEN];
    uint32_t *base;
    base = (uint32_t *)addr->s6_addr;

    snprintf (s_address, sizeof(s_address),
```

```
                        "%x%x%x%x", base[0], base[1], base[2], base[3]);

    return (s_address);

} // in6ToChar

int main (void)
{
    struct in_addr ipv4netAddr;
    struct in6_addr ipv6netAddr;
    char ipv4Address[INET_ADDRSTRLEN];
    char ipv6Address[INET6_ADDRSTRLEN];
    int result;

    // ---------------------------------------------------
    // first, IPv4 land

    // presentation to numeric
    strcpy (ipv4Address, "192.168.254.123");
    result = inet_pton (AF_INET, ipv4Address, &ipv4netAddr);

    if (result == 1) {
        printf ("address '%s' in binary: %x\n",
                ipv4Address, ipv4netAddr.s_addr);
    } else if (result == 0) {
        printf ("address '%s' not parsable\n\n", ipv4Address);
    } else {
        printf ("some other error happened: %d/%s\n",
                errno, strerror(errno));
    }

    // numeric to presentation
    const char *ntopResult;
    ntopResult = inet_ntop (AF_INET, &ipv4netAddr,
                            ipv4Address, sizeof(ipv4Address));

    if (ntopResult != NULL) {
        printf ("address '%x' presentation: '%s'\n",
                ipv4netAddr.s_addr, ipv4Address);
    } else {
        printf ("some other error happened: %d/%s\n",
                errno, strerror(errno));
    }

    // ---------------------------------------------------
    // now for IPv6

    strcpy (ipv6Address, "FE80:0000:0000:0000:0230:65FF:FE06:6523");
    result = inet_pton (AF_INET6, ipv6Address, &ipv6netAddr);

    if (result == 1) {
        printf ("address '%s'\n    in binary: %s\n",
                ipv6Address, in6ToChar(&ipv6netAddr));
    } else if (result == 0) {
        printf ("address '%s' not parsable\n\n", ipv4Address);
    } else {
        printf ("some other error happened: %d/%s\n",
```

```
                 errno, strerror(errno));
    }

    // numeric to presentation
    ntopResult = inet_ntop (AF_INET6, &ipv6netAddr,
                            ipv6Address, sizeof(ipv6Address));

    if (ntopResult != NULL) {
        printf ("address '%s'\n    presentation: '%s'\n",
                in6ToChar(&ipv6netAddr), ipv6Address);
    } else {
        printf ("some other error happened: %d/%s\n",
                errno, strerror(errno));
    }

    return (0);

} // main
```

And here is a sample run:

```
$ ./ptontoa
address '192.168.254.123' in binary: c0a8fe7b
address 'c0a8fe7b' presentation: '192.168.254.123'
address 'FE80:0000:0000:0000:0230:65FF:FE06:6523'
    in binary: fe800000023065fffe066523
address 'fe800000023065fffe066523'
    presentation: 'fe80::230:65ff:fe06:6523'
```

inet_ntop() is nice enough to render the IPv6 address in its minimal format, omitting extra zeros.

IPv4-specific functions

The functions described earlier can handle all of your address conversion needs. If you are working on an older platform that does not have those functions, or you are maintaining code that was written before IPv6, you may encounter a couple of other address conversion function.

These functions deal exclusively with 32-bit addresses and the dotted-quad presentation format. **inet_aton** converts from an ascii to a binary representation, and **inet_ntoa** converts going the other direction.

int **inet_aton** (const char *quadString, struct in_addr *address);

> Converts between an ascii representation of a dotted quad and returns the numeric address (hence a-to-n). It returns 1 if the conversion was successful, or 0 if the string is invalid.

char ***inet_ntoa** (struct in_addr address);

> Converts from the numeric address to an ascii representation. The string returned resides in a static memory area, so it will be clobbered on the next call to **inet_ntoa()**.

Domain Name Lookup

Human beings tend to prefer dealing with hostnames rather than working with raw IP addresses, even if the IP address is in a nice user-friendly presentation format. DNS, short for Domain Name Server or Domain Name Service, is the mechanism for translating human-readable hostnames, like www.bignerdranch.com into a corresponding IP address.

You will use struct hostent when looking up hostnames to resolve the address (via DNS, or local name resolution using configuration files or NetInfo):

```
struct hostent {
    char        *h_name;
    char        **h_aliases;
    int         h_addrtype;
    int         h_length;
    char        **h_addr_list;
    #define     h_addr  h_addr_list[0]
};
```

The element of the structure are:

h_name

> Official name of the host.

h_aliases

> A NULL-terminated array of alternate names for the host.

h_addrtype

> The type of address being returned. AF_INET for internet addresses.

h_length

> The length, in bytes, of the address.

h_addr_list

> A NULL-terminated array of network addresses (struct in_addr or struct in6_addr for the host, network byte order.

h_addr

> The first address in h_addr_list. Here for backward compatibility, or as a convenience if you just want to pick up the first address in the list.

gethostbyname2() looks up a hostname and returns a filled-in hostent, which like inet_ntoa is allocated in static space, so it will get clobbered on the next call, and is not thread-safe.

```
struct hostent *gethostbyname2 (const char *hostname, int
addressFamily);
```

> Returns a pointer to a struct hostent that contains the resolved address for hostname, using the specified addressFamily. There is also an older **gethostbyname()** function which takes a hostname argument, but no addressFamily

Note that **gethostbyname2()** does not return an error in errno. It provides its own variant of errno called h_errno, and you can use **hstrerror()** to get a human-readable message.

Example 11-2 is a program that exercises the address conversion functions.

Example 11-2. resolve.m

```
// resolve.m -- resolve an address using gethostbyname2()

/* compile with
cc -g -Wmost -o resolve resolve.m
*/

#import <sys/types.h> // random types
#import <sys/socket.h> // for AF_INET
#import <netinet/in.h> // constants and types
#import <arpa/inet.h> // for inet_ntop
#import <stdlib.h> // for EXIT_SUCCESS
#import <netdb.h> // for gethostbyname
#import <stdio.h> // for fprintf

int main (int argc, char *argv[])
{
    struct hostent *hostinfo;

    hostinfo = gethostbyname2 ("www.apple.com", AF_INET);

    if (hostinfo == NULL) {
        fprintf (stderr,
                "error with gethostbyname2 / apple.  error %s\n",
                hstrerror(h_errno));
    } else {
        // pointer used to step through hostent's arrays of pointers
        char **scan;

        printf ("gethostbyname www.apple.com\n");
        printf ("    official name: %s\n", hostinfo->h_name);

        // any aliases?  If so, print them out
        if (hostinfo->h_aliases[0] != NULL) {
            scan = hostinfo->h_aliases;
            printf ("    aliases:\n");
            while (*scan != NULL) {
                printf ("        %s\n", *scan);
                scan++;
            }
        } else {
            printf ("    no aliases\n");
        }

        printf ("    h_addrtype: %d (%s)\n",
                hostinfo->h_addrtype,
                (hostinfo->h_addrtype == AF_INET) ? "AF_INET"
                : (hostinfo->h_addrtype == AF_INET6) ? "AF_INET6"
                : "unknown");
```

```
            // additional addresses?  If so, print them out
        if (hostinfo->h_addr_list[0] != NULL) {
            scan = hostinfo->h_addr_list;
            printf ("    addresses:\n");
            while (*scan != NULL) {
                char addrBuffer[INET_ADDRSTRLEN];
                printf ("        %s\n",
                        inet_ntop(AF_INET, *scan,
                                  addrBuffer, sizeof(addrBuffer)));
                scan++;
            }
        } else {
            printf ("    no addresses\n");
        }
    }

    return (EXIT_SUCCESS);

} // main
```

and a sample run:

```
$ ./addresses
gethostbyname www.apple.com
    official name: www.apple.com.akadns.net
    aliases:
        www.apple.com
    h_addrtype: 2 (AF_INET)
    addresses:
        17.254.0.91
```

That weird official name for www.apple.com, that ends with akadns.net is the Akamai service to find the closest host to you when it serves up the page. The aliases entry of www.apple.com has the name that (for instance) a web browser would display when you go to the site.

Simple Network Programming

Server coding

Here is the set of calls and actions used when writing a server program:

1. Get a **socket()**.

2. Construct an address + port that the server will listen to.

3. **bind()** the address to the socket.

4. Tell the socket to start **listen()**ing for new connections.

5. **accept()** new connections.

6. Use **read()** and **write()** to receive and send data.

```
int socket (int domain, int type, int protocol);
```

This creates a socket and returns a file descriptor (just like the file descriptors from Chapter 8). You will not actually read or write through this particular file descriptor for a server, but instead use it as the focus for other networking calls. The **accept ()** call described later will give us a file descriptor you can read and write through.

For domain, use AF_INET for an internet socket. For type use SOCK_STREAM for a reliable connection, which means the bytes you send will be received in the same order you sent them and without error.

For protocol, just pass zero.

This returns -1 on errors and sets errno appropriately.

Constructing an address

To construct the address, create a struct sockaddr_in on the stack and fill out the various fields:

```
struct sockaddr_in address;

address.sin_len = sizeof (struct sockaddr_in);
address.sin_family = AF_INET;
address.sin_port = htons (2342);
address.sin_addr.s_addr = htonl (INADDR_ANY);
memset (address.sin_zero, 0, sizeof(address.sin_zero));
```

The family for Internet communications is AF_INET (AF for "address family"). INADDR_ANY means that any IP address can be used. This will cause the server program to listen on the network address of your machine. If you have multiple network addresses, it will listen on all of them. If you have a specific address you want to use, it can be specified here as well.

Note the port and address are put into network byte order, and the sin_zero portion of the structure is zeroed out.

bind

bind() brings together the address and the socket. The socket then owns that address/port pair.

```
int bind (int socket, const struct sockaddr *address, int addresslen);
```

Note that this takes a pointer to a struct sockaddr, not a struct sockaddr_in, so you need to cast. The addresslen parameter is the size of your struct sockaddr_in.

If the address/port pair is already in use **bind()** will return an error. This can be frustrating if your program has crashed but the previously bound socket still exists in the kernel (until a timeout of a couple of minutes). You should tell the socket to reuse the address using this **setsockopt()** call before the **bind()** will do that:

```
int yes = 1;
result = setsockopt (socket, SOL_SOCKET, SO_REUSEADDR,
                     &yes, sizeof(int));
```

setsockopt() is a generic interface for tweaking different socket parameters.

Both **setsockopt()** and **bind()** return -1 on errors and set errno.

listen

The **listen()** system call informs the kernel to start accepting connections to the address and port specified in the address passed to **bind()**.

```
int listen (int socket, int backlog);
```

The backlog parameter is the maximum length of the queue of pending connection requests. Once the queue fills any subsequent attempts to connect to the socket, it will get a "connection refused" error. The system will put a cap on the size of the backlog queue.

accept

The **accept()** call will wait for a new incoming connection. When a new connection is made, **accept()** will return with a file descriptor that can be read and write through. This file descriptor is just like any other. You can use functions like **read()**, **write()**, **send()**, **readv()**, and you can wrap it in a standard I/O FILE if you so desire. Some file operations (like seeking) will result in errors since you really cannot seek with a network connection.

```
int accept (int socket, struct sockaddr *address,
            socklen_t *addressLength);
```

Upon a successful **accept()**, the address parameter will be the address and port of the client making the request. This returns -1 on errors and sets errno appropriately.

Note that **accept()** will block until an incoming connection happens or an error happens. The socket can be set into a non-blocking mode so that accept does not block. You will read about that later with multiplexing connections.

Example 11-3 is a simple server that binds to port 2342 and listens for incoming connections. You can make such a connection using the telnet command. When a connection is made, the data from the other program is read and printed. Then it waits for another connection.

Example 11-3. simpleserver.m

```
// simpleserver.m -- listen on a port, and display any bytes
//                   that come through

/* compile with:
gcc -g -Wall -o simpleserver simpleserver.m
*/

#import <sys/types.h>    // random types
#import <netinet/in.h>   // for sockaddr_in
#import <sys/socket.h>   // for socket(), AF_INET
#import <arpa/inet.h>    // for inet_ntop
#import <errno.h>        // for errno
#import <string.h>       // for strerror
#import <stdlib.h>       // for EXIT_SUCCESS
#import <stdio.h>        // for fprintf
#import <unistd.h>       // for close

#define PORT_NUMBER 2342
```

```
int main (int argc, char *argv[])
{
    int fd = -1, result;
    int programResult = EXIT_FAILURE;

    // get a socket
    result = socket (AF_INET, SOCK_STREAM, 0);

    if (result == -1) {
        fprintf (stderr, "could not make a socket.  error: %d / %s\n",
                 errno, strerror(errno));
        goto bailout;
    }
    fd = result;

    // reuse the address so we do not fail on program launch
    int yes = 1;
    result = setsockopt (fd, SOL_SOCKET, SO_REUSEADDR,
                         &yes, sizeof(int));
    if (result == -1) {
        fprintf (stderr, "couldn't setsockopt to reuseaddr. %d / %s\n",
                 errno, strerror(errno));
        goto bailout;
    }

    // bind to an address and port
    {
        struct sockaddr_in address;
        address.sin_len = sizeof (struct sockaddr_in);
        address.sin_family = AF_INET;
        address.sin_port = htons (PORT_NUMBER);
        address.sin_addr.s_addr = htonl (INADDR_ANY);
        memset (address.sin_zero, 0, sizeof(address.sin_zero));

        result = bind (fd, (struct sockaddr *)&address,
                       sizeof(address));
        if (result == -1) {
            fprintf (stderr,
                     "could not bind socket.  error: %d / %s\n",
                     errno, strerror(errno));
            goto bailout;
        }
    }

    result = listen (fd, 8);

    if (result == -1) {
        fprintf (stderr, "listen failed.  error: %d /  %s\n",
                 errno, strerror(errno));
        goto bailout;
    }

    while (1) {
        struct sockaddr_in address;
        socklen_t addressLength = sizeof(address);
        int remoteSocket;
        char buffer[4096];
```

```
        result = accept (fd, (struct sockaddr*)&address,
                         &addressLength);
        if (result == -1) {
            fprintf (stderr, "accept failed.  error: %d / %s\n",
                     errno, strerror(errno));
            continue;
        }
        printf ("accepted connection from %s:%d\n",
                inet_ntop(AF_INET, &address.sin_addr,
                          buffer, sizeof(buffer)),
                ntohs(address.sin_port));
        remoteSocket = result;

        // drain the socket
        while (1) {
            result = read (remoteSocket, buffer, 4095);

            if (result == 0) {
                // EOF.
                break;
            } else if (result == -1) {
                fprintf (stderr, "could not read from remote socket.  "
                         "error %d / %s\n", errno, strerror(errno));
                break;
            } else {
                // null-terminate the string and print it out
                buffer[result] = '\000';
                printf ("%s", buffer);
            }
        }

        close (remoteSocket);

        printf ("\n---------------------------------------------\n");
    }

    programResult = EXIT_SUCCESS;

bailout:
    close (fd);
    return (programResult);

} // main
```

A sample run:

In one terminal window run `simpleserver`:

```
$ ./simpleserver
```

And in another run `telnet`:

```
$ telnet 10.0.1.142 2342
Trying 10.0.1.142...
Connected to 10.0.1.142.
Escape character is '^]'.
Here is some text I typed in.
```

```
Here is some more text.
(press control-] to get a telnet prompt)
telnet> quit
$
```

If you have not used `telnet` before, it makes a connection to the address indicated (the local machine at 10.0.1.142, but you can also use a domain name) and a port (2342 in this case). `telnet` will then send any text you enter to the program on the other side, and it will display any returned text (in this case there is not any). Here are the results from `simpleserver`:

```
$ ./simpleserver
accepted connection from 10.0.1.142:50605
Here is some text I typed in.
Here is some more text.

---------------------------------------------------
```

You can `telnet` again to the server and enter more text. To make the server exit, interrupt it with `control-C`.

Client Coding

Code on the client is very similar to the server:

1. Figure out the address information of the server.

2. Construct a `struct sockaddr_in` address.

3. Get a `socket()`.

4. `connect()` to the server.

5. Use `read()` and `write()` to receive and send data.

Note there is no `bind()` or `listen()` step for a client, but you do `connect()`.

connect

This is how a connection is made to the server. The file descriptor you got from `socket()` is what you will read and write with.

```
int connect (int socket, const struct sockaddr *name, int namelen);
```

Give it the address to connect to and it returns zero if the connection succeeds, or -1 for an error, with `errno` set.

Example 11-4 is a client that is a little more convenient than `telnet`:

Example 11-4. simpleclient.m

```
// simpleclient.m -- read from stdin and send to the simpleserver

/* compile with:
gcc -g -Wall -o simpleclient simpleclient.m
*/
```

```
#import <sys/types.h>    // random types
#import <netinet/in.h>   // for sockaddr_in
#import <sys/socket.h>   // for socket(), AF_INET
#import <netdb.h>        // for gethostbyname2, h_errno, etc
#import <errno.h>        // for errno
#import <string.h>       // for strerror
#import <stdlib.h>       // for EXIT_SUCCESS
#import <stdio.h>        // for fprintf
#import <unistd.h>       // for close

#define PORT_NUMBER 2342

int main (int argc, char *argv[])
{
    int programResult = EXIT_FAILURE;
    int fd = -1, result;
    struct sockaddr_in serverAddress;
    struct hostent *hostInfo;

    if (argc != 2) {
        fprintf (stderr, "usage: client hostname\n");
        goto bailout;
    }

    hostInfo = gethostbyname2 (argv[1], AF_INET);

    if (hostInfo == NULL) {
        fprintf (stderr, "could not gethostbyname for '%s'\n",
                 argv[1]);
        fprintf (stderr, " error: %d / %s\n",
                 h_errno, hstrerror(h_errno));
        goto bailout;
    }
    serverAddress.sin_len = sizeof (struct sockaddr_in);
    serverAddress.sin_family = AF_INET;
    serverAddress.sin_port = htons (PORT_NUMBER);
    serverAddress.sin_addr = *((struct in_addr *)(hostInfo->h_addr));
    memset (&(serverAddress.sin_zero), 0,
            sizeof(serverAddress.sin_zero));

    result = socket (AF_INET, SOCK_STREAM, 0);

    if (result == -1) {
        fprintf (stderr, "could not make a socket.  error: %d / %s\n",
                 errno, strerror(errno));
        goto bailout;
    }
    fd = result;

    // no need to bind() or listen()

    result = connect (fd, (struct sockaddr *)&serverAddress,
                      sizeof(serverAddress));

    if (result == -1) {
        fprintf (stderr, "could not connect.  error: %d / %s\n",
                 errno, strerror(errno));
```

```
            goto bailout;
        }

    do {
        char buffer[4096];
        size_t readCount;
        readCount = fread (buffer, 1, 4096, stdin);

        result = write (fd, buffer, readCount);

        if (result == -1) {
            fprintf (stderr, "error writing: %d / %s\n",
                    errno, strerror(errno));
            break;
        }

        // check EOF
        if (readCount < 4096) {
            if (ferror(stdin)) {
                fprintf (stderr, "error reading: %d / %s\n",
                        errno, strerror(errno));
            } else if (feof(stdin)) {
                fprintf (stderr, "EOF\n");
            }
            break;
        }

    } while (1);

    programResult = EXIT_SUCCESS;

bailout:
    close (fd);
    return (programResult);

} // main
```

Compile this, start the server running in one terminal window, then run the client in another.

```
$ ./simpleclient 10.0.1.142
hello
there
bork
bork
bork
(type control-D to send an EOF to the client)
```

When you send EOF to the client, the **fread()** will return, and the text will get written to the server.

On the server side you will see something like

```
accepted connection from 10.0.1.142:50610
hello
there
bork
bork
```

```
bork
```

You can do more than just type text. You can send the contents of a file too.

```
$ ./simpleclient 10.0.1.142 < /usr/share/dict/words
```

will send about 2 megs of words across the network to the server.

More Advanced Issues

Multiplexing connections

A one-connection-at-a-time server like `simpleserver` is OK for some applications, but to truly leverage the power of networking it is better to have a single server support many connections simultaneously. To do this, you need a way to multiplex multiple input and output streams, and to not block unless there is no work to be done.

The **select** () call is the Berkeley sockets way of doing this multiplexing. (You will see in Chapter 15 an alternate way of multiplexing connections, which is superior to **select** () in many ways, but is not available on many platforms) You give **select** () a set of file descriptors. If there is any data to be read, or if there is the ability to write on any of the descriptors, **select** () will tell you so. Otherwise it will block (with an optional time out) until network activity is possible.

```
int select (int nfds, fd_set *readfds, fd_set *writefds,
            fd_set *exceptfds, struct timeval *timeout);
```

nfds

> One more than the largest file descriptor number.

readfds

> A set of file descriptors to see if you can read data from without blocking.

writefds

> A set of file descriptors to see if you can write data to without blocking.

exceptfds

> A set of file descriptors to see if there are any error conditions.

timeout

> How long to wait for activity before breaking out of the select call. pass NULL for no timeout.

The `fd_set`s are modified by **select** (). You set the file descriptors you are interested in before calling **select** (), then examine the `fd_set`s to see which ones are interesting afterward.

What are `fd_set`s? They are an opaque bitvector that can be manipulated with this API:

```
    fd_set fdset;
```

```
FD_ZERO (&fdset);
```

Clear out the `fd_set`.

```
FD_SET (fd, &fdset);
```

Add a file descriptor to the set.

```
FD_CLR (fd, &fdset);
```

Remove a file descriptor from the set.

```
FD_ISSET (fd, &fdset);
```

Test to see if a file descriptor is in the set.

Usually a `fd_set` holds 1024 items. If you try to put more than that into an `fd_set`, you could end up writing over memory after the `fd_set`'s storage. You can alter this by putting a `#define FD_SETSIZE` before including `<sys/types.h>`. The **getdtablesize()** function will return the size of the file descriptor table for a process (but since it is a function call, it is not useful to send to `FD_SETSIZE`).

`struct timeval` is defined like this:

```
struct timeval {
    int32_t    tv_sec;      /* seconds */
    int32_t    tv_usec;     /* and microseconds */
};
```

You can specify the timeout in seconds and microseconds (but you are not guaranteed of microsecond granularity). Specify zero for both values to have **select()** return immediately. You can use this to have **select()** poll rather than block.

The usual way to use select is like this (say for reading):

```
fd_set readfds;
int maxFd = -1, result;
FD_ZERO (&readfds);

// add the listen socket
FD_SET (myListenSocket, &readfds);
maxFd = MAX (maxFd, myListenSocket);

// walk your data structure that has your open sessions
for (i = 0; i < whatever; i++) {
    FD_SET (session->fd, &readfds);
    maxFd = MAX (maxFd, session->fd);
}

result = select (maxFd + 1, &readfds, NULL, NULL, NULL);

if (result == -1) {
    ... handle error
}

// see if our accept socket is there
```

```
if (FD_ISSET (myListenSocket, &readfds)) {
    // call accept(), make a new session
}

// walk the data structure again looking for activity
for (i = 0; i < whatever; i++) {
    if (FD_ISSET(session->fd, &readfds)) {
        result = read (session->fd, ...);
    }
}
```

Figure 11-1. select()

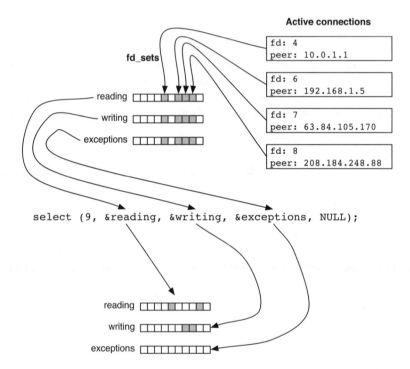

Note again that the first argument is one *more* than the largest file descriptor. A common mistake is to forget to do that. Also note that fd_sets can be copied and kept around. A common technique is to have a master fd_set that has all of the session file descriptors in it, then you can make a copy of it and pass the copy to select. This saves you from walking your data structures every time before a call to **select()**. It also means you have to keep that master set up to date when a session closes.

When a file descriptor is in the readfds set, it will appear in the set after **select()** returns when data is available. It will also appear when the connection closes (**read()** will return zero in that case). As seen above, you can also put the accept socket in there to know when new connections happen.

One thing you may notice is that **select()** does not tell you how much is available to read. If you just do a result = read (session->fd, buffer, bufferSize), the call to read will block until bufferSize data is read in, or an error happens. That is behavior you do not want in a busy server program. File descriptors can be put into a non-blocking mode. In this case, the **read()** will read however much data has appeared on the connection and then return. The return value from **read()** tells you how many bytes were read. To set a file descriptor to be non-blocking, use this **fcntl()** call:

```
result = fcntl (fd, F_SETFL, O_NONBLOCK);
```

(And of course error check the result. -1 is returned on error and errno set)

Message boundaries

Some networking protocols, like HTTP, are pretty easy to deal with. You can pretty much just read everything that comes on the socket, and then write out everything you need to. Other networking protocols are harder to deal with due to some of the "real world" issues regarding network communication and how the kernels on both sides of the connection buffer data.

Consider a little chat program where the client sends the server a message that looks like this:

length   : one byte
message : length bytes of text

Here are some scenarios:

One message from a **read()**

> This is pretty easy. Just look at the first byte for the length, and get the subsequent bytes of the message and send it out to the chat clients.

Multiple complete messages from a **read()**

> Since read does not know where the messages begin and end you have to walk the read buffer: get a length byte, process subsequent bytes, get another length byte, process those bytes, until you run out

A message straddles a **read()** boundary

> This is where things get complicated. Between calls to **read()** you need to remember that you only got half of a message. The first half waits around in a buffer until the second half gets in.

> Generally you will keep a buffer large enough to hold two or more complete messages and read into that buffer. When processing messages, you need to know whether you are picking up a resumed message or are starting with a new one.

Figure 11-2. Worst-case Scenario for Messages

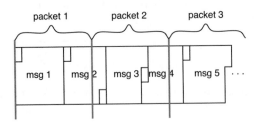

Example 11-5 is the `Chatter` server side. The more interesting parts are the select loop, and **readMessage()**, which handles the various pathological cases of incoming messages.

Example 11-5. chatterserver.m

```
// chatterserver.m -- chat server using standard sockets API

/* compile with:
gcc -g -Wall -o chatterserver chatterserver.m
*/

#import <sys/types.h>      // random types
#import <netinet/in.h>     // for sockaddr_in
#import <sys/socket.h>     // for socket(), AF_INET
#import <arpa/inet.h>      // for inet_ntop
#import <errno.h>          // for errno
#import <string.h>         // for strerror
#import <stdlib.h>         // for EXIT_SUCCESS
#import <stdio.h>          // for fprintf
#import <unistd.h>         // for close
#import <fcntl.h>          // for fcntl()
#import <syslog.h>         // for syslog and friends
#import <sys/uio.h>        // for iovec

/* message protocol
 * first message is:
 *
 * 1 byte : length of message, no more than 8
 * length bytes : the nickname of the user
 *
 * 1 byte : length of message
 * length bytes : message, not zero-terminated
 *
 * therefore, maximum message size is 256 bytes
 */
#define MAX_MESSAGE_SIZE        256
#define READ_BUFFER_SIZE        4096

// there is one of these for each connected user

typedef struct chatterUser {
    int     fd;             // zero fd == no user
    char    username[9];    // 8 character name plus trailing zero byte
```

```
    int     gotNickname;     // have we gotten the nickname packet?

    // incoming data workspace

    // what the length byte says we should get
    unsigned int currentMessageSize;

    // what we have read (not including length)
    int         bytesRead;
    char        buffer[READ_BUFFER_SIZE];
} chatterUser;

#define MAX_USERS 50
chatterUser g_users[MAX_USERS];

#define PORT_NUMBER 2342

int g_listenFd;

// returns fd on success, -1 on error
// (this is cut-and-paste from main() of simpleserver.m)

int startListening ()
{
    int fd = -1, success = 0;
    int result;

    // cut and pasted from main() in simpleserver.m

    result = socket (AF_INET, SOCK_STREAM, 0);

    if (result == -1) {
        fprintf (stderr, "could not make a scoket.  error: %d / %s\n",
                 errno, strerror(errno));
        goto bailout;
    }
    fd = result;

    {
        int yes = 1;
        result = setsockopt (fd, SOL_SOCKET, SO_REUSEADDR,
                             &yes, sizeof(int));
        if (result == -1) {
            fprintf (stderr,
                "unable to setsockopt to reuse address. %d / %s\n",
                errno, strerror(errno));
            goto bailout;
        }
    }

    // bind to an address and port
    {
        struct sockaddr_in address;
        address.sin_len = sizeof (struct sockaddr_in);
        address.sin_family = AF_INET;
        address.sin_port = htons (PORT_NUMBER);
        address.sin_addr.s_addr = htonl (INADDR_ANY);
```

```
        memset (address.sin_zero, 0, sizeof(address.sin_zero));

        result = bind (fd, (struct sockaddr *)&address,
                        sizeof(address));
        if (result == -1) {
            fprintf (stderr,
                        "could not bind socket.  error: %d / %s\n",
                        errno, strerror(errno));
            goto bailout;
        }
    }

    result = listen (fd, 8);

    if (result == -1) {
        fprintf (stderr, "listen failed.  error: %d /  %s\n",
                    errno, strerror(errno));
        goto bailout;
    }

    success = 1;

bailout:
    if (!success) {
        close (fd);
        fd = -1;
    }

    return (fd);

} // startListening

// our listening socket appeared in a readfd from select.  That means
// there is a connection there we can accept

void acceptConnection (int listenFd)
{
    struct sockaddr_in address;
    socklen_t addressLength = sizeof(address), result, fd, i;
    chatterUser *newUser = NULL;

    result = accept (g_listenFd, (struct sockaddr *)&address,
                    &addressLength);

    if (result == -1) {
        fprintf (stderr, "accept failed.  error: %d / %s\n",
                    errno, strerror(errno));
        goto bailout;
    }
    fd = result;

    // set to non-blocking
    result = fcntl (fd, F_SETFL, O_NONBLOCK);
    if (result == -1) {
        fprintf (stderr, "setting nonblock failed.  error: %d / %s\n",
                    errno, strerror(errno));
        goto bailout;
```

```
    }

    // find the next free spot in the users array
    for (i = 0; i < MAX_USERS; i++) {
        if (g_users[i].fd == 0) {
            // found it
            newUser = &g_users[i];
            break;
        }
    }

    if (newUser == NULL) {
        const char *gripe = "too many users.  try again later";
        write (fd, gripe, strlen(gripe));
        goto bailout;
    }

    // ok, clear out the structure, and get it set up
    memset (newUser, 0, sizeof(chatterUser));

    newUser->fd = fd;

    // log where the connection is from
    char buffer[INET_ADDRSTRLEN];
    syslog (LOG_NOTICE, "accepted connection from IP '%s' for fd %d",
            inet_ntop (AF_INET, &address.sin_addr,
                       buffer, sizeof(buffer)), fd);
bailout:
    return;

} // acceptConnection


// send a message to all the signed-in users

void broadcastMessage (const char *username, const char *message)
{
    chatterUser *scan, *stop;   // use a pointer chase for fun
    struct iovec iovector[4];   // use scattered writes just for fun too
    const char *seperator = ": ";

    printf ("Broadcast message: %s: %s\n", username, message);

    scan = g_users;
    stop = scan + MAX_USERS;

    while (scan < stop) {
        if (scan->fd != 0) {
            iovector[0].iov_base = (char *)username;
            iovector[0].iov_len = strlen (username);
            iovector[1].iov_base = (char *)seperator;
            iovector[1].iov_len = strlen (seperator);
            iovector[2].iov_base = (char *)message;
            iovector[2].iov_len = strlen (message);

            writev (scan->fd, iovector, 3);
        }
```

```
        scan++;
    }

} // broadcastMessage

// user disconnected.  Do any mop-up

void cleanUpUser (chatterUser *user)
{
    syslog (LOG_NOTICE, "disconnected user on fd %d\n", user->fd);

    // broadcast 'user disconnected' message
    close (user->fd);
    user->fd = 0;

    broadcastMessage (user->username, "has left the channel\n");

} // cleanUpUser

// the first packet is the user's nickname.  Get it

void readNickname (chatterUser *user)
{
    int result;

    // see if we have read anything yet
    if (user->currentMessageSize == 0) {
        unsigned char length;
        // we need to get the size

        result = read (user->fd, &length, 1);

        if (result == 1) {
            // we got our length byte
            user->currentMessageSize = length;
            user->bytesRead = 0;

        } else if (result == 0) {
            // end of file
            cleanUpUser (user);
            goto bailout;

        } else if (result == -1) {
            fprintf (stderr, "error reading.  error is %d / %s\n",
                     errno, strerror(errno));
            cleanUpUser (user);
            goto bailout;
        }

    } else {
        int readLeft;

        // ok, try to read just the rest of the nickname
        readLeft = user->currentMessageSize - user->bytesRead;

        result = read (user->fd, user->buffer + user->bytesRead,
                       readLeft);
```

```
        if (result == readLeft) {
            // have the whole nickname
            memcpy (user->username, user->buffer,
                    user->currentMessageSize);
            user->username[user->currentMessageSize] = '\000';
            printf ("have a nickname! %s\n", user->username);
            user->gotNickname = 1;

            // no current message, so clear it out
            user->currentMessageSize = 0;

            syslog (LOG_NOTICE, "nickname for fd %d is %s",
                    user->fd, user->username);
            broadcastMessage (user->username,
                              "has joined the channel\n");

        } else if (result == 0) {
            // other side closed the connection
            cleanUpUser (user);
            goto bailout;

        } else if (result == -1) {
            fprintf (stderr, "error reading.  error is %d / %s\n",
                     errno, strerror(errno));
            cleanUpUser (user);
            goto bailout;

        } else {
            // did not read all of it
            user->bytesRead += result;
        }
    }

bailout:
    return;

} // readNickname

// get message data from the given user

void readMessage (chatterUser *user)
{
    int result;
    char *scan, messageBuffer[MAX_MESSAGE_SIZE + 1];

    // read as much as we can into the buffer
    result = read (user->fd, user->buffer,
                   READ_BUFFER_SIZE - user->bytesRead);

    if (result == 0) {
        // other side closed
        cleanUpUser (user);
        // ok to skip message sending, since we have sent all complete
        // messages already
        goto bailout;
```

```
        } if (result == -1) {
            fprintf (stderr, "error reading.  error %d / %s\n",
                    errno, strerror(errno));
            goto bailout;

        } else {
            user->bytesRead += result;
        }

        // now see if we have any complete messages we can send out to
        // other folks the beginning of the buffer should have the length
        // byte, plus any subsequent message bytes

        scan = user->buffer;

        while (user->bytesRead > 0) {

            if (user->currentMessageSize == 0) {
                // start processing new message
                user->currentMessageSize = (unsigned char)*scan++;
                user->bytesRead--;
            }

            if (user->bytesRead >= user->currentMessageSize) {
                // we have a complete message
                memcpy (messageBuffer, scan, user->currentMessageSize);
                messageBuffer[user->currentMessageSize] = '\000';
                user->bytesRead -= user->currentMessageSize;
                scan += user->currentMessageSize;

                // slide the rest of the data over
                memmove (user->buffer, scan, user->bytesRead);
                scan = user->buffer;

                broadcastMessage (user->username, messageBuffer);

                // done with this message
                user->currentMessageSize = 0;
            } else {
                break;
            }
        }

bailout:
    return;

} // readMessage

// we got read activity for a user

void handleRead (chatterUser *user)
{
    if (!user->gotNickname) {
        readNickname (user);
    } else {
        readMessage (user);
    }
```

```
} // handleRead

int main (int argc, char *argv[])
{
    int programResult = EXIT_FAILURE;
    g_listenFd = startListening ();

    if (g_listenFd == -1) {
        fprintf (stderr, "could not open listening socket\n");
        goto bailout;
    }

    // block SIGPIPE
    signal (SIGPIPE, SIG_IGN);

    // wait for activity
    while (1) {
        fd_set readfds;
        int maxFd = -1, result, i;

        FD_ZERO (&readfds);

        // add our listen socket
        FD_SET (g_listenFd, &readfds);
        maxFd = MAX (maxFd, g_listenFd);

        // add our users;
        for (i = 0; i < MAX_USERS; i++) {
            if (g_users[i].fd != 0) {
                FD_SET (g_users[i].fd, &readfds);
                maxFd = MAX (maxFd, g_users[i].fd);
            }
        }


        // wait until something interesting happens
        result = select (maxFd + 1, &readfds, NULL, NULL, NULL);

        if (result == -1) {
            fprintf (stderr, "error from select(): error %d / %s\n",
                     errno, strerror(errno));
            continue;
        }

        // see if we have a new user
        if (FD_ISSET (g_listenFd, &readfds)) {
            acceptConnection (g_listenFd);
        }

        // handle any new incoming data from the users.
        // closes appear here too.
        for (i = 0; i < MAX_USERS; i++) {
            if (FD_ISSET(g_users[i].fd, &readfds)) {
                handleRead (&g_users[i]);
            }
        }
```

```
    }

        programResult = EXIT_SUCCESS;

bailout:
        return (programResult);

} // main
```

The client program, shown in Example 11-6 has a need for using **select ()** as well. It needs to be able to read from both the terminal (the user typing their words) as well as the server's connection for messages sent by other users. The protocol from server to client in this case is much simpler, the server just returns a bolus of text without size information.

Example 11-6. chatterclient.m

```
// chatterclient.m -- client side of the chatter world

/* compile with:
gcc -g -Wall -o chatterclient chatterclient.m
*/

/* message protocol
 * first message is:
 *
 * 1 byte : length of message, no more than 8
 * length bytes : the nickname of the user
 *
 * 1 byte : length of message
 * length bytes : message, not zero-terminated
 *
 * therefore, maxmimum message size is 256 bytes
 */

#import <sys/types.h>     // random types
#import <netinet/in.h>    // for sockaddr_in
#import <sys/socket.h>    // for socket(), AF_INET
#import <netdb.h>         // for gethostbyname, h_errno, etc
#import <errno.h>         // for errno
#import <string.h>        // for strerror
#import <stdlib.h>        // for EXIT_SUCCESS
#import <stdio.h>         // for fprintf
#import <unistd.h>        // for close
#import <fcntl.h>         // for fcntl()

#define PORT_NUMBER 2342

int writeString (int fd, const void *buffer, size_t length)
{
        int result;
        unsigned char byte;

        if (length > 255) {
                fprintf (stderr, "truncating message to 255 bytes\n");
                length = 255;
```

```
    }
    byte = (unsigned char)length;

    result = write (fd, &byte, 1);
    if (result <= 0) {
        goto bailout;
    }

    do {
        result = write (fd, buffer, length);
        if (result <= 0) {
            goto bailout;
        }
        length -= result;
        buffer += result;

    } while (length > 0);

bailout:
    return (result);

} // writeAll

int main (int argc, char *argv[])
{
    int programResult = EXIT_FAILURE;
    int fd = -1, result;
    struct sockaddr_in serverAddress;
    struct hostent *hostInfo;
    unsigned char length;

    if (argc != 3) {
        fprintf (stderr, "usage: chatterclient hostname nickname\n");
        goto bailout;
    }

    // limit nickname to 8 characters
    if (strlen(argv[2]) > 8) {
        fprintf (stderr, "nickname must be 8 characters or less\n");
        goto bailout;
    }

    hostInfo = gethostbyname2 (argv[1], AF_INET);

    if (hostInfo == NULL) {
        fprintf (stderr, "unable to gethostbyname2 for '%s'\n",
                 argv[1]);
        fprintf (stderr, "  %d / %s\n", h_errno, hstrerror(h_errno));
        goto bailout;
    }
    serverAddress.sin_len = sizeof (struct sockaddr_in);
    serverAddress.sin_family = AF_INET;
    serverAddress.sin_port = htons (PORT_NUMBER);
    serverAddress.sin_addr = *((struct in_addr *)(hostInfo->h_addr));
    memset (&(serverAddress.sin_zero), 0,
            sizeof(serverAddress.sin_zero));
```

```
result = socket (AF_INET, SOCK_STREAM, 0);

if (result == -1) {
    fprintf (stderr, "could not make a socket.  error: %d / %s\n",
             errno, strerror(errno));
    goto bailout;
}
fd = result;

// no need to bind() or listen()

// set standard in to non-blocking
result = fcntl (STDIN_FILENO, F_SETFL, O_NONBLOCK);
if (result == -1) {
    fprintf (stderr, "setting nonblock failed.  error: %d / %s\n",
             errno, strerror(errno));
    goto bailout;
}

result = connect (fd, (struct sockaddr *)&serverAddress,
                  sizeof(serverAddress));

if (result == -1) {
    fprintf (stderr, "could not connect.  error: %d / %s\n",
             errno, strerror(errno));
    goto bailout;
}

// first, send the nickname
length = strlen(argv[2]);
result = write (fd, &length, 1);

if (result == -1) {
    fprintf (stderr, "could not write nickname length.  "
             "error: %d / %s\n",
             errno, strerror(errno));
    goto bailout;
}

result = write (fd, argv[2], length);
if (result == -1) {
    fprintf (stderr, "could not write nickname.  error: %d / %s\n",
             errno, strerror(errno));
    goto bailout;
}

// now set to non-block
result = fcntl (fd, F_SETFL, O_NONBLOCK);
if (result == -1) {
    fprintf (stderr, "setting nonblock on server fd failed.  "
             "error: %d / %s\n",
             errno, strerror(errno));
    goto bailout;
}

do {
    fd_set readfds;
```

```
        char buffer[255];

        FD_ZERO (&readfds);
        FD_SET (STDIN_FILENO, &readfds);
        FD_SET (fd, &readfds);


        result = select (fd + 1, &readfds, NULL, NULL, NULL);

        if (result == -1) {
            fprintf (stderr, "error from select(): error %d / %s\n",
                    errno, strerror(errno));
            continue;
        }


        if (FD_ISSET (STDIN_FILENO, &readfds)) {

            result = read (STDIN_FILENO, buffer, 254);
            if (result == -1) {
                fprintf (stderr, "error reading from stdin.  "
                        "Error %d / %s\n",
                        errno, strerror(errno));
                goto bailout;
            } else if (result == 0) {
                // closed
                break;
            }
            length = result; // lop off the CR
            result = writeString (fd, buffer, length);
            if (result == -1) {
                fprintf (stderr, "error writing to chatterserver.  "
                        "error %d / %s\n",
                        errno, strerror(errno));
                goto bailout;
            }
        }
        if (FD_ISSET (fd, &readfds)) {
            char largeBuffer[4096];
            result = read (fd, largeBuffer, 4096);
            if (result == -1) {
                fprintf (stderr, "error reading from chatterserver.  "
                        "error %d / %s\n",
                        errno, strerror(errno));
                goto bailout;
            } else if (result == 0) {
                fprintf (stderr, "server closed connection\n");
                break;
            } else {
                largeBuffer[result] = '\000';
                printf ("%s", largeBuffer);
            }
        }
    } while (1);

    programResult = EXIT_SUCCESS;

bailout:
```

```
    close (fd);

    return (programResult);

} // main
```

The main thing of interest here is the writing of the string. Just calling **write()** is not sufficient. Once the buffer associated with the socket becomes full, **write()** is welcome to return a value smaller than what you told it to write. Here you have a loop that spins over **write()** until it completes.

For the More Curious:

Datagrams

What you have been talking about in this chapter have been "stream sockets." They are a connection-oriented, reliable form of network communication. Berkeley sockets also support "datagram sockets." These are a message-oriented, unreliable form of network communication. They are unreliable in the sense that datagrams may be lost in transit, and that the receiver might not get the datagrams in the same order in which they were sent. The data in the payload is checksummed, and so it will be correct. Stream sockets use the TCP protocol, and datagrams use the UDP protocol.

Figure 11-3. tcp vs. udp

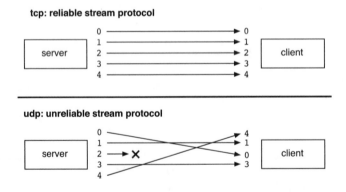

To create a datagram socket you use SOCK_DGRAM rather than SOCK_STREAM for the type parameter of **socket()**. For servers you would still **bind()** your address to the socket, but you do not call **listen()**. Clients do not have to **bind()**. They can just make a socket and then write through it.

To send and receive datagrams, you use **sendto()** and **recvfrom()**:

```
ssize_t sendto (int socket, const void *msg, size_t len, int flags,
                const struct sockaddr *to, int tolen);
```

The arguments:

`socket`

    The socket to write to

`msg, len`

    The data and its length

`flags`

    Just pass zero

`to, tolen`

    a `struct sockaddr_in` of the destination and the size of the structure

The return value is the number of bytes sent, -1/`errno` on error.

```
ssize_t recvfrom (int socket, void *buf, size_t len, int flags,
                       struct sockaddr *from, int *fromlen);
```

The arguments:

`socket`

    The socket to read from

`buf, len`

    Where to deposit the incoming data

`flags`

    Just pass zero (you can pass in `MSG_PEEK` to peek at an incoming data)

`from, fromlen`

    The address of the machine that sent the message

The return value is the number of bytes read, or -1/`errno` on an error.

Challenge

1. There is a problem with the use of **write()** in the chatterserver. None of the writes check the number of bytes actually written, meaning that a partial write could happen. Any remaining bytes will be lost. This could happen with a busy server and lots of messages coming in and being broadcast out. To address this, a technique similar to the incoming read bytes needs to be used. Keep a buffer of outgoing data and put the `fd` into the `writefds` argument of **select()**.

2. Change chatter to use datagrams. The messages are small enough to fit into a single datagram. Given the quality of discussion in most chat rooms, a lost packet here or there probably is not too much of an issue. Since the messages fit into packet boundaries, and **recvfrom()** will not coalesce packets like socket streams, this should simplify a lot of the code.

Chapter 12. CFRunLoop

Unix networking is based using file descriptors for reading and writing. Using file descriptors in server programs is pretty easy with the **select()** or **kevent()** functions. Using sockets in end-user GUI apps presents a problem, though. You cannot call **select()** to wait for network activity in your user interface. That will cause the UI to hang until there is something to be done on the network. Blocking the UI thread would cause your program to become unresponsive.

There are a couple of options available to you. You can put your blocking function into a new thread. That thread can then block to its heart's content until there is activity on the network, and then it can inform the UI thread that there is new data available for processing.

Another option is to take advantage of the *run loop*. A run loop is an event loop in a thread that looks for events, such mouse clicks, key presses, and timer firings, as shown in Figure 12-1. The run loop dispatches these events to interested parties and then goes to sleep waiting for more events. **NSRunLoop** from the Foundation framework has a high-level API for watching for activity on mach ports, timers, and distributed object connections. **NSRunLoop** is built upon **CFRunLoop**. We will be dealing with CFRunLoop here.

Figure 12-1. The Run Loop

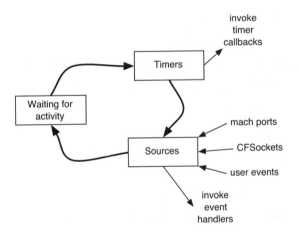

CFRunLoop is from CoreFoundation, which is a toolkit that provides a number of useful features, similar to what is provided by Cocoa's Foundation framework. Elements of CoreFoundation underly much of the Foundation framework, including the various collection classes.

CoreFoundation has a hybrid Cocoa/Carbon feel to it, with a quasi object-oriented programming model. Much of the time you del with CFReferences (which are like object pointers) and you need to retain and release them like Cocoa objects. Much of the work happens with C callbacks, which are more prevalent in the Carbon world.

CFRunLoop is where you can put the socket file descriptors to react to network traffic and not gum up the GUI works. There is one run loop per thread, whether it is created with **NSThread** or the pthread, so in a multithreaded application you can have multiple run loops, each handling multiple sockets.

CFSocket

CFSocket is the part of the **CFRunLoop** architecture that will let us place network sockets into the run loop. CFSocketRef is a pointer to an opaque type, and is created with **CFSocketCreateWithNative()**:

```
CFSocketRef CFSocketCreateWithNative (CFAllocatorRef allocator,
                                      CFSocketNativeHandle sock,
                                      CFOptionFlags callBackTypes,
                                      CFSocketCallBack callout,
                                      const CFSocketContext *context);
```

There are lots of CF data types here. For CFAllocatorRef you can pass kCFAllocatorDefault to get the default memory allocator. This will give you back a chunk of dynamically allocated memory that you should release by calling **CFRelease()**. Typically, you need to release memory obtained from a CoreFoundation function that has Create or Copy in its name. There are no autorelease pools in CoreFoundation.

CFSocketNativeHandle is your socket file descriptor, which is just an integer.

CFOptionFlags is one of these flags, which belong to an enum named CFSocketCallBackType:

kCFSocketNoCallBack

> No callback function is supplied.

kCFSocketReadCallBack

> Call the callback function when data can be read. The callback can get the data by calling **read()**.

kCFSockeWriteCallBack

> Call the callback function when there is space in the kernel buffers so that the socket is writable again. This is handy if you are writing large amounts of data to the socket.

kCFSocketAcceptCallBack

> Call the callback function when there is a new connection on a listening socket.

kCFSocketDataCallBack

> The data will be automatically read and packed into a **CFData** (similar to **NSData**). The callback will be called and be passed this **CFData**.

kCFSocketConnectCallBack

> The above constants are mutually exclusive. You can bitwise-OR kCFSocketConnectCallBack if you want your socket to connect to a remote machine in the background.

CFSocketContext is a pointer to a struct that looks like this:

```
typedef struct {
    CFIndex         version;
    void *          info;
```

```
    const void    *(*retain)(const void *info);
    void           (*release)(const void *info);
    CFStringRef    (*copyDescription)(const void *info);
} CFSocketContext;
```

Set everything to zero or NULL for all of these, unless you want to perform some custom memory management. info is a pointer to whatever data you want, such as an Objective-C object pointer if you are using Cocoa. You can see some of the Cocoa-flavored behavior with functions to perform retain and release on the context. Passing NULL for the function pointers indicates that the memory management for the item pointed to by info will be handled elsewhere, and that info will be valid at least as long as the life of the **CFSocket**.

The CFSocketCallBack is a function of the form

```
void (CFSocketRef s,
      CFSocketCallBackType type,
      CFDataRef address,
      const void *data,
      void *info);
```

CFDataRef is what you get if you registered a kCFSocketDataCallBack. data can be ignored if you don't need it, but it is used for the kCFSocketAcceptCallBack and kCFSocketConnectCallBack cases. info is the info pointer of the context structure given to **CFSocketCreateWithNative()**.

Here is some code that will register a socket, using self for the info pointer (assuming that the code is run from within an Objective-C method):

```
CFSocketContext context = { 0, self, NULL, NULL, NULL };

runLoopSocket = CFSocketCreateWithNative (kCFAllocatorDefault,
                                          serverSocket,
                                          kCFSocketReadCallBack,
                                          socketCallBack,
                                          &context);
```

If runLoopSocket is NULL, something went wrong.

Once you have the CFSocketRef from this call, it is time to create a **CFRunLoopSource** with the socket. A **CFRunLoopSource** wraps the CFSocketRef. A wrapped CFSocketRef can be added to the run loop.

```
CFRunLoopSourceRef CFSocketCreateRunLoopSource (CFAllocatorRef allocator,
                                                CFSocketRef runLoopSocket,
                                                CFIndex order);
```

Like you saw earlier, pass kCFAllocatorDefault to use the default allocator. The runLoopSocket parameter is the CFSocketRef you got from **CFSocketCreateWithNative()** earlier. The order parameter can control the order in which multiple callbacks are invoked. If you do not care about the order (which is usually the case), pass zero.

Here it is in action:

```
CFRunLoopSourceRef rls;
rls = CFSocketCreateRunLoopSource (kCFAllocatorDefault,
```

```
                                         runLoopSocket, 0);
```

If the return value is NULL, something went wrong.

Finally, add the RunLoopSourceRef to a runloop with **CFRunLoopAddSource()**:

```
void CFRunLoopAddSource (CFRunLoopRef rl,
                         CFRunLoopSourceRef source,
                         CFStringRef mode);
```

To get the current run loop, use **CFRunLoopGetCurrent()**. The source parameter is the **CFRunLoopSource** created above, and use the constant kCFRunLoopDefaultMode for the mode. If this in a UI thread, use kCFRunLoopCommonModes so that the socket doesn't get starved during some of the UI's runloop other modes, like when running a modal panel.

Add the socket to the run loop with

```
CFRunLoopAddSource (CFRunLoopGetCurrent(), rls, kCFRunLoopDefaultMode);
```

Since you created the run loop source, and the run loop itself retains the source, you need to use **CFRelease()** on the run loop source to keep the reference count correct.

GUI Chatter Client

chatterclient from the networking chapter works fine if you like living on the command line. Most Mac users (understandably) will want to use GUI programs. CFChatterClient is a GUI version of the chatterclient. It uses the CFRunLoop stuff we have been talking about so far.

In Xcode, create a new Cocoa Application project called CFChatterClient. Open up the MainMenu.nib file and layout the UI as shown in Figure 12-2

Figure 12-2. CFChatterClient User Interface

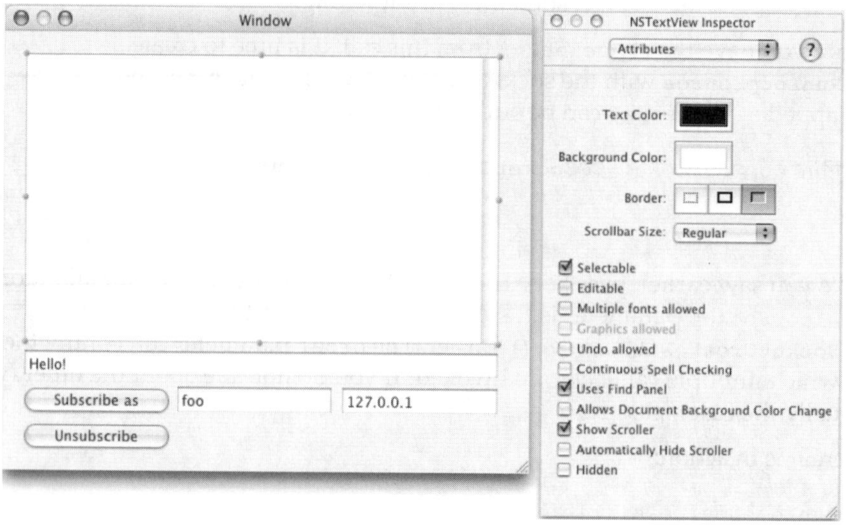

Create a subclass of **NSObject** and call it **AppController**. Add four IBOutlets to the class:

- **NSTextField** *hostField
- **NSTextField** *messageField
- **NSTextField** *nicknameField
- **NSTextView** *textView

Add three IBActions: **sendMessage:**, **subscribe:**, **unsubscribe:**. Create files for the class and create an instance of it. Figure 12-3 shows the object diagram for CFChatterClient.

Figure 12-3. CFChatterClient object diagram

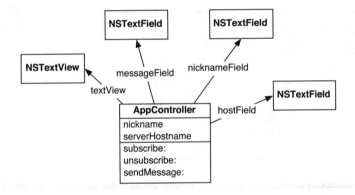

Set each outlet of the **AppController** to point to the appropriate view, as shown in Figure 12-4

Figure 12-4. Connecting Outlets

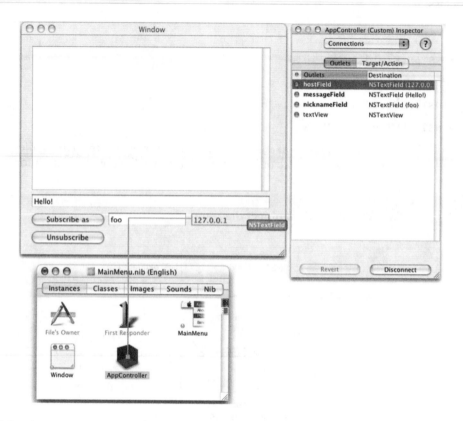

Make the **AppController** the target of the Subscribe button, the Unsubscribe button, and the message text field, as shown in Figure 12-5

Figure 12-5. Setting Message Target

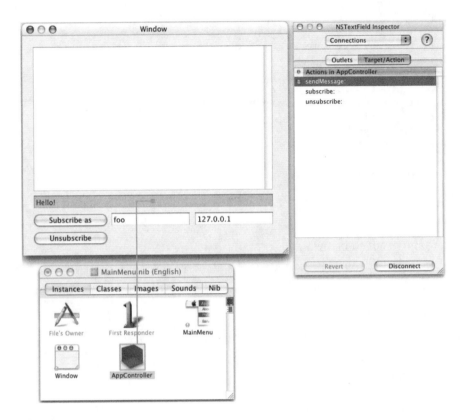

Save the nib file. Return to Xcode.

Edit the class **AppController**. Make the header look like Example 12-1 and make the body look like Example 12-2

Example 12-1. AppController.h

```
#import <Cocoa/Cocoa.h>

@interface AppController : NSObject
{
    IBOutlet    NSTextField      *hostField;
    IBOutlet    NSTextField      *messageField;
    IBOutlet    NSTextField      *nicknameField;
    IBOutlet    NSTextView       *textView;
                int              serverSocket;
                CFSocketRef      runLoopSocket;
}

- (IBAction)sendMessage:(id)sender;
- (IBAction)subscribe:(id)sender;
- (IBAction)unsubscribe:(id)sender;

@end // AppController
```

Example 12-2. AppController.m

```
#import "AppController.h"

#import <sys/types.h>    // random types
#import <netinet/in.h>   // for sockaddr_in
#import <sys/socket.h>   // for socket(), AF_INET
#import <netdb.h>        // for gethostbyname, h_errno, etc
#import <errno.h>        // for errno
#import <string.h>       // for strerror
#import <unistd.h>       // for close
#import <fcntl.h>        // for fcntl()

#define PORT_NUMBER 2342

int writeString (int fd, const void *buffer, size_t length)
{
    int result;
    unsigned char byte;

    if (length > 255) {
        fprintf (stderr, "truncating message to 255 bytes\n");
        length = 255;
    }
    byte = (unsigned char)length;

    result = write (fd, &byte, 1);
    if (result <= 0) {
        goto bailout;
    }

    do {
        result = write (fd, buffer, length);
        if (result <= 0) {
            goto bailout;
        }
        length -= result;
        buffer += result;

    } while (length > 0);

bailout:
    return (result);

} // writeString


@implementation AppController

- (id)init
{
    if (self = [super init]) {
        serverSocket = -1;
    }

    return (self);
```

```objc
} // init

- (void)updateUI
{
    // enable the message field if we are connected
    [messageField setEnabled: (runLoopSocket != NULL)];

} // updateUI

- (void)awakeFromNib
{
    [nicknameField setStringValue: NSUserName ()];
    [self updateUI];
} // awakeFromNib

- (void)closeConnection
{
    if (runLoopSocket != NULL) {
        CFSocketInvalidate (runLoopSocket);
        CFRelease (runLoopSocket);
    } else {
        close (serverSocket);
    }
    serverSocket = -1;
    runLoopSocket = NULL;

    [self updateUI];

} // closeConnection

- (void) dealloc
{
    [self closeConnection];
    [super dealloc];
} // dealloc

- (void)showErrorMessage:(NSString *)message
                sysError:(const char *)string
{
    NSString *errnoString = @"";

    if (string != NULL) {
        errnoString = [[NSString alloc] initWithCString:string];
        [errnoString autorelease];
    }

    (void) NSRunAlertPanel (message, errnoString, @"OK", nil, nil);

} // showErrorMessage

- (IBAction)sendMessage:(id)sender
{
    if (serverSocket != -1) {
        NSString *messageString;
        const char *message;
        unsigned char length;
        int result;
```

```
            // need to add newline to match behavior of the
            // command-line client
            messageString = [[messageField stringValue]
                                        stringByAppendingString:@"\n"];
            message = [messageString cString];
            length = strlen (message);

            if (length > 1) {

                result = writeString (serverSocket, message, length);

                if (result == -1) {
                    NSLog (@"error writing: %s\n", strerror(errno));
                }
                [messageField setStringValue:@""];
            }
        }

} // sendMessage


- (void)appendMessage:(NSString *)string
{
    NSRange range;
    range = NSMakeRange ([[textView string] length], 0);

    [textView replaceCharactersInRange:range withString:string];

    range = NSMakeRange ([[textView string] length],
                         [[textView string] length]);

    [textView scrollRangeToVisible:range];

} // appendMessage


- (void)readFromSocket
{
    int result;
    char buffer[5000];

    result = read (serverSocket, buffer, 5000 - 1);

    if (result == 0) {
        // other side closed
        [self closeConnection];
        NSLog (@"other side closed connection");
        [self showErrorMessage:@"Server closed the connection"
            sysError:NULL];

    } else if (result == -1) {
        [self showErrorMessage:@"Error reading from server"
            sysError:strerror(errno)];

    } else {
        [self appendMessage:[NSString stringWithCString:buffer
                                                length:result]];
    }
```

```
} // readFromSocket

void socketCallBack (CFSocketRef socketref, CFSocketCallBackType type,
                     CFDataRef address, const void *data, void *info)
{
    AppController *me = (AppController *) info;

    [me readFromSocket];

} // socketCallBack

- (void)addSocketMonitor
{
    CFSocketContext context = { 0, self, NULL, NULL, NULL };
    CFRunLoopSourceRef rls;

    runLoopSocket = CFSocketCreateWithNative (NULL,
                                              serverSocket,
                                              kCFSocketReadCallBack,
                                              socketCallBack,
                                              &context);
    if (runLoopSocket == NULL) {
        // something went wrong
        [self showErrorMessage:@"could not CFSocketCreateWithNative"
               sysError:NULL];
        goto bailout;
    }

    rls = CFSocketCreateRunLoopSource (kCFAllocatorDefault,
                                       runLoopSocket, 0);
    if (rls == NULL) {
        [self showErrorMessage:@"could not create a run loop source"
               sysError: NULL];
        goto bailout;
    }

    CFRunLoopAddSource (CFRunLoopGetCurrent (), rls,
                        kCFRunLoopDefaultMode);
    CFRelease (rls);

bailout:
    return;

} // addSocketMonitor

- (IBAction)subscribe:(id)sender
{
    NSString *errorMessage = nil;
    char *sysError = NULL;
    int result;
    struct sockaddr_in serverAddress;


    if (serverSocket != -1) {
        [self closeConnection];
    }
```

```
    // sanity check our nick name before trying to connect
    if ([[nicknameField stringValue] length] == 0 ||
        [[nicknameField stringValue] length] > 8) {
        errorMessage = @"Nickname should be between 1 and 8 characters";
        goto bailout;
    }


    {
        struct hostent *hostInfo;
        const char *hostname = [[hostField stringValue] cString];

        hostInfo = gethostbyname (hostname);
        if (hostInfo == NULL) {
            errorMessage = [NSString stringWithFormat:
                               @"Could not resolve host '%s'",hostname];
            sysError = hstrerror(h_errno);
            goto bailout;
        }

        serverAddress.sin_len = sizeof (struct sockaddr_in);
        serverAddress.sin_family = AF_INET;
        serverAddress.sin_port = htons (PORT_NUMBER);
        serverAddress.sin_addr = *((struct in_addr *)(hostInfo->h_addr));
        memset (&(serverAddress.sin_zero), 0,
                sizeof(serverAddress.sin_zero));
    }

    serverSocket = socket (AF_INET, SOCK_STREAM, 0);

    if (serverSocket == -1) {
        errorMessage = @"Could not create server socket.  Error is %s.";
        sysError = strerror (errno);
        goto bailout;
    }

    result = connect (serverSocket, (struct sockaddr *)&serverAddress,
                      sizeof(serverAddress));
    if (result == -1) {
        errorMessage = @"could not connect to server";
        sysError = strerror (errno);
        goto bailout;
    }

    // write out the nickname
    {
        const char *nickname;
        unsigned char length;
        nickname = [[nicknameField stringValue] cString];
        length = strlen (nickname);

        result = write (serverSocket, &length, 1);
        if (result == -1) {
            errorMessage = @"Could not write nickname length";
            sysError = strerror (errno);
            goto bailout;
        }
```

```
        result = write (serverSocket, nickname, length);
        if (result == -1) {
            errorMessage = @"could not write nickname.";
            sysError = strerror (errno);
            goto bailout;
        }
    }

    // set the serverSocket to non-blocking
    result = fcntl (serverSocket, F_SETFL, O_NONBLOCK);
    if (result == -1) {
        errorMessage = @"Could not make serverSocket nonblocking.";
        sysError = strerror(errno);
        goto bailout;
    }

    // yay!  We are done.
    [self addSocketMonitor];

bailout:
    if (errorMessage != nil) {
        [self showErrorMessage: errorMessage  sysError: sysError];
        [self closeConnection];
    }

    [self updateUI];

} // subscribe

- (void)unsubscribe: (id) sender
{
    [self closeConnection];

} // unsubscribe

@end // AppController
```

Run the `chatterserver` from the networking chapter. Build and run this client.

The System Configuration Framework

The user is free to change aspects of the system configuration at any time, such as changing their network location from "Office" to "Home". Changing the network location could change a number of lower-level settings, such as which IP addresses the machine has available and which DNS servers to use. There are also system parameters that change dynamically, such as the battery level in laptops. In some situations, your application needs to be able to react to these changes. For example, if you have a network socket listening on a particular IP address (as opposed to listening on all of them), you'll need to listen on the new IP if the user changes it.

In Mac OS X 10.1, Apple introduced the system configuration framework which provides an architecture for storing configuration and run-time information. Currently it only supports network configuration and the powerbook battery monitor, but in the future more information will be supported.

Architecture

At the heart of the system configuration framework is `configd`, the system configuration daemon. `configd` holds the dynamic store, which is an online database of configuration information consisting of key/value pairs. These pairs are arranged in a hierarchy, like nested dictionaries, and are addressed by paths similar to the URLs used to identify web pages. There are two major spaces, one for "setup" information (what is set in configuration applications) and one for "State" information (what is actually configured and running). The keys look like `State:/Network/Service/serviceID/IPv4` for the current IP state, and like `Setup:/Network/Service/serviceID/PPP` for PPP configuration.

Much of the persistent configuration information is stored in property lists that live in the `/Library/Preferences/SystemConfiguration/` directory. `configd` reads these files and places their contents into the dynamic store. There are also configuration agents, which are bundles that `configd` loads that provide configuration and notification services. Currently there are agents to monitor the preferences, to monitor the kernel and track the state of all network interfaces, as well as a PPP controller.

Basic API

The system configuration framework source code is included in Darwin if you are interested in poking around and seeing how things work. The API lives at the Core Foundation level, and so shares similarities to the rest of the Core Foundation API. The examples here that query the dynamic store will be primarily Cocoa based and take advantage of the toll-free bridging between Core Foundation data structures and the equivalent Cocoa data structures. Toll-free bridging lets you cast `CF*` pointers to their equivalent `NS*` types, such as `CFString` and `NSString`, or `CFArray` and `NSArray`, or `CFData` and `NSData`. Not all types are toll-free bridged. `CFBundle` and `NSBundle` are not, and neither are `CFNumber` and `NSNumber`.

For querying the dynamic store, perform these steps:

1. Connect to `configd`'s dynamic store with **`SCDynamicStoreCreate()`**.

2. Construct some access keys, either by explicitly constructing the paths or by supplying a regular expression to **`SCDynamicStoreCopyKeyList()`**.

3. Iterate over the keys and call **`SCDynamicStoreCopyValue()`** to fetch the value. Or you can use **`SCDynamicStoreCopyMultiple()`** to fetch the values for all keys at once. This second call provides a read-consistent view to the data. Use the `CopyMultiple` version of the function when you can to prevent possible race conditions when performing multiple calls to `CopyValue`.

4. If you want to be notified when a particular value changes, call **`SCDynamicStoreSetNotificationKeys()`** and tell it which keys you are interested in.

Here are the calls in more detail.

```
SCDynamicStoreRef
SCDynamicStoreCreate (CFAllocatorRef allocator,
                      CFStringRef name,
                      SCDynamicStoreCallBack callback,
```

```
SCDynamicStoreContext *context);
```

Creates a new session to talk to `configd`. The parameters are:

allocator

> The allocator used to allocate memory for the local object and for any storage it may need. Use `kCFAllocatorDefault` to use the default memory allocator.

name

> A string (which can be cast from an `NSString` pointer) that names the calling process.

callback

> A callback function that will get called when values change for the keys given to **SCDyanmicStoreSetNotificationKeys()**.

context

> A structure just like `CFSocketContext`, where you give the version, a pointer, and some function pointers to retain and release functions. In Cocoa, you can make one of these like this:

```
SCDynamicStoreContext context = {
    0, self, NULL, NULL, NULL
};
```

```
CFArrayRef
```
SCDynamicStoreCopyKeyList (SCDynamicStoreRef store,
                            CFStringRef pattern);

Returns an array of string keys that match a given regular expression. .

store

> The dynamic store reference that **SCDynamicStoreCreate()** returned.

pattern

> A regular expression (not the simple shell globs used elsewhere) that matches the keys you're looking for. For instance, `".*"` will match everything, and `"State:/Network/Service/[^/]+/IPv4"` will match IPv4 network service urls with for any service name.

```
CFPropertyListRef
```
SCDynamicStoreCopyValue (SCDynamicStoreRef store,
                           CFStringRef key);

Returns either a string or a dictionary with the value requested. .

store

> The dynamic store reference from **SCDynamicStoreCreate()**.

key

> The key representing the data you want, either specified explicitly or taken from `SCDynamicStoreCopyKeyList()`.

```
CFDictionaryRef
SCDynamicStoreCopyMultiple (SCDynamicStoreRef store,
                            CFArrayRef keys,
                            CFArrayRef patterns);
```

Like `SCDynamicStoreCopyValue()`, but returns the values for a set of keys. It returns a dictionary containing the values.

store

> The dynamic store reference from `SCDynamicStoreCreate()`.

keys

> The set of keys that indicate the values to return.

patterns

> Regular expression patterns to match keys in the dynamic store.

```
Boolean
SCDynamicStoreSetNotificationKeys (SCDynamicStoreRef store,
                                   CFArrayRef keys,
                                   CFArrayRef patterns);
```

This tells the dynamic store which keys and patterns of keys are interesting. When the values change, the callback function specified with `SCDynamicStoreCreate()` is called.

store

> The dynamic store connection.

keys

> The keys of interest.

patterns

> Regular expression indicating more keys of interest.

The callback function should look like this:

```
void storeCallback (SCDynamicStoreRef store, CFArrayRef changedKeys,
                    void *info);
```

store

> The dynamic store the callback has been associated with.

changedKeys

> An array of keys that have new values.

```
info
```

The pointer specified in the second field of the context passed to
`SCDynamicStoreCreate()`.

There are also some convenience functions like
`SCDynamicStoreCopyLocalHostName()` to get the current host name, and if you
want notifications on the current host name, you can call
`SCDyanmicStoreKeyCreateHostNames()` to get the key to pass to
`SCDynamicStoreSetNotificationkeys()`.

Seeing all values

Example 12-3 is a foundation tool that will show all of the keys and values in
`configd`'s dynamic store:

Example 12-3. scf-dump.m

```
/* scf-dump.m -- show all the live entries from the
 *               SystemConfiguration.framework
 */

/* compile with
cc -g -Wall -framework Foundation -framework SystemConfiguration \
   -o scf-dump scf-dump.m
*/

#import <Foundation/Foundation.h>
#import <SystemConfiguration/SystemConfiguration.h>

/* a little utility function to NSLog information, but without the
 * leading noise information like the current time and process ID
 */

void LogIt (NSString *format, ...)
{
    va_list args;
    va_start (args, format);

    NSString *string;
    // the string format stuff will expand %@, which regular v*printf
    // won't do
    string = [[NSString alloc] initWithFormat: format  arguments: args];

    va_end (args);

    printf ("%s\n", [string cString]);

    [string release];

} // LogIt


// print the contents of a dictionary (string keys, string values)

void dumpDictionary (NSDictionary *dictionary)
```

```
{
    NSArray *keys;
    NSArray *values;
    int i;

    keys = [dictionary allKeys];
    values = [dictionary objectsForKeys: keys  notFoundMarker: nil];

    for (i = 0; i < [keys count]; i++) {
        LogIt (@"    %@ : %@", [keys objectAtIndex: i],
                  [values objectAtIndex: i]);
    }

} // dumpDictionary


int main (int argc, const char *argv[])
{
    NSAutoreleasePool *pool = [[NSAutoreleasePool alloc] init];

    // make a connection to configd

    SCDynamicStoreRef store;
    SCDynamicStoreContext context = {
        0, NULL, NULL, NULL, NULL
    };

    store = SCDynamicStoreCreate (kCFAllocatorDefault,  // allocator
                                  CFSTR("SCF Dumper"),   // name
                                  NULL,                  // callback
                                  &context);         // DynStore ctx

    if (store == NULL) {
        NSLog (@"oops!  can't SCDynamicStoreCreate");
        goto bailout;
    }

    // get a list of all the keys.  the .* regexp should match everything
    CFArrayRef keys;
    keys = SCDynamicStoreCopyKeyList (store, CFSTR(".*"));

    if (keys == NULL) {
        NSLog (@"oops!  can't SCDynamicStoreCopyKeyList");
        goto bailout;
    }

    // walk the set of keys.  It returns a CFArrayRef, which is
    // toll-free-bridged to an NSArray, so we can use the
    // NSArray enumerator

    CFStringRef key;

    NSEnumerator *enumerator;
    enumerator = [((NSArray*)keys) objectEnumerator];

    while ((key = (CFStringRef)[enumerator nextObject])) {
```

```
        LogIt (@"key is %@", key);

        // get the value from configd
        CFPropertyListRef value;
        value = SCDynamicStoreCopyValue (store, key);

        // some values are keys, others are dictionaries withricher
        // result values
        if ([(id)value isKindOfClass: [NSDictionary class]]) {
            dumpDictionary ((NSDictionary *) value);
        } else {
            LogIt (@"    %@", (id)value);
        }

        LogIt (@"\n");
    }

bailout:
    [pool release];

    return (EXIT_SUCCESS);

} // main
```

and part of a sample run:

```
$ ./scf-dump
key is State:/Network/Global/DNS
    ServerAddresses : ("198.77.116.8", "198.77.116.12")

key is Setup:/Network/Service/5/DNS
    ServerAddresses : ("198.77.116.8", "198.77.116.12")

key is Setup:/System
    ComputerNameEncoding : 0
    ComputerName : iLamp

key is State:/Network/Service/4/IPv4
    Addresses : ("192.168.0.123")
    SubnetMasks : ("255.255.255.0")
    InterfaceName : en0

key is State:/Network/Interface
    Interfaces : (lo0, gif0, stf0, en0, en1)
...
```

SCFMonitor

The SCFMonitor application, shown in Figure 12-6, dispalys the current host name, the person logged in on the console, and the local IP address(es). Notifications are registered to keep the values up to date, although the console user won't change without a logout. The system configuration framework does not provide any notification or information about users logged in via the network.

Figure 12-6. SCFMonitor window

Local Host Name:	iLamp
Console User:	markd (501,20)
Local IP Address:	192.168.0.124 192.168.0.123

SCFMonitor

In Xcode, create a new Cocoa Application project called SCFMonitor. Add the system configuration framework by choosing **Add To Project** from the **Project** menu and selecting SystemConfiguration.framework. Then open the MainMenu.nib file and layout the UI as shown in Figure 12-7 by using 6 static text labels.

Figure 12-7. SCFMonitor static text labels

Local Host Name:	System Font Text
Console User:	System Font Text
Local IP Address:	System Font Text

SCFMonitor

Create a subclass of **NSObject** called **AppController**. Add three outlets to the class:

- **NSTextField** *hostnameField
- **NSTextField** *consoleUserField
- **NSTextField** *localIPField

There is no direct user action in this program, so there is no need to add any actions. Figure 12-8 shows the SCFMonitor object diagram.

Figure 12-8. SCFMonitor object diagram

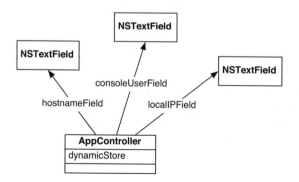

Set each outlet of the **AppController** to point to the appropriate text field.

Save the nib file and return to Xcode.

Edit the **AppController**.

Example 12-4. AppController.h

```
#import <Cocoa/Cocoa.h>
#import <SystemConfiguration/SystemConfiguration.h>

@interface AppController : NSObject
{
    IBOutlet    NSTextField    *hostnameField;
    IBOutlet    NSTextField    *consoleUserField;
    IBOutlet    NSTextField    *localIPField;

    SCDynamicStoreRef    dynamicStore;
}

- (void)refreshUI;

- (NSString *)hostname;
- (NSString *)consoleUser;
- (NSString *)localIPs;

@end // AppController
```

And then add the code to AppController.m:

Example 12-5. AppController.m

```
#import "AppController.h"

// result is a dictionary with Name, UID, and GID keys
#define CONSOLE_USER_KEY        (CFSTR("State:/Users/ConsoleUser"))

// result is a dictionary with a LocalHostName key.
// For illustration, this uses the convenience API for dealing
// with hostnames.  Change this by tweaking the Rendezvous Name
// in the Sharing preferences
#define HOSTNAME_KEY            (SCDynamicStoreKeyCreateHostNames(NULL))

// match any IPv4 service.  The "[^/]+" part of the pattern means
// "match one or more characters that are not slashes"
#define IP_PATTERN (CFSTR("State:/Network/Service/[^/]+/IPv4"))

// gets called when the dynamic store changes

void storeCallback (SCDynamicStoreRef store, CFArrayRef changedKeys,
                    void *info)
{
    NSLog (@"storeCallback: changedKeys is %@", changedKeys);

    AppController *controller = (AppController *)info;

    [controller refreshUI];
```

```
    } // storeCallback


@implementation AppController

- (NSString *) hostname
{
    CFStringRef hostname;

    hostname = SCDynamicStoreCopyLocalHostName (dynamicStore);

    return ((NSString *) hostname);

} // hostname

- (NSString *) consoleUser
{
    NSArray *keyList;
    keyList =
        (NSArray *) SCDynamicStoreCopyKeyList (dynamicStore,
                                               CONSOLE_USER_KEY);

    CFStringRef consoleValueKey;
    consoleValueKey = (CFStringRef) [keyList objectAtIndex:0];

    NSDictionary *consoleUserDict;
    consoleUserDict =
        (NSDictionary *) SCDynamicStoreCopyValue (dynamicStore,
                                                  consoleValueKey);

    NSMutableString *consoleUser;
    consoleUser = [[NSMutableString alloc] init];

    // make a string of the form "username (user-id, group-id)"
    [consoleUser appendString: [consoleUserDict objectForKey: @"Name"]];
    [consoleUser appendFormat:@" (%@, %@)",
                 [consoleUserDict objectForKey:@"UID"],
                 [consoleUserDict objectForKey:@"GID"]];

    return (consoleUser);

} // consoleUser

- (NSString *) localIPs
{
    NSMutableString *localIPs;

    localIPs = [[NSMutableString alloc] init];


    // make an array of stuff so we can use SCDynamicStoreCopyMultiple
    // and get a consistent snapshot, since there may be several IP
    // addresses, rather than several calls to SCDynamicStoreCopyValue

    NSArray *patternList;
    patternList = [NSArray arrayWithObject:(NSString *)IP_PATTERN];
```

```objc
    NSDictionary *dictionary;
    dictionary =
        (NSDictionary*)SCDynamicStoreCopyMultiple (dynamicStore,
                            NULL,  // keys
                            (CFArrayRef)patternList);
    // now walk the dictionary.
    // the key is an identifier, like State:/Network/Service/5/IPv4
    // the value is another dictionary, which has a key of "Addresses"
    // that is an array strings, which are the actual IP addresses

    NSEnumerator *enumerator;
    enumerator = [dictionary keyEnumerator];

    NSString *key;
    while ((key = [enumerator nextObject])) {
        NSDictionary *oneConfig;
        oneConfig = [dictionary objectForKey: key];

        NSArray *addresses;
        addresses = [oneConfig objectForKey: @"Addresses"];

        // now walk the addresses
        NSEnumerator *addressesEnumerator;
        addressesEnumerator = [addresses objectEnumerator];

        NSString *address;
        while ((address = [addressesEnumerator nextObject])) {
            [localIPs appendString: address];
            [localIPs appendString: @" "];
        }
    }

    return (localIPs);

} // localIP


- (void) refreshUI
{
    [hostnameField setStringValue:[self hostname]];
    [consoleUserField setStringValue:[self consoleUser]];
    [localIPField setStringValue:[self localIPs]];

} // refreshUI


- (void) awakeFromNib
{
    // create the dynamic store
    SCDynamicStoreContext context = {
        0, self, NULL, NULL, NULL
    };

    dynamicStore = SCDynamicStoreCreate (NULL,                  // allocator
                                CFSTR("SCFMonitor"), // name
                                storeCallback,       // callback
                                &context);      // context
    if (dynamicStore == NULL) {
        NSLog (@"could not create dynamic store reference");
```

347

```
        }

        // what are we interested in receiving notifications about?
        NSArray *noteKeys, *notePatterns;

        noteKeys = [NSArray arrayWithObjects:
                            (NSString *) HOSTNAME_KEY,
                            (NSString *) CONSOLE_USER_KEY,
                            nil];
        notePatterns = [NSArray arrayWithObject:
                                (NSString *) IP_PATTERN];
        // register those notifications
        if (!SCDynamicStoreSetNotificationKeys(dynamicStore,
                                               (CFArrayRef) noteKeys,
                                               (CFArrayRef) notePatterns)) {
            NSLog (@"could not register notification keys");
        }

        // create a run loop source
        CFRunLoopSourceRef runLoopSource;

        runLoopSource = SCDynamicStoreCreateRunLoopSource (NULL, // allocator
                                                           dynamicStore,
                                                           0);   // order
        // stick it into the current runloop

        CFRunLoopRef runLoop = CFRunLoopGetCurrent ();
        CFRunLoopAddSource (runLoop, runLoopSource, kCFRunLoopDefaultMode);

        CFRelease (runLoopSource);

        [self refreshUI];

    } // awakeFromNib

@end // AppController
```

Build and run it. If you have two IP addresses, they should both show up in the window. If you have an airport card and built-in ethernet, they can each have their own IP (but you may need to plug in an ethernet cable for the OS to acknowledge that the interface should be used).

If you change an IP you can see it disappear from the window for a couple of seconds and then reappear as the network interface is taken down and is brought back up to effect the change. You can change the hostname by editing the Rendezvous Name in the Sharing preferences.

For the More Curious

You can hook more stuff into the run loop, such as an observer. A run loop observer has its callback function invoked at a number of well defined places, shown Figure 12-9. These are the observation points:

- When the run loop is entered
- Before timers are fired

- After timers are fired
- Before sources (like the **CFSocket**) are checked
- Before the run loop waits for activity (blocking until it can do something)
- After it wakes up
- When the run loop exits

Figure 12-9. Run Loop Observation Points

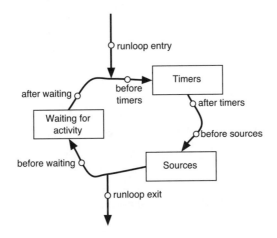

Here is a function that will register an observer:

```
void addRunLoopObserver ()
{
    CFRunLoopRef rl;
    CFRunLoopObserverRef observer;

    rl = CFRunLoopGetCurrent ();

    observer = CFRunLoopObserverCreate (kCFAllocatorDefault,
                        kCFRunLoopAllActivities, // activites
                        1, // repeats
                        0, // order
                        observerCallback,
                        NULL); // context

    CFRunLoopAddObserver (rl, observer, kCFRunLoopDefaultMode);

    CFRelease (observer);

} // addRunLoopObserver
```

This works in a very similar way to the CFSocketRef, except here you do not have to create an independent run loop source. You cannot use an observer for anything useful outside of a run loop, so the designers removed that step.

Here is an observer function which will print out what action is being observed:

```
typedef struct observerActivity {
```

```
    int          activity;
    const char *name;
} observerActivity;

observerActivity g_activities[] = {
    { kCFRunLoopEntry,          "Run Loop Entry" },
    { kCFRunLoopBeforeTimers,   "Before Timers" },
    { kCFRunLoopBeforeSources,  "Before Sources" },
    { kCFRunLoopBeforeWaiting,  "Before Waiting" },
    { kCFRunLoopAfterWaiting,   "After Waiting" },
    { kCFRunLoopExit,           "Exit" }
};

void observerCallback (CFRunLoopObserverRef observer,
                       CFRunLoopActivity activity,
                       void *info)
{
    observerActivity *scan, *stop;

    scan = g_activities;
    stop = scan + (sizeof(g_activities) / sizeof(observerActivity));

    while (scan < stop) {

        if (scan->activity == activity) {
            NSLog (@"%s", scan->name);
            break;
        }
        scan++;
    }

} // observerCallback
```

Challenge

1. Add the observer callback to your `CFChatterClient`.

2. If you run `scf-dump` on a laptop, you'll probably see something like this:

```
key is State:/IOKit/PowerSources/InternalBattery-0
    Max Capacity : 962
    Current Capacity : 962
    Name : InternalBattery-0
    Is Present : 1
    Is Charging : 0
    Time to Full Charge : 0
    Transport Type : Internal
    Time to Empty : 0
    Power Source State : AC Power
```

Extend the `SCFMonitor` application to monitor battery information, and display it in a tableview.

Chapter 13. Multiprocessing

All modern operating systems are multiprocessing, meaning that there are multiple independent programs running simultaneously and sharing the system's resources. The OS time-slices among the runnable programs, dividing the available CPU time among runnable processes (those that are not blocked by I/O). Using multiple processes allows multiple CPUs to be utilized as well.

Process Scheduling

The scheduler is the part of the OS that figures out what process should get the CPU next. It uses information such as process priority, how much CPU time a process has previously gotten, whether it has just completed an I/O operation, and other factors to decide what to run next.

Each process has a priority, an integer in the range from -20 to 20, where smaller values are actually higher priority than greater values. You can set the priority of a new program by running it with the `nice` command, while the `renice` command changes the priority of a running process. You can "nice down" (using a larger number for the priority, thereby making it lower priority) your own programs, but you cannot "nice up" a program unless you have superuser privileges.

Internally, the scheduler has a list of processes with their individual priorities, as shown in Figure 13-1. Those process that are not blocked are put into the run queue in order of their priority. When it is time to run a new process, the scheduler pulls a process off the front of the queue, lets it run until it blocks for some reason or its time slice expires, and then sticks it back in the queue.

Figure 13-1. The Scheduler

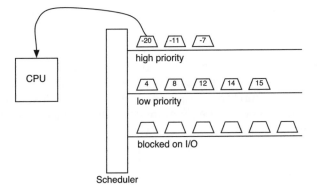

The load average of your machine can be shown by the `top` and `uptime` commands:

```
2:10PM  up 6 days, 16:28, 5 users, load averages: 0.36, 0.39, 0.36
```

The last three values are the load average, which is the average of the number of runnable processes (the depth of the run queue) over the last 1, 5, and 15 minutes. Here you can see that about a third of the time there is something in the run queue, and it is pretty constant over time. Mac OS X's load average just reports the depth of the run queue. It does not include the time blocked in disk I/O, which some Unix-like OSs (such as Linux) report.

A general rule of thumb is that a healthy machine, CPU-wise, has a load average at or less than two times the number of processors.

Convenience Functions

Starting new processes can be a powerful tool in your programming arsenal. Unix comes with a lot of little command-line utilities that perform useful functions. Sometimes it makes more sense to take advantage of these utilities rather than reimplementing their behavior. For example, you may have a Perl script that strips tags from HTML. If your application has a need for that kind of tag-stripping feature, it can be easier to start the perl script and feed it your HTML rather than playing around with regular expression code in Objective-C.

The easiest way to start another program is to use the **system()** function. This will start a program, wait until it finishes, and then return the result code. **system()** actually passes control to a new shell (/bin/sh) so you can use shell features like redirection.

```
int system (const char *string);
```

The return value from **system()** is the result value returned from the program, or else you get -1 and errno is set if there was an error before starting the shell. A return value of 127 means the shell failed for some reason (probably due to bad syntax in the command string). **system()** invokes the shell with the -c argument, passing in the command line as the next argument after the -c. You can use this too if you get this error and want to experiment with your command line using a shell in the Terminal.

If you want to actually read or write to the program you start, use **popen()** to start the program and open a pipe to it. **pclose()** closes the connection:

```
FILE *popen (const char *command, const char *type);

int pclose (FILE *stream);
```

Like **system()**, **popen()** invokes a shell to run the command. Example 13-1 is a little program that **popen**s the cal program to get a current calendar. Just for fun, the output from cal gets run through rev to reverse the lines (just to show that pipelines work in **popen()**). The program does the equivalent of a head -9 by only reading the first nine lines.

Example 13-1. pcal.m

```
// pcal.m -- display a calendar using popen

/* compile with:
cc -g -Wall -o pcal pcal.m
*/

#import <stdio.h>        // for popen, printf
#import <stdlib.h>       // for EXIT_SUCCESS

#define BUFSIZE    4096
#define NUM_LINES 9
```

```c
int main (int argc, char *argv[])
{
    int result = EXIT_FAILURE;
    FILE *pipeline = NULL;
    char buffer[BUFSIZE];
    int i;

    // reverse the lines just for fun
    pipeline = popen ("cal 2005 | rev", "r");

    if (pipeline == NULL) {
        fprintf (stderr, "error popening pipeline\n");
        goto bailout;
    }

    for (i = 0; i < NUM_LINES; i++) {
        if (fgets(buffer, BUFSIZE, pipeline) == NULL) {
            fprintf (stderr, "error reading from pipeline\n");
            goto bailout;
        }

        printf ("%s", buffer);
    }

    result = EXIT_SUCCESS;

bailout:

    if (pipeline != NULL) {
        pclose (pipeline);
    }

    return (result);

} // main
```

The man page for **popen()** claims that you can use a bidirectional channel. This is misleading, implying that you can both write and read from the pipeline. The program on the receiving end of **popen()** must be implemented specifically to support bidirectional channels.

Here is a sample run of pcal:

```
$ ./pcal
                                    5002

          hcraM                     yraurbeF                  yraunaJ
  S  F  hT  W  uT  M  S     S  F  hT  W  uT  M  S     S  F  hT  W  uT  M  S
  5  4   3  2   1           5  4   3  2   1           1
 21 11  01  9   8  7  6    21 11  01  9   8  7  6     8  7   6  5   4  3  2
 91 81  71 61  51 41 31    91 81  71 61  51 41 31    51 41  31 21  11 01  9
 62 52  42 32  22 12 02    62 52  42 32  22 12 02    22 12  02 91  81 71 61
        13 03  92 82 72           82 72  92 82              72 62  52 42 32
```

fork

To create a new process in Unix you must first make a copy of an existing process. That copy can continue to execute as an independent entity, or it can then be replaced with another program. The `fork()` system call is used to make this copy:

```
pid_t fork (void);
```

`fork()` makes a copy of the running process, and it is one of the few functions that can return twice. In the original process (known as the parent) `fork()` returns the process ID of the new process. In the child process, `fork()` returns zero. In the case of errors, `fork()` returns -1 and sets `errno`.

What is meant by making a copy of the process? All of the memory in the parent process is available to the child, as are open files, the real and effective user and group IDs, the current working directory, the signal mask, the file mode creation mask (umask), the environment, resource limits, and any attached shared memory segments. This copying behavior can be seen in Figure 13-2

Figure 13-2. Fork

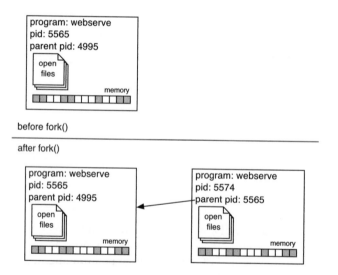

Mac OS X does not really make a deep copy (that is, make a duplicate) of the parent's memory space. It uses a technique called *copy on write*, as shown in Figure 13-3, where all the physical pages that relate to this process are marked as read-only. If either process tries to modify something in memory, the page being modified is first duplicated so that each process is given its own copy. The modifying process gets to make its changes, and the other process is none the wiser. This greatly reduces the amount of work the OS does on a `fork()`.

Figure 13-3. Copy On Write

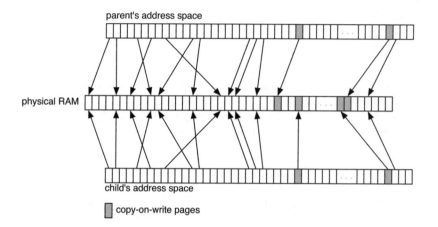

The convenience functions in the previous section (**system()** and **popen()**) call **fork()** under the hood, but for most purposes are rather heavy-weight and use more resources than a careful use of **fork()** would, particularly the invocation of a shell to run the new processes.

Example 13-2 shows a minimal program that makes a child:

Example 13-2. fork.m

```
// fork.m -- show simple use of fork()

/* compile with:
cc -g -Wall -o fork fork.m
*/

#import <sys/types.h>    // for pid_t
#import <unistd.h>       // for fork
#import <stdlib.h>       // for EXIT_SUCCESS
#import <stdio.h>        // for printf

int main (int argc, char *argv[])
{
    pid_t child;

    printf ("hello there");

    if ((child = fork())) {
        printf ("\nChild pid is %ld\n", (long)child);
        sleep (5);
    } else {
        printf ("\nIn the child.  My parent is %ld\n",
                (long)getppid());
        _exit (EXIT_SUCCESS);
    }

    exit (EXIT_SUCCESS);

} // main
```

and a sample run:

```
$ ./fork
hello there
Child pid is 2870
hello there
In the child.  My parent is 2869
```

As with just about everything in Unix-land, there are some gotchas that can catch the unwary. The first involves race conditions between the parent and the child: you are not guaranteed which will run first. You cannot depend on some code being run after the **fork()** in the parent before the child gets scheduled.

The other gotcha relates to how open files are shared between the two processes. Both the parent and child share the same file table entry in the kernel, as shown in Figure 13-4. This means that all of the attributes of the open file are shared, such as the current offset. This is commonly the desired behavior — when you want both child and parent to print to the same standard out, each process will increment the offset in the file when they print, so they'll avoid writing over each other. However, it can also be confusing when your file offsets move from underneath you and you were not expecting them to.

Related to the file table issue is the state of the buffers for buffered I/O. The buffered I/O buffers in the parent's address space get duplicated across the fork, also shown in Figure 13-4. If there is data in the buffer before the fork, both the child and the parent could print out the buffered data twice (like what happened in Example 13-2), which may not be what you want.

Figure 13-4. Files After Fork

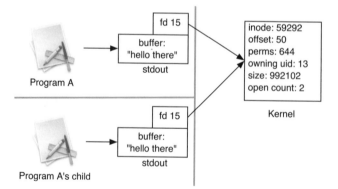

Also note the use of **_exit()** in Example 13-2. It behaves like **exit()**, closing file descriptors, generally cleaning up, but does not flush standard out, so you do not have to worry about **exit()** flushing a buffer for you that has duplicate data. In the example, though, the newline in the subsequent **printf**s flushed the buffer for us.

Parent And Child Lifetimes

Due to the nature of **fork()**, every process has exactly one parent process while a parent can have multiple child processes. Each process that terminates has a certain amount of state information associated with it, like its result code, system resource usage, and so on. This information gets reported to the parent. You use one of the **wait()** family of system calls to get this information. When you get this exit information, the child process can finally terminate. this is often called *reaping* the child process).

```
pid_t wait (int *status);

pid_t waitpid (pid_t wpid, int *status, int options);

pid_t wait3 (int *status, int options, struct rusage *rusage);

pid_t wait4 (pid_t wpid, int *status, int options, struct rusage *rusage);
```

In general, calling any one of the wait functions will collect the result code from the child. **wait()** will block until there is an exited child waiting to be reaped.. If there are multiple child processes that have exited, the **wait()** will return an arbitrary one of those. If you want to wait for a specific child process, use **waitpid()**. The options that **waitpid()** (and **wait3()** and **wait4()**) use are:

WNOHANG

Do not block waiting for a child. Return immediately if there are no exited children.

WUNTRACED

Report job-control actions on children (like being stopped or backgrounded).

wait3() is like **wait()**, and **wait4()** is like **waitpid()**. They either wait on an arbitrary child, or wait or a specific one. In addition tho this, **wait3()** and **wait4()** fill in a structure about resources consumed by the child. You can find the full struct rusage in /usr/include/sys/resource.h. The more interesting elements of this structure are:

```
struct rusage {
    struct timeval ru_utime;        /* user time used */
    struct timeval ru_stime;        /* system time used */
    long           ru_maxrss;       /* max resident set size */
}
```

You can see how much CPU was consumed by the child, as well as the child's high water mark of memory usage.

The return value from the child, along with a bunch of other useful bits of information, are encoded in the status result returned by all the **wait()** functions. Use these macros to pull out the items you are interested in:

WIFEXITED

True if the process terminated normally via a call to **exit()** or **_exit()**.

WEXITSTATUS

The low-order byte of the argument the child passed to **exit()** or **_exit()**. The return value from **main()** is used as the argument **exit()**. This assumes WIFEXITED(status) value is true.

WIFSIGNALED True if the process terminated due to receipt of a signal.

WTERMSIG

The number of the signal that caused the termination of the process. This assumes that WIFSIGNALED(status) is true.

WCOREDUMP

If true, the termination of the process was accompanied by the creation of a core dump.

WIFSTOPPED

True if the process has not terminated, but was just stopped due to job control in a shell (such as using control-Z to suspend a process).

WSTOPSIG

Returns number of the signal that caused the process to stop. This assumes that WIFSTOPPED(status) is true.

Example 13-3 shows these macros in action:

Example 13-3. status.m

```
// status.m -- play with various child exiting status values

/* compile with:
cc -g -Wall -o status status.m
*/

#import <sys/types.h>       // for pid_t
#import <sys/wait.h>        // for wait()
#import <unistd.h>          // for fork
#import <stdlib.h>          // for EXIT_SUCCESS
#import <stdio.h>           // for printf
#import <sys/time.h>        // for ru_utime and ru_stime in rlimit
#import <sys/resource.h>    // for rlimit
#import <errno.h>           // for errno
#import <string.h>          // for strerror

void printStatus (int status)
{
    if (WIFEXITED(status)) {
        printf ("program exited normally.  Return value is %d",
                WEXITSTATUS(status));

    } else if (WIFSIGNALED(status)) {
        printf ("program exited on signal %d", WTERMSIG(status));
        if (WCOREDUMP(status)) {
            printf (" (core dumped)");
        }

    } else {
        printf ("other exit value");
    }
    printf ("\n");
```

```
} // printStatus

int main (int argc, char *argv[])
{
    int status;

    // normal exit
    if (fork () == 0) {
        _exit (23);
    }

    wait (&status);
    printStatus (status);

    // die by a signal (SIGABRT)
    if (fork () == 0) {
        abort ();
    }

    wait (&status);
    printStatus (status);

    // die by crashing
    if (fork () == 0) {
        int *blah = (int *)0xFeedFace;   // a bad address
        *blah = 12;
    }

    wait (&status);
    printStatus (status);

    // drop core
    if (fork () == 0) {
        struct rlimit rl;

        rl.rlim_cur = RLIM_INFINITY;
        rl.rlim_max = RLIM_INFINITY;

        if (setrlimit (RLIMIT_CORE, &rl) == -1) {
            fprintf (stderr,
                    "error in setrlimit for RLIMIT_CORE: %d (%s)\n",
                    errno, strerror(errno));
        }
        abort ();
    }

    wait (&status);
    printStatus (status);

    return (EXIT_SUCCESS);

} // main
```

A sample run looks like this:

```
$ ./status
```

```
program exited normally.  Return value is 23
program exited on signal 6
program exited on signal 11
program exited on signal 6 (core dumped)
```

For the period of time between when the child program exits and the parent performs a **wait()**, the kernel needs to store the status and resource information somewhere. It does so by keeping the process in the process table. The kernel disposes of much of what the child allocated (memory, files, etc.), but still keeps this last piece of information around. The child process is known as a *zombie*. Zombies show up in the output of the ps command in parentheses:

```
root    2832    0.0   0.0      0  0 con-  Z+   31Dec69   0:00.00 (proctest)
markd   2834    0.0   0.0   4940  4 std   R+   10:42AM   0:00.00 grep 2832
```

Usually you do not have to worry too much about the occasional zombie (these zombies don't eat brains). You only need to worry if get a whole bunch of them, which is usually due to a programming error by not waiting on exited children. Uncontrolled zombie creation can fill up the process table and render the machine useless.

How do you know when to call **wait()**? You can adopt a polling model and call **waitpid()** occasionally, looking for children during idle time. Also, when a child exits, a SIGCHLD signal gets sent to the parent. You will not necessarily receive one SIGCHLD for each child process that exits, such as when two exit while the parent is waiting in the kernel's run queue. You can also use a kqueue to monitor for process termination and SIGCHLD signals.

One last issue dealing with parents and children: what happens to a child process when its parent goes away? Every child has to have a parent process ID, but now the original parent process is gone. init adopts it. The process with process ID 1 in every Unix system acts like an orphanage for these abandoned children. On most unix systems, process ID 1 is the init daemon, and on Mac OS X it is the launchd program, which are started by the kernel at the end of the bootstrap process, and is there (among other reasons) to be the parent of any orphaned children. So, when a parent dies, its children become children of init.

You can see the parent process ID by giving the ppid flag to the -o option of ps (more stuff added to make the output more useful):

```
$ ps -axo user,pid,ppid,vsz,tt,state,start,time,command
USER      PID   PPID     VSZ   TT  STAT  STARTED        TIME COMMAND
root        1      0    1308   ??  Ss    20Sep02    0:00.00 /sbin/launchd
root       51      1   15912   ??  Ss    20Sep02    0:02.45 kextd
root       73      1    1292   ??  Ss    20Sep02    0:20.98 update
...
root      429    397   14048   p2  Ss    21Sep02    0:00.84 login -pf markd
markd     430    429    5872   p2  S     21Sep02    0:00.05 -tcsh (tcsh)
markd     431    430   15840   p2  S+    21Sep02    2:34.63 emacs
markd     432    431    9952  std  Ss    21Sep02    0:01.10 -bin/tcsh -i (tcsh)
root     2894    432    5192  std  R+    11:18AM    0:00.00 ps -axo user pid pp
...
```

Here you can see some daemon processes with /sbin/launchd as the parent. There is also the login process (the parent pid 397 is Terminal.app), as well as some other programs like the shell and emacs.

exec

Most often after a fork you just want to run some other program. The **exec()** family of functions replace the current running process with a new one. You will typically hear of **fork()** and **exec()** spoken together since they are used a lot together.

There are number of variations of **exec()** depending on how you specify the file to run, how you specify the program arguments, and how you specify the environment variables for the new program.

Table 13-1. Variations of exec()

	Finding the Executable	**Program Arguments**	**Environment**
execl	given path	separate arguments	environ variable
execlp	PATH search	separate arguments	environ variable
execle	given path	separate arguments	array of strings
execv	given path	array of strings	environ variable
execvp	PATH search	array of strings	environ variable
execve	given path	array of strings	array of strings

How to decipher the names:

p

> If the given file name contains a slash, it is treated as a path to use. Otherwise, the call examines the PATH environment variable and locates the program.

v

> Program arguments are an array of strings.

l

> Program arguments are separate arguments in the **exec()** command.

e

> Environment variables are an array of strings of the form "VARIABLE=value".

If you do not use an 'e' version of **exec()**, the global variable environ will be used to construct the environment for the new process. The **execve()** function is the actual system call that all the other functions are based on.

If you use an array argument, you provide it an array of strings with a NULL pointer as the last element of the array.

A number of attributes are inherited across the **exec()**, such as:

- Open files
- Process ID, parent process ID, process group ID

- Access groups, controlling terminal, resource usages
- Current working directory
- Umask, signal mask

Pipes

Open files are inherited across an **exec()** unless you explicitly tell the file descriptors to "close on exec". This behavior forms the basis of building pipelines between programs. A process calls **pipe()** to create the communications channel between two programs before doing the **fork()**:

```
int pipe (int *fildes);
```

`fildes` is an array of two integers. **pipe()** fills in the `fildes` array with two file descriptors that are connected in such a way that data written to `fildes[1]` can be read from `fildes[0]`. If you wanted to **fork()** and **exec()** a command, and read that command's output, you would do something like this, which is illustrated in Figure 13-5:

1. Create the pipe
2. **fork()**
3. In the child, use **dup2()** to move `fildes[1]` to become standard out.
4. **exec()** the program you want to run.
5. In the parent, read the program's output from `fildes[0]`. When the child program has finished, it will exit, and reads in the parent from `fildes[0]` will cease when the pipeline data runs out.
6. The parent calls **wait()** on the child.

Figure 13-5. Pipe and Fork

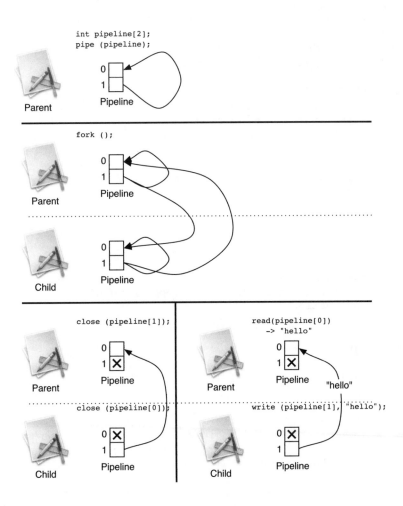

You can chain the input and output of multiple programs together using multiple pipes.

Example 13-4 is a program that builds a pipeline equivalent to

```
$ grep -i mail /usr/share/dict/words | tr '[:lower:]' '[:upper:]'
```

That is, get words from /usr/share/dict/words that contain "mail," and translate them to uppercase.

Example 13-4. pipeline.m

```
// pipeline.m -- manually create a pipeline to run the command
//     grep -i mail /usr/share/dict/words | tr '[:lower:]' '[:upper:]'

/* compile with:
cc -g -Wall -o pipeline pipeline.m
*/

#import <sys/types.h>    // for pid_t
```

```
#import <sys/wait.h>      // for waitpid
#import <unistd.h>        // for fork
#import <stdlib.h>        // for EXIT_SUCCESS, pipe, exec
#import <stdio.h>         // for printf
#import <errno.h>         // for errno
#import <string.h>        // for strerror

#define BUFSIZE 4096

int main (int argc, char *argv[])
{
    int result;
    int status = EXIT_FAILURE;
    int pipeline1[2];     // write on 1, read on zero
    int pipeline2[2];
    pid_t grep_pid = 0;
    pid_t tr_pid = 0;

    result = pipe (pipeline1);

    if (result == -1) {
        fprintf (stderr, "could not open pipe\n");
        goto bailout;
    }

    // start the grep

    if ((grep_pid = fork())) {
        // parent

        if (grep_pid == -1) {
            fprintf (stderr, "fork failed.  Error is %d/%s\n",
                        errno, strerror(errno));
            goto bailout;
        }
        close (pipeline1[1]); // we are not planning on writing

    } else {
        // child

        char *arguments[] = { "grep", "-i",
                                "mail", "/usr/share/dict/words", NULL };

        close (pipeline1[0]); // we are not planning on reading

        // set the standard out to be the write-side of the pipeline1

        result = dup2 (pipeline1[1], STDOUT_FILENO);
        if (result == -1) {
            fprintf (stderr, "dup2 failed.  Error is %d/%s\n",
                        errno, strerror(errno));
            goto bailout;
        }
        close (pipeline1[1]);

        // exec the child
        result = execvp ("grep", arguments);
```

```
        if (result == -1) {
            fprintf (stderr, "could not exec grep.  Error is %d/%s\n",
                    errno, strerror(errno));
            goto bailout;
        }
    }
}

// start the 'tr'

result = pipe (pipeline2);
if (result == -1) {
    fprintf (stderr, "could not open pipe\n");
    goto bailout;
}

if ((tr_pid = fork())) {
    // parent

    if (tr_pid == -1) {
        fprintf (stderr, "fork failed.  Error is %d/%s\n",
                errno, strerror(errno));
        goto bailout;
    }
    close (pipeline2[1]); // we are not planning on writing

} else {
    // child

    close (pipeline2[0]); // we are not planning on reading

    // set the standard out to be the write-side of the pipeline2

    result = dup2 (pipeline1[0], STDIN_FILENO);
    if (result == -1) {
        fprintf (stderr, "dup2 failed.  Error is %d/%s\n",
                errno, strerror(errno));
        goto bailout;
    }
    close (pipeline1[1]);

    result = dup2 (pipeline2[1], STDOUT_FILENO);
    if (result == -1) {
        fprintf (stderr, "dup2 failed.  Error is %d/%s\n",
                errno, strerror(errno));
        goto bailout;
    }
    close (pipeline2[1]);

    // exec the child

    result = execlp ("tr", "tr", "[:lower:]", "[:upper:]", NULL);

    if (result == -1) {
        fprintf (stderr, "could not exec tr.  Error is %d/%s\n",
                errno, strerror(errno));
        goto bailout;
    }
}
```

```
        }

        // this is only in the parent.   read the results
        FILE *blarg;
        char buffer[BUFSIZE];

        blarg = fdopen (pipeline2[0], "r");

        while (fgets(buffer, BUFSIZE, blarg)) {
        printf ("%s", buffer);
        }

        // and wait
        int childStatus;
        waitpid (grep_pid, &childStatus, 0);
        waitpid (tr_pid, &childStatus, 0);

        // *whew*, we're done.

        status = EXIT_SUCCESS;

bailout:
        return (status);

} // main
```

A sample run:

```
$ ./pipeline   | head
AIRMAIL
AUMAIL
BEMAIL
BLACKMAIL
BLACKMAILER
CAMAIL
...
UNMAIL
UNMAILABLE
UNMAILABLENESS
UNMAILED
```

Gotchas with Cocoa and fork()

There is one big huge issue involving **fork()** and Cocoa. Mac OS X is based on the Mach microkernel, and Mach ports are used for a lot of interprocess communications, particularly to the window server, and arevery important to Cocoa. These Mach ports get closed on a **fork()**, so you may run into problems if you try to use Cocoa after a **fork()**.

Also, when you are using threads (which Cocoa programs use implicitly), only the thread that calls **fork()** is running in the child. Unfortunately, all of the other thread stuff (mutexes and other data structures) still exist, and data structures that are protected by those mutexes are potentially still in an indeterminate state, which of course can lead to total mayhem. In general, if you are using threads or Cocoa, the only safe functions to call after a **fork()** are the **exec()** functions and any of the async-safe functions (the ones you can call in a signal handler). If you use any of the newer frameworks from Apple, be especially careful if you try to use them in the child program after a **fork()** without subsequently **exec()**ing. For example, the Disk Arbitration framework could do its work in a thread, and so could get confused in the child after a **fork()**.

For the More Curious

Despite the caveat with Cocoa and threaded programs, you can still do useful work after a **fork()**. For example, a web server could use **fork()** to do concurrent processing, especially if the processing is more than just I/O (such as CGI scripts for dynamic web pages).

The HTTP protocol

HTTP (the hypertext transport protocol) is what is used to exchange data between a web browser and the web server. In brief, the browser connects to a server listening on port 80 of whatever IP address is appropriate and sends a request. For an URL that looks like `http://www.bignerdranch.com/Classes/Core.html`, the server `www.bignerdranch.com` is contacted, and a GET request is made for `/Classes/Core.html`. Here is the full request made by `Mozilla`:

```
GET /Classes/Core.html HTTP/1.1
Host: www.bignerdranch.com
User-Agent: Mozilla/5.0 (Macintosh; U; PPC Mac OS X; en-US; rv:1.0) \
Gecko/20020510
Accept: text/xml,application/xml,application/xhtml+xml,text/html;\
q=0.9,text/plain;q=0.8,image/png,image/jpeg,image/gif;q=0.2,\
text/css,*/*;q=0.1
Accept-Language: en, pdf;q=0.50
Accept-Encoding: gzip, deflate, compress;q=0.9
Accept-Charset: ISO-8859-1, utf-8;q=0.66, *;q=0.66
Keep-Alive: 300
Connection: keep-alive
```

The above has the request:

```
GET /Classes/Core.html HTTP/1.1
```

and a bunch of headers that influence server behavior. For instance, the `Host` header

```
Host: www.bignerdranch.com
```

has the name of the host that was included in the URL. By inspecting the `Host` header, the web server can serve a bunch of domains off of a single IP address. Other headers can say what kind of data encoding (compressed or not) the browser supports, and what languages the user wants to see. Each line of the request is terminated with a `\r\n`, and a pair of `\r\n`'s is the end of the request. `\r\n` is affectionately known as "CRLF", short for "Carriage Return, Line Feed" after the ASCII terminal control characters of the same name. These are ASCII values 13 and 10. When interacting with a web server directly from a terminal, sending just a line feed character is sufficient to get things to work, but the HTTP specification says that you should use CRLF, especially when you are writing web browsers or servers.

First in the request is the method, such as GET (get a page), POST (post data in a form you filled out), or HEAD (just return the headers), followed by the resource you want to see, and then the protocol supported by the browser.

The server processes the request and sends a response that looks like this:

```
HTTP/1.1 200 OK
Date: Fri, 04 Oct 2002 16:43:55 GMT
Server: Apache
Last-Modified: Fri, 04 Oct 2002 14:50:19 GMT
Content-Length: 9023
Connection: close
Content-Type: text/html

<HTML>
<HEAD>
<title>Core Mac OS X and Unix Programming</title>
<link rel="stylesheet" type="text/css" href="/homepage_style.css">
...
```

The first line is the primary response, followed by a bunch of headers for the browser, followed by the actual data requested. The response

```
HTTP/1.1 200 OK
```

is the protocol the server will be talking with, the result code (200 for success, 404 for page not found, something in the 500s for an error) and a human-readable string whose actual value is ignored by the browser.

The headers have things like the time the server thinks it is, when the page was last modified (handy if you are caching pages), the content type (a MIME type that tells the browser how to handle the data), and how much data will be coming down the pipe. This last bit of data is optional. If no Content-Length header is returned, the browser will continually read new data from the network connection until it gets closed. Like the request, the header section is separated from the requested data by an extra \r\n.

The really nice thing about HTTP is that it is ubiquitous, and it is not that hard to write a working web server. Having a web server embedded in some applications can make sense, particularly for things like application servers and middleware pieces in a big distributed system. Stick in a little web server listening to port 80 and you can have ordinary web browsers contact them to get status information, change configurations, or perform diagnostics. No need to cook up your own network protocol to do that kind of stuff.

Example 13-5 is a little web server that uses **fork()** to handle the requests. In terms of efficiency, this is pretty bad, but it is simple and easy to write. The real life web servers will pre-fork a number of persistent children to handle requests and have a central process send the children requests to handle (like Apache), or will use threads to handle individual connections (like Apache 2 and AOLserver). In our example, the web server will **fork()**, handle the request in the new child process, then exit the child process. The parent process will begin waiting for another request immediately after forking off the child.

This architecture, though, has a couple of nice side benefits that simplify the implementation. There is no need for a select loop (and the resulting complexity) in either the parent or the child, but you still get parallel handling of requests. This is because the parent can block on **accept ()** waiting for a new connection while the child goes about its business. Setting system calls to be interruptible by signals makes **wait ()**ing for children simple, because the SIGCHLD indicating a child process exiting will break out of the **accept ()**.

Example 13-5. webserve.m

```
// webserve.m -- a simple web server using fork() to handle requests

/* compile with
cc -g -Wall -o webserve webserve.m
*/

#import <sys/types.h>        // for pid_t, amongst others
#import <sys/wait.h>         // for wait3
#import <unistd.h>           // for fork
#import <stdlib.h>           // for EXIT_SUCCESS, pipe, exec
#import <stdio.h>            // for printf
#import <errno.h>            // for errno
#import <string.h>           // for strerror
#import <sys/time.h>         // for struct timeval
#import <sys/resource.h>     // for struct rusage
#import <netinet/in.h>       // for sockaddr_in
#import <sys/socket.h>       // for socket(), AF_INET
#import <arpa/inet.h>        // for inet_ntoa
#import <unistd.h>           // for close
#import <arpa/inet.h>        // for inet_ntoa and friends
#import <assert.h>           // for assert

#define PORT_NUMBER 8080     // set to 80 to listen on the HTTP port

static int g_childSignaled;


// ----- child handling

// signal handler for SIGCHLD.  Just set a global value saying we've
// seen the signal.  We want to do more interesting stuff on child
// exits than are proper to do in a signal handler (runs in the
// parent) x

void childExited (int signalNumber)
{
    g_childSignaled = 1;

} // childExited


// wait for children and print out some resource usage
// (runs in the parent)

void reapChildren ()
{
    while (1) {
        pid_t childPid;
        int status;
        struct rusage resources;
```

```
            childPid = wait3 (&status, WNOHANG, &resources);

            if (childPid < 0) {
                // even though the man page says that we shouldn't get
                // this with WNOHANG as an option to wait3, it sometimes
                // happens
                if (errno != ECHILD) {
                    fprintf (stderr, "wait3 returned an error: %d/%s\n",
                             errno, strerror(errno));
                }
                break;

            } else if (childPid == 0) {
                // we've run out of children
                break;

            } else {
                // otherwise print some stuff to our log

                fprintf (stderr, "child %ld terminated %s\n",
                         (long)childPid,
                         WIFEXITED(status) ? "normally" : "abnormally");
                fprintf (stderr, "    user time: %d seconds %d msec\n",
                         (int)resources.ru_utime.tv_sec,
                         (int)resources.ru_utime.tv_usec);
                fprintf (stderr, "    system time: %d seconds %d msec\n",
                         (int)resources.ru_stime.tv_sec,
                         (int)resources.ru_stime.tv_usec);
                fprintf (stderr, "    max RSS: %ld\n",
                         resources.ru_maxrss);
            }
        }

    return;

} // reapChildren



// HTTP request handling

// these are some of the common HTTP response codes

#define HTTP_OK         200
#define HTTP_NOT_FOUND  404
#define HTTP_ERROR      500


// return a string to the browser

#define returnString(httpResult, string, channel) \
   returnBuffer((httpResult), (string), (strlen(string)), (channel))

// return a character buffer (not necessarily zero-terminated) to the
// browser (runs in the child)
```

```
void returnBuffer (int httpResult, const char *content,
                   int contentLength, FILE *commChannel)
{
    fprintf (commChannel, "HTTP/1.0 %d blah\r\n", httpResult);
    fprintf (commChannel, "Content-Type: text/html\r\n");
    fprintf (commChannel, "Content-Length: %d\r\n", contentLength);
    fprintf (commChannel, "\r\n");

    fwrite (content, contentLength, 1, commChannel );

} // returnBuffer


// stream back to the browser numbers being counted, with a pause
// between them.  The user should see the numbers appear every couple
// of seconds (runs in the child)

void returnNumbers (int number, FILE *commChannel)
{
    int min, max;
    min = MIN (number, 1);
    max = MAX (number, 1);

    fprintf (commChannel, "HTTP/1.0 %d blah\r\n", HTTP_OK);
    fprintf (commChannel, "Content-Type: text/html\r\n");
    fprintf (commChannel, "\r\n"); // no content length, dynamic

    fprintf (commChannel,
             "<h2>The numbers from %d to %d</h2>\n",
             min, max);
    int i;
    for (i = min; i <= max; i++) {
        sleep (2);
        fprintf (commChannel, "%d\n", i);
        fflush (commChannel);
    }

    fprintf (commChannel, "<hr>Done\n");

} // returnNumbers


// return a file from the file system, relative to where the webserve
// is running.  Note that this doesn't look for any nasty characters
// like '..', so this function is a pretty big security hole
// (runs in the child)

void returnFile (const char *filename, FILE *commChannel)
{
    const char *mimetype = NULL;

    // try to guess the mime type.  IE assumes all non-graphic files
    // are HTML
    if (strstr(filename, ".m") != NULL) {
        mimetype = "text/plain";
    } else if (strstr(filename, ".h") != NULL) {
        mimetype = "text/plain";
```

```
        } else if (strstr(filename, ".txt") != NULL) {
            mimetype = "text/plain";
        } else if (strstr(filename, ".tgz") != NULL) {
            mimetype = "application/x-compressed";
        } else if (strstr(filename, ".html") != NULL) {
            mimetype = "text/html";
        } else if (strstr(filename, ".htm") != NULL) {
            mimetype = "text/html";
        } else if (strstr(filename, ".mp3") != NULL) {
            mimetype = "audio/mpeg";
        }

        FILE *file;
        file = fopen (filename, "r");

        if (file == NULL) {
            returnString (HTTP_NOT_FOUND,
                          "could not find your file.  Sorry\n.",
                          commChannel);
        } else {
            fprintf (commChannel, "HTTP/1.0 %d blah\r\n", HTTP_OK);
            if (mimetype != NULL) {
                fprintf (commChannel, "Content-Type: %s\r\n", mimetype);
            }
            fprintf (commChannel, "\r\n");

#define BUFFER_SIZE (8 * 1024)
            char *buffer[BUFFER_SIZE];
            int result;

            while ((result = fread (buffer, 1, BUFFER_SIZE, file)) > 0) {
                fwrite (buffer, 1, result, commChannel);
            }
#undef BUFFER_SIZE
        }

} // returnFile


// using the method and the request (the path part of the url),
// generate the data for the user and send it back. (runs in the
// child)

void handleRequest (const char *method,
                    const char *originalRequest, FILE *commChannel)
{
    char *request = strdup (originalRequest);

    // we'll use strsep to split this
    if (strcmp(method, "GET") != 0) {
        returnString (HTTP_ERROR,
                      "only GETs are supported", commChannel);
        goto bailout;
    }

    char *chunk, *nextString;
    nextString = request;
```

```
        chunk = strsep (&nextString, "/");
        // urls start with slashes, so chunk is ""

        chunk = strsep (&nextString, "/");   // leading part of the url

        if (strcmp(chunk, "numbers") == 0) {
            int number;

            // url of the form /numbers/5 to print numbers from 1 to 5
            chunk = strsep (&nextString, "/");
            number = atoi(chunk);
            returnNumbers (number, commChannel);

        } else if (strcmp(chunk, "file") == 0) {
            chunk = strsep (&nextString, ""); // get rest of the string
            returnFile (chunk, commChannel);
        } else {
            returnString (HTTP_NOT_FOUND,
                          "could not handle your request.  Sorry\n.",
                          commChannel);
        }

bailout:
    fprintf (stderr, "child %ld handled request '%s'\n",
             (long)getpid(), originalRequest);

    free (request);

} // handleRequest



// read the request from the browser, pull apart the elements of the
// request, and then dispatch it.  (runs in the child)

void dispatchRequest (int fd, struct sockaddr_in *address)
{
#define LINEBUFFER_SIZE 8192
    char linebuffer[LINEBUFFER_SIZE];
    FILE *commChannel;

    commChannel = fdopen (fd, "r+");
    if (commChannel == NULL) {
        fprintf (stderr,
                 "could not open commChannel.  Error is %d/%s\n",
                 errno, strerror(errno));
    }

    // this is pretty lame in that it only reads the first line and
    // assumes that's the request, subsequently ignoring any headers
    // that might be sent.

    if (fgets(linebuffer, LINEBUFFER_SIZE, commChannel) != NULL) {
        // ok, now figure out what they wanted
        char *requestElements[3], *nextString, *chunk;
        int i = 0;
```

```
                    nextString = linebuffer;
                    while ((chunk = strsep (&nextString, " "))) {
                        requestElements[i] = chunk;
                        i++;
                    }
                    if (i != 3) {
                        returnString (HTTP_ERROR, "malformed request",
                                       commChannel);
                        goto bailout;
                    }

                    handleRequest (requestElements[0], requestElements[1],
                                    commChannel);
                } else {
                    fprintf (stderr, "read an empty request.  exiting\n");
                }

        bailout:
            fclose (commChannel);
            fflush (stderr);

            _exit (EXIT_SUCCESS);

        } // dispatchRequest



        // sit blocking on accept until either it breaks out with a signal
        // (like SIGCHLD) or a new connection comes in.  If it's a new
        // connection, fork off a child to process the request

        void acceptRequest (int listenSocket)
        {
            struct sockaddr_in address;
            socklen_t addressLength = sizeof(address);

            int result;
            result = accept (listenSocket, (struct sockaddr *)&address,
                              &addressLength);

            if (result == -1) {
                if (errno == EINTR) {
                    // system call interrupted by a signal.  maybe by SIGCHLD?
                    if (g_childSignaled) {
                        // yes, we had gotten a SIGCHLD.  clean up after the
                        // kids
                        g_childSignaled = 0;
                        reapChildren ();

                        // note that g_childSignaled is cleared before
                        // reapChildren is called, in case another sigchld
                        // happened during reapChildren, we won't lose it
                        goto bailout;
                    }
                } else {
                    fprintf (stderr, "accept failed.  error: %d/%s\n",
                              errno, strerror(errno));
```

```
        }
        goto bailout;
    }

    int fd;
    fd = result;

    // fork off a child to do the work

    // child sends output to stderr, so make sure it's drained before
    // moving on
    fflush (stderr);

    pid_t childPid;
    if ((childPid = fork())) {
        // parent
        if (childPid == -1) {
            fprintf (stderr, "fork failed.  Error: %d/%s\n",
                     errno, strerror(errno));
            goto bailout;
        }
        // close the new connection since the parent doesn't care
        // if we don't do this, the connection to the browser will
        close (fd);

    } else {
        // child
        dispatchRequest (fd, &address);
    }

bailout:
    return;

} // acceptRequest


// ----- network stuff


// this is 100% stolen from chatterserver.m
// start listening on our server port (runs in parent)

int startListening ()
{
    int fd = -1, success = 0;
    int result;

    result = socket (AF_INET, SOCK_STREAM, 0);

    if (result == -1) {
        fprintf (stderr, "could not make a scoket.  error: %d / %s\n",
                 errno, strerror(errno));
        goto bailout;
    }
    fd = result;

    int yes = 1;
```

```
        result = setsockopt (fd, SOL_SOCKET, SO_REUSEADDR,
                             &yes, sizeof(int));
    if (result == -1) {
        fprintf (stderr,
                 "could not setsockopt to reuse address. %d / %s\n",
                 errno, strerror(errno));
        goto bailout;
    }

    // bind to an address and port
    struct sockaddr_in address;
    address.sin_len = sizeof (struct sockaddr_in);
    address.sin_family = AF_INET;
    address.sin_port = htons (PORT_NUMBER);
    address.sin_addr.s_addr = htonl (INADDR_ANY);
    memset (address.sin_zero, 0, sizeof(address.sin_zero));

    result = bind (fd, (struct sockaddr *)&address,
                   sizeof(address));
    if (result == -1) {
        fprintf (stderr, "could not bind socket.  error: %d / %s\n",
                 errno, strerror(errno));
        goto bailout;
    }

    result = listen (fd, 8);

    if (result == -1) {
        fprintf (stderr, "listen failed.  error: %d /  %s\n",
                 errno, strerror(errno));
        goto bailout;
    }

    success = 1;

bailout:
    if (!success) {
        close (fd);
        fd = -1;
    }
    return (fd);

} // startListening


int main (int argc, char *argv[])
{
    int listenSocket;

    // install a signal handler to reap any children that have exited
    (void) signal (SIGCHLD, childExited);
    siginterrupt (SIGCHLD, 1);

    listenSocket = startListening ();

    while (1) {
        acceptRequest (listenSocket);
```

```
    }

    return (EXIT_SUCCESS);

} // main
```

The code is set to listen on port 8080 instead of HTTP's usual port 80. Listening to port 80 requires root access. Using port 8080 makes it easier to run and to test.

Here is a sample run where the server is started, and these two requests are performed using a web browser: `http://127.0.0.1:8080/file/webserve.m` `http://127.0.0.1:8080/numbers/23`

```
$ ./webserve
child 6514 handled request '/file/webserve.m'
child 6514 terminated normally
    user time: 0 seconds 0 msec
    system time: 0 seconds 0 msec
    max RSS: 0

child 6516 handled request '/numbers/23'
child 6516 terminated normally
    user time: 0 seconds 0 msec
    system time: 0 seconds 0 msec
    max RSS: 0
```

You can also use `telnet` to make requests. Type in the stuff in bold.

```
$ telnet 127.0.0.1 8080
Trying 127.0.0.1...
Connected to localhost.
Escape character is '^]'.
GET /bork HTTP/1.0

HTTP/1.0 404 blah
Content-Type: text/html
Content-Length: 38

could not handle your request.  Sorry.
Connection closed by foreign host.
```

Summary

Mac OS X is a multi-processing operating system. Independent processes are given slices of CPU time, giving the illusion that all of the programs on the system are running concurrently. Sometimes your programs need to create new processes to do their work. You can use one of the convenience functions like **system()** or **popen()** to run pipelines in a shell.

You can also use **fork()** and **exec()** yourself to create new child processes and run new programs in those processes. You can use **pipe()** to establish a communications channel between related processes.

Challenge:

1. Add some more URL handling types. Some ideas are:
   `/upcase/some/file/name`: similar to returnFile, but uppercases everything.

2. Design and implement a scheme to allow programmers to write plug-ins to handle different URLs.

3. In `pipeline.m`, if the parent does not close `pipeline[1]` (the write end of the pipe), the program will hang in the loop that reads results from the children. Why does it behave like that?

4. Fix the security hole in **returnFile()** so that it does not allow anyone to use multiple slashes or dots to access files above the directory where the web server is running.

Chapter 14. Using NSTask

In this section, you will learn:

- How to create new processes using **NSTask**.
- How to send data to the new process's standard in and read data from its standard out and standard error using **NSPipe** and **NSFileHandle**.
- How **NSProcessInfo** supplies the program with information about itself.

NSProcessInfo

Your application can access its own process information using the **NSProcessInfo** object. Here are some of the commonly used methods on **NSProcessInfo**:

+ (NSProcessInfo *)**processInfo**

You will use this class method to get hold of the shared instance of **NSProcessInfo** for the current process.

– (NSDictionary *)**environment**

Returns a dictionary containing all the environment variables as keys and their values.

– (NSString *)**hostName**

The name of the computer upon which the program is running.

– (NSString *)**processName**

The name of the program. This is used by the user defaults system.

– (NSString *)**globallyUniqueString**

This method uses the host name, process ID, and a timestamp to create a string that will be unique for the network. It uses a counter to ensure that each time this method is invoked it will create a different string.

NSTask

The **NSTask** object is used to create and control new processes. When the process ends, the object will post an NSTaskDidTerminateNotification notification. Before creating (or *launching*) the new process, you will set the attributes of the new process with these methods:

– (void) **setLaunchPath:** (NSString *)path

Sets the path to the code that will be executed when the process is created.

– (void) **setArguments:** (NSArray *)arguments

Takes an array of strings that will be the arguments to the program.

– (void)**setEnvironment:**(NSDictionary *)dict

>   You can use this to set the environment variables. If unset, the environment variables of the parent process will be used.

– (void)**setCurrentDirectoryPath:**(NSString *)path

>   Every process has a directory from which all relative paths are resolved. This is known as the current directory. If unset, the current directory of the parent process is used.

– (void)**setStandardInput:**(id)input

>   You can provide an object (either an **NSPipe** or an **NSFileHandle**) to act as a conduit to the new process's standard input.

– (void)**setStandardOutput:**(id)output

>   You can provide an object (either an **NSPipe** or an **NSFileHandle**) to act as a conduit from the new process's standard output.

– (void)**setStandardError:**(id)error

>   You can provide an object (either an **NSPipe** or an **NSFileHandle**) to act as a conduit from the new process's standard error.

There are also methods you will use when the new process is running. Here are the most commonly used:

– (void)**launch**

>   Creates the new process.

– (void)**terminate**

>   Kills the new process by sending it a SIGTERM signal.

– (int)**processIdentifier**

>   Returns the new process's process ID.

– (BOOL)**isRunning**

>   Returns YES if the the new process is running.

NSFileHandle

When reading a file, Cocoa programmers often read in an entire file and pack it into an **NSData** or **NSString** before parsing it. When writing a file, Cocoa programmers usually create a complete **NSData** or **NSString** which is then written to the file system. Sometimes you will want more control over reading from and writing to files. For example, you might read a file just until you find what you want and then close it. For more control over reading and writing from files, you will use **NSFileHandle**.

An **NSFileHandle** is used for reading and writing files. Some of the reading methods are blocking — that is, the application stops and waits for the data to become available— and others are non-blocking. We will discuss the non-blocking methods later in the chapter. Here are some commonly used methods for reading, writing, and seeking:

- (NSData *)**readDataToEndOfFile**
- (NSData *)**readDataOfLength:**(unsigned int)length

These methods read data from the file handle.

- (void)**writeData:**(NSData *)data;

A method for writing data to a file handle.

- (unsigned long long)**offsetInFile**
- (void)**seekToFileOffset:**(unsigned long long)offset

Methods for finding and changing your current location in a file.

- (void)**closeFile**

Closes the file.

NSPipe

The class **NSPipe** has two instances of **NSFileHandle**. One for input. The other for output.

- (NSFileHandle *)**fileHandleForReading**

- (NSFileHandle *)**fileHandleForWriting**

Creating an App that Creates a New Process

Unix systems have a program called sort that reads data from standard input, sorts it, and outputs it to standard output. You are going to write a program that invokes sort as a new process, writes data to its input and reads data from its output. The user will type in an **NSTextView**, click a button to trigger the sort, and read the result in another **NSTextView**. It will look like this:

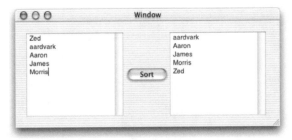

For the record, this is not how we would do a sort in a real application. The **NSArray** class has a couple of elegant ways to do sorting. This is just a simple example of using other processes.

Here is an object diagram of the nib file:

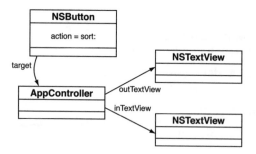

Create a new project of type Cocoa Application and name it SortThem. Open the MainMenu.nib file. Drop two **NSTextView** objects and an **NSButton** on the window. Make the text view on the right non-editable:

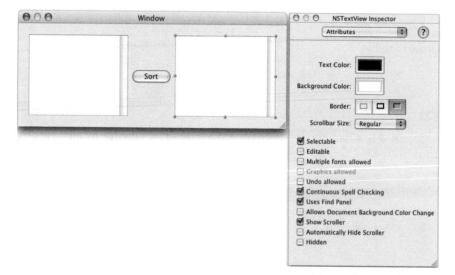

Under the Classes tab, create a new subclass of **NSObject** called **AppController**. Give it two outlets: inText and outText. Both outlets are pointers to **NSTextView** objects. Give it one action — **sort:**

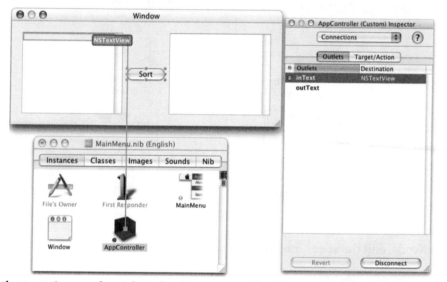

Create the files for the class and create an instance.

Control-drag from the **AppController** to set the text view on the left to be inText.

Set the text view on the right to be the outText. Set the target of the button to trigger
sort:.

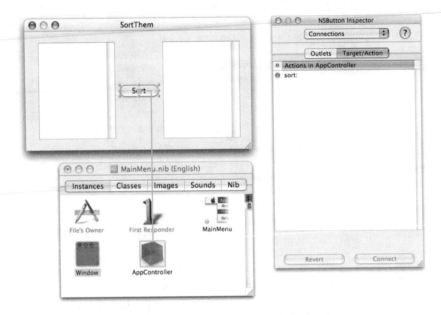

Before creating the code, here is an object diagram of the task:

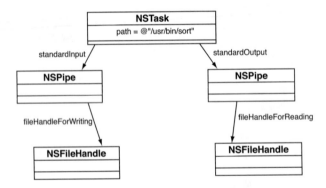

In Xcode, edit the **sort:** method in AppController.m:

```objc
- (IBAction)sort:(id)sender
{
    NSData *data;
    NSPipe *inPipe, *outPipe;
    NSFileHandle *writingHandle;
    NSTask *task;
    NSString *aString;
    task = [[NSTask alloc] init];
    inPipe = [[NSPipe alloc] init];
    outPipe = [[NSPipe alloc] init];

    // Set attributes of new process
    [task setLaunchPath:@"/usr/bin/sort"];
    [task setStandardOutput:outPipe];
    [task setStandardInput:inPipe];
    [task setArguments:[NSArray arrayWithObject:@"-f"]];
```

```
    // Start the new process
    [task launch];

    // Write ASCII to its standard in
    writingHandle = [inPipe fileHandleForWriting];
    [writingHandle writeData:[
            [inText string] dataUsingEncoding:NSASCIIStringEncoding]];
    [writingHandle closeFile];

    // Read ASCII from its standard out
    data = [[outPipe fileHandleForReading] readDataToEndOfFile];
    aString = [[NSString alloc] initWithData:data
                                encoding:NSASCIIStringEncoding];
    [outText setString:aString];
    [aString release];
    [task release];
    [inPipe release];
    [outPipe release];
}
```

Build and run your application.

Non-blocking reads

If a process takes a long time to return output, like the program traceroute, you will not want your application to stop while waiting for output from the program. You will want to create a file handle that does non-blocking reading. In particular, you will set up the file handle so that it posts a notification when there is data to be processed.

The notification created will be an NSFileHandleReadCompletionNotification. To start the file handle waiting for the data, you will send it the message **readInBackgroundAndNotify**. Each time you receive this notification, you will read the data using the **availableData** method of **NSFileHandle**. You will also need to call **readInBackgroundAndNotify** again to restart the wait for data.

In this example, you are going to create a task which runs traceroute. traceroute sends out packets to discover the routers between your machine and another host. The responses from the routers sometimes take a while to get back. You will read the data in the background and append it to the text view. The application will look like this:

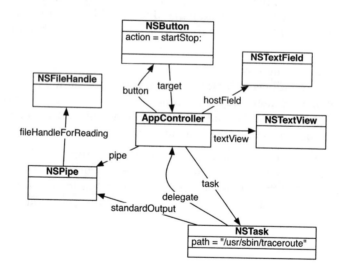

Edit the nib file

Create a new project of type Cocoa Application. Name it TraceRoute. Open
`MainMenu.nib` and create a new subclass of **NSObject** called **AppController**. Add
three outlets to **AppController**: `button`, `hostField`, and `textView`. Add one action
to **AppController** called **startStop:**.

Create the files for **AppController**.

Create an instance of **AppController**. Drop a text field, a text view, and a button on
the window. Make it look like this:

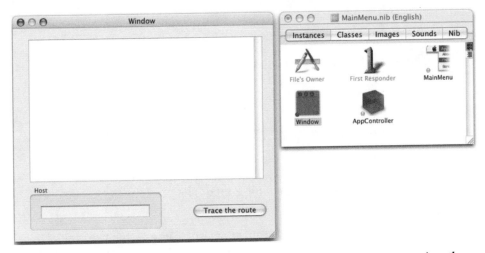

Connect the outlets of the **AppController** (button, hostField, textView) to the appropriate objects. Set the target of the button to point to the **AppController**, and set the action to be **startStop:**.

Edit the code

In Xcode, edit AppController.h:

```
#import <Cocoa/Cocoa.h>

@interface AppController : NSObject
{
    IBOutlet NSButton *button;
    IBOutlet NSTextField *hostField;
    IBOutlet NSTextView *textView;
    NSPipe *pipe;
    NSTask *task;
}
- (IBAction)startStop:(id)sender;
- (void)dataReady:(NSNotification *)note;
- (void)taskTerminated:(NSNotification *)note;
- (void)appendData:(NSData *)d;
- (void)cleanup;
@end
```

Open the AppController.m and add these methods to it:

```
#import "AppController.h"

@implementation AppController

// Append the data to the string in the text view
- (void)appendData:(NSData *)d {
    NSRange endRange = NSMakeRange([[textView string] length],0);
    NSString *string = [[NSString alloc] initWithData:d
                                encoding:NSUTF8StringEncoding];
    [textView replaceCharactersInRange:endRange
                        withString:string];
    [string release];
}
```

387

```
- (void)cleanup
{
    // Release the old task
    [task release];
    task = nil;

    // Release the pipe
    [pipe release];
    pipe = nil;

    // Change the title on the button
    [button setTitle:@"Trace the route"];

    // No longer an observer
    [[NSNotificationCenter defaultCenter] removeObserver:self];
}

- (void)taskTerminated:(NSNotification *)note
{
    NSData *leftInPipe;

    // Flush data still in pipe
    leftInPipe = [[pipe fileHandleForReading] readDataToEndOfFile];
    if (leftInPipe)
        [self appendData:leftInPipe];
    [self cleanup];
}

- (IBAction)startStop:(id)sender
{
    // Is the task already running?
    if ([task isRunning]) {

        // Stop it and tidy up
        [task terminate];
        [self cleanup];
    } else {

        // Create a task and pipe
        task = [[NSTask alloc] init];
        pipe = [[NSPipe alloc] init];

        // Set the attributes of the task
        [task setLaunchPath:@"/usr/sbin/traceroute"];
        [task setArguments:[NSArray arrayWithObject:
                                    [hostField stringValue]]];
        [task setStandardOutput:pipe];
        [task setStandardError:pipe];

        // Register for notifications
        [[NSNotificationCenter defaultCenter] addObserver:self
                    selector:@selector(dataReady:)
                        name:NSFileHandleReadCompletionNotification
                      object:[pipe fileHandleForReading]];

        [[NSNotificationCenter defaultCenter] addObserver:self
```

```
                    selector:@selector(taskTerminated:)
                        name:NSTaskDidTerminateNotification
                      object:task];
    // Launch the task
    [task launch];
    [button setTitle:@"Terminate"];
    [textView setString:@""];

    // Get the pipe reading in the background
    [[pipe fileHandleForReading] readInBackgroundAndNotify];
    }
}

- (void)dataReady:(NSNotification *)note
{
    NSData *data = [[note userInfo]
                valueForKey:NSFileHandleNotificationDataItem];
    if (data)
       [self appendData:data];

    // Must restart reading in background after each notification
    [[pipe fileHandleForReading] readInBackgroundAndNotify];
}

@end
```

Build and run the application.

Chapter 15. kqueues

Several of the functions you have seen so far date back to Unix's earlier days. Some of the APIs are awkward and difficult to use correctly, such as signal handling, and some are awkward and do not scale well, such as select().

Mac OS X 10.3 adopted a FreeBSD technology called Kernel Queues, abbreviated as "kqueues". kqueues are a unified notification mechanism used by the kernel which can inform your program about interesting events.

Inside the OS are a number of filters, shown in Figure 15-1, which are small pieces of code that live inside of the kernel. There is a filter associated with process handling, there is another filter associated with the network stack, and another one associated with the file system. Each of those filters watches for a set of interesting events that can happen, such as data appearing on a socket, a program has **fork()**ed, or a directory has had a file added to it.

Figure 15-1. kqueue in Action

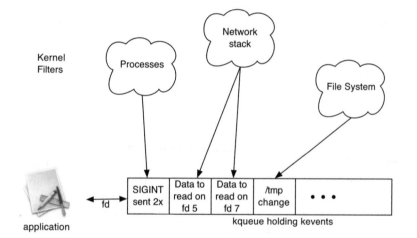

Your program registers its interest with the kernel about what entities it is interested in (which file descriptors or signal numbers), and what specific events associated with those entities it wants to know about, such as "I want to know about new data to be read on the socket, but I do not care if I can write to it or not." When any of those events occur, the program will be notified.

kqueue()

Before you can register interest in events with the kernel, you need to tell the kernel to create a new queue with the **kqueue()** function:

```
int kqueue ();
```

kqueue() returns a file descriptor that represents the queue. Your application can have any number of active kqueues, and it is perfectly OK for a library or framework to make kqueues for its own use. The thread-safety of kqueues is not documented, so do not use the same kqueue in multiple threads simultaneously. **kqueue()** returns -1 if an error occurred, and sets errno appropriately.

Even though **kqueue()** returns a file descriptor, do not **read()** or **write()** to it directly. Instead, you interact with the file descriptor via the **kevent()** function (described later). Because the kqueue is represented by a file descriptor, you can put it into a **select()** or **poll()** call (or even into another kqueue), and you can also put it into a runloop to see if there are any pending notifications. If there are, the kqueue file descriptor will appear as if you can read from it.

Events

The data structure you use to interact with kqueues is struct kevent:

```
struct kevent {
    uintptr_t ident;     /* identifier for this event */
    short      filter;   /* filter for event */
    u_short    flags;    /* action flags for kqueue */
    u_int      fflags;   /* filter flag value */
    intptr_t   data;     /* filter data value */
    void      *udata;    /* opaque user data identifier */
};
```

This structure is used both for communication from your program to the kernel and vice versa. When registering interest in an event, you fill in the fields of the structure. When responding to an event, you look at the fields to see what event happened, and to find any associated data about the event.

Here are the fields:

ident

> ident is the identifier for the event. You can only have one particular pairing of filter and identifier with a given kqueue. The identifier varies based on the filter. For most of the filters, a file descriptor is used, which is handy because a file descriptor can unambiguously identify a file in the file system, and file descriptors are what sockets use. For the signal filter, the signal number is used here (such as SIGINT or SIGHUP)

filter

> A constant is defined for each of the filters supplied by the kernel. Available filters include EVFILT_READ (data is available to be read on a file descriptor), EVFILT_WRITE (you can write to a file descriptor without blocking), EVFILT_VNODE (monitor changes to files and directories), EVFILT_PROC (trace process activity), and EVFILT_SIGNAL (receive signals in a synchronous manner). We will not be discussing the process filter.

flags

> flags is a bitmask that indicates the actions involving the event to perform when it is being registered. Valid flags include EV_ADD (adds the event to the kqueue), EV_ENABLE (start issuing notifications about the event), EV_DISABLE (stop issuing notifications about the event), EV_DELETE (remove the event from the kqueue), EV_ONESHOT (notify about the event only once, then delete it from the kqueue), and EV_CLEAR (reset the state of the event). flags is also set on an event notification.

fflags

> fflags is a bitmask that has arguments for a specific filter (fflags for "Filter Flags"). For the vnode filter there are flags for indicating interest in specific file operations (such as the file getting deleted, or the contents change, or the size increases, and so on). Some filters do not have any extra flags.

data

> data is an integer containing any filter-specific data. For an EVFILT_READ notification, for example, data would have the number of bytes pending in the kernel's read buffer. For EVFILT_WRITE, data would have the number of bytes you can write before blocking.

udata

> udata is a pointer that you can use for any purpose (it is short for "user data", sometimes known as a rock you can hide data under). You can use it to store a pointer to a string or a data structure that you want to associate with the event. You can also store a function pointer in here that you can use for a flexible event notification mechanism. The kernel passes this value back to you for each event so you can use it for your own purposes.

The EV_SET macro is provided for quick initialization of the structure:

```
EV_SET (&key, ident, filter, flags, fflags, data, udata);
```

You give the address to your struct kevent as the first argument, and then the subsequent arguments to the macro match the same-named entry in the kevent structure.

Registering and Handling Events

The **kevent()** function is what you use to register your interest in specific filters and events with a kqueue, and it is also the function used to block on a kqueue waiting for event notification. The signature of **kevent()** is a bit long because it lets you do both operations at the same time.

```
int kevent (int kqueue,
            const struct kevent *changeList, int numChanges,
                  struct kevent *eventList, int numEvents,
            const struct timespec *timeout);
```

The first argument to **kevent()** is the kqueue you want to manipulate. The change list holds the set of new events for the kqueue to monitor, as well as any changes to events the kqueue is already monitoring. If changeList is non-NULL and numChanges is greater than zero, then the events in changeList will be applied to the kqueue, saying "tell me about anything that happens about these".

The event list holds the events that **kevent()** is reporting. If eventList is non-NULL and numChanges is greater than zero, the event list gets filled in by **kevent()** with any pending events.

timeout is a struct timespec; its two fields specify how long you want to wait in seconds and nanoseconds.

```
struct timespec {
        time_t  tv_sec;         /* seconds */
        long    tv_nsec;        /* and nanoseconds */
};
```

The system will do its best to honor your timeout as accurately as possible, but the granularity of the system clock is much coarser than one nanosecond.

If the timeout parameter to **kevent ()** is NULL, the function will wait indefinitely, unless eventList is also NULL, in which case you are only registering new events (and not asking if any new events occurred), so **kevent ()** will return immediately. If you are waiting for events, **kevent ()** will block until an event happens. If you want to poll the kqueue to see if there is anything there, give it a timeout of {0, 0}.

kevent () returns the number of events it has written to eventList. It can return zero if there were no events prior to a timeout expiring. If an error happened while processing changeList, **kevent ()** tries to place an event with the EV_ERROR bit set in the flags field and the errno in the data field. Otherwise **kevent ()** returns -1 and errno will be set.

Here is how you would create a kqueue, register an event, and then block waiting for the event:

```
int kq = kqueue ();

if (kq == -1) {
    fprintf (stderr, "could not kqueue.  Error is %d/%s\n",
            errno, strerror(errno));
    // exit or goto an error handler
}

struct kevent event;
EV_SET (&event,       // event structure
        SIGINT,          // identifier
        EVFILT_SIGNAL, // filter
        EV_ADD | EV_ENABLE, // action flags
        0,               // filter flags
        0,               // filter data
        NULL);           // user data

// register the event
if (kevent(kq, &event, 1, NULL, 0, NULL) == -1) {
    fprintf (stderr, "could not kevent signal.  Error is %d/%s\n",
            errno, strerror(errno));
    // exit or goto an error handler
}

...

// block here until an event arrives
if (kevent(kq, NULL, 0, &event, 1, NULL) == -1) {
    fprintf (stderr, "could not kevent.  Error is %d/%s\n",
            errno, strerror(errno));
    // exit or goto an error handler
}

// look at change and handle the event
```

Here we are re-using `event`. You do not have hang on to the `struct kevent` you used to register the event. You just fill out the structure, hand it to the kernel via `kevent()`. The event structure is not needed after you register the event.

The `EV_ADD` and `EV_ENABLE` flags are necessary to have the event added to the kqueue, and to have event notification enabled. You can pass `EV_CLEAR` to say that you are not interested in any previous events that may be been recorded. The state of a kernel resource (such as data in a read buffer for a network socket) can also trigger an event. Using `EV_CLEAR` will suppress an event notification in this case.

kqueues for Signal Handling

Unix signals, due to their asynchronous nature, are difficult to handle correctly. There are all sorts of race conditions that can happen, plus you have to be aware of functions you can or cannot call at signal interrupt time. Most of the time, you really do not *have* to handle a signal the instant it is delivered. A frequent technique in a signal handler is to set a global variable and then wake up a `select()` call or an event loop.

You can use kqueues and `kevent()` to perform your signal handling. This saves you from the headaches caused by the signal handling API. Signals are also one of the simplest of the kqueue filters.

kqueue event handling can be used in tandem with the classic signal handling API. Calls like `signal()` and `sigaction()` have priority over events registered with a kqueue, so if someone has installed a signal handler (and even handlers left as `SIG_DFL`) it will get called and your kqueue event will not. Therefore you will need to do

```
signal (signum, SIG_IGN);
```

to remove any default signal handlers.

To handle a signal, place the signal number of interest into the `ident` portion of the `struct kevent`. Set `filter` to `EVFILT_SIGNAL`. When `kevent()` reports a signal-related event, the `data` member of the kevent structure will have a count of the number of times the signal has occurred since the last time it appeared on `kevent()`. This is a huge improvement over the traditional signal API, where you cannot know exactly how many times a signal has happened due to signal coalescing and race conditions.

Example 15-1 is a command-line tool that registers a number of signals with a kqueue and then blocks on `kevent()` waiting for signals to happen. When they do, the name of the signal is printed out along with the number of times that signal has happened since the last time it was seen in kevent(). A timeout of 5 seconds is used to show a heartbeat for the program, to show that it actually is alive and stays alive while signals get handled. A `SIGINT` signal will cause the program to exit cleanly.

Example 15-1. sigwatcher.m

```
// sigwatcher.m -- watch for signals happening

/* compile with
gcc -g -Wall -o sigwatcher sigwatcher.m
*/
```

```
#import <sys/event.h>    // for kqueue() etc.
#import <sys/signal.h>   // for SIGINT, etc
#import <sys/time.h>     // for struct timespec
#import <errno.h>        // for errno
#import <string.h>       // for strerror()
#import <stdio.h>        // for fprintf()
#import <unistd.h>       // for getpid()
#import <stdlib.h>       // for EXIT_SUCCESS

int main (int argc, const char *argv[])
{
    // program success/failure result
    int result = EXIT_FAILURE;

    // the queue to register the signal events with
    int kq;
    kq = kqueue ();

    if (kq == -1) {
        fprintf (stderr, "could not kqueue.  Error is %d/%s\n",
                 errno, strerror(errno));
        goto done;
    }

    // the list of events we're interested in (mostly just pulled
    // at random from <sys/signal.h>)

    int signals[] = { SIGHUP, SIGINT, SIGQUIT, SIGILL, SIGTRAP,
                      SIGABRT, SIGBUS, SIGSEGV, SIGPIPE, SIGTERM,
                      SIGCHLD };
    int *scan, *stop;
    scan = signals;
    stop = scan + sizeof(signals) / sizeof(*signals);

    // register each event with the kqueue

    while (scan < stop) {
        struct kevent event;
        EV_SET (&event, *scan,
                EVFILT_SIGNAL,
                EV_ADD | EV_ENABLE,
                0, 0, NULL);

        // kqueue event handling happens after the legacy API, so make
        // sure it doesn't eat the event before the kqueue can see it
        signal (*scan, SIG_IGN);

        // register the signal event; note that kevent()
        // will return immediately
        if (kevent(kq, &event, 1, NULL, 0, NULL) == -1) {
            fprintf (stderr,
                     "could not kevent signal.  Error is %d/%s\n",
                     errno, strerror(errno));
            goto done;
        }
        scan++;
```

```
    }

    printf ("I am pid %d\n", getpid());

    // now block and display any signals received

    while (1) {
        struct timespec timeout = { 5, 0 };
        int status;
        struct kevent event;
        status = kevent (kq, NULL, 0, &event, 1, &timeout);

        if (status == 0) {
            // timeout
            printf ("lub dub...\n");

        } else if (status > 0) {
            // we got signal!
            printf ("we got signal: %d (%s), delivered: %d\n",
                    (int)event.ident, strsignal((int)event.ident),
                    (int)event.data);

            if (event.ident == SIGINT) {
                result = EXIT_SUCCESS;
                goto done;
            }

        } else {
            fprintf (stderr, "could not kevent.  Error is %d/%s\n",
                     errno, strerror(errno));
            goto done;
        }
    }

done:
    return (result);

} // main
```

And here is a sample run. One terminal window is running the program, and another terminal window has the kill commands used to send signals to sigwatcher.

```
$ ./sigwatcher
I am pid 15341
lub dub...
we got signal: 11 (Segmentation fault), delivered: 1
we got signal: 11 (Segmentation fault), delivered: 1
lub dub...
we got signal: 11 (Segmentation fault), delivered: 3
lub dub...
lub dub...
we got signal: 2 (Interrupt), delivered: 1
```

And these commands were issued in the other terminal:

```
$ kill -s SEGV 15341
$ kill -s SEGV 15341
```

```
$ kill -s SEGV 15341 ; kill -s SEGV 15341 ; kill -s SEGV 15341
$ kill -s INT 15341
```

kqueues for Socket Monitoring

Like the signal handling API, the API for handling sockets (and other file descriptors) can be awkward and inefficient. **select()** is the function used most often on Mac OS X to determine the liveness of a socket (is it still connected?) and to see if there is any activity on a socket (can I read from it without blocking?)

The problem with **select()** (and its functionally equivalent counterpart **poll()**) is that it is a stateless call. Every time you call **select()** or **poll()**, you have to tell the kernel what file descriptors you are interested in. The kernel then copies this list of descriptors into its own memory space, does whatever work it does to test for liveness and activity, and then copies stuff back to the program's address space to let the program know what is going on.

The main problem with this is scalability. If you are dealing hundreds or thousands of file descriptors, you have to ask the kernel about *all* of them *every* time even if only a small percentage actually have anything interesting going on with them. High volume server applications can often find themselves spending a lot of CPU time on maintenance of the FD_SETs for **select()**.

The other problem with the **select()** technique is convenience. When **select()** tells you a file descriptor has data to be read, you have to loop over the returned FD_SET looking for the file descriptors of interest. Then you have to attempt a **read()** to see if the connection is still open. If the connection is still open, you do not know how much data is available to read. You have to guess how much to read, usually using a hard-coded argument, and looping if there is more than that amount.

Both of these problems are solved when using kqueues for monitoring your sockets. You register all of your sockets of interest with **kevent()**, and then subsequent **kevent()** calls will tell you exactly which sockets have activity. Included in the event is how much data is there to be read, which you can then slurp up with a single **read()**, rather than issuing multiple reads and stitching together the data.

For read operations on a socket (or file, or pipe), use the EVFILT_READ filter. It takes a file descriptor as the struct kevent identifier. You can use **listen()** sockets and sockets that have already been **accept()**ed. When **kevent()** returns, the data field of the event has the amount of data in the kernel buffers waiting to be read.

This is called a "level-triggered" event, because the event is triggered based on the level of data in the buffer. You will be notified by the EVFILT_READ filter if there is any data to be read from the socket. This allows you to read a convenient number of bytes from the socket (say the size of a message), and leave the rest of the data there. The next time **kevent()** is called, you will get a notification for the rest of the unread data.

Other filters are said to use "edge-triggered" events, whereby you get notifications when the entity of interest changes state. This is used more often with the EVFILT_VNODE filter, which you will see later.

Getting back to EVFILT_READ, if a socket has been shut down, the filter also sets the EV_EOF flag in the flags field, and returns any errno value in the event's fflags field. It is possible for EV_EOF to be set in the event flags and there still be data pending in the socket buffer.

The EVFILT_WRITE filter works in a similar manner. When a write event is received for a file descriptor, the data field of the event structure will contain the amount of space remaining in the write buffer, that is, how much you can write before blocking. This filter will also set EV_EOF when the reader disconnects.

kqueues for File System Monitoring

Usually when you hear kqueue being discussed on mailing lists and message boards, it is regarding monitoring the file system. Using EVFILT_VNODE, you can watch a file or a directory for changes and then react to those changes. You might want to watch a directory for changes and then pick up any files that have been placed in that directory, leading to "drop-box" functionality for the user. You could also implement an efficient tail -f feature by waiting for a file to have data written to it.

The filter used is EVFILT_VNODE. A vnode is a kernel data structure that contains information about a file or folder, and there is a unique vnode allocated in the kernel for each active file or folder. There are a number of events you can monitor on a vnode. These are bit flags you can bitwise-OR together in the filter flags of the event structure. When you receive a notification, you can bitwise-AND the filter flags to see what event(s) happened.

Here are some of the different events relating to EVFILT_VNODE:

NOTE_DELETE

The **unlink()** function was called on the file.

NOTE_WRITE

The contents of the file has been changed due to a **write()** operation.

NOTE_EXTEND

The file's size increased.

NOTE_ATTRIB

The file has had its attributes changed.

NOTE_LINK

The (hard) link count to the file has changed

NOTE_RENAME

The file has been renamed.

NOTE_REVOKE

Access to the file was revoked via the **revoke()** system call, or the underlying file system has been unmounted.

Example 15-2 is `dirwatcher`, a command-line tool that takes a set of directories as program arguments. Each of those directories is opened and the resulting file descriptor is placed in a kqueue using the NOTE_WRITE filter flag. When a directory changes, such as a file being added or removed, **kevent ()** will return saying which directory has changed. The program prints out the name of the directory that changed.

Mapping the change event to the directory name is really easy because dirwatcher puts a pointer to the directory's name into the event's user data pointer field. The program also catches SIGINT to do a clean shutdown. Many kinds of events can be mixed and matched in the same kqueue. You can use the user data field of the event structure to determine what kind of event it is (which is what dirwatcher does), or you can look at the filter field to see which filter generated the event.

Example 15-2. dirwatcher.m

```
// dirwatcher.m -- watch directories for changes

/* compile with
gcc -g -Wall -o dirwatcher dirwatcher.m
*/

#import <sys/event.h>   // for kqueue() etc.
#import <errno.h>       // for errno
#import <string.h>      // for strerror()
#import <stdio.h>       // for fprintf()
#import <stdlib.h>      // for EXIT_SUCCESS
#import <fcntl.h>       // for O_RDONLY

int main (int argc, const char *argv[])
{
    // program success/failure result
    int result = EXIT_FAILURE;

    // make sure there's at least one directory to monitor
    if (argc == 1) {
        fprintf (stderr, "%s directoryname [...]\n", argv[0]);
        fprintf (stderr, "    watches directoryname for changes\n");
        goto done;
    }

    // the queue to register the dir-watching events with
    int kq;
    kq = kqueue ();

    if (kq == -1) {
        fprintf (stderr, "could not kqueue.  Error is %d/%s\n",
                errno, strerror(errno));
        goto done;
    }

    // walk the set of directories provided by the user and
    // monitor them
    int i;
    for (i = 1; i < argc; i++) {
```

```
        // the vnode monitor requires a file descriptor, so
        // open the directory to get one
        const char *dirname = argv[i];
        int dirfd = open (dirname, O_RDONLY);

        if (dirfd == -1) {
            fprintf (stderr, "could not open(%s). Error is %d/%s\n",
                    dirname, errno, strerror(errno));
            continue;
        }

        // fill out the event structure.  Store the name of the
        // directory in the user data

        struct kevent direvent;
        EV_SET (&direvent,
                dirfd,                // identifier
                EVFILT_VNODE,         // filter
                EV_ADD | EV_CLEAR | EV_ENABLE,  // action flags
                NOTE_WRITE,           // filter flags
                0,                    // filter data
                (void*)dirname);      // user data

        // register the event
        if (kevent(kq, &direvent, 1, NULL, 0, NULL) == -1) {
            fprintf (stderr, "could not kevent.  Error is %d/%s\n",
                    errno, strerror(errno));
            goto done;
        }
    }

// register interest in SIGINT with the queue.  The user data
// is NULL, which is how we'll differentiate between
// a directory-modification event and a SIGINT-received event

struct kevent sigevent;
EV_SET (&sigevent,
        SIGINT,
        EVFILT_SIGNAL,
        EV_ADD | EV_ENABLE,
        0,
        0,
        NULL);

// kqueue event handling happens after the legacy API, so make
// sure it doesn't eat the event before the kqueue can see it
signal (SIGINT, SIG_IGN);

// register the signal event
if (kevent(kq, &sigevent, 1, NULL, 0, NULL) == -1) {
    fprintf (stderr, "could not kevent signal.  Error is %d/%s\n",
            errno, strerror(errno));
    goto done;
}

while (1) {
    // camp on kevent() until something interesting happens
```

```
        struct kevent change;
        if (kevent(kq, NULL, 0, &change, 1, NULL) == -1) {
            fprintf (stderr, "could not kevent.  Error is %d/%s\n",
                     errno, strerror(errno));
            goto done;
        }

        // the signal event has NULL in the user data.  Check it first.

        if (change.udata == NULL) {
            // we got signal!
            result = EXIT_SUCCESS;
            printf ("\nthat's all folks...\n");

            goto done;

        } else {
            // udata is non-null, so it's the name of the directory
            // that changed
            printf ("%s\n", (char*)change.udata);
        }
    }

done:
    return (result);

} // main
```

Here is a sample run that watches the the user's home directory and /tmp:

```
$ ./dirwatcher ~ /tmp
/tmp
/Users/markd
/Users/markd
/tmp
^C
that's all folks...
```

To get the different directories to appear in dirwatcher's output, files were created and deleted in each directory by using touch and rm in another terminal window. It will also notice changes that are made with the Finder. Finally, control-C (which generates a SIGINT) is used to shut down the program.

kqueues and Runloops

You can use kqueues in your Cocoa and Carbon applications to monitor OS events of interest. There are two techniques employed to do this: make a thread, or use the runloop.

You can create a thread that contains the **kevent()** call. **kevent()** will block the thread until something interesting happens. That thread, after it wakes up, can notify the application's main thread about what happened (or do whatever work is appropriate). A lot of kqueue wrapper code available on the internet uses this technique, and as does sample code from Apple.

The other technique is to put the file descriptor into the main thread's runloop. A kqueue is referenced by a file descriptor, and its behavior is such that **select()**, **poll()**, and **kevent()** can be used to see if there is an event notification waiting on a particular queue. You can wrap the kqueue file descriptor in a CFSocket just like you did with CFChatterClient and add it to the runloop. This is safe to do, so long as you do not try to actually read or write from the kqueue file descriptor.

CocoaDirWatcher, as shown in Figure 15-2, is a Cocoa application that watches three directories: /tmp, the user's home directory, and the user's preferences directory. When any of these change, the name of the directory is sent to the console via **NSLog()** and the directory is also added to the **NSTextView** in the window.

Figure 15-2. dirwatcherCocoa In Action

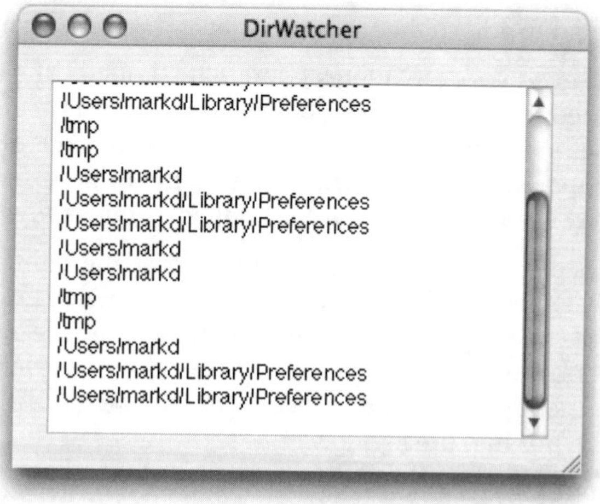

Create the CocoaDirWatcher project in Xcode, and add a new Objective-C class called AppController to the project. Make AppController.h look like Example 15-3

Example 15-3. AppController.h

```
// AppController.h -- CocoaDirWatcher's controller object

#import <Cocoa/Cocoa.h>

@interface AppController : NSObject
{
    // directory changed messages are appended to this
    IBOutlet NSTextView *logview;

    // file descriptor for the directory-watching kqueue
    int kqfd;

    // the socket placed into the runloop
    CFSocketRef  runLoopSocket;
}

// tell the user some activity has happened on the given
```

```
// path.  It NSLog()s the information, and appends it to
// the logView

- (void) logActivity: (NSString *) path;

@end // AppController
```

Open `MainMenu.nib`, drag over `AppController.h`, and instantiate a new
AppController. Put an **NSTextView** into the window and hook up the `logview`
outlet of the controller to point to the **NSTextView**. Tweak the window's layout to
look nice, and then close Interface Builder.

Example 15-4 shows `AppController.m`, which uses some code taken from
CFChatterClient. When **AppController**'s **awakeFromNib** method is called it
creates a new kqueue and starts a watch on the three directories. An **NSString** with
the directory name is put into the user data field of the kevent structure. That is how
we will know what to add to the logview when a directory changes.

After adding the events we are interested in to the kqueue, the kqueue's file
descriptor is added to the current runloop with the **addFileDescriptorMonitor:**
method. This method puts the file descrptor into a **CFSocket**, sticks that into a
CFSocketRunLoopSource, and then adds that to the runloop. `self`, the pointer to
the **AppController** object, is used for the context of the **CFSocket**.

When an event is placed in the kqueue by the kernel, the callback function will be
called. The callback then finds the pointer to the **AppController** object that had
been placed in the callback's context pointer. The kqueue file descriptor is read from
the **AppController** and used in a call to **kevent()**. A new event is pulled off of the
kqueue, which has the name of the directory in the user data pointer, and that
directory name is put into the logview.

There is one subtle Objective-C trick used in **socketCallBack()**. The function
accesses the kqueue file descriptor directly from the object by using the arrow (->)
operator. This file descriptor is purely an implementation detail, so there is no point
in creating a method to return the descriptor.

Ordinarily, if you try to access an object's fields directly using the arrow operator
you will get a warning saying that the fields are `@protected`. If you place
socketCallBack's definition before `@implementation AppController`, you will get
this warning. If you put the definition of the function *inside* of **AppController**'s
`@implementation` section, you will not get the warning.

Example 15-4. AppController.m

```
#import "AppController.h"

#import <errno.h> // for errno
#import <strings.h> // for strerror()
#import <sys/event.h> // for kqueue() and kevent()

@implementation AppController

// some activity has happened on the kqueue file descriptor.
// call kevent() to pick up the new event waiting for us

void socketCallBack (CFSocketRef socketref, CFSocketCallBackType type,
```

```
                    CFDataRef address, const void *data, void *info)
{
    AppController *me = (AppController *) info;

    struct kevent event;

    // because this function is inside of @implementation AppController
    // we can dig into the object structure without complaints from
    // the compiler

    if (kevent(me->kqfd, NULL, 0, &event, 1, NULL) == -1) {
        NSLog (@"could not pick up event.  Error is %d/%s",
                errno, strerror(errno));

    } else {
        [me logActivity: (NSString *)event.udata];
    }

} // socketCallBack


// add the given directory to the kqueue for watching

- (void) watchDirectory: (NSString *) dirname
{
    int dirfd;
    dirfd = open ([dirname UTF8String], O_RDONLY);

    if (dirfd == -1) {
        NSLog (@"could not open %@.  Error is %d/%s",
                dirname, errno, strerror(errno));
        return;
    }

    struct kevent direvent;
    EV_SET (&direvent,
            dirfd,
            EVFILT_VNODE,
            EV_ADD | EV_CLEAR | EV_ENABLE,
            NOTE_WRITE,
            0,
            [dirname copy]);

    // register event
    if (kevent(kqfd, &direvent, 1, NULL, 0, NULL) == -1) {
        NSLog (@"could not kevent watching %@.  Error is %d/%s",
                dirname, errno, strerror(errno));
    }

} // watchDirectory


// add the file descriptor to the runloop.  When activity happens
// (such as new data on a socket, or a new event in a kqueue()),
// call the socketCallBack function.

- (void) addFileDescriptorMonitor: (int) fd
```

```
    {
        CFSocketContext context = { 0, self, NULL, NULL, NULL };
        CFRunLoopSourceRef rls;

        runLoopSocket = CFSocketCreateWithNative (NULL,
                                                  fd,
                                                  kCFSocketReadCallBack,
                                                  socketCallBack,
                                                  &context);
        if (runLoopSocket == NULL) {
            NSLog (@"could not CFSocketCreateWithNative");
            goto bailout;
        }

        rls = CFSocketCreateRunLoopSource (NULL, runLoopSocket, 0);
        if (rls == NULL) {
            NSLog (@"could not create a run loop source");
            goto bailout;
        }

        CFRunLoopAddSource (CFRunLoopGetCurrent (), rls,
                            kCFRunLoopDefaultMode);
        CFRelease (rls);

bailout:
        return;

    } // addFileDescriptorMonitor


    // program is cranking up.  Watch a couple of directories

    - (void) awakeFromNib
    {
        kqfd = kqueue ();

        if (kqfd == -1) {
            NSLog (@"could not create kqueue.  Error is %d/%s",
                    errno, strerror(errno));
            return;
        }

        [self watchDirectory: @"/tmp"];
        [self watchDirectory: NSHomeDirectory()];
        [self watchDirectory:
                [@"~/Library/Preferences" stringByExpandingTildeInPath]];

        [self addFileDescriptorMonitor: kqfd];

    } // awakeFromNib


    // inform the user that something interesting happened to path

    - (void) logActivity: (NSString *) path
    {
        // log it to the console
```

```
        NSLog (@"activity on %@", path);

        // and also append the path to the textview
        NSAttributedString *astring;

        astring = [[NSAttributedString alloc] initWithString: path];
        [[logview textStorage] appendAttributedString: astring];
        [astring release];

        astring = [[NSAttributedString alloc] initWithString: @"\n"];
        [[logview textStorage] appendAttributedString: astring];
        [astring release];

        NSRange endPoint;
        endPoint = NSMakeRange ([[logview string] length], 0);

        [logview scrollRangeToVisible: endPoint];

} // logActivity

@end // AppController
```

Compile and run the program. Make some changes to the watched directories and see the program react. Opening and closing GUI applications (particularly applications like `iCal` can also cause activity in the `~/Library/Preferences` directory.

fsevents

As of Mac OS X 10.4, the `Finder` uses kqueues to monitor directories it is currently showing to the user. This is how it can react instantly to changes made to the directory by other programs. kqueues are great when you are monitoring a small number of files and directories.

kqueues are not as convenient for monitoring changes made to the entire disk, like what Spotlight does. Spotlight, and similar programs, open the special device `/dev/fsevents`, and receive notifications through that device about changes made to file systems. This is officially an undocumented API (as of Mac OS X 10.4), but it exists in the Darwin sources. If you download the XNU project and peer into the `bsd/sys/fsevents.h` and `bsd/vfs/vfs_fsevents.c` you can see some of the available functionality.

Chapter 16. Accessing the Keychain

A *keychain* is a file that holds passwords and certificates and information about those passwords and certificates. (For the purposes of this chapter, I will use "password" to mean "password or certificate.") Each user can have several keychains, but most people only have one: `~/Library/Keychains/login.keychain`. In the Security framework, there is a set of functions and data structures that allow you to read and write passwords and their associated data. A password and its associated data is known as a keychain item.

The user can inspect their keychain using the application `Keychain Access`:

Some data inside the keychain is encrypted and can only be accessed if the keychain is unlocked. The user unlocks a keychain by typing a password into a keychain panel:

Using the `Keychain Access` application, users can control access to individual keychain items.

Items and Attribute Lists

In a keychain, there are four types of items:

- *Internet* passwords are associated with some protocol, server, domain, and user.
- *AppleShare* passwords are used by the AppleShare system.
- *Certificate* items hold certificates, not passwords.
- *Generic* items are used for everything else.

The item has a password and a collection of attributes. The attributes are identified by a four-byte code. There are a few dozen of these codes. Refer to `/System/Library/Frameworks/Security.framework/Headers/SecKeychainItem.h` As examples, here are a few of four-byte of the codes:

`kSecCreationDateItemAttr`

> (`'cdat'`) Identifies the creation date attribute. You use this tag to set or get a value of type `UInt32` that indicates the date the item was created.

`kSecDescriptionItemAttr`

> (`'desc'`) Identifies the description attribute. You use this tag to set or get a value of type string that represents a user-visible string describing this particular kind of item (For example, "disk image password").

`kSecLabelItemAttr`

> (`'labl'`) Identifies the label attribute. You use this tag to set or get a value of type string that represents a user-editable string containing the label for this item.

kSecCustomIconItemAttr

> ('cusi') Identifies the custom icon attribute. You use this tag to set or get a value of type Boolean that indicates whether the item has an application-specific icon. To do this, you must also set the attribute value identified by the tag kSecTypeItemAttr to a file type for which there is a corresponding icon in the desktop database, and set the attribute value identified by the tag kSecCreatorItemAttr to an appropriate application creator type. If a custom icon corresponding to the item's type and creator can be found in the desktop database, it will be displayed by Keychain Access. Otherwise, default icons are used.

kSecAccountItemAttr

> ('acct') Identifies the account attribute. You use this tag to set or get a string that represents the user account. It also applies to generic and AppleShare passwords.

kSecSecurityDomainItemAttr

> ('sdmn') Identifies the security domain attribute. You use this tag to set or get a value that represents the Internet security domain. This is unique to Internet password attributes.

kSecServerItemAttr

> ('srvr') Identifies the server attribute. You use this tag to set or get a value of type string that represents the Internet server name or IP address. This is unique to Internet password attributes.

Use a SecKeychainAttributeList to read and write these attributes:

```
struct SecKeychainAttributeList
{
    UInt32 count;
    SecKeychainAttribute *attr;
};
```

count is the number of attributes in the list. And attr is a pointer to the first one.

```
struct SecKeychainAttribute
{
    SecKeychainAttrType tag;
    UInt32 length;
    void *data;
};
```

The tag is the four-byte code listed above. The length is the number of bytes in the data buffer. Usually, the data buffer is just a string.

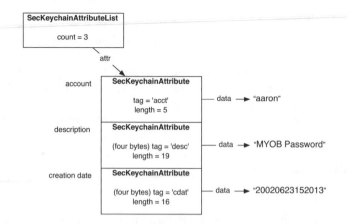

Searching for Items

Attribute lists are used in three ways:

1. To specify a search for items.
2. To read data from an item.
3. To set the data for an item.

For example, to create a search for all generic passwords that have *bignerdranch* as the account name, you would create an attribute list and invoke **SecKeychainSearchCreateFromAttributes()**.

```
OSStatus SecKeychainSearchCreateFromAttributes(CFTypeRef keychainOrArray,
                                   SecItemClass  itemClass,
                 const SecKeychainAttributeList *attrList,
                              SecKeychainSearchRef *searchRef);
```

Most of the functions in the Security framework deal well with NULLs. They do what you would hope. For example, if you can pass NULL as the first argument, the search will check all the user's normal keychains. Usually, this is what you want. For the second argument, you will pass one of the following:

- kSecInternetPasswordItemClass

- kSecGenericPasswordItemClass

- kSecAppleSharePasswordItemClass

- kSecCertificateItemClass

If you pass NULL as the attribute list, all items of that class will be returned. The final argument is a pointer to a search-specifying structure.

Here is a search that counts the number of Internet passwords on your keychain where the account name is *bignerdranch*. We will use just SecKeychainItemRef here and fill in the details in the next section:

Example 16-1. dumpem.m

```
// dumpem.m -- poke inside the keychain

/*
compile with:
cc -g -Wall -framework Security -framework CoreFoundation \
                                    -o dumpem dumpem.m
*/

#import <Security/Security.h>
#import <CoreFoundation/CoreFoundation.h>

#import <stdlib.h>        // for EXIT_SUCCESS
#import <stdio.h>         // for printf() and friends
#import <string.h>        // for strncpy

int main (int argc, char *argv[])
{
    SecKeychainSearchRef search;
    SecKeychainItemRef item;
    SecKeychainAttributeList list;
    SecKeychainAttribute attribute;
    OSErr result;
    int i = 0;

    // Create an attribute list with just one attribute specified
    // (You will want to change these to match a user name that you
    // have on your key chain)
    attribute.tag = kSecAccountItemAttr;
    attribute.length = 12;
    attribute.data = "bignerdranch";

    list.count = 1;
    list.attr = &attribute;

    result = SecKeychainSearchCreateFromAttributes
                (NULL, kSecGenericPasswordItemClass,
                 &list, &search);

    if (result != noErr) {
        printf ("status %d from "
                "SecKeychainSearchCreateFromAttributes\n",
                result);
    }

    // Iterate over the search results
    while (SecKeychainSearchCopyNext (search, &item) == noErr) {
        CFRelease (item);
        i++;
    }

    printf ("%d items found\n", i);
    CFRelease (search);

    return EXIT_SUCCESS;
```

```
} // main
```

Before building and running the program, launch `Keychain Access`. It is located in `/Applications/Utilities/`. Add at least one keychain item with the account name set to "bignerdranch". Then build and run the program.

Reading Data From an Item

Of course, once you have fetched the item, you can do all sorts of nifty things with it. For example, if you wanted to read the password, the account name, the description, and the modification date from an item, you would create an attribute list containing those attributes and call `SecKeychainItemCopyContent()`:

```
OSStatus SecKeychainItemCopyContent (SecKeychainItemRef   itemRef,
                                       SecItemClass *itemClass,
                           SecKeychainAttributeList *attrList,
                                          UInt32 *length,
                                          void **outData);
```

Note that here the `attrList` is specifying what data you want and is also acting as a receptacle. Add these functions to `dumpem.m`:

```
// given a carbon-style 4-byte character identifier,
// make a C string that can be given to printf

const char *fourByteCodeString (UInt32 code)
{
    // sick-o hack to quickly assign an identifier
    // into a character buffer
    typedef union theCheat {
        UInt32 theCode;
        char theString[4];
    } theCheat;

    static char string[5];

    ((theCheat*)string)->theCode = code;
    string[4] = '\0';

    return string;

} // fourByteCodeString

void showList (SecKeychainAttributeList list)
{
    char buffer[1024];
    SecKeychainAttribute attr;

    int i;

    for (i = 0; i < list.count; i++) {

        attr = list.attr[i];

        if (attr.length < 1024) {
```

```
                // make a copy of the data so we can stick on
                // a trailing zero byte
                strncpy (buffer, attr.data, attr.length);
                buffer[attr.length] = '\0';

            printf ("\t%d: '%s' = \"%s\"\n",
                    i, fourByteCodeString(attr.tag), buffer);
        } else {
            printf ("attribute %d is more than 1K\n", i);
        }
    }

} // showList

void dumpItem (SecKeychainItemRef item)
{
    UInt32 length;
    char *password;
    SecKeychainAttribute attributes[8];
    SecKeychainAttributeList list;
    OSStatus status;

    // list the attributes you wish to read
    attributes[0].tag = kSecAccountItemAttr;
    attributes[1].tag = kSecDescriptionItemAttr;
    attributes[2].tag = kSecLabelItemAttr;
    attributes[3].tag = kSecModDateItemAttr;

    list.count = 4;
    list.attr = attributes;

    status = SecKeychainItemCopyContent (item, NULL, &list, &length,
                                    (void **)&password);

    // use this version if you don't really want the password,
    // but just want to peek at the attributes
    //status = SecKeychainItemCopyContent (item, NULL, &list, NULL, NULL);

    // make it clear that this is the beginning of a new
    // keychain item
    printf("\n\n");
    if (status == noErr) {
        if (password != NULL) {

            // copy the password into a buffer so we can attach a
            // trailing zero byte in order to be able to print
            // it out with printf
            char passwordBuffer[1024];

            if (length > 1023) {
                length = 1023; // save room for trailing \0
            }
            strncpy (passwordBuffer, password, length);

            passwordBuffer[length] = '\0';
            printf ("Password = %s\n", passwordBuffer);
        }
```

```
        showList (list);

        SecKeychainItemFreeContent (&list, password);

    } else {
        printf("Error = %d\n", (int)status);
    }

} // dumpItem
```

When you call **SecKeychainItemCopyContent()**, if the keychain requires authentication, it will automatically bring up an authentication panel. If you only read publicly available data, no authentication panel will appear. The code above will probably trigger the panel for each item. If you change one line so that you are no longer fetching the password, the panel will not appear at all:

```
    SecKeychainItemCopyContent (item, NULL, &list, NULL, NULL);
```

Add a call to **dumpItem()** in **main()**:

```
    while (SecKeychainSearchCopyNext (search, &item) == noErr) {
        dumpItem (item);
        CFRelease (item);
        i++;
    }
```

Build and run the program. Note that if you choose **Always Allow**, the program will have access to the keychain item until you log out. However, if you recompile the program, you will have to re-authenticate. The security framework keeps checksums of the applications that have access.

Editing the Keychain

With the item, you can also make changes using an attribute list:

```
OSStatus SecKeychainItemModifyContent (SecKeychainItemRef  itemRef,
                   const SecKeychainAttributeList *attrList,
                                        UInt32  newPasswordLength
                             const void *newPassword)
```

The new attribute values would go into the attrList. A new password would go into newPassword.

To delete an item:

```
OSStatus SecKeychainItemDelete (SecKeychainItemRef itemRef)
```

Note that you would still have to call **CFRelease()** on the item to prevent a memory leak.

Getting Specific Keychains

As an argument to many of the keychain functions, you can specify a particular keychain. Usually, you will simply use the user's default keychain. For all of these functions, if you just supply NULL as the keychain, it will use the default keychain. However, if you want to explicitly get the default keychain you will use:

```
OSStatus SecKeychainCopyDefault(SecKeychainRef *keychain)
```

If you wanted to specify a different keychain (remember that it is just a file), you could use:

```
OSStatus SecKeychainOpen(const char *pathName,
                    SecKeychainRef *keychain)
```

When you are done with a keychain, make sure that you call **CFRelease()** to free it.

Keychain Access

Each keychain item defines how it may be accessed. The information about access privileges is kept in a SecAccessRef structure. To get the access structure for a particular keychain item, you will use the following function:

```
OSStatus SecKeychainItemCopyAccess(SecKeychainItemRef  item,
                                SecAccessRef *access);
```

To change the access on a keychain item, you edit the SecAccessRef and write it to the keychain item using:

```
OSStatus SecKeychainItemSetAccess(SecKeychainItemRef itemRef,
                                SecAccessRef access);
```

What, then, is a SecAccessRef? You can get a list of access control lists (ACLs) from it. Each access list has a list of trusted applications that are allowed to access the keychain item. Some applications can access the keychain item only after the user types in the keychain password.

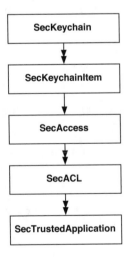

As an example of reading the ACLs for a keychain item, add the following code to **main()** in dumpem.m:

```
while (SecKeychainSearchCopyNext (search, &item) !=
                errSecItemNotFound) {
    dumpItem (item);
    // Get the SecAccess
    SecAccessRef access;
    SecKeychainItemCopyAccess(item, &access);
    showAccess(access);
    CFRelease(access);
    CFRelease(item);
    i++;
}
```

Add the following function:

```
void showAccess (SecAccessRef accessRef)
{
    int count, i;
    CFArrayRef aclList;
    CFArrayRef applicationList;
    SecACLRef acl;
    CFStringRef description;
    CSSM_ACL_KEYCHAIN_PROMPT_SELECTOR promptSelector;
    SecTrustedApplicationRef application;
    CFDataRef appData;

    // Get a list of access lists
    SecAccessCopyACLList(accessRef, &aclList);
    count = CFArrayGetCount (aclList);
    printf("%d access control lists\n", count);
    for (i = 0; i < count; i++) {
        char buffer[256];

        acl = (SecACLRef)CFArrayGetValueAtIndex(aclList, i);

        // Get the list of trusted applications
        SecACLCopySimpleContents(acl, &applicationList,
                        &description, &promptSelector);

        CFStringGetCString(description, buffer,
                                256, kCFStringEncodingASCII);
        CFRelease(description);

        // Does the apps on this list require the user
        // to type in the keychain passphrase?
        if (promptSelector.flags &&
                CSSM_ACL_KEYCHAIN_PROMPT_REQUIRE_PASSPHRASE) {
            printf("\t%d: ACL %s - Requires passphrase\n",
                                            i, buffer);
        } else {
            printf("\t%d: ACL %s - Does not require passphrase\n",
                                            i, buffer);
        }
        // Sometimes there is no application list at all
        if (applicationList == NULL) {
```

```
            printf("\t\tNo application list\n");
            continue;
        }
        int j, appCount;
        appCount = CFArrayGetCount(applicationList);
        printf("\t\t%d trusted applications\n", appCount);
        for (j = 0; j < appCount; j++) {
            application = (SecTrustedApplicationRef)
                    CFArrayGetValueAtIndex(applicationList, j);

            // Get the app data for the trusted application
            // (this is usually the path to the app)
            SecTrustedApplicationCopyData(application, &appData);
            printf("\t\t%s\n",CFDataGetBytePtr(appData));
            CFRelease(appData);
        }
        CFRelease(applicationList);
    }
    CFRelease(aclList);
}
```

Making a New Keychain Item

To create a new keychain item, you will use this function:

```
OSStatus SecKeychainItemCreateFromContent(SecItemClass   itemClass,
                              SecKeychainAttributeList *attrList,
                                            UInt32  passwdLength,
                                   const void *password,
                              SecKeychainRef  keychainRef,
                              SecAccessRef  initialAccess,
                              SecKeychainItemRef *itemRef);
```

Where the itemClass is kSecInternetPasswordItemClass,
kSecGenericPasswordItemClass, kSecApplesharePasswordItemClass, or
kSecCertificateItemClass. If you supply NULL as the keychainRef, the item will
be added to the default keychain. itemRef will be set to point to the newly created
item. To use the default access, just supply NULL as the initialAccess.

As an example, here is a short program that will insert a new item into your default
keychain.

Example 16-2. add_item.m

```
/*
compile with
cc -g -Wall -framework Security -framework CoreFoundation
            -o add_item add_item.m
*/

#import <Security/Security.h>
#import <CoreFoundation/CoreFoundation.h>
#include <stdio.h> // for printf()
```

```
int main (int argc, const char * argv[]) {
    SecKeychainAttribute attributes[2];
    SecKeychainAttributeList list;
    SecKeychainItemRef item;
    OSStatus status;

    attributes[0].tag = kSecAccountItemAttr;
    attributes[0].data = "fooz";
    attributes[0].length = 4;

    attributes[1].tag = kSecDescriptionItemAttr;
    attributes[1].data = "No Girls Allowed";
    attributes[1].length = 16;

    list.count = 2;
    list.attr = attributes;

    status = SecKeychainItemCreateFromContent(
                    kSecGenericPasswordItemClass, &list,
                    5, "budda", NULL,NULL,&item);
    if (status != 0) {
        printf("Error creating new item: %d", (int)status);
    }
    return 0;
}
```

After running this program, look at the keychain item in `Keychain Access`.

Also, note what "default access" is.

Convenience Functions

That is the whole story on keychains. There are some convenience functions that make common activities possible, but they simply use the functions that we have talked about already.

These functions allow you to create a new item without creating an attribute list:

```
OSStatus SecKeychainAddInternetPassword(SecKeychainRef keychain,
                        UInt32          serverNameLength,
                        const char      *serverName,
                        UInt32          securityDomainLength,
                        const char      *securityDomain,
                        UInt32          accountNameLength,
                        const char      *accountName,
                        UInt32          pathLength,
                        const char      *path,
                        UInt16          port,
                        SecProtocolType         protocol,
                        SecAuthenticationType authenticationType,
                        UInt32          passwordLength,
                        const void      *passwordData,
                        SecKeychainItemRef      *itemRef)

OSStatus SecKeychainAddGenericPassword(SecKeychainRef keychain,
                        UInt32          serviceNameLength,
                        const char      *serviceName,
                        UInt32          accountNameLength,
                        const char      *accountName,
                        UInt32          passwordLength,
                        const void      *passwordData,
                        SecKeychainItemRef *itemRef)
```

Note that neither of these can be used to change a password in an existing item. If you try this, the function will complain that the item already exists.

These methods allow you to find items without creating an attribute list:

```
OSStatus SecKeychainFindInternetPassword(CFTypeRef keychainOrArray,
                        UInt32      serverNameLength,
                        const char  *serverName,
                        UInt32      securityDomainLength,
                        const char  *securityDomain,
                        UInt32      accountNameLength,
                        const char  *accountName,
                        UInt32      pathLength,
                        const char  *path,
                        UInt16      port,
                        SecProtocolType protocol,
                        SecAuthenticationType authenticationType,
                        UInt32      *passwordLength,
                        void        **passwordData,
                        SecKeychainItemRef *itemRef)

OSStatus SecKeychainFindGenericPassword(CFTypeRef keychainOrArray,
                        UInt32      serviceNameLength,
                        const char  *serviceName,
                        UInt32      accountNameLength,
                        const char  *accountName,
                        UInt32      *passwordLength,
                        void        **passwordData,
                        SecKeychainItemRef *itemRef)
```

Notice that the protocol and authentication types are not strings. Here are the constants for the commonly used protocols:

- kSecProtocolTypeFTP

- kSecProtocolTypeFTPAccount

- kSecProtocolTypeHTTP

- kSecProtocolTypeIRC

- kSecProtocolTypeNNTP

- kSecProtocolTypePOP3

- kSecProtocolTypeSMTP

- kSecProtocolTypeSOCKS

- kSecProtocolTypeIMAP

- kSecProtocolTypeLDAP

- kSecProtocolTypeAppleTalk

- kSecProtocolTypeAFP

- kSecProtocolTypeTelnet

- kSecProtocolTypeSSH

There are several types of authentication, but you will almost certainly use `kSecAuthenticationTypeDefault`.

If you are writing a daemon or something else that should not be interrupting the user, you can prevent the authentication panel from appearing:

```
SecKeychainSetUserInteractionAllowed(NO);
```

Challenge

1. Write an app that saves a username and password to the default keychain.

2. Write an app that can read and change the saved password.

Chapter 17. Authorization

When you are trying to make sure someone is who they say they are, you are dealing with *authentication*. When you are checking to make sure that they are allowed to do what they want to do, you are dealing with *authorization*. The Security framework has functions which make authentication and authorization easier. The framework is extensible so that you can create your own modules for retinal scans and smartcards. In this chapter, we are going to talk about how to use the Security framework to do authentication and authorization, not how to extend it.

Let's say that you are writing an application called `Kama Sutra Coach`. You should only allow certain users in the household to run it. Even if one of those users is logged in, perhaps you should make the user re-authenticate when launching the app.

Here is the way the Security Server works: in your application, you ask for a right. A right is just a string, but it should relate to the task. In our example, you are writing the application for MegaCode Corporation. The name of the right might be `com.megacode.kamasutra.launch`.

The Security Server goes looking in its configuration file (`/etc/authorization`) for the right named `com.megacode.kamasutra.launch`. The configuration file is an XML property list containing one dictionary. The keys are rights, and the values are the rules by which those rights are authorized.

If you wanted everyone to have the right `com.megacode.kamasutra.launch`, you would add an entry like this:

```
<key>com.megacode.kamasutra.launch</key>
    <string>allow</string>
```

To prevent anyone from obtaining that right, you would change the entry:

```
<key>com.megacode.kamasutra.launch</key>
    <string>deny</string>
```

If you wanted to give the right to anyone who has authenticated as a member of the `parent` group within the last 700 seconds, you would make an entry like this:

```
<key>com.megacode.kamasutra.launch</key>
    <dict>
            <key>class</key>
            <string>user</string>
            <key>group</key>
            <string>parent</string>
            <key>shared</key>
            <true/>
            <key>timeout</key>
            <integer>700</integer>
    </dict>
```

(Note that you would also have to create a group called `parent` and add the user accounts of grown-ups in the house to that group.)

In `/etc/authorization`, there is an entry with an empty key. This is the default that gets used for all unrecognized rights. For your reference, here is the default policy:

```
<key>class</key>
<string>user</string>
```

```
<key>group</key>
<string>admin</string>
<key>shared</key>
<true/>
<key>timeout</key>
<integer>300</integer>
```

So, you get the default right for five minutes if you authenticate that you are a member of the admin group. Because the right is "shared", more than one application can have the right at the same time.

If the Security Server decides to grant the right, it returns a chunk of data to the application that requested the authorization. You can imagine this chunk of data as a ticket. Any process can present that ticket to the Security Server and ask, "Is this ticket good for the right com.megacode.kamasutra.launch?"

Notice the shared key in the entries in /etc/authorization. If that it is set to true, more than one valid ticket for the right can exist simultaneously.

The Security Framework API

The tickets representing rights that have been granted are held in an Authorization structure. To create an AuthorizationRef , you will use the function:

```
OSStatus AuthorizationCreate(const AuthorizationRights *rights,
                    const AuthorizationEnvironment *environment,
                             AuthorizationFlags  flags,
                               AuthorizationRef *authorization);
```

Typically, this is used just to create an empty structure, like this:

```
AuthorizationRef authorizationRef;
OSStatus status;
status = AuthorizationCreate(NULL,  kAuthorizationEmptyEnvironment,
             kAuthorizationFlagDefaults, &authorizationRef);
if (status != errAuthorizationSuccess)  {
   NSLog(@"Unable to create an empty authorization object");
```

The real work of getting approved for a set of rights usually happens in **AuthorizationCopyRights()**:

```
OSStatus AuthorizationCopyRights(AuthorizationRef authorization,
                     const AuthorizationRights *rights,
               const AuthorizationEnvironment *environment,
                       AuthorizationFlags  flags,
                         AuthorizationRights **authorizedRights);
```

An AuthorizationRights structure is just a set of AuthorizationItem structures:

```
typedef struct {
    AuthorizationString name;
    UInt32 valueLength;
    void *value;
    UInt32 flags;
} AuthorizationItem;
```

There are several things in the structure, but for acquiring rights, you will only set the name to be the name of the right you wish to aquire. The rest should just be set to zero.

To check for two rights, you would have a chunk of code like this:

```
// Create an array of rights to be acquired
AuthorizationItem rights[2];
rights[0] = { @"com.megacode.kamasutra.launch", 0, NULL, 0 };
rights[1] = { @"com.megacode.kamasutra.anotherright", 0, NULL, 0 };

// Pack them in a structure
AuthorizationRights rightSet = { 2, rights};

// Create the flags bitmap
AuthorizationFlags flags = kAuthorizationFlagDefaults |
                           kAuthorizationFlagInteractionAllowed |
                           kAuthorizationFlagExtendRights;

// Try to obtain a ticket for the rights from the security server
OSStatus status;
status = AuthorizationCopyRights(authorizationRef,
                                 &rightSet,
                                 kAuthorizationEmptyEnvironment,
                                 flags,
                                 NULL);
// If partial rights authorization were important, we would not pass NULL as
// the last argument. See the docs for details

// Did we fail to get the rights?
if (status != errAuthorizationSuccess) {
    fprintf(stderr, "No rights for you!\n");
    exit (EXIT_FAILURE);
}
```

If successful, the new rights are added to the `AuthorizationRef`.

Notice the flags. They say, "Bring up the authentication panel if necessary and extend the rights of this user if possible to include these two rights. "

Notice that the policy is defined by `/etc/authorization`, so the code does not have to be recompiled if the policy is changed. In reality, of course, very few users are going to edit their `/etc/authorization` to create a policy for `com.megacode.kamasutra.launch` and put all the adults in the household into a group called `parent`, so you should assume that the default policy is what will actually be used most of the time.

To free the `AuthorizationRef`:

```
OSStatus AuthorizationFree(AuthorizationRef authorization,
                           AuthorizationFlags flags);
```

In the flags argument, you can supply `kAuthorizationFlagDestroyRights`. If you do, the function tells the Security server to invalidate the ticket for the rights that have been authorized.

Passing authorization to a SUID tool

In Unix operating systems, if a process must be run with special privileges, the executable is owned by a privileged user and the SUID bit of the file permissions is set. When the SUID bit is set on an executable, the effective UID of a process created by running that executable is the UID of the owner of the file. (When the SUID bit is not set, the effective UID of the a process is the UID of the user that launched the executable.) So, for example, if you look at `passwd`, the SUID bit is set.

```
$ ls -l /usr/bin/passwd
-r-sr-xr-x  1 root   wheel   30492 Jul 27 23:00 /usr/bin/passwd
```

Thus, when you run `passwd`, it is being run as `root`.

```
$ whoami
rex

$ passwd
Changing password for rex.
Old password:
^Z
Suspended

$ ps -auxw | grep passwd
root   1309 0.0  0.1  1576   284 std  S  10:37AM  0:00.02 passwd
```

If you need to perform some privileged operation in your application, you will fork off a process and run an SUID tool. The tool can be embedded inside your app wrapper. All the dangerous stuff can be put into that tool. The tool should be as small, safe, and simple as possible.

But what keeps the bad people from going into my app wrapper and running the SUID tool? The answer is "Nothing!" So, we need to make sure that when the tool is run by an unauthorized user, it doesn't do anything.

Before launching your SUID tool from your application, you will preauthorize for a right and get a ticket. When the SUID tool is run, you will pipe the ticket to it. Before doing anything, the tool will check with the Security Server to make sure the ticket is good.

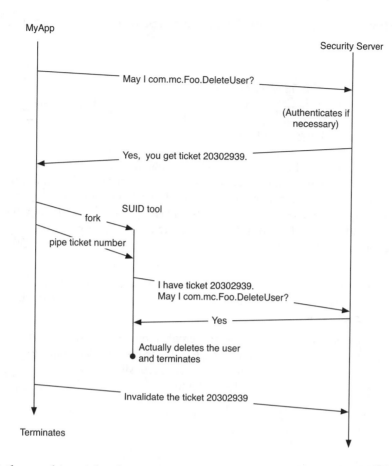

To pack the resulting ticket for sending to an external process, you will use:

```
OSStatus AuthorizationMakeExternalForm(AuthorizationRef authorization,
                           AuthorizationExternalForm *extForm);
```

To unpack the ticket in the SUID tool, you will use:

```
OSStatus AuthorizationCreateFromExternalForm(
                    const AuthorizationExternalForm *e,
                    AuthorizationRef *authorization);
```

Add Authentication to Remover

In this exercise, you will add the ability for `Remover` to read and delete any files on the system. Of course, you are going to make the user authenticate as a member of the admin group first.

Wrapping NSFileManager

You are going to write a replacement for **NSFileManager** called **AuthorizingFileManager** that will use **NSFileManager** when possible. If **NSFileManager**'s read or delete fails, **AuthorizingFileManager** will get authorization from the Security Server and run SUID tools to perform the forbidden operations.

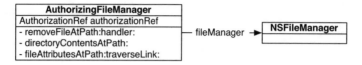

(Notice that we could have subclassed **NSFileManager**, but the class uses a shared instance. This brings up many questions: Should we replace the shared instance with our own? Or should there be two shared instances: one for **AuthorizingFileManager** and one for **NSFileManager**? Instead we will skip the questions and just create a completely seperate class -- a *proxy* for the **NSFileManager**. This will also be an opportunity to learn a couple of Objective-C tricks.)

You will also have to write three SUID tools: one that lists the contents of a directory, one that recursively deletes a directory and its contents, and one that determines if a path is a directory or a file.

Open the Remover project in Xcode and create a new Objective-C class called AuthorizingFileManager. We want it to be a drop-in replacement for **NSFileManager**, so it will have a shared instance. Alter your AuthorizingFileManager.m to look like this:

```
#import "AuthorizingFileManager.h"

static AuthorizingFileManager *_defaultAuthFileManager;

@implementation AuthorizingFileManager

+ (id)defaultManager
{
    if (!_defaultAuthFileManager) {
        _defaultAuthFileManager = [[self alloc] init];
    }
    return _defaultAuthFileManager;
}
```

The instance of **AuthorizingFileManager** will need a pointer to the **NSFileManager**, so add an instance variable to AuthorizingFileManager.h and declare the **defaultManager** method:

```
@interface AuthorizingFileManager : NSObject {
    NSFileManager *fileManager;
}
+ (id)defaultManager;
```

In AppController.m, initialize fileManager in **init** and release it in **dealloc**:

```
- (id)init
{
    [super init];
    fileManager = [[NSFileManager defaultManager] retain];
    return self;
}
```

```
- (void)dealloc
{
    [fileManager release];
    [super dealloc];
}
```

You want any message not understood by **AuthorizingFileManager** to be forwarded on to the shared instance of **NSFileManager**. Objective-C makes this possible. If a message is not recognized, it is bundled up into an **NSInvocation** object and the receiver is sent the message **forwardInvocation:**. So add the following methods to **AuthorizingFileManager**:

```
// This gets run as part of the creation of the NSInvocation object
// that is passed to forwardInvocation:
- (NSMethodSignature *)methodSignatureForSelector:(SEL)aSelector
{
    NSMethodSignature *result;
    result = [super methodSignatureForSelector:aSelector];
    if (!result){
        result = [fileManager methodSignatureForSelector:aSelector];
    }
    return result;
}

- (void)forwardInvocation:(NSInvocation *)invocation
{
    SEL aSelector = [invocation selector];
    if ([fileManager respondsToSelector:aSelector])
        [invocation invokeWithTarget:fileManager];
    else
        [self doesNotRecognizeSelector:aSelector];
}
```

Now just replace **NSFileManager** with **AuthorizingFileManager** in AppController.m and DirEntry.m. Build and run your app. It should work exactly the same as before. (Be sure to import AuthorizingFileManager.h at the beginning of AppController.m and DirEntry.m)

Preauthorizing

Now you will add the ability to delete directories that the user does not have write access to.

First, add an instance variable to hold onto our authorization object. Also, declare constants for the names of the rights. Make your AuthorizingFileManager.h file start like this:

```
#define LIST_RIGHT "com.bignerdranch.remover.readforbiddendirectories"
#define DELETE_RIGHT "com.bignerdranch.remover.deleteforbiddendirectories"

#import <Foundation/Foundation.h>
#import <Security/Security.h>

@interface AuthorizingFileManager : NSObject {
    AuthorizationRef authorizationRef;
    NSFileManager *fileManager;
```

```
    }
```

Open `AuthorizingFileManager.m`; initialize the `AuthorizationRef` in **init** and
free it in **dealloc**:

```
- (id)init
{
    OSStatus status;
    [super init];
    fileManager = [[NSFileManager defaultManager] retain];

    // Create an empty authorization structure
    status = AuthorizationCreate(NULL, kAuthorizationEmptyEnvironment,
                        kAuthorizationFlagDefaults, &authorizationRef);
    if (status != errAuthorizationSuccess) {
        NSLog(@"Failed to create the authref: %d.", status);
        [self release];
        return nil;
    }
    return self;
}


- (void)dealloc
{
    [fileManager release];
    AuthorizationFree(authorizationRef, kAuthorizationFlagDestroyRights);
    [super dealloc];
}
```

Create a method to preauthorize for a right:

```
- (BOOL)preauthorizeForRight:(const char *)rightName
{
    OSStatus status;
    AuthorizationItem right = { rightName, 0, NULL, 0 };
    AuthorizationRights rightSet = { 1, &right };
    AuthorizationFlags flags = kAuthorizationFlagDefaults |
                            kAuthorizationFlagPreAuthorize |
                            kAuthorizationFlagInteractionAllowed |
                            kAuthorizationFlagExtendRights;

    // This may cause the authorization panel to appear
    status = AuthorizationCopyRights(authorizationRef, &rightSet,
                        kAuthorizationEmptyEnvironment, flags, NULL);

    return (status == errAuthorizationSuccess);
}
```

Create a method that will pack your authorization ref into an **NSData**:

```
- (NSData *)authorizationAsData
{
    AuthorizationExternalForm extAuth;
    if (AuthorizationMakeExternalForm(authorizationRef, &extAuth))
        return nil;
    return [NSData dataWithBytes:&extAuth length:sizeof(extAuth)];
}
```

Create a method that will **alloc** and **init** an **NSTask**, set its launch path to an exectuable in the app wrapper, and connect pipes to its input and output:

```
// Create a task with pipes for input and output
- (NSTask *)taskForExecutable:(NSString *)execName
                    argument:(NSString *)arg
{
    NSString *executablePath;
    NSPipe *inPipe, *outPipe;
    NSTask *task;

    // Create a task for the requested executable
    task = [[NSTask alloc] init];
    executablePath = [[NSBundle mainBundle] pathForResource:execName
                                        ofType:@""];
    [task setLaunchPath:executablePath];
    [task setArguments:[NSArray arrayWithObject:arg]];

    // Set up the inPipe
    inPipe = [[NSPipe alloc] init];
    [task setStandardInput:inPipe];
    [inPipe release];

    // Set up the outPipe
    outPipe = [[NSPipe alloc] init];
    [task setStandardOutput:outPipe];
    [outPipe release];

    [task autorelease];
    return task;
}
```

Now, create a method that tries to use **NSFileManager**'s **removeFileAtPath:handler:** method. If that fails, then create a task that will run an executable called remover_deletor.

```
- (BOOL)removeFileAtPath:(NSString *)path handler:handler
{
    BOOL successful = [fileManager removeFileAtPath:path handler:self];
    if (!successful) {
        NSFileHandle *inFile;
        NSTask *task;
        NSData  *authData;

        // preauthorize
        if (![self preauthorizeForRight:DELETE_RIGHT]) {
            NSLog(@"Unable to preauthorize delete");
            return NO;
        }

        // Pack authorization for piping to tool
        authData = [self authorizationAsData];

        // Create a task
        task = [self taskForExecutable:@"remover_deletor"
                          argument:path];
        if (!task) {
            NSLog(@"Unable to create task");
```

```
        return NO;
    }

    // Get filehandle for writing
    inFile = [[task standardInput] fileHandleForWriting];

    // Launch the task
    [task launch];

    // Pipe the authData to the tool and send EOF
    [inFile writeData:authData];
    [inFile closeFile];

    // Was it successful?
    [task waitUntilExit];
    successful = ([task terminationStatus] == 0);
}

return successful;
}
```

You may declare all these methods in `AuthorizingFileManager.h` if you wish.

Creating the SUID tools

Now, it is time to create the tool `remover_deletor`. First add a new target (using the **Project** menu in `Xcode`) called **remover_deletor** of type **BSD Shell Tool** to your project. While you are at it, create targets for the other two tools also: **remover_lister** and **remover_statter**. `Remover` has a dependency on all three of the tools, so drag them under `Remover` in the target tab.

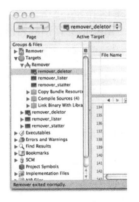

Create a BSD C file called `remover_deletor.c` add it to the **remover_deletor** target.

This will be the tool that will remove the file or directory.

```c
#include <unistd.h>
#include <stdlib.h>
#include <sys/stat.h>
#include <stdio.h>
#include <Security/Security.h>
#include <dirent.h>


#define RIGHT "com.bignerdranch.remover.deleteforbiddendirectories"

// remove_tree recursively removes a directory and its contents
void remove_tree(const char *path){
    DIR *dir;
    struct dirent *entry;
    char childPath[PATH_MAX];
    if (unlink(path) == 0)
        return;

    // Open the directory
    dir = opendir(path);
    if (!dir) {
        fprintf(stderr, "Cannot open %s\n", path);
        return;
    }

    // Read all the entries
    while (entry = readdir(dir)) {
        // Skip . and ..
        if (strcmp(entry->d_name, "..") == 0) {
            continue;
        }
        if (strcmp(entry->d_name, ".") == 0) {
            continue;
        }
        snprintf(childPath, PATH_MAX, "%s/%s", path, entry->d_name);
        remove_tree(childPath);
    }

    // Close the directory
    closedir(dir);

    // Delete the now-empty directory
```

```
        rmdir(path);
    }


int main(int argc, char *argv[])
{
    OSStatus status;
    AuthorizationRef auth;
    char *path;

    AuthorizationExternalForm extAuth;

    // Is this process running as root?
    if (geteuid() != 0) {
        fprintf(stderr, "Not running as root\n");
        exit(-1);
    }

    // Was there one argument?
    if (argc != 2) {
        fprintf(stderr, "Usage: remove_deletor <dir>\n");
        exit(-1);
    }

    // Get the path
    path = argv[1];

    // Read the Authorization data from our input pipe.
    if (fread(&extAuth, sizeof(extAuth), 1, stdin) != 1) {
        fprintf(stderr, "Could not read authorization\n");
        exit(-1);
    }

    // Restore the externalized Authorization back
    // to an AuthorizationRef
    if (AuthorizationCreateFromExternalForm(&extAuth, &auth)) {
        fprintf(stderr, "Unable to parse authorization data\n");
        exit(-1);
    }

    // Create the rights structure
    AuthorizationItem right = { RIGHT, 0, NULL, 0 };
    AuthorizationRights rights = { 1, &right };
    AuthorizationFlags flags = kAuthorizationFlagDefaults |
                               kAuthorizationFlagExtendRights;

    fprintf(stderr, "Tool authorizing right %s for command.\n", RIGHT);

    // Check the authorization
    status = AuthorizationCopyRights(auth,
                                     &rights,
                                     kAuthorizationEmptyEnvironment,
                                     flags,
                                     NULL);
    if (status != 0) {
        fprintf(stderr,
                "Tool authorizing command failed authorization: %ld.\n",
                status);
```

```
        exit(-1);
    }

    // Unlink the path
    remove_tree(path);

    // Terminate
    exit(0);
}
```

To link against the `Security.framework`, add the framework to the the project and all four targets.

Now make sure that the tool gets copied into the application's bundle resources. To do this, drag the remover_deletor executable under the Products group into the Copy Bundle Resources under the Remover target.

Build the application.

After building the application, you will need to make sure that the file's owner is changed to `root` and the SUID bit is set on `remover_deletor` when it is installed. You can set the SUID bit and the file's owner on the executables using Terminal commands:

```
$ sudo -s
Password:
# chmod 6555 build/Debug/Remover.app/Contents/Resources/remover_*
# chown root:admin build/Debug/Remover.app/Contents/Resources/remover_*
```

Now run the application. If you try to delete a protected file or directory, the authorization panel should appear and force you to supply the username and password for a user in the admin group. After this, you should be able to delete protected directories for 300 seconds without reauthorizing. For testing purposes, I'd suggest that you create some protected directories as `root` in `/tmp`. Be careful with this application; an erroneous delete can cause much misery.

If that works, you are ready to add listing of protected files and directories. Add these two methods to `AuthorizingFileManager.m`:

```
- (NSArray *)directoryContentsAtPath:(NSString *)path
{
    NSFileHandle *inFile, *outFile;
    NSArray *result = nil;
    NSTask *task;
```

```
        NSData *output = nil, *authData = nil;
        NSString *outputAsString = nil;

        // Can we do it the easy way?
        if ([fileManager isReadableFileAtPath:path]) {
            // List the directory with using NSFileManager
            result = [fileManager directoryContentsAtPath:path];
            return result;
        }

        // Preauthorize
        if (![self preauthorizeForRight:LIST_RIGHT]) {
            NSLog(@"Unable to preauthorize");
            return nil;
        }

        // Pack authorization for piping to tool
        authData = [self authorizationAsData];

        // Create a task
        // Pass the path of the directory to the tool as argv[1]
        task = [self taskForExecutable:@"remover_lister" argument:path];
        if (!task) {
            NSLog(@"Unable to create task");
            return nil;
        }

        // Get filehandles for reading and writing
        inFile = [[task standardInput] fileHandleForWriting];
        outFile = [[task standardOutput] fileHandleForReading];

        // Launch the task
        [task launch];

        // Pipe the authData to the tool and send EOF
        [inFile writeData:authData];
        [inFile closeFile];

        // Read the listing of the directory from the tool's
        // standard output
        output = [outFile readDataToEndOfFile];

        if ([output length] == 0) {
            result = [NSArray array];
        } else {
            // Convert to an NSString
            outputAsString = [[NSString alloc] initWithData:output
                                    encoding:NSUTF8StringEncoding];

            // Break into components
            result = [outputAsString componentsSeparatedByString:@"\n"];

            // Release the string
            [outputAsString release];
        }
        return result;
    }
```

```
// This is sort of a cheap solution.  For the exercise,  we only
// need to know if it is a directory and the size.  I should really
// put together an entire dictionary of file attributes.
// This is left as an exercise for the reader.

- (NSDictionary *)fileAttributesAtPath:(NSString *)path
                          traverseLink:(BOOL)willTraverse
{
    NSDictionary *result;

    // Try to use NSFileManager
    result = [fileManager fileAttributesAtPath:path
                                  traverseLink:willTraverse];

    // Was it successful?
    if (result) {
        return result;
    }

    // Stat the file the hard way
    NSFileHandle *inFile, *outFile;
    NSTask *task;
    NSData *output, *authData;
    NSString *outputAsString;

    // Preauthorize
    if (![self preauthorizeForRight:LIST_RIGHT]) {
        NSLog(@"Unable to preauthorize");
        return nil;
    }

    // Pack authorization for piping to tool
    authData = [self authorizationAsData];

    // Create a task
    task = [self taskForExecutable:@"remover_statter"
                          argument:path];
    if (!task) {
        NSLog(@"Unable to create task");
        return nil;
    }

    // Get filehandles for reading and writing
    inFile = [[task standardInput] fileHandleForWriting];
    outFile = [[task standardOutput] fileHandleForReading];

    // Launch the task
    [task launch];

    // Pipe the authData to the tool and send EOF
    [inFile writeData:authData];
    [inFile closeFile];

    // Read the listing of the directory from the tool's
    // standard output
    output = [outFile readDataToEndOfFile];
```

```
    // Convert to an NSString
    outputAsString = [[NSString alloc] initWithData:output
                                    encoding:NSUTF8StringEncoding];

    // Break into components
    NSArray *outputArray = [outputAsString componentsSeparatedByString:@"\

    // Release the string
    [outputAsString release];

    NSMutableDictionary *statResult = [NSMutableDictionary dictionary];

    // Is there less than two lines of data?
    if ([outputArray count] < 2) {
        NSLog(@"no stat");
        return statResult;
    }

    NSString *fileType = [outputArray objectAtIndex:0];
    int fileSize = [[outputArray objectAtIndex:1] intValue];
    [statResult setObject:fileType
                forKey:NSFileType];
    [statResult setObject:[NSNumber numberWithInt:fileSize]
                forKey:NSFileSize];
    return statResult;
}
```

Of course, you have to create the `remover_lister.c` and `remover_statter.c` files and add them to their respective targets. Here is `remover_lister.c`:

```
#include <unistd.h>
#include <stdlib.h>
#include <dirent.h>
#include <stdio.h>
#include <Security/Security.h>

#define RIGHT "com.bignerdranch.remover.readforbiddendirectories"

int
main(int argc, char * argv[])
{
    OSStatus status;
    AuthorizationRef auth;
    char *path;
    DIR *dir;
    struct dirent *entry;
    int firstTime = 1;

    AuthorizationExternalForm extAuth;

    // Is this process running as root?
    if (geteuid() != 0) {
        fprintf(stderr, "Not running as root\n");
        exit(-1);
    }
```

```
// Was there one argument?
if (argc != 2) {
    fprintf(stderr, "Usage: remove_lister <dir>\n");
    exit(-1);
}

// Get the path
path = argv[1];

// Read the Authorization "byte blob" from our input pipe.
if (fread(&extAuth, sizeof(extAuth), 1, stdin) != 1) {
    fprintf(stderr, "Unable to read authorization\n");
    exit(-1);
}

// Restore the externalized Authorization
// back to an AuthorizationRef
if (AuthorizationCreateFromExternalForm(&extAuth, &auth)) {
    fprintf(stderr, "Unable to parse authorization data\n");
    exit(-1);
}

// Create the rights structure
AuthorizationItem right = { RIGHT, 0, NULL, 0 };
AuthorizationRights rights = { 1, &right };
AuthorizationFlags flags = kAuthorizationFlagDefaults |
                           kAuthorizationFlagExtendRights;

fprintf(stderr, "Tool authorizing right %s for command.\n", RIGHT);

// Check the authorization
if (status = AuthorizationCopyRights(auth, &rights,
                  kAuthorizationEmptyEnvironment, flags, NULL)) {
    fprintf(stderr, "Tool command failed authorization: %ld.\n",
                  status);
    exit(-1);
}

// Open the directory
dir = opendir(path);
if (dir == NULL) {
    fprintf(stderr, "Cannot open %s\n", path);
    exit(-1);
}

// Read all the entries
while (entry = readdir(dir)) {

    // Skip . and ..
    if (strcmp(entry->d_name, "..") == 0) {
        continue;
    }
    if (strcmp(entry->d_name, ".") == 0) {
        continue;
    }

    // Put \n before each line except the first
```

```
            if (firstTime) {
                firstTime = 0;
            } else {
                fputc('\n',stdout);
            }

            // Write out the filename
            fputs(entry->d_name,stdout);
    }

    // Close the directory
    closedir(dir);

    // Close output
    fclose(stdout);

    // Terminate
    exit(0);
}
```

Here is `remover_statter.c`:

```c
#include <unistd.h>
#include <stdlib.h>
#include <sys/stat.h>
#include <stdio.h>
#include <Security/Security.h>

#define RIGHT "com.bignerdranch.remover.readforbiddendirectories"

int
main(int argc, char *argv[])
{
    OSStatus status;
    AuthorizationRef auth;
    char *path;
    struct stat statbuf;
    char *typeAsString;

    AuthorizationExternalForm extAuth;

    // Is this process running as root?
    if (geteuid() != 0) {
        fprintf(stderr, "Not running as root\n");
        exit(-1);
    }

    // Was there one argument?
    if (argc != 2) {
        fprintf(stderr, "Usage: remove_statter <dir>\n");
        exit(-1);
    }

    // Get the path
    path = argv[1];

    // Read the Authorization "byte blob" from our input pipe.
    if (fread(&extAuth, sizeof(extAuth), 1, stdin) != 1) {
```

```
        fprintf(stderr, "Unable to read authorization\n");
        exit(-1);
    }

    // Restore the externalized Authorization back
    // to an AuthorizationRef
    if (AuthorizationCreateFromExternalForm(&extAuth, &auth)) {
        fprintf(stderr, "Unable to parse authorization data\n");
        exit(-1);
    }

    // Create the rights structure
    AuthorizationItem right = { RIGHT, 0, NULL, 0 };
    AuthorizationRights rights = { 1, &right };
    AuthorizationFlags flags = kAuthorizationFlagDefaults |
                               kAuthorizationFlagExtendRights;

    fprintf(stderr, "Tool authorizing right %s for command.\n", RIGHT);

    // Check the authorization
    if (status = AuthorizationCopyRights(auth, &rights,
                    kAuthorizationEmptyEnvironment, flags, NULL)) {
        fprintf(stderr, "Tool failed authorization: %ld.\n",
                    status);
        exit(-1);
    }
    // Stat the path
    if (stat(path, &statbuf)) {
        fprintf(stderr, "Unable to stat %s", path);
        exit(-1);
    }

    // Write out stat info
    if (S_ISDIR(statbuf.st_mode))
        typeAsString = "NSFileTypeDirectory";
    else
        typeAsString = "NSFileTypeRegular";

    fprintf(stdout, "%s\n%lu", typeAsString, (unsigned long)statbuf.st_size);
    fclose(stdout);

    // Terminate
    exit(0);
}
```

These tools also need to be copied into the application's bundle resources. Drag the remover_statter and remover_lister executables under the Products group into the Copy Bundle Resources under the Remover target.

Once again, build it and set the SUID bit and owner for the tools. Run the application. You will now be able to browse protected directories.

For the More Curious: AuthorizationExecuteWithPrivileges()

Notice that in the case above, everything works nicely because the owner and the SUID bits are set on the tool. The question so many installers would have is, "How do I get the owner and SUID bits set?" (You can see the chicken-or-egg nature of the problem: you have no privileges with the SUID bit, and you can't set the SUID bit or change the owner to `root` without privileges.)

The solution is **AuthorizationExecuteWithPrivileges()**. It calls a tool in a manner that is similar to what you've done in this exercise. The difference is that the effective UID is changed *before* the tool is called. Actually, the way it works is that there is an SUID tool on every system called `/usr/libexec/security_authtrampoline` which reads the name of another tool (let's call it "Tool X") from its command line and reads an authorization from its standard input. It checks to make sure that the authorization includes the right `system.privilege.admin`. It then starts Tool X and pipes the authorization into the Tool X's standard input. Since Tool X was started by a process that has root's UID as its effective UID, Tool X also has root's UID as its effective UID.

The right associated with **AuthorizationExecuteWithPrivileges()** is called `system.privilege.admin`. The entry in `/etc/authorization` looks like this:

```
<key>system.privilege.admin</key>
    <dict>
            <key>class</key>
            <string>user</string>
            <key>group</key>
            <string>admin</string>
            <key>shared</key>
            <false/>
            <key>allow-root</key>
            <true/>
            <key>timeout</key>
            <integer>300</integer>
    </dict>
```

(The `allow-root` means "allow anyone running as root to have this right without authentication".)

Notice that **AuthorizationExecuteWithPrivileges()** is really easy to use. In one simple call it preauthorizes, forks, and packs up the authorization and sends it to the trampoline which checks the authorization. The trampoline pipes that authorization to the tool that it starts. If, for some reason, your tool needs to read rights from that authorization, use the function **AuthorizationCopyPrivilegedReference()**.

Because it is so easy to use, many programmers are using **AuthorizationExecuteWithPrivileges()** anytime they need to do something as a privileged user. This is flawed because they are creating many apps and many types of operations that use the exact same right: `system.privilege.admin`. This is an invitation to evil doers to create trojan horses. A user may authenticate in an app that is supposed to do something relatively harmless. The generated ticket could be used to run a tool that does something much more violent.

Moral: Name your rights something unique. Do not use **AuthorizationExecuteWithPrivileges()** unless absolutely necessary. Typically, it is only necessary in installers. (For example, installing applications and then setting the SUID bit on them.)

If you are writing an installer, here is the information you will need to run
AuthorizationExecuteWithPrivileges():

```
OSStatus AuthorizationExecuteWithPrivileges(AuthorizationRef authorization,
                                const char *pathToTool,
                     AuthorizationFlags options,
                          char * const *arguments,
                               FILE **communicationsPipe);
```

The first argument is an authorization structure. It will be filled in if necessary by bringing up the authentication panel. The second argument is the path to the tool. The third argument is always zero. The fourth argument is an `argv`-like array of command-line arguments to be passed to the tool. The final argument is a pointer. A new pipe that will be attached to the new process for bidirectional communcations will be created. This pointer will be set to point to it.

For the More Curious: Computing a Checksum

If you are going to be running a tool via the trampoline, it is a good idea to make sure that no one has replaced your tool with something unpleasant. A checksum (or message digest) is a fingerprint for a file. One common algorithm for creating a checksum is called *SHA1*. SHA1 is part of the OpenSSL library (`/usr/lib/libssl.dylib`). Here is an example of how to get a checksum using **NSData**.

```
#include <openssl/evp.h>
...
// Map the file into memory
NSData *d = [NSData dataWithContentsOfMappedFile:path];

// Create a buffer to hold the checksum
unsigned char buffer[EVP_MAX_MD_SIZE];
unsigned int size = EVP_MAX_MD_SIZE;

// Process the file and fill the buffer
EVP_Digest((void *)[d bytes], [d length], buffer, &size, EVP_sha1(), NULL);

// Create an NSData containing the signature
NSData *output = [NSData dataWithBytes:buffer
                                length:size];
```

Real and effective UID

While the SUID bit will set your process's *effective* user ID, it does not set your process's *real* user ID. Some tools are sensitive to this and may refuse to run without the real user ID of a privileged user. If you run into this problem, the fix is to explicitly set your real user ID:

```
setuid(geteuid());
```

Chapter 18. Distributed Objects

Distributed Objects (or DO) is a technology that allows an object in one process to send a message to an object in another. In fact, the objects communicating may be on different machines. This is a rather nifty way to create client/server applications: the client sends messages to an object in the server process and gets back a response. It is also a way for one application to be informed of changes in another. Distributed Objects is part of Cocoa's Foundation framework.

DO integrates very neatly with the run loop that makes event handling work. Thus, while your app is waiting for messages to arrive from other processes via DO, it can continue to handle user input. For this reason, DO is also used to send messages between threads in a single application. Using DO between threads will be discussed in Chapter 23

Distributed Objects Concepts

Here is the basic idea: Let us say that there is a client process and a server process. The server process makes a server object available to the world. The client process asks for that server object, but gets an instance of **NSDistantObject**. The **NSDistantObject** is a proxy for the server object (it is, in fact, a subclass of **NSProxy**). When messages are sent to the proxy, the message (including the arguments) are packed up and sent across the network to the server object. The server object executes the method, and the result is packed up and sent back to the client process. The proxy returns the result as if it had done the computation.

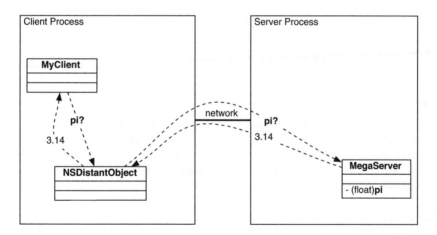

The dream, then, is that you get the proxy object and treat it just like you would the server object. The reality is not as simple because many things can go wrong with the client, the server, or the network in between. There are also performance issues to consider; you will want to keep the amount of data that you send across the network to a minimum.

Notice that when the client asks for the server, it gets a proxy. The proxy represents the server object. On the client side, the proxy is attached to an **NSConnection**, which handles its communications. On the server side, the corresponding server object is also attached to an **NSConnection**. You can ask a connection for its distant objects and it will return an array of the proxies for which it is responsible. You can ask a connection for its local objects, and it will return an array of server objects.

More specifically, the local objects are objects which have been vended out as proxies in other processes.

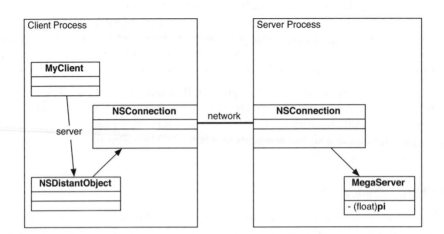

NSPort

An **NSConnection** object has two instances of **NSPort**: one receives data and the other sends data. There are several subclasses of **NSPort** which enable the connection to handle its communcations in different ways.

NSPort

This is the superclass of all other ports. Concrete instances are only useful when the proxy and the object it represents are in the same process. Instances of **NSPort** are commonly used when DO is used for communications between two threads in the same process.

NSMachPort

This port uses Mach messaging. Instances of **NSMachPort** are only useful when the proxy and the object it represents are on the same machine. Instances of **NSMachPort** are commonly used for communcations between two applications running on the same machine. If two mach ports are connected, when one stops working, the other is informed immediately.

NSSocketPort

This port uses sockets. Instances can communicate even when the proxy and the object it represents are on different machines.

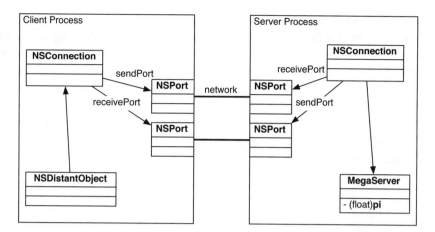

Create a DO Server

In this chapter, you will create a simple chat client and server using Distributed Objects. Create a new Foundation Tool Project. Name it chatterd. This is will be the server.

Clients will subscribe and unsubscribe with the server. Clients will send messages to be distributed to the server. The server will then send the message to the clients for display.

Whenever you are sending messages between two processes, it is a good idea to create a protocol that contains the messages that will be sent. This is an important step in design, and later you will see that the protocol can actually be used to increase performance.

Create an empty file called ChatterServing.h.

```
#import <Foundation/Foundation.h>

// Messages the client will receive from the server
@protocol ChatterUsing

- (oneway void)showMessage:(in bycopy NSString *)message
            fromNickname:(in bycopy NSString *)nickname;

- (bycopy NSString *)nickname;

@end


// Messages the server will receive from the client
@protocol ChatterServing

- (oneway void)sendMessage:(in bycopy NSString *)message
            fromClient:(in byref id <ChatterUsing>)client;

// Returns NO if someone already has newClient's nickname
- (BOOL)subscribeClient:(in byref id <ChatterUsing>)newClient;

- (void)unsubscribeClient:(in byref id <ChatterUsing>)client;

@end
```

Notice that this file has some Objective-C keywords that you may never have seen before. Remember when I said "packs up the message (including the arguments) and sends it to the server?" These keywords control specifically how the arguments and return values should be packed up.

`oneway void`

> If a method has a return type of `oneway void`, the client does not wait for a response. If the return type is anything else, the proxy blocks until the response comes from its corresponding object.

`in`

> If an argument has `in` in its type, it is assumed that the receiver is going to read the value, but not change it. The argument is thus sent from the requestor to the the receiver, but not returned. This minimizes network traffic.

`out`

> If an argument has `out` in its type, it is assumed that the reciever is going to change the value, but not read it. The argument is thus not sent from the requestor to the receiver, but is returned to requestor.

`inout`

> If an argument has `inout` in its type, it is assumed that the receiver is going to both read and change the value. This is the default if you supply neither `in` nor `out`.

`bycopy`

> If an argument has `bycopy` in its type, the argument is archived before it is sent to the receiver and unarchived in the receiver's process space.

`byref`

> If an argument has `byref` in its type, the argument is represented by a proxy in the receiver's process space.

That last keyword explains how our server will work: It will have an array of proxies. Each proxy will represent one client. When a client subscribes, its proxy will be added to the array. When the server receives a message, it will send that message to each of its proxies for display. When a client unsubscribes, it will be removed from the array of proxies.

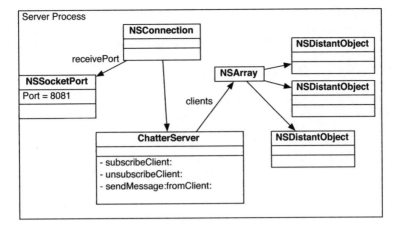

Create a new class called **ChatterServer**. Edit the header file:

Example 18-1. ChatterServer.h

```
#import <Foundation/Foundation.h>
#import "ChatterServing.h"

@interface ChatterServer : NSObject <ChatterServing> {
    NSMutableArray *clients;
}
@end
```

Implement the methods in the implementation file:

Example 18-2. ChatterServer.m

```
#import "ChatterServer.h"
@implementation ChatterServer

- (id)init
{
    [super init];
    clients = [[NSMutableArray alloc] init];
    return self;
}

// Private method
- (id)clientWithNickname:(NSString *)string
{
    id currentClient;
    NSEnumerator *enumerator;
    enumerator = [clients objectEnumerator];
    while (currentClient = [enumerator nextObject]) {
        if ([[currentClient nickname] isEqual:string]) {
            return currentClient;
        }
    }
    return nil;
}
```

```objc
// Methods called by clients
- (oneway void)sendMessage:(in bycopy NSString *)message
                fromClient:(in byref id <ChatterUsing>)client
{
    NSString *senderNickname;
    id currentClient;
    NSEnumerator *enumerator;
    senderNickname = [client nickname];
    enumerator = [clients objectEnumerator];
    NSLog(@"from %@: %@", senderNickname, message);
    while (currentClient = [enumerator nextObject]) {
        [currentClient showMessage:message fromNickname:senderNickname];
    }
}

- (BOOL)subscribeClient:(in byref id <ChatterUsing>)newClient
{
    NSString *newNickname = [newClient nickname];

    // Is this nickname taken?
    if ([self clientWithNickname:newNickname]) {
        return NO;
    }
    NSLog(@"adding client");
    [clients addObject:newClient];
    return YES;
}

- (void)unsubscribeClient:(in byref id <ChatterUsing>)client
{
    NSDistantObject *clientProxy = (NSDistantObject *)client;
    NSConnection *connection = [clientProxy connectionForProxy];
    [clients removeObject:client];
    [connection invalidate];
    NSLog(@"client removed");
}

- (void)dealloc
{
    [clients release];
    [super dealloc];
}
@end
```

Notice that in **unsubscribeClient**: you explicitly invalidated the connection. This ensures that the connection and its ports get freed. This is because for each client that subscribes, the server will create a proxy and a connection for that client.

Each connection can have a delegate. Each time the connection spawns a new "child" connection, the child will have its delegate outlet set to point to the parent's delegate. The delegate gets informed each time a new connection is spawned and when the connection dies. Create a new class to be the delegate of your connections. Create a class **ConnectionMonitor** to log these:

Example 18-3. ConnectionMonitor.m

```
#import "ConnectionMonitor.h"

@implementation ConnectionMonitor

- (BOOL)connection:(NSConnection *)ancestor
              shouldMakeNewConnection:(NSConnection *)conn
{
        NSLog(@"creating new connection: %d total connections",
                         [[NSConnection allConnections] count]);
        return YES;
}

- (void)connectionDidDie:(NSNotification *)note
{
    NSConnection *connection = [note object];
    NSLog(@"connection did die: %@", connection);
}
@end
```

You can leave `ConnectionMonitor.h` as-is.

Now edit `chatterd.m` so that it creates a connection, a server, and a monitor before starting the runloop.

Example 18-4. chatterd.m

```
#import "ChatterServer.h"
#import "ChatterServing.h"
#import "ConnectionMonitor.h"
#include <sys/socket.h>

#import <Foundation/Foundation.h>

int main (int argc, const char * argv[]) {

    NSAutoreleasePool * pool = [[NSAutoreleasePool alloc] init];
    NSRunLoop *runloop = [NSRunLoop currentRunLoop];
    ConnectionMonitor *monitor = [[ConnectionMonitor alloc] init];
    ChatterServer *chatterServer = [[ChatterServer alloc] init];

    // Create the receive port
    NSSocketPort *receivePort;
    @try {
        // This server will wait for requests on port 8081
        receivePort = [[NSSocketPort alloc] initWithTCPPort:8081];
    }
    @catch (NSException *e) {
        NSLog(@"unable to get port 8081");
        exit(-1);
    }

    // Create the connection object
    NSConnection *connection;
    connection = [NSConnection connectionWithReceivePort:receivePort
                                                sendPort:nil];
```

```
        // The port is retained by the connection
        [receivePort release];

        // When clients use this connection, they will
        // talk to the ChatterServer
        [connection setRootObject:chatterServer];

        // The chatter server is retained by the connection
        [chatterServer release];

        // Set up the monitor object
        [connection setDelegate:monitor];
        [[NSNotificationCenter defaultCenter]
                addObserver:monitor
                    selector:@selector(connectionDidDie:)
                        name:NSConnectionDidDieNotification
                      object:nil];

        // Start the runloop
        [runloop run];

        // If the run loop exits (and I do not
        // know why it would), cleanup
        [connection release];
        [monitor release];
        [pool release];
        return 0;
}
```

Note that we are using new-style Objective-C exceptions, so you will need to enable those on the C compiler.

Build and run your server. It will not do much until you've created a client.

Create a Client Using DO

Create a new Cocoa Application project called ChatterClient. Open up the
MainMenu.nib file and layout the UI as shown:

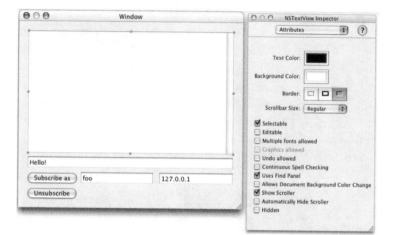

Create a subclass of **NSObject** called **AppController**. Add four outlets to the class:
NSTextField *hostField, **NSTextField** *messageField, **NSTextField**
*nicknameField, **NSTextView** *textView. Add three actions: **sendMessage:,**
subscribe:, unsubscribe:. Create files for the class and create an instance of it.

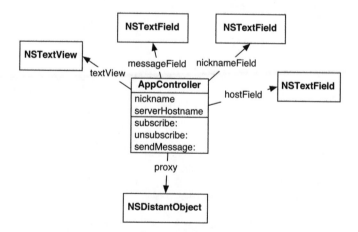

Set each outlet of the **AppController** to point to the appropriate view.

Make the **AppController** the target of the Subscribe button, the Unsubscribe button, and the message text field.

Make the **AppController** the delegate of **NSApplication**.

Save the nib file. Return to Xcode.

Add the file ChatterServing.h to the ChatterClient project.

Edit the class **AppController**.

Example 18-5. AppController.h

```
#import <Cocoa/Cocoa.h>
#import "ChatterServing.h"

@interface AppController : NSObject <ChatterUsing>
{
    IBOutlet NSTextField *hostField;
    IBOutlet NSTextField *messageField;
    IBOutlet NSTextField *nicknameField;
    IBOutlet NSTextView *textView;
    NSString *nickname;
    NSString *serverHostname;
    id proxy;
}
- (IBAction) sendMessage: (id) sender;
- (IBAction) subscribe: (id) sender;
- (IBAction) unsubscribe: (id) sender;
@end
```

Example 18-6. AppController.m

```
#import "AppController.h"

@implementation AppController

// Private method to clean up connection and proxy
- (void) cleanup
```

```objc
{
    NSConnection *connection = [proxy connectionForProxy];
    [[NSNotificationCenter defaultCenter] removeObserver:self];
    [connection invalidate];
    [proxy release];
    proxy = nil;
}

// Show message coming in from server
- (oneway void)showMessage:(in bycopy NSString *)message
            fromNickname:(in bycopy NSString *)n
{
    NSString *string = [NSString stringWithFormat:@"%@ says, \"%@\"\n",
                                                    n, message];
    NSTextStorage *currentContents = [textView textStorage];
    NSRange range = NSMakeRange([currentContents length], 0);
    [currentContents replaceCharactersInRange:range
                                   withString:string];
    range.length = [string length];
    [textView scrollRangeToVisible:range];
    // Beep to get user's attention
    NSBeep();
}


// Accessors
- (bycopy NSString *)nickname
{
    return nickname;
}

- (void)setNickname:(NSString *)s
{
    [s retain];
    [nickname release];
    nickname = s;
}

- (void)setServerHostname:(NSString *)s
{
    [s retain];
    [serverHostname release];
    serverHostname = s;
}

// Connect to the server
- (void)connect
{
    BOOL successful;
    NSConnection *connection;
    NSSocketPort *sendPort;

    // Create the send port
    sendPort = [[NSSocketPort alloc] initRemoteWithTCPPort:8081
                                            host:serverHostname];

    // Create an NSConnection
    connection = [NSConnection connectionWithReceivePort:nil
```

```
                                            sendPort:sendPort];

    // Set timeouts to something reasonable
    [connection setRequestTimeout:10.0];
    [connection setReplyTimeout:10.0];

    // The send port is retained by the connection
    [sendPort release];

    @try {
        // Get the proxy
        proxy = [[connection rootProxy] retain];

        // Get informed when the connection fails
        [[NSNotificationCenter defaultCenter] addObserver:self
                                selector:@selector(connectionDown:)
                                    name:NSConnectionDidDieNotification
                                  object:connection];

        // By telling the proxy about the protocol for the object
        // it represents, we significantly reduce the network
        // traffic involved in each invocation
        [proxy setProtocolForProxy:@protocol(ChatterServing)];

        // Try to subscribe with chosen nickname
        successful = [proxy subscribeClient:self];
        if (successful) {
            [messageField setStringValue:@"Connected"];
        } else {
            [messageField setStringValue:@"Nickname not available"];
            [self cleanup];
        }
    }
    @catch (NSException *e) {
        // If the server does not respond in 10 seconds,
        // this handler will get called
        [messageField setStringValue:@"Unable to connect"];
        [self cleanup];
    }
}

// Read hostname and nickname then connect
- (IBAction)subscribe:(id)sender
{
    // Is the user already subscribed?
    if (proxy) {
        [messageField setStringValue:@"unsubscribe first!"];
    } else {
        // Read the hostname and nickname from UI
        [self setServerHostname:[hostField stringValue]];
        [self setNickname:[nicknameField stringValue]];

        // Connect
        [self connect];
    }
}
```

```objc
- (IBAction)sendMessage:(id)sender
{
    NSString *inString;

    // If there is no proxy,  try to connect.
    if (!proxy) {
        [self connect];
        // If there is still no proxy, bail
        if (!proxy){
            return;
        }
    }

    // Read the message from the text field
    inString = [messageField stringValue];
    @try {
        // Send a message to the server
        [proxy sendMessage:inString fromClient:self];
    }
    @catch (NSException *e) {
        // If something goes wrong
        [messageField setStringValue:@"The connection is down"];
        [self cleanup];
    }
}

- (IBAction)unsubscribe:(id)sender
{
    @try {
        [proxy unsubscribeClient:self];
        [messageField setStringValue:@"Unsubscribed"];
        [self cleanup];
    }
    @catch (NSException *e) {
        [messageField setStringValue:@"Error unsubscribing"];
    }
}

// Delegate methods

//  If the connection goes down,  do cleanup
- (void)connectionDown:(NSNotification *)note
{
    NSLog(@"connectionDown:");
    [messageField setStringValue:@"connection down"];
    [self cleanup];
}

// If the app terminates,  unsubscribe.
- (NSApplicationTerminateReply)applicationShouldTerminate:
                                        (NSApplication *)app
{
    NSLog(@"invalidating connection");
    if (proxy) {
        [proxy unsubscribeClient:self];
        [[proxy connectionForProxy] invalidate];
    }
```

```
    return NSTerminateNow;
}

- (void)dealloc
{
    [self cleanup];
    [super dealloc];
}

@end
```

Once again, enable Objective-C exceptions on the C compiler.

With your server running, build and run the client.

For the more curious: NSPortCoder

When a message is being sent to a remote object, the arguments are archived using an **NSPortCoder**. Each object that would be sent is first sent the message:

```
- (id)replacementObjectForPortCoder:(NSPortCoder *)aCoder
```

The object that comes back is the one that is put into the archive. This method is defined in **NSObject**. As defined in **NSObject**, the method returns an **NSDistantObject**. Thus, by default, proxies instead of objects are sent. In objects that would be willing to send copies of themselves (**NSString**, for example) `replacementObjectForPortCoder:` is overridden to return themselves.

An **NSPortCoder** knows whether the argument to the method is bycopy or byref, and you can ask it. Here is a reasonable way to override `replacementObjectForPortCoder:` in an object that conforms to the **NSCoding** protocol:

```
- (id)replacementObjectForPortCoder:(NSPortCoder *)c {
    if ([c isBycopy])
        return self;
    else
        return [NSDistantObject proxyWithLocal:self
                                    connection:[encoder connection]];
}
```

Bindings and Distributed Objects

Key-value coding, key-value observing, and bindings were not designed to work with Distributed Objects. There are some sneaky tweaks in these technologies for convenience and performance that makes them DO-incompatible.

Chapter 19. Bonjour

Zeroconf is a very compelling idea. It extends the idea of DNS so that things on the network can declare their intentions. For example, when a zeroconf-compliant device is plugged into a network, it can declare "I am bozo.local, and my IP address is 168.254.32.1!" If another device already has that IP address, it can complain. The new device will then change its address. Thus, a network device can get in IP address without a DHCP server. This capability is known as *link local addressing*.

However, the beauty of Zeroconf does not end at devices and IP addresses. It also allows services to declare their name, type, address, and port number. Thus, the local network is informed of new devices and services as they are added. Furthermore, it adds the ability for the services to be browsed. That is, if you are looking for a type of service, you can ask for all the information about all the individual servers on a particular network.

The DNS standard actually already had a mechanism by which a service could be advertised. The idea was that, for example, to find all the ftp servers in the `bignerdranch.com` domain, your ftp client would ask for the SRV record for `_ftp._tcp.bignerdranch.com`. There are two reasons why you have probably never heard of the SRV record:

1. No one uses it.
2. Only a DNS server can advertise the service.

To make it possible for many, many machines to advertise services on a network, Multicast DNS was created. Essentially, every machine is running a Multicast DNS server. This daemon is `/usr/sbin/mDNSResponder`.

Thus, Zeroconf is a clever marriage of link local addressing and multicast DNS. Zeroconf is a proposed standard, and Bonjour is Apple's implementation of that standard. There are three different APIs for dealing with Bonjour:

1. The mach-level API called DNSServiceDiscovery is what all the other APIs are based upon.
2. The C API in the CoreServices framework uses DNSServiceDiscovery but integrates more easily with the rest of Core Foundation.
3. The Objective-C classes **NSNetService** and **NSNetServiceBrowser** are part of the Foundation framework.

In this chapter, we will use the Objective-C API to let our chatter server declare its availability and let our chatter client browse for servers.

Publishing an NSNetService

In a server, you will advertise the availability of your service by creating an instance of **NSNetService** and publishing it. You will give the server a name, you will tell it what service it provides, what port it runs on, and the name of the network it is part of (the domain). The important methods are:

```
- (id) initWithDomain: (NSString *) domain
             type: (NSString *) type
             name: (NSString *) name
             port: (int) port
```

This is the initializer that you will use when creating a service to be published. You may pass in @"" as the domain, and the host's default domain will be used. The type is a string of the form "service_type.protocol". As a convention, host names are not prepended with an underscore, whereas service and protocols are. The protocol is usually either _tcp or _udp. For our example, the type will be @"_chatter._tcp.". You can use any Unicode string as the name. The only tricky bit is that your name may conflict with another's. The port is the port number upon which the server is waiting.

```
- (void) publish
```

This method advertises the service on the network. It returns immediately, and the delegate is informed later if it was a failure.

The delegate can implement:

```
- (void) netService: (NSNetService *) sender
    didNotPublish: (NSDictionary *) errorDict
```

Notifies the delegate that the service offered by sender could not be published. You can use the dictionary keys NSNetServicesErrorCode and NSNetServicesErrorDomain to determine the cause of the error. A common error is that the name of your server was already claimed by another server in the same domain.

Make chatterd Zeroconf-compliant

Open the chatterd project. In **main()**, add the lines to read the first argument into a string. Also, declare a variable for the **NSNetService**:

```
int main (int argc, const char * argv[]) {
    NSAutoreleasePool *pool = [[NSAutoreleasePool alloc] init];
    if (argc != 2) {
        NSLog(@"Usage: chatterd <servicename>");
        exit (-1);
    }
    NSString *serviceName = [NSString stringWithUTF8String:argv[1]];
    NSNetService *netService;
```

Immediately before the run loop starts, create and publish the **NSNetService**:

```
    netService = [[NSNetService alloc] initWithDomain:@""
                                    type:@"_chatter._tcp."
                                    name:serviceName
                                    port:8081];

    [netService setDelegate:monitor];
    [netService publish];
    NSLog(@"service published = %@", netService);
```

```
    [runloop run];
```

In `ConnectionMonitor.m`, add a method to indicate if the publish has failed:

```
- (void)netService:(NSNetService *)sender
    didNotPublish:(NSDictionary *)errorDict
{
    NSLog(@"failed to publish = %@", errorDict);
}
```

Voila! A Bonjour-aware server. Build and run it. It must be run with one argument -- the name of the service. You can set the argument in the inspector for the chatterd executable:

Browsing Net Services

When a client needs to find a service, it multicasts a message onto the network. The published servers respond. Notice, however, that with busy servers on a busy or slow network, this might take some time. So a browser is told to start a search, and then, as responses come in, the delegate is informed.

NSNetServiceBrowser has the following method:

```
- (void)searchForServicesOfType:(NSString *)type
                       inDomain:(NSString *)domainString
```

This method kicks off the search for services of the given type in the given domain. Once again, @"" can be supplied as the domain.

The delegate gets sent these messsages:

```
- (void)netServiceBrowser:(NSNetServiceBrowser *)aNetServiceBrowser
         didFindService:(NSNetService *)aNetService
           moreComing:(BOOL)moreComing
```

This method gets called as net services are discovered. If there are several to be processed, the `moreComing` flag will be YES. Thus, you will know to wait before updating your user interface.

```
- (void)netServiceBrowser:(NSNetServiceBrowser *)aNetServiceBrowser
       didRemoveService:(NSNetService *)aNetService
           moreComing:(BOOL)moreComing
```

This method gets sent if a server disappears.

Make ChatterClient browse for servers

Open the ChatterClient project.

First, we are going to replace the hostname text field with a combo box. Open AppController.h. Change the type of the pointer, add a mutable array for the discovered services, and add an **NSData** to hold the address of the selected service:

```
#import <Cocoa/Cocoa.h>
#import "ChatterServing.h"

@interface AppController : NSObject <ChatterUsing>
{
    IBOutlet NSTextField *messageField;
    IBOutlet NSTextField *nicknameField;
    IBOutlet NSTextView *textView;
    NSString *nickname;
    id proxy;
    NSData *address;
    NSNetServiceBrowser *browser;
    NSMutableArray *services;
    IBOutlet NSComboBox *hostField;
}
- (IBAction)sendMessage:(id)sender;
- (IBAction)subscribe:(id)sender;
- (IBAction)unsubscribe:(id)sender;
- (void)cleanup;
- (void)setAddress:(NSData *)a;
// Combo box data source methods
- (int)numberOfItemsInComboBox:(NSComboBox *)aComboBox;
- (id)comboBox:(NSComboBox *)aComboBox
            objectValueForItemAtIndex:(int)index;
- (unsigned int)comboBox:(NSComboBox *)aComboBox
            indexOfItemWithStringValue:(NSString *)string;
@end
```

Save AppController.h and parse it into MainMenu.nib. Add a combo box and set its datasource to be the **AppController**. Set the **AppController**'s hostField to point at the combo box.

Select the combo box. In the inspector, check the box that says, "Uses data source". Save the nib file and close `Interface Builder`.

Create an **awakeFromNib** method in `AppController.m` that creates a browser and starts the search:

```
- (void)awakeFromNib
{
    browser = [[NSNetServiceBrowser alloc] init];
    services = [[NSMutableArray array] retain];
    [browser setDelegate:self];
    [browser searchForServicesOfType:@"_chatter._tcp."
                            inDomain:@"local."];
    NSLog(@"begun browsing: %@", browser);
}
```

Before using a discovered net service, you will want to resolve it — that is, look up an address for it. This is another method that returns immediately but actually waits in the background for success.

If the net service has not resolved, when you ask it for its array of addresses (yes, there might be more than one) it will return an empty array.

Add these browser delegate methods to `AppController.m`:

```
- (void)netServiceBrowser:(NSNetServiceBrowser *)aNetServiceBrowser
         didFindService:(NSNetService *)aNetService
            moreComing:(BOOL)moreComing
{
    NSLog(@"Adding new service");
    [services addObject:aNetService];
    if (!moreComing) {
        [hostField reloadData];
    }
}

- (void)netServiceBrowser:(NSNetServiceBrowser *)aNetServiceBrowser
       didRemoveService:(NSNetService *)aNetService
            moreComing:(BOOL)moreComing
```

```
    {
        NSLog(@"Removing service");
        NSEnumerator *enumerator = [services objectEnumerator];
        NSNetService *currentNetService;
        while (currentNetService = [enumerator nextObject]) {
            if ([[currentNetService name] isEqual:[aNetService name]] &&
                    [[currentNetService type] isEqual:[aNetService type]] &&
                    [[currentNetService domain] isEqual:[aNetService domain]]) {
                [services removeObject:currentNetService];
                break;
            }
        }
        if (!moreComing) {
            [hostField reloadData];
        }
    }
```

Add methods for the combo box data source:

```
- (int)numberOfItemsInComboBox:(NSComboBox *)aComboBox
{
    return [services count];
}


- (id)comboBox:(NSComboBox *)aComboBox
              objectValueForItemAtIndex:(int)index
{
    NSNetService *item;
    item = [services objectAtIndex:index];
    return [item name];
}


- (unsigned int)comboBox:(NSComboBox *)aComboBox
                indexOfItemWithStringValue:(NSString *)string
{
    unsigned int k, max;
    NSNetService *item;
    max = [services count];
    for (k = 0; k < max; k++) {
        item = [services objectAtIndex:k];
        if ([string isEqual:[item name]]) {
            return k;
        }
    }
    return 0;
}
```

Create an accessor for the address instance variable:

```
- (void)setAddress:(NSData *)a
{
    [a retain];
    [address release];
    address = a;
}
```

In the **connect** method, use that address when you create the send port, rather than the static port you used before:

```
sendPort = [[NSSocketPort alloc]
              initRemoteWithProtocolFamily:AF_INET
                                 socketType:SOCK_STREAM
                                   protocol:INET_TCP
                                    address:address];
```

To get these constants defined, add the following at the beginning of
`AppController.m`:

```
#include <sys/socket.h>
```

In **subscribe:**, get the address from the selected service:

```
- (IBAction)subscribe:(id)sender
{
    NSNetService *currentService;

    // Is the user already subscribed?
    if (proxy) {
        [messageField setStringValue:@"unsubscribe first!"];
    } else {

        // What is the selected service in the combobox?
        currentService = [services objectAtIndex:
                                     [hostField indexOfSelectedItem]];
        [currentService setDelegate:self];

        // Try for 30 seconds to get address of the selected service
        [currentService resolveWithTimeout:30];
    }
}

- (void)netServiceDidResolveAddress:(NSNetService *)currentService
{
    NSArray *addresses;
    addresses = [currentService addresses];

    // Just take the first address
    [self setAddress:[addresses objectAtIndex:0]];
    [self setNickname:[nicknameField stringValue]];

    // Connect to selected server
    [self connect];
}

- (void)netService:(NSNetService *)sender
      didNotResolve:(NSDictionary *)errorDict
{
    NSString *errString;
    errString = [NSString stringWithFormat:@"Unable to resolve %@",
                                            [sender name]];
    [messageField setStringValue:errString];
}
```

That is it, build it and run it. If your server is running, its name should appear in the combo box. If you have several servers running, you should be able to choose among them.

For the More Curious: TXT Records

Besides the standard information for a service (host, port, name), the DNS record used to publish the services has a TXT record. This is a place where you can put any sort of data that clients might want to know about. For example, your chatter server might want to advertise the number of users already connected. It could use the TXT record to do this. **NSNetService** has a method that would be used on the server side:

```
- (BOOL) setTXTRecordData: (NSData *)d;
```

On the client side, you would ask the **NSNetService** for the data using:

```
- (NSData *) TXTRecordData;
```

Of course, the server might change the TXT record. (For example, if more people subscribe, your chatterd server would want to change the advertised number of subscribers.) On the client, you would become a delegate of the NSNetService. When the TXT record is changed, you will be sent:

```
- (void) netService: (NSNetService *) sender
       didUpdateTXTRecordData: (NSData *) data;
```

Challenge

Using the TXT record, have the chatterd server advertise the number of subscribers. On the client, display the number of subscribers for each server in the server list pop-up.

Chapter 20. Daemons and launchd

Unix was designed to be a system of independent processes that cooperate with each other. Mac OS X is no exception. If you run the `ps -aux` command in the terminal, you will see a lot of processes running. There are a number of processes that run as root, such as `coreaudiod`, the system sound server and manager of the sound hardware, `syslogd`, the system logger, and `cupsd`, the print server.

You will also see a number of background user processes, such as `SystemUIServer`, which is the window server, `ATSServer`, which is used for typography services, `pbs`, the pasteboard server, `mdimportserver`, which is used for spotlight, and any other user background stuff from Apple and third party products. Every logged in user (via Fast User Switching) has their own copies of these user processes. If there are three users logged in, there are three `SystemUIServers`, three `pbs` servers, and so on.

In Apple terminology, the root background processes are called daemons, and the user background processes are called agents, as shown in Figure 20-1

Figure 20-1. Daemons and Agents

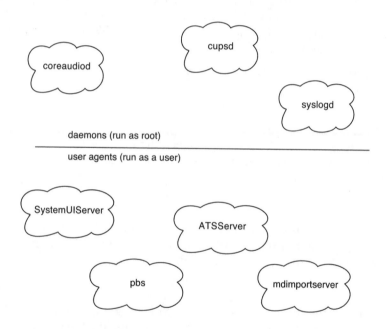

Traditionally, writing daemons for Unix is not a straightforward task. There are numerous mechanisms for starting daemons, such as `init`, which keeps certain daemons running all the time. There is also `inetd`, short for "Internet Daemon", and an enhanced version called `xinetd`, which launch daemons on-demand. There is also the DaemonTools package which provides services similar to `init`. The `/etc/rc` script can also start up background processes. Mac OS X 10.3 also introduced Startup Items, which handle some of the daemon startup and shutdown duties.

There are also programming issues involved when writing a traditional Unix daemon, such as having to disconnect from the controlling terminal (whether by using two **fork()** calls or using the **daemon()** function). You also typically need to save your process ID into a file so that system administrators can easily track down your daemon process. Unfortunately there are error conditions that can happen, such as the daemon crashing before it has a chance to clear its pid file, and then a system administration tool using the stale pid and killing an unrelated user process.

Mac OS X 10.4 introduced `launchd`, a system-wide and per-user daemon and agent manager. `launchd` is a unified mechanism for automatically starting background processes, whether at launch time, on-demand, or at a particular point in time. It subsumes the other unix daemon starting technologies, and it takes over some of the duties of `cron`, which starts programs at particular times.

Programming daemons that are run by `launchd` is a great deal simpler than with traditional Unix systems. `launchd` also runs as process id 1, meaning that orphaned processes become children of `launchd`. It replaces `init` as pid 1.

launchd Configuration

Many things in Mac OS X are configured via property lists (commonly referred to by the moniker "plist"), and `launchd` follows suit. Individual daemon and agent processes (also collectively called "jobs") are controlled by property lists. There are a large number of property list keys available that allow you to customize how `launchd` treats your daemon. All of the keys are case-sensitive, so double-check the capitalization of the keys if something is not working. Most of the keys are optional, but a few are required, as noted below.

The first group of configuration keys identify the program to `launchd`, and specify what to run:

Label

> (Required) This is a string that uniquely identifies the job to `launchd`. Use the reverse-DNS nomenclature for this, like `com.bignerdranch.groovyDaemon`, to generate a unique identifier.

ProgramArguments

> (Required) This is an array of strings which are used as arguments for the program. `launchd` executes the daemon using **execvp()**, and passes this array to **execvp()** in the `argv[]` parameter.

Program

> This is a string that specifies the path of the program to run and will be used as the first argument of **execvp()**. If this key is missing, the first element of the `ProgramArguments` array will be used for the program name.

ServiceDescription

> This is a string that gives a human-readable (or at least system administrator readable) non-localized description of the job to be run.

ServiceIPC

> This boolean tells `launchd` that the daemon is `launchd`-aware. When this value is set to YES, you can query `launchd` for information using the API specified in `/usr/include/launch.h`. This API allows you to get the values of

configuration plist entries and is also the mechanism by which the daemon can get the file descriptors for new network connections.

Debug

This is a boolean value that tells launchd to adjust its syslog mask so that it logs additional information (as LOG_DEBUG) when dealing with your daemon. Look in your /var/log/system.log for output from launchd.

This batch of keys control how the job is to be run:

Disabled

This boolean value controls whether the daemon should be run (with a NO value) or not run (a YES value). It defaults to NO, so the daemon will be run when appropriate. You have to think of this setting in a double-negative frame of mind.

OnDemand

This boolean value, if set to YES, will cause the daemon to only be run when someone wants to use its services. This is similar to how [x]inetd works. If set to NO, the daemon will be kept continuously running, which is similar to how init and DaemonTools control daemons on other unix platforms. OnDemand defaults to NO. You can also think of this flag as a "keep alive" flag. If it is set to NO, and launchd discovers the daemon has stopped, it will get restarted. Too many restarts in a short period of time will make launchd think your daemon is crashing, so it will stop running the daemon for awhile. A good rule of thumb is to make sure your daemon stays alive for at least 10 seconds before exiting.

RunAtLoad

This boolean value, if set to YES, cause the daemon to be launched immediately when its plist is loaded. If set to NO, the job will be run later. If OnDemand is NO, the job will be launched when the plist is loaded, even if RunAtLoad is set to NO

inetdCompatibility

This is a dictionary, which if it exists, tells launchd that the daemon expects to be run as if it were launched from inetd. The dictionary takes a single key, Wait, which is a boolean flag. YES corresponds to the wait (datagram sockets) inetd option, and NO corresponds to the nowait (stream sockets) inetd option. This setting controls whether launchd waits for a job that uses datagrams to release the socket before launchd goes to listen to the socket again.

The next group of keys control the running environment of the job. If the job is run in a login context, the jobs will run as the user and group as the owner of the login context. If the job is run in a root context, these keys control who the daemon will actually be running as.

UserName

This string tells launchd the name of the user that should own the daemon process. If you do not specify a value, the job will be run as the user who submitted the job to launchd.

GroupName

This string tells `launchd` the groupname to run the daemon as. If you do not specify a value, the job will be run as the group of the user who submitted the job to `launchd`.

InitGroups

This boolean controls whether `launchd` calls **initgroups()** before running the job. When **initgroups()** is called for a specific user, any extra groups that the user belongs to (outside of their primary group) is added to the process' control list. For example, user `markd`'s primary group is `markd`, and secondary groups are `appserveradm`, `appserverusr`, and `admin`. With `InitGroups` set to NO, only the `markd` group will be engaged and any attempts to group-access files as `admin` will not work. With `InitGroups` set to YES, the daemon can access those files.

RootDirectory

This string tells `launchd` which directory it should **chroot()** to before running the daemon. **chroot()** is a system call that causes a process to hoists a particular directory and treat it like is was / as far as the running program is concerned. This provides a great deal of security since the program cannot escape the **chroot** "jail" and access files outside of the directory.

WorkingDirectory

This string tells `launchd` to call **chdir()** before running the daemon. This directory will become the current working directory of the daemon, meaning any relative paths will be resolved relative to this directory.

EnvironmentVariables

This dictionary of strings is a set of key/value pairs to add to the environment the job runs in. Use this to set any environment variables the job needs in order to run.

Umask

This integer controls the daemon's umask.

Nice

This integer sets the nice value (process priority) under which the job will run.

LowPriorityIO

This boolean, if set to YES, tells the kernel to treat I/O performed by the daemon to be scheduled at a low priority when doing file system I/O. You probably do not want this if your daemon slurps large quantities of movie data from the hard drive, but if your daemon does a lot of logging and tracing, you might want to use low priority I/O to be nicer to the rest of the system.

SoftResourceLimits and HardResourceLimits

These are dictionaries that specify the resource limits imposed on the daemon. They contain the same values you can tweak with the **setrlimit()** function. Each dictionary contains string keys and numeric values. The available keys are: Core (max core file size, in bytes), CPU (time in seconds), Data (RAM consumption in bytes), FileSize (max file size, in bytes), MemoryLock (**mlock()** limit, in bytes), NumberOfFiles (max number of open files), NumberOfProcesses (max number of simultaneous processes), ResidentSetSize (max size on physical memory, in bytes), and Stack (max size of the program's call stack, in bytes).

The next two keys cause launchd to redirect a stream to go to a file instead. These can be absolute paths, or they can be relative to the setting in the WorkingDirectory key. You cannot use Indirect reference using the tilde (~). This is a planned enhancement, but it is not supported as of Mac OS X 10.4.2. If you need to refer to something in a particular user's home directory (such as ~/Library/Logs), you will either need to construct the path in your daemon, or process the plist file to use the proper full path.

StandardOutPath

> This string tells launchd what file should be used to store any data the daemon writes to the standard out stream.

StandardErrorPath

> This string tells launchd what file should be used to store any data the daemon writes to the standard error stream. stream.

The next four keys control how launchd starts your service (other than from a request on a network socket).

StartInterval

> Setting this integer causes the daemon to be started every N seconds.

StartCalendarInterval

> This dictionary causes the job to be started every calendar interval as specified by the integer values for these keys (which act like crontab values): Minute, Hour, Day, Weekday (0 and 7 represent Sunday), and Month. Missing arguments are considered to be a wildcard (like * in crontab) You cannot specify multiples of any setting, such as multiple minutes settings allowing your daemon to run every 5 minutes. You can use StartInterval to get this kind of behavior, though.

WatchPaths

> An array of strings containing paths to files and/or directories in the file system. The job will be started if any one of them is modified.

QueueDirectories

> This array of strings contains paths to directories. The daemon will be started if a directory is not empty. You can use this to create a "drop-box" directory. Users can drop files in a directory for further processing.

The last key deals with specifying what sockets launchd should listen to. When a new connection is made to the socket, launchd will launch your daemon. If the inetdCompatibility setting exists, launchd will hook up the network socket to standard in and standard out. Otherwise `launchd` will message you with the new socket.

`Sockets`

This can be an array of dictionaries, or it can be a dictionary of dictionaries. If you supply a dictionary of dictionaries, the dictionary keys immediately under Socket can be anything meaningful to your daemon. If you do not need to identify each socket with a name, you can just provide a simple array of dictionaries.

You can use the following keys in each socket-specific dictionary to control what the sockets are bound to. Many of these correspond to inputs to the **getaddrinfo()** function. All of the entries in the `Sockets` dictionary are optional.

`SockType`

This string instructs `launchd` what type of socket to create. Valid values are `dgram` (UDP), `seqpacket` (sequenced packets, corresponding to SOCK_SEQPACKET, which is a reliable connection-based communication channel with a maximum message size), or `stream` (TCP). `stream` is the default.

`SockPassive`

This boolean controls what `launchd` does to the socket. If this is set to YES (the default), `launchd` calls **listen()** on the socket. If set to NO, `launchd` calls **connect()**. This **connect()** behavior is new to `launchd` over existing unix daemon handling. This allows a daemon to use `launchd` to establish a connection to a server (such as a mail server). If there is any activity on the socket, `launchd` will then start the daemon, which can then handle the new activity.

`SockNodeName`

This string is the node (address or hostname) to **bind()** to if `SockPassive` is set to YES, or to **connect()** to if `SockPassive` is set to NO.

`SockServiceName`

This string is the service (port) to **bind()** or **connect()** to. This can be a service name, like "http", or a port number, like 80 (for http).

`SockFamily`

This string allows you to specifically request that `IPv4`, `IPv6`, or `Unix` sockets be created.

`SockProtocol`

This string is the protocol to be passed to the **socket()** system call. As of Mac OS X 10.4.2, the only valid value is `TCP`.

`SockPathName`

This string is only valid if `SockFamily` is set to "Unix". It is a path that `launchd` will use to **connect()** or **bind()** to.

`Bonjour`

> This boolean, string, or array of strings tells `launchd` to register the service with Bonjour. If you specify a boolean (with a YES value), `launchd` will infer the service name from the `SockServiceName` setting. If you specify a string (or strings), they are used to construct the service name(s). `ssh`, for instance, has "ssh" and "sftp-ssh" as its Bonjour names.

Starting Daemons

There are two mechanisms for getting your configuration plist onto `launchd`'s list of daemons. The first is putting your plist into one of a number of pre-defined directories, and the other is via the `launchctl` command-line utility.

Well-known Directories

`launchd` looks in a number of well-known directories to find daemon plists:

`/System/Library/LaunchDaemons`

> This directory holds the plists for the Mac OS X system-wide daemons. This is Apple's territory, so hands-off. You can poke around there and see what services are available, and see what their plists look like, but do not touch.

`/System/Library/LaunchAgents`

> This directory holds the plists for the Mac OS X per-user agents. This is also Apple's territory, but you can poke around here too. As of Mac OS X 10.4.2, this directory is empty.

`/Library/LaunchDaemons`

> This directory holds the plists for system-wide daemons provided by the machine's system administrator. You can also have an installer place your daemon's plist in this directory if you are supplying a system-wide service.

`/Library/LaunchAgents`

> This directory holds the plists for per-user agents provided by the machine's system administrator.

`~/Library/LaunchAgents`

> This directory holds the plists for per-user agents provided by the user. You are welcome to make your own plist and place them in this directory. The jobs will run automatically when you log in.

launchctl

You can use the `launchctl` program to feed plists into `launchd`. You can run `launchctl` as an interactive program. Even though you run the `launchctl` program, you will be given a `launchd%` prompt.

```
$ launchctl
launchd% help
usage: launchctl <subcommand>
        load        Load configuration files and/or directories
        unload      Unload configuration files and/or directories
        start       Start specified jobs
        stop        Stop specified jobs
        list        List jobs and information about jobs
        setenv      Set an environmental variable in launchd
        unsetenv    Unset an environmental variable in launchd
        getenv      Get an environmental variable from launchd
        export      Export shell settings from launchd
        limit       View and adjust launchd resource limits
        stdout      Redirect launchd's standard out to the given path
        stderr      Redirect launchd's standard error to the given path
        shutdown    Prepare for system shutdown
        reloadttys  Reload /etc/ttys
        getrusage   Get resource usage statistics from launchd
        log         Adjust the logging level or mask of launchd
        umask       Change launchd's umask
        help        This help output
launchd%
```

The most interesting commands include `load`, which reads a plist or a directory and registers the specified services. Any non-on-demand services are started automatically. `unload` will unregister the service and stop any of that plists's jobs by sending them the `SIGTERM` signal. This is a good command to have handy if your service is running amok, which can happen during development. `list` will show you the currently registered jobs. Use control-D to exit from `launchd` (as of Mac OS X 10.4.2, there is no `exit` or `quit` command).

You can also specify the subcommands on the command line:

```
$ launchctl load ./sample.plist
$ launchctl list
com.bignerdranch.daemonsample

$ launchctl unload ./sample.plist
$ launchctl list
```

Making Your Own Daemons

Thanks to `launchd`, making your own daemons under Mac OS X 10.4 is much easier than on other unix systems and previous versions of Mac OS X. Much of the hassle of writing daemons for other unix flavors is the bookkeeping involved, such as disconnecting from the controlling terminal, saving off the pid, and writing scripts to handle startup, shutdown, and reloading.

There are some rules involved when writing a `launchd` capable daemon. There are things that you must not do, such as **fork()** and then have the parent call **exit()** or **_exit()**. If you **fork()** and **exit()**, launchd will think your program has died, and will try to relaunch it. You should also not call the **daemon()** function, which will also make `launchd` think that the daemon has died. These will cause your daemon to not operate correctly when run from `launchd`.

Things you should not do include explicitly setting the user ID or group ID, setting the working directory, setting the session ID (with **setsid()**), or call **chroot()**. Do not close stray file descriptors, change the standard input or output streams to /dev/null, or manually set resource limits with setrusage() or change the program's scheduling priority. You also should not ignore the SIGTERM signal. Your daemon will still run, but it may not behave correctly.

On a more positive note, you should catch SIGTERM; it is sent to daemons on system shutdown and to user agents on logout, allowing you to do any kind of appropriate cleanup and perform a clean shutdown of your service.

Some daemons use TCP Wrappers to enhance their security when dealing with requests from over the network. TCP Wrappers are a security aid that gives an additonal layer of protection to network services by defining which remote machines are allowed, or not allowed, to use the service. Usage of TCP Wrappers comes for free if the daemon is using launchd's inetd compatibility mode. Native daemons (that is, launchd-aware daemons) will need to link against libwrap.a and use the TCP Wrappers API.

A Minimal Daemon

Example 20-1 shows the code for a minimal daemon. It prints some stuff to stdout just so we can see it running. For a proper daemon, you would use syslog or ASL to log stuff.

Example 20-1. minimal-daemon.m

```
// minimal-daemon.m -- a minimal daemon that runs under launchd

/* compile with
gcc -g -Wall -o minimal-daemon minimal-daemon.m
*/

/* schedule with
launchctl load ./minimal-daemon.plist
launchctl unload ./minimal-daemon.plist
*/

#import <stdio.h>      // for printf()
#import <signal.h>     // for signal()
#import <stdlib.h>     // for exit()
#import <unistd.h>     // for write()
#import <strings.h>    // for strlen()

void handleSigTerm (int signal)
{
    // cannot use printf() within a signal handler
    char *message = "we got signal!\n";
    int len = strlen (message);

    write (1, message, len);

} // handleSigTerm

int main (void)
{
```

```
        printf ("starting!\n");
        fflush (stdout);

        signal (SIGTERM, handleSigTerm);

        sleep (100);

        exit (0);

} // main
```

Example 20-2 shows the property list for minimal-daemon. This is not in any real plist format, but it shows the keys and their relationships without being too wordy like the XML format. The development tools come with `Property List Editor` that provides a GUI interface for creating property lists. Be aware that if you misspell something in the property list, or you have a malformed path, the daemon may not work right. So be sure to double-check your property lists if your daemon does not start correctly.

Example 20-2. minimal-daemon.plist

```
Root:
    Label:                com.bignerdranch.daemontest
    OnDemand:             No
    StandardErrorPath:    /Users/markd/stderror.txt
    StandardOutPath:      /Users/markd/stdout.txt
    ProgramArguments:
        0:                /Users/markd/minimal-daemon
```

Compile the program and schedule it. Cat the file `stdout.txt` to see the "starting!" line. Then unschedule the job. The running daemon is sent a `SIGTERM`.

```
$ launchctl load ./minimal-daemon.plist
$ cat stdout.txt
starting!
$ launchctl unload ./minimal-daemon.plist
$ cat stdout.txt
starting!
we got signal!
```

A Minimal Service

The next program has `launchd` listening on a socket. A new connection on the socket causes the daemon to be launched. The daemon works in `inetd` compatibility mode, meaning that a new instance of the daemon will be created for each connection, and the daemon communicates with its client via stdin and stdout.

Example 20-3 is a Perl script that reads input from the stdin stream, and writes a reversed version of it to the stdout stream. There is one gotcha when writing `inetd-compatible` daemons: the standard out stream needs to be flushed before the client will see any data. Call `fflush()` when using stdio in C, or use the perl idiom $| = 1.

Example 20-3. minimal-service.pl

```perl
#!/usr/bin/perl

# schedule with
# launchctl load ./minimal-service.plist
# launchctl unload ./minimal-service.plist

# force auto-flush on standard out
$| = 1;

while (<>) {
    chomp;
    print scalar reverse $_;
    print "\n";
}
```

The `minimal-service.plist` looks like Example 20-4. It specifies port 2342 on all network interfaces as the place for `launchd` to listen on. When a connection happens, `launchd` will automatically start the perl script.

Example 20-4. minimal-service.plist

```
Root:
    inetdCompatibiity:
         Wait:              No
    Label:                  com.bignerdranch.minimalservice
    OnDemand:               Yes
    ProgramArguments:
         0:                 /Users/markd/minimal-service.pl
    Sockets:
        Listeners:
            SockServiceName:   2342
```

Here is a sample run:

```
$ launchctl load ./minimal-service.plist
$ telnet localhost 2342
Trying ::1...
Connected to localhost.
Escape character is '^]'.
hello
olleh
i seem to be a verb
brev a eb ot mees i
very well, have a nice day.
.yad ecin a evah ,llew yrev
^]
telnet> quit
Connection closed.
$ launchctl unload ./minimal-service.plist
```

Talking to launchd

The information in your `launchd` configuration plist is available to your daemon. Sometimes the plist contains information that is useful for your daemon's operation, such as the timeout interval. `launchd` can also tell you when new connections have appeared on your daemon's sockets and will feed the daemon new file descriptors for it to communicate over. To do this you need to take advantage of `launchd`'s "advanced communication" facility. You enable this by specifying the `ServiceIPC` boolean in your daemon's plist and setting it to YES.

Accessing Configuration Information

As of Mac OS X 10.4.2, the `launchd` access API is officially undocumented, so you need to go spelunking in the `/usr/include/launch.h` header file to find the available functions. This section will give you a flavor of the API and the most common usage, which should be enough information to let you figure out the rest of the API.

The fundamental data type for `launchd` communication is `launch_data_t`. It is an opaque pointer type that can point to many different kinds of data values. You use the API to create and access those values. `launchd` provides fundamental data structures like arrays and dictionaries, which are also accessed with `launch_data_t` pointers.

So why yet another aggregate data API? The designers of `launchd` were aiming for a very portable code base. Existing APIs, like Core Foundation, pull in a lot of extra baggage which reduces the portability of the code. `launchd` also runs as process ID 1 (which is `init` on most other Unix systems), and is one of the fundamental running processes in the OS. Having a simpler code base to deal with in that situation is an advantage.

Before you can access your property list information, you have to "check in" with `launchd`. You do that by creating a new string with `launch_data_new_string()` that holds the check-in message, and then using the `launch_msg()` function to send the message and get a response. `launch_data_free()` is used to release values you have created that you are no longer using.

```
launch_data_t launch_data_new_string (const char *string);
```

Creates a new string data object that represents the value of `string`. You are responsible for calling `launch_data_free()` to clean up after it.

```
launch_data_t launch_msg (launch_data_t message);
```

Sends `message` to `launchd`. You can pass NULL as the message to receive any pending messages to the daemon. You can also use a `kqueue` to receive messages from `launchd` (this will be shown later). If no message is received, NULL is returned and `errno` set to zero. If there were problems, NULL is returned and `errno` set. The response to a `LAUNCH_KEY_CHECKIN` message is a dictionary containing the configuration data specified in the daemon's plist. This dictionary also contains the file descriptors for any open sockets that `launchd` has opened. Be sure to `launch_data_free()` the configuration dictionary when you are done.

```
void launch_data_free (launch_data_t data);
```

Releases any resources consumed by the data parameter. You only need to release objects you have created via the **launch_data_new*** functions and any responses from **launch_msg()**.

Here is how you check in with launchd:

```
launch_data_t message, configDict;
message = launch_data_new_string (LAUNCH_KEY_CHECKIN);

configDict = launch_msg (message);

launch_data_free (message);
// .. process the message
launch_data_free (configDict);
```

The configDict response will either be an errno reporting an error, or a dictionary consisting of the property list data. Use **launch_data_get_type()** to get the type of data a particular object holds.

```
launch_data_type_t launch_data_get_type (launch_data_t data);
```

Returns the type of the data pointed to by data, as specified by this enumeration:

```
typedef enum {
    LAUNCH_DATA_DICTIONARY = 1,
    LAUNCH_DATA_ARRAY,
    LAUNCH_DATA_FD,
    LAUNCH_DATA_INTEGER,
    LAUNCH_DATA_REAL,
    LAUNCH_DATA_BOOL,
    LAUNCH_DATA_STRING,
    LAUNCH_DATA_OPAQUE,
    LAUNCH_DATA_ERRNO
} launch_data_type_t;
```

You would check the response for an error from launchd like this:

```
if (launch_data_get_type(configDict) == LAUNCH_DATA_ERRNO) {
    // get the error value using launch_data_get_errno()
}
```

If you get a "permission denied" error, it most likely means you forgot to set ServiceIPC to YES in your plist. If your response is not an errno, it should be a dictionary and you can start pulling information out of it using **launch_data_dict_lookup()**.

```
launch_data_t launch_data_dict_lookup
                (launch_data_t dictionary, const char *key);
```

Looks up key in the dictionary, returning a data pointer if the key is found or NULL if the key is not in the dictionary. A number of constants corresponding to the property list keys are provided. Consult launch.h for the full list.

If you were looking for the timeout configuration, you would access it by looking up LAUNCH_KEY_TIMEOUT in the configuration dictionary:

```
    struct timespec timeout = { 60, 0 }; // 60 second default
```

```
    int timeoutValue = launch_data_dict_lookup (configDict,
                                                LAUNCH_JOBKEY_TIMEOUT);
    if (timeoutValue != NULL) {
        timeout.tv_sec = launch_data_get_integer (timeoutValue);
    }
```

The above code uses another function, **launch_data_get_integer()** which extracts an integer value out of a piece of launch data. There are similar functions to get a file descriptor (**launch_data_get_fd()**), real, bool, string, and opaque data values.

The launchd API also has array operators. The Sockets configuration information in the plist, for example, is augmented with an array of file descriptors representing IPv4 and IPv6 sockets. You can access these file descriptors in their array by using **launch_data_array_get_count()** and **launch_data_array_get_index()**:

size_t **launch_data_array_get_count** (launch_data_t array);

Returns the number of elements in the array referenced by data.

launch_data_t **launch_data_array_get_index** (launch_data_t array,
                                               size_t index);

Returns the data living in array at the given index.

You typically use these in a loop to walk through an array:

```
launch_data_t sockets, listeners;

sockets = launch_data_dict_lookup (configDict, LAUNCH_JOBKEY_SOCKETS);
listeners = launch_data_dict_lookup (sockets, "SampleListeners");

size_t i;
for (i = 0; i < launch_data_array_get_count (listeners); i++) {
    launch_data_t tempi = launch_data_array_get_index (listeners, i);
    int fd = launch_data_get_fd (tempi);
    // do something with the file descriptor
}
```

A "Proper" Daemon

Example 20-5 shows a "proper" daemon, that is, one that checks in with launchd, queries its configuration information, and receives new network connections from launchd. It is a network daemon that is launched on demand to respond to requests on port 2342. The daemon checks in with launchd and gets its configuration dictionary, which contains file descriptors to use with **select()** or a kqueue to react to new connections.

When a new connection happens on the daemon's sockets, launchd takes the connecting socket and sends the file descriptor to the daemon (via the file descriptors provided in the configuration dictionary). The daemon can then do an **accept()** and start talking. To handle the communication with launchd, sampled uses a kqueue to receive notifications for the new connections. The original version of this code is courtesy of Apple.

Example 20-5. sampled.m

```
#include <sys/time.h>      // for struct timespec
#include <sys/socket.h>    // for sockaddr_storage, etc
#include <syslog.h>        // for openlog() and syslog()
#include <stdlib.h>        // for getprogname(), EXIT_SUCCESS, etc
#include <sys/event.h>     // for kqueue(), kevent()
#include <errno.h>         // for errno
#include <stdio.h>         // for fprintf(), fdopen(), etc
#include <unistd.h>        // for close()
#include <launch.h>        // for launch_data*

/* compile with
gcc -g -Wall -o sampled sampled.m
*/

/* schedule with
launchctl load ./sampled.plist
launchctl unload ./sampled.plist
*/

int main(void)
{
    // program success/failure result
    int result = EXIT_FAILURE;

    // send interesting messages out through syslog.  Also send
    // messages to standard error, log the process ID, write to
    // the console if syslog isn't available, and we'll be using
    // the daemon facility for logging.
    openlog (getprogname(),
            LOG_PERROR | LOG_PID | LOG_CONS, LOG_DAEMON);

    // values gotten from launchd data query functions
    launch_data_t message = NULL, configDict = NULL;

    // make the checkin message
    message = launch_data_new_string (LAUNCH_KEY_CHECKIN);

    // and check in with launchd
    if ((configDict = launch_msg(message)) == NULL) {
        syslog (LOG_ERR,
                "launch_msg(\"" LAUNCH_KEY_CHECKIN "\") failure: %m");
        goto done;
    }

    // see if launchd returned an errno.  If you get "permission
    // denied" make sure you have ServiceIPC=true in your plist
    if (launch_data_get_type(configDict) == LAUNCH_DATA_ERRNO) {
        errno = launch_data_get_errno (configDict);
        syslog (LOG_ERR, "Check-in failed: %m");
        goto done;
    }

    // see if any specific timeout has been requested in plist.
    // default to a minute if not
    struct timespec timeout = { 60, 0 };
```

```
launch_data_t timeoutValue;
timeoutValue = launch_data_dict_lookup (configDict,
                                        LAUNCH_JOBKEY_TIMEOUT);
if (timeoutValue != NULL) {
    timeout.tv_sec = launch_data_get_integer (timeoutValue);
}


// get the socket(s) configured
launch_data_t sockets;
sockets = launch_data_dict_lookup (configDict,
                                   LAUNCH_JOBKEY_SOCKETS);
if (sockets == NULL) {
    syslog (LOG_ERR, "No sockets found to answer requests on!");
    goto done;
}


// currently only support one configured socket, but you're
// welcome to support more if you wish
if (launch_data_dict_get_count (sockets) > 1) {
    syslog (LOG_WARNING, "Some sockets will be ignored!");
}


// dig into the Sockets dictionary to get the SampleListeners
// dictionary
launch_data_t listeners;
listeners = launch_data_dict_lookup (sockets, "SampleListeners");
if (listeners == NULL) {
    syslog (LOG_ERR, "No known sockets found to answer requests!");
    goto done;
}


// make a queue we'll use to get new connection fd's from launchd
int kq;
if ((kq = kqueue()) == -1) {
    syslog (LOG_ERR, "kqueue(): %m");
    goto done;
}


// register a read event with the kqueue
struct kevent kev;
size_t i;
for (i = 0; i < launch_data_array_get_count (listeners); i++) {
    launch_data_t tempi;
    tempi = launch_data_array_get_index (listeners, i);

    EV_SET (&kev,               // struct to fill in
            launch_data_get_fd(tempi),  // identifier
            EVFILT_READ,   // filter
            EV_ADD,        // action flags
            0,             // filter flags
            0,             // filter data
            NULL);         // context

    if (kevent(kq, &kev, 1, NULL, 0, NULL) == -1) {
        syslog (LOG_DEBUG, "kevent(): %m");
        goto done;
    }
```

```
        }

        while (1) {
            int status;

            // wait until we get a new event, or the timeout
            status = kevent (kq, NULL, 0, &kev, 1, &timeout);

            if (status == -1) {
                syslog (LOG_ERR, "kevent(): %m");
                goto done;

            } else if (status == 0) {
                // timed out, time to go home
                result = EXIT_SUCCESS;
                goto done;
            }

            // fetch info on the new socket waiting for us from launchd
            struct sockaddr_storage ss;
            socklen_t slen = sizeof(ss);

            int fd;
            fd = accept (kev.ident, (struct sockaddr *)&ss, &slen);
            if (fd == -1) {
                syslog (LOG_ERR, "accept(): %m");
                continue; /* this isn't fatal */
            }

            // read the request and write the response
            FILE *stream;
            stream = fdopen (fd, "r+");

            if (stream != NULL) {
                char buffer[1024];
                buffer[0] = '\0';

                char *gotten;
                gotten = fgets (buffer, 1024, stream);

                fprintf (stream, "hello world!\n");
                fprintf (stream, "you said '%s'\n", buffer);
                fclose (stream);

            } else {
                syslog (LOG_ERR, "could not fdopen(): %m");
                close (fd);
            }
        }

done:
    // finally clean up after ourselves.
    if (message != NULL) launch_data_free (message);
    if (configDict != NULL) launch_data_free (configDict);

    closelog ();
```

```
      return (result);
```

```
} // main
```

And Example 20-6 contains the property list value used to control `sampled`:

Example 20-6. sampled.plist

```
Root:
    Label: com.bignerdranch.sampled
    OnDemand: Yes
    ProgramArguments:
        0: /Users/markd/sampled
    ServiceIPC: Yes
    Sockets:
        SampleListeners:
            SockServiceName: 2342
    StandardErrorPath: /Users/markd/stderror.txt
    StandardOutPath: /Users/markd/stdout.txt
```

Chapter 21. Directory Services

A network needs a database to hold information about host configuration (like IP addresses and shared directories) and user information (like the user's encrypted password). Other types of information (like contact information) might also be put into this database. We would call this database a *directory server*. This is a confusing name because it has nothing to do with filesystem directories, but rather relates to a directory that you would find in the lobby of a tall building.

In a perfect world, this database would:

- be an open standard
- be distributed and hierarchical (like DNS)
- use encryption to keep the data from prying eyes
- use public keys to ensure the users requesting the data and the returned data are both authentic
- have good performance and reliability

This is, however, the real world. As we have been slouching towards a real solution, different vendors have supplied us with half-baked ones. First, Unix systems used utilities like `rsync` to make copies of text files on every machine on the network. Then, Sun developed the Network Information Service (NIS) which was a very simple, reliable database. Then, NeXT developed NetInfo which was better than NIS in that it was hierarchical and distributed. Sun responded with NIS+, which was similar to NetInfo, but encrypted data before sending it across the network. With NT, Microsoft introduced its Primary Domain Controller. Novell built a company on its directory server. And the OSI gave us the Lightweight Directory Access Protocol (LDAP).

While most of OSI's ideas have been abandoned, LDAP is rapidly gaining popularity. It is also rapidly being revised to include the items on our dream list. It is likely that some mutation of LDAP is the future of directory servers. For example, Microsoft's "Active Directory" is an implementation of LDAP.

The constant struggle for dominance in the directory server world makes a problem obvious: As a programmer, how do you create an application that reads from or writes to a directory server without having to make a new release of your application every time a new breed of directory server is introduced. The answer is Mac OS X's DirectoryServices framework -- one API that enables your app to access any sort of directory server.

This is a nice idea, but several things have gone wrong along the way. First problem: Mac OS X already had a way of dealing with files versus NIS versus NetInfo. In Mac OS X, every machine runs a local NetInfo server by default. There is also a daemon called `lookupd` that figures out where to get data from. There is also an API for dealing with `lookupd`.

For some reason, it was decided that these existing servers and the corresponding API could not be extended to deal with the future of directory servers. So, a new `lookupd`-like daemon was created: the `DirectoryService` daemon. And a new API was created: `DirectoryService.framework`. The source for both were released as part of the Darwin project. For backwards compatibility, by default your machine now runs a local NetInfo server, `lookupd`, and the `DirectoryService` daemon.

Second problem: It seems that Apple let the summer intern write the API. `DirectoryService.framework` is the most awkward-to-use framework in the entire system.

Directory Server Concepts

A directory server has nodes. Each node is identified by a path, and each node has some records. Each record has some attributes. An attribute is a key-value pair. For example, by default, the information about the users on your system are kept in a NetInfo directory server. The path to the node that holds this information is `/NetInfo/root`. This node has lots of records of different types: groups, aliases, mount points, and users. There is a user record for each user. Each record has serveral attributes like `realname`, `home`, and `shell`. The easiest way to browse this information is to use `NetInfo Manager`.

If you wanted your system to use an LDAP server instead of NetInfo, you could configure the system using `Directory Access`. You can list several different nodes (which can be different types of servers) to check for information.

To make this configuration invisible to the developer, the DirectoryServices server provides your application with several pseudo-nodes. `/Search`, for example, is the psuedo-node that you can query for authentication information: users, groups, and aliases.

Of course, editing user data is a privileged activity. Before you could edit the node, you would have to authenticate yourself with the node. After authenticating, you could edit the records in that node.

This introduces the idea of a Directory Service session. How long is your authentication good for? As long as the session lasts.

Open Directory Data Structures

All data structures in the DirectoryService framework have the following traits: The names of types are prefixed with 't'. The names of fields in a structure are prefixed with 'f'. Function names are prefixed with 'ds'. Any list-like data structure begins at index 1, not zero like nearly everything else in the C world.

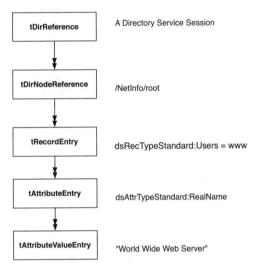

tDirReference

A tDirReference structure keeps track of the information for your session. It is the first argument for many functions in the Open Directory APIs. You create one using the function **dsOpenDirService()** like this:

```
tDirReference dirRef;
dsOpenDirService(&dirRef);
```

And closing the session looks like this:

```
dsCloseDirService(dirRef);
```

During the session you can access many different nodes on different directory servers.

tDataBuffer

A `tDataBuffer` is used primarily as a string. It is actually defined like this:

```
typedef struct
{
   unsigned longfBufferSize;
   unsigned longfBufferLength;
   char       fBufferData[1];
} tDataBuffer;
```

The 1 is misleading. The buffer is often more than one character long.

You could initialize a 1k data buffer like this:

```
dataBuffer = dsDataBufferAllocate(dirRef, 1024);
```

And release it like this:

```
dsDataBufferDeAllocate(dirRef, dataBuffer);
```

(Note the odd capitalization of "DeAllocate".)

tDataList

A `tDataList` is a list of `tDataBuffers`. For example, let's say you have a string that you want broken up into components. The following would put each component into a data buffer and put all the data buffers into a data list.

```
tDataListPtr nodeName;
char *myString;
myString = "/NetInfo/root";
nodeName = dsBuildFromPath(dirRef, myString, "/");
```

To free it, you would use **dsDataDeallocate()**:

```
dsDataListDeallocate(dirRef, nodeName);
```

(Note that "Deallocate" is now capitalized correctly.)

tDirNodeReference

When you open a node, you will get a `tDirNodeReference`.

```
tDirNodeReference nodeRef;
long dirStatus;

dirStatus = dsOpenDirNode(dirRef, nodeName, &nodeRef);
if (dirStatus != eDSNoErr) {
    fprintf(stderr, "Unable to open node. Error %ld\n", dirStatus);
}
```

To close it:

```
dsCloseDirNode(nodeRef);
```

tRecordEntry and tAttributeList

When you get a record from a node, you will get a `tRecordEntry` and a list of attribute data in the form of a `tAttributeList`.

However, getting a record is a little tricky. You do a search based on the type of record, the name of the record, and which attributes you want. To do this search, you need to create a datalist of the names, types, and attributes.

```
tDataList recordNames;
tDataList recordTypes;
tDataList attributeTypes;
unsigned long recordCount;
tDataBufferPtr dataBuffer;
tContextData context = NULL;

// Specify fetch: get me all the attributes for all users named "www"
// These can put many strings in the list, so terminate with NULL
dsBuildListFromStringsAlloc (dirRef, &recordNames, "www", NULL);
dsBuildListFromStringsAlloc (dirRef, &recordTypes,
                             kDSStdRecordTypeUsers, NULL);
dsBuildListFromStringsAlloc (dirRef, &attributeTypes,
                             kDSAttributesAll, NULL);

// Create a buffer to hold the results of the fetch
dataBuffer = dsDataBufferAllocate(dirRef, 1024 * 32);

// Getting all the records may require multiple calls
// to dsGetRecordList()
do {

    // Do the fetch
    // dataBuffer gets the result
    // recordCount gets the number of records fetched
    // context is non-null if and only if there are more
    // records to fetch
    dirStatus = dsGetRecordList(nodeRef, dataBuffer, &recordNames,
                                eDSExact, &recordTypes,
                                &attributeTypes, 0,
                                &recordCount, &context);

    if (dirStatus != eDSNoErr) {
        fprintf(stderr, "Unable to read records: Error %ld", dirStatus);
        exit(EXIT_FAILURE);
    }
    // Read the records
    for (i = 1; i <= recCount; i++) {
        tRecordEntry *recEntry;
        tAttributeListRef attrList;

        // Get record and list of attributes
        dirStatus = dsGetRecordEntry(nodeRef, dataBuffer, i,
                                     &attrList, &recEntry);

        // Print record information
        printf("\tRecord %lu has %lu attributes\n", i,
                              recEntry->fRecordAttributeCount);
```

```
        // Process the attributes here (See next section)

        // Clean up
        dsCloseAttributeList(attrList);
        dsDeallocRecordEntry(dirRef, recEntry);
    }
} while (context != NULL)

dsDataListDeallocate(dirRef, &recNames);
dsDataListDeallocate(dirRef, &recTypes);
dsDataListDeallocate(dirRef, &attrTypes);
dsDataListDeallocate(dirRef, nodeName);
```

tAttributeValueList, tAttributeEntry, and tAttributeValueEntry

As mentioned above, each record can have several attributes. Each attribute has one name, but may contain many values. Once you have a tRecordEntry and tAttributeList, you will want to read the name of each attribute and its values. The attribute data (like its name) will be put into a tAttributeEntry, and the values will be put into a tAttributeValueList. When reading individual values, they will be put into a tAttributeValueEntry.

```
for (j = 1; j <= recEntry->fRecordAttributeCount; j++) {

    tAttributeEntry *attrEntry;
    tAttributeValueEntry *valueEntry;
    tAttributeValueListRef valueList;

    // Get the information for one attribute out of the data buffer
    dsGetAttributeEntry(nodeRef, dataBuffer, attrList, j,
                                  &valueList, &attrEntry);

    // Print the name of the attribute
    printf("\t\t%s = ", attrEntry->fAttributeSignature.fBufferData);

    // Step through each value
    for (k = 1; k <= attrEntry->fAttributeValueCount; k++) {

        // Read the value
        dsGetAttributeValue(nodeRef, dataBuffer, k, valueList,
                                &valueEntry);

        // Print the value
        printf("%s, ", pValueEntry->fAttributeValueData.fBufferData);

        // Deallocate the value
        dsDeallocAttributeValueEntry(dirRef, pValueEntry);
    }
    // Put in a newline character before printing the next value
    fprintf(stderr,"\n");

    // Clean-up list
    dsCloseAttributeValueList(valueList);
    dsDeallocAttributeEntry(dirRef, attrEntry);
}
```

There is a command-line tool called `dscl` for reading and editing your directory servers. You can get this same data on the command-line like this:

```
$ dscl /NetInfo/root -read /Users/www
```

UserPictureBrowser

As a simple example of using the concepts that we have covered so far, you will create an application that will list the user name and real name of every user on your system. When you select a user name, you will see the image that appears on the login panel for that user.

Create a new Cocoa Application called UserPictureBrowser. Right-click on the **Frameworks** group to add the existing framework `DirectoryService.framework`.

Open the `MainMenu.nib` file. Add a table view with two columns and an image view as shown:

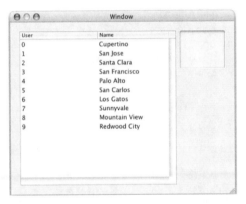

Set the identifier on the columns to be `userName` and `realName`. Create a subclass of **NSObject** called **AppController**. **AppController** needs two outlets: `imageView` of type **NSImageView**, and `tableView` of type **NSTableView**. Create the files for **AppController** and create an instance of **AppController** in the nib file.

Make the **AppController** the `dataSource` and the `delegate` for the table view. Set the **AppController**'s outlets to point to the table view and the image view. Save the nib file.

In `Xcode`, create a class called **User**. After fetching the data for a user from the directory server, you will store it in a **User** object. **User** will have instance variables for the `userName`, `realName`, and `picturePath`. All will be strings. After fetching an image, the **User** will keep a reference to that image. The instance variable will be `_imageCache` and it will be of type **NSImage**. `User.h`, then, will look like this:

```
#import <Cocoa/Cocoa.h>

@interface User : NSObject {
    NSString *userName;
    NSString *realName;
    NSString *picturePath;
    NSImage *_imageCache;
}
```

```
-  (id)initWithUserName:(NSString *)un
                realName:(NSString *)rn
             picturePath:(NSString *)pp;
-  (NSString *)userName;
-  (NSString *)realName;
-  (NSImage *)picture;
-  (NSString *)picturePath;

@end
```

Implement these methods in `User.m`:

```
#import "User.h"

@implementation User

-  (id)initWithUserName:(NSString *)un
                realName:(NSString *)rn
             picturePath:(NSString *)pp
{
    [super init];
    userName = [un copy];
    realName = [rn copy];
    picturePath = [pp copy];
    _imageCache = nil;
    return self;
}

-  (NSString *)userName
{
    return userName;
}

-  (NSString *)realName
{
    return realName;
}

-  (NSImage *)picture
{
   if (!_imageCache) {
       _imageCache = [[NSImage alloc] initWithContentsOfFile:picturePath];
   }
   return _imageCache;
}

-  (NSString *)picturePath
{
    return picturePath;
}

-  (void)dealloc
{
    [userName release];
    [_imageCache release];
    [picturePath release];
    [realName release];
    [super dealloc];
```

```
}
@end
```

In **AppController**, you are going to actually use the DirectoryService framework to fetch an array of **User** objects. Here is AppController.h:

```
#import <Cocoa/Cocoa.h>

@interface AppController : NSObject
{
    IBOutlet NSImageView *imageView;
    IBOutlet NSTableView *tableView;
    NSMutableArray *users;
}

- (void)fillUsersWithData;
- (void)tableViewSelectionDidChange:(NSNotification *)note;
- (int)numberOfRowsInTableView:(NSTableView *)tableView;
- (id)tableView:(NSTableView *)tableView
        objectValueForTableColumn:(NSTableColumn *)tableColumn
                               row:(int)row;
@end
```

Here is AppController.m:

```
#import "AppController.h"
#import "User.h"
#include <stdlib.h>
#include <stdio.h>
#include <DirectoryService/DirServices.h>
#include <DirectoryService/DirServicesUtils.h>
#include <DirectoryService/DirServicesConst.h>

@implementation AppController

- (void)fillUsersWithData
{
    long dirStatus;
    tDirReference dirRef;
    tDirNodeReference nodeRef;
    tDataListPtr nodeName;
    tDataList recNames;
    tDataList recTypes;
    tDataList attrTypes;
    tRecordEntry *recordEntry;
    unsigned long recCount, i, j;
    tAttributeListRef attributeList;
    tAttributeValueListRef valueList;
    tAttributeValueEntry *valueEntry;
    tAttributeEntry *attributeEntry;
    tDataBufferPtr dataBuffer;
    unsigned long bufferCount;
    tContextData context = NULL;
    char * pPath;

    // Start a directory service session
    dsOpenDirService(&dirRef);
```

```
        // Allocate a data buffer
        dataBuffer = dsDataBufferAllocate(dirRef, 32 * 1024);

        // Find the node for looking up users, pack the list in dataBuffer
        dirStatus = dsFindDirNodes(dirRef, dataBuffer, NULL,
                eDSAuthenticationSearchNodeName, &bufferCount, &context);

        if (dirStatus != eDSNoErr) {
            NSLog(@"Finding Authentication Node Failed: %d", dirStatus);
            return;
        } else {
            NSLog(@"Found %d nodes for authentication", bufferCount);
        }

        // Get the name of the first node in dataBuffer
        nodeName = dsDataListAllocate(dirRef);
        dirStatus = dsGetDirNodeName(dirRef, dataBuffer, 1, &nodeName);
        if (dirStatus != eDSNoErr) {
            NSLog(@"Getting Node Name Failed: %d", dirStatus);
            return;
        }

        // Display node name as path
        pPath = dsGetPathFromList(dirRef, nodeName, "/");
        NSLog(@"Node = %s", pPath);
        free(pPath);

        // Open the node and store in nodeRef
        dirStatus = dsOpenDirNode(dirRef, nodeName, &nodeRef);
        if (dirStatus != eDSNoErr) {
            NSLog(@"Opening Node Failed: %d", dirStatus);
            return;
        }

        // Describe what you are looking for as three lists of strings
        dsBuildListFromStringsAlloc (dirRef, &recNames,
                                        kDSRecordsAll, NULL);
        dsBuildListFromStringsAlloc (dirRef, &recTypes,
                                        kDSStdRecordTypeUsers, NULL);
        dsBuildListFromStringsAlloc (dirRef, &attrTypes,
                        "dsAttrTypeStandard:RecordName",
                        "dsAttrTypeStandard:RealName",
                        "dsAttrTypeStandard:Picture", NULL);
        do
        {
            // Get the list of all the records
            // Call this until context is null.
            dsGetRecordList(nodeRef, dataBuffer, &recNames, eDSExact,
                        &recTypes, &attrTypes, 0, &recCount, &context);
            printf("dsGetRecordList returned %lu entries\n", recCount);
            for (i = 1; i <= recCount; i++)
            {
                // Get a record from the list
                dsGetRecordEntry(nodeRef, dataBuffer, i, &attributeList,
                            &recordEntry);

                NSString *userName = nil;
```

```objc
        NSString *realName = nil;
        NSString *picturePath = nil;
        for (j = 1; j <= recordEntry->fRecordAttributeCount; j++)
        {
            NSString *key;
            NSString *value;

            // Read the attribute
            dsGetAttributeEntry(nodeRef, dataBuffer,
                                attributeList, j,
                                &valueList, &attributeEntry);
            key = [NSString stringWithUTF8String:
                    attributeEntry->fAttributeSignature.fBufferData];

            // Read the first value for the attribute
            dsGetAttributeValue(nodeRef, dataBuffer, 1, valueList,
                                &valueEntry);
            value = [NSString stringWithUTF8String:
                        valueEntry->fAttributeValueData.fBufferData];

            // Tidy up attribute-level data
            dsDeallocAttributeValueEntry(dirRef, valueEntry);
            valueEntry = NULL;
            dsDeallocAttributeEntry(dirRef, attributeEntry);
            attributeEntry = NULL;
            dsCloseAttributeValueList(valueList);

            // Put the data in the right variable
            if ([key isEqual:@"dsAttrTypeStandard:Picture"]) {
                picturePath = value;
            }
            if ([key isEqual:@"dsAttrTypeStandard:RealName"]) {
                realName = value;
            }
            if ([key isEqual:@"dsAttrTypeStandard:RecordName"]) {
                userName = value;
            }


        }
        // Create a user object
        User *newUser = [[User alloc] initWithUserName:userName
                                            realName:realName
                                          picturePath:picturePath];
        [users addObject:newUser];

        // users will retain newUser
        [newUser release];

        // Tidy up record-level data
        dsCloseAttributeList(attributeList);
        attributeList = (tAttributeListRef)NULL;
        dsDeallocRecordEntry(dirRef, recordEntry);
        recordEntry = NULL;
    }

// Loop until all of the data has been obtained.
```

```
        } while (context != NULL);

        // Tidy up node-level data
        dsDataListDeallocate(dirRef, &recNames);
        dsDataListDeallocate(dirRef, &recTypes);
        dsDataListDeallocate(dirRef, &attrTypes);
        dsDataListDeallocate(dirRef, nodeName);
        dsCloseDirNode(nodeRef);

        // Tidy up session-level data
        dsCloseDirService(dirRef);
}

- (id)init
{
    [super init];
    users = [[NSMutableArray alloc] init];
    [self fillUsersWithData];
    return self;
}

- (void)tableViewSelectionDidChange:(NSNotification *)notification
{
    int newSelection = [tableView selectedRow];
    if (newSelection >= 0) {
        NSImage *i = [[users objectAtIndex:newSelection] picture];
        [imageView setImage:i];
    }
}

- (int)numberOfRowsInTableView:(NSTableView *)tableView
{

    return [users count];
}

- (id)tableView:(NSTableView *)tableView
      objectValueForTableColumn:(NSTableColumn *)tableColumn
                          row:(int)row
{
    User *u = [users objectAtIndex:row];
    NSString *identifier = [tableColumn identifier];
    return [u valueForKey:identifier];
}

@end
```

Build it and run it. You should be able to browse users and see their login picture.

Authenticating

The exercise begs the question: I can see the user's picture, how do I change it? Before you can change important information like this, you need to authenticate yourself to the node.

There are many types of directory servers and each can be configured to require different types of authentication. When you want to authenticate with a node, you ask it what types of authentication it supports. Looking at the list of supported authentication methods, you will choose one and pack up a buffer with the required authentication data in the appropriate format. Then you will ask the node to authenticate with the preferred method using the supplied buffer. Depending on the method, you may get a buffer of data back from the node.

For most of the methods, you pack the buffer with the following:

- A 4-byte integer representing the length of username
- The username in UTF8 encoding
- A 4-byte integer representing the length of password
- The password in UTF8 encoding

Here are the currently supported authentication methods:

`dsAuthMethodStandard:dsAuthClearText`

Sends the user name and password as clear text.

`dsAuthMethodStandard:dsAuthCrypt`

Run the password through crypt before sending.

`dsAuthMethodStandard:dsAuthSetPasswd,dsAuthMethodStandard:dsAuthChangePasswd`

Used to change the password for a user. Does not require prior authentication. The buffer is packed as follows:

- A 4-byte integer representing the length of username
- The username in UTF8 encoding
- A 4-byte integer representing the length of old password
- old password in UTF8 encoding
- A 4-byte integer representing length of new password
- The new password in UTF8 encoding

`dsAuthMethodStandard:dsAuthSetPasswdAsRoot`

Used to change the password for a user. Does not require prior authentication. The buffer is packed as follows:

- A 4-byte integer representing the length of username
- The username in UTF8 encoding
- A 4-byte integer representing the length of the root password
- old password in UTF8 encoding
- A 4-byte integer representing length of new password
- The new password in UTF8 encoding

`dsAuthMethodStandard:dsAuthNodeNativeCanUseClearText`

Whatever authentication the node does most naturally.

`dsAuthMethodStandard:dsAuthNodeNativeCannotUseClearText`

Whatever authentication excepting clear text that the node does most naturally.

`dsAuthMethodStandard:dsAuth2WayRandomChangePasswd`

Change the password for a user using the two-way random method. The buffer is packed as follows:

- A 4-byte integer representing the length of username
- A username in UTF8 encoding
- A 4-byte integer representing the length of old password encrypted with new (should be 8)
- The old password encrypted with new
- A 4-byte integer representing the length of new password encrypted with old (should be 8)
- The new password encrypted with old

`dsAuthMethodStandard:dsAuthAPOP`

`dsAuthMethodStandard:dsAuth2WayRandom`

`kDSStdAuthSMB_NT_Key`

`kDSStdAuthSMB_LM_Key`

`kDSStdAuthCRAM_MD5`

`kDSStdAuthDIGEST_MD5`

To figure out which are supported for a given node, you need to read the `dsAttrTypeStandard:AuthMethod` attribute of the node using **`dsGetDirNodeInfo()`**. (Yes, nodes and records can both have attributes.)

```
tDataList attributeTypes;
tDataBufferPtr dataBuffer;
unsigned long k;
tAttributeListRef attrListRef;
tContextData context;
tAttributeValueListRef valueList;
tAttributeValueEntry *valueEntry;
tAttributeEntry *attributeEntry;

// Create a buffer
dataBuffer = dsDataBufferAllocate(dirRef, 32 * 1024);
```

```
    // Prepare to fetch the Authorization attributes
    dsBuildListFromStringsAlloc (dirRef, &attributeTypes,
                                    kDSNAttrAuthMethod, NULL);

    // Fetch the authorization attribute
    dsGetDirNodeInfo(nodeRef, &attributeTypes, dataBuffer, 0,
                        &count, &attributeList, &context);

    // There should be just one.  Read it into a value
    // list and attribute entry
    dsGetAttributeEntry(nodeRef, dataBuffer, attrList, 1,
                                    &valueList, attributeEntry);

    // Print the name of the attribute
    printf("\t%s = ", j, attributeEntry->fAttributeSignature.fBufferData);

    // Iterate through its values
    for (k = 1; k <= attributeEntry->fAttributeValueCount; k++) {

        // Read the value into valueEntry
        dsGetAttributeValue(nodeRef, dataBuffer, k,
                                        valueList, &valueEntry);

        // Print it
        printf("%s, ", valueEntry->fAttributeValueData.fBufferData);

        // deallocate the valueEntry
        dsDeallocAttributeValueEntry(dirRef, valueEntry);
    }
    printf("\n");
    dsCloseAttributeValueList(valueList);
    dsDeallocAttributeEntry(dirRef, attributeEntry);
    dsDeallocList(dirRef, &attributeTypes);
```

Note that if you run this against the /Search node, it will return no authentication
methods. Remember that it is a pseudo-node. You can not edit the /Search. Instead,
you would fetch the dsAttrTypeStandard:AppleMetaNodeLocation when you
fetch dsAttrTypeStandard:RecordName, dsAttrTypeStandard:RecordName and
dsAttrTypeStandard:Picture. AppleMetaNodeLocation contains the name of the
node where the record *really* lives.

Here is an example of how you might do node-native authentication. It assumes
that you have already opened a directory services session and the node for which
you want to authenticate:

```
int DoNodeNativeAuthentication (const tDirNodeReference  nodeRef,
                                        const char *username,
                                        const char *password)

{
    tDataNodePtr authType;
    tDataBufferPtr dataBuffer;
    tDataBufferPtr responseBuffer;
    tDirStatus aDirErr;
    tContextData aContinueData = NULL;
    long aDataBufSize = 0;
    long aTempLength = 0;
    long aCurLength = 0;
```

```
        int result;

        // First, specify the type of authentication.
        authType = dsDataNodeAllocateString(dirRef,
                          kDSStdAuthNodeNativeClearTextOK);

        // Calculate the size and allocate a buffer
        // for the authentication data
        aDataBufSize += sizeof(long) + strlen(username);
        aDataBufSize += sizeof(long) + strlen(password);
        dataBuffer = dsDataBufferAllocate(dirRef, aDataBufSize);

        // Allocate a response buffer in case we get one from the
        // node when we try to authenticate
        responseBuffer = dsDataBufferAllocate(dirRef, 512);

        // Copy the length of the username into the buffer
        aTempLength = strlen(username);
        memcpy(dataBuffer->fBufferData, &aTempLength, sizeof(long));
        aCurLength += sizeof(long);

        // Copy the actual username into the buffer
        memcpy(&(dataBuffer->fBufferData[aCurLength]), username, aTempLength);
        aCurLength += aTempLength;

        // Copy the length of the password into the buffer
        aTempLength = strlen(password);
        memcpy(&(dataBuffer->fBufferData[aCurLength]), &aTempLength,
            sizeof(long));

        // Copy the actual password into the buffer
        aCurLength += sizeof(long);
        memcpy(&(dataBuffer->fBufferData[aCurLength]), password, aTempLength);

        // Tell the buffer how long it is
        dataBuffer->fBufferLength = aDataBufSize;

        // Do the authentication
        aDirErr = dsDoDirNodeAuth(nodeRef, authType, 0, dataBuffer,
                          responseBuffer, &aContinueData);

        // Were we successful?
        if (aDirErr == eDSNoErr) {
            result = 1;
        } else {
            printf("NodeAuth failed: %d\n", aDirErr);
            printf("response = %lu,%s\n", responseBuffer->fBufferLength,
                                responseBuffer->fBufferData);
            result = 0;
        }

        // Clean up allocations.
        aDirErr = dsDataBufferDeAllocate(dirRef, dataBuffer);
        aDirErr = dsDataBufferDeAllocate(dirRef, responseBuffer);
        aDirErr = dsDataNodeDeAllocate(dirRef, authType);

        // Return the result of the authentication
```

```
        return result;
    }
```

Editing Records

Once you have autheticated, you can insert, delete, and edit records. Deleting a record a simple. After you've opened the record, just call **dsDeleteRecord()**:

```
tRecordReference record;
tDataNodePtr recordName;
tDataNodePtr recordType;
recordName = dsDataNodeAllocateString(dirRef, "www");
recordType = dsDataNodeAllocateString(dirRef, kDSStdRecordTypeUsers);

// Open the record using its name and type
dirStatus = dsOpenRecord(nodeRef, recordType, recordName, &record);

if (dirStatus != eDSNoErr) {
    fprintf(stdout, "Unable to open record: %ld\n", dirStatus);
} else {
    dirStatus = dsDeleteRecord(recordEntry);

    if (dirStatus != eDSNoErr) {
        // Print a message to show failure
        fprintf(stdout, "Unable to delete record: %ld\n", dirStatus);

        // Close the record you were unable to delete
        dirStatus = dsCloseRecord(record);
    } else {
      printf("Deleted record\n");
    }
}
dsDataNodeDeAllocate(dirRef, recordType);
dsDataNodeDeAllocate(dirRef, recordName);
```

If you have an open node, here is how you would create a new record in that node and add an attribute to it:

```
void CreateRecord (const tDirNodeReference nodeRef)
{
    long dirStatus;
    tDataNodePtr recordName;
    tDataNodePtr recType;
    tDataNodePtr attrName;
    tDataNodePtr attrValue;
    tRecordReference record;

    // Create the name and type of the record to be created
    recordName = dsDataNodeAllocateString(dirRef, "NewUserRecordName");
    recType = dsDataNodeAllocateString(dirRef, kDSStdRecordTypeUsers);

    // Create and open the record
    dirStatus = dsCreateRecordAndOpen(nodeRef, recType,
                                recordName, &record);

    // Was it successful?
    if (dirStatus == eDSNoErr){
```

```
                    printf("Successfully created and opened record\n");

            // Prepare an attribute to add to the record
            attrName = dsDataNodeAllocateString(dirRef,
                                        kDS1AttrDistinguishedName);
            attrValue = dsDataNodeAllocateString(dirRef,
                                        "User Record's Display Name");
            // Add the attribute to the record
            dirStatus = dsAddAttribute(record, attrName, NULL, attrValue);
            if (dirStatus != eDSNoErr) {
                    printf("Error adding attribute:%ld\n", dirStatus);
            } else {
                    printf("Successfully set attribute\n");
            }
            // Cleanup
            dsDataNodeDeAllocate(dirRef, attrValue);
            dsDataNodeDeAllocate(dirRef, attrName);
            dirStatus = dsCloseRecord(record);
        } else {
            printf("Unable to create record:%ld\n", dirStatus);
        }
        dsDataNodeDeAllocate(dirRef, recType);
        dsDataNodeDeAllocate(dirRef, recordName);
    }
```

If you have an open record with an attribute that you would like to change, you can use **dsSetAttributeValue()**.

```
OSStatus setRecordAttribute(tDirReference   dirRef,
                        tDirNodeReference   nodeRef,
                      tDirRecordReference   recRef,
                                    char *attribute,
                                    char *value )
{
    OSStatus dirStatus = eDSNoErr;
    tDataNodePtr attrType = NULL;
    tAttributeValueEntry *pValueEntry = NULL;
    tAttributeValueEntry *pNewValueEntry = NULL;

    attrType = dsDataNodeAllocateString(dirRef, attribute);
    if (attrType != NULL) {
        dirStatus = dsGetRecordAttributeValueByIndex(recRef, attrType, 1, &
        if (dirStatus == eDSNoErr) {
            pNewValueEntry = dsAllocAttributeValueEntry(dirRef, pValueEntry
                                                value, strlen(value
            if (pNewValueEntry != NULL) {
                dirStatus = dsSetAttributeValue(recRef, attrType, pNewValue
            }

            dsDeallocAttributeValueEntry(dirRef, pValueEntry);
            pValueEntry = NULL;

            dsDeallocAttributeValueEntry(dirRef, pNewValueEntry);
            pNewValueEntry = NULL;
        }
        dsDataNodeDeAllocate(dirRef, attrType);
        attrType = NULL;
    }
```

```
    return dirStatus;
}
```

Challenge

1. Extend `UserPictureBrowser` to allow the deletion of users.

2. Extend `UserPictureBrowser` to allow the picture to be changed.

3. Extend `UserPictureBrowser` to allow new users to be added to the system.

Chapter 22. Multithreading

Multithreading is another method for achieving concurrency in your application. While multiprocessing uses multiple independent processes with their own address spaces and resources, threads are multiple execution streams that all execute within a single application, with a single address space, all sharing the available resources.

Multithreading, like multiprocessing, can take advantage of multiple CPUs. You can also use it to simplify some kinds of programming. Each thread can go on its merry way, computing values and calling functions that block, while other threads can run independently and are unaffected. One very common use of threads is handling requests in a network server (like a web server). A new connection is **accept()**ed and a thread is created to handle the request. This thread can then use **read()** to get the request and **write()** to send data back. It can also open files and perform loops, so there is no need to multiplex the I/O using **select()**, and there is no need to go through contortions to do computations piecemeal.

Posix Threads

Mac OS X uses the Posix thread API, more commonly known as "pthreads," for its native threading model. Unfortunately, pthreads have a different convention for reporting error conditions than the rest of the Unix API. While it returns zero on success like you would expect, it returns the error code on error, rather than returning -1 and setting errno.

Creating threads

pthread_create() is used to create a new thread:

```
int pthread_create (pthread_t *threadID, const pthread_attr_t *attr,
                    void *(*startRoutine)(void *), void *arg);
```

which returns zero on success and an error value on failure. These are the arguments it takes:

threadID

> A pointer to a pthread_t. The thread ID for the new thread will be written here.

attr

> A set of attributes. Pass NULL to use the default attributes. Specific attributes are not discussed (they tend to confuse discussions about the basics of threaded programming).

startRoutine

> A pointer to a function with a signature of

> void ***someFunction** (void *someArg);

This is where execution in the thread will start. The thread will terminate when this function returns. The someArg parameter is the value of the arg parameter passed to **pthread_create()**. The return value is some pointer to return status. You can pass whatever data structure you want for these two values.

`arg`

> The argument given to the `startRoutine`.

The system allocates a private stack (similar to the main function call stack) for a thread when it gets created, as shown in Figure 22-1. The thread uses this stack for function call housekeeping and local variable storage.

Figure 22-1. Thread Stacks

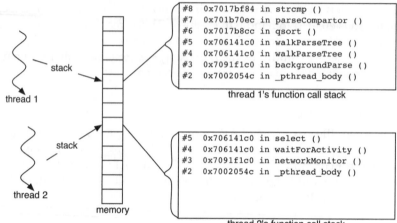

```
#8   0x7017bf84 in strcmp ()
#7   0x701b70ec in parseCompartor ()
#6   0x7017b8cc in qsort ()
#5   0x706141c0 in walkParseTree ()
#4   0x706141c0 in walkParseTree ()
#3   0x7091f1c0 in backgroundParse ()
#2   0x7002054c in _pthread_body ()
```
thread 1's function call stack

```
#5   0x706141c0 in select ()
#4   0x706141c0 in waitForActivity ()
#3   0x7091f1c0 in networkMonitor ()
#2   0x7002054c in _pthread_body ()
```
thread 2's function call stack

Threads are like processes because they have a return value that could be of interest to whomever created the thread. Using a mechanism similar to **waitpid()** for processes you can use **pthread_join()** to rendezvous with a particular thread:

```
int pthread_join (pthread_t threadID, void **valuePtr);
```

pthread_join() will block until the indicated thread exits. The return value will be written into the `valuePtr`.

To determine your own `threadID`, use **pthread_self()**;

Sometimes you want to detach a thread so that you do not have to **pthread_join()** it. The thread will run to completion, and then exit. To do that, use **pthread_detach()**:

```
int pthread_detach (pthread_t threadID);
```

Detached threads are sometimes called "daemon threads", since they run independently of their parents like daemons.

A common idiom is for a thread function to call

```
pthread_detach (pthread_self());
```

to turn itself into a daemon thread.

Example 22-1 is a little program that spins off a couple of threads that all count from zero to some value. Some are detached, and some are not and should be waited on:

Example 22-1. basics.m

```
// basics.m -- basic thread creation

/* compile with:
cc -g -Wall -o basics basics.m
*/

#import <stdio.h> // for printf
#import <pthread.h>        // for pthread_* calls
#import <string.h>         // for strerror()
#import <unistd.h>         // for usleep()
#import <stdlib.h>         // for exit

#define THREAD_COUNT 6

// information to tell the thread how to behave

typedef struct ThreadInfo {
    pthread_t   threadID;
    int         index;
    int         numberToCountTo;
    int         detachYourself;
    int         sleepTime;      // in microseconds (1/1,000,000)
} ThreadInfo;

void *threadFunction (void *argument)
{
    ThreadInfo *info = (ThreadInfo *) argument;
    int result, i;

    printf ("thread %d, counting to %d, detaching %s\n",
            info->index, info->numberToCountTo,
            (info->detachYourself) ? "yes" : "no");

    if (info->detachYourself) {
        result = pthread_detach (pthread_self());
        if (result != 0) {
            fprintf (stderr, "could not detach thread %d. %d/%s\n",
                     info->index, result, strerror(result));
        }
    }

    // now to do the actual "work" of the thread

    for (i = 0; i < info->numberToCountTo; i++) {
        printf ("  thread %d counting %d\n", info->index, i);
        usleep (info->sleepTime);
    }

    printf ("thread %d done\n", info->index);

    return (NULL);

} // threadFunction

int main (int argc, char *argv[])
```

```
    {
        ThreadInfo threads[THREAD_COUNT];
        int result, i;

        // initialize the ThreadInfos:
        for (i = 0; i < THREAD_COUNT; i++) {
            threads[i].index = i;
            threads[i].numberToCountTo = (i + 1) * 2;
            threads[i].detachYourself = (i % 2); // detach odd threads
            threads[i].sleepTime = 500000 + 200000 * i;
            // (make subseuqent threads wait longer between counts)
        }

        // create the threads
        for (i = 0; i < THREAD_COUNT; i++) {
            result = pthread_create (&threads[i].threadID, NULL,
                                     threadFunction, &threads[i]);
            if (result != 0) {
                fprintf (stderr,
                        "could not pthread_create thread %d. %d/%s\n",
                        i, result, strerror(result));
                exit (EXIT_FAILURE);
            }
        }

        // now rendezvous with all the non-detached threads
        for (i = 0; i < THREAD_COUNT; i++) {
            void *retVal;
            if (!threads[i].detachYourself) {
                result = pthread_join (threads[i].threadID, &retVal);
                if (result != 0) {
                    fprintf (stderr, "error joining thread %d. %d/%s\n",
                            i, result, strerror(result));
                }
                printf ("joined with thread %d\n", i);
            }
        }

        exit (EXIT_SUCCESS);

    } // main
```

The sample run is much more interesting in real life. Here is a part of it:

```
$ ./basics
thread 0, counting to 2, detaching no
  thread 0 counting 0
thread 1, counting to 4, detaching yes
  thread 1 counting 0
thread 2, counting to 6, detaching no
  thread 2 counting 0
...
  thread 2 counting 1
thread 0 done
joined with thread 0
  thread 3 counting 1
  thread 4 counting 1
```

```
    . . .
    thread 4 counting 9
    thread 5 counting 8
thread 4 done
joined with thread 4
```

There are a couple of things to note. The first is there is no predefined order that the threads will run. They are at the mercy of the OS scheduler. The other is that the main thread (where **main()** runs) is special. Once the main thread exits, the program terminates immediately even if there are other threads still running. This is why thread five sometimes does not finish its work by the time the program exits.

Synchronization

Remember the discussion about race conditions and concurrency when talking about signals? Threads have the same kinds of problems. There is something mentioned above that bears repeating: There is no predefined order that the threads will run. They are at the mercy of the OS scheduler.

This can cause a lot of problems and introduces a lot of complexity to make sure that this (possibly) random order of execution will not corrupt data.

For example, in basics.m above, you made an array of the ThreadInfo structure and gave each thread a pointer to its own array element. Compare to this:

```
ThreadInfo info;

for (i = 0; i < THREAD_COUNT; i++) {
    info->index = i;
    info->numberToCountTo = (i + 1) * 2;
    . . .
    result = pthread_create (&threads[i].threadID, NULL,
                            threadFunction, &info);
}
```

Then threadFunction would copy the data it wanted.

There are three cases to consider:

1. *threadFunction starts executing immediately.* The thread copies the data out of its argument pointer and goes on its merry way. Things work OK in this mode.

2. *threadFunction starts executing a little later, like at the top of the loop.* The thread gets created when the i loop variable is 2. The loop then goes to index 3 and creates a thread, and now is about to do loop number 4. The "2 thread" finally gets scheduled and starts executing, looks at the memory for its control information, and uses the same configuration information intended for thread four.

3. *threadFunction starts executing a little later, in the middle of the loop.* This is the worst-case scenario: corrupted data. If the "2 thread" wakes up while index and numberToCountTo have been updated for i = 4, but detachYourself and sleepTime still have i = 3's values, it will get half the data of the "3 thread" and half from the "4 thread" info.

Along the same lines, unprotected manipulations to data structures in a threaded environment can lead to corruption. Imagine a linked list that is in the middle of the pointer manipulations for adding a new node. This thread gets preempted by another thread that tries to add something of its own to that list. Best case you will crash because a pointer being modified is pointing to a bad address. Worst case is that one or the other insertions gets lost and you have slightly corrupted data, an error that will only manifest itself later, far away from the race condition that caused it.

Getting synchronization right is hard to do, and can be very hard to debug. There is a fine line between safe data access and efficient data access, and this is the primary reason threaded programming is much harder than people think it is.

To help address these problems, the pthread API provides some synchronization mechanisms, specifically mutexes (mutual exclusion locks) and condition variables.

Mutexes

Mutexes are used to serialize access to critical sections of code, meaning that when mutexes are used properly, only one thread of execution can be executing that section of code, as shown in Figure 22-2. All other threads wanting to run there will be blocked until the original thread finishes. After that an arbitrary thread will be picked to run that piece of code.

Figure 22-2. A Mutex

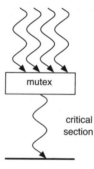

The use of a mutex over a section of code eliminates any concurrency that code may have (which is the general motivation for using threads), so you want the duration of a mutex lock to be as short as possible. Be aware that although mutexes control access to *code*, you are just using that to control access to *data*.

The datatype for a mutex is `pthread_mutex_t`. You can declare them as local variables, global variables, or **malloc()** memory for them. There are two ways to initialize a mutex. The first way is to use a static initializer, which is handy for a singleton mutex that you want to stick outside of a function:

```
static pthread_mutex_t myMutex = PTHREAD_MUTEX_INITIALIZER;
```

The other is to get a chunk of memory the size of `pthread_mutex_t` and use **pthread_mutex_init()** on that memory:

```
int pthread_mutex_init (pthread_mutex_t *mutex,
                            const pthread_mutexattr_t *attr);
```

Like with **pthread_create()**, specific attributes aren't discussed.

You would use **pthread_mutex_init ()** when you have a mutex per data structure (like you create a new tree, and create a mutex just for that tree).

When you are done with a mutex you initialized with **pthread_mutex_init ()**, use **pthread_mutex_destroy ()** to release its resources:

```
int pthread_mutex_destroy (pthread_mutex_t *mutex);
```

To acquire a mutex use **pthread_mutex_lock**:

```
int pthread_mutex_lock (pthread_mutex_t *mutex);
```

If the mutex is unavailable, this call will block until it becomes free. When execution resumes after this call (with a zero return value), you know you have sole possession of the mutex.

To release a mutex, use **pthread_mutex_unlock ()**:

```
int pthread_mutex_unlock (pthread_mutex_t *mutex);
```

If you do not want to block when acquiring a mutex, use **pthread_mutex_trylock ()**:

```
int pthread_mutex_trylock (pthread_mutex_t *mutex);
```

If this returns with zero, you have locked the mutex. If it returns EBUSY, the mutex is locked by another party and you need to try again.

Example 22-2 shows mutexes in action.

Example 22-2. mutex.m

```
// copy basic.m to mutex.m first, then change threadFunction to this:

pthread_mutex_t g_mutex = PTHREAD_MUTEX_INITIALIZER;

void *threadFunction (void *argument)
{
    ThreadInfo *info = (ThreadInfo *) argument;
    int result, i;

    printf ("thread %d, counting to %d, detaching %s\n",
            info->index, info->numberToCountTo,
            (info->detachYourself) ? "yes" : "no");

    if (info->detachYourself) {
        result = pthread_detach (pthread_self());
        if (result != 0) {
            fprintf (stderr,
                    "couldn't detach thread %d. Error: %d/%s\n",
                    info->index, result, strerror(result));
        }
    }

    // now to do the actual "work" of the thread

    pthread_mutex_lock (&g_mutex);
```

```
    for (i = 0; i < info->numberToCountTo; i++) {
        printf ("  thread %d counting %d\n", info->index, i);
        usleep (info->sleepTime);
    }

    pthread_mutex_unlock (&g_mutex);

    printf ("thread %d done\n", info->index);

    return (NULL);

} // threadFunction
```

And now see that execution has been serialized:

```
$ ./mutex
  thread 0 counting 1
thread 0 done
  thread 1 counting 0
joined with thread 0
  thread 1 counting 1
  thread 1 counting 2
  thread 1 counting 3
thread 1 done
. . .
```

Also notice how much slower the entire program runs now that the critical section (the counting loop) is serialized.

Deadlocks

If you are dealing with multiple mutexes for a single operation (such as locking two data structures before manipulating them together) and you are not careful about acquiring the mutexes in the same order every time you use them, you could be open for a deadlock situation.

Suppose thread one has

```
    pthread_mutex_lock (mutexA);
    pthread_mutex_lock (mutexB);
```

and thread two has

```
    pthread_mutex_lock (mutexB);
    pthread_mutex_lock (mutexA);
```

Figure 22-3 shows an execution path like this:

- Thread one locks A. It gets pre-empted.
- Thread two locks B. It gets pre-empted.
- Thread one attempts to lock B. It blocks.
- Thread two attempts to lock A. It blocks.

Figure 22-3. Deadlock

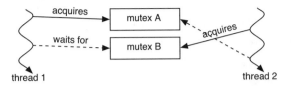

Both threads are now deadlocked, each waiting on the other to release its resource, and there is no way to break it. Each thread instead should do something like:

```
while (1) {
    pthread_mutex_lock (mutexA);
    if (pthread_mutex_trylock(mutexB) == EBUSY) {
        pthread_mutex_unlock (mutexA);
    }
}
```

That is, lock the first mutex and try locking the second. If it is locked, someone else has it, so release the first lock and try all over again, just in case someone has `mutexB` held and is waiting for `mutexA`.

Condition Variables

Mutexes are great for what they do, protecting critical regions of code. Sometimes, though, you have situations where you want to wait until some condition is true before locking your mutex (like a queue has an item in it before you process a request). If you use mutexes for this, you will end up writing loops to test the condition and then release the mutex. In other words, this is a polling operation, which is wasteful of CPU time.

Condition variables (`pthread_cond_t`) address this problem. Condition variables let interested parties block on the variable. The blocking will stop via a signal from another thread. (*Signal* is an unfortunate choice of words, since this signaling has no relation to the Unix signals that were discussed earlier.)

Like the mutex, you can initialize them statically with `PTHREAD_COND_INITIALIZER`, or use

```
int pthread_cond_init (pthread_cond_t *cond,
                       const pthread_condattr_t *attr);
```

Similarly, if you initialize a condition variable, destroy it it with

```
int pthread_cond_destroy (pthread_cond_t *cond);
```

A mutex and a condition variable are associated. To use a condition variable, you lock the associated mutex, then while the condition you are interested in is false, call **pthread_cond_wait()**:

```
int pthread_cond_wait (pthread_cond_t *cond, pthread_mutex_t *mutex);
```

The mutex is automatically unlocked and the call blocks. When another thread calls **pthread_cond_signal()**:

```
int pthread_cond_signal(pthread_cond_t *cond);
```

a single thread that is currently blocked on **pthread_cond_wait()** will wake up (use **pthread_cond_broadcast()** to wake up all blocked threads). Be aware that **pthread_cond_wait()** can spuriously return. You should always check the value of your condition before moving on.

OK, so what is this "value of your condition"? Consider Figure 22-4, the request queue for a web server:

Figure 22-4. Server Request Queue

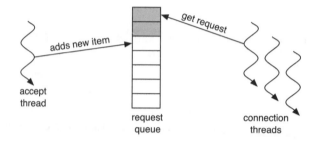

A single thread blocks on the **accept()** call waiting for new connections. When a new connection comes in, it gets put at the end of the request queue. At the same time, connection threads are hanging around, pulling the topmost entry off of the queue and processing them. (This is a version of the classic "producer/consumer" problem that just about every concurrent programming book talks about.)

For both the "accept" and "connection" threads, there are two states they can be in with respect to the queue. Accept thread accepts a new connection:

The queue has free space to put a new request

```
put request on queue
signal a connection thread to wake up
```

The queue is full:

```
block on a condition variable until there is space in the queue
when it wakes up, put the request in the queue
```

and in pseudo code:

```
pthread_mutex_lock (queueLock);
while (queue is full) {
    pthread_cond_wait (g_queueCond, queueLock);
}
put item on the queue;
pthread_mutex_unlock (queueLock);
signal a connection thread
go back to accept()
```

The **pthread_cond_wait()** will only happen when the queue is full, and you hang around in that loop until there is free space in the queue. The while loop is to protect against spurious returns.

Connection thread:

The queue has a request on it:

```
get the request from the queue
if the queue had been completely full, signal the accept() thread
that there is now space available, in case it is blocked waiting
for free space in the queue
```

The queue is empty:

```
block on a condition variable until there is space in the queue
when it wakes up, get the request from the queue
```

Likewise

```
pthread_mutex_lock (queueLock);
while (queue is empty) {
    pthread_cond_wait (g_queueCond, queueLock);
}
get item from the queue;
pthread_mutex_unlock (queueLock);
signal the accept thread
process the request.
```

If you do not want to block indefinitely, you can specify a timeout for waiting on a condition variable by using **pthread_cond_timedwait()**:

```
int pthread_cond_timedwait (pthread_cond_t *cond,
                            pthread_mutex_t *mutex,
                            const struct timespec *abstime);
```

The timeout is specified by filling out this structure:

```
struct timespec {
    time_t  tv_sec;       // seconds
    long    tv_nsec;      // nanoseconds
};
```

pthread_timed_condwait() differs from similar calls (like **select()**) in that the timeout is an absolute time, not a relative time. This makes it easier to handle the case of spurious wake-ups since you do not have to recalculate the wait time each time.

Example 22-3 is the webserver program from the multiprocessing chapter modified to use threads instead of **fork()** (new or changed code is in bold). You will notice that all of the child process-handling code is gone, and that there is now a request queue that uses condition variables. The code to set up networking and to handle requests is identical to the previous version.

Example 22-3. webserve-thread.m

```
// webserve-thread.m -- a very simple web server using threads to
//                      handle requests

/* compile with:
```

```
cc -g -Wall -o webserve-thread webserve-thread.m
*/

#import <sys/types.h>       // for pid_t, amongst others
#import <sys/wait.h>        // for wait3
#import <unistd.h>          // for fork, close
#import <stdlib.h>          // for EXIT_SUCCESS, pipe, exec
#import <stdio.h>           // for printf
#import <errno.h>           // for errno
#import <string.h>          // for strerror
#import <sys/time.h>        // for struct timeval
#import <sys/resource.h>    // for struct rusage
#import <netinet/in.h>      // for sockaddr_in
#import <sys/socket.h>      // for socket(), AF_INET
#import <arpa/inet.h>       // for inet_ntoa
#import <arpa/inet.h>       // for inet_ntoa and friends
#import <assert.h>          // for assert
#import <pthread.h>         // for pthread_*

#define PORT_NUMBER 8080         // set to 80 to listen on the HTTP port

#define MAX_THREADS 5            // maximum number of connection threads

// ----- queue for handling requests

#define QUEUE_DEPTH 10

typedef struct Request {
    int                 fd; // file descriptor of the incoming request
    struct sockaddr_in  address;
} Request;

static Request g_requestQueue[QUEUE_DEPTH];
static int g_queueEnd = -1; // 0 is the head. end == -1 for empty queue
static pthread_mutex_t g_queueMutex = PTHREAD_MUTEX_INITIALIZER;
static pthread_cond_t g_queueCond = PTHREAD_COND_INITIALIZER;

void getRequest (int *fd, struct sockaddr_in *address)
{
    int doSignal = 0;

    pthread_mutex_lock (&g_queueMutex);
    while (g_queueEnd == -1) { // queue is empty
        pthread_cond_wait (&g_queueCond, &g_queueMutex);
    }

    // copy the request to the caller
    *fd = g_requestQueue[0].fd;
    memcpy (address, &g_requestQueue[0].address,
            sizeof(struct sockaddr_in));

    if (g_queueEnd == QUEUE_DEPTH - 1) {
        // going from full to not quite so full
        doSignal = 1;
    }

    // shift up the queue
```

```
    if (g_queueEnd > 0) {
        memmove (g_requestQueue, g_requestQueue + 1,
        sizeof(Request) * g_queueEnd);
    }
    g_queueEnd--;

    pthread_mutex_unlock (&g_queueMutex);

    if (doSignal) {
        pthread_cond_signal (&g_queueCond);
    }

} // getRequest

void queueRequest (int fd, struct sockaddr_in *address)
{
    pthread_mutex_lock (&g_queueMutex);

    assert (g_queueEnd <= QUEUE_DEPTH);

    while (g_queueEnd == QUEUE_DEPTH - 1) { // queue is full
        pthread_cond_wait (&g_queueCond, &g_queueMutex);
    }

    assert (g_queueEnd < QUEUE_DEPTH - 1);

    g_queueEnd++;
    g_requestQueue[g_queueEnd].fd = fd;
    memcpy (&g_requestQueue[g_queueEnd].address, address,
            sizeof(struct sockaddr_in));

    pthread_mutex_unlock (&g_queueMutex);

    pthread_cond_signal (&g_queueCond);

} // queueRequest

// HTTP request handling
// these are some of the common HTTP response codes

#define HTTP_OK        200
#define HTTP_NOT_FOUND 404
#define HTTP_ERROR     500

// return a string to the browser

#define returnString(httpResult, string, channel) \
      returnBuffer((httpResult), (string), (strlen(string)), (channel))

// return a character buffer (not necessarily zero-terminated) to
// the browser (runs in the child)

void returnBuffer (int httpResult, const char *content,
                   int contentLength, FILE *commChannel)
{
    fprintf (commChannel, "HTTP/1.0 %d blah\n", httpResult);
```

```
        fprintf (commChannel, "Content-Type: text/html\n");
        fprintf (commChannel, "Content-Length: %d\n", contentLength);
        fprintf (commChannel, "\n");
        fwrite (content, contentLength, 1, commChannel );

} // returnBuffer


// stream back to the browser the numbers being counted, with a pause
// between them.  The user should see the numbers appear every couple
// of seconds (runs in the child)

void returnNumbers (int number, FILE *commChannel)
{
    int min, max, i;
    min = MIN (number, 1);
    max = MAX (number, 1);

    fprintf (commChannel, "HTTP/1.0 %d blah\n", HTTP_OK);
    fprintf (commChannel, "Content-Type: text/html\n");
    fprintf (commChannel, "\n");

    // no content length since this is dynamic

    fprintf (commChannel, "<h2>The numbers from %d to %d</h2>\n",
            min, max);

    for (i = min; i <= max; i++) {
        sleep (2);
        fprintf (commChannel, "%d\n", i);
        fflush (commChannel);
    }

    fprintf (commChannel, "<hr>Done\n");

} // returnNumbers


// return a file from the file system, relative to where the webserver
// is running.  Note that this does not look for any nasty characters
// like '..', so this function is a pretty big security hole
// (runs in the child)

void returnFile (const char *filename, FILE *commChannel)
{
    FILE *file;
    const char *mimetype = NULL;

    // try to guess the mime type.
    // IE assumes all non-graphic files are HTML
    if (strstr(filename, ".m") != NULL) {
        mimetype = "text/plain";
    } else if (strstr(filename, ".h") != NULL) {
        mimetype = "text/plain";
    } else if (strstr(filename, ".txt") != NULL) {
        mimetype = "text/plain";
    } else if (strstr(filename, ".tgz") != NULL) {
        mimetype = "application/x-compressed";
    } else if (strstr(filename, ".html") != NULL) {
```

```
        mimetype = "text/html";
    } else if (strstr(filename, ".html") != NULL) {
        mimetype = "text/html";
    } else if (strstr(filename, ".xyz") != NULL) {
        mimetype = "audio/mpeg";
    }

    file = fopen (filename, "r");

    if (file == NULL) {
        returnString (HTTP_NOT_FOUND,
                     "could not find your file. Sorry\n.",
                     commChannel);
    } else {
#define BUFFER_SIZE (8 * 1024)
        char *buffer[BUFFER_SIZE];
        int result;
        fprintf (commChannel, "HTTP/1.0 %d blah\n", HTTP_OK);
        if (mimetype != NULL) {
            fprintf (commChannel, "Content-Type: %s\n", mimetype);
        }
        fprintf (commChannel, "\n");
        while ((result = fread (buffer, 1, BUFFER_SIZE, file)) > 0) {
            fwrite (buffer, 1, result, commChannel);
        }
#undef BUFFER_SIZE
    }

} // returnFile

// using the method and the request (the path part of the url),
// generate the data for the user and send it back. (runs in
// the child)

void handleRequest (const char *method, const char *originalRequest,
                    FILE *commChannel)
{
    //strsep used to split this
    char *request = strdup (originalRequest);
    char *chunk, *nextString;

    if (strcmp(method, "GET") != 0) {
        returnString (HTTP_ERROR, "only GETs are supported",
                     commChannel);
        goto bailout;
    }

    nextString = request;
    chunk = strsep (&nextString, "/");
                // urls start with slashes, so chunk is ""
    chunk = strsep (&nextString, "/");
                // the leading part of the url

    if (strcmp(chunk, "numbers") == 0) {
        int number;

        // url of the form /numbers/5 to print numbers from 1 to 5
```

```
                    chunk = strsep (&nextString, "/");
                    number = atoi(chunk);
                    returnNumbers (number, commChannel);

            } else if (strcmp(chunk, "file") == 0) {
                    chunk = strsep (&nextString, ""); // get rest of the string
                        returnFile (chunk, commChannel);
            } else {
                    returnString (HTTP_NOT_FOUND, "could not handle request.\n.",
                                  commChannel);
            }

    bailout:
        fprintf (stderr, "child %ld handled request '%s'\n",
                 (long)pthread_self(), originalRequest);

        free (request);

    } // handleRequest

    // read the request from the browser, pull apart the elements of the
    // request, and then dispatch it.  (runs in the child)

    void dispatchRequest (int fd, struct sockaddr_in *address)
    {
    #define LINEBUFFER_SIZE 8192
        char linebuffer[LINEBUFFER_SIZE];
        FILE *commChannel;

        commChannel = fdopen (fd, "r+");
        if (commChannel == NULL) {
            fprintf (stderr, "could not open commChannel. Error:%d/%s\n",
                     errno, strerror(errno));
        }

        // this is pretty lame in that it only reads the first line and
        // assumes that is the request, subsequently ignoring any headers
        // that might be sent.

        if (fgets(linebuffer, LINEBUFFER_SIZE, commChannel) != NULL) {
            // ok, now figure out what they wanted
            char *requestElements[3], *nextString, *chunk;
            int i = 0;
            nextString = linebuffer;
            while ((chunk = strsep (&nextString, " "))) {
                requestElements[i] = chunk;
                i++;
            }
            if (i != 3) {
                    returnString (HTTP_ERROR, "malformed request",
                                  commChannel);
                goto bailout;
            }

                handleRequest (requestElements[0], requestElements[1],
                               commChannel);
        } else {
```

```
            fprintf (stderr, "read an empty request.  exiting\n");
        }

bailout:
    fclose (commChannel);
// removed fflush (stderr);  _exit EXIT_SUCCESS);

} // dispatchRequest

// sit blocking on accept() until a new connection comes in.  queue the
// connection (which should eventually wake up a connection thread to
// handle it)

void acceptRequest (int listenSocket)
{
    struct sockaddr_in address;
    socklen_t addressLength = sizeof(address);
    int result, fd;

    printf ("before accept\n");
    result = accept (listenSocket, (struct sockaddr *)&address,
                    &addressLength);
    printf ("after accept\n");

    if (result == -1) {
        fprintf (stderr, "accept failed.  error: %d/%s\n",
                errno, strerror(errno));
        goto bailout;
    }
    fd = result;

    queueRequest (fd, &address);

bailout:
    return;

} // acceptRequest

// ----- network stuff

// this is 100% stolen from chatterserver.m
// start listening on our server port (runs in parent)

int startListening ()
{
    int fd = -1, success = 0;
    int result;


    result = socket (AF_INET, SOCK_STREAM, 0);

    if (result == -1) {
        fprintf (stderr, "could not make a socket.  error: %d / %s\n",
                errno, strerror(errno));
        goto bailout;
    }
    fd = result;
```

```
    {
        int yes = 1;
        result = setsockopt (fd, SOL_SOCKET, SO_REUSEADDR,
                                &yes, sizeof(int));
        if (result == -1) {
            fprintf (stderr,
                        "could not setsockopt to reuse address. %d/%s\n",
                        errno, strerror(errno));
            goto bailout;
        }
    }

    // bind to an address and port
    {
        struct sockaddr_in address;
        address.sin_len = sizeof (struct sockaddr_in);
        address.sin_family = AF_INET;
        address.sin_port = htons (PORT_NUMBER);
        address.sin_addr.s_addr = htonl (INADDR_ANY);
        memset (address.sin_zero, 0, sizeof(address.sin_zero));

        result = bind (fd, (struct sockaddr *)&address,
                        sizeof(address));
        if (result == -1) {
            fprintf (stderr, "could not bind socket.  error: %d/%s\n",
                        errno, strerror(errno));
            goto bailout;
        }
    }

    result = listen (fd, 8);

    if (result == -1) {
        fprintf (stderr, "listen failed.  error: %d /  %s\n",
                    errno, strerror(errno));
        goto bailout;
    }

    success = 1;

bailout:
    if (!success) {
        close (fd);
        fd = -1;
    }
    return (fd);

} // startListening

// ----- thread functions

// there is just one of these. It is the producer of new requests

void *acceptThread (void *argument)
{
    int listenSocket = *((int *)argument);
```

```
    while (1) {
        acceptRequest (listenSocket);
    }

} // acceptThread

// there are N of these to handle requests

void *requestThread (void *argument)
{
    int fd;
    int result;

    // spin out on our own
    result = pthread_detach (pthread_self());

    if (result != 0) {
        fprintf (stderr, "could not detach connection thread.  "
                         "error %d/%s\n", result, strerror(result));
        return (NULL);
    }

    struct sockaddr_in address;

    while (1) {
        getRequest (&fd, &address); // this will block until
                                    // request is queued
        dispatchRequest (fd, &address);
    }

} // requestThread

// ----- get things started in main
int main (int argc, char *argv[])
{
    int listenSocket, result;
    int i;
    pthread_t acceptThreadID;
    int status = EXIT_FAILURE;

    listenSocket = startListening ();

    if (listenSocket == -1) {
        fprintf (stderr, "startListening failed\n");
        goto bailout;
    }

    // block SIGPIPE so we do not croak if we try writing to a closed
    // connection
    if (signal (SIGPIPE, SIG_IGN) == SIG_ERR) {
        fprintf (stderr, "could not ignore SIGPIPE.  error is %d/%s\n",
                errno, strerror(errno));
        goto bailout;
    }

    // start our accept thread
```

```
        result = pthread_create (&acceptThreadID, NULL, acceptThread,
                                    &listenSocket);
    if (result != 0) {
        // pthread_* does not use errno :-|
        fprintf (stderr,
                    "could not create accept thread. Error:%d/%s\n",
                  result, strerror(result));
        goto bailout;
    }


    // start our connection threads
    for (i = 0; i < MAX_THREADS; i++) {
        pthread_t connThreadID;
        result = pthread_create (&connThreadID, NULL,
                                    requestThread, NULL);
        if (result != 0) {
            fprintf (stderr, "could not create connection thread.   "
                        "error is %d/%s\n", result, strerror(result));
            goto bailout;
        }
    }


    pthread_join (acceptThreadID, NULL);

    status = EXIT_SUCCESS;
bailout:
    return (status);

} // main
```

Compile and run the program. You can use `telnet` to commuicate with the server, or fire up a web browser and use URLs like `http://localhost:8080/file/webserve-thread.m` to return a file, or `http://localhost:8080/numbers/37` to see the numbers. Safari does some aggressive caching of data before displaying, so you may not see the individual numbers being display until they are all generated. Other browsers, like `FireFox` or `Camino` will show the numbers as they are generated.

Cocoa and Threading

You can use multiple threads in a Cocoa program. As usual, Cocoa brings a nice set of clean APIs that provide the threading features. All of the caveats above regarding race conditions and performance apply when using Cocoa, as well as some additional gotchas.

NSThread

NSThread is the class that abstracts threads. To create a new thread, use the class method

```
+ (void) detachNewThreadSelector: (SEL) aSelector
                        toTarget: (id) aTarget
                      withObject: (id) anArgument;
```

aSelector is a selector that describes a method that aTarget can receive. The signature of aSelector should be

- (void) **aSelector**: (id) anArgument;

anArgument is what gets passed to this method. This call works just like **pthread_create()** in that the thread starts executing with the first instruction of aSelector and the thread terminates when the method exits. This is a daemon thread so there is no need to do any kind of waiting for it to finish.

When the first **NSThread** object is created the **NSThread** class posts an NSWillBecomeMultiThreadedNotification. Afterward, calls to [NSThread isMultiThreaded] will return YES. You can use this call and the notification to decide whether you need to use synchronization for your data structures. (If you are single threaded, using synchronization will just slow you down for zero benefit.) **pthread_create()** does not post this notification, nor does it cause **–isMultiThreaded** to return YES, so be aware of this if you mix pthreads and **NSThread**.

When you create an **NSThread**, you get an **NSRunLoop** along with it which you can use for event handling and DO operations. If you are going to be using any Cocoa calls in the thread, you should create an **NSAutoreleasePool**. **NSApplication**'s **+detachDrawingThread:toTarget:withObject** method is a convenience for making a new thread and setting up an autorelease pool. And you are not constrained to only doing drawing in that thread.

The **NSLock** class behaves very much like a pthread_mutex_t. You can lock and unlock it, try the lock, and have a lock timeout. Likewise, **NSConditionLock** fills the role of pthread_cond_t. The Cocoa condition lock API hides the loop that you had to use when using **pthread_cond_wait()**. Instead, it is a little state machine that keeps track of what state it is in (all programmer definable), and you can tell it to wait until a particular state occurs, as well as tell it what state to move to.

Prior to OS X 10.2, child threads could not draw into Cocoa views. Jaguar added this ability. You need to call – **(BOOL) lockFocusIfCanDraw** before doing your drawing. You also have to explicitly flush the window before the window server will show the updated contents:

```
if ([drawView lockFocusIfCanDraw]) {
    // set colors, use NSBezierPath and NSString drawing functions
    [[drawView window] flushWindow];
    [drawView unlockFocus];
}
```

Here is a program that draws random colored lines into an **NSView** from multiple threads:

1. Create a new Cocoa Application project (call it ThreadDraw).

2. Create AppController.h and AppController.m:

Example 22-4. AppController.h

```
#import <Cocoa/Cocoa.h>

@interface AppController : NSObject
{
```

```
        IBOutlet NSView *drawView;
}

@end // AppController
```

Example 22-5. AppController.m

```
#import "AppController.h"
#import <unistd.h> // for sleep

@implementation AppController

- (NSPoint) randomPointInBounds: (NSRect) bounds
{
    NSPoint result;
    int width, height;
    width = round (bounds.size.width);
    height = round (bounds.size.height);
    result.x = (random() % width) + bounds.origin.x;
    result.y = (random() % height) + bounds.origin.y;
    return (result);

} // randomPointInBounds

- (void)threadDraw:(NSColor *)color
{
    NSAutoreleasePool *pool = [[NSAutoreleasePool alloc] init];
    NSPoint lastPoint = [drawView bounds].origin;

    while (1) {

        if ([drawView lockFocusIfCanDraw]) {
            NSPoint point;
            point = [self randomPointInBounds:[drawView bounds]];
            [color set];
            [NSBezierPath strokeLineFromPoint:lastPoint
                                      toPoint:point];
            [[drawView window] flushWindow];
            [drawView unlockFocus];
            usleep (random() % 500000); // up to 1/2 second
            lastPoint = point;
        }
    }
    [pool release];
} // threadDraw

- (void)awakeFromNib
{
    [drawView setNeedsDisplay:YES];

    [NSThread detachNewThreadSelector:@selector(threadDraw:)
             toTarget:self
             withObject:[NSColor redColor]];

    [NSThread detachNewThreadSelector:@selector(threadDraw:)
             toTarget:self
```

```
                withObject:[NSColor blueColor]];

    [NSThread detachNewThreadSelector:@selector(threadDraw:)
            toTarget:self
            withObject:[NSColor greenColor]];

    [NSThread detachNewThreadSelector:@selector(threadDraw:)
            toTarget:self
            withObject:[NSColor yellowColor]];

} // awakeFromNib

@end // AppController
```

3. Open `MainMenu.nib` in `Interface Builder`.

4. Drag over `AppController.h` from `Xcode` to `Interface Builder` and instantiate an **AppController** object.

5. Open the Window and drag over a plain **NSView**. Connect **AppController**'s `drawView` outlet to the view.

6. Build and run.

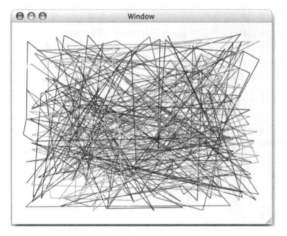

Cocoa and thread safety

Parts of the Foundation and AppKit frameworks are thread safe, and some are not. In general, immutable objects are thread safe and can be used by multiple threads. Mutable objects are not thread safe and should not be used by multiple threads. You have to be careful about how you create an object before making assumptions about mutability of an object — for instance, a method that takes an **NSString**. **NSString**s are generally immutable. Given inheritance though, a caller can legally create an **NSMutableString** and give it to a method that takes an **NSString**. Similarly, immutable containers are safe to share amongst threads, but mutable containers are not. The file `/Developer/Documentation/Cocoa/TasksAndConcepts/ ProgrammingTopics/ Multithreading/Tasks/foundation.html` has a list of thread-safe and thread-unsafe functions.

Objective-C @synchronized Blocks

When you tell the compiler to use native Objective-C exceptions, whether with the checkbox in Xcode or by giving the compiler the -fobjc-exceptions flag, you also get to use a new Objective-C thread synchronization operator.

The @synchronized() directive locks a section of code that operates on a particular object. Only a single thread can manipulate that object in this chunk of code at a time. Other threads using the same object will be blocked until the @synchronized block is exited.

@synchronized() takes a single argument which can be any Objective-C object. You can use an object that is stored in an instance variable, or you can use self, or you can even use a class object. If you are using @synchronized(self) inside of a class method, you will be @synchronized with the class object. @synchronized(someObject) acts like a recursive mutex, so a thread can use the same object in different blocks that are synchronized with the same object. Exceptions thrown from within a @synchronized() block will automatically release the lock.

Example 22-6 is a program that has multiple threads, each adding new **NSNumbers** to an **NSMutableArray** using **insertObject:atIndex:**. **insertObject:atIndex:** is not a thread-safe operation, so *anything* can happen if two threads try to do this at the same time. If you run the program without any command line arguments it performs the object insertions without any thread protection. If you give it a command-line argument (it does not matter what you give it), the @synchronized() directive will be used around the manipulations of the array.

Example 22-6. synchronized.m

```
// synchronized.m -- use the @synchronized() directive to protect
//                   mutable array object insertion

#import <Foundation/Foundation.h>

/* compile with:
gcc -g -fobjc-exceptions -framework Foundation \
    -o synchronized synchronized.m
*/

// tweak these so that things break on your system.

// how many threads to run
#define THREAD_COUNT 10

// how many items each thread adds to the array
#define ITEM_COUNT 5000

// how long to wait for the threads to complete
#define SLEEP_TIME 3


// a ThreadRunner object is the target object for each of the threads

@interface ThreadRunner : NSObject
{
    NSMutableArray *array;  // array too add NSNumbers to
```

```
        BOOL synchronized;          // use @synchronized?
}


- (void) runThread: (id) object;
- (void) setSynchronized: (BOOL) yOrN;
- (int) arrayCount;

@end // ThreadRunner


@implementation ThreadRunner

- (id) init
{
    if (self = [super init]) {
        array = [[NSMutableArray alloc] init];
        // synchronized defaults to NO
    }

    return (self);

} // init


- (void) dealloc
{
    [array release];
    [super dealloc];

} // dealloc


- (void) setSynchronized: (BOOL) yOrN
{
    synchronized = yOrN;
} // setSynchronized


- (void) runThread: (id) object
{
    int i;

    if (synchronized) {
        for (i = 0; i < ITEM_COUNT; i++) {
            NSNumber *number = [[NSNumber alloc] initWithInt: i];

            // this is a thread-safe operation
            @synchronized (array) {
                [array insertObject: number  atIndex: i];
            }
        }

    } else {
        for (i = 0; i < ITEM_COUNT; i++) {
            NSNumber *number = [[NSNumber alloc] initWithInt: i];

            // this is not thread-safe
```

```
                [array insertObject: number   atIndex: i];
        }
    }

    NSLog (@"done!");

} // runThread


- (int) arrayCount
{
    return ([array count]);
} // arrayCount

@end // ThreadRunner


int main (int argc, const char *argv[])
{
    NSAutoreleasePool *pool = [[NSAutoreleasePool alloc] init];

    // make a single object to be abused by multiple threads
    ThreadRunner *runner = [[ThreadRunner alloc] init];
    if (argc != 1) {
        [runner setSynchronized: YES];
    }

    // spin off the threads
    int i;
    for (i = 0; i < THREAD_COUNT; i++) {
        NSThread *thread;
        [NSThread detachNewThreadSelector: @selector(runThread:)
                  toTarget: runner
                  withObject: nil];
    }

    // hang out for awhile
    sleep (SLEEP_TIME);

    // should be THREAD_COUNT * ITEM_COUNT
    NSLog (@"count is %d", [runner arrayCount]);

    [pool release];

    return (0);

} // main
```

First are a couple of sample runs that do not use the @synchronized() directive.
The program either falls over with a hard crash, or it generates the wrong result
(which should be 50000):

```
$ ./synchronized
2005-06-22 20:54:05.756 synchronized[383] done!
2005-06-22 20:54:05.826 synchronized[383] done!
2005-06-22 20:54:05.880 synchronized[383] done!
2005-06-22 20:54:05.982 synchronized[383] done!
```

```
Segmentation fault
```

```
$ ./synchronized
2005-06-22 20:54:07.369 synchronized[385] done!
2005-06-22 20:54:07.422 synchronized[385] done!
2005-06-22 20:54:07.474 synchronized[385] done!
2005-06-22 20:54:07.526 synchronized[385] done!
2005-06-22 20:54:07.617 synchronized[385] done!
2005-06-22 20:54:07.767 synchronized[385] done!
2005-06-22 20:54:07.780 synchronized[385] done!
2005-06-22 20:54:07.800 synchronized[385] done!
2005-06-22 20:54:07.815 synchronized[385] done!
2005-06-22 20:54:07.832 synchronized[385] done!
2005-06-22 20:54:10.731 synchronized[385] count is 37255
```

Telling the program to to use the @synchronized() directive makes it behave correctly:

```
$ ./synchronized -x
2005-06-22 21:08:21.721 synchronized[408] done!
2005-06-22 21:08:22.533 synchronized[408] done!
2005-06-22 21:08:23.539 synchronized[408] done!
2005-06-22 21:08:23.556 synchronized[408] done!
2005-06-22 21:08:23.557 synchronized[408] done!
2005-06-22 21:08:23.563 synchronized[408] done!
2005-06-22 21:08:23.564 synchronized[408] done!
2005-06-22 21:08:23.569 synchronized[408] done!
2005-06-22 21:08:23.589 synchronized[408] done!
2005-06-22 21:08:23.599 synchronized[408] done!
2005-06-22 21:08:24.789 synchronized[408] count is 50000
```

For the More Curious: Thread Local Storage

Sometimes it is very handy to have storage that is private to a thread. In the basics.m program above, you could stash the contents of the ThreadInfo stack into thread local storage instead of on the function call stack. Thread local storage behaves like global variables, but are private to the thread. errno is stored in thread local storage so that every thread has its own errno.

To use thread local storage, initialize a pthread_key_t using **pthread_key_create()**:

```
int pthread_key_create (pthread_key_t *key, void (*destructor)(void *));
```

This creates an abstract key. Usually you name a variable with a descriptive name, or associate this key with a descriptive string in a dictionary, as shown in Figure 22-5. The destructor function is called when the thread exits, so that dynamic memory (or other resources) can be cleaned up.

Set a thread-local value by using pthread_setspecific():

```
int pthread_setspecific (pthread_key_t key, const void *value);
```

and get the value by using **pthread_getspecific()**: void *pthread_getspecific (pthread_key_t key);

Figure 22-5. Thread Local Storage

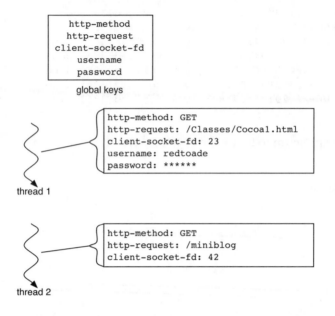

If you are using **NSThread**, you can use

- (NSMutableDictionary *)**threadDictionary**

To put stuff into thread local storage, just store stuff into the dictionary. This is an **NSThread** instance method, so you need to find your current **NSThread** object by using [NSThread currentThread].

For the More Curious: Read/Write Locks

Both Cocoa and pthreads provide read/write locks. These allow a data structure to be read by a number of readers simultaneously, but only allow one thread write access at a time.

pthread_rwlock_t works just like pthread_mutex_t, but with a couple of extra calls. Here are the details:

pthread_rwlock_init (pthread_rwlock_t *lock,
                        const pthread_rwlockattr_t *attr);

(OS X does not define PTHREAD_RWLOCK_INITIALIZER, so you cannot create them statically)

int **pthread_rwlock_destroy** (pthread_rwlock_t *lock);

Rather than use **lock()**, you specify which kind of locking you want:

- `int` **`pthread_rwlock_rdlock`** `(pthread_rwlock_t *rwlock);`

- `int` **`pthread_rwlock_tryrdlock`** `(pthread_rwlock_t *rwlock);`

- `int` **`pthread_rwlock_wrlock`** `(pthread_rwlock_t *rwlock);`

- `int` **`pthread_rwlock_trywrlock`** `(pthread_rwlock_t *rwlock);`

And unlock by using

`int` **`pthread_rwlock_unlock`** `(pthread_rwlock_t *rwlock);`

In general, using read/write locks is a bad idea, since the number of actual lock operations are doubled. (Read/write locks can be implemented with a mutex and two condition variables.) Unless you have some really expensive data structures, the overhead of the read/write lock operations will be more than the operation you are protecting. Given that caveat, there are some times when they are quite useful, especially when there are a lot of readers, not many modifications, and accessing the data structure is time consuming.

Challenge

1. Tweak `basics.m` to use Thread Local Storage to store the index, number to count to, and the sleep time.

2. Make `nodepool.m` from the Memory chapter thread safe so that multiple threads can allocate stuff out of the same pool.

Chapter 23. Using Distributed Objects Between Threads

In Chapter 18 (Distributed Objects), you used DO to communicate between two processes. Part of the reason DO is an elegant way to do this is because it plays nicely with the run loop -- messages coming in waited in the queue until the process was ready to handle them. This same mechanism can be very handy in multithreaded applications.

When a thread is created with **NSThread**, it gets its own runloop and its own autorelease pool stack. All messages sent via DO from another thread will be queued in the runloop until the thread is idle again. This queuing can often alleviate the need for locking. Many developers find that DO enables them to more easily create high-performance multithreaded applications.

"Each Server In Its Own Thread" Design

In Cocoa, drawing is usually done from the main thread. So a very common idiom is to create one or more server objects. Each server runs in its own thread and has its own run loop. The main thread communicates with these servers via DO. While the app is multithreaded, each object is manipulated only in a single thread. Thus, you can code them as if they are single threaded.

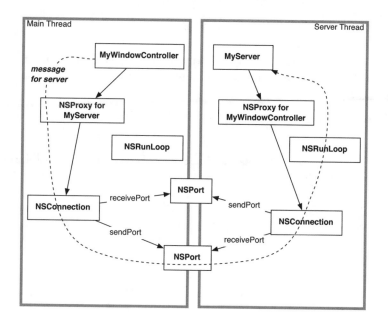

The server typically has a `oneway void` method that does some time-consuming operation. After dispatching the message via DO, the main thread immediately returns to doing whatever it would normally do (usually it sits around waiting for user events). The server calls back the client after it has completed the operation.

Generate the Mandelbrot set

The trickiest part of this design is getting the server, **NSConnection**, and **NSThread** objects set up correctly. The easiest way to demonstrate this is with an example. Our example will be an application that runs in five threads: the main thread and four server objects, each in its own thread. When a view in the main thread wants to fill a bitmap with the Mandelbrot set, it will ask each of the servers to fill in a quarter of the image. As each finishes, it will make a callback to the view. When all the servers are done, the view will composite the image map onto the window.

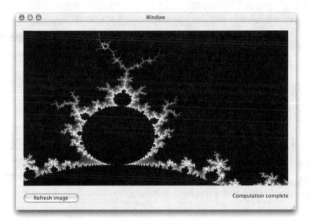

Notice the two benefits to this design:

- The main thread does not stop checking for events while the Mandelbrot set is being calculated. The user interface remains responsive and the user does not get the wait cursor.
- If the user has multiple processors, they will be fully utilized.

The view class will be called **MandelbrotView**. The server class will be called **MandelbrotServer**.

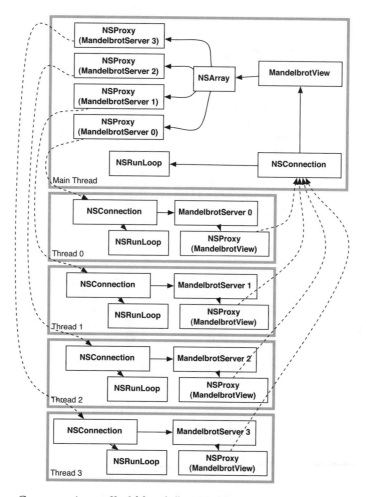

Create a new Cocoa project called Mandelbrotter. Open `MainMenu.nib` and create subclass of **NSView** called **MandelbrotView**. It should have one action (**refreshImage:**) and two outlets (`refreshButton` and `progressTextField`). Create an instance on the window. Also, drop a button and a textfield on the window. Set the button to be disabled.

Make the view the target of the button. Set the view's outlets to point to the button and the text field. Create the files for **MandelbrotView**.

In `Xcode`, create an empty file named `MandelbrotProtocols.h` to hold the protocols for the client and the server. The protocols act as hints to the DO system. I recommend that whenever possible, you define protocols for the messages sent over

DO. Add the following to `MandelbrotProtocols.h`:

```
#import <Cocoa/Cocoa.h>

@protocol MandelbrotServerMethods

// Fill buffer with the colors for the region defined by
// minX, minY, maxX, and maxY.
// The buffer represents RBG data that is w pixels x h pixels
- (oneway void)fill:(uintptr_t)buffer
               minX:(float)minX
               minY:(float)minY
               maxX:(float)maxX
               maxY:(float)maxY
              width:(int)w
             height:(int)h;
@end

@protocol MandelbrotClientMethods

// Called when a new server object is created
- (void)addServer:(id)newServer;

// Called when a server reaches the end of
// fill:minX:minY:maxX:maxY:width:height:
- (oneway void)serverIsDone;

@end
```

Now the tricky part. Open up `MandelbrotView.h` and make it look like this:

```
#import <Cocoa/Cocoa.h>
#import "MandelbrotProtocols.h"

@class MandelbrotServer;

@interface MandelbrotView : NSView <MandelbrotClientMethods>
{
    // The array of Mandelbrot servers
    NSMutableArray *servers;

    // The imageRep that is displayed
    NSBitmapImageRep *imageRep;

    // This will be a count of all the servers
    // are done with their work
    int serversThatAreDone;

    // UI stuff
    IBOutlet NSTextField *progressTextField;
    IBOutlet NSButton *refreshButton;

    // Region to be drawn
    NSRect region;
}

- (id)initWithFrame:(NSRect)rect;
- (void)createServer;
```

```
-  (IBAction) refreshImage: (id) sender;
@end
```

Now add the following to `MandelbrotView.m`:

```objc
#import "MandelbrotView.h"
#import "MandelbrotServer.h"
#define SERVER_COUNT 4

@implementation MandelbrotView

- (id)initWithFrame:(NSRect)frameRect
{
    [super initWithFrame:frameRect];

    // Create and retain an array to hold the servers
    servers = [[NSMutableArray alloc] init];
    imageRep = nil;

    // Start with a nice high-level view of the set
    region = NSMakeRect(-2.0, -1.2, 3, 2.4);
    return self;
}


- (void)awakeFromNib
{
    int i;

    // Create the servers
    for (i = 0; i < SERVER_COUNT; i++) {
        [self createServer];
    }
}

- (void)createServer
{
    NSPort *port1;
    NSPort *port2;
    NSArray *portArray;
    NSConnection *clientConnection;

    // Create two ports (one incoming, one out)
    // These actually create NSMachPort objects
    port1 = [NSPort port];
    port2 = [NSPort port];

    // Create an NSConnection on this end
    clientConnection = [[NSConnection alloc] initWithReceivePort:port1
                sendPort:port2];

    [clientConnection setRootObject:self];

    portArray = [NSArray arrayWithObjects:port2, port1, nil];

    // Create a new thread and send a message in the new thread
    [NSThread detachNewThreadSelector:@selector(connectWithPorts:)
                toTarget:[MandelbrotServer class] withObject:portArray];
}
```

```
@end
```

So at this point, we have created a thread to send the message **connectWithPorts:**
to the **MandelbrotServer** class with the array of **NSPort**. Before adding any more to
the **MandelbrotView** class, create the files for **MandelbrotServer**. Make
MandelbrotServer.h look like this:

```objc
#import <Cocoa/Cocoa.h>
#import "MandelbrotProtocols.h"

@interface MandelbrotServer : NSObject <MandelbrotServerMethods> {
    // This is a proxy that represents the view
    id client;
}
+ (void)connectWithPorts:(NSArray *)portArray;
- (id)initWithClient:(id)obj;
@end
```

In MandelbrotServer.m, implement the methods that will initialize the servers:

```objc
#import "MandelbrotServer.h"

void mandelbrot(double x, double y, unsigned char *buffer);

@implementation MandelbrotServer

// This is called when the new thread is created
+ (void)connectWithPorts:(NSArray *)portArray
{
    NSAutoreleasePool *pool;
    MandelbrotServer *serverObject;
    NSRunLoop *runLoop;
    NSConnection *serverConnection;
    id proxy;

    pool = [[NSAutoreleasePool alloc] init];

    // This connection uses the same ports as the client connection, but
    // reversed: the client's receive is the server's send.
    serverConnection = [[NSConnection
            connectionWithReceivePort:[portArray objectAtIndex:0]
                            sendPort:[portArray objectAtIndex:1]] retain]

    // Get a proxy for the view
    proxy = [serverConnection rootProxy];

    // Create a new Mandelbrot server
    serverObject = [[self alloc] initWithClient:proxy];

    // Everything works better if you tell the proxy its protocol
    [proxy setProtocolForProxy:@protocol(MandelbrotClientMethods)];

    // Tell the view to add the new server to its list
    [(id)[serverConnection rootProxy] addServer:serverObject];

    // The server is retained by its connection
    [serverObject release];
```

```
    // Start up the run loop
    runLoop = [NSRunLoop currentRunLoop];
    [runLoop run];
    [pool release];

    return;
}

- (id)initWithClient:(id)obj
{
    [super init];
    client = [obj retain];
    return self;
}
@end
```

Note that the client gets told to add the new server object.

Back in `MandelbrotView.m`, implement this method:

```
// This method will be called by the server via DO.
// anObject is really an NSProxy
- (void)addServer:(id)anObject
{
    [anObject setProtocolForProxy:@protocol(MandelbrotServerMethods)];
    [servers addObject:anObject];
    NSLog(@"added a server");

    // If all the servers are created, generate the image
    if ([servers count] == SERVER_COUNT) {
        [self refreshImage:nil];
    }
}
```

Look over the code you've just typed in and the diagram for this application. You've already done everything that is necessary to get the servers, the threads, the **NSConnections,** and the proxies configured correctly; What follows now is just the stuff to make pretty pictures.

We are going to need the C functions that calculate the value of the Mandelbrot set at any point and figure out the color for that value. Create a C file called `MandelbrotFunctions.c`:

```
#include <math.h>
#include <complex.h>
#define LOOP 150
#define LIMIT 128

// gradient() determines what colors go with which values.
// I have set it up for a red scheme
void gradient(int value, unsigned char *buffer) {
    unsigned char *ptr = buffer;
    value = value * 4;
    if (value > 255)
        value = 255;
    *ptr++ = value;    // Red
    *ptr++ = 0;        // Green
    *ptr = 0;          // Blue
```

```
    }

    // (x, y) is the point to be dealt with
    // buffer is a pointer to the three bytes that will hold
    // the resulting color
    void mandelbrot(double x, double y, unsigned char *buffer) {
        int i;
        complex z,c;

        c = x + (y * 1.0i);
        z = 0;

        for (i = 0; i < LOOP; i++) {
            z = (z * z) + c;
            if ( cabs(z) > LIMIT ) {
                gradient(i, buffer);
                return;
            }
        }
        // If z never escaped, color it as zero.
        gradient(0, buffer);
    }
```

In `MandelbrotServer.m`, we are going to write the method that calls **mandelbrot()**:

```
    // Notice that buffer is basically an int,  even though we know it is
    // an unsigned char *.  DO cleverness caused trouble,  so we sent the
    // pointer as an int.

    - (oneway void)fill:(uintptr_t)buffer
                    minX:(float)minX
                    minY:(float)minY
                    maxX:(float)maxX
                    maxY:(float)maxY
                   width:(int)w
                  height:(int)h
    {
        unsigned char *ptr;
        int x, y;
        float regionH, regionW;
        float regionX, regionY;

        NSLog(@"Server %p: starting", self);

        // What is the size of the region?
        regionW = maxX - minX;
        regionH = maxY- minY;

        ptr = (unsigned char *)buffer;

        // Loop through each row
        for (y = 0; y < h; y++) {
            // Calculate where on the set this y is
            regionY = maxY - (regionH * (float)y) / (float)h;

            // Loop through each column
            for (x = 0; x < w; x++) {
                // Calculate where on the set this x is
```

```
            regionX = minX + (regionW * (float)x) / (float)w;

            // Do the calculation and color the pixel.
            mandelbrot(regionX, regionY, ptr);

            // move the next pixel
            ptr += 3;
        }
    }
    NSLog(@"Server %p: done", self);

    // Tell the view that our part is done
    [client serverIsDone];
}
```

Note that the method is declared as oneway void. Thus, the client will not block waiting for this method to end. At the end of the method, we call back to the client via DO to tell it that the buffer of data is ready.

Add these methods to MandelbrotView.m:

```
- (void)drawRect:(NSRect)rect
{
    NSRect bounds = [self bounds];

    // Draw a white background
    [[NSColor whiteColor] set];
    [NSBezierPath fillRect:bounds];

    // If the image is ready,  draw it.
    if (serversThatAreDone == SERVER_COUNT) {
        [imageRep draw];
    }
}


- (IBAction)refreshImage:(id)sender
{
    unsigned long rowsPerServer;
    float maxY, maxX, deltaY;
    int i;
    unsigned char *ptr;
    [progressTextField setStringValue:@"Computation starting"];
    [refreshButton setEnabled:NO];

    // Clear the serversThatAreDone to show that
    // none of the servers are done
    serversThatAreDone = 0;
    NSRect bounds = [self bounds];
    int pixelsHigh = bounds.size.height;
    int pixelsWide = bounds.size.width;

    // The image maybe a few pixels shorter than the view.
    // Benefit:  all servers draw the same number of rows.
    int remainder = pixelsHigh % SERVER_COUNT;
    pixelsHigh = pixelsHigh - remainder;
    rowsPerServer = pixelsHigh / SERVER_COUNT;

    NSLog(@"Image will be %d x %d", pixelsWide, pixelsHigh);
```

```
        [imageRep release];

        // Create the image rep the servers will draw on
        imageRep = [[NSBitmapImageRep alloc]
                        initWithBitmapDataPlanes:NULL
                                        pixelsWide:pixelsWide
                                        pixelsHigh:pixelsHigh
                                    bitsPerSample:8
                                    samplesPerPixel:3
                                            hasAlpha:NO
                                            isPlanar:NO
                                    colorSpaceName:NSCalibratedRGBColorSpace
                                        bytesPerRow:pixelsWide * 3
                                        bitsPerPixel:0];

        // Get the pointer to the raw data
        ptr = [imageRep bitmapData];
        maxY = NSMaxY(region);
        maxX = NSMaxX(region);
        deltaY = region.size.height / SERVER_COUNT;

        // Ask each server to draw a set of rows.
        for (i = 0; i < SERVER_COUNT; i++){
            // Assign a region to the server
            [[servers objectAtIndex:i] fill:(uintptr_t)ptr
                                        minX:region.origin.x
                                        minY:maxY - deltaY
                                        maxX:maxX
                                        maxY:maxY
                                        width:pixelsWide
                                        height:rowsPerServer];

            // Move down the image
            maxY = maxY - deltaY;

            // Move jump to next region in bitmapData
            ptr = ptr + (pixelsWide * rowsPerServer * 3);
        }
        [progressTextField setStringValue:@"Computation started"];
    }

- (oneway void)serverIsDone
{
    serversThatAreDone++;
    [progressTextField setIntValue:serversThatAreDone];
    NSLog(@"%d servers are done", serversThatAreDone);
    if (serversThatAreDone == SERVER_COUNT) {
        [progressTextField setStringValue:@"Computation complete"];
        [refreshButton setEnabled:YES];
        [self setNeedsDisplay:YES];
    }
}
```

Build and run your application. You should see a lovely image. If you have multiple processors, you should see the image much faster than the people with single processors. Regardless, you should see that the menus are still useable while the image is being calculated.

Add Zooming

For those of you who want to be able to select regions to zoom in on, adding this to the **MandelbrotView** is quite easy. First, you will need a few more instance variables and a method in MandelbrotView.h:

```
    BOOL dragging;
    NSPoint downPoint, currentPoint;
}
-(NSRect)selectedRect;
```

Also, you will need to override the **mouseDown:**, **mouseDragged:**, and **mouseUp:** methods:

```
- (void)mouseDown:(NSEvent *)event
{
    // Ignore drags while servers are working
    if (serversThatAreDone == SERVER_COUNT) {
        dragging = YES;
        NSPoint p = [event locationInWindow];
        downPoint = [self convertPoint:p fromView:nil];
        currentPoint = downPoint;
    }
}


- (void)mouseDragged:(NSEvent *)event
{
    if (dragging) {
        NSPoint p = [event locationInWindow];
        currentPoint = [self convertPoint:p fromView:nil];
        [self setNeedsDisplay:YES];
    }
}


- (void)mouseUp:(NSEvent *)event
{
    NSRect r, bounds;
    NSRect newRegion;
    if (dragging) {
        dragging = NO;
        NSPoint p = [event locationInWindow];
        currentPoint = [self convertPoint:p fromView:nil];
        bounds = [self bounds];
        r = [self selectedRect];

        // Calculate newRegion as if in the unit square
        newRegion.origin.x = r.origin.x / bounds.size.width;
        newRegion.origin.y = r.origin.y / bounds.size.height;
        newRegion.size.width = r.size.width / bounds.size.width;
        newRegion.size.height = r.size.height / bounds.size.height;

        // Scale to region's size
        newRegion.origin.x = region.origin.x +
                            newRegion.origin.x * region.size.width;
        newRegion.origin.y = region.origin.y +
                            newRegion.origin.y * region.size.height;
        newRegion.size.width = region.size.width * newRegion.size.width;
        newRegion.size.height = region.size.height * newRegion.size.height;
```

```
        region = newRegion;
        [self refreshImage:nil];
    }
}


- (NSRect)selectedRect
{
    float minX = MIN(downPoint.x, currentPoint.x);
    float maxX = MAX(downPoint.x, currentPoint.x);
    float minY = MIN(downPoint.y, currentPoint.y);
    float maxY = MAX(downPoint.y, currentPoint.y);

    return NSMakeRect(minX, minY, maxX-minX, maxY-minY);
}
```

Finally, let the user see the region they are selecting by adding the rectangle to the drawRect: method:

```
- (void)drawRect:(NSRect)rect
{
    NSRect bounds = [self bounds];

    // Draw a white background
    [[NSColor whiteColor] set];
    [NSBezierPath fillRect:bounds];

    // If the image is ready, draw it.
    if (serversThatAreDone == SERVER_COUNT) {
        [imageRep draw];
    }
    // If the user is dragging, show the selected rect
    if (dragging) {
        NSRect box = [self selectedRect];
        [[NSColor redColor] set];
        [NSBezierPath strokeRect:box];
    }

}
```

performSelectorOnMainThread:

In a multithreaded Cocoa application, it is common to have heavy computation going on in one thread while the main thread continues handling events and updating the screen. One way to communicate with the main thread is to use Distributed Objects as you did in this exercise. Another technique is to use the following method:

```
- (void)performSelectorOnMainThread:(SEL)aSelector
                         withObject:(id)obj
                      waitUntilDone:(BOOL)wait;
```

This method is defined on **NSObject**, so you can send it to any object. Basically, the method packs up an invocation (the receiver is the target and obj is the only argument) and queues it the run loop of the main thread to be executed as soon as possible. If wait is true, this method will block until the invocation has been executed.

In a single-threaded application, this method is used when you are thinking, "As soon as the current event has been handled and all the necessary redrawing has occurred, I'd like a message sent." Thus, if you call this method from the main thread with `wait` as NO, it will execute the invocation the next time through the run loop. If you call this method from the main thread with `wait` as YES, it will execute the invocation immediately.

Challenge 1

Make it so that if the user closes the window, the connections, proxies, servers and their run loops are destroyed.

Challenge 2

1. Make the **MandelbrotServer** run in a daemon that can be accessed from other machines. It will require that you change the protocol a bit. I suggest that this be the method on the server that begins the calculation:

```
- (oneway void) calculateMinX: (float) minX
                         minY: (float) minY
                         maxX: (float) maxX
                         maxY: (float) maxY
                        width: (int) w
                       height: (int) h
                          tag: (int) serverTag;
```

The callback to the client would be:

```
- (oneway void) doneWithData: (NSData *) calculatedData
                      forTag: (int) serverTag;
```

Notice that the client does not send the data buffer, but it will send a tag so that it knows which response came from with which server. Thus, the client will be able to assemble a single image from all the data that arrives.

2. Allow the server processes to be found via Bonjour, and make your client utilize all the server processes on the local network.

Chapter 24. Subversion

Version control (also known as "source code control" and "revision control") is a system that keeps a history of the changes you make to a set of files, whether they be Objective-C or Java source files for a program, HTML and CSS files for a website, system configuration files, or even the contents of your home directory. When you make a change to your files that you want to make permanent, you tell the version control system about the change. The system then remembers what the change is, who made it, and when it was made.

Subversion is an open-source version control system designed to address many of the problems with the venerable CVS (another popular version control system, featured in the first edition of this book). We will only be touching on the highlights of Subversion, and the full documentation can be found on the web at `http://svnbook.org/`.

The Mac OS X developer tools come with CVS, but not Subversion, so you will need to acquire Subversion from a third party. There are number of people on the internet that provide an installer package with all of the different bits and pieces needed to make Subversion work. See this book's website for links to installable packages.

Subversion has a flexible architecture allowing you to have a Subversion repository on your own machine for single-developer change tracking, all the way up to having the repository on a webDAV-based server solution supporting hundreds of users. The repository is the database where Subversion stores its past and current versions of files.

Multiple people can interact with a repository at the same time, and all of these people can contribute to the same body of work. Subversion keeps track of who changed files when, and what those changes were. In essence, it is an electronic paper trail. This is handy for figuring out who broke the build so you can tell them not to make that mistake again. Version control systems help multiple people contribute to the same project without stumbling on each other too often.

A version control system is a very powerful tool to have in your programming arsenal, whether it is CVS, Subversion, or another system. Using version control is very useful even if you are the only one working on a project. If you put your files under version control you can use it like a big undo mechanism. Unhappy with your latest refactoring of the code? Just revert to the previously checked-in version. Tracking down a nasty bug? Feel free to hack and slash the code knowing you can fall back to an unmodified version once you figure out where the problem is. Every project that will release more than one version of a program can benefit from tagging and branching to ease maintenance of old and new versions of the program.

You can also use a version control system as a time machine, to see how your files looked at any point of time in the past. This can be handy for doing project postmortems, or if you just want to see how your program has evolved over time.

Figure 24-1 shows the revision tree for a file called `BigParse.m`, part of the `BigShow` program. The main trunk of development is called the HEAD. That is where all new development goes. Coming off of the main trunk are two branches, for two different released versions of `BigShow`. By having a branch like this for a released version, the maintenance crew can make bug fixes to `BigShow` 1.0 and ship them out to customers without impacting the work (possibly a rewrite or major refactoring) that is happening on the HEAD line.

Figure 24-1. Revision Tree for `BigParse.m`

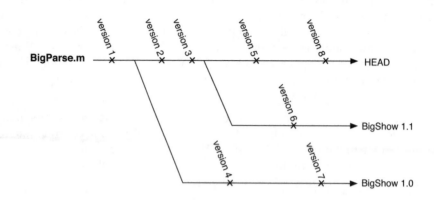

The version of `BigParse.m` in `BigShow` 1.0 includes changes made in versions 1, 4, and 7. `BigParse.m` in `BigShow` 1.1 is composed of the changes made to versions 1, 2, 3, and 6, and the HEAD includes changes made in versions 1, 2, 3, 5, and 8. Subversion can merge changes that happen on a branch into other versions, allowing code to be fixed just once, and then merged over.

Version control systems usually work in one of two ways. The first is "lock, edit, unlock". If you want to change a file, you first lock it, thereby preventing other people from changing the file. You make your changes (and test them, hopefully) and then tell the version control system to accept your changes and unlock the file. The next person can then lock the file and make their changes.

While Subversion supports this model, it is most often used with an "edit, merge" model. The idea is that every person is working on their own personal copy of the program (or website, or whatever). You are free to edit any file at any time. Once you are done editing you ask Subversion to merge the changes into the original. If there are not any conflicts, Subversion merges the changes into the original. If there are conflicts, like Andrew makes a change, checks it in, and then Lisa makes a different change at the same spot, Subversion would ask Lisa to resolve the conflict. This model scales up much better with larger, more distributed teams than the locking model. Plus you avoid the problem of someone locking a file and then flying to Aruba for a couple of weeks.

Subversion Commands

Subversion commands take this form:

```
svn <command> <command-options> <file-name(s)>
```

Subversion commands are based on CVS commands, so people familiar with CVS can get up to speed with Subversion very quickly. `svn help` will give you usage information including the list of commands. `svn help <command>` will give you help on a particular command.

The common commands you will regularly use are:

```
add
```

Add a new file or directory to the repository.

`checkout`

Check out sources for editing. This creates a working copy you can work with.

`commit`

Send changes to files to the repository.

`diff`

Show differences between revisions.

`log`

Print out differences between revisions.

`update`

Sync the working copy with the repository.

`status`

See which files you have modified in your working copy, and which files have been changed in the repository by others, since your last update.

Some common command options include

`--dry-run`

Go through the motions of running a command, but without making any changes to the files in your working copy or in the repository. This flag is handy when experimenting with Subversion commands. Subversion will not change anything on disk and potentially mess up your work.

`--verbose / -v`

Provide extra output. Handy for seeing what Subversion is doing.

`--quiet / -q`

Only essential information is displayed when performing a command.

`--message / -m`

A message to be logged with the file or directory. Log messages tell others why a particular change was made to a file.

`--revision / -r`

Indicate a particular revision of interest. Very useful with the log and diff commands.

Getting Started

Creating the Repository

Before you can put any of your files under Subversion control, you will need to create a repository. A repository is the database that Subversion uses to keep track of your files' contents and the changes made to them.

Subversion has two different ways of managing its repository data store. One uses the BerkeleyDB to store files and their changes, the other, called FSFS, uses a hierarchy of directories and files to keep track of this information. In general, you will want to use the FSFS version. It is easier to maintain and backup than the Berkeley DB version, and it will work on a networked file system. A number of people have had corruption issues with using a Berkeley DB repository. Subversion 1.2 and later defaults to creating new repositories with FSFS, but it is good to explicitly indicate you want to use FSFS in case you are using an older version.

To create the repository, use the `svnadmin` command:

```
$ svnadmin create --fs-type fsfs /usr/local/svnroot/
```

`svnadmin create` creates a new repository in the directory `/usr/local/svnroot` (make sure it exists first). You can have multiple repositories on a single machine, and you can put repositories into your home directory if you do not have write access to `/usr/local`. Repositories are just directories that contain the revision history information.

Importing a Project

An empty repository is not very useful without some projects to work with. Importing an already-existing hierarchy of files is a common next step. You might already have a pile of files from a current project, or you might have a freshly-built template from `Xcode`.

There are two decisions to make before importing files for a project: do you want to keep more than one project in the repository, and will you be doing tagging and branching (discussed below). If either is the case, you will need to tweak the directory hierarchy of the project you are importing.

Multi-Project Repositories

By default, repositories are single-project. Each new project requires a separate repository. Often, however, repositories are set up to hold multiple projects. You might even have multiple repositories containing multiple projects.

Many repositories are set up to hold multiple projects. It is OK to have a setup that includes multiple repositories, each with multiple projects. A consulting shop might keep each client's projects in their own repository. That way all of a client's materials are in one place, but one client's information will not be intermixed with another.

To support multiple projects in a repository, you first create a pair of special sub-directories in the repository for each project. Here are two projects that are going into the new repository: `BigShow` and `BigSql`. Make two directories in the repository:

```
$ svn mkdir -m "initial revision" \
file:///usr/local/svnroot/bigshow
```

```
$ svn mkdir -m "initial revision" \
file:///usr/local/svnroot/bigsql
```

The `file:///usr/local//svnroot/` stuff tells Subversion where to look for its repository. Subversion supports different repository access mechanisms, such as via WebDAV (using the `http://` or `https://` protocols), and it also has its own server protocol (`svn://` or `svn+ssh://`), discussed later.

Project Directory Layout

The next step is to create a directory layout. Figure 24-2 is what the `BigShow` directory layout looks like before importing into the repository.

Figure 24-2. BigShow Directory Layout

```
BigShow/
    AppController.h
    AppController.m
    ...
    English.lproj/
        InfoPlist.strings
        MainMenu.nib/
        ...
    Typeface.h
    Typeface.m
    logo.gif
    main.m
```

With other revision control systems (like CVS) you would just import these files directly. With Subversion, you will need to tweak the directory layout a bit. You will put the source files and directories into a directory called `trunk`. Then make two empty directories on the same level as `trunk` called `tags` and `branches`, like this:

```
$ cd ~/Projects
$ mv BigShow trunk
$ mkdir branches
$ mkdir tags
$ mkdir BigShow
$ mv trunk tags branches BigShow
```

You will end up with something like Figure 24-3

Figure 24-3. BigShow Project Layout

```
BigShow/
     tags/
     branches/
     trunk/
          AppController.h
          AppController.m
          ...
          English.lproj/
               InfoPlist.strings
               MainMenu.nib/
               ...
          Typeface.h
          Typeface.m
          logo.gif
          main.m
```

This layout works out well with how Subversion handles tagging and branching, so this will be covered in a later section.

Performing the Import

Now with the preliminaries out of the way (making directories in the repository and creating the appropriate directory hierarchy), it is time to add files to the repository using the `svn import` to import the files:

```
$ cd /Path/To/BigShow
$ svn import -m "initial import" . \
file:///usr/local/svnroot/bigshow
```

`svn import` recursively adds files to the repository, starting from a given directory; the dot is used to specify the current directory. The `file:///` url tells the `svn` command which repository to use. The `/usr/loca/svnroot` is the location on the disk to find the repository, and `/bigshow` is the virtual folder within the repository to put the new files. The `-m` flag lets you specify a comment explaining why this group of files were imported.

Subversion emits some output telling you what it is doing when it runs the command:

```
Adding          trunk
Adding          trunk/MyDocument.m
Adding          trunk/main.m
Adding          trunk/BigWindow.h
...
Adding          trunk/PrefsController.m
Adding          branches
Adding          tags
Committed revision 2.
```

You can ignore the revision number for now. This is a monotonically increasing integer, global to the repository, that changes with each change to the repository.

Some Subversion bookkeeping can increase the revision number when you are not expecting it.

The same steps are used to import BigSql (assuming that we have already created the branches / tags / trunk directories in the BigSql project):

```
$ cd /Path/To/BigSql
$ svn import -m "initial import" . \
file:///usr/local/svnroot/bigsql
```

`svn import` adds the files and their contents to the repository, but does not change the current directory into a working copy that is under Subversion control (this works like importing files into CVS). To actually make a working copy of the project, you need to check it out:

```
$ cd ~/Development/Projects
$ svn checkout file:///usr/local/svnroot/bigshow/trunk BigShow
```

Like `svn import`, you will get some output telling you what Subversion has done:

```
A   BigShow/MyDocument.m
A   BigShow/BigWindow.h
A   BigShow/main.m
...
A   BigShow/Image.m
A   BigShow/PrefsController.m
Checked out revision 2.
```

The "A" means that a file has been added to your working copy.

Take a look at the command again:

```
$ svn checkout file:///usr/local/svnroot/bigshow/trunk BigShow
```

Notice that the url given to checkout includes the name of the project as well as the trunk. The "BigShow" at the end of the line tells subversion what to name the directory it creates to hold your working copy. Without that, you would have a directory named `trunk`, which is not very descriptive. You could also rename the `trunk` directory after the checkout has completed if you do not want to specify a file name at the end of the checkout command.

When checking out a project, always be sure to include the `trunk` directory at the end of your repository URL. If you leave out `trunk` you will bring down the tags and branches directories, which can unnecessarily consume a lot of local disk space.

Daily Workflow

Now that you have a working copy of your project, it is time to look at the Subversion commands you will use daily.

svn commit

To edit a file, you just edit the file. No need to ask anyone for permission to edit it. Open it up in `Xcode` or `emacs` or `vi` and hack away. When you have made and tested your changes and are ready to add them to the repository, use `svn commit`:

```
$ svn commit -m "Fixed dereference of NULL in para tag handler" \
    BigParse.m
Sending         BigParse.m
Transmitting file data .
Committed revision 3.
```

Subversion tells you what it is doing as it does it. The -m flag gives Subversion the log message you want to attach to the change. If you do not provide a commit message, Subversion will launch a text editor for you. It is a good idea to create detailed commit messages. That way your peers (or even yourself) can tell why particular changes have been made.

You can use svn commit with multiple files at one time, just specify the file names on the command line. If you do not supply any file names, Subversion will perform a commit with any modified file in the current directory and any subdirectories.

Commits in Subversion are atomic. If you commit multiple files at once they will all have the same revision number (and the same log message). All of the files will commit, or none of them will. This behavior has a number of benefits: Your coworkers will not ever catch you in "mid-commit", where you have half of your changed files committed and half still left to go. This is a common problem using CVS: if your peers update their world in the middle of your commit, the program will probably be in a broken state. For example, if they update their copy at a time when one of your changed .h file has been committed, but the corresponding .m file has not been committed yet, their project is now broken. Subversion avoids this problem.

You can also roll back changes in one operation if you discover a problem with the commit. You can examine the repository to see all changed files for a particular revision. This is handy in conjunction with a bug tracking system to match bug fixes with modified files.

svn diff

If you have made changes to files, you will frequently want to know what those changes are before you commit them. Nothing is more embarrassing than accidentally leaving in a pile of caveman debugging NSLog() statements. svn diff will compare your working copy of a file with the revision it came from and show you the differences between the two. For example:

```
$ svn diff BigParse.m
Index: BigParse.m
===================================================================
--- BigParse.m   (revision 9)
+++ BigParse.m   (working copy)
@@ -49,17 +49,17 @@
        case kCFXMLNodeTypeEntityReference:
            theText = CFXMLNodeGetString(node);
            if ([(NSString *)theText isEqual:@"lt"])
+               return @"<";
+           if ([(NSString *)theText isEqual:@"gt"])
                return @">";
-           if ([(NSString *)theText isEqual:@"gt"])
-               return @"<";
            if ([(NSString *)theText isEqual:@"t"])
                return @"\t";
```

```
-            if ([(NSString *)theText isEqual:@"bork"])
-                return @":-)";
+            if ([(NSString *)theText isEqual:@"spc"])
+                return @" ";

             NSLog(@"Unknown entity:%@", theText);
             return NULL;
```

Subversion uses what is known as a "Unified Diff" format, showing what lines were added (a plus sign in the margin) and removed (a minus sign in the margin). Changed lines have both a plus and a minus sign.

You can see in the listing that the `lt` and `gt` cases had their angle brackets reversed in the previous version, and are now using the correct one. This can be a little bit hard to visualize (but still easier to visualize than the CVS diff format).

The `spc` case has also been added, and the `bork` case has been removed. Subversion also shows you some lines of code around the change so you can see the change in context. One of the very nice features of Subversion is that `svn diff` does not need to connect to the repository (if you are using a repository across the network) to do the difference operation. You can be working on your code in a nice secluded spot, away from all network connections, and still be able to diff your changes. How Subversion manages this magic is discussed in the section about `.svn` Directories.

svn add

You can add new files and directories to your working copy at any time. When you are ready to add them to the repository, use `svn add`. It will schedule the files to be added (not they will not actually be added until the next `svn commit` command, as shown below).

For example, you may decide that `BigParse.m` is too big and needs to be split into two files. You would add the new files like this:

```
$ svn add BigParse2.[hm]
A         BigParse2.h
A         BigParse2.m
```

This schedules the two files to be added to the repository, but does not actually add them yet. (The `[hm]` in the command is a shell expression that will match the two files `BigParse2.h` and `BigParse2.m`). The "A" next to each file name means that the file will be added. You would do a `svn commit` to actually commit the addition of the new files to the repository.

```
$ svn commit -m "Split BigParse into two parts."
Adding         BigParse2.h
Adding         BigParse2.m
Transmitting file data ..
Committed revision 4.
```

You can commit both the addition of new files and changes to other files all at the same time. Because commits are atomic, everything will happen under one revision number, just like committing changes to multiple files. And do not worry if you edit the file between adding it and committing it. The add operation just schedules the addition of the file, and it does not care about the contents of the file.

Directories can be added as well as files, and the directories are versioned along with the files. This is an improvement over CVS, which doesn't version directories, it just keeps track of whether there is a directory or not.

svn rm

You can remove files from the repository. You may discover you did not need a particular file or directory. svn rm will schedule a file for removal:

```
$ svn rm BigParse2.[hm]
D          BigParse2.h
D          BigParse2.m
```

(The "D" beside each file name means the file is scheduled for removal / deletion.) And then, like the other commands, use svn commit to actually make the changes permanent:

```
$ svn commit -m "Didn't really need these files anyway."
Deleting        BigParse2.h
Deleting        BigParse2.m

Committed revision 5.
```

svn status

Say you have made a changes to a number of files. You can use svn status to get a listing of what Subversion will do on the next commit:

```
$ svn status
M       BigParse.h
M       BigParse.m
A       BigParse2.h
A       BigParse2.m
D       test-case23.txt
```

Here svn status shows that the BigParse.[hm] files were modified (indicated by the leading M), BigParse2.[hm] are scheduled to be added (the leading A), and test-case23.txt is scheduled to be deleted (the leading D).

Subversion can make these determinations without accessing the repository, so if you are using Subversion across a network, and are without network access, you can still use svn status and svn diff to see your changes. Committing your work of course will require you to be hooked up to the network.

If you want to see what files others have changed since you last updated your working copy, use svn status:

```
$ svn status --show-updates
        *       11    BigParse.m
        *       11    Slide.m
```

This says that someone else has made changes to BigParse.m and Slide.m, and the changes were made with a revision number of 11. This will hit the network if your repository is on another machine.

svn update

`svn update` is used to update your working copy with any changes that have been made to the repository. When other people commit changes to the repository, your working copy remains untouched. This way you can keep working on your stuff and not be affected by other's changes until you are ready for them. When you are ready to bring your working copy into sync with the repository, use `svn update`:

```
$ svn update
U  BigParse.m
U  Slide.h
Updated to revision 11.
```

The output says that someone else has updated `BigParse.m` and `Slide.h`. Your working copy now reflects the state of the repository as it is at revision 11. You may see other letters like A for newly added files, D for removed files, and G for changes that have been merged into files you have modified.

CVS users will need to break the habit of using "update" to see what local files have been modified. Instead, use `svn status`. Also, unlike CVS, `svn update` does not list locally modified files.

Updates and conflicts

When you `svn update` your working copy, Subversion tries its best to merge all the changes that everyone has made into your working copy. If you made a change at the start of a file and another person made a change at the end of the file, Subversion can merge these two changes automatically. But when you are working with other people on the same project, there is the possibility of conflicts. A conflict happens when you have made a change to a file at the same place someone else also made a change. Perhaps you changed a line but your peer deleted that line, or you both made different changes to the same line. In such cases, Subversion cannot figure out what to do without your help.

```
$ svn update
C  BigParse.m
Updated to revision 12.
```

The C indicates that a conflict happened. If you look in the file, you will see a conflict marker:

```
        break;
    case kCFXMLNodeTypeProcessingInstruction:
<<<<<<< .mine
        theClass = [Show classForElementName:
                        (NSString *)CFXMLNodeGetString(node)];
=======
        theText = CFXMLNodeGetString(node);
        return (void*)theText;
>>>>>>> .r12
        break;
    case kCFXMLNodeTypeComment:
        return NULL;
```

In this code, I made a change to the `kCFXMLNodeTypeProcessingInstruction` case that wants to get a class for element name, but my peer wants to return the node's string. Between the $<<<<<<<$ .mine part and ======= is the text as it exists in my working copy (which happens to be revision 11). In the next section of the above listing is the text as it exists in the repository (revision 12). To fix the conflict, edit the file between the markers so that the file is in the correct state (hopefully coordinating with the other programmer to work out the cause of the conflict).

In addition to adding these markers to the file, Subversion creates three files, BigParse.m.mine, BigParse.m.r11, and BigParse.m.r12. The .mine file is a copy of BigParse.m (with your changes in it) before the conflict markers have been added. The .r11 file is how the file exists in the repository for the revision that your working copy of BigParse.m is based on, and the .r12 file is the most recent version in the repository. Neither the .r11 and .r12 files have conflict markers in them. If you find that editing the conflict markers is inconvenient (like there are dozens of them), you can copy one of these three files over your copy of BigParse.m, or use them with a diff tool to solve the conflict.

After you have solved the conflict, tell Subversion that it is resolved using svn resolved:

```
$ svn resolved BigParse.m
Resolved conflicted state of 'BigParse.m'
```

This will remove the extra files Subversion created. You need to do this step before you commit your changes:

```
$ svn commit -m "Revised node type processing" BigParse.m
Sending        BigParse.m
Transmitting file data .
Committed revision 13.
```

Note to CVS users: svn resolved is an extra step required by Subversion when resolving conflicts.

svn annotate

The svn annotate will annotate a file so that every line shows what revision last changed that line and who made the change. This can be handy to see when a particular change (whether a bug was removed, or one was introduced) happened. Most often this is used in the latter setting, so the Subversion developers (who have a sense of humor) call it the svn blame command too. (svn praise is another way of running the same command). svn annotate is the emotionally neutral version of the concept, so I will be using that (plus it parallels the cvs annotate command). By default svn annotate sends the output to standard out, so you will usually want to redirect the output to a file:

```
$ svn annotate BigParse.m > BigParse.m-annotated
```

And a portion of that file looks like this:

```
    . . .
        2        markd            break;
        2        markd            case kCFXMLNodeTypeProcessingInstruction:
       13        markd                theClass = [Show classForElementName:
       13        markd                    (NSString *)CFXMLNodeGetString(node)];
        2        markd            break;
```

```
6       bork        case kCFXMLNodeTypeComment:
6       bork            return NULL;
6       bork            break;
2       markd       case kCFXMLNodeTypeText:
```

Here you can see the result of the conflict resolution in revision 13, and see also that the bork user added the nodeTypeComment section in revision 6.

svn log

Earlier it was mentioned that you should use good check-in comments. These comments are displayed by `svn log` to show you the revision history of a file.

```
$ svn log BigParse.m
------------------------------------------------------------------
r13 | markd | 2005-03-27 23:44:42 -0500 (Sun, 27 Mar 2005) | 1 line

Revised node type processing
------------------------------------------------------------------
r12 | bork | 2005-03-27 23:09:35 -0500 (Sun, 27 Mar 2005) | 1 line

Added new logic to node type processing
------------------------------------------------------------------
r4 | markd | 2005-03-26 16:48:15 -0500 (Sun, 27 Mar 2005) | 1 line

Split BigParse into two parts.
------------------------------------------------------------------
r3 | markd | 2005-03-26 16:48:15 -0500 (Sat, 26 Mar 2005) | 1 line

Fixed dereference of NULL in para tag handler
------------------------------------------------------------------
r2 | markd | 2005-03-26 15:38:31 -0500 (Sat, 26 Mar 2005) | 1 line

initial import
------------------------------------------------------------------
```

For each committed revision, the information shown is the revision number the change happened in, the user responsible for the change, when it happened, how many lines are in the revision comment, followed by the revision comment. It does not show you how many lines were actually changed in the revision.

Specifying Revisions

Several Subversion commands (like `diff`, `annotate`, `update`, `log`) can take an optional flag, `--revision` / `-r` to specify a particular revision the command should take a look at. You can specify a particular revision:

```
$ svn log -r 12 BigParse.m
------------------------------------------------------------------
r12 | bork | 2005-03-27 23:09:35 -0500 (Sun, 27 Mar 2005) | 1 line

Added new logic to node type processing
------------------------------------------------------------------
```

If a file was not changed in a particular revision, (such as revision 5), you will get an empty log message:

```
$ svn log -r5 BigParse.m
------------------------------------------------------------------------
```

You can specify a range of revisions by separating the start and end of the range (inclusive) with a colon:

```
$ svn log -r2:4 BigParse.m
------------------------------------------------------------------------
r4 | markd | 2005-03-26 16:48:15 -0500 (Sun, 27 Mar 2005) | 1 line

Split BigParse into two parts.
------------------------------------------------------------------------
r3 | markd | 2005-03-26 16:48:15 -0500 (Sat, 26 Mar 2005) | 1 line

Fixed dereference of NULL in para tag handler
------------------------------------------------------------------------
r2 | markd | 2005-03-26 15:38:31 -0500 (Sat, 26 Mar 2005) | 1 line

initial import
------------------------------------------------------------------------
```

You can also specify a date in curly braces:

```
$ svn log -r {2005-03-27} BigParse.m
------------------------------------------------------------------------
r4 | markd | 2005-03-26 16:48:15 -0500 (Sun, 27 Mar 2005) | 1 line

Split BigParse into two parts.
------------------------------------------------------------------------
```

When you specify a date, Subversion shows you the log file of the revision of the file as it existed at that point in time. The date format also works with `svn annotate`, and with `svn update` to bring down the revision as of a particular date. (Note that csh users users will need to escape the curly braces with backslashes.)

You can specify a time as well. You need to quote the date and time because of the space in there (otherwise the shell gets confused):

```
$ svn log -r { "2005-03-27 16:48:00" } BigParse.m
```

There is one gotcha, if you do not specify a time, like `-r { "2005-03-26 16:48:15"}`, the date is interpreted as midnight on that date. Doing `svn log -r {2005-03-26}` will show the latest revision as of midnight that starts the 26th, not showing any changes that were made for the rest of the day.

If you want to see what a file looked like a particular revision or point in time, use `svn update`:

```
$ svn update -r 4 BigParse.m
U  BigParse.m
Updated to revision 4.
```

To get back to the HEAD revision, use the HEAD keyword for the revision name:

```
$ svn update -r HEAD BigParse.m
U  BigParse.m
Updated to revision 13.
```

This will override the file in your working copy.

There are a number of useful keywords you can use for revisions:

HEAD

> latest version in the repository

BASE

> pristine version of revision of the file in the working copy.

COMMITTED

> last revision which the file changed before (or at) BASE.

PREV

> The revision just before the last revision in which an item changed. You can think of it as COMMITTED - 1.

So, if BigParse.m is at version 14, and the last modified version was version 10, then BASE would be version 14, COMMITTED would be version 10, and PREV would be version 9.

Using these keywords, you can do some handy operations:

Show the last change committed to BigParse.m:

```
$ svn diff -r PREV:COMMITTED BigParse.m
```

Show the checkin message for the most recent commit:

```
$ svn log -r HEAD BigParse.m
```

Compare the working revision to the latest version in the repository:

```
$ svn diff -r HEAD BigParse.m
```

If you use svn diff without the -r HEAD option, the diff will happen against the revision your working copy is based on. If revision 13 is the version your working copy is based on and the repository has had a change to BigParse.m checked in at revision 16, svn diff BigParse.m will compare against version 13. Using svn diff -r HEAD BigParse.m, the diff will compare the local BigParse.m with version 16.

The previous command compares the current working copy (including any local modifications) with the HEAD version. If you want to see what change were made to the file, without considering your local changes, use this command:

```
$ svn diff -r BASE:HEAD BigParse.m
```

This tells `svn diff` to fetch the BASE version (what the working copy is based on) and the HEAD version (most recent committed version) and compare them.

To see the commit log messages since the last update, use

```
$ svn log -r BASE:HEAD
```

Tagging and Branching

Tagging

One common operation in revision control systems is associating a human-readable tag with a particular set of versions of a set of files. For example, you have been working on BigShow for awhile and you are ready to release version 1.0 to the world. You would want to tag the source files so you could go back and rebuild version 1.0 (say to fix bugs), as well as to figure out what changes have been made from version 1.0 in later versions.

In Subversion, making a tag is actually a copy operation that happens in the repository. The current versions of the files of the project are copied into the tags directory in the repository. (Now you see why the tags directory was created before importing the project.)

The easiest way to make a tag off of the HEAD revision is to use `svn copy`, supplying an URL for the project's trunk, and the destination in the tags directory:

```
$ svn copy file:///usr/local/svnroot/bigshow/trunk \
       file:///usr/local/svnroot/bigshow/tags/release-1.0 \
       -m "Tag for BigShow 1.0"

Committed revision 20.
```

If you get an error like `svn: Out of date: 'bigshow' in transaction '18-1'`, that usually means that you do not have a tags directory, or misspelled part of one of the source or destination urls for the copy command.

Now, any time in the future, you can check out the code that went into BigShow 1.0:

```
$ svn checkout \
     file:///usr/local/svnroot/BigShow/tags/release-1.0 \
     bigshow-1.0
A   bigshow-1.0/MyDocument.m
A   bigshow-1.0/BigWindow.h
A   bigshow-1.0/main.m
...
A   bigshow-1.0/Image.m
A   bigshow-1.0/PrefsController.m
Checked out revision 27.
```

The "Checked out revision" number can be ignored. It just shows what the current revision count (which is global to the repository) is, and isn't the revision the tag was checked in as.

And if you wanted to see the tags that have already been made for the BigShow project, use the `svn ls` command, which lists files in the repository:

```
$ svn ls file:///usr/local/svnroot/bigshow/tags
release-1.0/
release-1.1/
```

Repository URLS

You have seen some commands that include a reference to the repository (such as the `file:///` URLs in the `svn ls` and `svn copy` commands above), and sometimes commands are done without directly referencing the repository. When you explicitly mention the repository, you are performing an operation directly on the files and revisions in the repository. You do not need to have a working copy to do your work against. So, the command you saw earlier:

```
$ svn copy file:///usr/local/svnroot/bigshow/trunk \
        file:///usr/local/svnroot/bigshow/tags/release-1.0 \
        -m "Tag for BigShow 1.0"
```

Means "copy the trunk, in the repository in the bigshow project, into the `tags` directory of the big show project, naming it release-1.0". You can run this command from anywhere - from your home directory, from a working copy, or from some unrelated project.

Other commands, like the `svn log` commands are usually used against a local copy:

```
$ svn log BigParse.m
```

But you can use these commands on the repository, in case you do not have a working copy handy.

```
$ svn log \
file:///usr/local/svnroot/bigshow/trunk/BigParse.m
```

Branching

Another common operation performed with revision control systems is branching. A branch is made when you want to perform work on a file in parallel. Say that `BigParse.m` in version 1.0 of `BigShow` had some errors that are causing problems for an Important Customer. You want to fix the errors and give the customer an updated version. Problem is, `BigParse.m` is in the middle of a re-write for version 1.1. If it was a car, it would be up on blocks leaking oil. You do not want to undo all of the work that's been done for version 1.1 just so you can fix the 1.0 errors, but you also do not want to use the half-rewritten version as the basis for the fix for `BigShow` 1.0.

Branching solves this difficulty. By making a branch based on the 1.0 version of `BigShow`, work can be done there to fix the problems in `BigParse.m`, and the re-write can continue on the HEAD for `BigShow` 1.1.

Making a branch is just like making a tag, you just stick it into the branches directory of the project in the repository:

```
$ svn copy \
    file:///usr/local/svnroot/bigshow/tags/release-1.0 \
```

```
file:///usr/local/svnroot/bigshow/branches/branch-1.0 \
-m "Branch for BigShow 1.0"
Committed revision 22.
```

And then you can check out the branch and make modifications:

```
$ svn checkout \
  file:///usr/local/svnroot/BigShow/branches/branch-1.0
A  branch-1.0/MyDocument.m
A  branch-1.0/BigWindow.h
A  branch-1.0/main.m
...
A  branch-1.0/Image.m
A  branch-1.0/PrefsController.m
Checked out revision 22.
```

`branch-1.0` is now a working copy, so you can go into it, make changes, and `svn commit` them back to the repository. Work done in this branch will not affect the work that is being done on the `HEAD`.

Branching vs. Tagging

Both branching and tagging are done with `svn copy`, so what is the difference? There is actually no difference between branches and tags as far as Subversion is concerned (which is different from many other version control systems, including CVS). By convention, tagged revisions usually do not get changed - only work done in the branch gets committed, but that is just a convention.

You may also be thinking "with all that copying going on, won't my repository get huge?" Subversion is actually very smart about making copies. The developers call the technology "Smart Copies". Only the differences are kept between files in the branch and the version the branch is based off of. For changed files, only the changes are kept around. For unchanged files, only a pointer to the original version of the file is kept. This is only a handful of bytes, no matter how big the file actually is. Feel free to make as many tags or branches as are appropriate.

Properties

Subversion lets you store arbitrary metadata on your files and directories. Some of this metadata information (which is versioned along with the file's contents) is used by Subversion, and some can be used for your own purposes.

Subversion calls this metadata "properties". Properties are textual key/value pairs. You could use a property to store a quick to-do list for a file by using the `svn propset` command:

```
$ svn propset "todo" \
"need to reflux the frobulator" BigParse.m
property 'todo' set on 'BigParse.m'
```

You can also use `propedit`, which cranks up your configured editor program to let you edit the properties.

Because properties are versioned you will need to commit them before they become visible to others. `svn status` shows the modification state for properties:

```
$ svn status
  M     BigParse.m
```

Notice that the M (for modification) is in the second column of the output. The first column of svn status output regards changes to the file itself, the second column shows the status of properties. Here it shows that BigParse.m has had a property change, but not any changes to the file. Had there been changes to the file, the line would have had MM before it. Commit the file to send the property change to the repository:

```
$ svn commit -m "updated todo" BigParse.m
Sending        BigParse.m
Committed revision 25.
```

Use svn propget to retrieve the value of a property:

```
$ svn propget todo BigParse.m
need to reflux the frobulator
```

When you are done with a property, use svn propdel:

```
$ svn propdel todo BigParse.m
property 'todo' deleted from 'BigParse.m'.
```

```
$ svn commit -m "removed todo property" BigParse.m
Sending        BigParse.m
```

There are some properties that are meaningful to Subversion which you can set:

svn:executable

> Use this to control the executable bit for a file. Set it to a non-empty value ("*" is good) so that Subversion will ensure that the executable bit stays set for this file.

svn:mime-type

> Indicates the kind of content stored in the file. If the mime-type is non-empty, and is not a text mime type (text mime types are things like as text/plain or text/html), then Subversion will treat the file as a binary file, not attempting to do line-based merging. Also, the Subversion Apache module will use the mime-type to set the Content-Type HTTP header. Subversion automatically sets the mime-types for some files when doing an import:

```
$ svn propget svn:mime-type logo.gif
application/octet-stream
```

svn:keywords

> Controls the substitution of keywords in files. Users of RCS and CVS are familiar with keywords, such as $LastChangedBy: $ and $Id: $, which get expanded when a file is checked in. $LastChangedBy: $ becomes $LastChangedBy: markd $ when I check in a file. Likewise $Id: $ expands to a line of information about the check-in. RCS and CVS expand keywords by default, requiring you to turn off expansion for files that might be corrupted by them.

Subversion, on the other hand, does not expand keywords by default. You turn them on by setting the property `svn:keywords` to a space-separated list of keywords to substitute. For `BigParse.m`, we want to an `$Id: $` and `$HeadURL: $`, which will give id information and the full url of the file in the repository.

```
// BigParse.m
// $Id: $
// $HeadURL: $

#import <CoreFoundation/CFXMLParser.h>
...
```

Then the property is set on the file, and the file committed:

```
$ svn propset svn:keywords "Id HeadURL" BigParse.m
property 'svn:keywords' set on 'BigParse.m'

$ svn commit -m "added keyword property" BigParse.m
Sending          BigParse.m
Transmitting file data .
Committed revision 28.
```

Then when you look at `BigParse.m`, the keywords have been expanded:

```
// BigParse.m
// $Id: BigParse.m 28 2005-04-03 02:30:34Z markd $
// $HeadURL: file:///usr/local/svnroot/BigShow/trunk/BigParse.m $

#import <CoreFoundation/CFXMLParser.h>
...
```

`svn:externals`

Lets you specify additional projects to include in the working copy when a checkout is made. Say that `BigShow` uses a third-party library. You could download their source code using their subversion repository directly and import the code into your working copy. If you do this, you won't pick up any changes made to the external code.

If you use `svn:externals`, you can include infrastructure components, such as utility frameworks, and to make umbrella projects, where checking out a single project can pull down the source code for a bunch of other projects.

To use `svn:externals`, set that property on the directory which will hold the third-party (or framework) files. The value is a multi-line table of directory names, and Subversion repository URLS.

For example, `BigShow` may decide to use a third-party animation package for doing slide transitions and start using a Ranch-wide framework of utilities. Use `svn propset` or `svn propedit` to set the `svn:externals` property. You will probably want to use `svn propedit` to crank up your favorite editor, because this property involves multiple lines. This is what the property would look like after setting it:

```
$ svn propget svn:externals BigShow
transitions http://svn.groovymation.net/repos/transitions
frameworks      file:///usr/local/svnroot/frameworks
```

Now, when you do a `svn checkout` or a `svn update`, these repositories will be consulted too, and their contents downloaded. `BigShow/`transitions will have the slide transitions stuff, and frameworks will have the common frameworks.

Subversion knows that these directories are external, so it won't automatically recurse into the directories when doing commits. `svn status` shows a status code of x for the externals directories.

System Administration Issues

There are some administrative issues to be aware of when using Subversion. Even if someone else is doing all of the system administration for you, it is good to be aware of these.

.svn Directories

The first involves disk space. Luckily in today's world of mammoth hard drives, disk space usually is not a problem. Subversion is designed with today's large drives in mind. Inside of each directory of every working copy is a hidden directory called `.svn`. This contains a number of administrative files that help Subversion know what particular versions of files are being used in the working copy. Complete copies of all the files under Subversion control are kept here as well. So if `BigParse.m` is 10K, there will be 10K consumed in the repository for that file (along with any changes made), plus 10K for `BigParse.m` in your local copy, plus another 10K for a copy of `BigParse.m` in the `.svn` directory. For small files on big disks, that is not a big deal. If you are keeping a 500 megabyte QuickTime movie file in Subversion with a local repository on a cramped disk, you may run into disk space problems.

So why waste that space keeping copies of files in the `.svn` directory? It is actually a pretty useful feature. The copy of each file that is kept in the `.svn` directory is the pristine version of that file's current revision. This is how `svn status` (see what is different) and `svn diff` (against the version the changes are based on) are able to work without hitting the repository. When you are working with a networked repository, being able to do a lot of work remotely (including doing status and diffs) is really nice. You can take the laptop to that beach in Aruba and get some work done without having to be on the network.

Making Backups

Anyone who cares about their data wants to make sure things are kept backed up. If you are using the FSFS style of Subversion repository, you can just use the typical operating system tools to back up the files (such as `dump`, `tar`, `rsync`, `ditto`, and so on). Changes to the Subversion repository are atomic, so you do not have to worry about an important file changing while you are making a copy of it, leaving you with a corrupt version of the file. Backing up BerkeleyDB repositories is more work (which is another reason to use FSFS)

Remote Repositories

One of the nice things about Subversion is that it is equally facile with a repository that is located across the network as it is with a local repository. Having a network-available repository is very useful for collaborative projects where multiple people are using the same repository and making changes to the same sets of files. It is also handy for single-programmer projects, having a repository on a central "server" machine, and using that repository from your laptop in the back yard.

Apache

Subversion currently has two different forms of remote repositories. One uses the Apache web server and WebDAV file system. You can use existing Apache modules that add advanced features (such as sophisticated authentication schemes). You talk to the repository using `http://` (standard web protocol) or `https://` (secure encrypted web protocol) URLS:

```
$ svn checkout \
    https://svn.bignerdranch.com/bnr/bigshow/trunk bigshow

Checked out revision 22
```

Actually setting up Apache to serve remote Subversion repositories is beyond the scope of this book, but there are walkthrough guides available on the internet (see the resources section of the book website for pointers.)

svnserv

`svnserv` is a lightweight, easy to set up server included with Subversion. You can run `svnserv` on the machine that hosts the repository, and have the server listen on a network port through which you can checkout files and commit changes. There are instructions for configuring svnserv in the Subversion documentation. You access `svnserv` repositories using the `svn://` URL format.

svn+ssh

For single users of Subversion, or for small groups in one company or on a LAN, you can quickly set up a networked repository using `svnserv` and `ssh` (secure shell). If you have a login available by `ssh` on the remote machine, you can access a Subversion repository there by using `svn+ssh://` URLS. Using this, Subversion will initiate an `ssh` connection, and then on the remote side start a private `svnserv` which accesses the repository. For instance:

```
 $ svn checkout \
svn+ssh://192.168.254.42/Users/markd/junk/svnroot/BigShow/trunk \
BigShow-remote
 markd@192.168.254.42's password:
 A  BigShow-remote/MyDocument.m
 A  BigShow-remote/BigWindow.h
 A  BigShow-remote/main.m
 ...
 A  BigShow/Image.m
 A  BigShow/PrefsController.m
 Checked out revision 28.
```

Subversion will ask for your password each time you perform an operation that needs to access the repository. Local operations, such as some `svn diffs` and `svn status` just access the local `.svn` directory rather than over the network. You can avoid having to enter your password each time by creating an `ssh` keypair or using `ssh-agent` to do passwordless `ssh` connections. Check the man pages for `ssh` and `ssh-agent` for more details.

Mac OS X Weirdness

Not surprisingly, Subversion under Mac OS X has some issues that other Unix platforms do not have.

Bundled Files

The first involves file bundles, the directories that act like files under Mac OS X, such as `Interface Builder` nib files or `Xcode` project files. Subversion does not treat these bundles as individual files. Instead, the directory for the bundles is checked in, as are the individual files inside of it. Once it is checked in, you can use Interface Builder and `Xcode`, and check in changes. Just be aware when you do operations on bundles that you will be seeing the moving parts of the bundle's contents in the `svn` output:

```
$ svn commit -m "added new AppController class and instance" \
   MainMenu.nib
Sending          MainMenu.nib/classes.nib
Sending          MainMenu.nib/info.nib
Sending          MainMenu.nib/objects.nib
Transmitting file data ...
Committed revision 23.
```

There is one gotcha relating to bundled files and Subversion. Recall the `.svn` metadata directory which lives in every directory of your working copy. Therefore there is a `.svn` directory in the `MainMenu.nib` directory. The programs that edit bundled files have to be aware that there is a `.svn` directory, and the programs need to preserve it when they save changes to the file. `Interface Builder` and `Xcode` preserve the `.svn` directory, so life is groovy.

Applications targeted more to end-users apps, like `TextEdit`'s RTFD files, and `Keynote` will not preserve the `.svn` directory, so if you want to keep these kinds of bundled files in Subversion, you will need to make sure to preserve the `.svn` directory. You could write a shell script to move the `.svn` directory to a safe place before you open a Keynote file, and then have another script restore the `.svn` directory right before you commit your changes.

Xcode

`Xcode` has support for basic Subversion commands from the **SCM** (Source Code Management) menu. You can update your projects, see differences between versions, and commit new version. If `Xcode`'s **SCM** menu has just one item that says

"SCM Unavailable" you will need to enable it in the inspector for the top-level project in the Groups & Files panel, as shown in Figure 24-4

Figure 24-4. Project Inspector

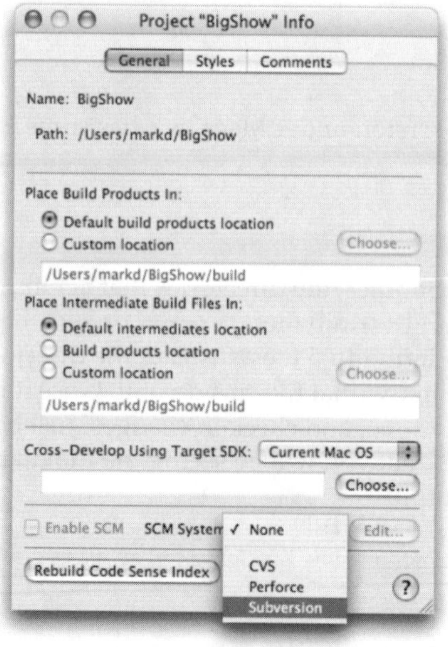

You first need to choose an SCM system, then check the Enable SCM check box. You may want to click the Edit button as well, which tells Xcode where to find the svn program. By default, Xcode looks in /usr/local/subversion/bin/svn. Most Subversion packages place the executable at /usr/local/bin/svn.

Once SCM is active, the Xcode project window will grow an SCM item which shows files that are modified or unknown, as shown in Figure 24-5, which shows that BigParse.m has been modified, as has project.pbxproj.markd.pbxuser has not been added to the repository, so it is marked with a question mark. The main file pane also grows an SCM column which shows this information.

Figure 24-5. Xcode with SCM Display

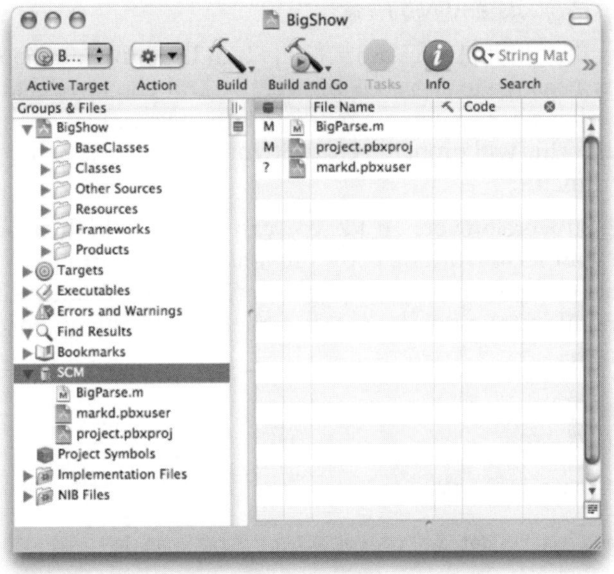

To commit the changes, select one or more files and choose Commit Changes from the SCM menu. Xcode will prompt you for a commit message. If you want to see the log of changes to the file, select the file, open the file's inspector, and click the SCM tag, as shown in Figure 24-6. You can also see the difference between version, and get an annotation.

Figure 24-6. Xcode File Inspector

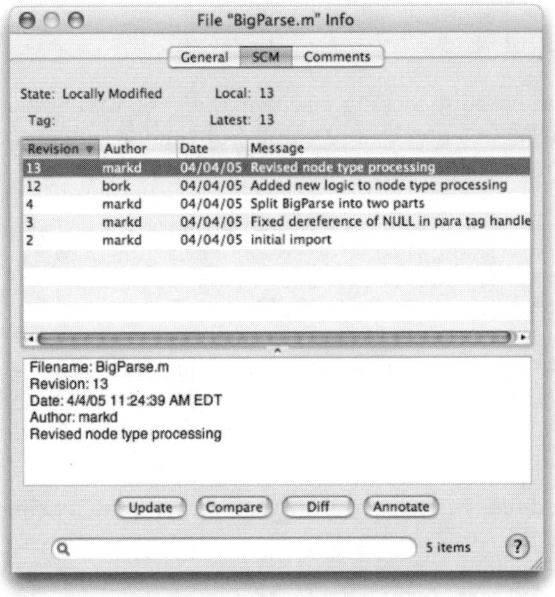

Conflicts with Projects and Nib Files

Xcode project files and nib files are actually bundles containing opaque files. If your peer commits a change to an Xcode project file, and you have changed it locally too, Subversion will insert text conflict markers into the changed opaque files within the project bundle. This will probably corrupt your project file, or at least make undoing the changes difficult.

Starting with Subversion version 1.2, you can lock files (in the repository) while you edit them in your local working copy, preventing others from checking in changes until yours are committed. Xcode project files, Interface Builder nib files, and any other bundled files (frameworks, for example) should always be locked while making changes.

Subversion Locking

To lock a file, use svn lock:

```
$ svn lock -m "Updating treewalking" BigParse.h
'BigParse.h' locked by user 'markd'.
```

If another user tries to lock the file, they will get an error:

```
$ svn lock -m "Doing some work" BigParse.h
svn: Path 'BigParse.h' is locked by user 'markd'
     in filesystem '/usr/local/svnroot/db'
```

Unfortunately, Subversion does not let you lock directories, so to lock a nib bundle, you will need to lock each of the individual files:

```
$ svn lock -m "Adding Debug menu" MainMenu.nib/*
'objects.nib' locked by user 'markd'.
'info.nib' locked by user 'markd'.
'classes.nib' locked by user 'markd'.
```

To make a bundle require locking, use svn propset to set the svn:needs-lock proeprty. When set to a non-empty value, Subversion will make the files within the bundle read-only until a lock is taken out on it.

```
$ svn propset svn:needs-lock "" MainMenu.nib/*
property 'svn:needs-lock' set on 'classes.nib'
property 'svn:needs-lock' set on 'info.nib'
property 'svn:needs-lock' set on 'objects.nib'
```

After setting this property, the next time anyone performs an svn update, their MainMenu.nib files will become read-only. If they open the nib in Interface Builder, it will let them know it is read-only. (To edit the nib, they would need to take out lock on it.)

To see the locked files in your repository, along with the locking comment, use svnadmin lslocks:

```
$ svnadmin lslocks /usr/local/svnroot
Path: /BigParse.h
```

```
UUID Token: opaquelocktoken:2eca0ee4-dff3-0310-9e24-b4399cd8fbf9
Owner: markd
Created: 2005-04-03 18:37:39 -0400 (Sun, 03 Apr 2005)
Expires:
Comment (1 line):
Updating treewalking
```

.svn Directory in Built Applications with Xcode *1.5 and Earlier*

The .svn directory, even though it is a Subversion implementation detail, is
something you have to be aware of if you are using Xcode 1.5 or earlier (this is fixed
in Xcode 2.0). Because the .svn control files exist in all directories, they exist in all
bundled files, including nib files. So, when you build your application, your nib files
are copied into the Application bundle, and those nib files carry along the .svn
directories too. If your nib files are large, they will be even larger if they carry the
.svn directories along. You can fix this by adding a shell script build phase.

In Xcode, choose **Project->New Build Phase->New Shell Script Build Phase**. A new
shell script will be added to your target. Select the shell script files phase, open the
inspector, and use this script (all on one line, even though it is on two lines here):

```
find "$BUILD_DIR/$WRAPPER_NAME" -name .svn -exec rm -rf {} \;
    >& /dev/null
```

This will walk the directories in the built application removing any .svn directories
it finds there.

Summary

Subversion is a powerful, easy to use, open-source revision control system. It can be
used for single-programmer projects, as well as for large projects with hundreds of
developers spread across the globe.

Chapter 25. Performance Tuning

It is happened to all of us: We have written our program, subjected it to real world data, and discover that performance is sub-optimal (ranging from "could be faster" to "locks up instantly"). Finding out what the performance problem is can be a difficult task. Many times we think we know where the problem is, but the initial idea turns out to be wrong. Luckily there are a number of tools available to give definite metrics of where the program spends its time, and what kind of pressure it puts on the OS in general.

End to Free Performance is Nigh!

Over the last several decades, computer performance has been doubling about every 18 months, a figure attributable to Moore's Law. There are lots of versions of Moore's law, but the one I will invoke here is "The number of transistors in microchips will double about every 18 months" We have been seeing doublings of performance figures over that time period which has been helped along with increases in the clock frequency of the processors (from megahertz to gigahertz)

As software developers, we have (as an industry) had the luxury of writing sub-optimal code while improvements in computer hardware have masked inefficiencies. This has allowed us to tackle larger, more interesting problems without having to obsess over every cycle; and let us use simpler algorithms with more expensive orders of complexity.

The major chip manufacturers have hit a hard barrier in the race to crank up clock speeds. Moore's Law regarding those transistors is still in force, though. Manufacturers are still cramming more and more transistors into their processors, but these transistors are being used in other places. In particular, they are being used to increase parallelism.

Newer chips of the PowerPC and Intel varieties take advantage of internal parallelism, having multiple integer and floating point units to do calculations in parallel, plus the Altivec and SSE2 (Streaming SIMD Extensions, while SIMD is an acronym for Single Instruction / Multiple Data) vector processors which also work in parallel with the other processing units.

Processors these days are also going to mutlicore and hyperthreaded architectures. Multicore chips have several distinct CPUs on one physical chip. The processors operate in parallel to each other and have their own logic units. Hyperthread processors have two or more threads operating in parallel in a single CPU. Hyperthreads still share stuff like processor cache and math units, but it still allows the processor to chew through more instructions in a given time period.

The design decisions occurring on the hardware side of the world are going to have an impact on us living on the software side of the world. Writing efficient code is coming back into style because we cannot count on processors "just getting faster" to help us.

Parallel code will become more and more prevalent to take advantage of these muticore and hyperthreaded architectures (not to mention multiple CPUs in a single computer). Parallel code usually is the domain of the more advanced programmers because of of the difficulty in the writing correct concurrent programs. As you saw in Chapter 22 (Multithreading), there are a lot of issues that make parallel development difficult. More programmers will be needing to learn about this world and its problems so that we (as an industry) can continue developing software that behaves correctly and has the performance the users have come to expect.

The fact that users are dealing with ever-growing sets of data does not help the problem either. As computers got more powerful, users were using them to do more stuff to larger sets data. Take a look at iPhoto. People first used iPhoto to manage small libraries of relatively small photos. Now that we have bigger hard drives, faster machines, and cheap digital cameras that take high resolution pictures, users create huge photo libraries of enormous images. Users will also expect to be able to sling around ever larger sets of data as time goes on. They will not particularly care to hear any excuses about the megahertz barrier.

Approaches To Performance

Programmers are notoriously bad at being able to locate performance problems, most likely all of the readily apparent performance issues have already been addressed. I know I am usually surprised at the cause of my performance problems. Sometimes it looks obvious in retrospect, but it sure was not obvious at the time.

The key to keeping on top of your performance is to use profiling tools. Profile early, and profile often. Catch performance issues early in your development so you do not build a lot of code around an inefficient core.

But be careful to not totally contort your design early-on in the quest for Optimal Performance. You might be addressing performance issues that might not have a real impact on your final product. If you use Shark (or other performance tools) regularly, you can see possible performance issues on the horizon before they come close and bite you.

Be sure to profile with each new revision of the OS, and on new hardware. As Apple changes Mac OS X under the hood, things that were optimal may now be suboptimal, and vice-versa. Hardware changes can change the game performance-wise. As we will see later, the G5 processor changes the game when it comes to look-up tables. On G4 and older processors, using a look-up table can still be faster than calculating a value, but on the G5 the reverse is often the case. Having situations like this can be a real problem if you have to support older versions of the OS, or if you are wanting to optimally target vastly different hardware.

Reports from profilers are not gospel. It may highlight a performance problem, but the problem may be something you do not need to fix. If a problem highlighted by a profiler will not affect the user experience of your program, or is something that happens only once in a long while, you can put your energies into optimizing something else.

Finally, do not just profile your development builds. If you use different compiler flags for deployment builds (particularly when using higher optimization levels), you will want to do some profiling on your final build, so that you do not waste time fixing some code paths that will change with compiler optimizations.

Major Causes of Performance Problems

Performance problems typically come from one or more of 5 major areas: algorithms, memory usage, CPU usage, disk usage, and graphics. Granted, that is pretty much everything your program interacts with in the computer, and is a bit like saying "Everything gives you cancer." You can use performance tools to look at each aspect of computer performance in isolation to get a better handle on your overall performance issues, even if one problem is causing problems in a several categories.

Memory

Even though modern machines have large amounts of memory, RAM is still a scarce resource. Macintosh systems historically have had slower memory busses than their PC brethren, and low-end consumer Macs have slower memory access than their high-end workstation siblings. This makes memory operations slow.

Typically, when optimizing, if you optimize to reduce your memory usage (optimizing for space) you will also get speedups as well since the processor is not waiting for all that extra data to arrive from memory. Also, since Mac OS X is a shared system with daemons running, with each user running lots of programs of their own, and potentially multiple users logged in, it is good to be conservative with your memory usage. This can be a tough discipline, since each process has its own wide-open address space to play in.

Locality of Reference

Locality of reference is a term that means that memory accesses happen near each other. Reading a hundred bytes off of one 4k page is faster than reading one byte from a hundred different pages scattered across the address space. The processor grabs a sequence of bytes every time it goes to memory, so if you set up your loops to operate on memory sequentially, you can see a performance boost.

Example 25-1 creates a large two dimensional global array and accesses it in two different ways.

Example 25-1. locality.m

```
// locality.m -- time the effect of locality of reference

/* compile with
cc -g -Wall -o locality locality.m
*/

#include <stdio.h>    // for printf
#include <time.h>     // for time_t, time()
#include <stdlib.h>   // for EXIT_SUCCESS

#define ARRAYSIZE (10000)
int a[ARRAYSIZE][ARRAYSIZE]; // make a huge array

int main (int argc, char *argv[])
{
    int i = 0, j = 0;
    time_t starttime;
    time_t endtime;

    starttime = time(NULL);

    // walk the array in row-major order, so that once we're done
    // with a page we never bother with it again
```

```
for (i = 0; i < ARRAYSIZE; i++){
    for(j = 0; j < ARRAYSIZE; j++){
        a[i][j] = 1;
    }
}

endtime = time(NULL);

printf("%d operations in %d seconds.\n", i * j,
        (int)(endtime - starttime));

starttime = time(NULL);

// walk the array in column-major order. We end
// up touching a bunch of pages multiple times

for (j = 0; j < ARRAYSIZE; j++){
    for(i = 0; i < ARRAYSIZE; i++){
        a[i][j] = 1;
    }
}

endtime = time(NULL);

printf("%d operations in %d seconds.\n", i * j,
        (int)(endtime - starttime));

return (EXIT_SUCCESS);

} // main
```

Here is a sample run:

```
$ ./locality
100000000 operations in 21 seconds.
100000000 operations in 106 seconds.
```

A simple reversal the for loops can give you a 5x performance penalty! The first loop follows the way that C has the array's memory organized, as shown in Figure 25-1. That is, the loop accessing adjacent bytes. As the loop works through the array it has good locality of reference. Memory pages are accessed only once, and after the loop has stopped manipulating memory on a page that page is no longer used.

Figure 25-1. Good memory access pattern

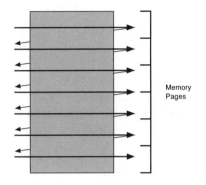

The second loop works "across the grain", as shown in Figure 25-2. It ends up hitting every page used by the array every time through the loop. This puts a lot of pressure on the virtual memory system and causes it to waste time manipulating its internal data structures.

Figure 25-2. Bad memory access pattern

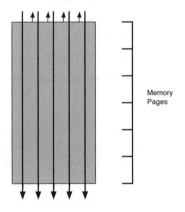

Caches

One technique that is often suggested when there are performance problems (especially when there are disk I/O problems) is to perform aggressive caching. The thought behind caching is you can save on disk I/O by doing it once and keeping the results in memory.

This technique can have some drawbacks in system like Mac OS X that employs virtual memory and paging. Recall that memory that has not been accessed in a while, and that could be used by other processes can be paged out to disk.

If do you choose to cache information, it is best to split up your cache data and the metadata that describes the cached data. You do not want to use an architecture like Figure 25-3 which intermixes the cache data and the metadata.

Figure 25-3. Bad Locality of Reference

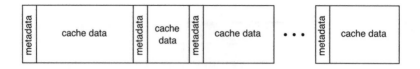

Instead, organize your data as shown in Figure 25-4 Keep your metadata together because you will have good locality of reference when walking your cache looking for expired objects.

Figure 25-4. Good Locality of Reference

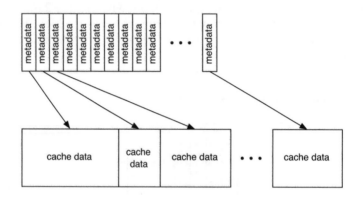

Memory is the New I/O

The motivation that drives programmers to cache data from disk is because I/O to disk is hideously expensive. One disk I/O can cost hundreds of thousands (or more) CPU cycles that could be put to better use.

With today's processors, memory subsystems, and bus architectures, RAM has become I/O too. Sometimes accessing memory can be horrifically slow compared to CPU speed. For example, according to an Apple tech note, a G5 can do 16 to 50 vector adds in the time it takes to load a cacheline (a sequence of bytes) from memory.

Sometimes the "precalculate and store in memory" technique can become a bottleneck, compared to brute-force calculations. The CPU can grind through some calculations faster than the fetch from memory, and the look-up table can force more important data from the CPU caches. The tech note goes on to say "In one example, vector code that converts unsigned char data to float and then applies a 9th order polynomial to it is still marginally faster than hand tuned scalar code that does a lookup into a 256 entry lookup table containing floats." Unfortunately, for G4-class processors, look-up tables can still be a performance win, and at the time of writing, the Macs based on Intel processors have not been released, so performance characteristics of those machines are unknown.

The Level-1 Cache (The cache memory nearest the CPU logic units) has an area for instructions, but it is only 32Kb, so optimizations that increase code length (like loop unrolling, and running 64-bit code) can blow this cache requiring code to be continually brought in from RAM. It becomes a balancing act between the size of code, what you calculate, and what you store and retrieve. Sometimes trial-and-error is the way to go to see what technique results in the best performance, especially if you have high-performance scientific modeling that will have long runtimes, or are dealing with large volumes of data quickly, such as processing video.

Sometimes the C language can get in our way performance-wise, especially with regards to memory because of necessary, but hidden memory accesses that cannot be optimized. C has pointers, so there can be aliasing problems, which is where multiple pointers can point to the same place in memory.

When using a data structure through a pointer or a global variable in a loop, the compiler will emit code to reload that location in memory each time through the loop, just in case it got changed by someone else, either in another thread or by a function called inside the loop. By making a local variable to hold the global's value, the compiler can figure out that this value is not going to change, and can avoid having to have the memory hit each time through the loop.

CPU

CPU usage is the metric that most folks think of first when confronted with an optimization issue. "My app is pegging the CPU and I need to speed it up". Typically when CPU usage becomes a dominant factor, the root cause is a slow algorithm, whether it has a high level of complexity, or it might just be a poor implementation. In almost all cases changing your algorithm will give you more speedups than most other kinds of code or system tweaking. The classic example is changing from a bubble-sort (an order $O(N^2)$ algorithm) to a quicksort or merge sort ($O(n \log n)$).

Sometimes a bad implementation of an algorithm can wreak havoc. A programming error turned **strstr()** in one version of SunOS 4.1.x from an O(N) operation to a worthless $O(N^2)$ one:

```
while (c < strlen(string)) {
    // do stuff with string[c]
}
```

Because there is no length that is stored with C strings, **strlen()** has to traverse the entire string counting characters. In this particular case, the length of the string is not going to change, so there is no reason to take the length every time through the loop.

Luckily high CPU usage can be pretty obvious to discover (by noticing that the CPU meter is pegged, or `top` is showing your app consuming 99% of the available CPU power). The sampling and profiling tools discussed later are ideal for tracking down the cause of these problems.

Disk

Disk access is very slow, many orders of magnitude slower than accessing memory. In general, if you can avoid disk I/O, do so. When dealing with caching data from disk, be aware that the virtual memory system also uses the disk. If you cache a large amount of data you could end up causing the VM system to do disk I/O. This is a very bad situation because you have now exchanged one disk read (from disk into memory) into a read, a write (paging it out), and another read (paging it back in from the disk into memory).

Locality of reference plays a part when optimizing disk access when there is VM paging involved. With bad locality of reference you end up touching lots of pages. These pages cause other pages to "age out" of the VM cache and get sent to disk. Eventually you will touch them again which could cause disk I/O to retrieve the data on those pages.

You can avoid some of the expense of disk I/O by not doing the work at all. Putting windows into different .nib files and loading them on demand is a common technique. If you do not need to show the window, there is no reason to load it in memory.

Similarly, If you have a large database of information, accessing it piecemeal can yield significant speedups over loading the whole thing into memory. Using memory mapped files can avoid disk activity because only the parts of the file being touched will make their way into memory.

Graphics

The Quartz graphics engine in Mac OS X puts a lot of pressure on the memory system. There are large graphic buffers, one used for each window visible on the screen. There are also compositing operations that happen with those buffers to render the user's desktop. Quartz also puts a lot of pressure on the CPU to do all of the fancy drawing effects, although many of these operations are being migrated to the graphics processing unit that lives on the graphics card.

The key to optimizing drawing is to avoid doing drawing when you can. Use the Quartz Debug utility to see where you are doing unnecessary drawing. Quartz Debug will highlight areas in yellow that will be redrawn by an application, and highlight areas in red that are duplicate drawing. It can also automatically flush drawing so that you can see drawing as it happens, before the drawing is flushed to the screen.

Figure 25-5. Quartz Debug

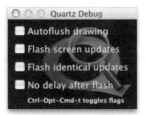

NSView has some features that let you decide what parts of the view need to be redrawn, and which ones do not. You can hit-test the rectangle that is passed to NSView's drawRect: method and only perform drawing calls for items that live in that rectangle. This rectangle tends to be the union of all of the area that needs redrawing, so you can consult **getRectsBeingDrawn:** and **needsToDrawRect:** to hit-test against the areas that need to be redrawn.

One aspect of Quartz drawing that catches some programmers off-guard is that overlapping lines in a single path are very expensive. A lot of work happens at line crossings, such as anti-aliasing the intersections, as well as making sure that transparent colors do not get "painted" multiple times at the crossings and appear darker. If you need to do lots of overlapping lines, especially if you are using opaque colors and do not care about antialiasing, you can get much better performance by drawing a bunch of small paths.

Before using any of the profiling tools

When doing optimizations, forget any assumptions you may have about where the performance problems may be. Programmers are notoriously bad about predicting where performance problems are, otherwise the problems would already be fixed. One programmer I know was convinced that file loading and disk I/O was the slow part of his program when loading files. After a session with the performance tools, the problem actually turned out to be the marshaling of data into a tree so that **NSOutlineView** could use it. The time spent in actual file I/O was very small

Keep good notes on what you do and the measurements you make so that you can apply the optimizations to other situations. By keeping a record of execution times (for instance) you can tell if your optimization attempts are actually making the problem worse.

When tracking down performance problems, throw a large data set at your application. Like with the file-loading issue, some of the test data were 5K files that took a second or two to load. That is too small a window in which to figure anything out. If your application is designed to edit 50 page research papers then throw a 500 or 5000 page document at it. If you have an order N^2 algorithm in there, the larger data set should make it stand out like the proverbial sore thumb. If you can make your program responsive with 5000 page documents, it should give the user a really nice experience when they are just using it to edit the 50 page documents.

There is some debate over when you should optimize. One school of thought is "premature optimization is the root of all evil", where you should wait until the end of your development cycle to identify and fix performance problems. Unfortunately that can require re-engineering large chunks of the product if it is a deeply rooted bottleneck. Another school of thought is to act like you are on a diet and adopt a constant discipline about performance. The down side to that is that premature optimization can obscure the design and the code, and make it harder to track down program errors before shipping.

As with everything in programming, the middle ground is a good place to live. Keep an eye out for algorithms that can be improved, but do not obfuscate code too early in the development process. Throw large datasets at your program often. Do not wait until right before launch to subject your program to what the customer is going to be throwing at it. Keep an eye on your memory usage so that it does not grow too large too quickly. Also be sure to often run the program in the user's environment. If you are writing a desktop app, be sure to have Safari and iTunes running, since the user probably will be using those apps. If your application is a memory pig and makes iTunes skip, you will definitely get some user complaints.

Command-Line Tools

Mac OS X comes with a number of command line tools for tracking down particular types of performance problems. The nice thing about the command line tools is that you can remotely log into a machine and watch things as they happen, and not bother with having the tool's interface interfere with your application's user interface, or interfere with the system in general.

time

The simplest tool is time. It times command execution and shows you clock time, CPU time in userspace, and CPU time spent in the kernel. Here is a run of /usr/bin/time on BigShow, the Big Nerd Ranch slide show program. The time measured was the time starting BigShow up, loading a big set of slides, and then paging through them.

```
$ /usr/bin/time build/BigShow.app/Contents/MacOS/BigShow
       128.35 real          3.07 user          0.80 sys
```

This is 128 seconds of clock time, three seconds in user space, and less than a second in the kernel. Pretty good performance characteristics.

The C shell has its own version of time that gives some more information:

```
% time build/BigShow.app/Contents/MacOS/BigShow
3.300u 0.800s 1:44.78 3.9% 0+0k 0+22io 0pf+0w
```

This is 3.3 seconds in user space, 0.8 seconds in kernel space, one minute, 44 seconds clock time. The 3.9% is a utilization percentage : ratio of user + system times to real time. After the time information is memory information: shared + unshared memory usage, input + output operations, number of pagefaults and swaps. OS X seems not to report the shared + unshared memory usage.

time is very handy when comparing optimizations. Run a baseline or two with time, make the optimization, then try time again. If you are optimizing CPU usage and discover CPU time figures going up, you should reconsider that particular optimization.

ktrace

Many Unix systems have a utility that will show all of the system calls a program makes. On Solaris it is called truss, on Linux it is strace. Mac OS X has ktrace (kernel tracing).

The tracing of system calls is a two-stage process. Run your program with ktrace (or tell ktrace to attach to an already running program). ktrace will start logging system calls, their arguments, and return values. ktrace writes this information (in an unreadable format) to a file named ktrace.out. The kdump program takes this file and turns it into something readable.

For example:

```
$ ktrace ls
$ kdump
```

This generates a couple hundred lines of output, including stuff like this:

```
17477 ktrace    CALL    execve(0xbffff7b0,0xbffffd9c,0xbffffda4)
17477 ktrace    NAMI    "/bin/ls"
17477 ktrace    NAMI    "/usr/lib/dyld"
17477 ls        RET     execve 0
17477 ls        CALL    open(0x1460,0,0)
17477 ls        NAMI    "/usr/lib/libSystem.B.dylib"
17477 ls        RET     open 3
```

The columns are process ID, program name, action performed, and the system call + arguments.

The first three lines are `ktrace` doing an **exec()** of the `ls` program. `CALL` indicates the system call invocation. `NAMI` are certain interesting arguments being printed out. `RET` is the return code. Following the **exec()**, `ktrace` turns into `ls`, and **open()** is called on a system shared library. The return value of **open()** is 3, file descriptor number three. This is the correct value, since file descriptors 0, 1, 2 are used for the standard streams.

A little later on is something like this;

```
17477 ls        CALL    write(0x1,0x48000,0x4b)
17477 ls        GIO     fd 1 wrote 75 bytes
      "CVS            objectalloc-bs.pdf      sampler-bs-default.pdf
      "
17477 ls        RET     write 75/0x4b
```

This is a **write()** system call. The arguments to **write()** are 0x1 (file descriptor number 1), which is standard out. The last argument 0x4b is the number of bytes written (75 bytes). `GIO` is the input/output data. By looking at the string you can tell this is one line of `ls`'s output.

You can also watch a `ktrace` trace in real time using the `kdump -l`. You will either need to put the traced program into the background or run the `kdump` program in a new terminal window. `kdump -l` acts like `tail -f`. It will will continually read from `kdump.out` and display the results.

Being able to see the system call traffic can be a great debugging aid, especially if you have a program that will not start. You can see if the program is trying to load a missing shared library, or if it needs some configuration file that is not supplied.

System call tracking can be a performance tuning aid too. You might discover a lot of one-byte writes that can be coalesced into a single operation, or you may have given a bad timeout to **kevent()** so that it returns a lot sooner than you expect, or to see why your program blocks unexpectedly.

fs_usage and sc_usage

`fs_usage` and `sc_usage` are programs run as the root user which also show system call activity. `fs_usage` shows file system information while `sc_usage` shows system call information.

Here is `BigShow` about to start paging through slides:

```
$ sudo fs_usage
password:
18:38:06 open   /Preferences/com.apple.dock.plist 0.00005   BigShow
18:38:06 fstat                                     0.00000   BigShow
```

```
18:38:06 read                                              0.00029   BigShow
18:38:06 close                                             0.00002   BigShow
18:38:06 open   com.apple.dock.0003931024a6.plist 0.00015   BigShow
18:38:06 PAGE_IN                                           0.00070 W BigShow
18:38:06 open   /Library/Preferences/Network     0.00008   BigShow
18:38:06 open   com.apple.systempreferences.plist 0.00005   BigShow
```

Part of Cocoa is looking at the plist for the dock (presumably for getting size and location information so that it can properly place a window). You can see the open, the stat (to get the size of the file), the read of the file, and its close. Unlike ktrace, there is not an easy way to correlate specific calls (like a **read()**) with the file descriptor it is using, but fs_usage does show you how much time it took. fs_usage can be run on a system-wide basis, which can be handy if you have a problem that is slowing the entire machine down. fs_usage is also very useful when you have a program that is accessing the hard drive unexpectedly, and you want to track down who is responsible.

One really snazzy feature of fs_usage is when it is used on applications that make Carbon file-system calls. If you set the environment variable DYLD_IMAGE_SUFFIX to _debug, fd_usage will show the Carbon calls being made. Here is a peek at Mozilla running:

```
18:34:38 GetCatInfo                                   0.000174   LaunchCFMApp
18:34:38 PBMakeFSSpec  (0, 0x0, 0x0, 0x0)                        LaunchCFMApp
18:34:38 getattrlist   .vol/280763/Mozilla.app 0.000032   LaunchCFMApp
18:34:38 PBMakeFSSpec                              0.000064   LaunchCFMApp
18:34:38 GetCatInfo    (-100, 0x0, 0x0, 0x0)                     LaunchCFMApp
18:34:38 getattrlist   .vol/280763/Mozilla.app 0.000046   LaunchCFMApp
```

sc_usage shows system calls for a program in a manner like top, with a continually updating display. Here is a snapshot from BigShow:

```
BigShow       0 preemptions  0 context switches  1 thread    18:41:43
              0 faults        0 system calls                 0:00:52

TYPE                       NUMBER    CPU_TIME   WAIT_TIME
-------------------------------------------------------------------
System      Idle                                0:37.893(0:00.019)
System      Busy                                0:07.969(0:01.118)
BigShow     Usermode                0:01.333

zero_fill                  1549      0:00.045   0:00.000
pagein                       16      0:00.005   0:00.329
cache_hit                   174      0:00.005   0:00.000

mach_msg_trap              4398      0:00.113   0:27.360(0:01.137) W
vm_deallocate             1100      0:00.054   0:00.000
vm_allocate                105      0:00.002   0:00.000
vm_copy                     99      0:00.020   0:00.000
getattrlist                 18      0:00.000   0:00.000
mk_timer_arm               105      0:00.003   0:00.000
mach_port_insert_member    103      0:00.001   0:00.000
write                        2      0:00.000
```

The CPU_TIME column is the amount of cpu time consumed, and WAIT_TIME is the absolute time the process waits.

If you think you have I/O performance problems, these two programs can help you track down the specific calls that could be causing problems.

top

Unix systems are complex, being composed of multiple programs interacting. Sometimes performance problems manifest themselves as overall system slowness while each program looks fine in isolation. The ktrace and sc_usage utilities are useful for monitoring system calls in a particular program, while the top program can be used to monitor all the programs on the system. Running top without arguments will show the familiar OS information (memory distributions, load average). By default, it orders programs by launch order (most recent program listed first). This is useful if you are monitoring a recently launched program. The -u flag will sort things by CPU usage.

top can also count and show system-wide events. top -e shows VM (virtual memory), network activity, disk activity, and messaging stats:

```
$ top -e

Processes:  74 total, 3 running, 71 sleeping... 198 threads
Load Avg: 0.52, 0.57, 0.58  CPU usage:  9.4% user, 5.9% sys, 74.7% idle
Networks:    967607 ipkts/552961K      1198784 opkts /445769K
Disks:       318661 reads/3531419K      464932 writes/5488572K
VM:           89751 pageins             99649 pageouts

  PID COMMAND %CPU  TIME    FAULTS PAGEINS COW_FAULTS MSGS_SENT MSGS_
17550 top      1.8% 0:00.52 4180   0       72         21555     21504
17536 tcsh     0.0% 0:00.06 271    0       24         54        50
17535 login    0.0% 0:00.75 281    0       51         145       135
17534 ssh      0.0% 0:00.61 300    14      20         60        49
17533 tcsh     0.0% 0:00.05 267    0       24         53        49
17532 login    0.0% 0:00.68 565    0       50         145       135
17526 Preview  0.0% 0:02.78 5741   29      169        8114      5338
17523 tcsh     0.0% 0:00.03 283    0       22         45        44
17520 emacs    0.9% 0:17.94 2680   125     536        59        54
17494 tcsh     0.0% 0:00.09 337    0       24         60        56
17493 login    0.0% 0:00.80 385    0       52         145       135
17436 iCal     0.0% 0:05.12 4725   27      184        4979      4188
17428 Mozilla  4.6% 8:41.23 57963  38      317        477036    40587
17231 tcsh     0.0% 0:00.04 267    2       24         53        49
17230 login    0.0% 0:00.69 488    10      53         145       135
```

top -e shows cumulative output, while top -d will show things in a delta mode. The update interval is one second. That can be changed by using the -s flag to control the number of seconds between intervals.

Stochastic profiling

One of my favorite low-tech tools is stochastic profiling. You run the program in the debugger, interrupt it every now and then and see what is on the call stack. If you see the same function(s) on the stack over and over again, you know you have a place to start looking. This technique is handy if you are on a platform or in a situation where traditional performance tools are not available or do not work. Plus it is fast and easy, especially if you are already running your program in a debugger.

sample

You can do some profiling from the command-line to perform quick-and-dirty "what is happening here?" kinds of questions. The sample program will sample a process at 10 millisecond intervals, and then build a snapshot of what the program was doing. You can give sample a pid, or give it the partial name of a program:

```
$ sample iTunes 5
Sampling process 216 each 10 msecs 500 times
Sample analysis of process 216 written file /tmp/iTunes_216.sample.txt
```

The resulting trace file shows you a bunch of call stacks, one for each thread, along with the number of times it found those particular functions on a call stack. Like this is one thread that is waiting in a run loop.

```
434 Thread_1103
  434 _pthread_body
    434 dyld_stub_binding_helper
      434 CFRunLoopRun
        434 CFRunLoopRunSpecific
          434 __CFRunLoopRun
            434 mach_msg
              434 mach_msg_trap
                434 mach_msg_trap
```

And there are other deeper call stacks that show the functions being used to decode the mp3s. The trace files created by sample can be read by the `Sampler` application so you can explore the stack traces with a GUI interface.

Precise Timing with mach_absolute_time()

I am a fan of writing little command-line tools as benchmarks for those cases where you can isolate an algorithm or a programming technique out of your full application. A dozen-line or a couple hundred-line command line tool is a much more tractable problem than a million-line application. Not every problem can be put into a little benchmark, but enough can to make it a useful technique.

The nice thing about command-line programs is you can use the `time` command to get absolute figures of the running time of the program, making it easy to compare and contrast changes you make to your target program.

Sometimes the `time` command is not good enough because you want more precise timing, or you are just interested in timing a specific part of your program. You might not be interested in the time it takes to load the data to feed your algorithm. If that takes 3 times as long as it takes the algorithm to run, you will want to do timing inside of the program yourself.

Mach, Mac OS X's kernel, provides some functions you can use for precise timing. **mach_absolute_time()** reads the CPU time base register and reports the value back to you. This time base register serves as the basis for other time measurements in the OS:

```
uint64_t mach_absolute_time (void);
```

`mach_absolute_time()` returns values based on the CPU time, and is not directly usable as-is for getting accurate counts because you don't know what time span each each increment of the counter represents.

To translate `mach_absolute_time()`'s results to nanoseconds, use `mach_timebase_info()` to get the scaling of `mach_absolute_time()`'s values:

```
kern_return_t mach_timebase_info (mach_timebase_info_t info);
```

Where `mach_timebase_info_t` is a pointer to this struct:

```
struct mach_timebase_info {
    uint32_t numer;
    uint32_t denom;
};
```

`mach_timebase_info()` fills in the struct with the fraction to multiply the result of `mach_absolute_time()` against to calculate nanoseconds. Multiply the result of `mach_absolute_time()` by `numer` and divide by `denom`.

Example 25-2 shows how to use these two functions. The code times how long it takes to call `mach_timebase_info()` and **printf()**. For real-life code, you would want to put something more interesting in there to time.

Example 25-2. machtime.m

```
#import <mach/mach_time.h>   // for mach_absolute_time()
#import <stdio.h>            // for printf()
#import <stdlib.h>           // for abort()

/* compile with
gcc -g -Wall -o machtime machtime.m
*/

int main (void)
{
    mach_timebase_info_data_t info;

    uint64_t start, end, elapsed;
    start = mach_absolute_time ();

    if (mach_timebase_info (&info) == KERN_SUCCESS) {
        printf ("%u %u\n", info.numer, info.denom);
    } else {
        printf ("mach_timebase_info failed\n");
  abort ();
    }

    end = mach_absolute_time ();
    elapsed = end - start;

    uint64_t nanos;
    nanos = elapsed * info.numer / info.denom;

    printf ("elapsed time was %lld nanoseconds\n", nanos);
```

```
        return (0);

} // main
```

And here it is in action:

```
$ ./machtime
1000000000 24965716
elapsed time was 1247150 nanoseconds
$ ./machtime
1000000000 24965716
elapsed time was 279423 nanoseconds
$ ./machtime
1000000000 24965716
elapsed time was 274135 nanoseconds
$ ./machtime
1000000000 24965716
elapsed time was 337302 nanoseconds
```

On my Powerbook (Ti500) the numerator of the conversion is 1,000,000,000 and the denominator is 24,965,716, resulting in a value of 40.05. So there are about 40 nanoseconds for each increment of **mach_absolute_time()**.

Outside of the first run, it takes about 297,000 nanoseconds, or 297 microseconds to do the work between the two timings. So what is up with that first run? It is an order of magnitude larger than the other runs. When you are dealing with time values this short, *anything* can perturb them. Maybe some dynamic library lookup was necessary for the first run. Maybe iTunes was running and was loading a new track. For a real benchmark, you would have it run for a larger period of time to hide some of those small one-time-only blips. And of course run the benchmark a couple of times to get a good average and iron out the noise.

GUI Tools

Mac OS X comes with a number of GUI performance tools, which are a good deal more powerful and easier to use than the command-line tools. The GUI performance tools live in /Developer/Applications/Performance Tools.

ObjectAlloc

Memory issues are frequently performance hot spots. Too many allocations and deallocations can chew up time that could be saved by reusing a memory buffer or reusing some objects. The ObjectAlloc application can be used for Objective-C programs to keep a tally of allocations and deallocations of objects, along with the stack traces of each of these operations. If you see a couple million allocs/deallocs when opening a small file, you have a good idea where to start looking.

ObjectAlloc lets you set a "mark" at a point in time to restrict the set of allocations you are evaluating to be the objects that have been allocated since the mark was set. This is used to screen out all the overhead work that happens on program startup.

Here is BigShow with a mark set after program start, showing the result of loading a really big slide show (a couple hundred slides) XML File. Artificially inflating the data you are processing can make performance issues stand out more.

You can see that a lot of **CFString** action has gone on. Looking at CFString (immutable), there are currently 10,667 of them floating around. At the high point, there were 12,676 in existence, with a total of 22,895 allocations.

If you see a particular kind of allocation that looks interesting, the Call Stacks tab will give you an opportunity to see who was responsible for allocations.

Here the CFString (mutable) entry has been expanded. The count column is a cumulative summation of the number of **CFString**s that have been allocated. Note the difference between the selected line and the next line. **parseTag** was responsible for 4683 (14203 - 9520) allocations. Likewise, **parseAttributes** contributed 2911 (3797 - 886) allocations.

Sampler

Sampling is a profiling technique where the program being sampled is interrupted periodically and the stack traces of the threads are recorded. Once the sampling stops, the sampler program accumulates the data it recorded and determines which functions were most active during the sampling period. One of the nice things about sampling is that it shows time spent blocked in system calls. Function call profilers typically do not calculate that time. Sampler is one such profiling utility.

Here is a sampling of BigShow after paging through a hundred or so slides:

The tree browser portion of the window lets you navigate stack traces to see where the samples are distributed. Unfortunately the browser portion is not easily resizable, so function call names get cut off. In this case, **mach_msg_send()** was on the top of the stack for 48% of the samples. If you want to see who called all those **mach_msg_send()**s, you can re-root the call tree. Select the **mach_msg_send()** and set the root. You will then see something like this:

So the calls **SendFontM***, **_CGSynch**, **__CFRunLoop** are the big callers. The first two imply that there is a lot of text (font stuff) and graphics (CG for Core Graphics).

`Sampler` is an OK profiler. These days I mainly use it for consuming trace files created by the command-line `sample` utility. `Shark`, part of the CHUD tools, is the premiere sampler for the Mac.

CHUD

CHUD is Apple's profiling framework. Apple says that CHUD stands for "Computer Hardware Understanding Development kit," but it is probably just a fun code name that stuck. CHUD is a kernel extension plus a framework that gives access to the Performance Monitor Counters (PMC) of the CPU, the memory controller, and certain OS counters. There are a number of pre-built programs that are useful for getting performance metrics both system wide and for a particular program. The framework those programs are built on are available for your use as well.

Shark

`Shark` is CHUD's profiling tool, replacing the `Shikari` program that appeared in the first edition of this book. The `Shark` can be found in `/Developer/Applications/Performance Tools`.

`Shark` works like other samplers, interrupting your program (and other programs on the system) on a regular basis, inspecting the call stack, and then building a profile of your program's performance characteristics based on what it saw.

`Shark` does not just profile your application, it profiles the entire system. You can use this to find out if your program is putting a lot of pressure on the window server, for example. `Shark` can also be used to record events that happen on the hardware and OS's PMI (Performance Monitor Interrupt) registers.

`Shark` comes with two excellent tutorials accessible from `Shark`'s Help menu. One is the Profiling Tutorial, which is not really a tutorial, but more of a "Here is how we used `Shark` to optimize the Flurry screen saver" document, and the `Shark` Data Mining Tutorial, which shows a number of `Shark` features for sifting through the data from a sampling run.

Starting With Shark

When you start up `Shark`, you are presented with a window similar to what is shown in Figure 25-6. Items in `Shark` get moved around just about every release, so the screen shots here are just approximations of what you currently have.

Figure 25-6. Shark's Greeting Window

Starting from the left is the **Start** button. That tells `Shark` to start gathering samples. You can use the option-Escape hotkey to start and stop sampling even if `Shark` is not the front-most application. Usually you will want to use the hotkey so that more time is spent sampling your app rather than sampling the time it takes to bring your application to the front and start exercising it.

Next to the start button is a pop-up menu that shows the different Shark configurations. Time Profile is one of the easiest to use, and one of the most useful, so it is the one chosen by default. You can pop up that menu to see some of the other options, such as a Malloc Trace (record each time dynamic memory is allocated or released), a general Function Trace (record a stack trace each time a particular function is called), VM system tracing, and even some Java monitoring. We will be dealing with the Time Profile here.

Finally there is a pop-up menu that lets you choose between sampling the entire system, or just sampling a particular application. Some other configurations will grow an additional menu letting you select a particular process to interact with.

After you have started Shark up, go to your application and get it set up so you can exercise the portions you are interested in getting information about. For example, load a very wide spreadsheet if you are wanting to profile scrolling speed. In this walk-through, a cross-stitch chart editor, shown in Figure 25-7 is being profiled because drawing of individual stitches gets really sluggish after awhile.

Figure 25-7. The Application Being Profiled

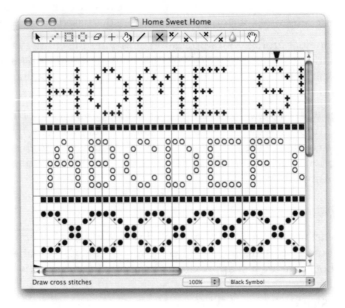

Type option-escape to start sampling and exercise your program. Shark will interrupt the system every 10 milliseconds for 30 seconds, for a maximum of 30,000 samples. You can change the sampling rate and sampling duration if you want. Shark automatically adds some fuzz to the sampling interval, injecting a little bit of randomness to the sampling frequency. This helps avoid situations where the code being profiled is in harmony with the sampling frequency, causing misleading results.

Interpreting Results

When Shark runs out of sample time, or when you tell it to stop by typing option-escape again (or even clicking Shark's **Stop** button), Shark will process all the samples, and show a window like Figure 25-8

Figure 25-8. First Round of Results

!	Self ▼	Total	Library	Symbol
	35.2%	35.2%	libobjc.A.dylib	▶ objc_msgSend
	13.7%	13.7%	BorkGraph	▶ -[BWCrossStitchStorage isSymbolAtRow:column:]
!	12.5%	12.5%	Foundation	▶ -[NSCFArray objectAtIndex:]
	11.8%	11.8%	CoreFoundation	▶ _CFArrayCheckAndGetValueAtIndex
!	8.1%	8.1%	BorkGraph	▶ -[BWCrossStitch row]
	6.4%	6.4%	BorkGraph	▶ dyld_stub_objc_msgSend
	3.0%	3.0%	Foundation	▶ dyld_stub__CFArrayCheckAndGetValueAtIndex
	0.9%	0.9%	mach_kernel	▶ ml_set_interrupts_enabled
	0.7%	0.7%	BorkGraph	▶ -[BWGridGeometry rectForRow:column:]
	0.6%	0.6%	BorkGraph	▶ -[BWCrossStitchLayer drawRect:]
	0.3%	0.3%	Foundation	▶ NSIntersectsRect
!	0.3%	0.3%	BorkGraph	▶ -[BWCrossStitch column]
	0.2%	0.2%	libSystem.B.dylib	▶ szone_free
	0.2%	0.2%	commpage [libob...	▶ objc_msgSend_rtp
!	0.2%	0.2%	BorkGraph	▶ -[BWCrossStitchStorage symbolAtIndex:]
	0.2%	0.2%	libobjc.A.dylib	▶ objc_msgSend_stret
	0.2%	0.2%	CoreFoundation	▶ CFArrayGetCount
	0.2%	0.2%	libSystem.B.dylib	▶ szone_calloc
!	0.1%	0.1%	BorkGraph	▶ -[BWCrossStitchChangeList isChangeAtRow:column:]
	0.1%	0.1%	libSystem.B.dylib	▶ szone_malloc
	0.1%	0.1%	CoreGraphics	▶ vecCGSColorMaskCopyARGB8888
	0.1%	0.1%	libSystem.B.dylib	▶ szone_size
	0.1%	0.1%	commpage [libSy...	▶ __pthread_getspecific
!	0.1%	0.1%	BorkGraph	▶ -[BWCrossStitch topThread]

Session 1 – Time Profile of Everything

Profile   Chart

Heavy (Bottom–Up)

24013 of 24013 (100.0%) process samples displayed

Process: (83.3%) BorkGraph [5263]   Thread: All   View: Heavy (Bottom–Up)

At the bottom are pop-up menus that let you choose what parts of the world to see. On the left-side is the **Process** pop-up menu. This lets you choose amongst the different processes that were running at the time of the sampling. Figure 25-9 shows the **Process** menu for this run. This shows BorkGraph (the program under scrutiny) took about 83% of the total run time, followed by the kernel and the window server. You can also see that I was running Classic (the TruBlueEnvironment), Camino, Pages, and other goodies.

Figure 25-9. The Process Pop-Up Menu

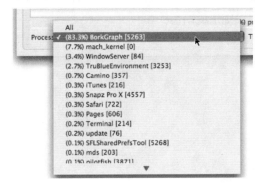

Next to the process pop-up is one that lets you choose to look at a particular thread. The target app is not heavily threaded, so looking at all threads is OK. There is also a pop-up menu that lets you choose between the different Shark views.

Getting Heavy

There are three ways to show information in the main window. Shark starts out with its "Heavy" view, showing the functions and methods that appeared most often in the samples. In this sample run, **objc_msgSend()** is at the top of the stack, indicating that this function appeared most often in the samples, followed closely by the method **isSymbolAtRow:column:** from the class **BWCrossStitchStorage** (these are domain objects of the application.)

To better see how the heavy view works, change the stats display to show counts rather than percentages. To do this, open Shark's drawer drawer by choosing the **Advanced Settings** menu item under the **View** menu. The drawer will change contents based on what Shark is displaying in its window. Right now look at the **Profile Analysis** panel, as shown in Figure 25-10. Under stats display, choose **Value** rather than **% of Scope**.

Also enable **Color By Library**. That will help differentiate where different symbols come from. The application's symbols will be one one color, Foundation's symbols will be another, AppKit in yet another. If you see your app's colors most often, you know that your app's code and algorithms probably have the problem. If you see mainly system frameworks, then your apps usage of those frameworks is probably suboptimal.

Figure 25-10. Profile Analysis Advanced Settings Panel

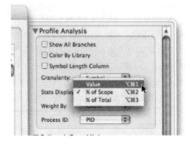

The heavy view colorized will look like Figure 25-11. It probably does not look very impressive in black-and-white print, but you can probably still tell that the functions are colored differently.

Figure 25-11. Results Showing Counts and Library Colors

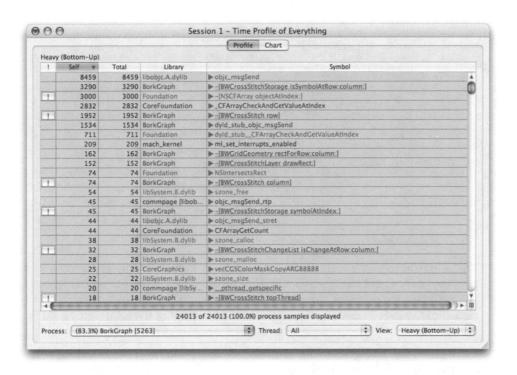

Looking again at the heavy view, you can see that **objc_msgSend()** was found in 8459 samples. This function is how Objective-C method dispatch is done. The message send syntax [object method] gets turned into an **objc_msgSend()** call by the compiler.

If you open the disclosure triangle, Shark will show you everyone that called **objc_msgSend()**. Well, everyone that Shark saw samples for. It will not show you every single **objc_msgSend()** because most of them happen rapidly enough to not get caught. In the case of our program, there must be someone calling **objc_msgSend()** a whole lot. Opening the disclosure triangle will show you something like Figure 25-12

Figure 25-12. Seeing objc_msgSend()'s callers

Self ▼	Total	Library	Symbol
8459	8459	libobjc.A.dylib	▼ objc_msgSend
0	7929	BorkGraph	▶ -[BWCrossStitchStorage isSymbolAtRow:column:]
0	371	BorkGraph	▶ -[BWCrossStitchLayer drawRect:]
0	54	BorkGraph	▶ -[BWCrossStitchChangeList isChangeAtRow:column:]
0	31	BorkGraph	▶ -[BWCrossStitchStorage symbolAtIndex:]
0	27	Foundation	▶ -[NSCFArray objectAtIndex:]
0	23	BorkGraph	▶ -[BWGridLayer drawGridInRect:lightLines:heavyLines:]
0	9	BorkGraph	▶ drawLightLine
0	2	libSystem.B.dylib	▶ free
0	2	BorkGraph	▶ -[BWLayerView drawRect:]
0	2	BorkGraph	▶ -[BWCrossStitchStorage removeSymbolAtRow:column:]
0	1	BorkGraph	▶ -[BWSymbol pathInRect:]
0	1	BorkGraph	▶ -[BWLayer okToRenderRow:column:]
0	1	BorkGraph	▶ -[BWLayer bounds]
0	1	BorkGraph	▶ -[BWGridLayer drawRect:]
0	1	BorkGraph	▶ -[BWGridAttributes colorForKind:]
0	1	BorkGraph	▶ -[BWCrossStitchLayer drawThread:inRect:]
0	1	BorkGraph	▶ -[BWCrossStitchLayer drawStitch:atRow:column:]
0	1	BorkGraph	▶ -[BWBackStitchLayer drawRect:]
0	1	AppKit	▶ +[NSBezierPath fillRect:]
3290	3290	BorkGraph	▶ -[BWCrossStitchStorage isSymbolAtRow:column:]
3000	3000	Foundation	▶ -[NSCFArray objectAtIndex:]

Take a look at the Total column. `objc_msgSend()` has 8459 samples, next down is `isSymbolAtRow:column:`, with 7929. That most likely will be our smoking gun for this performance problem. After that `drawRect:` had 371 samples, then 54 for `isChangeAtRow:column:`, and so on. If you add up all of the total figures, you will get 8459.

The heavy view also goes by the name "Bottom-Up". It finds the functions with the most samples, and then builds up from there, seeing who called those functions, and how often they were found on the call stacks.

Branching Out

The second `Shark` view is the Tree view, also called the "Top-Down" view. (The third `Shark` view shows both the heavy and tree views at the same time.) The tree view is a view of the samples from the beginning of the stack. Figure 25-13 shows the tree view. Everything starts out with `start()`, then down to `main()`, then to

`NSApplicationMain()`, and so on.

Figure 25-13. Shark's Tree View

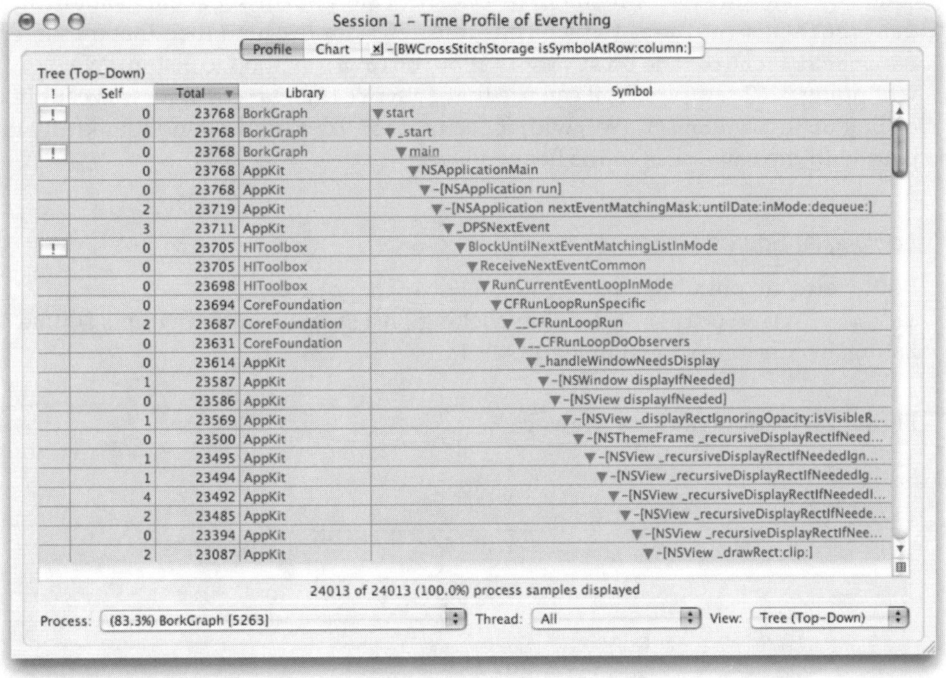

!	Self	Total	Library	Symbol
!	0	23768	BorkGraph	▼start
	0	23768	BorkGraph	▼_start
!	0	23768	BorkGraph	▼main
	0	23768	AppKit	▼NSApplicationMain
	0	23768	AppKit	▼-[NSApplication run]
	2	23719	AppKit	▼-[NSApplication nextEventMatchingMask:untilDate:inMode:dequeue:]
	3	23711	AppKit	▼_DPSNextEvent
!	0	23705	HIToolbox	▼BlockUntilNextEventMatchingListInMode
	0	23705	HIToolbox	▼ReceiveNextEventCommon
	0	23698	HIToolbox	▼RunCurrentEventLoopInMode
	0	23694	CoreFoundation	▼CFRunLoopRunSpecific
	2	23687	CoreFoundation	▼__CFRunLoopRun
	0	23631	CoreFoundation	▼__CFRunLoopDoObservers
	0	23614	AppKit	▼_handleWindowNeedsDisplay
	1	23587	AppKit	▼-[NSWindow displayIfNeeded]
	0	23586	AppKit	▼-[NSView displayIfNeeded]
	1	23569	AppKit	▼-[NSView _displayRectIgnoringOpacity:isVisibleR...
	0	23500	AppKit	▼-[NSThemeFrame _recursiveDisplayRectIfNeed...
	1	23495	AppKit	▼-[NSView _recursiveDisplayRectIfNeededIgn...
	1	23494	AppKit	▼-[NSView _recursiveDisplayRectIfNeededIg...
	4	23492	AppKit	▼-[NSView _recursiveDisplayRectIfNeededI...
	2	23485	AppKit	▼-[NSView _recursiveDisplayRectIfNeede...
	0	23394	AppKit	▼-[NSView _recursiveDisplayRectIfNee...
	2	23087	AppKit	▼-[NSView _drawRect:clip:]

This view can be a bit hard to use because of deep nesting of the calls. Scrolling down shows you where things start getting interesting, as shown in Figure 25-14

Figure 25-14. Farther Down the Call Tree

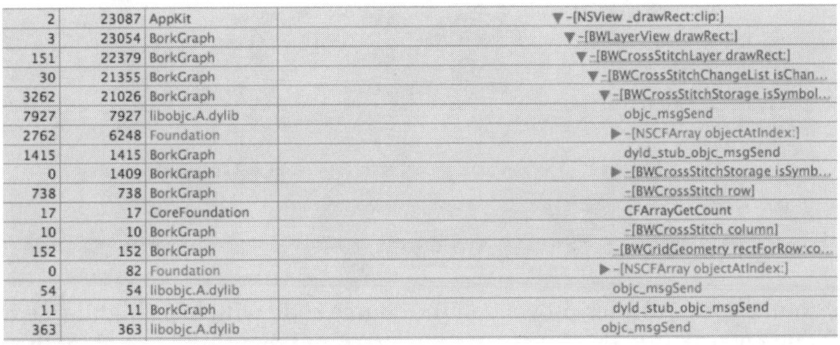

2	23087	AppKit	▼-[NSView _drawRect:clip:]
3	23054	BorkGraph	▼-[BWLayerView drawRect:]
151	22379	BorkGraph	▼-[BWCrossStitchLayer drawRect:]
30	21355	BorkGraph	▼-[BWCrossStitchChangeList isChan...
3262	21026	BorkGraph	▼-[BWCrossStitchStorage isSymbol...
7927	7927	libobjc.A.dylib	objc_msgSend
2762	6248	Foundation	▶-[NSCFArray objectAtIndex:]
1415	1415	BorkGraph	dyld_stub_objc_msgSend
0	1409	BorkGraph	▶-[BWCrossStitchStorage isSymb...
738	738	BorkGraph	-[BWCrossStitch row]
17	17	CoreFoundation	CFArrayGetCount
10	10	BorkGraph	-[BWCrossStitch column]
152	152	BorkGraph	-[BWGridGeometry rectForRow:co...
0	82	Foundation	▶-[NSCFArray objectAtIndex:]
54	54	libobjc.A.dylib	objc_msgSend
11	11	BorkGraph	dyld_stub_objc_msgSend
363	363	libobjc.A.dylib	objc_msgSend

The left-hand column is the Self column, the next is the Total column. Self shows the number of samples that were found inside of the code of the function. The Total column shows the number of samples that were also found in the functions that the function calls.

For example, `-[BWCrossStitchLayer drawRect:]` (third line down) has a self value of 151, while its total is 22379. That means that 151 samples were found in the code of this **drawRect:** method. In the other 22228 samples **drawRect:** was on the call stack but not the active (top-most) function. This means this method took a noticeable chunk of time, but the stuff that it calls are the big huge time wasters.

Because this is a tree view, things indented underneath a symbol are things that were called by that function or method. **drawRect:** calls **BWCrossStitchChangeList**'s **isSymbolAtRow:column:** (which consumed 30 samples), and then that method calls **BWCrossStitchStorage**'s **isSymbolAtRow:column:** method, consuming a whopping 3262 samples. You can see that **isSymbolAtRow:column:** was caught calling **objc_msgSend()** a lot, with it occupying 7927 samples (and thankfully this jibes with the value seen in the heavy view).

Looking At Source Code

Both views are pointing us to -[BWCrossStitchStorage isSymbolAtRow:column:]. Double-clicking on a symbol will bring up a source code listing, like the one shown in Figure 25-15

Figure 25-15. Source Code Viewer

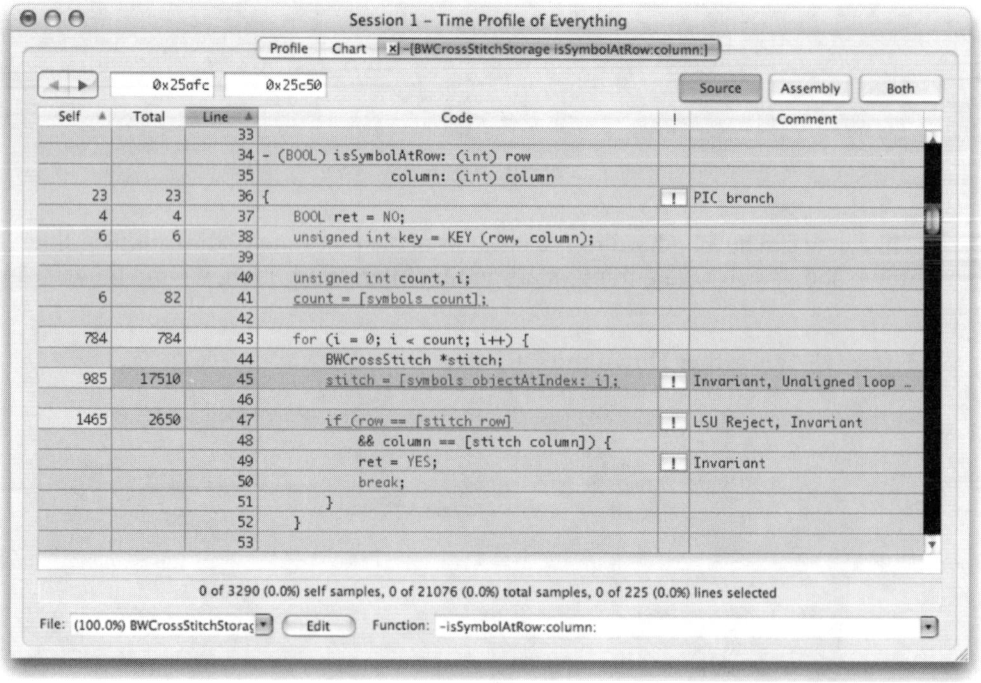

The source code browser shows you the source code with lines highlighted with different colors based on density of samples found there. The trough of the scroll bar will show you where hot spots are as you are browsing through the code.

The Self and Total columns work just like in the tree view. For example, the [symbols objectAtIndex:] call and assignment consumed 985 samples, in this method, and **objectAtIndex:** (and descendants) consumed 17510 samples.

The little exclamation point buttons shown here (and seen elsewhere) highlight things that Shark thinks are problems based on a static analysis of the code. Click on the button and get a talk balloon that describes the problem, and what Shark thinks you should do about it. Figure 25-16 shows one of the helpful hints from Shark. You can have Shark perform a static analysis without having to run your program.

Figure 25-16. Handy Hints from Shark

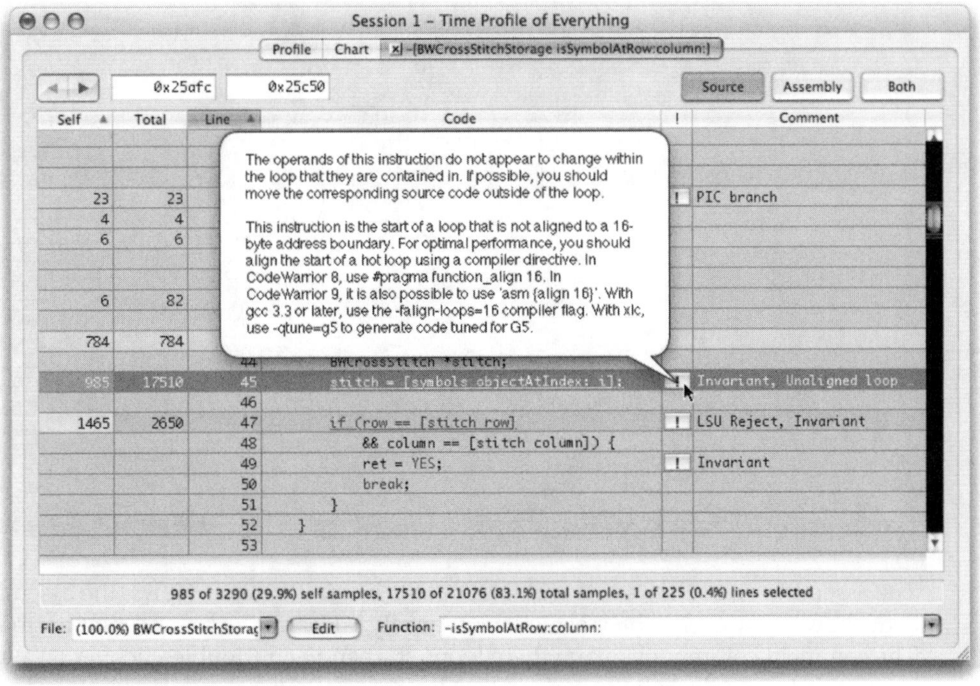

Sometimes you have to take some of the hints with a grain of salt, such as this one saying the operands of the instruction do not change within the loop, even though it seems obvious that the index variable is going to be changing. You cannot depend on the `objectAtIndex:` method to always return the same result.

If you are more curious, you can click the Assembly button to see the assembly-language version of your code. The Both button shows them side-by-side, which is a great way to explore how the compiler converts your code to object code. Figure 25-17 shows the assembly listing after double-clicking on the line of code that calls `objectAtIndex:`.

Figure 25-17. The Assembly Window

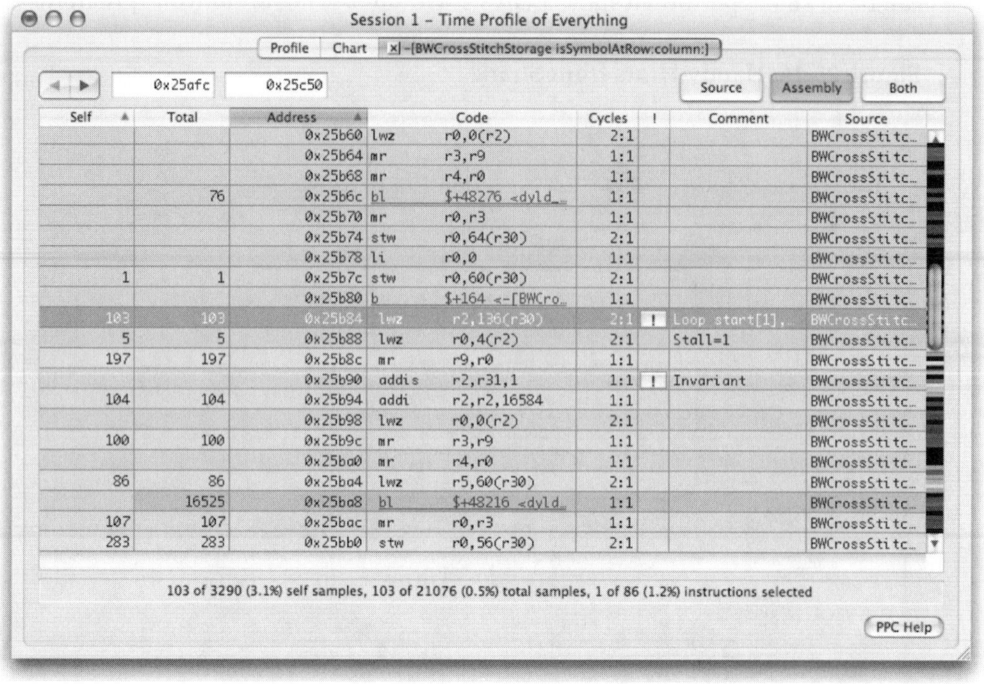

The assembly view shows self and total counts like in the other views, the assembly code, how many cycles the instructions typically take and the helpful-hint buttons. The comment column tells you where loops start and end (double-clicking on a loop start or end will select all the code in that loop). Shark also shows you pipeline stalls, which is where data used by subsequent instructions will have to wait for this instruction to complete. Finally the Source column shows you the file and line of source code that the line of assembly relates to. When you have narrow windows with long file names, it is kind of hard to tell what goes where (as shown here). The **PPC Help** button at the bottom brings up reference material the for PowerPC assembly language.

Charts

Shark will also show you a chart of samples it made over time. Figure 25-18 shows the stack depth over time. For this application, the stack depth is pretty uniform, implying that a small number of functions are consuming all the samples

Figure 25-18. Shark's Chart View

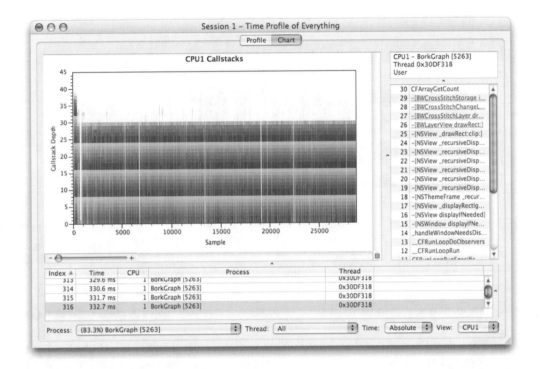

You can click in the graph to select particular call stacks, and `Shark` will update the call-stack list on the right-hand part of the window to show the stack of the sample you clicked on. If you do not see the stack window, click the box at the intersection of the chart's scroll bars. The slider on the left lets you zoom in on parts of the chart, and you can drag out a rectangle to zoom in on interesting sections. Figure 25-19 shows the chart zoomed in

Figure 25-19. Shark's Chart View, Zoomed In

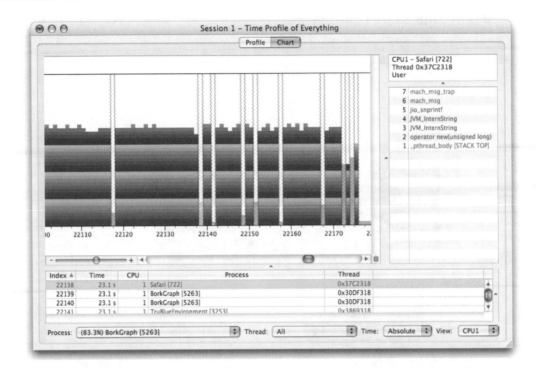

The wavy lines in the chart show where samples from other applications happened. A sample from Safari is selected showing that Safari was doing some Java VM stuff while it was idling in the background. Not terribly germane to our app's performance problems, but still interesting.

Figure 25-20 shows Shark's idea of stack frame tenure. The mouse was clicked where the pointer is shown in the figure. The selected stack frame (which runs vertically) is highlighted in yellow. Any stack frame contents in common with the selected stack frame are also highlighted in yellow. For this entire group of samples in this block, all of the bottom elements of the stack frame are the same, showing that the functions near the top of the stack are the ones that are consuming the most time. Looking at the stack window, a CFArray bounds checking method is first (that is the block at the very top), followed by an **objectAtIndex:** call, and then there is our friend **isSymbolAtRow:column:**. It is a good sign when everything is pointing to the same area.

Figure 25-20. Call Stack Tenure

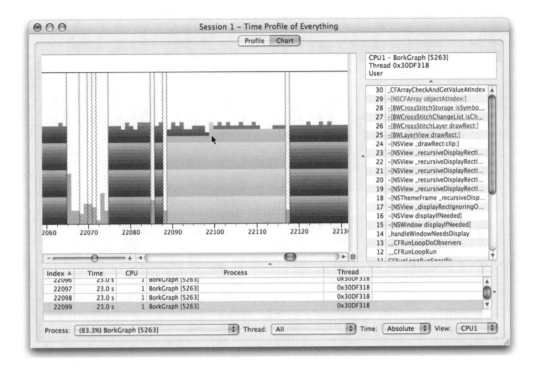

Data Mining

The problem with **isSymbolAtRow:column:** that Shark pointed us to turned out to be an O(N²) algorithm, with an array being traversed over and over again looking for a particular object.

After that got fixed, the program was re-Sharked to see if there are any additional issues that can be addressed. Figure 25-21 shows the heavy view for the second run.

Figure 25-21. Another Shark Session

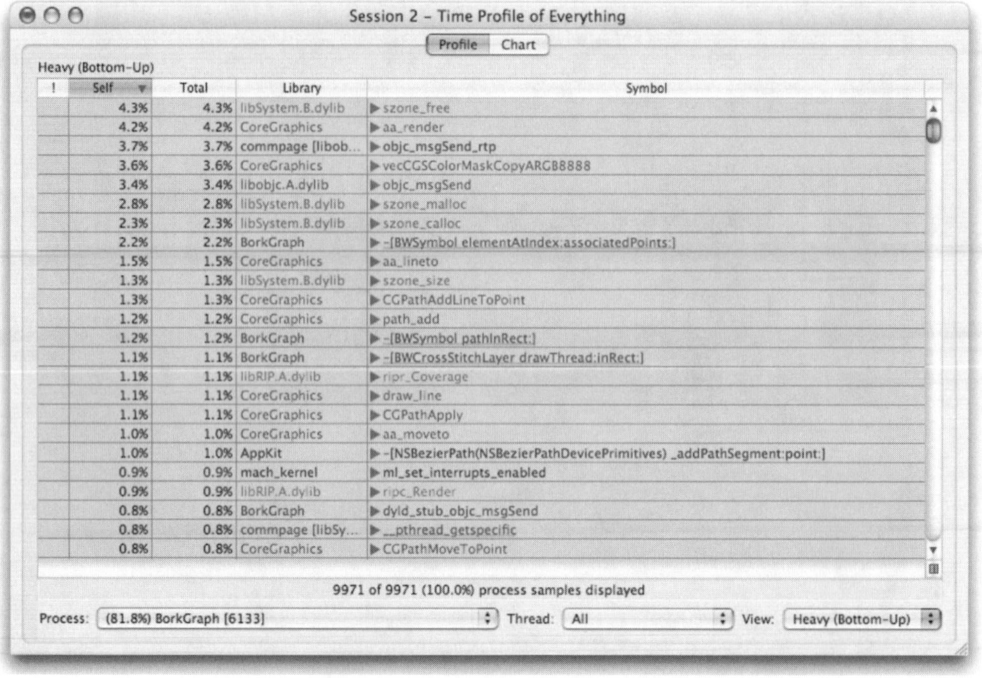

There is no smoking gun in this one. There are functions from all sorts of different libraries in there. Shark has a number of "data mining" features that lets you tweak how the data is presented so you can explore your application's performance characteristics.

Living in the **Advanced Settings** drawer is a panel called Callstack Data Mining, as shown in Figure 25-22.

Figure 25-22. Callstack Data Mining Panel

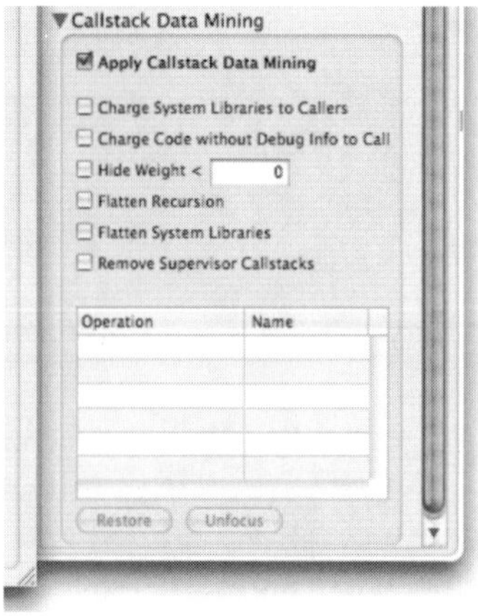

The call stack data mining panel contains 4 items of interest. The first item (located in the middle of the checkbox group) is a way to hide items that fall below a particular threshold. Sometimes Shark displays get cluttered up by a whole bunch of functions with one or two samples in them. Hiding these small-sample functions can give you more space to look at interesting data.

The next involves flattening. By default, Shark shows you everything that gets called. You can end up seeing a bunch of functions that are implementation details in a system framework, such as a bunch of the CoreGraphics functions (**path_add**, **draw_line**, etc). By checking Flatten System Libraries, only the public entry points into the library are shown. Any samples found in the functions called by the library entry points are charged back to that entry point. No sampling information is lost, you just lose some of the detail in the system frameworks, which in this case is fine.

After flattening system libraries, the heavy window looks like Figure 25-23. (The stats display has been changed to show count instead of percentages too.)

Figure 25-23. Heavy View After System Library Flattening

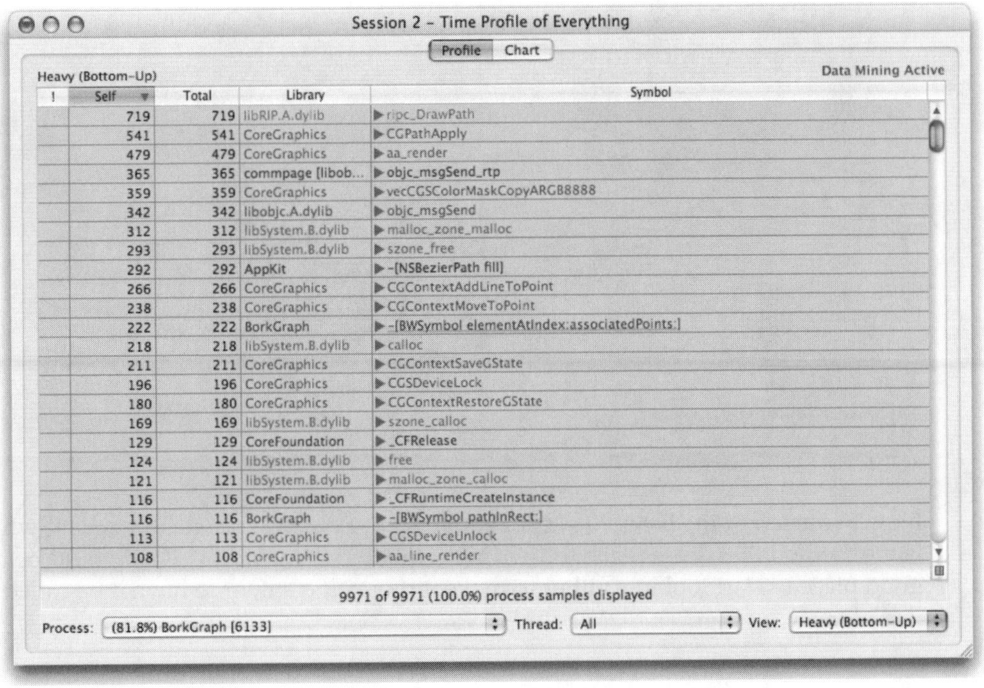

Now at the top of the list are a number of drawing calls. **CGPathApply**, **aa_render** (rendering something Anti-Aliased), and **-[NSBezierPath fill]**. Path drawing looks like a good place to start looking for problems. Peering underneath **-[NSBezierPath fill]** line would be a good place to start looking.

In addition to flattening the system libraries, you can also flatten recursion. Recursive algorithms can lead to headaches when using Shark because the recursion can push some of details way off the right side of the window. By flattening recursion, all recursive calls are hidden and samples found in the recursive calls are charged back to a single instance of that function.

The last bits of call stack data mining involve charging samples to different places than were they were found. The Charge Code without Debug Info to Caller option causes any samples found in code without debug symbols (like some library calls) to be considered counted in the function called it. Dealing with code without debug symbols can be difficult, and for casual profiling it is not necessary to deal with.

The more interesting charge-back is **Charge System Libraries to Callers**. This causes any samples found in system frameworks to be charged back to the application. If any samples were found in a system library, that sample would instead be counted as if it came from application code. Turning on this option gives us Figure 25-24

Figure 25-24. Heavy View After Library Chargeback

!	Self ▼	Total	Library	Symbol
	6291	6291	BorkGraph	▶ -[BWCrossStitchLayer drawThread:inRect:]
	1550	1550	BorkGraph	▶ -[BWSymbol pathInRect:]
!	526	526	BorkGraph	▶ main
	331	331	BorkGraph	▶ drawLightLine
	222	222	BorkGraph	▶ -[BWSymbol elementAtIndex:associatedPoints:]
	204	204	BorkGraph	▶ -[BWCrossStitchLayer drawRect:]
	93	93	BorkGraph	▶ -[BWCrossStitchStorage isSymbolAtRow:column:]
	84	84	BorkGraph	▶ dyld_stub_objc_msgSend
	57	57	BorkGraph	▶ scalePoint
!	57	57	BorkGraph	▶ -[BWCrossStitchStorage symbolAtIndex:]
	57	57	BorkGraph	▶ -[BWCrossStitchLayer drawStitch:atRow:column:]
	56	56	BorkGraph	▶ -[BWGridGeometry rectForRow:column:]
	41	41	BorkGraph	▶ drawHeavyLine
	36	36	BorkGraph	▶ -[BWLayerView drawRect:]
!	26	26	BorkGraph	▶ -[BWCrossStitch tag]
!	23	23	BorkGraph	▶ -[BWCrossStitchChangeList isChangeAtRow:column:]
	23	23	BorkGraph	▶ -[BWCrossStitchChangeList changeEnumerator]
	21	21	BorkGraph	▶ -[BWCrossStitchStorage addStitch:]
!	21	21	BorkGraph	▶ -[BWCrossStitch row]
	17	17	BorkGraph	▶ -[BWCrossStitchStorage removeSymbolAtRow:column:]
!	12	12	BorkGraph	▶ -[BWLayer active]
!	10	10	BorkGraph	▶ -[BWThread symbol]
	10	10	BorkGraph	▶ -[BWCrossStitchStorage addStitchWithThread:atRow:column:tag:]
	9	9	BorkGraph	▶ -[BWLayer okToRenderRow:column:]

9868 of 9868 (100.0%) process samples displayed

Process: (96.9%) BorkGraph [6133]   Thread: All   View: Heavy (Bottom-Up)

Now at the top of the list is `-[BWCrossStitchLayer drawThread:inRect:]`, which is the method that draws each individual symbol in the window. That would be a good place to start looking, either to make it more efficient, or to have it be called less often.

Saturn

Another CHUD tool is `Saturn`, a performance tool like `Shark`, but it uses instrumented profiling along with sampling. Rather than being limited to a short time period of sampling like with `Shark`, `Saturn` analyzes an entire run of a program. `Saturn` uses profiling code (instrumentation that records function entries and exits) generated by the compiler and linker to build a call graph, and it also uses sampling to determine how much time individual functions consume.

To use `Saturn`, you will need to turn on Generate Profiling Code in Xcode (or use the `-pg` option with your compiler). Figure 25-25 shows the Xcode setting to to get this profiling instrumentation.

Figure 25-25. Xcode's Generate Profiling Code

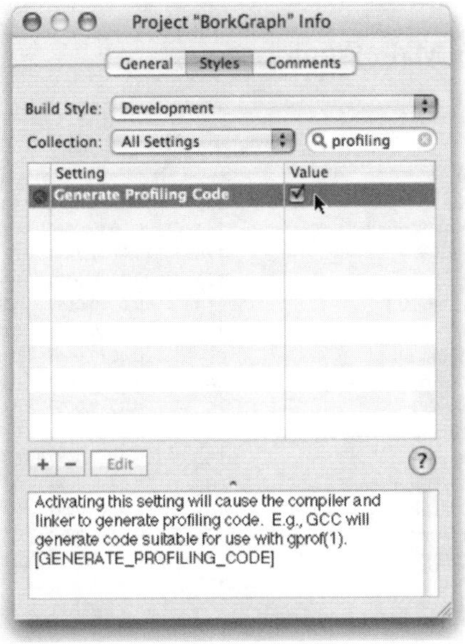

After you have recompiled your project, start up `Saturn`, which lives in `/Developer/Applications/Performance Tools/CHUD`.

`Saturn` is not as fancy as its bigger brother `Shark`, so you will not get any windows on start-up with `Saturn`. Under the `Saturn` menu, choose **Launch Process**. You will get a dialog like in Figure 25-26. Here you can choose your program, pick a working directory, which will also be where the profiling results will be placed, as well as any launch arguments for the application. `Saturn` fills in a number of environment variables it needs, and you can add your own.

Figure 25-26. Saturn's Launch Window

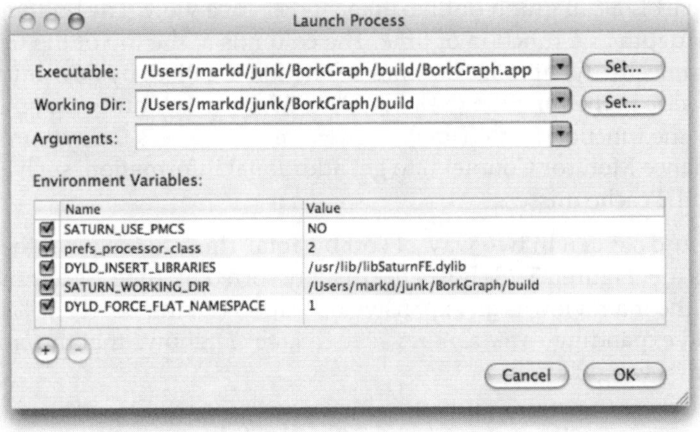

Click **OK**, and then `Saturn` launches your program. Exercise your app, and quit it. You can hear your hard drive percolating as `Saturn` records the program's activity. Once you quit your app, `Saturn` comes back and asks you to open the data file.

After it chews through the data (which can take awhile on slower machines), you will see a window like Figure 25-27

Figure 25-27. Saturn's Main Window

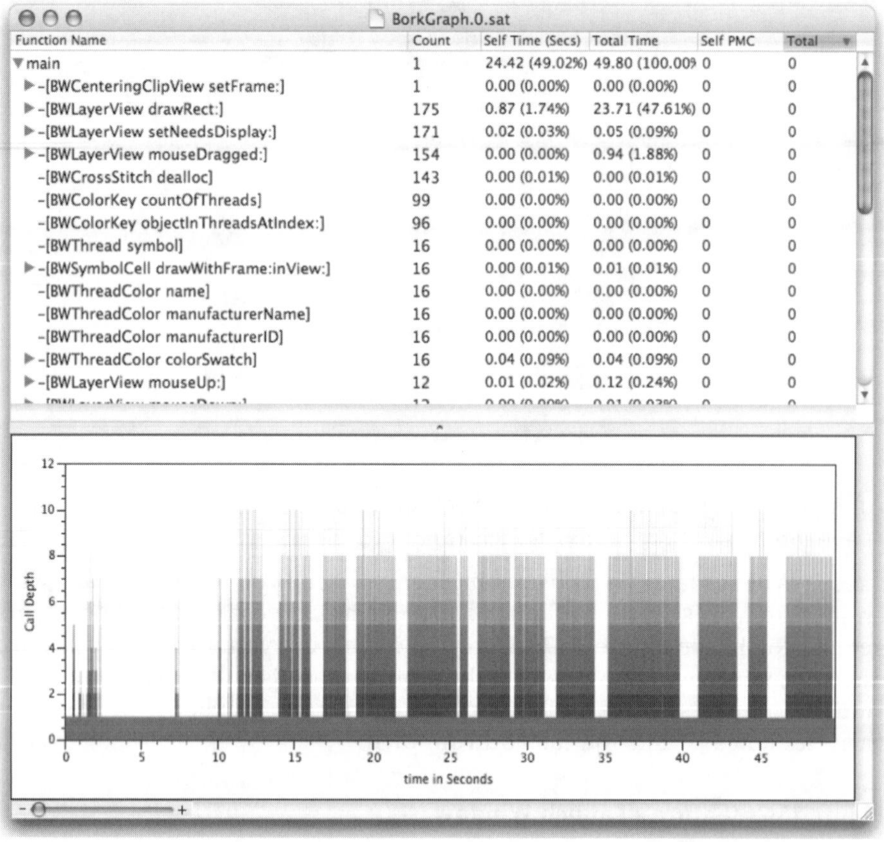

The top part is a call graph outline, like Shark's tree view. The bottom part shows call stack depth as a function of time. The columns at the top of the tree view let you sort by name, by the number of times a function is called, by how much time was spent in code in the function (**Self Time**), and how much time was spent in functions called by the function (**Total Time**). Saturn can also access the system's PMCs (Performance Monitor Counters) to get additional information, such as CPU cycles used and L2 cache misses.

I usually use Saturn in two ways. I sort by Total Time, to see what the heavy-weight functions are. Figure 25-28 shows the display sorted by time, and shows that drawing the main view is an expensive operation (taking nearly 50% of the run time), and expanding -[BWLayerView drawRect:] shows that the cross-stitch layer is the heavy-weight.

Figure 25-28. Saturn Sorted by Time

Function Name	Count	Self Time (Secs)	Total Time
▼main	1	24.42 (49.02%)	49.80 (100.00%)
▼-[BWLayerView drawRect:]	175	0.87 (1.74%)	23.71 (47.61%)
▶-[BWCrossStitchLayer drawRect:]	522	1.66 (3.34%)	18.07 (36.29%)
▶-[BWGridLayer drawRect:]	174	0.01 (0.02%)	4.75 (9.54%)
-[BWLayerSet reverseLayerEnumerator]	174	0.01 (0.03%)	0.01 (0.03%)
▶-[BWBackStitchLayer drawRect:]	348	0.00 (0.00%)	0.00 (0.01%)
-[BWLayer visible]	1218	0.00 (0.00%)	0.00 (0.00%)
-[BWLayerView isFlipped]	350	0.00 (0.00%)	0.00 (0.00%)

Next I expand the main disclosure triangle all of the way (by option-clicking on it) and then sorting by Count. This is a good way to make sure that operations happen in the proportions you think they should be. If you are writing a file browser, and see that `lastModificationTime()` was called ten times but `fileName` was called ten thousand times, you may have an opportunity for optimization.

Sort by Count is not a pure sort. It tries to get the most expensive stuff at the top, but if a method has been called inside of another method, the more heavy-weight method will be further down in the list. Figure 25-29 shows this run, looking at counts.

Figure 25-29. Saturn Sorted by Count

Function Name	Count	Self Time (Secs)	Total Time (Secs)
▼main	1	24.42 (49.02%)	49.80 (100.00%)
-[BWLayerView isFlipped]	1425	0.00 (0.00%)	0.00 (0.00%)
▼-[BWLayerView drawRect:]	175	0.87 (1.74%)	23.71 (47.61%)
-[BWLayer visible]	1218	0.00 (0.00%)	0.00 (0.00%)
▼-[BWCrossStitchLayer drawRect:]	522	1.66 (3.34%)	18.07 (36.29%)
-[BWCrossStitch row]	247916	0.17 (0.34%)	0.17 (0.34%)
-[BWCrossStitch column]	247916	0.23 (0.45%)	0.23 (0.45%)
-[BWCrossStitchStorage symbolAtIndex:]	79019	0.16 (0.32%)	0.16 (0.32%)
▼-[BWCrossStitchChangeList isChangeAtRow:column:]	79019	0.19 (0.37%)	0.33 (0.67%)
-[BWCrossStitchStorage isSymbolAtRow:column:]	79019	0.15 (0.30%)	0.15 (0.30%)
▼-[BWCrossStitchLayer maybeDrawStitch:atRow:column:]	78463	0.45 (0.91%)	13.43 (26.96%)
▼-[BWCrossStitchLayer drawStitch:atRow:column:]	78463	0.53 (1.06%)	12.61 (25.32%)
▼-[BWCrossStitchLayer drawThread:inRect:]	78463	8.75 (17.56%)	11.90 (23.89%)
▼-[BWSymbol pathInRect:]	78463	2.24 (4.50%)	3.03 (6.09%)

This shows that the **BWLayerView** was redrawn 175 times, and isFlipped was called 1425, about 8 times per draw. This is called by Cocoa, so there is not a lot we can do about it (and it is not an expensive call), but it is interesting it is being called at 8x the rate of drawing.

-[BWLayer visible] is called about 7 times the rate of drawing, which makes sense because there are 7 layers to be drawn for this particular document.

What is interesting is how often the accessors -[BWCrossStitch row] and its column counterpart is called. There were only a couple of hundred stitches, which comes out to about 2500 calls per stitch. At over 175 layerView drawings, that is about 14 calls per stitch, assuming every stitch was drawn every time through. That is a more reasonable value, even though every stitch getting drawn every time is kind of bad. (That is actually what this performance problem was - bad handling of setNeedsDisplayInRect:)

You can see in this listing that I seem to have fixed the `isSymbolAtRow:column:` performance issue. It was called 79,000 times here, or about 4 times per stitch per drawing, with a total consumed time of a quarter of a second.

Both `Shark` and `Saturn` are excellent tools. `Shark` was perfect for finding the first problem with the O(N^2) algorithm. Finding the drawing issue took some data mining in `Shark`, but was immediately apparent in `Saturn`. `Quartz Debug` was used to verify the results from `Saturn`, that indeed too much drawing was happening. Apple provides lots of very good performance tools. It is well worth using them all.

Using the CHUD Frameworks

You can access some of CHUD's features from within your application, such as starting a remote performance monitor (like `Shark`) so you have control over what `Shark` samples. If you have expensive one-time set-up code, you might not want to sample that. Instead you would want to only profile your number-crunching code. You need to include the CHUD framework in your application (it lives in `/System/Library/PrivateFrameworks`). You will need to download the CHUD installer from Apple to get the CHUD headers. It is not a published and supported API, so it can change, which is why Apple took the header files out of the framework.

```
#import <CHUD/chud.h>

chudInitialize ();
chudSetErrorLogFile (stderr);
chudUmarkPID (getpid(), TRUE);
chudAcquireRemoteAccess ();
```

Then before your code of interest, invoke:

```
result = chudStartRemotePerfMonitor ("SomeIdentifier");
// zero for success, a code on error
```

Do your code, then call:

```
chudStopRemotePerfMonitor ();
chudReleaseRemoteAccess ();
```

Before running this part of your code, go into `Shark` and choose **Programmatic (Remote)** from the **Sampling** menu. `Shark` will wait for another program to signal it before it will start working. Once you execute **chudStartRemotePerfMonitor ()**, `Shark` turns on the counters and starts sampling your program.

CHUD also includes programs like `MONster`, which shows many details of system-wide performance; `amber`, which captures the entire instruction and data streams from a program; and `acid`, which takes the trace from `amber` and analyzes it. `BigTop` is like the `top` command on steroids. There are also some examples living in `/Developer/Examples/CHUD/`.

Summary

Performance is a never-ending game. The rules change constantly as new OS revisions and new hardware comes out. We are nearing the end of free performance gains from hardware, at least for applications that can only take advantage of one

CPU. Efficiency in coding and in algorithms, as well as parallel processing, will become more and more important as time goes on.

Luckily we have a number of good tools to profile our code and highlight the areas where we should focus our attention. Shark is a sampling profiler with data mining and analysis features. Saturn is a profiler that will build a call graph. Both are good tools and worth getting comfortable with.

Index